The World's Religions

Part of a relief from Brauron, c.400 B.C.E., showing
Zeus, Leto (a Titaness and mother of Artemis),
Apollo and Artemis. Brauron, to the south of Athens,
was a center for the veneration of Artemis. National
Museum, Athens.

THE
World's Religions

Second Edition

Ninian Smart

For Luisabel

PUBLISHED BY THE PRESS SYNDICATE OF THE UNIVERSITY OF CAMBRIDGE
The Pitt Building, Trumpington Street, Cambridge, United Kingdom

CAMBRIDGE UNIVERSITY PRESS
The Edinburgh Building, Cambridge, CB2 2RU, UK http://www.cup.cam.ac.uk
40 West 20th Street, New York, NY 10011-4211, USA http://www.cup.org
10 Stamford Road, Oakleigh, Melbourne 3166, Australia

First published 1989
First paperback edition 1992
Second edition 1998

A catalogue record for this book is available from the British Library

Library of Congress Cataloguing in Publication data applied for

ISBN 0 521 63139 4 hard covers
ISBN 0 521 63748 1 paperback

This book was designed and produced by
Calmann and King Ltd, London

Layout by Andrew Shoolbred
Printed in Slovenia

Contents

Preface to the second edition

This book needed revision primarily because of the collapse of the Soviet Union and the subsequent emergence of "new" states from under the imperial aegis of Russian-based Communist rule. There were, in addition, those under a wider Stalinist conquest who once again saw independence: the nations of Eastern Europe, together with Mongolia. The Communist system established by Tito in Yugoslavia also dissolved into messy and often warring nations. All this changed the political and religious landscape. In Europe varying forms of Christianity, notably Catholicism in Poland, where it had a decisive part in the disintegration of the Soviet empire, reemerged: in the Caucasus, varieties of Orthodoxy and Islam; in Central Asia, also Islam; and in Mongolia, Buddhism. Judaism was also able to be itself again in Russia. And so we have here taken some pains to record these events: the latter part of the chapter on Eastern Europe and the Soviet Union has been rewritten.

A new final chapter (25) has been composed, to reflect on the twentieth century, now that it is coming to a close. This takes into account the pluralism of the scene in the latter half of the century particularly. It emphasizes the way the facts of religion (and ideology) should be taught — through informed empathy, and in an open manner. At last we humans are beginning seriously to stress the way religions should be *understood*, rather than presented in a dogmatic and narrow manner. But there is still a large struggle for so many so-called religious people are more interested in dogmatizing their opinions than in illuminating how people actually behave, and how traditions develop.

The religions are a wonderful resource for humanity. But they live together now: they have to, as our global civilization emerges out of the jet and the Internet. In reflecting at the end on the uses of religious studies, I of course want to show how a book like this has a small part to play.

The main theme remains how traditions have responded to the modern era, and that chiefly a colonial era, in which every culture has undergone a profound shock.

I wish to thank particularly Melanie White of Calmann and King, the London publishing house that saw this book through its birth and adolescence, and have done a fine job, particularly in view of the beautifully illustrated character of the text. Also, I thank Max Leeming, Amy Cooper and Ellen Posman of ULSB for their fine assistance. The pictures, incidentally, have been somewhat changed for this edition. They are beautiful: their only disadvantage is that readers may neglect the text. It is, however, serious and contains a serious theory about the modern transformation of religions.

Ninian Smart, Tremezzo, Lake Como, Italy, 20 August 1997

Introduction

The Importance of Understanding the World's Worldviews

Understanding the world's religions and ideologies is important in three ways. First, they are a vital ingredient in the varied story of humankind's various experiments in living. The religions and ideas of ancient Greece or of the Maya are worth our recapturing, so far as we can, as part of the great heritage of human civilization. Second, and of more immediate importance, is the fact that in order to grasp the meanings and values of the plural cultures of today's world, we need to know something of the worldviews which underlie them. To understand the Middle East you need to know something about Islam, not to mention Christianity and Judaism; and to understand Japan you need some insight into Buddhism, Shinto, and the Confucian heritage. Third, we may as individuals be trying to form our own coherent and emotionally satisfying picture of reality, and it is always relevant to see the great ideas and practices of various important cultures and civilizations. To make judgments about philosophies and ways of life we need a comparative perspective—to know something of the quest of the Christian mystic and the Hindu yogin, and of the spirituality of the Hasidic Jew and the Mahāyāna Buddhist. In a number of ways, the individual cultures of the world contribute to human civilization, and the religions and ideologies permeating those cultures are not to be neglected.

In undertaking a voyage into the world's religions we should not define religion too narrowly. It is important for us to recognize secular ideologies as part of the story of human worldviews. It is artificial to divide them too sharply from religions, partly because they sometimes function in society like religions, and partly because the distinction between religious and secular beliefs and practices is a modern Western one and does not represent the way in which other cultures categorize human values. Essentially, this book is a history of ideas and practices which have moved human beings.

To understand religious and secular worldviews and their practical meaning we have to use imagination. We have to enter into the lives of those for whom such ideas and actions are important. As the Native American proverb says, "Never judge a person until you have walked a mile in his moccasins." Much of this book will be in a broad way informative; but it will also, I hope, convey something of the spirit of the human quest for crosscultural communication.

Once a Christian theologian complained to me in a public discussion because I had dealt among other themes with Buddhist attitudes to creation: "What need do we have to consider Buddhism, since it is incompatible with the Gospel, and the Christian Gospel is all the truth we need?" It seems to me inappropriate to be so defensive, and a limitation on this man's knowledge of the forces animating different parts of humanity. Anyway, I craftily replied: "You must indeed have read a lot, to know that Buddhism is incompatible with the Christian Gospel."

The voyage into other folks' beliefs and practices may turn out to be a journey into your neighborhood. It is common today for varieties of people to live together in the great cities. In London, New York, Los Angeles, Sydney, Singapore, Frankfurt, and Paris, most of the great religions and ideologies are present. This pluralism is the richer because each of the traditions includes many forms: Catholics, Orthodox, Lutherans, Baptists; Shi'a and Sunni Muslims, and Muslims from Morocco, Indonesia, and Egypt; Buddhists from Sri Lanka, Vietnam, and Korea, as well as Anglo converts; and so on. It often happens, then, that cities are microcosms of the whole world. This is an added reason why it is important to know something of others, so that mutual understanding, though maybe not agreement, may animate community relations.

Inevitably the Vietnamese migrant to Corpus Christi, Texas, and the Indian villager listening to a radio are affected to some degree by modernity and in a measure by Western values. The tremendous impact of the West has helped to shape the old religions in their voyage into the contemporary world. They have cherished their roots, but they have also adapted. The Hinduism of today bears deeply the imprint of its struggle against the imperial mentality, and the same is true, much more clearly, of the way smaller-scale cultures have bent to the winds of Western-dictated change. Consequently in this book the period of Western navigation, exploration, exploitation, and imperial rule marks a watershed in the story. Before, there is the narrative of the rise and fall of religious cultures in differing parts of the globe; afterwards, we see patterns of interaction, and eventually the emergence of a global civilization, in which inevitably religious and secular worldviews have to learn to adapt to one another.

The Nature of a Religion

In thinking about religion, it is easy to be confused about what it is. Is there some essence which is common to all religions? And cannot a person be religious without belonging to any of the religions? The search for an essence ends up in vagueness—for instance in the statement that a religion is some system of worship or other practice recognizing a transcendent Being or goal. Our problems break out again in trying to define the key term "transcendent." And in answer to the second question, why yes: there are plenty of people with deep spiritual concerns who do not ally themselves to any formal religious movement, and who may not themselves recognize anything as transcendent. They may see ultimate spiritual meaning in unity with nature or in relationships to other persons.

It is more practical to come to terms first of all not with what religion is in general but with what *a* religion is. Can we find some scheme of ideas which will help us to think about and to appreciate the nature of the religions?

Before I describe such a scheme, let me first point to something which we need to bear in mind in looking at religious traditions such as Christianity, Buddhism, or Islam. Though we use the singular label "Christianity," in fact there are a great many varieties of Christianity, and there are some movements about which we may have doubts as to whether they count as Christian. The same is true of all traditions: they manifest themselves as a loosely held-together family of subtraditions. Consider: a Baptist chapel in Georgia is a very different structure from an Eastern Orthodox church in Romania, with its blazing candles and rich ikons; and the two house very diverse services—the one plain, with hymns and Bible-reading, prayers and impassioned preaching; the other much more ritually anchored, with processions and chanting, and

The ritual dimension: Easter celebrations in Moscow led by Russian Orthodox bishops.

mysterious ceremonies in the light behind the screen where the ikons hang, concealing most of the priestly activities. Ask either of the religious specialists, the Baptist preacher or the Orthodox priest, and he will tell you that his own form of faith corresponds to original Christianity. To list some of the denominations of Christianity is to show something of its diverse practice— Orthodox, Catholic, Coptic, Nestorian, Armenian, Mar Thoma, Lutheran, Calvinist, Methodist, Baptist, Unitarian, Mennonite, Congregationalist, Disciples of Christ—and we have not reached some of the newer, more problematic forms: Latter-Day Saints, Christian Scientists, Unificationists, Zulu Zionists, and so forth.

Moreover, each faith is found in many countries, and takes color from each region. German Lutheranism differs from American; Ukrainian Catholicism from Irish; Greek Orthodoxy from Russian. Every religion has permeated and been permeated by a variety of diverse cultures. This adds to the richness of human experience, but it makes our tasks of thinking and feeling about the variety of faiths more complicated than we might at first suppose. We are dealing with not just traditions but many subtraditions.

It may happen, by the way, that a person within one family of subtraditions is drawn closer to some subtradition of another family than to one or two subtraditions in his or her own family (as with human families; this is how marriage occurs). I happen to have had a lot to do with Buddhists in Sri Lanka and in some ways feel much closer to them than I do to some groups within my own family of Christianity.

The fact of pluralism inside religious traditions is enhanced by what goes on between them. The meeting of different cultures and traditions often produces new religious movements, such as the many black independent churches in Africa, combining classical African motifs and Christianities. All around us in Western countries are to be seen new movements and combinations.

Despite all this, it is possible to make sense of the variety and to discern some patterns in the luxurious vegetation of the world's religions and subtraditions. One approach is to look at the different aspects or dimensions of religion.

The Practical and Ritual Dimension

Every tradition has some practices to which it adheres—for instance regular worship, preaching, prayers, and so on. They are often known as rituals (though they may well be more informal than this word implies). This *practical* and *ritual* dimension is especially important with faiths of a strongly sacramental kind, such as Eastern Orthodox Christianity with its long and elaborate service known as the Liturgy. The ancient Jewish tradition of the Temple, before it was destroyed in 70 C.E., was preoccupied with the rituals of sacrifice, and thereafter with the study of such rites seen as equivalent to their performance, so that study itself becomes almost a ritual activity. Again, sacrificial rituals are important among Brahmin forms of the Hindu tradition.

Also important are other patterns of behavior which, while they may not strictly count as rituals, fulfill a function in developing spiritual awareness or ethical insight: practices such as yoga in the Buddhist and Hindu traditions, methods of stilling the self in Eastern Orthodox mysticism, meditations which can help to increase compassion and love, and so on. Such practices can be combined with rituals of worship, where meditation is directed toward union with God. They can count as a form of prayer. In such ways they overlap with the more formal or explicit rites of religion.

The Experiential and Emotional Dimension

We only have to glance at religious history to see the enormous vitality and significance of experience in the formation and development of religious traditions. Consider the visions of the Prophet Muhammad, the conversion of Paul, the enlightenment of the Buddha. These were seminal events in human history. And it is obvious that the *emotions* and *experiences* of men and women are the food on which the other dimensions of religion feed: ritual without feeling is cold, doctrines without awe or compassion are dry, and myths which do not move hearers are feeble. So it is important in understanding a tradition to try to enter into the feelings which it generates—to feel the sacred awe, the calm peace, the rousing inner dynamism, the perception of a brilliant emptiness within, the outpouring of love, the sensations of hope, the gratitude for favors which have been received. One of the main reasons why music is so potent in religion is that it has mysterious powers to express and engender emotions.

Writers on religion have singled out differing experiences as being central. For instance, Rudolf Otto (1869–1937) coined the word "numinous." For the ancient Romans there were *numina* or spirits all around them, present in brooks and streams, and in mysterious copses, in mountains and in dwelling-places; they were to be treated with awe and a kind of fear. From the word, Otto built up his adjective, to refer to the feeling aroused by a *mysterium tremendum et fascinans*, a mysterious something which draws you to it but at the same time brings an awe-permeated fear. It is a good characterization of many religious experiences and visions of God as Other. It captures the impact of the prophetic experiences of Isaiah and Jeremiah, the theophany through which God appeared to Job, the conversion of Paul, the overwhelming vision given to Arjuna in the Hindu Song of the Lord (*Bhagavadgītā*). At a gentler level it delineates too the spirit of loving devotion, in that the devotee sees God as merciful and loving, yet Other, and to be worshiped and adored.

But the numinous is rather different in character from those other experiences which are often called "mystical." Mysticism is the inner or contemplative quest for what lies within—variously thought of as the Divine Being within, or the eternal soul, or the Cloud of Unknowing, emptiness, a dazzling darkness. There are those, such as Aldous Huxley (1894–1963), who have thought that the imageless, insight-giving inner mystical experience lies at the heart of all the major religions.

There are other related experiences, such as the dramas of conversion, being "born again," turning around from worldly to otherworldly existence. There is

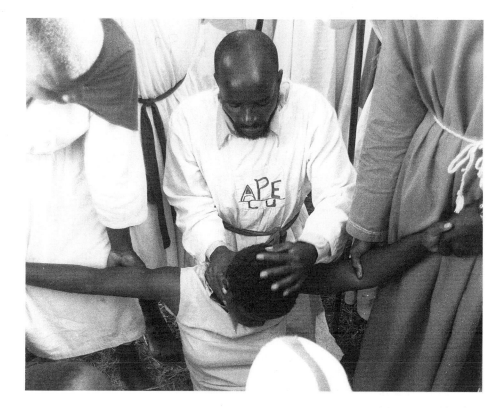

The experiential dimension: casting out demons in Zimbabwe.

also the shamanistic type of experience, where a person goes upon a vision quest and acquires powers to heal, often through suffering himself and vividly traveling to the netherworld to rescue the dying and bring them to life again. Shamans are common to many small-scale societies and peoples that make their living by hunting, but many of the marks of the shamanistic quest have been left upon larger religions.

The Narrative or Mythic Dimension

Often experience is channeled and expressed not only by ritual but also by sacred narrative or myth. This is the third dimension—the *mythic* or *narrative*. It is the story side of religion. It is typical of all faiths to hand down vital stories: some historical; some about that mysterious primordial time when the world was in its timeless dawn; some about things to come at the end of time; some about great heroes and saints; some about great founders, such as Moses, the Buddha, Jesus, and Muhammad; some about assaults by the Evil One; some parables and edifying tales; some about the adventures of the gods; and so on. These stories often are called myths. The term may be a bit misleading, for in the modern study of religion there is no implication that a myth is false.

The seminal stories of a religion may be rooted in history or they may not. Stories of creation are before history, as are myths which indicate how death and suffering came into the world. Others are about historical events—for

The mythic dimension: a Brahmin worshiping Kṛṣṇa, the eighth incarnation of the god Viṣṇu.

instance the life of the Prophet Muhammad, or the execution of Jesus, and the enlightenment of the Buddha. Historians have sometimes cast doubt on some aspects of these historical stories, but from the standpoint of the student of religion this question is secondary to the meaning and function of the myth; and to the believer, very often, these narratives *are* history.

This belief is strengthened by the fact that many faiths look upon certain documents, originally maybe based upon long oral traditions, as true scriptures. They are canonical or recognized by the relevant body of the faithful (the Church, the community, Brahmins and others in India, the Buddhist Sangha or Order). They are often treated as inspired directly by God or as records of the very words of the Founder. They have authority, and they contain many stories and myths which are taken to be divinely or otherwise guaranteed. But other documents and oral traditions may also be important—

the lives of the saints, the chronicles of Ceylon as a Buddhist nation, the stories of famous holy men of Eastern Europe in the Hasidic tradition, traditions concerning the life of the Prophet (ḥadīth), and so forth. These stories may have lesser authority but they can still be inspiring to the followers.

Stories in religion are often tightly integrated into the ritual dimension. The Christian Mass or communion service, for instance, commemorates and presents the story of the Last Supper, when Jesus celebrated with his disciples his forthcoming fate, by which (according to Christians) he saved humankind and brought us back into harmony with the Divine Being. The Jewish Passover ceremonies commemorate and make real to us the events of the Exodus from Egypt, the sufferings of the people, and their relationship to the Lord who led them out of servitude in ancient Egypt. As Jews share the meal, so they retrace the story. Ritual and story are bound together.

The Doctrinal and Philosophical Dimension

Underpinning the narrative dimension is the *doctrinal* dimension. Thus, in the Christian tradition, the story of Jesus' life and the ritual of the communion service led to attempts to provide an analysis of the nature of the Divine Being which would preserve both the idea of the Incarnation (Jesus as God) and the belief in one God. The result was the doctrine of the Trinity, which sees God as three persons in one substance. Similarly, with the meeting between early Christianity and the great Graeco-Roman philosophical and intellectual heritage it became necessary to face questions about the ultimate meaning of creation, the inner nature of God, the notion of grace, the analysis of how Christ could be both God and human being, and so on. These concerns led to the elaboration of Christian doctrine. In the case of Buddhism, to take another example, doctrinal ideas were more crucial right from the start, for the Buddha presented a philosophical vision of the world which itself was an aid to salvation.

The doctrinal dimension: the Buddha in his form as teacher.

In any event, doctrines come to play a significant part in all the major religions, partly because sooner or later a faith has to adapt to social reality and so to the fact that much of the leadership is well educated and seeks some kind of intellectual statement of the basis of the faith.

It happens that histories of religion have tended to exaggerate the importance of scriptures and doctrines; and this is not too surprising since so much of our knowledge of past religions must come from the documents which have been passed on by the scholarly elite. Also, and especially in the case of Christianity, doctrinal disputes have often been the overt expression of splits within the fabric of the community at large, so that frequently histories of a faith concentrate upon these hot issues. This is clearly unbalanced; but I would not want us to go to the other extreme. There are scholars today who have been much impressed with the symbolic and psychological force of myth, and have tended to neglect the essential intellectual component of religion.

The ethical dimension: Zen monks exhibit discipline and the desire for orderly work as they set out to tidy the grounds of their monastery.

The Ethical and Legal Dimension

Both narrative and doctrine affect the values of a tradition by laying out the shape of a worldview and addressing the question of ultimate liberation or salvation. The law which a tradition or subtradition incorporates into its fabric can be called the *ethical* dimension of religion. In Buddhism, for instance, there are certain universally binding precepts, known as the five precepts or virtues, together with a set of further regulations controlling the lives of monks and nuns and monastic communities. In Judaism we have not merely the Ten Commandments but a complex of over six hundred rules imposed upon the community by the Divine Being. All this Law or Torah is a framework for living for the Orthodox Jew. It also is part of the ritual dimension, because, for instance, the injunction to keep the Sabbath as a day of rest is also the injunction to perform certain sacred practices and rituals, such as attending the synagogue and maintaining purity.

Similarly, Islamic life has traditionally been controlled by the Law or *shar 'a*, which shapes society as both a religious and a political society, as well as shaping the moral life of the individual—prescribing that he should pray daily, give alms to the poor, and so on, and that society should have various institutions, such as marriage, modes of banking, etc.

Other traditions can be less tied to a system of law, but still display an ethic which is influenced and indeed controlled by the myth and doctrine of the faith. For instance, the central ethical attitude in the Christian faith is love. This springs not just from Jesus' injunction to his followers to love God and their neighbors: it flows too from the story of Christ himself who gave his life out of love for his fellow human beings. It also is rooted in the very idea of the Trinity, for God from all eternity is a society of three persons, Father, Son and Holy Spirit, kept together by the bond of love. The Christian joins a community which reflects, it is hoped at any rate, the life of the Divine Being, both as Trinity and as suffering servant of the human race and indeed of all creation.

The Social and Institutional Dimension

The dimensions outlined so far—the experiential, the ritual, the mythic, the doctrinal, and the ethical—can be considered in abstract terms, without being embodied in external form. The last two dimensions have to do with the incarnation of religion. First, every religious movement is embodied in a group of people, and that is very often rather formally organized—as Church,

The social dimension: a Jewish family celebrating their first Passover since arriving in Israel.

19

The material dimension: the holy city of Benares on the banks of the river Ganges. The Hindu temples are overshadowed by the mosque, which was built by the Mogul emperor Aurangzeb (1618–1707) as a sign of the ultimate triumph of Islam.

or Sangha, or *umma*. The sixth dimension therefore is what may be called the social or *institutional* aspect of religion. To understand a faith we need to see how it works among people. This is one reason why such an important tool of the investigator of religion is that subdiscipline which is known as the sociology of religion. Sometimes the social aspect of a worldview is simply identical with society itself, as in small-scale groups such as tribes. But there is a variety of relations between organized religions and society at large: a faith may be the official religion, or it may be just one denomination among many, or it may be somewhat cut off from social life, as a sect. Within the organization of one religion, moreover, there are many models—from the relative democratic governance of a radical Protestant congregation to the hierarchical and monarchical system of the Church of Rome.

It is not, however, the formal officials of a religion who may in the long run turn out to be the most important persons in a tradition. For there are charismatic or sacred personages, whose spiritual power glows through their demeanor and actions, and who vivify the faith of more ordinary folk—saintly people, gurus, mystics, and prophets, whose words and example stir up the spiritual enthusiasm of the masses, and who lend depth and meaning to the rituals and values of a tradition. They can also be revolutionaries and set religion on new courses. They can, like John Wesley, become leaders of a new denomination, almost against their will; or they can be founders of new groups which may in due course emerge as separate religions—an example is Joseph Smith II, Prophet of the new faith of Mormonism. In short, the social dimension of religion includes not only the mass of persons but also the outstanding individuals through whose features glimmer old and new thoughts of the heaven toward which they aspire.

The Material Dimension

This social or institutional dimension of religion almost inevitably becomes incarnate in a different way, in *material* form, as buildings, works of art, and other creations. Some movements—such as Calvinist Christianity, especially in the time before the present century—eschew external symbols as being potentially idolatrous; their buildings are often beautiful in their simplicity, but their intention is to be without artistic or other images which might seduce people from the thought that God is a spirit who transcends all representations. However, the material expressions of religion are more often elaborate, moving, and highly important for believers in their approach to the divine. How indeed could we understand Eastern Orthodox Christianity without seeing what ikons are like and knowing that they are regarded as windows onto heaven? How could we get inside the feel of Hinduism without attending to the varied statues of God and the gods?

Also important material expressions of a religion are those natural features of the world which are singled out as being of special sacredness and meaning—the river Ganges, the Jordan, the sacred mountains of China, Mount Fuji in Japan, Ayers Rock in Australia, the Mount of Olives, Mount Sinai, and so forth. Sometimes of course these sacred landmarks combine with more direct human creations, such as the holy city of Jerusalem, the sacred shrines of Banaras, or the temple at Bodh Gaya which commemorates the Buddha's Enlightenment.

Uses of the Seven Dimensions

To sum up: we have surveyed briefly the seven dimensions of religion which help to characterize religions as they exist in the world. The point of the list is so that we can give a balanced description of the movements which have animated the human spirit and taken a place in the shaping of society, without neglecting either ideas or practices.

Naturally, there are religious movements or manifestations where one or other of the dimensions is so weak as to be virtually absent: nonliterate small-scale societies do not have much means of expressing the doctrinal dimension; Buddhist modernists, concentrating on meditation, ethics, and philosophy, pay scant regard to the narrative dimension of Buddhism; some newly formed groups may not have evolved anything much in the way of the material dimension. Also there are so many people who are not formally part of any social religious grouping, but have their own particular worldviews and practices, that we can observe in society atoms of religion which do not possess any well-formed social dimension. But of course in forming a phenomenon within society they reflect certain trends which in a sense form a shadow of the social dimension (just as those who have not yet got themselves a material dimension are nevertheless implicitly storing one up, for with success come buildings and with rituals ikons, most likely).

If our seven-dimensional portrait of religions is adequate, then we do not need to worry greatly about further definition of religion. In any case, I shall now turn to a most vital question in understanding the way the world works, namely to the relation between more or less overtly religious systems and those which are commonly called secular: ideologies or worldviews such as scientific humanism, Marxism, Existentialism, nationalism, and so on. In examining these worldviews we shall take on some of the discussion about what count as religious questions and themes. It is useful to begin by thinking out whether our seven-dimensional analysis can apply successfully to such secular worldviews.

The Nature of Secular Worldviews

Nationalism

Although nationalism is not strictly speaking a single worldview or even in itself a complete worldview, it is convenient to begin with it. One reason is that it has been such a powerful force in human affairs. Virtually all the land surface of the globe, together with parts of the world's water surface, is now carved up between sovereign states. Nationalism has given shape decisively to the modern world, because its popularity in part stems from the way in which assembling peoples into states has helped with the processes of industrialization and modern bureaucratic organization. Countries such as Britain, France, the United States, Germany, and Italy pioneered the industrial revolution, and the system of national governments spread from Western to Eastern Europe after World War I and from Europe to Asia, Africa, and elsewhere after World War II. Ethnic identity was sometimes demarcated by language and therefore cultural heritage, sometimes by religion, sometimes by both, and sometimes simply by shared history. Examples of each of these categories can be seen in the cases of Germany (shared language), the two parts of Ireland (distinctive religion), Poland (both distinctive language and religion), and Singapore (shared history of Chinese, Malay, and other linguistic groups). Colonialism often helped to spread nationalism by reaction: the British conquest of India fostered an Indian nationalism, and there are signs of national awakening in parts of the former Soviet Union, once colonized by Tsarist Russia, and in Tibet, conquered by China.

The nation-state has many of the appurtenances of a religion. First of all (to use the order in which we expounded the dimensions of religion in the previous section), there are the *rituals* of nationhood: speaking the language itself; the national anthem; the flying and perhaps saluting of the flag; republic and memorial days, and other such festivals and holidays; the appearance of the Head of State at solemn occasions; military march-pasts; and so on. It is usual for citizens to make secular pilgrimages to the nation's capital and other significant spots—Washington (the Lincoln Memorial, the Vietnam Memorial, the White House, and so on); Plymouth Rock; Mount Rushmore; natural beauties exhibiting "America the Beautiful." Memorials to the nation's dead are of special significance, and often religious language is used about the sacrifices of the young on the altar of national duty.

The experiential or *emotional* side of nationalism is indeed powerful—for the sentiments of patriotism, pride in the nation, love of its beauties and powers, and dedication to national goals, can be very strong. Especially in times of national crisis, such as war, such sentiments rise to the surface. But they are reinforced all the time by such practices as singing the national anthem and other patriotic songs.

A Japanese naval officer indicates his nationalist dedication by wrapping his country's flag around his head as he prepares for combat in World War II.

The *narrative* dimension of nationalism is easily seen, for it lies in the history of the nation, which is taught in the schools of the country, and which in some degree celebrates the values of the great men and women of the nation—for Italians, such great forebears as Julius Caesar (Giulio Cesare), Dante, Galileo, Leonardo, Garibaldi, Cavour, Verdi, Leopardi, Alcide de Gasperi, and others. History is the narrative that helps to create in the young and in citizens at large a sense of identity, of belonging, of group solidarity.

Of *doctrines* nationalism is somewhat bereft, unless you count the doctrine of self-determination. But often, too, nations appeal to principles animating the modern state, such as the need for democracy and the rights of the individual in a freedom-loving nation, etc.; or a nation may appeal to the doctrine of a full-blown secular ideology, such as Marxism. Or it may hark back to the teachings of its ancestral religion, and so represent itself as guarding the truths and values of Christianity, or of Buddhism, or of a revived and revolutionary Islam.

The *ethical* dimension of nationalism consists in those values which are inculcated into citizens. Young people are expected to be loyal people, taxpayers, willing to fight if necessary for the country, law-abiding, and hopefully good family people (supplying thus the nation with its population). There is of course a blend between ethical values in general and the particular obligations to one's own kith and kin, one's fellow-nationals.

The *social* and *institutional* aspect of the nation-state is of course easily discerned. It culminates in a head of state who has extensive ceremonial functions—especially with monarchy, as in Britain, where the Queen is an important ritual object—and on whom sentiments of patriotism also focus. The state has its military services which also perform ceremonial as well as fighting tasks. There are the public schools, with the teachers imparting the treasured knowledge and rules of the nation. Even games come to play an institutional role; loyalty is expressed through the Olympics and various other contests, and the ethos of the athlete comes to be blended with that of the ideal citizen. In some countries loyalty to religion or to a secular ideology blends with loyalty to one's nation, and those who do not subscribe to it are treated as disloyal. State occasions are shown on television, which itself comes to have a role in transmitting and focusing the values of the nation.

Finally, there is of course much *material* embodiment of the nation in its great buildings and memorials, its flag, its great art, its sacred land, its powerful military hardware.

In all these ways, then, the nation today is like a religion. If you have a relative who has died for a cause, it is not like the old days when he might have died for his religion, maybe at the stake; now he is most likely to have died for his country.

It is, then, reasonable to treat modern nationalism in the same terms as religion. It represents a set of values often allied with a kind of modernism, which is natural to the thinking of many of our contemporaries, and which stresses certain essentially modern concerns: the importance of economic development; the merits of technology; the wonders of science; the importance of either socialism or capitalism, or some mixture, in the process of modernization; the need for the state to look after the welfare of its citizens; the importance of universal education; and so on.

There are some growing limitations on nationalism: the fact that in many countries which were once reasonably homogeneous there are now increasing ethnic mixes, the growth of transnational corporations, the developing economic interdependence of nations, the impossibility of older ways of conceiving sovereignty in the context of modern warfare, and so on. Nevertheless, nationalism remains a very strong and alluring ingredient in the world, and many of the trouble spots are so because of unfulfilled ethnic expectations and ethnic rivalries—in Cyprus, Northern Ireland, Israel and Palestine, South Africa, Sri Lanka, Kurdistan, Afghanistan, and elsewhere.

The Dimensions of Marxism

It is because Marxism has itself become more than a movement of ideas but has become embodied in many states that its analysis too needs to follow the general outlines I have sketched. It has a coherent set of *doctrines*, modified variously by leaders such as Stalin, Mao, Hoxha, and Ceauşescu; it has a mythic dimension in the analysis of historical events in accordance with the principles of the dialectic (so that then the history of the Russian Revolution or the German Democratic Republic gets fitted into a more general salvation-history of the human race). Its *rituals* combine with those of nationalism but have their own symbolisms, such as the widespread use of the color red, the adoption of festivals such as May Day and the anniversary of the October Revolution, the adulation of the Party leader, etc. The *emotions* it encourages are those of patriotism, internationalism, and revolutionary commitment; its *ethics* those of solidarity; its *institutions* those of the Party; and its *artistic* style is that of socialist realism, which glorifies the ideals of the Party, state, and country, with more than a hint of that pietism which can characterize religious painting. Its music is heroic and rousing. State Marxism, then, has a distinctly religious-type function, and moves men by theory, symbols, rituals, and Party energy. Like many religions it may not ultimately prove to be successful, for the people may not be inwardly and deeply moved by the embodied values of Marxism as an ideology: indeed the collapse of the Soviet system shows the hollowness of Marxism in a number of Eastern European countries, and in the Soviet Union. It was always faced with the struggle against local patriotisms, against religions, against the humanist desire for freedom of inquiry, and so on.

Some other secular worldviews are less clearly like traditional religions insofar as they tend not to wield the symbols of power: for instance, scientific humanism, which is influential in one form or another among many intellectuals in the West, and which in rather inarticulate form expresses something of the worldview of ordinary folk in secularized circumstances. It holds to human and democratic values, and it stresses science as the source of knowledge. It repudiates the doctrines of religion, especially of Jewish and Christian theism. It sees human individuals as of ultimate value. But it does not, as I have said, embody itself in a rich way as a religious-type system. Its rituals are slight, beyond those which reinforce other aspects of modernity. Perhaps the modern passion for games and sports is one sign of a kind of persistence of interest in activities pursued according to ritual rules. Its myths are not extensive, beyond a feel for the clash between science and religion during the modern period from Galileo Galilei (1564–1642) onward. Its *doctrines* can be complex, especially in the formulations of contemporary humanistic (analytical and linguistic) philosophy. Its profoundest *experiences* are maybe those of culture, such as music and the arts. Its *ethics* are generally speaking those of utilitarianism, which sees morality as maximizing happiness and minimizing suffering. Its *institutions* are found in secular education. Its *material* symbols are perhaps the skyscraper and the stadium. But it is hard to disentangle its manifestations from many other aspects of modern living.

Though to a greater or lesser extent our seven-dimensional model may apply to secular worldviews, it is not really appropriate to try to call them religions, or even "quasi-religions" (which by implication demotes them below the status of "real" religions). The adherents of Marxism and humanism wish to be demarcated strictly from those who espouse religions—they conceive of themselves, on the whole, as antireligious. However, we have seen enough of the seven-dimensional character of the secular worldviews (especially nationalism and state Marxism) to emphasize that the various systems of ideas and practices, whether religious or not, are competitors and mutual blenders, and can thus be said to play in the same league. They all help to express the various ways in which human beings conceive of themselves, and act in the world.

Roots, Formation, and Reformation

We are here concerned with the history of the worldviews of the world. It has been conventional to look at the founders and first scriptures as being the points of origin of the faiths: as though Judaism had sprung in all its complexity from the mouth of Moses; as if Hinduism were all there in the Vedas; and as if Christianity had been fully sketched out, so to speak, in the mind of Christ. While it remains most important to evaluate founders and early scriptures, we also need to be sensitive to the ways in which religious traditions evolve and form. It does not take long to reflect that some vital features of Hinduism, for instance, are absent from the early Vedic writings, even from the great texts known as the Upanishads: for instance, the whole complex of temple religion, the cult of images, pilgrimages, and so on. It may be that materials for the construction of the Trinity doctrine or the Eastern Orthodox liturgy are to be found in the New Testament, but formally speaking that doctrine and that liturgy are not there. In short, religions may be rooted in their early texts, but they do not form and develop simply on a scriptural basis. There may indeed be a later development—such as the Reformation in Christianity—that demands a return to absolute origins and seeks to base everything on scripture; but even here modern elements, undreamed of by Jesus' disciples or by Paul, are blended into the new and reformed patterns of religion.

We may be the more aware of this because of the way in which contemporary traditions, whether East or West or North or South, reflect attempts to deal with the revolutionary changes which have overcome the world—the rise of science, the emergence of nationalisms, Western-style imperialism and colonialism, the interplay of cultures. These events have led necessarily to changes in worldviews. To some extent nearly all of the religions of the world, except in the remotest spots, have undergone Western and modern influences. And so, even if the modern Western-educated Hindu, for instance, may draw upon ancient motifs and old philosophies, and quote texts of three thousand years ago, she will cast her exposition of the faith in forms which owe much to the seminal period of nineteenth- and twentieth-century thought and struggle. She will be influenced by Vivekananda (1862–1902) and Radhakrishnan (1888–1975), not to mention Mahatma Gandhi (1869–1948) (see Chapter 16).

Because of the evolving and changing character of the traditions and subtraditions of the world, I shall not oversimplify by treating religions as if there were a neat origin for each. Of course, there are some, such as Islam or Mormonism, where the founding Prophet and his period are of immense, even overwhelming, importance. But generally we may distinguish between the period or periods of *roots* and those of *formation*. Thus early classical Christianity of course had its roots in the New Testament and the theology of Paul. But it is not until the fourth century C.E. that its formation is (roughly speaking) completed, with the formulation of crucial doctrines, such as that of the Trinity, the full elaboration of the communion or liturgy, the creation of a complex priestly hierarchy, the beginnings of mysticism and the monastic impulse, the new ethos of being both a good Christian and a good citizen, the emergence of Eastern and Western forms based on linguistic and political differences.

Judaism had a similar period of formation, which culminated in the period of the Diaspora or dispersion of the people after the destruction of the Temple in 70 C.E. The classical features of rabbinic scholarship, synagogue worship, conception of the oral Torah, the study of the Temple rituals as a substitute for conducting them, dispersal of the community, belief in an afterlife, and so forth, had their antecedents before this period; but it was really not until the emergence of Christianity and the perceived need to regroup after the disaster of 70 C.E. and persecutions in the Empire that Judaism finally pulled together in a form recognizable still to us today. Then there was a second great period of formation, that of modern Judaism in its disjunct modes, as Orthodox, Reform, and Conservative (with other variations too), during the nineteenth century after the thrill and trauma of emancipation.

Of course, religions reflect on their own history, and it is natural to project supposed origins back onto roots. The oral Torah is ascribed to the time of Moses; the doctrines and rites of classical Christianity are seen in the New Testament. By contrast, modern scholarship tends to tug at these projections and cause them to disintegrate, and this is a potent source of tension between piety and scholarship. Insofar as this book is a modern history, it has to be somewhat skeptical of some pious beliefs; but in thinking of a tradition as having a "root" period and a period of classical formation, as well as other times of major reformation, we may seek to avoid unnecessary conflicts.

In some degree traditions have to change in order to stay the same. This is paradoxical; but if you stay frozen in the customs and interpretations of a given period, then changed circumstances will make you look old-fashioned, when that was not your original intention. Riding in buggies, like the Amish of Pennsylvania, means something quite different in an age before there are cars from what it means when there are actually automobiles to reject. So it is natural enough that, although some aspects of a tradition may indeed be traditional (like the mitres worn by Catholic bishops), not all of them can be ancient, for the tradition will have had to adapt in some degree in order to continue to be intelligible and meaningful.

There is also some variation in the time of the "watershed" which has altered the face of religious history. For the West it was the period of the Reformation and its scientific and artistic aftermath. For Judaism it was the period of emancipation, namely the first part of the nineteenth century. For the Hindu and Buddhist traditions it was the nineteenth century, with European penetration into the relevant cultures of Asia. For African religions it was likewise the nineteenth century, but a bit later. For the Native American religions of North and South America, it was essentially earlier, with the vast shock, especially, of the Spanish and Portuguese conquests in the sixteenth and seventeenth centuries. Basically, the countries of the world (and I have not here listed all regions or religions) came to be deeply affected by the expansion of Europe, and the subsequent spread of various political and scientific ideas, jointly with the spread of missionary Christianity. Obviously there had been other shocks and watersheds: the Muslim conquest of much of India had, of course, affected Islam before the British Raj. Islamic forces also transformed parts of Africa before the European "scramble for Africa." The Mongol conquests of Genghis Khan and his successors had been a shock, from China to Europe. But nothing ultimately has matched the effects of European conquest, for it introduced a whole variety of challenges across the world and spread ideas as heady as democracy, liberation, modernity, and the need for higher education in the Western mode. It was impossible that religious and other worldviews could be unaffected. It is out of the turbulences born of these conquests and of the two great wars of the twentieth century that the contemporary world has been created.

Part I

	GENERAL	TRADITIONAL, AMERICAN, AFRICAN, SHAMANISTIC, ETC	HINDUISM AND JAINISM	BUDDHISM	CONFUCIANISM
before 3000 BCE	Sumerian urban settlements in Mesopotamia (4500) Cultivation established along Nile (4000) Unification of Upper and Lower Egypt (c.3100)	Lascaux Caves, France (c.15,000) Volp Caves, Ariège, France (12,000–11,000) Çatal Hüyük, Turkey (c.6000–c.5500) Saharan rock painting (6000–1000) Lapita culture of Oceania (c.3500) Indus Valley civilization (3000–1600)	Vedas heard by *rishis*, carried orally (8000–6000) Harappan civilization (3500–1500) Viṣṇu incarnates as Vyasa, who writes down Vedas (c3102)		
3000 BCE	"Royal" graves at Ur (2500) Pyramids at Giza (c.2560) Sumerians overrun by Sargon (2330)	Stonehenge, England, built from c.2800) *Epic of Gilgamesh* compiled (2212–2004)			
2000 BCE	Minoan civilization in Crete (c.2000) Sumerian civilization collapses (2000) Hittites arrive in Anatolia (1850) Shang dynasty, China (1766–1122) Mycenean civilization (1600–1200) Hittite empire collapses (1200) Zhou dynasty, China (1122–256)	Adoption of Linear B in Mycenean culture (1400) Akhenaton (r.1378–62) introduces monotheism to Egypt	Aryan invasion of north India (2000–900) Series of Tirthankaras Early Vedas written down (1500)		
1000 BCE	Egypt reunited under Libya (950) Nubians conquer Egypt (750) Assyrian control Egypt (from 664) Cyrus I (r.560–530) founds Achaemenid empire Persians conquer Egypt (525)	*Iliad* and *Odyssey* attributed to Homer (750–700)	Vyasa systematizes the *Upanishads* (c.1000–500) Brahmanas written down (c.900–700) Parsvanatha, 23rd Tirthankara Mahāvīra (Vardhamāna; c.599–527) last of the 24 Tirthankaras	Gautama Siddhartha (c.563–483)	Confucius (c.551–479)
500 BCE	Athens leading Greek city-state under Pericles (c.495–429)	Nok settlements in central Nigeria (5th–3rd centuries) Parthenon rebuilt (447–438) Zapotecs (300BCE–300CE) Moche culture in Peru (200BCE–600CE) Hopewell Indians in Ohio and Illinois (100BCE–500CE)	*Rāmāyana* (400BCE–200CE) *Mahābhārata* (400BCE–400CE) Patanjali systematizes Yoga Sūtras (by 200BCE)	King Aśoka begins dissemination of Buddhism from India (c.258) Development of Theravāda Buddhism begins (to 200CE) Pali canon written down (c.80)	Mengzi (c.371–c.289) refines theory and introduced mystical element Hsün-tzu (c.298–c.230) stressed importance of tradition and ritua Qin dynasty (221–206) educational system based on Confucian class (205)
0 CE	Interregnum (Wang Mang) 8–23 Claudius (r.42–54) Eastern Han dynasty, China (25–220)		Split of the Jain community into Digambaras ("Sky-Clad") and Svetambaras ("White-Clad") (79)	Buddhism transmitted to China and thence to East Asia (c.50)	
100 CE	Trajan (r.98–117) expands Roman Empire	Kingdom of Axum in Ethiopia (100–1000) Berber (Mandingo) tribes begin to dominate Sudan (c.150)		Development of Mahāyāna Buddhism (2nd century)	
200 CE	Three Kingdoms Period, China (220–280) Western Jin dynasty, China (266–317) Diocletian (r.284–305)	Nascas in Peru (c.200–c.500) Mayans (200–850)		Nāgārjuna expounds concept of voidness (c.200)	
300 CE	Constantine I (r.306–337) Eastern Jin dynasty, China (318–420)		Tantras written down (c.300)		
400 CE	Sack of Rome by Goths (410) Sack of Rome by Vandals (455) End of Western Roman Empire (476)	Towns in sub-Saharan Africa at Jenne-jeno (c.400)			
500 CE	Justinian I (r.527–565), Byzantine emperor Sui dynasty, China (581–618)		Sankara reorganizes Vedānta (c.500–800)	Zhii (538–597) develops Tiantai sect	Japan imports Confucianism to u tribes (500–600)
600 CE	Tang dynasty, China (618–907)	Tiahuanaco culture in Bolivia (600–1000) Mixtecs (c.600 to present)	Bhakti movement flourishes (600–1800)	Peak of Chinese Buddhism (618–907) Buddhism introduced to Tibet (640)	T'ai Tsung (r.626–649) orders buil of Confucian temple in each pr fecture (630)
700 CE	Battle of Talas river (751) sets boundary of China & Abbasid caliphate	Kingdom of Ghana (8–11th centuries)	Muslim invasions of India begin (711)	Songstan declares Buddhism national religion of Tibet First Buddhist monastery in Tibet (749)	
800 CE	Charlemagne (r.768–814)		*Purana of the Lord* written down (c.800–900)		
900 CE	Five Dynasties and Ten Kingdoms Period, China (907–960) Song dynasty, China (960–1279)	Toltec in Mesoamerica (900–1100) Thule in Alaska (900–1300)			Sung dynasty (960–1280) revive ritualistic Confucianism, espec under Chao Heng (r.997–1022
1000 CE	Norman conquest of England (1066)	Chimu culture in Peru (1000–1470)	Jains influential in Gujarat	Milarepa (1079–1153)	Chang Tsai (1020–77) writes *Ch meng*, which becomes basis o Neo-Confucianism
1100 CE	Florence a free republic (1115) Jin dynasty, China (1122–1234)	Ife in southern Nigeria (1100–1450) Aztec (c.1170–1521		Eisai (1141–1215) brings back Rinzi school of Zen	"Five Classics" collated (1130–12
1200 CE	Yuan dynasty, China (1279–1368)	Incas (1200–1532)		Dogen (1200–53) Nichiren (1222–82) Qan Buddhism to Japan as Zen	
1300 CE	100 Years' War (1337–1453) Black Death in Europe (1350) Ming dynasty (1368–1644)				
1400 CE	Columbus lands at San Salvador (1492)	Owo in eastern Nigeria (1400) Songhay empire in west Africa (15–16th centuries)		Buddhism declines in southern India (15th century)	

SHINTO AND DAOISM	JUDAISM	CHRISTIANITY	ISLAM	ZOROASTRIANISM
Shinto begins in pre-history as local nature- and ancestor-based tradition				
				Early elements in Indo-Iranian tribes
Origins of Daoism in shamanistic religion prevalent during Shang dynasty (1766–1122)	Abraham, first patriarch (?1900–1700), leads Hebrews from Mesopotamia to Canaan Moses leads the Israelites out of Egypt (12th century) Joshua invades Canaan (c.1274) first mention of Israelites (1200)			
Shinto name adopted Laozi (c.600–500) Concept of Yin and Yang developed in 6th century Daode Jing compiled Zhuangzi (c.389–286)	David, King of Israel (?1010–970) First Temple built (950) Nebuchadnezzar II (c.630–562) takes Jerusalem (597) First Temple destroyed (586) Second Temple built (515)			Zoroaster (c.628–c.551 or earlier) Cyrus II, the Great (c.585–529) makes Zoroastrianism state religion of Achaemenid dynasty in Persia
Chang Ling (c.34–c.156) founds organized religion Daoism of the Celestial Master founded by Zhang Dao Ling Daoist rebellion (184)	Torah established (430) Alexander destroys Achaemenid empire and Palestine becomes part of Ptolemies' kingdom Palestine under Seleucid rule (198) revolt of Maccabees (165) Hillel the Elder (c100bce–10ce)			Oral tradition obliterated under Alexander the Great Parthians under Mithradates I (r.171–138) make Z'm state religion Becomes official religion of Sassanid dynasty and state religion of Iranian Empire (131)
	Rabbinic tradition (1st–4th c) Jerusalem falls to Romans (70) Jewish canon fixed (c.90) Jewish revolt (132–135) after Hadrian founds Roman colony in Jerusalem	Jesus (0–27/33) Letters of Paul (c.50–60) Gospels written down (c.73–83)		Mithraism introduced into Roman empire (c.60)
	Rabbi Judah (c.135–220) codifies traditional law in Mishnah (c.200)	New Testament used at Rome (200) persecution of Christians in Roman Empire by Decius (r.249–251) New Testament used by Origen (250)		Mani (c.217–c.277) Ardashir (r.224–241) founds Sassanian empire with state religion
	Palestinian Talmud adds the Gemara to the Mishnah (c.375)	Constantine declares toleration of Christianity (313) in Roman Empire Council of Nicaea (325)		
T'ao Hung-ching (451–536) edited work of Daoist writers and producing compendia, Chen Kao and Teng-chen	Intellectual leadership passes to descendants of Babylonian exiles (4–5th centuries)	Council of Carthage (450) Council of Chalcedon (451) St Benedict (c.480–542)		
			Muhammad (c.570–632)	Avesta compiled from earlier texts
		Synod of Whitby (664)	Hegira from Mecca (622) Written text of Qur'an established (650) Sunni-Shi'ite split (c.682)	
	"Golden age" (8–13th centuries)		Muslim invasion of Spain (711) Islam at cultural peak under Abbasid caliphs (750–1258)	
	Saadia ben Joseph (882–942)	Centralization of papal power (800–1100)	Abbasid capital is moved to Samarra (836)	
Most of canon, Tay-tzang, written during Song dynasty (960–1279)		Cluny monastery founded (910)	al-Hallaj killed (922) Text of the Qur'an is finalized (935)	Emigration of Parsis to India during 10th century
	Judah ha-Levi (c.1075–1141)	Great Schism (1054) Crusades (1095–1272)	Muslims desecrate Holy Sepulchre, Jerusalem (1009) al-Ghazali (1058–1111)	
	Moses Maimonides (1135–1204)	St Francis (1182–1226)	Saladin recaptures Jerusalem from Crusaders (1171)	
Ch'ang-ch'un (1148–1227), Daoist monk, travels to Genghis Khan (1219)		Inquisition begins in Europe (1233)	Sultanate of Delhi founded (1206) Mongols sack Baghdad (1258) Mamlukes capture Acre (1291)	
	As Christianity becomes dominant, Jews are increasingly segregated	Proliferation of monastic orders		
Daoist canon is printed in its totality Onin War (1467–78) in Japan	Jews expelled from Spain (1492)	Spanish Inquisition established (1478)	The Ottoman Turks take Constantinople (1453)	

CHAPTER 1

Earliest Religion

The Problem of Origins

It is most likely that the first humans came from Africa. Once that continent, together with Europe, was covered with forests. As it thinned out, and the trees were interspersed with grasslands and swamps, so its game became most plentiful; and in this favorable milieu there emerged hominids who became progressively closer to modern humans. There was *Homo habilis*, the tool-user, and *Homo erectus*, the upright type, walking like us on two feet; and then, perhaps 250,000 years ago, *Homo sapiens*, the knowledgeable one. Later we discover Neanderthal humans, of the same or parallel stock, with thick limbs and heavy bones. Their name, drawn from a valley in West Germany where the first remains were found, is sometimes associated with beetle-browed thugs, in the modern caricature; but they were bright people who, like other modern humans, gained their advantage through social cooperation, of which language is a key factor. And there is evidence—from red ocher used in staining bones, which has survived in some Neanderthal burial grounds—that they may have believed in some kind of survival after death. Even before this, in the deep reaches of the prehistory of *Homo erectus*, there are telltale signs of beliefs about the afterlife.

Naturally, as we push back our knowledge further into human prehistory, we speculate about the lives of these our predecessors; and so ultimately we speculate about the origin of human religion. But thoughts are hard to infer from bones, or feelings from chiseled flint, or wishes from fragments of animal skeletons partly touched by fire. Some scholars have wished to infer beginnings from the religions of hunter-gatherers today, like the Australian aboriginals or the Tierra del Fuegans. Yet such a move is risky, for every people extant today has lived over many, many centuries and has necessarily

Opposite Part of the paintings from the caves at Lascaux, southern France, dating from c.15,000 B.C.E. In addition to buffalo, the symbolic and realistic paintings depict horses and deer as well as what are thought to be shamanistic symbols.

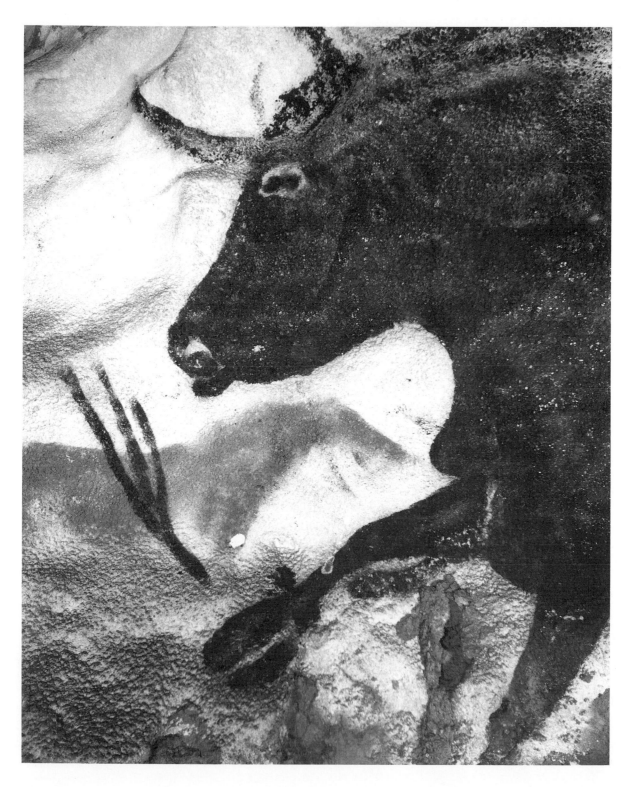

undergone change. Once, too, such a move was likely to be part of a racist ideology that treated hunter–gatherers as essentially "primitive." There used to be a vogue for thinking that there was something called "primitive religion," and such a view implied that the contemporary aboriginal was at some kind of arrested stage of evolutionary development. This was a convenient ideology for those who came into their regions to deprive them of their lands.

Of course, we can learn something from hunting and gathering societies. If early humans lived in the same way, we can obviously hear the echoes reverberating into prehistory. Basically, however, early humans were just like us in basic character and intelligence: where we differ is only in cultural style, and in the greater organizational complexity of the world today. Further, modern hunting and gathering societies are in some respects diverse, so we should bear in mind that the pursuit of something called "prehistoric religion" in the singular is no doubt misconceived. There must have been very divergent patterns of ritual and belief through the varied cultures that were developing after 30,000 B.C.E. in Siberia, Australia, Africa, Europe, and, a little later, the Americas. In some of them, ranging in time and space from southwest France and northern Spain to the Urals and southern Africa, and from 20,000 B.C.E. to relatively modern times, there is a brilliant display of rock and cave paintings. Amber bison, black and white cows, horses, crows, and eagles vibrate off ancient surfaces, and so sometimes do the figures and arrows of the hunters. These pictures are mysterious to interpret, and sometimes they are buried in deep recesses of the ground, like painted wombs in mother earth.

One of the cave paintings of wild animals, in this instance a horse, from the extensive Volp Caves at Ariège in the French Pyrenees, dating from about 12,000 B.C.E.

Old wicker lamps dimly lit these wondrous exhibitions of the mimic skill of ancient humans. But we possess no records and can only guess at the ideas and rituals that underpinned these great artistic endeavors.

So it is that questions about the origin of religion are guesswork. It is no longer fashionable to create such theories at all, but in late Victorian times it was all the rage. Thus Sir James Frazer (1854–1941), famous author of *The Golden Bough*, saw a certain evolution of ideas, beginning with the use of magic, which used sacred formulae to try to coerce and bend the operations of nature, and leading on to religion proper, which sought to propitiate unseen forces rather than compel them. In his view these ways of dealing with the world were replaced in modern times by science, which is the most rational and effective way of harnessing the powers of Nature. Edward Tylor (1832–1917), an early anthropologist, saw primitive religion as consisting entirely in a belief in, and practice toward, unseen spirits: such religion he dubbed "animism" (a term which most scholars nowadays reject, but which is still used popularly and in censuses to refer to classical or indigenous religions in small-scale societies). Another anthropologist, R. R. Marett (1866–1943) proposed the idea of "preanimism" or "dynamism" as even more basic and early, in which nature is seen as pervaded by nonpersonal forces, to which humans can relate through various rites. Often these powers were referred to by using the Melanesian term *mana*, a kind of sacred power inhering in anything unusual—in a strange rock, a peculiar mountain, an unusual human, a chief, a beautiful woman, a ferocious bear, or whatever. It was theorized that religion first started with belief in *mana*, then progressed to belief in more personal spirits, then moved into polytheism, where the gods are even more fully personalized, and then into monotheism and (this extra option depended on the ideology of the theorist) atheism.

Such evolutionary schemes can be challenged. Wilhelm Schmidt (1868–1954), a Catholic priest and anthropologist, detected widespread belief in a High God existing "behind" or "above" the multitude of gods, spirits, and powers of many small-scale societies. He thought that this indicated a substratum of theism—belief in a personal God—which derived from a primordial revelation and was subsequently overlain by belief in many spirits and gods. He wished to save the traditional idea of a revelation at the beginning of human history, reflecting the account in *Genesis* of God's dealings with the first humans.

There may be some truth in such ideas, but hardly anyone now would subscribe to any of these accounts; nor would we adhere in any literal fashion to the account given by Sigmund Freud (1856–1939) in his *Totem and Taboo*, which made too much of totemism, that is, the belief in and practice of a sacramental relationship with some animal species or other entities on the part of diverse segments of a group. It is not anywhere near universal in small-scale religion as was once thought. Freud's account was based on his psychoanalytic theory, drawing on the dynamics of the nuclear family in modern Vienna.

The Patterns of Prehistoric Life

If we are to speculate about motifs in prehistoric religion, we need to think about the differing ingredients in the life of the hunters and gatherers of Stone Age times and earlier. Such ingredients are: the need for group activity in hunting the larger and more agile animals, and in fishing; the discovery and use of fire, going back to the epoch of *Homo erectus*; the importance of stories in the cultural life of any group, with (moreover) quite a lot of leisure to while away in the periods between big chases; reflection on the inner life—the role of dreams and visions, and possibly early forms of meditation and yoga; the wondrous sky and its rhythmic relations to earthly cycles, e.g. the menstrual; the feeling that humans, who can talk and hunt so well, are a special breed apart from the animals with whom they live; the vital role of ritual and etiquette in interpersonal relations; the magic of representation and the success in painting and sculpture, where this occurred; the great human dependence on nature, and on the animals and plants in particular; the mysteries of birth and fecundity, both in human beings and elsewhere; the reality of sickness and concern with maintaining health; the universal character of death; storms and violence in the sky and environment; and the beginning powers of music.

The Dimensions of Prehistoric Religion

From reflection on the above motifs, and from archaeological discoveries, it is possible to hazard some guesses about early humans' religious life. Let us begin with the *ritual* dimension. The first thing to consider is that religious ritual and ceremonious behavior continuous with the kind of stylized actions and words which we use in treating each other as persons. Human language is replete with performance utterances, to use a word coined by the philosopher John Austin (1911–60): that is, by uses of language which perform or do things—such as cursing, promising, thanking, pleading, or saluting—rather than simply inform. Every fully fledged performative utterance has, in the broad sense of the term, a ritual aspect. It is thus when people say to each other "Good morning." Such a greeting is a little ceremony in which two persons acknowledge each other's presence at the beginning of a new day, and take up their relationship from previous days.

Early humans, making use of language and bodily gestures, were aware of how the coherence of each group was vital to its survival, since the human ability to deal with more powerful animals, for instance the bear, stems from cooperative effort. It is not unreasonable for humans to think of ceremonious behavior, so effective in keeping groups together and shaping their strategies of hunting and gathering, as effective beyond the group, in relationship to animals, natural forces and broadly the whole universe which lies unfolded before the human being. It is thus likely that rituals addressed to these entities formed part of the fabric of the life of early humans from the time of *Homo erectus* onward, but especially among the Neanderthal strain and its relation, our own direct ancestor *Homo sapiens sapiens*.

An animal from the Vogelherd cave in Württemberg, southwest Germany, possibly indicating some form of magic associated with hunting, and dating from c.26,000 B.C.E. Other carved ivory figurines from the cave depict mammoths, horses and bison.

We have evidence of this in remains of burials and in the cult of skulls and in the mysterious paintings in caves such as Lascaux in France and Altamira in Spain. In a cave in eastern Switzerland are various smaller caves, including one with bear skulls in niches in the wall. It seems hard to explain this except in terms of some rituals directed toward the bear. Some have seen the paintings as having to do with hunting magic; and the brilliant depictions of bison and other beasts, both here and on bone decorations, suggest a connection with these people's source of food. And yet the inaccessibility of some of the caves, the discovery of beautifully made lamps, and the painting or engraving of various abstract signs, suggest something more.

Since it was not until much later in human cultural history that a purely nonpersonal idea of causation came to be established, it is quite probable that in speculating about their surroundings early humans thought of changes as brought about by personal causation of some kind. Early humans could not have known much about the past, save what was handed on in each group. Their cosmology had to proceed outward from their own experience. It was thus reasonable for them to try to establish potent relations with various forces through ritual means.

Some of the burial rites suggest too a kind of ceremonial to somehow ensure safe passage to the next world: the bones of the Neanderthal dead, smeared with red ocher, may have reflected some ritual reintroduction of blood to symbolize revived flesh. There are hints of concern with human survival in the bones of *Homo erectus* at Zhougoutian outside Beijing. At Le Moustier in the Dordogne in France, a young Neanderthal man was buried, on his right side, with his head pillowed with flat stones; and by his body were charred animal bones and a hand axe. All this suggests some belief in life beyond death. But at any rate, here is evidence of ritual behavior concerned with reverence for and no doubt love for the dead.

Another factor about which we may speculate is symbolic thinking. A symbol is something which stands for or represents something else. Among instances of symbolic thinking the most obvious and powerful is when one member of a species or kind is taken to stand for the whole. It suggests a shadowy but real collective being or spirit lying behind and pervading all members of that species or kind. The one bison stands for the collective; and by extension the image stands for what it is an image of. Such an attitude is echoed in modern times by what philosophers call "realism" as opposed to "nominalism" (nominalism being the idea that all that holds together individuals of the same kind is the common name; realism being the theory, stemming from Plato, that the individuals share the same "real" universal).

Such a conception allows people to think of their symbolic rituals as causing them to participate in the power inherent in the being toward whom their sacrifice or communion is directed. It may even be that the marvelous art of Altamira, Lascaux, and elsewhere was itself seen as a kind of offering to the sacred forces inherent in the herds of bison and in the other animal species represented.

There is a famous picture (left) in the cave at Les Trois Frères in France of a figure dressed, so it seems, in animal skins and antlers, who may represent a great sorcerer and possibly a shaman—that is, a religious specialist who has great powers derived from ecstatic experiences in which he or she has contact with sacred forces. At Star Carr in England, by a lake, there has been found an antlered skull with holes drilled in it suggesting it was worn as a headdress. This is reminiscent of some forms of headdress worn by modern shamans in Siberia and elsewhere. To this question of shamanism in prehistory I shall return. Let us turn briefly to speculate about the worldviews held by ancient humans.

The hunter and gatherer has a lot of leisure, especially when resources are plentiful. It is not like the long drudgery of much of agricultural life, still less like the clocked-in hours of industrial humanity. With the invention of techniques for preserving and kindling fire, humans had a natural focus of warmth and sociability; it is thus inevitable that the telling of stories should occupy much of their time. Narrative has a powerful grip on the human imagination, and is a way of imagining the past, bringing to the forefront of imagination some selected contents of the past and explaining how things too in nature came to be. Again, it is reasonable to think that prehistoric thinking proceeded from the microcosm to the macrocosm, from the human situation to the delineation of the whole environment. Together with the notions to which we have already alluded—that personal causation works in nature as well as in human events, and that similar things are animated by the same substance—the preference for the story form will have generated a whole range of myths: how sky and earth perform together; the way the moon waxes and wanes, and how woman reflects this moonishness; how the spirit of the bison or the fox was created; how humans can turn into animals, and one species into another; the cause of the mountains over there; how the sea was formed; how a spirit below the sea brings the sole to multiply. The concern with fertility, and the analogy of the earth as a woman, no doubt grew in importance as settled agriculture developed in such regions as north China, Thailand, the Indus Valley, Mesopotamia, and Egypt.

The celebrated dancing sorcerer (if that is what it is) or shaman figure that dominates a profusely engraved "sanctuary" within Les Trois Frères Cave at Ariège in the south of France.

The story form, laced with symbols, could be well integrated into the rituals whereby early humans celebrated and coaxed the powers about them. Underlying the stories, however, there could be speculative answers to questions of creation, and such thinking is reflected in some of humankind's early texts. There could be a Spirit who produced an egg, out of which other beings could come. Or it might be that the thought that the First Being needed an Other led to the evolution of the world. Or maybe the world was produced by a number of beings (but whence did they come, and whence came the one Spirit?—there were unanswerable riddles about ultimate origins). Or perhaps there was always something there, like water, which needed stirring up before the world could condense or form.

There were questions about pain and suffering, no doubt, too. How did these come to us? Where did Death come from? Perhaps it was because of some primeval alienation between humans and the Spirit. It was easy to think that humans had become distanced from their world, for they (we) were thinking about other beings, and *they* showed no signs of fully comprehending the future and the nature of death. But we humans faced that terror.

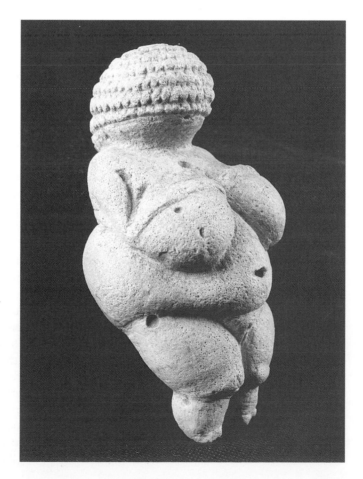

The so-called Venus of Willendorf, from Willendorf in Austria. Carved in limestone it dates from c.30,000–25,000 B.C.E. Several smililar sculptures have been found which suggests that a female fertility goddess played a vital role in Paleolithic life.

39

Was death, moreover, the end? This was another question which might rate as an expression of early humankind's *doctrinal* dimension. We have seen hints in practice of belief in some future life. There were rituals to send off the dead, and maybe for revering the ancestors. If so, early humans must have also been wondering about the other life: was it hunting in some other realm, or perchance rebirth in animal or human or spiritual form? And there may have been the beginnings of epistemology: reflection about how to know things, with a reliance on vivid dreams and bright visions induced in quests and dancing, and in self-control. It may have been that the visions of the shaman prepared the way for the later refined forms of yoga. Men and women noticed their own powers, and saw that with language they could think in ways that were locked away even from the divine and clever bear.

The hints of shamanism may tell us something of the *experience* of prehistoric humans. The special people who had strong visions and dreams would also have affinity with some animal kind or other—with the bison, the serpent, the crow, the tiger: and they would have special knowledge of which direction to go in the hunt. And they would, too, have knowledge of the cure of souls and bodies. In their visionary episodes they would skim into the lower world where dead people went, and would rescue the sick person by undergoing his pain and travail. This would rest on the perception that mind and body are intertwined, and rock and spirit, and tree and god. The spirit could be seen as the essence of the human or animal: but so also could bones. The shaman's fate was to have his bones de-fleshed (like the dead) and to be put back together again.

Because of the important representation of female figures in Paleolithic art and religion it is tempting to speculate about its meaning. In Siberia, near Lake Baikal, no less than twenty figurines of a goddess have been found. From a similar time representations of goddesses have been found in Liguria in Italy, Austria and France. Sometimes these emphasize strongly the breasts, and often the legs are fused together, tapering downward (suggesting that they were stuck upright in the ground). It looks therefore as if a female fertility goddess played a vital role in paleolithic life. Of course, climatic and other conditions may have been selective in what has been preserved for us, and also stone (rather than, say, straw) persists and so may give us a skew in our knowledge of such early societies. Even so, it is reasonable to think that the goddess was important, and judging by comparison with hunting and gathering societies still (just) extant, it is probable that a vital role was played by the concept and symbolization of fertility in these early cultures. We may note, too, that the use of caves, not just for shelter but also for rituals related to the brilliant paintings, suggests that these caves were viewed as wombs. The feminine figure could have played various roles: as creator of the world, as mistress of the animals (on whom humans were mysteriously dependent), as helper in the location and killing of animals. It would not have gone unnoticed that the woman mimicked the moon in her cycles, and in general more clearly reflected the rhythms of the seasons and of life and death. In many ways the female was more strangely potent than the male. We also may note that humans no doubt were aware of their own difference from the other animals, part of which lay in their mental furniture. So, as we might now say, the powers of human beings were lodged partly in their religion.

We may also accept that the feeling of awe before powerful sacred forces— the numinous experience—will have occurred, as described in the classic account of Rudolf Otto (1869–1937). This may have contributed to self-consciousness, human beings feeling themselves apart from the world around them, as they stalked zebra through the savannah, or plotted together the next hunt of the elephant, or lazily stirred by the side of the fire at the memory of how they had fared as a group. They would have felt terror and awe at the fierce thunderstorms round Mount Kilimanjaro or among the foothills of the Alps; and they would have cowered at great hailstorms. They would have felt, though, their own solidarity, and the beginnings too of affinity with other human groups. And so in self-consciousness they would have wondered at the Creation. Some of them, no doubt, would have conceived of the world as a whole, and made a myth about its origin: partly because having knowledge of origins is a way of having power over that whose origins you know.

About the *ethical* dimension we know scarcely anything. There are signs of human violence in some remains, and no doubt warfare between groups was not infrequent, though the landscapes were vast and human populations probably rather scattered and small. With the beginning of large settlements and cities, which depended on food surpluses and agriculture, wider systems of *social* political organization were required. Already such developments are starting to merge into history, in Egypt, Mesopotamia, the Indus Valley, northern China, and so on.

We can only guess at the nature of the ethical and institutional dimensions of the many societies which constituted early humankind; but we can see that some of the influential early theories were both right and wrong. They were wrong in imposing too orderly an evolutionary sequence upon events, and certainly wrong to think that so-called "primitives" were in basic constitution less developed than ourselves. They were wrong to neglect ways in which so-called "primitive" thought can be found among moderns. They often generalized too much, finding (for instance) totemism everywhere. There were probably here and there the various elements held at one time or another to be characteristic of early religion, but blended together into untidy wholes. Thus, it is plausible to think that prehistoric men and women in some groups combined the ideas of monotheism, belief in a High God, with ideas of many more or less personalized powers (polytheism and animism) and with notions of sacred forces with less personal attributes (dynamism). They may have believed in a life after death, and they may have begun to practice self-control in the transition to a form of primeval yoga.

What is sure is that in their engraved bones and cave paintings some very ancient groups produced some of the most splendid kinds of art. The *material* dimension of their life, insofar as it has come down to us, is spectacular. This is

One of a series of prehistoric "plastered skulls" found at Jericho. The real skull was covered with plaster, which was painted to represent the features of the dead person. Many of the skulls had cowrie shells set within the eye sockets. The skulls may have indicated belief in the continued life of the individual, but they are evidence that heads were severed from bodies before burial.

41

a further good indication that it is unwise to think that they were essentially different from ourselves.

They also pioneered the marks and signs which are the precursors of writing. Some of these may record the phases of the moon, and others may have had some use in rituals addressed to ancestors. It would not be surprising if they had a relatively sophisticated knowledge of the behavior of the heavenly bodies. If there is an evolution in human beings it is a cumulative cultural advance, as the tentacles of language spread ever wider, and a gallery of concepts is built up with which to understand and manipulate our world.

There are other aspects of prehistory which I shall not touch on here—for instance, the Megalithic culture of northern Europe and the enigmatic remains of the Indus Valley culture. I shall leave this urban and stone-building prehistory to be developed on a regional basis. This in itself will help to dispel the illusion of a single prehistory, to which it is easy to fall prey in the absence of much information to guide us in judging the spiritual life of early human beings.

We need also to remember that we are talking about very long periods—perhaps over two million years ago for the emergence of *Homo erectus*. Caves could be occupied and worked on for one or two millennia. In the evolutionary "rise" to *Homo habilis*, and through *Homo erectus* to *Homo sapiens*, and to ourselves, we have already the proliferation of cultures which characterizes later human civilizations. But there can be no doubt that human beings through all these developments had an awareness of that unseen world which they have in diverse ways striven to understand. They perceived their affinity with the animals, and yet were conscious of their distance from them too. If they could feel communion with the bear or stag whose flesh they ate, they also knew how to manipulate life somewhat, and to begin their long march toward the technological mastery of nature, including—in aspiration, at least—their own nature. But similar hatreds and loves, and a like sense of identity in a group, no doubt animated them as us; and we have become much more dangerous than they.

South Asia

India's Diversity

India is often referred to as a subcontinent. Its area is fairly well defined, because it resulted from the drift of part of the old continent of Gondwanaland northward, where it slowly but inexorably collided with the southern part of what was then Asia. By consequence the great ranges of the Himalayas rose up, to form a barrier, scarcely penetrable except to the northwest, which was to enable Indian culture to emerge largely on its own. In thinking about the area we should not be mesmerized by modern political divisions. India, in the historical sense of the term, comprises everything now included in the modern states of Pakistan, India, Bangladesh, Nepal, Bhutan, and Sri Lanka. Also in this treatment it is convenient to include Tibet, for it was permeated by Buddhist culture from India.

The top and the bottom of the region—Tibet and Sri Lanka—are predominantly Buddhist. Much of the subcontinent at one time was also Buddhist; but over time, Hinduism has become the main force in Indian life, together with Islam. During the most glorious period of Indian civilization, roughly speaking during the first thousand or more years of the Common Era, there was a mixed Hindu-Buddhist Indic culture, with other smaller religious elements, such as Jainism and, in the far southwest, Christianity, woven into its fabric. This Indic civilization had within it fabulous diversity, made richer by the fact that only at certain periods was India under the domination of a single major empire, and that it was typically fragmented into various states and tribal enclaves. Its diversity partly came from its languages, ranging from the Indo-European tongues of north India (such as Gujerati, Hindi, and Bengali) to the Dravidian languages (Tamil, Telugu, Kannada, Malayalam) of the south. As these languages developed they became vehicles of differing kinds of piety. And beyond the variety of tongues there

Map 1 South Asia.

were differences of climate and terrain, from the mountains and green forests of Sri Lanka and Kerala to the dry deserts of Rajasthan, and from the steamy heat of the monsoons to the colder drizzles and snows of the Himalayan foothills.

Even to talk of a single something called Hinduism can be misleading, because of the great variety of customs, forms of worship, gods, myths, philosophies, types of ritual, movements, and styles of art and music contained loosely within the bounds of the religion. Some scholars would like to jettison the term. Yet in modern times there is a much better defined sense than before of what is in the Hindu tradition. It is as if many Hinduisms had merged into one. It is now much more like the trunk of a single mighty tree; but its past is a tangle of most divergent roots.

Regarding the formation of religious ideas and practices there are periods into which the history of the subcontinent can be divided: the early period of the Indus Valley civilization and its aftermath lasted from about 3000 B.C.E. down to the culture reflected in the early sacred text known as the *Rig Veda*, around 1000 B.C.E.

The next phase, which may be called preclassical, covers the formative and creative recasting and development of worldviews, including the composition of the texts known as Upanishads (800–400 B.C.E.), the teachings of Mahāvīra the Jain and Gautama the Buddha (c.500 B.C.E.), and the spread of the religions of the Brahmins, the Buddhists, the Jains, and others. Roughly speaking, this is the period of a thousand years from 1000 B.C.E. to near the turn of the millennium (say 100 C.E.).

Then we come to the great classical period of Indic civilization, lasting until about 1000 C.E., which contains the development of most of the patterns of classical Hindu religiosity and the great flourishing and then the decline (in India) of Mahāyāna Buddhism and indeed of Buddhism generally. It was a Hindu-Buddhist civilization, with many other motifs woven into it.

Then, from 1000 onward till the dawn of the modern period (roughly 1750), we have the formation of a Hindu and Muslim civilization in the Indian subcontinent: it saw the reign of the great Mughals from Delhi, the consolidation of traditional Hinduism, the final withering of Buddhism in India, the rise of the Sikhs, and the attempt by Akbar (ruled 1562–1605) to establish a pluralistic ideology accepting the truth of India's many faiths. This "medieval" period ended with the increased incursions of Europeans, above all the British, who came to dominate the area.

The modern era, after 1750, saw the coming of missionaries, the founding of the British Rāj, and the development of railroads, higher education, modern industry, and a relatively centralized administration. It saw the renewal of Hinduism, Islam, and other religions, and the struggle for independence which ended with the partition of India into the states of India and Pakistan, and the subsequent splitting of Pakistan into (West) Pakistan and Bangladesh. It saw the resurgence of Buddhism in Sri Lanka and the forcible modernization of Tibet by China. Above all it brought a new understanding of Hinduism.

During the various periods there arose empires which sometimes unified most of India and sometimes did not—such as the Indus Valley civilization which lasted till about 1500 B.C.E. in the early period; the Mauryan empire toward the end of the preclassical period, especially under the pro-Buddhist emperor Aśoka (reigned 269–232 B.C.E.); the Gupta and Kushan empires during the classical period; and the Mughal empire during premodern times. Especially during the Gupta period, the spread of Sanskrit culture across the whole of India helped unify the subcontinent. Even among the Buddhists, who rejected the authority of the Brahmins—the primary bearers of Sanskrit culture—the language was used in the composition of sacred texts and commentaries. In Sri Lanka the texts were written in Pali, and in Tibet they were translated into Tibetan. This linguistic difference came to be a chief marker of the difference between Indic, Tibetan, and Sinhala cultures.

In all sorts of ways, however, it is not possible to look on South Asia—the Indian subcontinent—as a single unit. Regional empires and monarchies and other groupings were quite as normal as the unitary state.

The Ingredients of Indian Religion

If the history of India and its neighbors up to the modern period has been complex, so have the many doctrines, rituals, experiences, and customs which characterize Indian thinking. To a Western reader in particular, and to many South Asians who have been alienated from their heritage by modern education, they are in part unfamiliar. So it is useful to list some of the main ingredients of Hindu and Buddhist, and other, practices and beliefs during the classical period. This will make it useful to survey these ingredients in advance of our discussion of the history: it will constitute the grammar of Indian religions, just as the gods, holy figures, temples, and statues constitute their vocabulary.

If we were miraculously transported back to the sacred cities along the holy river Ganges during the classical age of Indian culture, we would be struck, doubtless, by the splendor of temples, the variety of human types, from proud Brahmins, with their partly shaved heads, to recluses with matted hair; from women in white, widowed and immersed in piety, to monks and nuns belonging to the Jain and Buddhist orders. Let us analyze the ingredients by reference to our seven dimensions.

Of the *ritual* and *practical* dimension, three important elements are: yoga, or self-training; worship or *pūjā*; and sacrifice. The first is ancient in the tradition, and forms the basis of an inward search, and a training of the mind, taking somewhat differing forms according to the school or movement to which one belongs. Much later, during the premodern period, it was supplemented by that kind of gymnastics which in this century became popular in the West and which often is identified with yoga, although it is in fact far less significant than the spiritual side. The inward search is to discover the true Self or to attain liberation. It has been one of the main preoccupations of the Indian spiritual tradition.

Worship was in classical India directed toward a large number of gods, of whom Viṣṇu and Śiva emerged as dominant. Buddhist *pūjā* was at first little more than the ceremonial remembrance of a great teacher, but later, as the faith flowered into the high Mahāyāna or Great Vehicle, it embodied fervent devotion or *bhakti* toward the Buddha conceived as a kind of God.

Sacrifices of all sorts existed in earliest India. Later, under the influence of Buddhism and Jainism—both religions with a deep respect for animal life— sacrifice came to be largely confined to plant life and melted butter (ghee) and the like. The people in charge of sacrificial ritual were the Brahmins, who were the highest of the four classes which supplied the skeleton of the later

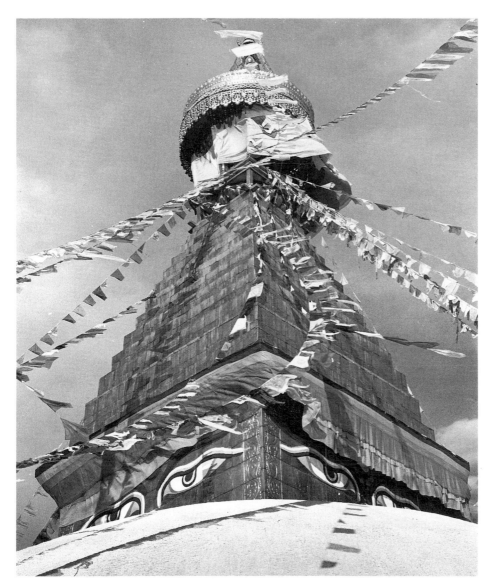

Bodnath *stūpa* in Nepal, in characteristic Nepalese style, shows the eyes of the Buddha gazing out from the stone, signifying his presence.

fully elaborated caste system. From their expertise in sacrifices, the Brahmins came to dominate the rituals of temples, which did not exist in the earliest recorded Brahmin religion, i.e. in the Vedas. Temples were houses of the gods, in which their daily life was enacted, and where festivals abounded.

Pilgrimage is a less important element in the ritual dimension, but it was integral to Jainism, Buddhism, and the religion of the Brahmins, taking the faithful to sacred rivers, to holy temples, to the birthplaces of the great, or to the Bodhi Tree under which the Buddha attained his great illumination. There were treks, too, to the great mountains, to the source of the Ganges, and to the places where holy persons would meditate and practice austerities.

The doctrinal dimension: for many centuries it was customary to represent the Buddha by his absence. Here the seat and the Bodhi Tree signify his presence. This no doubt helped to convey the doctrine that after his decease it is incorrect to say either that the Buddha exists, or that he does not exist. Similarly, it is incorrect to state that he both does and does not, or that he neither does nor does not.

The Sanskrit for austerity is *tapas*, literally "heat," for austere self-mortification creates heat in the body, and with it power. *Tapas* as a practice came to form a vital part of some religious movements, notably Jainism. It is the polar opposite of Tantra, which uses magical and esoteric means of gaining liberation, sometimes through the performance of that which is normally forbidden—extramarital sex, meat-eating, and so forth—to express the ways in which the Tantric adept is above ordinary social laws.

So we can list as important practices, among the welter of Hindu, Buddhist, and other rituals, yoga, worship, sacrifice, pilgrimage, austerity, and Tantra. On the *experiential* and *emotional* level, the spirit behind such ritual practices varied. Poets and others expressed the feelings of devotional religion or *bhakti*, associated both with temple worship and with the fervor of pilgrimages and festivals. Behind yoga there was the spirit of meditation or *dhyāna*, with the hope of inner peace, bliss, insight, and what was called liberation. For the ascetic there was the sense of independence and power, so that the adept frightened the gods, according to myth: for the ascetic would gain more power than they.

The *mythic* dimension of Indian classical culture revolves around a thousand themes. There are millions of gods (traditionally 330 million), but the famous trio of Brahmā, Viṣṇu, and Śiva emerged as the most important. Also vital are their female consorts, conceived as personal manifestations of *śakti* or creative force. In Indian civilization the female is thought of as active, the male as more passive. Sometimes, in the religious movement known as Śaktism (from *śakti*), the Supreme Being is conceived as female (Durgā or Kālī). Another theme is that of the *avatār* or human incarnation of God, mostly of Viṣṇu, a theme which plays some part in the vast epics known as the *Mahābhārata* and the *Rāmāyana*. It is thought that the *avatār* figure comes down to restore proper teachings and behavior at the end of a period of decline, a theme which is found in the three major traditions of the Brahmins, Buddhism, and Jainism. In the case of the Buddha, he is not precisely a "descent" of God, but rather a superhuman person who enters the world to restore the Truth to humans.

God is described in numerous narratives as taking many forms, and gradually there grew up the view that the different gods were so many manifestations of the One Divine Being. This idea, first expressed in the *Rig Veda*, was among other things a way of synthesizing the myriad myths.

In all the major systems of belief in Indian culture there prevailed a sense of decline. The present age, or Kaliyuga, latest of the vast and endless cycles of time which go to make up the fabric of human existence, is one of increasing chaos and evil; and in the Buddhist cosmology there is a sense that religion declines the farther you get in time from the age of the Buddha himself.

These ideas were to be interpreted in terms of the *doctrinal* and *philosophical* themes which characterize classical Indian culture. Pervasive is the theme of rebirth or reincarnation. Each individual living being traverses virtually endless time through many, many lives. The person's destiny is shaped by the deeds she has performed both before and in this life. This "law of *karma*" (action) binds living beings to the round of existence or *saṃsāra*. The desire to leave *saṃsāra*, or at least to overcome its cloying effects, calls for great efforts, which eventually may yield liberation of *mokṣa* when the individual leaves *saṃsāra*, or at least overcomes it by superior insight into the nature of the world. Such liberation is often called *nirvāṇa* in the Buddhist tradition, and is referred to as *kevala* or isolation in the Jain tradition.

God as creator is also implicated in the processes of *saṃsāra*: but he or she (or It) is often conceived also as lying beyond all description. This unspeakable Brahman lies beyond even God as she appears as a person. So in some philosophies there is that higher side of the Divine which has a correspondence with the inner side of the soul, the eternal *ātman* or Self which lies within every individual. By turning inward and practicing meditation a person may come to experience that inner eternal Self and at the same time achieve unity with the one Divine Being, Brahman. Many forms of belief in India have not accepted the idea of God, and so in them liberation is not communion with God but a lonely disappearance from the round of rebirth.

So there are various dominant doctrines of Indian culture during the classical age: the idea of reincarnation or rebirth, the possibility of ultimate liberation, the idea of a personal God who creates and recreates the cosmos, and for that matter destroys and redestroys it, the notion of an indescribable Brahman lying so to speak beyond the personal God, and the idea of an eternal "something" within the migrating individual. The various philosophies of the Indian tradition are expressed through variations of the ways in which these ideas are put together.

As to the *ethical* dimension; the Jain and Buddhist traditions place much, though differently slanted, emphasis on the practice of non-injury to living beings. This had its effects on the Brahmins, who came to be vegetarian. It was part of an ethos of asceticism which permeated parts of classical Indian civilization. Such "giving up" often took the form of leaving the world to become a monk or nun; but an alternative was the system of four stages of life, which was often held up as the ideal of the pious householder. According to this scheme a man in his early life is a celibate student, learning at the feet of a Brahmin teacher; then he becomes a householder; thirdly, he begins to withdraw from family and public life; and finally he becomes a wandering, homeless recluse, or *sannyāsin*. This allows an ethic of compromise between living in the world and outside society. Increasingly, a person's moral and ritual duties came to be determined by his particular circumstances in life.

The pervasive belief in rebirth had its effects of course on the whole interpretation of moral life. It was typically thought in popular Indian traditions that one could improve one's position in life in the future—even to the extent of going to heaven—by accumulating merit. Such merit could be attained by charitable giving (to holy persons and for pious purposes, such as contributing to the beautification of temples); but above all by good deeds.

In brief, from an ethical angle, there are a number of fairly constant elements in Indian civilization: a tendency to respect the sanctity of all forms of life; a sense of the special character of the ascetic life; an emphasis on merit-making; and the idea that much, in the practical life, depends on a person's place in life.

All this was integrated into the *social* and *institutional* dimension of classical Indian culture, of which the caste system came to be the most striking and pervasive feature. Its skeletal structure was formed during the early days of the Indo-European invasion of India, around 1500 B.C.E. The invaders, like others of the Indo-European linguistic group, were divided into three classes: the priests (Brahmins), the warriors (Kṣatriyas), and the artisans and others who served the top two classes (Vaiśyas). As they conquered the indigenous peoples a fourth class of servants and underlings (Śūdras) was added. Eventually, even further down, a fifth class of "untouchables" came to be recognized. Because Hindu ritual was much concerned with purity, the four- or five-class system itself came to be reinforced by the practical application of the concepts of purity and impurity: the upper-class Indian could be contaminated by contact with those lower down, and especially by the untouchables. This last class came to include a whole variety of tribal peoples who were absorbed into the fabric of the wider society. The first four classes are known as the *varṇas* or (literally) "colors." This name probably derives from racial distinctionns, the Indo-European invaders being originally of light complexion. This *varṇa* system was later reinforced and rendered much more complicated by subgroups known as *jātis* ("births" or "lineages").

The vast mosaic known as the caste system represents a great hierarchy into which Indian society is formed; but the Buddhists and others never recognized the system, especially because, when men and women entered the monastic order, the Sangha, they were supposed to leave social distinctions behind them. This Order was, with its Jain counterpart, an important ingredient in Indian society in the classical period. Monasticism had some place in Hinduism also, as in the organization founded by the great reformer Śankara (late eighth century C.E.).

Various other kinds of holy persons were socially important too: the priestly Brahmins, who were highest in the Indian hierarchy; Buddhist and other monks, dressed in brown, gray, or pink robes symbolizing rags; naked holy men and Jain monks whose nudity indicated the absolute rejection of worldly things; gurus or teachers of various kinds; *sannyāsins* or recluses of varying persuasions. Also, animals, above all the cow, could be a source of holy power and cleansing efficacy. Yet if many of these figures signified renunciation, erotic acceptance of the world was also part of the fabric of India. The family was a vital center of life and of domestic cults.

On the *material* and *artistic* level, the classical period saw the emergence of that typical feature of the Indian scene, the temple. (In the early period Brahmin religion used only temporary sacred grounds and structures.) As well as the shrines to the many gods, there were Buddhist and Jain temples. There were also sacred rivers, sources of purity and founts of merit; and holy mountains, homes of gods and sacred teachers. In the temples were images and icons—images of the Buddha, of Mahāvīra and other great figures of the Jain tradition, or of Hindu gods—and in houses too there were little shrines. Some of the carvings of the classical period are sublime, whether of the Buddha preaching, teaching, and—in reclining pose—at the time of his decease, or of Śiva dancing. In Sri Lanka the golden ages of the cities of Anuradhapura and Polonnaruwa were particularly productive of great art. In Tibet there evolved wonderful paintings which depicted the great celestial beings of the Buddhist tradition. Many images were small and cheap, for the villager or the poor person; and some were made of clay and used temporarily for some great feast in the calendar of Indian religious life. They were "throwaway" sculptures. Perhaps most powerful of all symbols was a stone pillar with a rounded top, the *lingam*. In its simplicity and suggestive strength, it expressed and promised the fertile power of God.

We can schematize all this as follows:

DIMENSION	ITEMS
Ritual, practical	yoga, worship, sacrifice, pilgrimage, austerity, and tantra
Experiential, emotional	*bhakti*, *dhyāna*, sense of empowerment
Narrative, mythic	myriad gods, the religious hero who restores the Truth, times in decline
Doctrinal, philosophical	rebirth, possibility of liberation, God as personal, Brahman as nonpersonal, an eternal soul or freedom-seeking nature within each person
Ethical, legal	reverence for animals, ascetic ethos, merit-making, ethics of one's station in life
Social, institutional	caste system, Sangha system, varieties of sacred or holy persons, sacred cow, family
Material, artistic	holy places (mountains and rivers), temples, images, *lingam*

These ingredients, combined in differing ways, represent many of the varieties of Indian religion. It was out of this classical material that the idea of Hinduism as such was composed in the modern, colonial period.

The Early Period

In 1924 there began a series of discoveries which has revealed a remarkable ancient culture, known as the Indus Valley civilization. It has deepened our understanding of Indian religions, for it contains suggestive features foreshadowing later developments. This great and uniform civilization stretched from Gujarat in the south to the eastern Punjab in the north and from Sind in the west to the edges of Uttar Pradesh in the east. Its chief cities were at Mohenjo-Daro on the Indus and Harappa on the Ravi (or near it, for the riverbed has changed its course). They were rather uniformly laid out in grids of streets, with villas, houses, and small lanes occupying the various blocks; and with a higher acropolis containing what seems to be a temple complex and a granary, dominated by a large tank or bath. The whole of each city was laced with an excellent sewage system. Outside the main walls of each city (walls designed no doubt to resist flooding) were areas for the farmers and others who supplied services to the merchants and priests who, we may infer, controlled the civilization.

There are affinities to, and there were some contacts with, the Elamite and Sumerian cultures to the west; and from Elam the Indus Valley civilization may have derived its writing system. Alas, this is as yet not deciphered, or at least not in any agreed manner. The most likely thing is that the language was an early version of Dravidian, and that Dravidian-speakers, probably pastoralists, had moved southward from Central Asia to the Indus region, where on the basis of villages an urban and mercantile civilization had gradually been built up. The Indus Valley civilization lasted essentially from about 2500 to 1500 B.C.E. It ended rather suddenly, possibly through some great natural disaster combined with conquest by outsiders. Many scholars have held that it was destroyed by the invading Aryans, speaking an Indo-European language, who came into India around 1500 B.C.E.

From the Indus Valley culture we have a wonderful harvest of seals, inscribed clearly with the ideographic script whose decipherment remains controversial. The seals lead us into a world of goddesses, snakes, tigers, water buffaloes, a unicorn, sacred peepul trees, bulls, and elephants. There is a cross-legged figure sometimes thought to be a forerunner of the Hindu god Śiva. There are also small figures of gods and goddesses, sometimes dancing. But what these seals and figurines mean is obscure. There are some mixed animal-human figures, and a wonderful figure of a priest or shaman, perhaps, with a neat beard and a band around his head. Many of these figures are suggestive: they link up with later Dravidian conceptions of a fertility goddess with both benign and fierce attributes. There are suggestions that perhaps sacrifice on the high places in the cities was important. There may have been great processions of the goddess and other deities, and maybe pilgrimages to the mountains from where the inhabitants of the civilization had come. It may be, too, that the figure often identified with Śiva was a fertility god. Perhaps there were myths of the divine couple. The buffalo also seems to have been the consort of the Great Goddess.

We have too little evidence to be sure of anything about the worldview or political structure of this great civilization. We can imagine that once the streets and alleyways of the cities teemed with life, each household no doubt engaging in domestic rites before sculptured figures, and that religious life also involved ablutions and perchance, among the more prosperous, the sacrifice of animals. Out in the surrounding countryside there were wide fields of grain, part of which was tribute to the city granaries. All this is likely to have been organized through religious allegiance rather than force, for we do not, strange to say, find evidence of weapons. On great feast days doubtless the high platforms with their bathing tanks would witness a priesthood skilled in sacrificial ritual, parading before the Goddess from whom the earth and the prosperities of the farming life emanated. From her too, no doubt, came domestic animals, and she gave protection against the tigers and snakes who lurked on the earth and on the fringes of the villages.

The Preclassical Period

As time passed, the Dravidians moved south, and in due course made other powerful contributions to Indian religion and culture. The great Indus Valley civilization died. In its place there slowly arose a new mixture, composed of Aryan and various other ingredients. The invaders came from the northwest and settled in the region between the Indus, flowing southwest, and the Ganges, going east. Eventually the heartland of this Aryan culture, of which Sanskrit was the sacred and later the literary language, spread down along the Ganges, where, by the sixth century B.C.E., various mercantile cities arose, such as Benares (or Varanasi) and Pataliputra (modern Patna). Republics and kingdoms were in the making; and in this exciting climate of economic advancement and political consolidation there was a creative welter of religious movements. The Aryan priests, the Brahmins, brought with them a repertory of sacred lore and hymns composed over a period of five hundred years. The ascetic traditions were revitalized in the same period by Mahāvīra and the Buddha; and other worldviews, typically propounded by wandering teachers, contended both with these and with Brahmin orthodoxy. Among these doctrines were materialism, rejecting all ideas of transcendent powers and goals, and skepticism, rejecting all positions.

The Brahmins and Ascetics

Brahmin culture turned out to be the most persistent element in all Indian civilization. The Brahmins, who thought of themselves as animated by the power *brahman*, enjoyed tremendous prestige, and shared preeminence with other sacred persons, collectively known as *śramaṇas* or wandering ascetics. *Śramaṇas* thought of themselves as beyond ordinary social obligations: they had left the world behind. But the Brahmins were necessarily tied to the concerns of ordinary life in a rather direct way: many of them made their living by their expertise in ritual. This ritual, increasingly complicated, could bring for the person who paid for the sacrifice (in cows and other expensive commodities) prosperity and the assurance of worldly success. And the tradition of ritual which they brought with them was derived from the timeless past, from the beginning of the cosmos, from everlasting authority, from the age of the seers (*ṛṣis*) who heard the ultimate sacred sounds and brought them forth by a creative process to compose the collections of hymns known as the Three

Vedas (to which a fourth, magical collection, the *Atharva Veda*, was added in the preclassical period, after 600 B.C.E.). Masters of the holy hymns and the sacred language, skilled in the intricacies and long performance of sacrificial rites, whether for kings and princes or for ordinary householders, the Brahmins were one of the main forces in the creation of Indian religion. So much so indeed that even today what we mean by "Hinduism" is largely their creation: Hindu orthodoxy is defined as the acceptance of the authoritative value of the revelation (*śruti*) which includes the Vedas.

The Early Vedic Period

In voyaging to the ancient past we are necessarily indebted mainly to texts. We have seen how hard it is to interpret the rich archaeological findings of the Indus Valley civilization without the benefit of a deciphering of the script. In the case of the early Aryans in India, who infiltrated there in waves during the period from about 1500 B.C.E. onward, having originated (probably) in the region of southern Russia, we have texts which reflect their existence during the period of settlement. There are of course problems, for the texts, orally transmitted over many centuries, were gathered together subsequently for ritual purposes, and not in order to give us an historical record of early times. We have to make inferences from the hymns, and it is not always easy to do so. Imagine trying to reconstruct American or British life from a Catholic hymnbook. We could pick up hints, but often the references to Zion and Calvary would baffle us: were they contemporary references or not?

The hymns look back to a time when the plains of north India were being subdued by those who called themselves Aryans or "Noble People." Arrogant with horses and chariots, aggressive and confident, these folk were able to conquer the native Dasyus, who were dark people, living in citadels, venerating *lingams*, tied in no doubt to a plethora of rituals to increase their crops and pastoral wealth. They were many of them descendants of those who had once occupied the Indus Valley cities. Much of their lore, and elements of their speech, were to enter the habits of the Aryans.

Some of the many gods of the *Rig Veda* reflect the period of aggrandisement. There is the fierce, towering Indra, great warrior leader, incarnated in the thunderstorm and the lightning bolt. Over a quarter of the hymns in the collection are addressed to him. His main function is in leading the warriors, the Kṣatriya class, the second of the fourfold list of Vedic society. He fights not only human enemies but also the wicked demons, the antigods, who support them. But Indra is also in some sense creator, for in primordial times he prises apart heaven and earth, and frees from a cave the cows imprisoned there, the main symbol of Aryan wealth. In his creative act he discovers the Sun, which brings light and vision to all creatures.

Indra in his violence and creativity—and his exuberance, too, in drinking great drafts of the sacred and hallucinogenic drink of *soma*—gives us a feel for the rough warriors who led the migrations out of the plains southward and westward in search of new pasturelands and places to conquer. It hints at the ethos of the distant past, before the Aryans became settled in and integrated into the landscape of north India, with its warm and rich forests, its cleared areas for cultivation, its expanding villages, and its cities in the making.

Indra's parting of the sky and earth sets the scene for conflicts between good and evil gods. The latter are often associated with human enemies; but even the divine Vedic world itself is riven with conflict, so that there are strains between a number of the mighty forces which are envisioned in the hymns. Even sacrifice, the central ritual, is seen as a mode of conflict: sacrificial rituals often incorporated contests of riddles and chariot races, as if inner combats were continuous with the ongoing struggle between the mobile horsemen of the Aryans and the settled culture of the despoiled indigenous inhabitants.

If Indra is rambunctious and somewhat chaotic, the god Varuṇa is, much of the time, the model of order. He presides over the orderliness of the cosmos, summed up as *ṛta*, an idea somewhat like the later Hindu concept of *dharma* as the sacred pattern underlying both cosmic and social life. He displaces Dyaus, the old sky-god, who is the Vedic counterpart of the Greek Zeus and the Roman Jupiter. Varuṇa rules the heavens and especially the night sky, where the stars are perceived as his innumerable eyes. And so it is that he knows everything. He is the moral judge, since he knows all the secrets of human beings, and with his companion, Mitra, he presides over promises and contracts. He upholds truth. But he has dark and earthly associations too, and these become more vital in the later mythology of the classical period.

An important ritual god, personifying the phenomenon that is central to sacrifice, is Agni, god of fire. As the representative of earthly fire, Agni is the lowest of a threesome that also includes atmospheric fire or lightning (Indra) and the heavenly fire of the Sun (Surya). Alternatively, he may be identified with the fiery aspect of all three. By a splendid act of imagination, the people who defined their society through the Vedic hymns saw the continuity between the three levels of heaven, atmosphere, and earth. A night storm, especially in the warm climate of India, is numinous and terrifying; and earthly fire can be unpredictable and elusive, even hard to maintain, especially when people are on the move.

Fire is important sacrificially in many cultures. The reason is that it performs at least two functions: it consumes or (in the case of roasting) transforms that which is offered; and it wafts the offering upward to the gods, conceived as being "up there." When a person offers that which is valuable, it is important that he gives it away: it has to leave his zone and enter the god's zone. This is done by the smoke of offerings burnt as sacrifice. Already something is done, of course, in the case of animals; their life is destroyed, for instance by the letting of blood.

In the sacrifice, fire is created by one stick twirling in a hole in another. The sexual symbolism to be seen in this—phallus in vagina—makes the making of fire like the stimulating of fertility in animals and human beings. So in many ways fire is crucial to cosmic processes. But above all it is the consumer and conveyor of what is sacrificed, whether it be the horses of the ancient kingly sacrifices or the ghee and milk poured out daily in domestic rituals. It is the necessary adjunct of the long and complex Brahmin-controlled sacrifices that are made to bring prosperity. So it is not surprising that Agni the fire god appears so frequently in the Vedic hymns.

Another important god in Vedic times, who later faded in actual religious practice, was Soma, god of the intoxicating juice that was prepared and consumed as part of the ritual. It stimulated visions, and it may be that some of the imagery of the hymns comes from the contents of such visions.

By comparison the gods who are so great later—Viṣṇu and Śiva—are minor. But Viṣṇu's importance is foreshadowed in the myth in which he takes three steps across the universe, establishing its bounds; the last step is indeed beyond human ken, for it paces out heaven. Those who reenact this creative act in ritual attain to a mastery of the cosmos. His companion Rudra, the Red One, is uncontrolled fire, dwelling in mountains and jungles, wild. Later he is to become the great god Śiva.

The hymns indicate that within the framework of a given celebration many of the gods—the more important ones described above, as well as others—were regarded each as supreme. It is like a painting: the perspective and the frame isolate the painting from all others. So in a given hymn the given god is God. This has been called henotheism, from the Greek, meaning "one-God-at-a-time-ism." It is one way of combining a kind of theism or belief in God with the existence of different cults of gods; and it has been a characteristic of Indian religion since these early times.

The hymns of the *Rig Veda* and the other collections do not yield enough information for us to trace anything of the history of the early period, or indeed of anything before about 600 B.C.E. Their importance is less as historical data than as sacred texts, which came to be part of the later canonical revelation. Though there are continuities between the hymns and the more developed classical religion of India, there were also considerable transformations, which were brought about by the Brahmins' seeking control over, and being influenced by, non-Aryan forces in Indian society which brought with them new religious ideas. It was a series of blends between the Vedic tradition and such forces which prepared the way for the creation of classical Hinduism.

A New Beginning

In the hundred years or so around 500 B.C.E., a whole new constellation of ideas and practices was moved into the forefront of attention. Most important was the idea of *saṃsāra*, the cycle of rebirth, which led to a quest for liberation through the practice of austerity or mediatation or both. To be saved we need to wipe out the effects of our past actions or *karma*. It is this set of beliefs that formed the background of many of the new religious movements; and it was a set of ideas that penetrated into Brahmin religion as a new and great secret, in the teachings of the speculative texts known as the Upanishads.

This was a period when, evidently, many *śramaṇas* or wandering recluses and teachers had gained vast respect and were often coupled in the texts with Brahmins. The region of India in which this ferment was occurring was to the east of the area around modern Delhi which constituted the Aryan heartland. It was a region centered on the Ganges, and on such newly great cities as Benares and Patna. Because of economic and political forces, including the emergence of strong kingdoms and republics, a new mercantile class was becoming more important, and this was attracted to some of the new movements that were springing up, especially that of the Buddha.

Buddhism

All dates in early Indian history are the subject of scholarly debate. But it was probably in the sixth century B.C.E. that the Buddha was born and various other major figures flourished. Some scholars date such events later: the Buddha, for instance, in the fourth century. But we shall stay with a more traditional scheme.

The Buddha's story is legendary: onto some historical facts were glued some wondrous stories. This fact means that it is hard for us to get to what may be called the "historical Buddha." But the legendary account of the Buddha's

Part of the 3-mile waterfront at Benares, Uttar Pradesh, northern India, which has sacred stairways to the water for those seeking purification through bathing in the sacred river Ganges. The building visible in the center is the Visvanath temple.

Buddhism some key terms

Bodhisattva Buddha-to-be who puts off his final liberation to work tirelessly for the sake of other living beings. The most famous bodhisattva figure is Avalokiteśvara, who became Guanyin in China and Kannon in Japan.

Buddha An enlightened being who has seen the truth of dharma.

Dhyāna Meditation: usually in eight stages of ascending purity of consciousness.

Nirvāṇa Final liberation when the saint will no longer be reborn.

Prajñā Insight or wisdom concerning the nature of the cosmos.

Pratītyasamutpāda Codependent origination of events, the law which links together all the events of the world in sequences of samsāra.

Saṃsāra The living flux of existence in which individuals are involved in the process of rebirth.

Sangha The order of monks and nuns founded by the Buddha to carry on the teaching of the Dharma.

Śīla Virtue or a precept encouraging a virtue, such as the five precepts summing up Buddhist morality.

Stūpa A mound for containing relics, formalized into the central feature of temples and pagoda.

Śūnyatā Emptiness, the pervading characteristic of all events, in that they are empty of self-subsistence and are relative.

Tantra A ritual text or method in the so-called Vajrayana form of Buddhism (chiefly now in Tibet) for acquiring sacramental power, usually through the instruction of a guru.

life is important, for it is that on which the remembrance and piety of Buddhists through the ages has fastened. Moreover, it has served as a kind of model for analogous lives, such as that of his supposed contemporary Mahāvīra, who founded or refounded the Jain tradition.

Later Buddhists were to have the creed: "I take refuge in the Buddha; I take refuge in the Dharma; I take refuge in the Sangha." We can translate this as "I take refuge in the Enlightened One; I take refuge in the Teaching; I take refuge in the Order" (that is, of monks and nuns). This summary of loyalty pinpoints the three most vital ingredients in the Buddhist tradition: the narrative of the Buddha; the doctrinal or philosophical worldview presented; and the institution that carried on the practical path to liberation, namely the body of dedicated followers of the Buddha. Beyond this simple credo Buddhism was to take many forms, and it is useful here to give a small sketch of that history of divergence.

The History of Buddhism in Brief

First, there is the early period, in which the Buddha lived and the teachings and practice were consolidated. This period can be said to last from about 500 B.C.E. down to the first century C.E., by which time the canon of scriptures was already written down in Pali, in Sri Lanka, and was taking a fixed form in the shape of what is known as Theravāda or the Doctrine of the Elders. This stream of Buddhism still carries on in Sri Lanka and Southeast Asia, though not without admixture from the other great branch, the Mahāyāna or Greater Vehicle. The Mahāyāna, which had roots parallel to those of the Theravāda in early Buddhism, emerged in India in about the third century B.C.E.

Second, from the first century C.E. onward, Buddhism spread into China and eventually into Korea and Japan. Both in Indian Mahāyāna and in the Theravāda, Buddhism achieved high articulation, and we can call this the classical period.

Third, from the seventh century C.E., there developed a form of Buddhism, sometimes called the Vajrayāna (Diamond Vehicle) and sometimes the Mantrayāna (Vehicle of Sacred Utterance), with much emphasis upon magical and sacramental rites, in which spiritual consequences were thought to flow from the recitation of *mantras* or sacred formulae. This was gradually assimilated into the Hindu practices of the era, and was one reason for the ultimate virtual disappearance of Buddhism from subcontinental India. On the other hand it became the dominant form of Buddhism in Nepal and Tibet, where the religion spread during this period. We may call the era from the seventh century C.E. till the eighteenth century the medieval period.

Fourth, there came the modern period, which eventually affected Buddhism not only in South Asia but in the rest of Asia whither it had spread. The impact of colonialism will be discussed in the second part of this book.

All these periods—early, classical, medieval, and modern—apply primarily to Buddhism in South Asia, and differing periodization will be used in regard to East Asia and elsewhere.

In sketching Buddhist roots, I shall deal with its different dimensions as follows. First, the *narrative* dimension, telling the story of the Buddha and the world out of which he came. Second, the *doctrines* he taught: these philosophical ideas are geared to the practical life, but are especially important in the Buddhist tradition, which has a strong emphasis—for reasons which will become clear—upon analysis of the world and of human nature. Third, the ritual or *practical* dimension, so central in the quest for liberation. With this we shall connect the *ethical* dimension. Then we shall look to the inward *experiences* of both the Buddha and his followers. We shall move on to sketch the *social* organization of the religion. Finally we shall look at the *material* dimension of early Buddhism.

The Narrative Dimension

Where indeed should one begin to tell the story of the man who came to be called the Buddha? His life as an individual never really began, for, like us all, he was, in the Buddhist view, a beginningless wayfarer in the round of *saṃsāra*. There are many wondrous and edifying tales told of him in the scriptures about how he was a snake, or a hare, or a king, or whatever, in previous births. These so-called Jataka tales were a great source of instruction in social life and compassion for the peoples who came to follow the Buddha. Immediately before his birth in this world as a human and more-than-human teacher and liberator, the Buddha-to-be, or Bodhisattva, resided for millions of years in a heaven, called Tuṣita, enjoying great happiness like a god. But he had to give this up to help living beings to relieve and ultimately to get rid of their sufferings.

It was possibly in 586 B.C.E. that he was born into this world as Siddhartha Gautama, on the periphery of the new civilization emerging along the river Ganges. He was born into a people known as the Śākyas, and came to be known as Śākyamuni, the sage of the Śākyas. They were under the general suzerainty of the kingdom of Kosala. His father Suddhodana was a ruler, and his mother was Mahāmāyā. It was predicted at his birth that he was destined to become a world ruler, but it was uncertain whether this was to be in a political or a spiritual sense. The birth itself was miraculous, according to legend. His mother dreamed that the Buddha-to-be took the form of a white elephant and entered her womb, and she ceased to have any wish for sex. So though she was not a virgin, having borne other children, it was in a loose sense a virgin birth; and it occurred at the time of the full moon in May at a park called Lumbini.

The young Siddhartha grew up in some luxury, but eventually, after he married and had become father of a son, he was impelled to leave the worldly life, and to take up that of the wandering recluse. He had been struck by the four sights of a very old man, a sick person, a corpse being taken to the burning-ground, and finally a holy beggar. He left his wife and baby and lived a nomadic life of severe austerity and reflection. He studied and practiced for a while with a group of six fellow *śramaṇas*. Eventually, on his own, and at a place now called Bodh-Gaya, under a sacred fig tree or pipal, he attained full insight into the nature of the world and of the way to overcome suffering and tribulation. As Enlightened One, he was henceforth to be called the Buddha.

He returned to Benares, to a deer park outside the city at a place called Sarnath, where he had left his companions, and delivered to them his first Sermon in which he expounded his insight. It was referred to as the Sermon of the Turning of the Wheel, in which he set the wheel of Dharma in motion. They became his first disciples and core of the new order of Sangha. Thereafter, for forty-five years, until he was eighty, he traveled around, teaching and consolidating the organization of the Sangha. He visited the great new cities of the region—Benares, Uruvela, Rajagriha, Vaisali, Sravasti, Kausambi, and his own town Kapilavastu. According to Sri Lankan chronicles, the Buddha made three journeys to the island in his lifetime, one being to the peak of Sumanakata, later called Adam's Peak, where he left a huge footprint which became the focus of the island's most important pilgrimage. He consorted with princes and kings, courtesans and smiths. He preached his saving doctrine of the Way to Liberation.

At last, he died of a digestive complaint. As with other major events in his life there were heavenly and earthly portents—earthquakes and showers of flowers. His decease was one of insight and peace: all compound things are impermanent and sooner or later the death of the physical Gautama Buddha had to take place. He had fought off more than once the wiles of Māra the Tempter, who would have liked the Buddha not to have gained insight, and not to have kept on in the world to deliver his message. He had overcome the forces of death, and now he would be no more reborn. He came to be called the Tathagata, or Thus-Gone, and his final state was mysterious. He would not be reborn, but it was wrong to think of him as either existing or not existing, or both or neither. His followers cremated his body, and his relics were installed under cairns in various places.

The grief of his followers at the passing of the Buddha—he had told them, however, that all compound things are impermanent and that the Teaching would remain: "When I am gone the doctrine I have preached will be your Master. Watch and pray without respite."

This was the life of the most recent in the line of Buddhas. In the Pali Canon, various others are listed, such as the Buddhas Vipassi, Sikhi, Vessabhu, Kakusandha, Konagamana, and Kassapa. It is thought that the Buddha did not found the faith, but restored it.

The Doctrinal Dimension

The Buddha's doctrines belonged to the general pattern of śramanic religion of the time, but he gave that a radical new interpretation. The primary questions turned around the problem of rebirth and how to gain liberation from an unsatisfactory world. Like the contemporary Jain and Ājīvika groups (see pp. 68–72), he was attracted to the practice of austerity; but in the end he found mere austerity too negative. He learned from others the arts of yoga, and evolved a system of meditation; but he thought that meditation without understanding was blind, and understanding without meditation was without fruits. You had to combine the two, and for this a right orientation to philosophical questions was vital.

His central insight was of the impermanence and interdependence of everything. He sought the causes of every event, and especially those which directly concern the human being: so we need to train ourselves in self-awareness to perceive the nature of events taking place inside us and their conditions. But he rejected determinism (as preached by the Ājīvikas, for instance). We are free to reshape our destinies, even though we inherit from previous lives tendencies which, if unchecked, will lead to other existences, each one impregnated with *dukkha* or illfare (usually translated as "suffering"). Indeed, in the popular view of the nature of the universe which Buddhism adapted and reshaped, there are many heavens—though even in these the good life must come to an end—and many purgatories of a horrifying kind; while humans could become ghosts, or worms, or any other kind of living being, in accordance with their deeds.

Because nothing in the universe is permanent, no satisfaction can last for ever; and its disappearance is painful. All life therefore is permeated by suffering. This was the first of the Four Noble Truths which the Buddha enunciated. The second is that the cause of suffering is craving or thirst for existence (Pali: *taṇhā*). The third is that this cause can be eliminated. And the fourth is that the mode of doing this is by treading the Noble Eightfold Path.

This path has eight aspects, and is an expansion of a more fundamental idea, that there are three elements in the Way, namely trust, ethical conduct, and meditation. The first two aspects of the Path concern trust: they are Right Belief and Right Attitude. The next three are to do with ethical conduct: Right Speech, Right Bodily Action, and Right Livelihood (that is, not engaging in an occupation which would necessarily cause the infringement of the Buddhist ethic, such as butchering). The last three, to do with yoga or self-training, are: Right Effort, Right Self-Awareness, and Right Meditation.

The Path was thought of by the Buddha as "Middle," that is, as centered between extremes: between the extremes of self-indulgence and self-mortification, and between the extremes of thinking that the soul is eternal and that it is cut off at death. It is in various other ways a moderate faith.

The Path leads to a condition in this life of complete insight and serenity, such as the Buddha himself achieved at his Enlightenment; on death the saint disappears like a flame going out or a spark disappearing in the darkness. It is not extinction, but it is not continued individual existence either. So the Tathagata was seen as having no further relations with this world. The best way to point to his transcendent condition is by silence.

The best way to go for salvation is by becoming a nun or a monk. Such a life of spiritual community, with periods of solitude, is best for meditation. Lay followers not yet ready for the relative severity of the Sangha might through ethical living and by giving to the order attain a future in some better or heavenly state, and might thereafter come back to earth ready to assume the ocher robe.

The idea of impermanence, the rejection too of a permanent soul in the individual, the concept of universal causation, and the goal of an ineffable ultimate state—*nirvāṇa*—are the bare bones of the Buddha's message. We shall see later how these notions came to be developed. Underpinning the worldview was the thought of rebirth and the pervasive power of *karma*. It was original in its substance and presentation and had a strong appeal in the areas where the Buddha taught.

It rejected the appeal to revelation, and in particular Brahmin claims for the Vedas. The Buddha had directly experienced the truths he taught, and the Brahmins (he argued) relied on mere tradition and authority. They had not seen the gods they called upon. The true Brahmin was not the one born into a priestly class, but the person who followed virtue and self-control.

The Practical Dimension

The most important practice invoked in the Buddha's teachings is that of yoga, in which an individual, seated in some serene spot, tries to control his mind, and is eventually able to climb up through the various stages of *dhyāna* (Pali: *jhāna*). He might begin with some simple object such as a blue flower and learn to see it just as a patch of blue. Then he might discard such a device and ascend through various levels of increasing purity of consciousness. The adept does not by such exercises alone attain to *nirvāṇa* and sainthood; but they form an integral part of the earliest pictures we have of Buddhism. It is above all a faith of meditation and self-training.

The structure of the Sangha prevents, however, too great an individualism, since the Buddha envisaged his followers as living together according to the rule or *vinaya*. At each phase of the moon, they would make a mutual public confession of faults; and at the end of the rainy season there would be a larger and more formal occasion for such confession and mutual forgiveness.

Another important aspect of early life was that like other śramanic groups Buddhist monks and nuns would get their food by begging. It was an exchange: they received food, the lay folk got merit. This giving (*dāna*) was the

Dependence and the Middle Path: Saṃyutta Nikāya

On ignorance depends karma;

On karma depends consciousness;

On consciousness depend name and form;

On name and form depend the six organs of sense;

On the six organs of sense depends contact;

On contact depends sensation;

On sensation depends desire;

On desire depends attachment;

On attachment depends existence;

On existence depends birth;

On birth depend old age and death, sorrow, lamentation, misery, grief, and despair. Thus does this entire aggregation of misery arise.

But on the complete fading out and cessation of ignorance ceases karma;

On the cessation of karma ceases consciousness;

On the cessation of consciousness cease name and form;

On the cessation of name and form cease the six organs of sense;

On the cessation of the six organs of sense ceases contact;

On the cessation of contact ceases sensation;

On the cessation of sensation ceases desire;

On the cessation of desire ceases attachment;

On the cessation of attachment ceases existence;

On the cessation of existence ceases birth;

On the cessation of birth cease old age and death, sorrow, lamentation, misery, grief, and despair. Thus does this entire aggregation of misery cease.

primary lay duty toward the order. Early on, the important sites of the Buddha's life may have been thought worth visiting to gain merit: where he was born, where he gained his Vision, where he preached the first sermon, and where he died; at Lumbini, Bodh-Gaya, Sarnath, and Kusinagara. In the treatment of Gautama's relics, at his death, lay the germs of later devotion and indeed worship (though in a sense the Tathagata was "not there" to worship: only his memory served as a spur to good deeds and self-salvation).

The Ethical Dimension

As a Middle Path, the Way emphasized that intentions count, rather than a literal application of the rules. Our actions should be controlled by the Five Precepts (*pancaśīla* in Sanskrit and in Pali). One should refrain from taking life, from taking what is not given, from wrong sex, from wrong speech, and from drugs (substances which obstruct self-awareness). To these basic rules were added a set for controlling more narrowly the life of the nun or monk: for example, rules about not using a high bed, or money, and following the conditions of the Order. Such morality was to be suffused by certain great virtues, such as compassion. This was one of the Four Divine Dwelling Places in which the good person should reside—friendliness, compassion, sympathy, and equanimity.

The Experiential Dimension

What kind of inner experiences did earliest Buddhism aim toward? We can learn something from the accounts of yogic practice. The supreme point in the ascending scale of purifying consciousness is a kind of tranquil bliss, from which height the adept looks down, when he comes out of trance, at ordinary

Opposite A twelfth-century carving at Polonnaruwa in Sri Lanka, showing on the right the Buddha having attained final *nirvāṇa*.

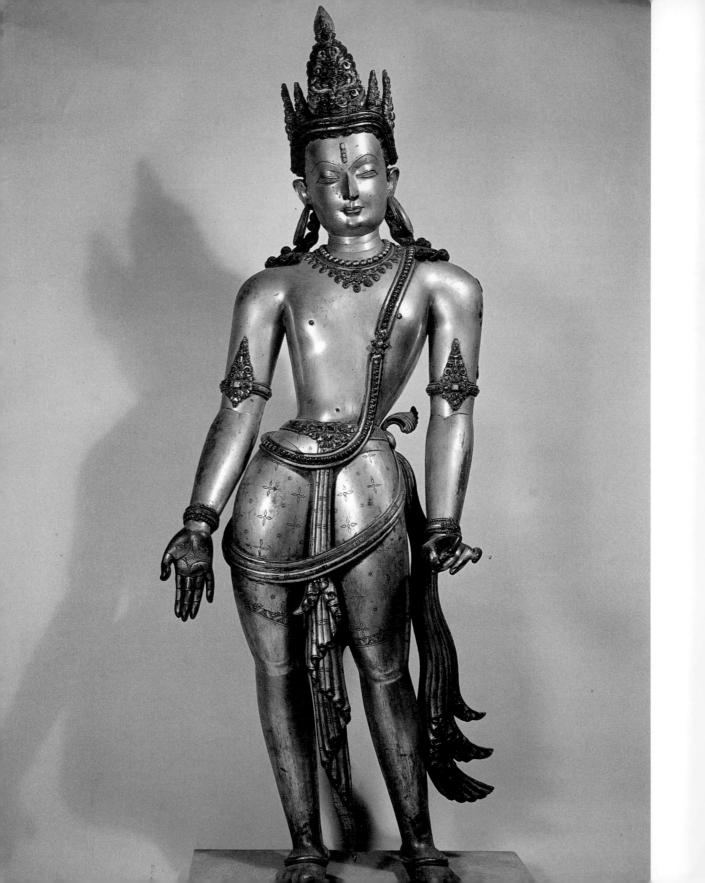

experience as being mundane and yet itself, in tranquility, suffused by a kind of joy and assurance.

Such illuminated consciousness is sometimes referred to as mystical experience; but in the Buddhist case there is no question of seeing it as a union with the Ultimate, such as a personal God. Buddhism does not deny the gods, even the great god Brahmā, creator of the world according to Brahmins (though not according to the Buddha: he is merely the first god to come into existence at the beginning of a new cycle in the universe's existence). But the gods too, however splendid, are impermanent. So the supreme bliss and insight of *nirvāṇa* are beyond all words and all ideas of being united with Anyone.

This seems the central experience of the Buddha and of his saintly followers—that is, those who attained *nirvāṇa*. But such high consciousness is accompanied by an intellectual realization that all things are impermanent. Such a realization could occur in a flash, in a pregnant moment of understanding. We have accounts of such moments in some of the autobiographical poems of the early monks and nuns which were incorporated into the Pali canon. It took time for a more fervent devotional religion aimed at celestial Buddhas to come about. But there is plenty of recognition in the early Canon of the keen appreciation of Nature and the poignancy of life, and such sentiments form a fine counterpoint to the depths and glories of Buddhist meditation.

The Social Dimension

The Sangha was at first perhaps much more loosely brought together than it later became. Many monks and nuns were hermits over much of the year, camping in caves and by river banks in huts, save for the wet season when they would congregate and live in some of the centers given by rich laity in and around the cities and larger villages. Though the Buddha acted as monarch of the Sangha in his lifetime, thus being a spiritual world-conqueror and imperial figure, he made no provision for a successor. He preferred the republican model of some of the peoples now being absorbed into the kingdoms burgeoning along the valley of the Ganges. The new leader would be the Dharma, the teaching. After I am gone, said the Buddha, there will remain the Teaching.

Similarly organized were some of the other śramanic movements, notably those of the Jains and Ājīvikas, led by Mahāvīra Vardhamāna and Makkhali Gosāla respectively. So we can see the Buddhist Sangha alongside its rivals, and surrounded at the periphery by a miscellaneous population of wandering recluses, some shaven, some naked, some with matted hair, some weird and frightening, others gentle. It was also a rival to the hereditary priests or Brahmins. The civilization was mixed, and the Brahmins, recluses, and monks of the various traditions had to live together. Buddhism had lots of rich support, from kings and merchants. It was modernizing and subtle, and gave opportunities for lay people to use their wealth and clean living in ways which promised better things for the future, and possibly heaven.

Opposite A bronze figure from Nepal of the great Bodhisattva Avalokiteśvara, who looks down in compassion. Avalokiteśvara, who remained in this world for the salvation of creatures, is often represented with a pink lotus flower in his left hand.

It was also a period of political change. Some of the tribal republics were being absorbed into the kingdoms which dominated the region. The Sangha offered an alternative life when so many social changes were occurring.

The Material Dimension

The relics of the Buddha were distributed at his death. They were installed in cairns, which were the precursor of the great mound or *stūpa* of the classical Buddhist temple. Such concern with relics was to prefigure much else. But it was some time before Buddhist monasteries, with all their accompanying art, were to be created. Only later was there to be the wonderful development of statuary and paintings which made Buddhist art one of the glories of human civilization. In the beginning, there was perhaps a strong sense that by the doctrines taught by the Buddha there was "nothing there" to portray. The Teacher was trackless, like a rhinoceros or a bird in the sky.

Śramanic Alternatives

From these early beginnings, Buddhism started to spread. We should note the success, too, of some of its rivals. In the period following 400 B.C.E. we have some consolidation indeed of all the major strands of religious practice. The Brahmins had developed far beyond the Three Vedas which were so severely chastised in the Buddhist texts. By the time of the Buddha, or not long after it, there were in existence the principal classical Upanishads. These discourses, originally handed down orally, contain ideas which became seminal for some of the innovative theologies of classical Hindu thought. Within the wider context of the consolidation of kingdoms, such as that of Magadha, the Brahmin class had new opportunities; and when the old Āryavarta or Aryan region around Delhi was absorbed by the vigorous mercantile states of the Ganges valley, the Brahmin theories were brought into direct conflict and coexistence with the newer śramanic ideologies. As we move on through a period which also saw the invasion of India by Alexander the Great in 327–324 B.C.E., with stimulating effects on Indian culture, we may survey the religious traditions which formed alternatives to early Buddhism. The major ones are Jainism, Ājīvika, and Brahmin thought itself, or Brahmanism.

Jainism

Jainism, like Buddhism, claimed immemorial antiquity: the leader, Mahāvīra, merely restored an ancient faith and did not originate it. It has a more severe character than Buddhism, and its central virtue is *ahiṃsā* or non-injury to living beings, practiced in a very comprehensive way. Monks should tread the ground softly for fear of squashing insects and smaller forms of life. They should sweep the terrain with peacock feathers to clear away such beings. They should strain their drinking water, wear masks, and so on, to prevent the accidental taking of life, since such actions, even when not intended, bring bad karmic consequences. The monks, nuns, and dedicated lay followers practice severe austerity, or *tapas*.

The religion involves mental training; but physical austerities lie at its heart. The noblest ideal is for the saint, when he is ready, to starve himself to death.

Vardhamāna, or Mahāvīra ("Great Hero"), was born, according to Jain tradition, in 599 B.C.E.—but some scholars put the date fifty or more years after this—in a village near Vaiśālī in what is now the state of Bihar. At the age of thirty he, like the Buddha, renounced the world, and plucked out all his hair, to lead the life of the wandering holy man. After twelve years of fasting and penances he gained release and the sense of omniscience. He went on to gather disciples and refounded in a fuller form the religion of his predecessor, Pārśva, the previous Tīrthamkara (or "Fordmaker," i.e. person who shows the crossing to the other shore of existence), who may have lived in the eighth century B.C.E. At seventy-two Mahāvīra gained final *nirvāṇa*.

He was thought to be the last of twenty-four Fordmakers. The Jain religion came to be quite influential in medieval times, but its numbers now in India

Jainism some key terms

Ahiṃsā Non-violence toward all living beings, a virtue central to Jainism, and important in aspects of Hinduism and in Buddhism, as well as in Gandhi's thought.

Ajīva Non-living matter, including human and other bodies: everything which is not *jīva* (soul).

Anekāntavāda Perspectivism or non-one-sidedness: the doctrine that no one perspective gives you the whole truth.

Angas The earliest texts in the Jain tradition.

Digambara Sky-clad ones, that is, Jains who keep to the rule of nudity for monks, as a sign of ultimate lack of possessions.

Jina Victor or conqueror, the main title of the great Jain teachers, notably Mahāvīra: from it is derived the name *Jaina* or follower of the Jina.

Kevala State of liberation in which the *jīva* exists motionless at the summit of the universe, pictured as a colossal human.

Mahāvrata Great vow taken by a monk or nun, pledging to practice *ahiṃsā*, and to avoid lying, sex, stealing, or owning anything.

Śvetambara White-clad ones: those Jains belonging to the group which does not practice monastic nudity. Each monk or nun has three pieces of white cloth to wear.

Tapas Austerity, widely practiced in India, but especially by Jains.

Tīrthamkara Ford-maker, that is, a great leader such as Mahāvīra who makes a way across the stream of life to salvation.

Non-Injury and the Path: Sūtrakṛtāṅga

This is the quintessence of wisdom: not to kill anything. Know this to be the legitimate conclusion from the principle of the reciprocity with regard to non-killing.

He should cease to injure living beings whether they move or not, on high, below and on earth, for this has been called the Nirvāṇa, which consists in peace.

Master of his senses and avoiding wrong, he should do no harm to anybody, neither by thoughts, nor by words, nor by acts.

A wise man who restrains his senses and possesses great knowledge should accept such things as are freely given him, being always circumspect with regard to the accepting of alms, and abstaining from what he is forbidden to accept.

The ethical dimension: as part of their non-violent practice toward all living things, the concept of *ahiṃsā*, Jain ascetics wear masks so that they do not inadvertently inhale insects.

are less than three million. Because followers could not take up agriculture and other death-dealing professions they came to populate the merchant and artisan classes, and are a relatively prosperous community. They feel that the religion, as we get away from Mahāvīra's time, and as history goes on in a downward direction, is in decline. They are divided into two denominations, the chief difference between them being that one demands that monks and nuns be unclothed and the other that they wear robes. The one is called the Digambaras or "Sky-Clad" and the other the Svetambaras or "White-Clad."

Jainism has no doctrine of a creator. The universe is roughly in the shape of a huge person, we being at the waist. Above are various heavens and below are hells. The liberated *jīva* or soul rises, free of the weight of its depressing *karma*, to the top of the universe where it remains, free from pain and motionless. Every soul is in itself omniscient, but due to defilements it loses this knowledge; through emancipation its original omniscience is regained.

These beliefs, seemingly archaic, have provided the framework for the practice of a religion which through the centuries has had important influences on Indian civilization as a whole. In the Buddhist texts it comes out, with the Brahmins, as the chief rival to Buddhism.

The Ājīvikas

The leader of the important Ājīvika movement was Maskarin Gośāla (Sanskrit) or Makkhali Gośāla (Pali), who conformed to the general śramanic pattern. He too was thought of as the twenty-fourth Fordmaker of the present age. Born in Magadha, he took up the mendicant life and for six years was indeed a follower of Mahāvīra. He claimed to have advanced beyond the latter in his practice of austerity and acquisition of magical powers, and set up his headquarters at Sravasti in northwestern Magadha. Eventually he died of self-starvation in about 487 B.C.E.

According to Ājīvika teachings, which we have to reconstruct from outside sources such as Jain and Buddhist scriptures, the Ājīvika monks and nuns

Jaina cosmology: the cosmos is seen in this Jaina manuscript as a huge human. Liberated souls eventually rise to the top of the universe and stay motionless forever. The Jain universe is usually represented in the form of a cosmic man.

underwent severe austerities. In the first two or three centuries of the religion's existence it was a primary rival to Buddhism and Jainism. In one of his inscriptions, the emperor Aśoka (after 268 B.C.E.) names the Ājīvikas third after Buddhists and Brahmins (maybe third in size or third in his approbation).

The Ājīvika teachings centered on the idea of *niyati* or fate. No virtuous act or austerity can help an individual to be released from the sufferings of this world, although such actions are presumably indications that a person is close to liberation. Every soul, indeed, must traverse eight million four hundred thousand lives. Even then it may be that she is not finally released but comes back from blissful existence to resume transmigrations. There is, then, nothing that an individual can do to alter his destiny or fate. This idea was most strenuously resisted by the Buddha and Mahāvīra. The Buddhists regarded the fatalism of the Ājīvikas as particularly threatening.

After about 100 B.C.E. their influence seems to have dwindled, though we have references to them in south India as late as the fourteenth century. In the Tamil country they seem eventually to have merged with the Digambara denomination of the Jains and with devotional Vaiṣṇavas (followers of Viṣṇu).

It is interesting to see the relative destinies of the three main śramanic movements. Buddhism died out in India almost completely, but established itself throughout nearly all the rest of South and East Asia. It became one of the three great missionary religions of the world. The Ājīvikas died out completely. The Jains flourished but eventually shrank, surviving significantly in India but not becoming a missionary religion like Buddhism. A major reason for Buddhism's success was its cultural adaptability; and that in a sense too was the cause of its demise in India, since it merged so successfully with Hindu culture that the latter took it over.

Brahmanism, or the Religion of the Upanishads

Meanwhile, in the centuries up to the time of the Buddha, the religion of the Brahmins had been evolving. Long periods of settlement in the Āryavarta had made the thundering and conquering religion of Indra the Warrior less relevant. To the east of the main Aryan area, the new religious revival represented by Buddhism, Jainism, and other movements was a challenge from a region where Brahmin control and presence were less fully felt. There was in Brahmin life a certain dilemma. The reason why Brahmins were in demand from kings and wealthy folk was their expertise in ritual: that implied secrecy. On the other hand, their doctrines needed to develop in debate with outsiders, such as these sophisticated new movements. They were scarcely in a position to speak too openly, beyond instructing those members of the community who belonged to the upper three classes (priests, warriors, and artisans): the "twice-born" who were born again through an initiation with the sacred thread and the status of full-fledged Aryans.

In some measure Brahmin ideas were opened up through the composition of the texts known as Upanishads. The principal ones were composed perhaps

Brahmins reciting a fire ritual to ensure a good harvest.

between 800 and 400 B.C.E., and in parallel with some of the new ideas prevalent in the śramanic movements. These works, partly verse and partly prose, were attached to the growing corpus of works in turn affixed to the Vedic hymn collections, and known as Brāhmaṇas and Āraṇyakas (Holy and Forest Treatises). The Upanishads are concerned essentially with the meaning of the sacrificial rites, and in the process they introduce profound metaphysical and religious ideas.

When we refer to "the Upanishads" we mean those original ones which form part of the revealed corpus of the Veda. In fact, Upanishads as a kind of literature continued to be composed right down to the sixteenth century. The term means "Secret Teachings," and it is assumed that they originated in oral interpretations of the sacred tradition imparted by gurus within the context of initiation.

The central concept in the Upanishads is that of *brahman*. This is sacred or divine power operative in the sacrifice and indeed within the Brahmin class itself. What power? The new insight of these texts is that the whole cosmos is as it were a sacrifice, and *brahman* is the holy power which informs and animates the whole of reality. Consequently the word came to be used as a name of the divine Ultimate, or of God, and is commonly written in English with a capital, as Brahman. No longer was the sacred expertise of the Brahmins seen as something restricted to the operations of sacred liturgy. It was now seen in principle as knowledge about the whole universe. Some of the Upanishads see Brahman as a personal Lord or Īśvara, as in the *Īśa Upaniṣad*. Sometimes it is seen as without personal qualities, but lying "beyond" qualities and the reach of speech. Much of later Indian philo-

Īśa Upaniṣad

By the Lord all this universe must be enveloped,
Whatever moving thing there is in this moving
world.
Renounce this and you may enjoy existence.
Do not covet anyone's wealth.
Even while doing deeds here
One may wish to live a hundred years;
Thus on thee – this is how it is –
The deed adheres, not on the person.

Those worlds are named after the antigods
Which are covered over by blind darkness.
Those people who kill the Self
Go to them, on descending.

Unmoving, the One is swifter than the mind.
The senses do not reach it, as it hurries on
before,
Running past others. It goes, while standing
still.
In it Mātariśvān places activity.

It moves, it moves not;
It is far and it is near;
It is within this universe
And it is outside of all this.

Now he who looks on all things
As in the Self, and on the Self
As in all beings – he
Does not shrink away from Him.

sophizing concerns the question as to whether the Ultimate is personal or nonpersonal. Sometimes it is seen as both: nonpersonal in its own nature, but personal in relation to the universe and creatures.

Into the sacred world of Brahman and the Brahmin ideology there penetrated that other complex of ideas which I have called śramanic: ideas of reincarnation, liberation, yoga, and *tapas*. So many times we hear in ancient texts of Brahmins and *śramaṇas* coupled together: they were the two classes of holy persons in the society of the sixth and fifth centuries B.C.E. It is not surprising that the Brahmins made a move toward synthesis. The results of such a move are to be found in the Upanishads.

First, there is presented as a new and secret teaching the idea of rebirth—or redeath as it is more grimly called—the thought that the individual who has not gained the Ultimate will be subjected to repeated death.

Second, in the Upanishads we find the remarkable act of identification in which the inner, yogic quest is coupled by implication to the rituals of sacrifice through which Brahmins tried to control cosmic events. This act of identification is to say that Brahman is the same as the *ātman* or eternal Self which lies within the person. As the formula which is used has it, "That art thou": in other words, that ultimate being out there, which lies behind and pervades the visible world as its ground and creator, is the same as that eternal something within you.

So the two paths, of ritual action and inner self-control, converge. The Upanishads, moreover, stress the unity of the world and with it the sacred Lord who controls it. But the many gods of the Vedic tradition are not simply swept aside: they are so many refractions of the One. The texts also make use of ideas which were later or at about the same time worked up into the philosophical system known as Sāṃkhya, which was closely associated with the practice of yoga and the Hindu tradition of thought known as the Yoga Philosophy.

Though yoga in the general sense crosses the boundaries of tradition, a particular formulation of its philosophy came to be accepted as orthodox and Hindu; and it was this system which coalesced in the medieval period with Sāṃkhya.

Sāṃkhya thought had affinities with the śramanic systems. It saw the world in terms of a unitary cosmos, known as *prakṛti* or nature, and many souls wandering through transmigration and so impaled on suffering. There was no God as such in this viewpoint, but the Upanishads saw the quest for liberation in terms of the attainment of unity with or close communion with the One Holy Power or Brahman.

If the central ritual idea in Brahmanism was *yājña* or sacrifice, the central idea of the inner quest was that of direct experience through meditation. A third ingredient can be seen glimmering through the texts. The beginnings of devotion are to be seen as directed toward a supreme Lord. This motif was to be taken up much more powerfully later on in the Indian traditions, both Buddhist and Hindu, as *bhakti*. The reliance on the Lord also foreshadows the message of the *Bhagavadgītā*. And so the main themes of the Hindu tradition are perceived at least in principle.

In the *Īśa Upaniṣad* (Secret Teaching of the Lord) there is a famous vision of the cosmic Lord standing outside the cosmos, and a vision of the One somehow within us. The question which was later to exercise thinkers was whether Brahman and soul are strictly identical, in which case we all share the one Self, and the fact that we seem to be many individuals is no more than an illusion; or whether we have separate selves in which the one Lord indwells. But we still have some way to go from the Upanishads to classical Hinduism.

Theravāda Buddhism

The Mauryan Empire and Aśoka

Of the states arising in the Ganges region in the period of the Buddha the most vital was Magadha, which eventually became the basis for the Mauryan empire, named after Candragupta Maurya, who came to the throne in 326 B.C.E. He expanded the empire to cover most of north India, defeating the Greek successor of Alexander, Seleucus, in the process and acquiring large swaths of territory in the northwest. Of those who followed him the most important was Aśoka, who came to the throne probably in 268 B.C.E. A few years later he conquered Kaliṅga, a troublesome eastern kingdom. The massacres and miseries consequent upon this action afflicted his conscience, and he became a lay follower of Buddhism. The rock edicts he inscribed in various parts of his dominions testify to his concern for religious tolerance and the values of the Dharma. This Dharma was an extrapolation from the full Buddhist teaching, but it enjoined virtue and discouraged practices such as meat-eating. The moderating effects of Buddhist values were brought into Aśoka's practice of statecraft. In 258 B.C.E. he celebrated a great festival of

Buddhism in his vast capital of Pātaliputra on the Ganges (the largest city of its time in the world), and began to send out missionaries and ambassadors to distant regions, including Greece and the successor states to Alexander's empire. Partly thanks to his energy, Buddhism spread into Central Asia, whence in due course it was to be taken along the silk route into China. Aśoka gave an example of the virtuous king, which was to remain an important ideal both in Hindu and Buddhist tradition.

One of his most lasting achievements was the spread of Buddhism to Sri Lanka, carried there by his son (or nephew), Mahinda. It was in Sri Lanka that the Pali scriptures were written down, and there a major form of Buddhism, Theravāda, had its apogee in the civilization which flowered first and most strikingly in Anuradhapura.

Classical and Medieval Theravāda

The coming of Mahinda, and the importance of Aśoka in the legendary past of Buddhism, added to the belief that the Buddha had set foot in Sri Lanka during his lifetime. For the Sinhalese people, who spoke a language derived from north India, it seemed as if their blessed isle was singularly favored to carry on the Dharma (Pali: Dhamma) of the Buddha. It was a rich place, especially because of the development of irrigation in the dry north-central region. In the capital, as Buddhism came to be firmly established as the royal religion, there arose the great monastic settlement known as the Mahāvihāra, with its huge relic mound or *stūpa*, known as the Ruanväli. Later another monastic settlement known as the Abhayagiri was established, which was more hospitable than the conservative Mahāvihāra to non-Theravādin forms of Buddhism. In the third century C.E. the penetration of too many unorthodox elements (as the rebels saw it) brought the hiving off of a third great settlement, the Jetavana.

Though some Mahāyāna and Hindu elements in the end got incorporated into the fabric of orthodox Theravāda—such as the use of Buddha statues (which for obscure reasons were not favored in early Buddhism) and the building of shrines to the gods inside temple complexes—Theravāda remained remarkably unchanged in the long period from King Dutthagamini in the first century B.C.E. until the advent of the British. It became a civilizational religion, both forming and being formed by the culture of the island. A solid bond related monarchy to the Sangha. The king was to keep an eye on the monastic community, in case moral and spiritual abuses became too widespread. The Sangha ensured the prosperity and order of the kingdom. Monarchy contributed in a worldly way to the spiritual health of religion, and religion in a spiritual way to the worldly health of monarchy. Such a pattern was to be followed in Thailand and other Buddhist societies of South and Southeast Asia. Theravāda of course also flourished over a long period in India itself; but it is convenient for us to trace its shape through the living tradition of an Indic civilization outside of mainland India proper. Let us look to its various dimensions.

Theravāda: Ritual and Practical Dimensions

We have seen that meditation was a central part of early Buddhism. In theory this was a main occupation of monks and nuns. Also increasingly important, as the Pali Canon of scriptures came to be written down, was study, with a growing body of commentaries. The complexities of Buddhist analysis were considerable: there were analyses of the material and psychological constituents of the individual, from blood, pus, and semen to mental dispositions and states of consciousness; and of forms of perception; and of rules of conduct; and so on. There was, then, fertile ground for commentarial work. Monks also had a duty to preach to the laity and instruct them in the values of social life. Then, as time went on there were increasingly elaborate public festivals, for instance at Vesak, the full moon in May, celebrating the birth, Enlightenment, and final decease of the Buddha. The clergy were also in demand to perform rites for the sick, and to protect households, and the like. In theory nuns and monks got their food by begging, but modern excavation has revealed arrangements for serving the monastic inhabitants with large quantities of food, doubtless ultimately supplied by the king and other laity. At the end of Vassa, the rainy season of retreat, lay folk presented new robes to the monks, and this was an occasion of joyful ceremonial.

What made the great monasteries possible was high income from food-growing, and orderly government to control a society which had to maintain large irrigation works. Naturally, over the centuries there were attempts at reform of a religion which risked becoming self-satisfied in a very rich environment. There were those who became *araññika* or forest-monks, and who revived the practice of the hermit life, dwelling alone in caves and huts in the jungle, and carrying on with strict meditation. They were relevant to outlying village life, for their reputation for merit made the villagers' offerings especially potent.

For the laity, various works of piety were the norm: feeding the monks and nuns, sending a son or daughter into the Order, going to the monasteries to circumambulate the *stūpa* or relic-mound, often huge and white, its plaster surface shining against the greens of the tropical landscape. There were gifts which the poorest and the richest might give to the Sangha. All such deeds brought merit which might help an individual to attain heaven next time, or at least a more favorable station in life. For the laity perhaps heaven was the dominant hope; but, as still today, they were able to distinguish between the desire for enjoyment, of which rebirth in one of the many heavens would be the greatest example, and spiritual growth, of which *nibbāna* (*nirvāṇa*) would be the culminating point. In their lives the monks and nuns stood as constant reminders of the ideal of "giving up" and looking to a goal beyond all ordinary goals.

Largely under outside (Mahāyāna) influence, there came to be shrines at the temples which included Buddha statues, some of enormous size. These became objects of piety, and again merit and mental purification could be had by making offerings to the Buddha. And surrounding Buddhist practice and commingling with it were the various gods and spirits, to whom the villagers still turned for help with harvest, possession, sickness, and other concerns. This interface with ordinary culture has been characteristic of Buddhism throughout its spread.

Theravāda: the Experiential Dimension

One of the reasons why the classical Theravāda is so important in the history of religions is that it is the prime example of mysticism without God, and even without some all-pervading Absolute such as Brahman. The monk, nun, or pious layperson who follows the prescriptions of one of the famous manuals, for instance Buddhaghosa's *Visuddhimagga* (*Path of Purity*, fourth—fifth century C.E.), is doing something very like those Sufis and Christian contemplatives who empty their minds of thoughts and imaginings to make way for a divine vision. But here the ultimate experience is seen as realizing or (so to speak) touching *nibbāna*: coming in contact with that unborn, ineffable, transcendental state which for the Buddha is the Ultimate. The training of one who takes this path to the Highest includes much besides the purification of consciousness—it involves moral improvement, for instance—but at its heart is the practice of the *jhāna* (Sanskrit: *dhyāna*), to which we referred earlier. But since the Buddha did not believe in anything Beyond in the form of God or Absolute, mysticism in the Theravāda tradition does not involve any kind of sense of union, which many other branches of mysticism speak about.

Though the Theravāda has no place for a numinous Supreme Being, its practice has tended to invest its ceremonies and artifacts with something of that sense of the sacred. So the layperson might feel awe at a Buddha statue, as well as in connection with the lesser deities of daily life. In popular cults, too, there were aspects of shamanism in the healing ceremonies for those possessed by demons. But the gods and spirits were outside the Sangha's ambit of organization. For the spiritual path itself there was emphasis upon purity of life and self-training through meditation. It was through this that holy monks and nuns exuded a strange power.

Theravāda: the Narrative Dimension

It became a commonplace that the story of the Buddha's life could be traced through many generations. His previous lives were edifying; and after his decease his influence still lived. For monks and laity alike in Sri Lanka this tale was continued in the various chronicles, which saw the island as creating a fine Buddhist civilization and as battling (against Tamil Hindu dynasties, for instance) for the preservation of this spiritual heritage. This was reinforced by the pilgrimage to Adam's Peak, which emphasized a sense of the holy presence of the Buddha in the island. There was also the shrine at Mihintale, recalling Mahinda's coming at the behest of the legendary great emperor, Aśoka. In these ways, the story of the Buddha was extended to history, giving the assurance of the central place of Sri Lanka, blessed island, in the whole story of Liberation.

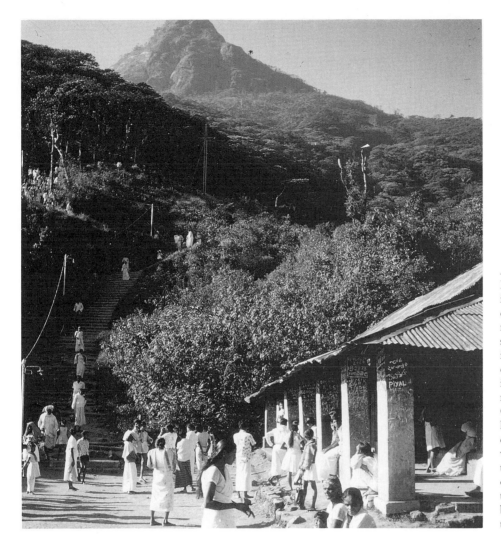

Adam's Peak, Sri Lanka, is sacred to the island's Buddhists. A depression near the mountain's peak is shaped like the impression of an enormous foot, and it is believed that it was made by Siddhartha Gautama. Hindus, however, attribute the depression to Śiva, while Muslims hold that Adam stood on the spot for a thousand years after being expelled from the Garden of Eden.

Theravāda: the Doctrinal Dimension

Though there was plenty of the miraculous in the scriptural accounts of the Buddha, Theravāda saw him primarily as a great human being, who, in attaining a full understanding of the Dhamma, came to embody it. So there was a transcendental side to his nature. But believers adhered to the view that it was unwise to go beyond what the Buddha had said, so that though analysis could be elaborated, no large-scale development of doctrine was possible. Little could be said as to the nature of *nibbāna*, except that it was beyond the perishable events of this world. They stuck to the fourfold negation enunciated in this matter by the Buddha. As to the question of whether a Tathagata existed after death, he said: "It is not correct to say that he does, or does not, or both does and does not, or neither does nor does not." Such comprehensive negation pointed to the idea that the question was wrongly put: *nibbāna* as a condition escapes our ordinary language.

Great emphasis was placed on the *anattā* or nonself doctrine. Individuals transmigrate, but there is no permanent soul. What use is an unchanging soul? It can explain nothing by the very fact that it is unchanging: to cause something a thing has to change. It merely stands as a symbol for the possibility of salvation, and that was sufficiently taken care of by use of the concept of *nibbāna*.

The world of the Theravāda is vast: there are many world systems apart from ours, and each "galaxy" has its own heavens and hells and earth, its own gods, including Brahmā, and its own Satan, Māra, the death-dealing Tempter. The universe is virtually unending and beginningless, and exists in vast dimensions of space and time. The individual transmigrates through this vast system, now going to heaven, now assuming human, animal, or ghostly form, now suffering torments in one of the hells, now rising to the insect class, and so on and so on, till hopefully he may be reborn as a monk and approach final liberation: *nibbāna*. Then he will no longer be reborn. Pure selflessness in spirit will ensure that he will not regret the final disappearance of his individuality.

The Buddhist analysis of persons was designed to reinforce this sense of "selflessness": a person was made up of five types of events—bodily events, perceptions, feelings, dispositions, and states of consciousness. These five groups of events were dispersed at death and reassembled because of the continued impulses contained in the dispositions. So if you still have a craving for this or that, you will be reborn. What holds one part of your life together with another is just a complex chain of causes, similar to what holds one life together with another. The person, then, is a temporary amalgamation of five kinds of impermanent events.

Much of the close doctrinal analysis in the Theravāda is in the third portion of the Tripitaka, that is, the threefold canon of scriptures. This, known as the *Abhidhamma* portion (the name means "Analysis of the Dhamma": Sanskrit *Abhidharma*), was the last to be assembled, after the two other portions, the *Sutta* (supposed discourses or *sūtras* of the Buddha) and *Vinaya* (Rule).

Theravāda: Institutions and other matters

The Vinaya rules control in great detail the daily life of the monk and nun. They can in theory be altered by majority vote, since the Sangha is constitutionally based on a republican form of government extant in the Buddha's time. But on the whole the conservative tendencies of the Theravāda have held the system fairly tight. The scriptures are shared, of course, by other Theravādin communities in other countries, such as Burma and Thailand, and there has been much interaction over the centuries between the Theravādin countries.

The brilliant capital of Anuradhapura came to be replaced by the glories of Polonnaruwa (p. 65) to the east, the center of a renewed irrigation-based civilization in the eleventh and twelfth centuries C.E. At this period there was greater integration between Buddhist and Hindu rites, and shrines to the gods were brought inside the temple complexes. We find, then, in Theravādin Sri Lanka a rich Indic civilization, which had a strong feeling of its glorious destiny in the spiritual life of the human race.

The Rise of the Mahāyāna

In parallel with the full formation of the Theravādin tradition there came into existence a type of Buddhism which regarded itself as a Mahāyāna, a Greater Vehicle toward salvation than the more narrowly conceived Theravāda and other "Lesser Vehicle" schools. Its roots relate to the ethical, ritual, and philosophical dimensions. At the ethical level, there was felt to be an increasing strain in the conventional interpretation of Buddhism: if a person strove through the practice of *dhyāna* and the like to better himself and ultimately to attain *nirvāṇa*, was not this essentially selfish and ego-oriented? The ideal of the serene *arhant* or Theravādin saint was in the final analysis as egoistic as the pursuits of the wealth-gaining merchant. The problem was the tension between insight and compassion, and was resolved, said the proponents of these ideas, in the ideal of the Bodhisattva, or Buddha-to-be, who out of compassion puts off his own final salvation till all are saved. This was a development of ideas implicit in the Jātaka stories and in the career of the Buddha himself, who was tempted to leave the world but stayed to preach the liberating, but subtle and difficult, Dharma.

In the ritual dimension, there was a growth in northwest India, from about the second century B.C.E., of the use of Buddha statues. It was not a long step from this to the idea that Buddhas continue to be present to us and so can be worshiped. This generated a type of Buddhism in which *bhakti* (warm devotion) came to supplement and even displace the austerer form of self-training, and mysticism. Out of this arose mythological innovations: stories about great Bodhisattvas such as Avalokiteśvara (p. 66), the Lord Who Looks Down (with compassion), and Amitābha, the Buddha of Infinite Light. Already about the third century B.C.E., a group known as the Mahāsanghikas had begun to break away from the Sthaviravādin (Theravādin) tradition in India, arguing for a more open community, and for a less rigid adherence to the words of the historical Buddha. They regarded the Buddha as *lokottara*, beyond the world and transcendent, and yet somehow still present. All these tendencies came together from the first century B.C.E. onward in the worship of a multiplicity of Buddha and Bodhisattva figures. This gave Buddhism a rich *bhakti* dimension. It also developed ideas of merit, so that the laity, and indeed monks and nuns, could gain merit by *pūjā*, the worship of these semidivine beings; and this in turn paved the way for a doctrine of grace, that is, salvation granted from above.

In some ways the philosophical changes were even more dramatic, though they are not always easy to grasp. Parallel developments occurred in the writings known as *Prajñāpāramitā Sūtras*, or *sūtras* of the Perfection of

Nāgārjuna

Nāgārjuna probably lived in the second century C.E. It was not until 405 C.E. that his biography was written, by the famous Chinese scholar Kumārajīva. Not only does this check with other accounts, both Chinese and Tibetan, but it tallies too with other evidence. He was born into a Brahmin family in South India. As a boy he showed considerable powers of understanding; and it seems that he converted at a young age when he first encountered Mahāyāna teachings. This squares with the way his philosophy carried on the tradition of the *Prajñāpāramitā* (*Perfection of Wisdom*) literature, then evolving in South India. According to Kumārajīva, a bodhisattva belonging to the Nāga tribe furnished him with the most profound Mahāyāna verses. Nāgārjuna digested these swiftly and preached the truth based on them. Since the Nāgas lived in South India, the stories more or less fit together. Much of his subsequent life, which was a long one, was spent in composing various philosophical and religious works, of which the most important was the *Mūlamadhyamakakārikā* (*Basic Verses on the Middle Way*).

Nāgārjuna's influence proved considerable. His teaching about the emptiness (*śūnyatā*) and relativity of every event and his holding that there are two levels of truth (ordinary or everyday truth and higher truth) put their stamp on the Mahāyāna tradition, while his extension of the application of the Buddha's fourfold negation to apply to all claims was daring. Later his philosophy was to have a profound influence on the Advaita Vedānta of Saṃara. He also saw firmly the connection between this apparently more theoretical or philosophical side of Buddhism and the practicalities of everyday compassion and piety.

Opposite The ritual dimension: Benares the greatest of India's holy cities, is a focus of pilgrimage and piety, and it is believed that those who die in the city will automatically go to heaven. Here a Brahmin washes in the river Ganges.

Wisdom, and in the writings of the philosopher Nāgārjuna of the early second century C.E.. It may be noted that scriptures (*sūtras*) of various kinds were being composed in this period in Sanskrit or what is called Buddhist Hybrid Sanskrit. The writings are not cryptic and secretive, like Hindu parallels (where *sūtras* cannot be understood without a teacher or commentary); Buddhist writings are generally long and open, to the point of being prolix and repetitive. But the fact that new scriptures were being composed was important: it was a period when writing was becoming more universal, and something of the mystique which writing possesses for those who are still being weaned from oral traditions rubbed off on such literature. Texts were even to be put in *stūpas* and so reverenced like relics. The words describe the Truth and participate in the Truth; so in reverencing texts you reverence the Truth, and in doing this you reverence the Buddha, whose body is Truth. Naturally the Theravāda resisted the introduction of what it regarded as new and unwarranted "scriptures" into the canon. But the composers of the new texts thought of themselves as drawing out the essence of the Buddha's message, and so the writings could be ascribed to the Buddha himself.

The fundamental teaching of the Perfection of Wisdom is that all things in the world are relative to one another. They are mutually conditioned. Nothing has its own nature in itself. Intrinsically all things are "empty." If there is any ultimate truth it is this: the truth of emptiness, which is ineffable and can only be realized through direct experience—the mystical experience of the Buddhas.

Nāgārjuna's Mādhyamika or "Middle" philosophy is very similar and is argued in a more explicitly philosophical manner, refuting alternative theories. It can be shown, according to Nāgārjuna, that certain fundamental concepts which pervade all our thinking and talking, such as the idea of cause, are contradictory. If causes are short-lived events, then they go out of existence before their effects arrive; and this implies that the existent is caused by the nonexistent, which is absurd. And so on with all theories. If our fundamental ideas are vitiated by contradictions, so then are all accounts of the world. At best our language is a convenience, but it cannot "get at" the nature of reality, which is relative, empty, unspeakable. So we follow the Buddha, for he pointed the way through the contradiction, to the experience of liberation which can replace all philosophy, including the Buddha's own. This approach of Nāgārjuna's implies a two-level theory of truth: a distinction between ordinary pragmatic truth and ultimate, experienceable Truth.

These notions from the Perfection of Wisdom and the Mādhyamika combined with religious ones. In attaining Truth we in effect become Buddhas, just as at the ethical level in treading the path of the Bodhisattva we are indeed Buddhas-to-be, and the Buddha nature resides in each one of us. In worshiping Buddhas and Bodhisattvas we are still at the lower level and, as it were, worshiping our future state. The whole apparatus of celestial Buddhas and belief in the earthly Buddha eventually can be discarded when we enter the Beyond, in ineffable enlightenment.

There was another twist to the tale. If you recognize with Nāgārjuna that our usual conceptual distinctions between one thing and another are merely provisional, then so is our conventional distinction between *nirvāṇa* and *saṃsāra*. In other words, we already are in the realm of *nirvāṇa*, but do not know it until we have the "higher" point of view. All this fitted together with a new role for the layperson who could as well tread the Bodhisattva path in the ordinary life of *saṃsāra*.

The Mahāyāna Pure Land

Three centuries or more after Nāgārjuna's work there was the philosophy of the brothers Asanga and Vasubandhu, who propounded the so-called Vijñānavāda or Consciousness school. It is often thought to teach the unreality of the world out there and its origin in the mind. It is in the philosophical sense "idealist," according to this way of looking at it. But more strictly it teaches that everything which we claim as the truth or knowledge is qualified by consciousness: that is, it is reality as interpreted by consciousness and language. It is always seen through the lens of the subject-object structure of consciousness. In itself, however, reality does not have this subject-object

Opposite, above The narrative dimension: an episode from the *Mahābhārata*, one of Hinduism's two great epics, and a vast source of entertainment and spiritual instruction. This scene shows Arjuna overcoming Karna, with various gods looking on. This was an episode in the great civil war depicted in the epic.

Opposite, below The doctrinal dimension: much of Hindu tradition envisaged the cosmos as being periodically created and re-created. In between were periods of rest, symbolized here by Viṣṇu lying on the serpent Ananta ("Endless"), representing eternity. Viṣṇu, accompanied here by his consort, Lakṣmi, awaits his next burst of creative activity. In the upper section of the painting are Viṣṇu riding on Garuda, Brahma, and Śiva.

character. We can seek to obtain a unitive consciousness without duality through the higher experience of Buddhism.

More important in the life of ordinary people was the Sukhāvatī or Pure Land school, which arose about the time of Nāgārjuna; it holds that the Buddha Amitābha has constructed a Pure Land far to the west, full of splendors and joys, such as rivers which run as deep or as warm as you want and trees composed wholly of jewels. This place is highly conducive to the ultimate attainment of *nirvāṇa*; but its glories tended to dominate the imagination and it became for many an end in itself, like the Christian or Islamic Paradise. Just by calling on the name of Amitābha, the faithful were assured of translation at death to the Pure Land.

We shall return to these forms of the Mahāyāna when we are dealing with Chinese and Japanese experience, for there they had their full flower. They and many other schools of Buddhism flourished in India during the first millennium C.E. They flourished in such study centers as Nalanda in the north and Nagarjunikonda in the south; and were interwoven with the fabric of growing Hinduism. There still remains one more phase of the life of Buddhism in South Asia, before the modern period; and that is its journey into Tibet and life there. This is tied in with those developments known as Tantra. Meanwhile let us turn to see how classical Hindu practices and ideas were taking shape just before and during the first millennium C.E.

Below A typical southern *gopuram* (temple tower) decorated with depictions of the gods near Kanchipuram, Tamil Nadu, southern India.

Below, right The descent from heaven to earth of the river Ganges, with various mythic figures, is depicted at Mahabalipuram in Tamil Nadu, southern India. The Hindu religious complex in the southern Indian port dates from the seventh century.

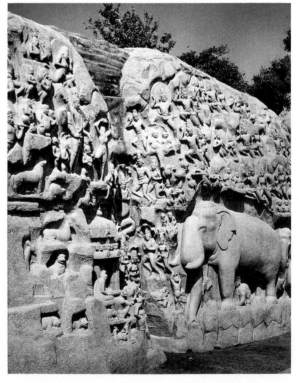

Classical Hinduism: its Main Shape

Devotion

Various forces were coalescing to provide a shape for the heterogeneous religions over which the Brahmins came to prevail. The cult of gods and goddesses, probably always important in modest circumstances inside the home, began to acquire more permanent public form. Perhaps in part under the stimulus of Buddhism, the Hindu temple came to play a leading role in Indian life. It provided a focus for ceremonial and a place for meeting with the great and lesser gods. The Brahmanical heritage in the old days had been without such ikons and buildings. The place of sacrifice had to be laid out, constructed, as befitted an originally nomadic way of life. There was no necessity that Brahmins should be involved in the *pūjā* of the temple; but it was an advantage to the priestly class that it should control so potent a means of focusing the people's piety and impulses to giving. So images and temples

Hinduism some key terms

Arca Image which is occupied by a God once it is consecrated.

Ātman The self of an individual which is eternal and in Advaita is regarded as identical with Brahman (see below).

Avatāra Descent or incarnation of God (notably Viṣṇu) in such figures as Rama, Kṛṣṇa and the future Kalki.

Bhakti Warm devotion to God.

Brahman The sacred Power which is both in the sacrificial process and in the cosmos: hence the term is used of the Divine Being.

Dharma The pattern underlying the cosmos and manifest in the ethical and social laws of humankind.

Īśvara The Lord, that is, God, considered as a person and (typically) as creator.

Jāti Caste, a group with whom the individual identifies in marriage and in eating: the fabric of *jātis* makes up the caste system.

Karma The law which governs the effects of deeds both in this life and in subsequent lives within the operation of rebirth or reincarnation.

Pūjā Worship.

Sannyāsin Holy person who has left ordinary duties as determined by *dharma* and *jāti* behind, often as a wanderer.

Yoga Methods of meditation, sometimes involving physical as well as mental discipline.

were the outer manifestation of a wider role for priests in the developing Hindu society.

This was a symptom of the growing importance not just of worship but more particularly that fervent sharing in the life of the God known as *bhakti* religion. Its features are already portrayed in one book of the great epic *Mahābhārata*, known as the Song of the Lord or *Bhagavadgītā*. This was composed possibly as early as 300 B.C.E. It has in it—as the most famed of India's philosophers, S ánkara, said—the essence of the Vedas. Its popularity gave it immense influence, and it inspired many imitations on behalf of Śiva and other gods. It came to be recognized as part of the sacred tradition or *smṛti*, which continues the more strictly authoritative *śruti* or revelation, consisting of the Vedic hymns and appended works down to the main classical Upanishads; in fact, in its conditioning of Indian religion, the *Gītā* is actually more influential than the Vedic hymn collections.

In the *Bhagavadgītā*, Viṣṇu as Lord and numinous creator of the universe reveals himself as also loving. His avatar Kṛṣṇa declares at the end: "Those who worship me with complete discipline and who contemplate me, whose thoughts are constantly on me—these I soon raise up from the sea of death and rebirth." Arjuna, awaiting battle against his relatives, is given a firmer mind after his confusions and despair about the dread effects of battling against his

A youthful Kṛṣṇa plays his flute to various women, who symbolize the souls of his devotees, near Brindaban.

kith and kin. There are many riches in the *Gītā* ("song"), as it is often called for short; but the central value is that of loyalty and devotion to God, namely *bhakti*.

Viṣṇu, with his incarnations, and Śiva, great Yogin and destroyer of the world, stimulator of the divine *śakti* or power, emerge during this time as the twin great manifestations of the divine Being. They displace some of the older deities important in the Vedic scriptures. Followers of Viṣṇu were called *Vaiṣṇavas* and of Śiva were called *Śaivas* and included the important movements of Kashmiri and Tamil Śaivism. They are enclosed together in the world of traditional religion (*smārta*) as both rivals and cooperators. Viṣṇu is gentler, and much concerned with the periodic restoration of the Dharma through sending down his incarnations, of whom Rāma and Kṛṣṇa are the two most important—Rāma the ideal king, Kṛṣṇa the glorious lover. Śiva is more numinous, wrathful and destructive, but potent through yoga, and indissolubly linked to the Goddess.

The third main divinity of later Hinduism, the Goddess was beginning to emerge into general recognition by the fourth century C.E., in such texts as the *Devīmahātmyam*. She was always there, of course: already in the Indus Valley civilization, and in the villages and undercurrents of life below the surface of the rather macho society of the Vedic hymns; and in the many myths of the consorts of the gods, above all of the great Gods. In Tantric Hinduism she was destined to flower further. But we may say that for much of the Hindu tradition the three great deities are Śiva, Viṣṇu, and the Goddess, under her various names such as Dūrgā, Kālī, and Parvatī.

Below the ultimate Gods are the many deities of the incredibly rich narrative corpus of the Hindus: the two vast epics; the *Harivaṃśa* (about Kṛṣṇa); the *Purāṇas*, and the oral traditions of the various regions of the subcontinent.

The mythic dimension: an eighth-century Pala bronze of Viṣṇu.

Philosophies

Behind the stories were erected the philosophies, above all those systems of belief known as Vedānta, which contains several great variations. There is the doctrine of the aphoristic scripture known as the *Brahmasūtra*, which sets forth Vedānta, "The End or Final Part of the Veda." Its doctrine is probably a version of that system known as Bhedābhedavāda or "Difference-in-Nondifference": Brahman is both different from and not different from the world and souls. The most influential in modern times has been the Advaita, or Nondualistic Vedānta, of Śankara (eighth century C.E.) and his later followers, which sets forth the identity of the soul and Brahman, and the illusoriness, therefore, of the world as multiplicity. There was in the eleventh century the *bhakti*-oriented theism of Rāmānuja's Viśiṣtādvaita or Qualified Nondualism, which sees the world and souls as God's body and instruments of his will. In the thirteenth century there was Madhva's Dvaita or Dualism, in which an eternal difference between soul and soul, soul and world, soul and Brahman, and world and Brahman is affirmed: again a kind of theism. These philosophies underpinned spiritual practice: Śankara could only assign *bhakti* to second

Śankara

Śankara (otherwise known as Śankarācāryaor, "Sankara the Teacher") is the most influential teacher of Hindu traditional theology, at least in the modern period. He is conventionally assigned the dates of 788–820, but details of his biography are highly unreliable, having been composed relatively late.

According to later sources he was born in Kerala in south India, in a village called Kāladi. His parents were childless, but then brought forth a son, Śankara. He was a marvel of precocity. When he was about seven he resolved to bypass the householder state (which was the second main stage of orthodox Hindu progression through life) and immediately become a *sannyāsin* or ascetic. He then left home to sit at the feet of Govindanātha, a guru who dwelt beside the river Narmada. He was in turn a disciple of the more famous Gaudapāda, to whom Śankara in his writings assigns the status of guru of his own guru. These were teachers of Advaita or Nondualistic Vedānta (Vedānta means, roughly, Hindu theology). Śankara did not therefore originate the system which he made famous; but he did produce a viewpoint which was highly articulate and at the same time original in its particular shape.

From the Narmada he moved north to the sacred city of Benares, where he acquired his first disciple: and from there to Badarī in the Himalayan mountains. He was already composing some of his famous works, notably his commentary on the *Brahmasūtra* ("Aphorisms on the Divine Power") and on the *Bhagavadgītā* ("Song of the Lord"). He continued his travels, debating with various rival theologians. He established four or five monastic centers in Sṛngeri in the south, one at Badarī in the north, one at Puri in the east, one at Dvāraka in the west, and maybe one at Kāñchipuram, in Tamil Nadu. He also founded an order of monks. The heads of these various centers carry on his teaching, and are ecclesiastically powerful. His life was miraculously short considering his achievements, and he probably died in the Himalayas, as some hold in Kāñchipuram.

place, as something fit for the unenlightened person still mired in the world of magical illusion (*māyā*). Mystical intuition of identity with the One is the fruit of the higher path.

Commonly these philosophies are held to conduce to liberation or *mokṣa*, which was the last of the four ends of life laid down in classical Hinduism—the others being *kāma*, pleasure (sex being the most intense of the pleasures, the word also stands for this as in the famous *Kāmasūtra*), *artha* or economic gain, and *dharma*, virtue or action in accord with the Dharma. This last was summed up in the law books of Manu, which set down the varieties of duties of Hindus within the structure of the caste system.

Social Existence in the Classical Period
In the early classical period it was thought necessary to fight the challenge

posed to orthodoxy by Buddhism and the other śramanic movements. There was evolved the theory of the four stages of life or *varṇāśramadharma*: student, householder, parent of adult son, ascetic; and Hinduism developed its own monastic orders, one of which was founded by Śankara.

Classical Hinduism saw the increasing articulation of the caste system. Caste groups married within each group, and ate only with that group. These practices of endogamy and commensality were the framework for various castes based upon occupation, traditional God, region, and history. The framework of the four *varṇas* was filled in with a vast mosaic of more refined distinctions, in a social hierarchy topped by the Brahmins and undergirded by the "fifth class" or untouchables, whose occupations were specially polluting (leather work, butchering, brewing, cleaning latrines, fishing, etc.).

And so during the Gupta period, a most florid episode in Indian history, from the fourth to the sixth centuries C.E., we can imagine the glories and complexities of classical Hinduism—the temples, the great rivers, the pilgrims, the parades of gods, the recitations of the epics, the fervor of *bhakti*, the wandering *sannyāsins*, the yogins in meditation, the pandits exploring metaphysics, the elaboration of caste, the sacrifices for princes and emperors, the chanting of vastly ancient verses, the household rites, the pomp of weddings, the countless villages, the wandering of sacred cows, the smell of cowdung burning, the hovels of untouchables, the pride of Brahmins, the rites of the Goddess, the *lingam* of Śiva, the tales of Kṛṣṇa—a great amalgam which yet through the Brahmins had a loose orthodoxy. Hinduism by now had a loose federal existence through the idea that those who accepted the *śruti*, whatever else they did not accept—God, Viṣṇu, *karma*, rebirth, virtue— accepted the primordial authority of the Veda, coeval with time.

And in our mental picture of the times we should recall too, mingled in with the Hindu conglomeration, the shaven-headed monks and nuns of the Buddhists, the various ascetics, the angular temples of the Jaina tradition, the *stūpas* and Bo trees of Buddhist compounds, the cells of monks, the flags of unorthodox festivities, the Buddha statues and the Jātaka tales, the moral discourses, the huge scriptures, the *bhakti* to Amitābha, the giving of protective spells, wives who followed the wise teachings of the Buddha, households of Jains gentle toward animals and insects—in short the whole mingling of the unorthodox traditions with the religion where the Brahmins held sway. India then was a glorious jumble of customs and beliefs, as indeed it is to a lesser extent today.

Buddhism Spreads North: the Tibetan Experience

The cultural region which stretches from Ladakh and Nepal up over the mountains into Tibet, and east beyond today's Tibet into western China, can conveniently be called the Tibetan region; it came gradually to absorb influences both from China and from India. In the end Indian, and in particular Buddhist, influence was predominant. The area assumed very great

Left In the Himalayan region, as in Sikkim, the Vajrayāna or "Diamond Vehicle" predominates. This old Buddhist woman uses a prayer wheel to express her piety.

significance, for the destruction of Buddhist centers in north India by Turkish Muslim pillagers left Tibet as the great repository of Mahāyāna texts, as well as of a whole assemblage of esoteric or secret Tantric texts. The form of Buddhism which had developed in northern Bihar, Bengal, and Kashmir was naturally accessible to Tibet. And it included what is often referred to as the Vajrayāna or "Diamond Vehicle," sometimes also called the Mantrayāna or "Sacred Formula Vehicle." The reason for this last name was because of the great emphasis put in this form of Buddhism on the use of ritual utterances.

The Vajrayāna was concerned with new ways of transforming consciousness, typically in conjunction with the guidance of a guru, through the practice of relating both to sacred formulae and to the visualized figures of various Buddhas and deities. Equations between the different aspects of individual life, the cosmos, and the deities led to a fusion of inner and outer magical and psychological methods. Sometimes Tantric initiates used forbidden practices, such as meat-eating and sexual intercourse, to help them to rise "beyond morality" and so beyond the world. Such methods, by the use of secret rituals and the breaking of taboos in a ritual context, were pioneered also in the Hindu environment of north India. But though they were an element in the kind of Buddhism which came to be established in Tibet, Tibetan Buddhism could also more broadly be defined as Mahāyāna. The texts that they studied, much of the yoga they practiced, and much of the spirit of

Tibet could be said to be "Greater Vehicle" in character.

The "Diamond" of the name of the Vajrayāna refers to the eternal Buddhahood resident in all beings, unsplittable and achieved through the cutting edge of wisdom (*prajñā*). The spiritual exercises of Tantra aimed at identification with this Buddhahood here and now, and conceived of the individual as being of the same nature as the universe. So by self-purification, usually using earlier Buddhist methods of meditation, an adept could visualize his chosen deity or Buddha-figure and thus attain unity with him. The use of magical diagrams or *maṇḍalas* combined the elements of sacred formulae, since the diagrams contained sacred syllables, and the internal use of the visual imagination. Various equations occurred: the five *skandhas* or groups of events which make up the individual (bodily events, perceptions, feelings, dispositions, and states of consciousness) were equated with five Buddhas—Vairocana, Akṣobhya, Ratnasambhava, Amitābha, and Amoghasiddhi (their names mean: Illuminator, Imperturbable, Jewel-Born; Boundless Light, and Infallible Success). These in turn correspond to the five directions of the cosmos (center, east, south, west, and north), and to five kinds of evil and five kinds of wisdom. By imagining brilliantly your deity, you gain unity with him and he with you. This nondual unification is often symbolized by the sexual bond, where two bodies become fused into one.

Female deities took on great importance as consorts or *śaktis* of Buddhas; the greatest of them, Tārā, the Savioress, is the consort of the great Bodhisattva

Below, left A Tibetan painting of Avalokiteśvara as a meditation Buddha-to-be. In China Avalokiteśvara was known as Kuan-yin (Guanyin), the goddess of mercy.

Below, right A *maṇḍala* (ritual diagram) displaying Akṣobhya, the Eastern Buddha, one of the Buddhas of the five directions (north, south, east, west, and center). Probably Tibetan, 18th century.

Avalokiteśvara. Though gentler in nature and purer in appearance than the somewhat fierce representation of the numinous Goddess in the Hindu tradition, the Goddess here is part of a very old stream of sentiment going back to the beginnings of Indic civilization, but here translated to Tibet. Avalokiteśvara and Tārā, incidentally, are thought to have procreated monkeys who transformed themselves over generations into the Tibetan people. (No emotional problems here over the theory of evolution!)

The first monastery in Tibet was founded near the end of the eighth century C.E. There was some resistance to the new religion from the indigenous religion, commonly referred to as Bön (but to its nature and identity we shall return). It was in the eleventh century that there was a second and more vigorous diffusion of Buddhism. It was in this period that the great teacher Atīṣa, who had been to Sumatra to advise the court over there, came to Tibet at the insistence of the Buddhist rulers of west Tibet. One of his disciples founded the religious order of bKa'-gdams-pa. In the same century, in consequence of the teaching of Marpa, a famous Tibetan monk who had studied at one of the great north Indian universities, the Sa-skya order was started. A third order, the bKa'-rgyud-pa, was host to Tibet's most beloved religious teacher, Mila Raspa (or Milarepa, 1079–1153).

On the whole the reason for the importation of Buddhism into Tibet by its secular rulers seems to have been political, to provide a "modern" ideology of rule and to open up to Tibet the advantages of literacy and philosophy. In the ensuing centuries it became more important due to the conversion of many Mongols, especially the emperor of China, Kublai Khan. The grand lamas of the Sa-skya order were nominated in effect as viceroys, under Mongol suzerainty; eventually, after political conflict, sometimes armed (so we have the spectacle of Buddhist orders fighting one another as monks of war, but overwhelmingly for political and not ideological reasons), the chief rule passed in the seventeenth century C.E. to the head of the reformed Dge-lugs-pa order, which had been founded by the great Tson-kha-pa in the fourteenth century. The succession of the Dalai Lamas, as they are still called, is by a process of identifying a reincarnation of a deceased Dalai Lama. This was a method of succession which had been used by other orders in Tibet since the twelfth century.

Thus we have established in Tibet a kind of theocracy—one could call it a Buddhocracy. Though it was a country thoroughly infused with varieties of the Vajrayāna, it also contained something of its own indigenous Bön tradition. But this too had undergone a transformation over the years as a result of Buddhist influence. Ascribing its founding to the legendary Gsen-rab, who came from a country far to the west, was a fully enlightened being at birth, and spent his life as a prince propagating the Bön religion, the religion formed its own corpus of scriptures corresponding to those of the Buddhists. Just as the Tibetan Buddhists believe that the scriptures in their corpus, the Tanjur, were expounded by the Buddha Śākyamuni himself, so the Bön-po think of *their* Tanjur as having been uttered by Gsen-rab himself. Also like the Buddhists, they have a body of commentaries and other works, known as the Kanjur. The Bön-po have their own monasteries, order, *stūpas*, and so on: they have produced a sort of mirror image of Buddhism. They circumambulate their *stūpas* and other holy objects counterclockwise, and likewise spin their prayer wheels; but they teach that the Buddha was a fraud, and that the coming of Buddhism to Tibet was a great disaster, the cause of evil *karma*. Even so, their aims and methods and popular piety are much the same as those of Buddhism, and the two religions live side by side amicably enough.

The Goddess and Hindu Tantra

Though the roots of the worship of the Goddess go right back to the Indus Valley civilization, it was in the late classical and medieval periods that it achieved a central importance in the Indian tradition. It was especially important in the northeast, in Bengal and Assam; but everywhere in India, scattered through villages and in domestic rites, there were varieties of goddesses, who came to be seen as diverse manifestations of one Goddess, who represents the creative power or *śakti* of the Ultimate. There is of course no reason in doctrine why we should think of God as female or as male, since she/he is neither, strictly. It is only human imagery that needs to make the decision. But there are powerful connections with the idea of the supreme Female, with the earth as being our Mother, with fertility, with motherly love, with falling in love. A devotee could see the Goddess under so many disguises, as provider of food, of great creatrix of the world, as object of affection and devotion, as lover of my soul, as all-devouring Time or Death, as bringer of smallpox and cholera, and so on.

Śaktism could be connected in practice with Hindu Tantra. The main thoughts behind this magico-spiritual outlook have been in part touched upon in regard to Buddhist Tantra: but in the Hindu context it especially is expressed through the thought of harnessing magical and spiritual energy— the *śakti* which the female both personifies and wields. Another motif is secrecy, mimicking the restrictions which apply to Vedic knowledge, but here devoted to keeping apart the techniques and initiations of those adept in harnessing the energy. Like a number of other religious movements, Tantrism broke down caste barriers, as it indeed could violate other taboos.

Islam in India

Though Islam came to Sind in the seventh century, and Muslim traders also settled in various places, it was not really till the eleventh century that substantial inroads were made into the traditional heartlands of Indian culture. Islam and Indic religions were on the whole in conflict. Islam rejected, with a kind of pious horror, the use of images; and this provided the excuse for invaders to smash up statues and temples, whether Hindu, Buddhist, or Jain.

A popular Muslim story tells of an ascetic visited in the desert by his former beloved. The painting shows Hindu influences on Islamic spirituality.

However, Islam was by no means wholly alien. There were other movements in India which were largely without images; the *sant* tradition of poets and preachers emphasized devotion toward the *nirguṇam* form of God, that is, his nature seen as without visible attributes or images. Moreover, Islam had the great advantage that it was not fettered by the caste system. It was not spread chiefly by the sword, but by the conversion of men and women, and here missionary Sufis were important in India. Their mystical path was congenial to many Hindus, and their sanctity could combine with the more evident social justice in Islam to attract many to convert. The Islamic shaykhs and pirs as holy leaders had analogies to Hindu holy men; while the influential work of Ibn al-Arabi (1185–1240), with its emphasis on the unity of all being, had similarities to Advaita Vedānta. There were less orthodox holy men, *qalandars*, who closely resembled some of the wandering ascetics, going round smeared in ashes, begging, performing austerities, smoking hashish: they were inclined to sit loose to orthodox Islamic practice, but they could mediate belief in Allah to the Hindu population.

From the sixteenth century on, the pressures of state also moved toward conversion under the great Mughal Empire, ruled from Delhi. It is true that the emperor Akbar (1556–1605) tried to establish a new, syncretic religion, combining the best, as he saw it, in Islam and the Hindu and other traditions; but under his successor there was a rather rigid imposition of Islamic law.

Mughal culture gave much to India—a framework in which a new kind of piety could flourish, and the brilliance of architecture and art which provided a model for later princes, whether Hindu, Muslim, or Christian. But it was surrounded by a rich civilization that had its own new impulses to religious creativity, some of which had their roots in the classical period.

Regional Movements

In examining the varieties of Hinduism in the medieval epoch I shall be necessarily selective, and shall choose four from differing regions; Śrī Vaiṣṇavism from Tamil Nadu; the Lingayats of south central India; Kashmiri Śaivism from the far north; and the Caitanya tradition from the northeast. To this I shall add the Sikhs, who though they became a separate religion displayed some characteristic features of *bhakti* Hinduism.

Śrī Vaiṣṇavism and Tamil Poetry

The greatest thinker in the Vaiṣṇava tradition was undoubtedly Rāmānuja, who lived around 1000 C.E. His great synthesis reconciled the Tamil Vaiṣṇava and Vedānta traditions. His motives were not primarily philosophical but religious. He found the Nondualism (Advaita) of Śankara to be a great danger, mainly because with its theory of levels of truth and reality it assigned the Lord, and the worship of the Lord, to the lower level, below the mystical intuition of Oneness. It cut at the root of devotional religion. It also cut at the root of sacrificial Brahmin practice; but that was less serious. Rāmānuja wished to express a fervid devotion to the Lord which at the same time could be seen as a good interpretation of the *śruti* or revealed truth of the Hindu faith, notably as expressed in the Upanishads and the *Brahmasūtra*, and as shown forth in the *Gītā*, which was the jewel of *smṛti* or holy memory.

For five centuries the great poets of Tamil Nadu had been composing sacred songs to both Viṣṇu and Śiva. These poets were known as the Ālvārs (Vaiṣṇavas) and the Nayanars (Saivas). Twelve Ālvār poets are found in the tenth-century collection known as "The Four Thousand Divine Verses." The works of the sixty-three Nayanars, of whom the most important was Māṇikkavāçagar, were incorporated in the Śaiva Canon (*Āgamas*) which expressed an alternative to the Veda (sometimes it was called a fifth Veda) for the followers of the Tamil movement known as Śaiva Siddhānta.

After Rāmānuja, Śrī Vaiṣṇavism became a very powerful force in the south, splitting into two schools, based on Sanskrit and Tamil scriptures and sources respectively, and holding different views on the subject of God's grace. Both stressed that salvation from the ocean of rebirth flows from God's love; the debate centered on the interpretation of this—whether the devotee has to do nothing, like the kitten being transported by the scruff of its neck by its mother, or to reach out, as the little monkey uses its arms to cling to its mother—but the essence of the faith was loving devotion to and reliance upon the Lord. The Lord's mythic deeds and goodness were to be celebrated in song, in the rites of clothing and feeding him (present in his image), and in pilgrimage to the sacred sites commemorating his glory. Socially, Śrī Vaiṣṇavism was egalitarian before the Lord. Since it is not by works that you are saved, your status—arrived at through *karma*—does not matter. Thus, as elsewhere, *bhakti* could be a protest against the hierarchical nature of Indian society. The *bhaktas* or devotees of south India picked up some of the ethos of Buddhism and Jainism which they had done so much, by their fervid missionary spirit, to phase out.

Rāmānuja thought of the cosmos and the souls which transmigrated within it as being God's body. By "body" he meant that which subserves a soul. God, being perfect, perfectly controls his body; we do so with ours only imperfectly. He guides us also from within each individual soul as the *antaryāmin* or "inner controller." *Karma* is merely the working out of God's will; and if we call on God in faith we shall be rewarded by being born in God's glorious heaven, close to him. By the metaphor of the body Rāmānuja preserves the sense of intimate unity between God and the world, as expressed in the Upanishads themselves.

The Lingāyata Contrast

Lingāyata was founded in the twelfth century by an intellectual and reformer called Bāsava. Its other name is Vīraśaiva or heroic Śaivism. It has a certain austerity, deriving ultimately from the Jain tradition. The Lingāyats are called "*lingam*-carriers," the meaning of their name, because each person is supposed to carry a small phallic symbol in a tube fastened around the neck or to the arm, and this is virtually the sole ikon in their faith. It is useless to go on pilgrimage or worship in temples or perform any other ritual actions, and for the major part of life the sole practice enjoined by Bāsava was the reverencing of the *lingam*, symbol of Śiva, twice a day. Some other rites and the use of holy water, ashes, rosaries, and so on also came into Lingāyata practice, which concentrates in other respects on the paying of homage to Śiva, through the formula *Namaḥ Śivāya*, and the inner recollection of the God.

Striking features of Lingāyata are its rejection of the caste system, its condemnation of child marriage, and its proclamation of the equality of the sexes. Though it has a hereditary priesthood of its own, it avoids all the rituals of the Brahmins, and in some respects seems a protest against Brahmin domination. Though it rejected caste at the outset, the inevitable of course happened: it itself was treated by the other castes as a caste. There is little escaping the embracing arms of the system in Hindu India. Its ethics are those of equality and humility, as befits those who follow the great God. Honesty and hard work in one's daily occupation were deemed important; and in some ways the group seems like a Hindu counterpart of Protestant Christianity.

Kashmiri Śaivism: a Synthesis

Very different in emphasis from the two regional movements we have looked at is the so-called Trika (Triad) Śaivism of Kashmir, which started as a Tantric movement directed at absorbing and utilizing the energy of a threesome or triad of goddesses, later seen as three manifestations of Śiva's powerful consort Kālī (probably the most potent of all Indian representations of the Goddess). Mostly the movement had its base in Kashmir; and its chief exponent and theologian was the philosopher Abhinavagupta (975?–?1035). He wrote important works on aesthetics, partly because there was emphasis in the rites of this kind of Śaivism on dance, song, and poetry. Abhinavagupta argued against various positions, though he was sympathetic to their general sense, such as Śaiva Siddhānta (the theology of south Indian Śaivism), the Yogācāra school of Buddhism, and Advaita Vedānta. In combining elements from the orthodox tradition of Śankara and the unorthodox Tantric Śaivism, which involved sexual intercourse as a means of attaining the highest state of interior bliss and knowledge, he claimed to teach the most catholic of Śaiva doctrines and practices. He saw the world as a triadic unity between the individual, the divine Śakti or Goddess, and Śiva as the underlying being behind the Goddess. This "new triad" was intended to give a positive view of the notion of Nondualism: the nondual experience could be had in ecstatic participation in the world, and not (as with Śankara) by some kind of withdrawal to a higher level of Truth.

Kṛṣṇa Devotion and Caitanya

Late in the premodern period of Hinduism, in the sixteenth century, we have in Bengal and elsewhere in the northeast (Orissa and Assam) the revival of an intense form of Kṛṣṇa devotion and Vaiṣṇava *bhakti* through the life and work of Caitanya. At the age of twenty-two, while on pilgrimage to Bodh-Gaya to perform rites for the death of his first wife, Caitanya had an intense conversion to loyalty and love toward Kṛṣṇa. As a consequence, he changed his name to Kṛṣṇa-Caitanya ("he whose consciousness is Kṛṣṇa"—hence his modern followers refer to their movement as "Krishna Consciousness"). The chief practice of devotees, whether they be mendicants or householders— and the movement made powerful headway among the middle classes—was the utterance of Kṛṣṇa's name, calling on him for divine mercy. Love of Kṛṣṇa was often modeled after the loves that Kṛṣṇa himself had with the milkmaids of Brindavan or with his divine mistress Rādhā. Separation from him was pain, and the individual *bhakta* clung to Kṛṣṇa with passion. Persons were, as elsewhere in the main Hindu tradition, caught up in a cycle of rebirth; but by God's grace and mercy they would be delivered and restored to communion with Viṣṇu, from whom, like sparks, they had originally emanated. In this latter age, the Kaliyuga, it is not easy at all for people to undertake religious duties: it is therefore fortunate that God in his love makes salvation available to those who throw themselves upon him in faith and love.

Sikhism and the Bhakti Tradition

There were some obvious affinities between the *bhakti* movements—especially the *niruṇam* form which stressed the imageless and formless God—and the Islamic heritage of devotion to the one God, Allah. The similarity was perceived with great clarity by Nānak (1469–c.1539), who came to be recognized as the first Guru in the Sikh tradition. In the traditional accounts of his life he underwent a dramatic experience when bathing in a stream, in which he received a call from God. When he reappeared after three days' absence, his first words were: "There is no Hindu; there is no Muslim." Thereafter he became a wandering recluse and undertook long journeys, even according to Sikh tradition as far as Mecca. Before his experience, however, he had already moved in this direction of providing a faith which transcended external barriers between religions. He and a Muslim minstrel called Mardana had composed hymns together, which became a vital part of later Sikh

Sikhism some key terms

Amrit Initiation by baptism in sweetened water stirred by a two-edged sword, in which the initiate swears to abide by the code or Rahit.

Granth or *Adi Granth* or *Guru Granth* The sacred scriptures of Sikhism which, since Guru Gobind Singh, serve as the teacher or Guru.

Gurdwara or *Gurudwara* The Sikh temple housing, primarily, a copy of the Granth.

Guru One of the ten leaders and preceptors of Sikhism, from Nānak to Gobind Singh.

Janamsakhi Punjabi writings celebrating the life of Guru Nānak.

Khalsa The Sikh community or order, the "pure ones" started by Gobind.

Mool Mantra The "basic verse," a brief statement of belief composed by Nānak affirming the oneness of God.

Panth The community of the Sikhs, literally the "path."

Rahit The code of ethics and rituals laid upon Sikhs, including the wearing of the five K's: uncut hair, dagger, breeches, comb, iron bangle.

Sant A member of a devotional tradition of north India, picturing God as without attributes or *nirguṇan* rather than more personally as among Vaiṣnavas. The two most important members were founders of Sikhism, Nānak and Kabir. A Sant is a preceptor or guru within the tradition.

Sat Guru The name most given to God in Sikhism, "Being, the Teacher."

Sikh Literally "disciple," member of the Sikh Panth.

> ### Guru Nānak's Japjī
>
> There is but one God whose name is true, the Creator, devoid of fear and
> enmity, immortal, unborn, self-existent; by the favor of the Guru.
>
> The True One was in the beginning; the True One was in the primal age.
>
> The True One is now also, O Nānak; the True One also shall be.
>
> By thinking I cannot obtain a conception of Him, even though I think
> hundreds of thousands of times.

worship. On Nānak's journey to Mecca he is reported to have fallen asleep in
error with his feet pointing toward Mecca, and so showing disrespect to the
Muslim faith. A mullah had woken him angrily, but Nānak's comment was
devastating: "Then turn my feet in a direction where God is not."

A feature of the religious movement set in motion by Nānak was the
importance of the guru. The teacher, who is not thought of in any way as an
incarnation or manifestation of God, is important for guiding people in the
way of Truth or God. The framework of Nānak's theology was Hindu in that
he affirmed reincarnation and that the best symbol of the divine was the
mysterious syllable Oṃ of Vedic origin. He referred to God as creator of
Brahman and the Vedas. But he dispensed with the idea of a priesthood (he
himself was a Kṣatriya, of the warrior caste).

Nānak's successors as leaders of the new community were a line of nine
further Gurus, culminating in Guru Gobind Singh, who died in 1708, and
who nominated the scriptures of the community, the Ādi Granth, henceforth
to be the Guru. Of the other Gurus perhaps Arjun is the most important. He
led the community from 1581 to 1606. He founded the Golden Temple at
Amritsar, collected the scriptures, and came into conflict with the emperor
Jehangir—a conflict which led to clearer self-definition of the Sikhs as a
militant and outwardly distinguishable group. But this side of the Sikh story
comes later, in the modern period. It may be noted that there has long been
fluidity at the edges of Sikhism. Quite a few followers of the Nānak
tradition—and that of his elder contemporary Kabīr (1440–1518), some of
whose poems were incorporated into the Sikh scriptures—remain within the
definitely Hindu framework, as followers of a path which emphasizes *bhakti*
and the unity of religions.

Some Traditional Minorities

It must not be forgotten in drawing a picture of the mainstream traditions of
the Indian classical and medieval periods that there were also some significant
minorities—for instance there were the religions of the various tribal groups
who peppered the subcontinent and who in many cases were gradually
assimilated into the fabric of mainstream culture. We can ascribe some of the

Opposite The narrative dimension: Rāma, the avatār of Viṣṇu, and Lakṣmana shooting arrows at Ravana, the demon king of Lanka. Hanuman and the monkeys are in the background, while Sita waits within Ravana's compound, guarded by the king's demons. The scene from the *Rāmāyaṇa* is depicted in a late nineteenth-century painting.

great richness of the Hindu mythic corpus to the assimilation of varied stories from such diverse groups.

There were also Christians in India throughout these later periods—the followers of St. Thomas the Apostle in south India. He is supposed to have preached there and to have been eventually martyred; his tomb is displayed in Mylapore, on the outskirts of Madras. Whether or not the tradition is true, the Thomas Christians are certainly very ancient, going back at least to the third century C.E.

There were two communities of Jews, so-called White and Black, on the coast of Kerala, and they claim origins going back to the fall of the Temple in 70 C.E.; but we have historical records only from about the year 1000.

Also settled on the west coast, from the eighth century onward, were Zoroastrians (or Parsees, "Persians," as they came to be known), who remain a small but influential element in Indian society.

The Indian Tradition in the Classical and Medieval Periods

The story we have told is only a sample of the full unfolding of events which are immensely complicated. If we look for a moment to the dimensions of religion we can rehearse some of the many patterns.

First, as to *ritual* and *practice*, we have seen varying types of yoga—Hindu, Buddhist, and Jain. We have seen the persistence of the Brahmins with their sacrificial rites and their takeover of the temples, which housed gods who were treated to worship and *bhakti*. We see how sometimes the inward devotion becomes much more important than any outward observance, as among the Lingāyats and in the Sikh religion of Nānak. We see India drawn together by great pilgrimages, at Benares and at the vast Kumbh Mela fair at Prayag, where the rivers Jumna and Ganges meet the invisible river Sarasvatī. We see great regional divergences of practice, from Tamil Nadu to Kashmir and from Kerala to Assam. We see coming into this complex the Muslims, who helped to knock out Buddhism in north India and contributed to its demise in the whole of India. We see everywhere villages, and at a more basic level households. Each household was likely to have its little shrine, and such domestic rites remained a vital part of the fabric of Indian religions.

In *experience* we have the patterns of inner meditation and strenuously achieved bliss and equanimity; the numinous awe before great and fierce goddesses and gods; the devotion and sense of peace bestowed by loving deities; the securities bestowed by local and domestic gods; the sexual ecstasies of Tantra; and the luminous inner visions got in the Vajrayāna. There are mergings with Tārā in Tibet; there is the lofty path of inner purity in Sri Lanka; and there is still shamanism in villages and healing cults. All such experiences are impregnated with ideas and symbols drawn from doctrine and myth.

Śiva dancing and so signifying the effortless joy of the act of creation. The Lord of the Dance is represented in a bronze statuette from southern India.

In *philosophy* there is Emptiness and the imageless (*nirguṇam*) Brahman, the creative Lord, dim liberation from the color and miseries of rebirth, there is Dualism and Nondualism and all the mysterious variations in between, there is the One Self of Advaita, the No-Self of Buddhism, and the many selves of the *bhakti* cults. There are the Six Viewpoints of the orthodox Brahmin schools, the semi-orthodox Śaiva Siddhānta and other systems, the many schools of Buddhism, the Jain metaphysics, and the negations of the Materialists. All these patterns of thought are woven into classical and medieval Indian civilization. To complicate further, there are the varied speculations of Sufis and Muslim philosophers.

At the *narrative* level, there are immense riches in medieval Hinduism: the great Sanskrit epics of the *Rāmāyana* and the *Mahābhārata*, translations in later vernaculars, the storehouse of myth known as the *Purānas*, the birth stories, of Buddhism and the tales concerning the various Buddhas and Bodhisattvas, the Jain narratives, the bewildering variety of local legend; and with all this there was *doctrinal* belief in many forms of God. The multiple manifestations of the gods gave the Hindu scene a confusing multiplicity, and as yet there was not yet the clear step to saying that the gods, however many, were really One; or at least this motif was only sporadically observed. Presiding over the many, though, were Śiva and Viṣṇu and the Goddess, and as a strong and relentless rival conception the Allah of the Muslims.

By medieval times the *social* grip of the caste system was inexorable. With Buddhism fading and Jainism not so strong, it was possible for small rivals to be swallowed up and themselves treated as castes (this happened to Jews and Christians). The system imposed a kind of overall pattern on the varieties of customs and legal obligations and even ethical standards of the various groups: from those who sacrificed goats to those who were strict in harmlessness toward animals; and from celibacy to the glorification of sex; from those who searched for complete freedom to those who imposed the obligation of suicide for widows. There were also the types of holy persons on the fringes of society to consider—the naked ascetics, the *sannyāsins*, the wandering gurus, the monks of Hindu orders, and the monks of Buddhism and Jainism. There were the tribal groups trapped like islands within the sea of Indian culture.

And as a *material* sign of regional variety and religious plurality there were the many shrines, from the high temples of the south to the *stūpas* of Nepal, and from the Jain temples of Mount Abu to the wondrous painted walls of Ajanta. In all these outer manifestations of the spirit of Indian culture, perhaps the statues of the meditating Buddha and the dancing Śiva stand out—the one replete with lovely calm, the other expressing a dynamism of beauteous exuberance. These were the twin polarities of Indian civilization. One cannot anymore quite go back to the Middle Ages, but the nearest thing perhaps is the Kathmandu Valley, with its medieval carved balconies and old streets, and its quiet blending of Buddhist and Hindu ways of life. It gives us a hint at least, amid the new diesel fumes, of what that ancient and diverse culture was like well before the British were poised to transform at least the surface of the subcontinent.

CHAPTER 3

China

A General Perspective

Westerners have often been confused about religion in China. They have assumed that Chinese religious and philosophical ideas can be classified in a Western way, so that we can speak of three religions of China, namely Confucianism, Daoism, and Buddhism; but often these are not so much three as parts of a single functioning system. Also, the words themselves which we use can be misleading. Is "Confucianism" a word meaning the philosophical stream of thought that started with Confucius? Is Daoism the teaching of Lao-tzu? If so, then the religions labeled by these nouns are something very different from the "philosophical" teachings, though overlapping with them. Moreover, the state cult which is sometimes labeled "Confucianism," though it rested on an ideology of ritual which can be traced to Confucius—and though temples to the memory of the Sage himself were incorporated into it—was a rather artificial construction. It was not strictly speaking the religion of anyone, except that people were expected to observe it in connection with the ongoing welfare of the State. Also there is so-called "popular religion," meaning the general and usually very localized religion of the people, which also is sometimes loosely referred to as Confucianism, but is actually a set of practices and ideas which draws on various aspects and institutions of Daoism, Buddhism, and the state religion. All this, from a Western angle, is rather messy and muddled. It seems clearer for us to make some stipulations about words.

First, what we are dealing with as a single roughly organic, but also very localized and varied phenomenon, is Chinese religion. Now because of substantial organizational facts we can point fairly clearly to Buddhism and Daoism, both of which have well defined monastic embodiment and a class of religious specialists; and when we refer to these traditions by these names, we shall mean these religions as separately embodied. In parallel with this we shall

Map 2 China and Japan.

use "Confucianism" to refer to the official cult which disappeared with the revolution of 1911, and has had no basic significance since then. To refer to the philosophical tradition from the time of Confucius (and indeed before) we shall speak of "Confucian thought." This includes a strong strand of ethical theory and prescriptions, so one should not take the word "thought" in too austerely intellectual a sense. Similarly we shall refer to the Daoist intellectual tradition, which begins with the anthology known as the *Daode Jing (Tao-te Ching)*, ascribed to the legendary Laozi (Lao-tzu), and the treatise known as the *Book of Zhuangzi (Chuang-tzu)*, as "Daoist thought." Themes from Daoist

---

Confucius: Analects

Kong said, "The ruler who governs the state through virtue is like the pole star, which stays put while the other stars revolve around it."

Kong said, "All of the three hundred odes in the Classic of Poetry can be summed up in one of its lines, 'Have no wrong thoughts.'"

Kong said, "If you control the people by government acts and keep them in line with law and order, they will refrain from doing wrong, but they will not have a sense of honor or shame.

But if you lead them through virtue and regulate them by the laws of propriety, then they will have a sense of shame and will attain goodness."

Kong said, "At fifteen my mind was fixed on learning. By thirty my character had been formed. At forty I had no more confusions. At fifty I understood the Mandate of Heaven. At sixty it was easy for me to hear the truth. At seventy I could follow my desires without transgressing what was right."

thought were to be incorporated, as one element, into "Daoist religion." But neither Laozi nor Zhuangzi, even if they really existed as historical persons, was responsible for the later faith, with all its complexities, which used the name of Dao to describe itself.

Although the Chinese in fact managed to integrate rites from the three strands into their local practice, there were of course also rivalries for state patronage between the three organizations—the class of *ju* or Confucian-trained scholars, the Buddhist order, and the Daoist monasteries. We may also mention that at varying periods certain Western religions made some impact on China: Nestorian Christianity, once quite powerful; Manichaeism; Zoroastrianism; Judaism; and Islam. Of these, Islam remains the most potent. In modern times Christian missions have made an impact, especially in the educational field.

Important Periods of Chinese Religious History

Shortly before 1000 B.C.E. the old Shang dynasty came to an end, to be replaced by the Zhou (Chou), under the regent who became an ideal figure in later times, the Duke of Zhou. It was from the eighth century B.C.E., under the rule of the Eastern Zhou (771–221 B.C.E.), that Chinese culture as we know it began to form. The classics which Confucius was to edit as part of his educational and philosophical task date from this time. Confucius himself, or Master Kong (K'ung) as his name says ("Confucius" being a Latinized reflection of Kongfuzi (K'ung-Fu-tzu)), lived from 551 to 479 B.C.E. The legendary Laozi was supposedly an older contemporary of his; but the anthology which he is supposed to have composed is doubtless somewhat later. The succeeding centuries saw some important figures in the traditions of Confucian and Daoist thought, such as Zhuangzi and Mengzi (Mencius).

By the first century C.E. Buddhism was starting to establish itself in China. In the second century Dao (Tao) as a religious system was founded (or at least one main branch of it) by Zhang Daoling (Chang Tao Ling). It seems therefore reasonable to look on the period before the second century C.E. as the formative or early period. Then we can look on the Sui and Tang dynasties, up to the tenth century, as the classical period, during which the three religious traditions took their main form, and when great contributions were made by specifically Chinese Buddhism to the corpus of Buddhist thought and practice. And finally, from the eleventh to the end of the eighteenth century we may nominate the medieval or premodern period, before the full and somewhat fatal impact of the West made itself felt in China.

During the classical period, particularly, the effects of Chinese culture were perceived abroad, especially in Vietnam, in Korea, and in Japan. China was the foremost world civilization, and was creating a new synthesis of cultures in Chinese Buddhism. In the nineteenth century substantial migrations occurred under the influence of a growing colonialist world economy, and in consequence Chinese culture and religion are to be found in the U.S.A., the West Indies, Indonesia, Malaysia, Singapore, and elsewhere.

Some Fundamental Ideas and Practices

Since we are dealing with a single civilization which can be held to incorporate a single, but loosely knit, religion, it is reasonable to try to single out its chief ideas and practices. At the *ritual* level, there is that most general and important concept of *li (li)*, roughly meaning due ceremonial behavior, or ritual at the broadest, including music. This *li* played a vital role in Kong's whole philosophy. Of immediate significance also were the offerings directed toward ancestors—a kind of cult that occurred in the emperor's reverence toward his ancestors, in clan temples, and in the home. The cult of ancestors ties in with funerary rites, designed to transfer the dead happily to their resting-places, so that they are not consigned to the sad status of restless ghosts.

Chinese Religion some key terms

Chiao A religious movement, teaching or sect.

Dao Way or principle through which nature works.

Jing A classical text, usually used for the ancient Confucian collection of five classics, but also applied to some other fundamental sources such as the Platform Sutra of Qān tradition.

Li Principle or the spiritual substance or energy which combines with *qi*.

Li Rituals, ceremonial, rules of propriety, good behavior: a central concept in Confucian education.

Qān Meditation (a Chinese version of Sanskrit *dhyāna*) and name of an important school known in Japanese as Zen.

Qi The idea of material energy, which combines with *li* or principle to make up things in the world, according to Neo-Confucian philosophy.

Ren Human-heartedness, or loving benevolence toward other humans: a pivotal ethical notion in Confucianism.

Taizhi The Supreme Ultimate in the *Ijing* and in Neo-Confucianism or Source of all things.

Taiping The heavenly peace or eschatological kingdom looked forward to in some Daoist literature: the name given to the revolutionaries of 1850–64 who tried to establish a new order in central and north China.

Tian Heaven or personalized God residing above, whose cult was that of the Emperor.

Yang The male principle in the world, whose interplay with Yin forms the basis of much Chinese thinking.

Yin The female principle in dialectical interplay with Yang.

The doctrinal dimension: various motifs important in Chinese thought are symbolized here – the Yin and the Yang, the Buddhist swastika, the basic trigrams that, when combined, form the hexagrams of the *Ijing* (*Book of Changes*), and stylized dragons, alluding to the fertility of nature and the emperor.

A third important ritual motif was divination, extensively practiced from before the time of the classic *Book of Changes* or *Ijing* (*I Ching*). Geomancy, or the practice of harmonizing human activity—such as building a house—with the spirit (and the spirits) of the landscape, is worth mention too. Chinese religion also made its contributions to forms of mysticism and Yoga, through Daoist breath control and the novel methods of the Qān (Ch'ān) or meditation school of Buddhism.

At the *experiential* level, a characteristic idea was the goal of experiencing harmony or identity with nature through following the Way of Nature, the Dao. Mediumistic religion in the form of being possessed by the god was important in popular religion, and much attention was paid to visions of the divine realm.

Doctrinally, importance was always attached to the concept of Heaven, sometimes treated rather abstractly as Providence, and sometimes more personally as God. Rulers were thought of as receiving, or not receiving, the Mandate of Heaven which justified (or failed to justify) their governance. In later thought there was also the notion of the Great Ultimate, a sort of God beyond God. In cosmology much was made throughout Chinese history of the interplay between the Yang (Yang) and the Yin (Yin) (the male and female principles, and active and passive polarities). There was a whole system of classifying phenomena according to the Yin and Yang and Five Elements or processes: wood, fire, earth, metal, and water.

The *narrative* and mythic dimension of Chinese culture was peculiarly rich. From our perspective we need to note the story of Kong's life, the tale of Laozi, and the stories of the divine immortals as especially significant. *Socially*, the ideal of the scholar or *ju* was important; but still more vital was the figure of the sage. Much of Confucian *ethics* revolved around family relationships, but at the same time Buddhist and Daoist monasticism provided an escape from the family's structures, through the monastic vocation. Throughout there is a corresponding ethical contrast between the morality to be displayed by the benevolent person in the world, summed up in *ren (jen)* or human-heartedness, and that of the Daoist or Buddhist who is concerned with *wu wei*, that is, not-acting, or acting through not acting.

These then are some of the principal motifs of Chinese religious culture. If one were to point to anything at the *material* level it would perhaps be the

The social dimension: Chinese women mourning at a grave are burning imitation money as an offering. Ancestors remain important members of the society they have left behind.

painting scroll. For the Chinese painter there is no frame. It is not as if nature can be framed: the scene painted wanders off beyond the dimensions of the scroll itself. And it is common to bind together the arts: the poem or inscription is an integral part of the painting and vice versa. A certain dynamic boundlessness gives fluidity to Chinese culture: it is less concerned with analysis, than either Western or Indian philosophy and religion.

The Early Period

Kong's Life and Teachings

Because of the total imprint which he placed upon Chinese culture, it is right for us to start with Kong, whose discourse has come down to us in the book known as *Analects* and whose spirit was to be followed by many generations of China's scholars and administrators. Kong was born, probably in 551 B.C.E., in what is now Shandong Province, in the small state of Lu. He was perhaps from a minor aristocratic family. At any rate, he received an education, which until his time was normally reserved for the elite. One of the revolutionary aspects of his teaching was to throw open his academy to everyone; this helped, with his teachings, to create the notion of the true gentleman (*xunzi* or *hsün-tzu*) whose high class is not a matter of birth but rather of moral behavior. Kong was perturbed by the chaotic state of political and social life in his times. In theory the royal house of Zhou was supreme in north China, but in fact there was a variety of independent feudal rulers. He saw that good rule should occur not by force but by moral suasion: and for this reason he paid a lot of attention to rites and ceremonies, since he perceived in them the characteristic way of inculcating right behavior and loyal service. He pondered the meaning of tradition, and though a reformer, he was also highly committed to older ways. He had a vision of the past, refined and redefined, as playing a vital role in shaping the nonviolent means whereby the good ruler maintains his power.

At about the age of fifty, by which time, so Kong avers in the *Analects*, he "knew Heaven's decree," he took service as a minister or official in the state of Lu; but in the event his political intervention was not a success. He left Lu in wandering exile for some thirteen years in neighboring states, with a band of his disciples. He went back to Lu around the time of his sixty-eighth birthday. By seventy, he said, "he could follow his heart's desire without overstepping the line." He had reached full maturity of judgment. He died at seventy-three, saddened by the loss of his son and two disciples who predeceased him. But his influence lived on; and eventually his ideal of the scholar as administrator became the norm for about two thousand years.

He is credited (probably wrongly) with having edited the Six Classics, actually now five: the *Shijing* (*Shi Ching*) or Classic of Poetry, the *Ijing* or Classic of Changes, the *Shujing* (*Shu Ching*) or Classic of History, the *Lizhi* (*Li Chi*) or Book of Ritual, the *Qungqiu* (*Ch'un-ch'iu*) or Spring and Autumn Annals, and the now lost *Yuejing* (*Yüeh Ching*) or Classic of Music. At any rate, his name came to be associated with these major literary works, which

Confucius (551–479 B.C.E.), from an anonymous seventeenth-century Chinese painting in the Bibliothèque Nationale, Paris.

together with some other writings came to form the curriculum for the imperial civil service examinations. And so, indirectly at least, Kong was responsible for the creation of a class of bureaucrats who had deep literary skills, knew about the ceremonial side of life, and were brought up in the ideals not only of correct formal behavior but also of the necessary sincerity which has to lie behind it. They were also infused with the moral ideal of *ren* or human-heartedness. The official ruler must be correct, sincere, and humane. It was a fine vision, which placed classical education at the heart of politics. The Confucian ideals were to serve China well.

There was nothing greatly speculative in Kong's thought. It is clear from various references that, although he did not talk about it much, he respected belief in Heaven as a kind of personal God. He did not talk about miracles and such events, it is reported; and he was not without a gently rationalistic tone in what he said about religion. It is partly from this that later "official" Confucians were often dismissive of what they saw as the superstitions of popular religion. There came to develop an elitist poise about the scholarly gentleman in China; but this seems to have been foreign to Kong's own thinking. He underlined the importance of treating all people well and the sanctity of ancient rites, including offerings to ancestors and to Heaven. His was not a combative nature, but one of humility and grave courtesy, not without a sense of humor. A nice touch is that when out shooting he would not shoot at a sitting bird, thus showing a sense of fair play.

Kong set the agenda of much later Chinese thought, concerned as he was with political rule, right conduct, and human nature. In the following century we see the pendulum swinging toward a much less formal view of virtue and government. Mozi (Mo-tzu) argued vigorously for the importance of universal love and applied utilitarian tests to all policies, which should be in the interests of the people, conducing to their wealth and safety. He found a sanction for his doctrines in the will of a Supreme God, Heaven (Tian or T'ien), who had under his command a host of lesser spirits. His personalist ethic and frugality in living did not appeal to all, and the movement which he founded gradually died out, though there was a revival of interest in the eighteenth century C.E.

Mengzi, Xunzi, Hanfeizi

The greatest of the successors to Kongfuzi was Mengzi, known in the West as Mencius, who lived c.371–289 B.C.E. or perhaps two decades earlier. He advocated rule by a kingly sage, whose policies would be informed with virtue. His path should be the Wangdao (Wang-tao) or Emperor's Way; and people were entitled to rise up against an evil monarch who would have forfeited the Mandate of Heaven. Despite this he was strongly pacifist, partly because of the disturbed and bloody period during which he lived. Conquest should only proceed by the desire of other peoples to join the country of a supremely benevolent ruler. The most important part of his teaching, however, has to do with his concept of *xin* (*hsin*), or "heart," "mind." This is the power within each person which contains dispositions, which should be encouraged to sprout and grow, toward *ren* or humaneness, *i* or dutifulness, *li* or proper behavior, and *xhi* (*chih*) or knowledge of right and wrong. This inner sense is essentially oriented therefore toward goodness. In other words human nature is essentially good. In this Meng was defending the Confucian tradition against those–Daoists, for instance–who saw the human heart as egoistic and obstructive of harmonious living, and on the other hand against those like Mozi who had a superficial idea of goodness, defining it in outer and material terms. It followed also from his idea of *hsin* that both moral education and political policy should be designed to bring out the innate tendencies toward virtue.

By contrast Xunzi (Hsün-tzu) (third century B.C.E.), who lived to see the unification of the states of China under the Qing (Ch'in) regime (221 B.C.) and was upset to observe its harsh nature, especially since two of his own disciples served as officials at court, took a different and more pessimistic line from that of Mencius. In his view human nature was inherently chaotic and bad and needed the forces of education to tame it. He strongly emphasized the *li* aspect of the Confucian tradition: ceremonial and behavioral propriety was something that involved both inner feeling and outer act, but it was instrumental in teaching individuals how to act well, and was crucial therefore in moral education. In practice, then, Xunzi, though breaking with the moral optimism of the earlier Confucian tradition, adopted a very similar view of the shape and point of education. Some of his writings also give *li* a cosmic role. Thus he says:

> Indeed it is through *li* that Heaven and earth are in harmony, that the sun and

moon are splendid, that the four seasons succeed each other, that the stars follow their motions, that the rivers and streams maintain their flow, that all things and creatures enjoy prosperity, and joy and wrath are controlled.

He also rather movingly writes, in defence of reverence for the dead, so central a value in Chinese culture:

When man's end and beginning are both well treated, the Dao of humanity is fulfilled. Hence the superior individual respects the beginning and attends to the end. To treat them alike is the Dao of the superior individual and the refinement of *li* and *i*. To exalt the living and belittle the dead is to respect one who has consciousness and neglect one who has lost it—this is the way of the evil man...

Xunzi came at the end of a creative period, that of the so-called "hundred philosophers." There were various schools apart from the Confucian, of course—Daoists, legalists or authoritarian writers, and others. The Confucian tradition had already established itself as an educational force, and it was not

The mythic dimension: the legendary Laozi, "founder" of Daoism, with his disciples en route to the far West (some Daoists thought of Buddhism as a distorted form of Daoism brought back into China).

Opposite A Tibetan figure of the Buddha, bringing the earth to bear witness of his Enlightenment.

long before Confucian literature became the staple of a centralized education system through the establishment of a Great Academy. Yet this was after a traumatic period for Chinese thought and scholarship, when in 213 B.C.E. all controversial books were burned.

Legalism (Fajia or Fa-chia) had as its chief exponent Hanfeizi (Han Fei-tzu), who had studied with Xunzi but rejected the latter's Confucian morality. The main point about Fajia was what it rejected: it saw written law as opposed to traditional moral values as the best way of controlling people. Hanfeizi 's book is a witty exercise in expounding for a ruler the best methods of dominating people and controlling a bureaucracy. A person's title should be defined in terms of the work he was expected to perform and his actual success in this should be measured. The central fact about government is the use of power, and Hanfeizi has a lot of good advice on this front. For instance, the effective ruler should not make his desires or prejudices known, or otherwise his ministers will distort information and advice to him. He should delegate action, and so should sit at the center of power not acting (somewhat in the Daoist manner). The two handles of government are reward and punishment, and these should be used systematically. Method will triumph over virtue: you do not need to wait for a sage to get effective rule, since heeding Hanfeizi 's methods will accomplish much, and mediocre talent will be able to make good use of them. But his rather cynical way of writing and his emphasis on human-created law rather than traditionally sanctioned morality gave him a Machiavellian reputation.

Laozi and the Daoist Tradition

Meanwhile the main anti-Confucian tradition of this early period had already begun to take shape in the book known as the *Daode Jing*, the Classic of the Way and its Virtue. This wonderful and mysterious text has exercised a fascination down the centuries, and not for nothing are there over forty English translations published. It is ascribed in the Daoist tradition to the sage Laozi (Lao Tan), who supposedly was an older contemporary of Kong, whom he instructed in various matters, including *li*, so claim later texts. Modern scholars are skeptical as to whether there was such an historical person; but he is vivid nevertheless in Chinese imagination, and for vast numbers of Chinese through the ages he has been real enough. Eventually he was seen as an incarnation of a transcendental Laozi, supreme Immortal. But of such legendary developments we shall speak later, when we come to describe Daoism as a religion during the classical period. For the moment we are dealing with Daoist thought, in the *Daode Jing* and the later book the *Zhuangzi*.

The justly famous opening words of the Classic of the Way and its Virtue have many resonances. They read:

> The way that can be followed is not the eternal way;
> The name that can be named is not the eternal name;
> That which is without name is of heaven and earth the beginning;

Left A red lacquer panel, with Yin and Yang surrounded by the Eight Symbols used in divination, which was used to ward off evil spirits that might enter the house.

Below The mythic dimension: the Chinese transformation of Avalokiteśvara, Kuan-yin, guide of souls and savior deity. A tenth-century painting on silk. British Museum, London.

That which is nameable is of the ten thousand things the mother.
He who is eternally without desire perceives the spiritual side of it:
He who is permanently with desire perceives the limit of it.
These two things are the same in origin but different in name;
Calling them the same is a mystery —
Indeed it is the mystery of mysteries; of all spirituality it is the gate.

These words suggest that the underlying but ineffable principle which pervades the universe (and is indeed the origin of the cosmos) is the Dao, the Way. It is a fundamental idea in the classical work that this Way is something to which we should conform: but since nature acts with complete spontaneity, so in conforming to her we need spontaneity and complete naturalness. It is not something which can be striven for. That is why it is not a way which can be followed. It is not a way which can be taught. From this perspective Confucian thought with its stress on complex and learned *li* was on the wrong track. This is why according to the legend Kong needed instruction from Laozi. So the person who lives in accord with the way of all things sees the way in all things—and so the nameable world is also an unnameable Reality. As later was to be realized, there are profound similarities between these teachings and those of Buddhism, especially Mahāyāna Buddhism in the works of the *Prajñāpāramitā* and of Nāgārjuna. These resemblances were to be exploited both by Buddhists, in their evolution of Ch'ān or Zen Buddhism, and by Daoists, who saw Buddhism as deceptive and derivative.

There is in the *Daode Jing* an array of analogies which were used to suggest the power of the empty Dao, the power of *wu-wei*, of "acting through not acting": there is the valley which is the "active" space between the mountains; there is water which is so strong in its formless fluidity; there is the space in the pot—the whole point of a pot is that its space should be filled, but that point is constituted by a kind of nothingness. In brief, Daoist thought emphasizes not-acting, naturalness, spontaneity, passivity. It is a quietist tradition, emphasizing peace and meditation, and it looks, in its experiential dimension, to the achievement of a contemplative inner stillness. By contrast Confucianist thought is active, pragmatic, conventional. Daoist thought is quietistic, anarchistic, and intuitive: in fact, ultimately it is not thought.

These motifs were carried on in the book known after its supposed author Zhuangzi. He is supposed to have lived from about 369 B.C.E. to about 286 B.C.E. There are not many details of his life available, but we do have the fine and poetic book named for him. Again, he sees the Dao as the quiet spirit pervading everything. Since all the dualities which we use, such as health and sickness, life and death, pleasure and pain, brightness and darkness, are artificial—made up by us, and not ultimately true in telling about the Dao the way it really is—we should overcome them: we should treat sickness and health, good and bad, alike. We should cultivate utter serenity. This mystical quest is finally something very private. Zhuangzi's doctrines were thus viewed by Confucian thinkers with deep suspicion as being subversive.

We may note that Daoist thinking was important in later Chinese contexts in its providing an ideology of rebellion, so maybe the Confucians were right in pointing toward its subversive nature as a movement. Zhuangzi also, in describing the freedom of the Dao-conforming sage, writes of great flights through the air and immense longevity. Later in the Daoist tradition much attention is paid to the search for an elixir of life to stave off death, and to other miraculous powers that the Daoist follower might acquire. In these ways Zhuangzi foreshadows later developments.

We have sampled some of the thinkers of the early period. China was moving toward unification. Buddhism was expanding into Central Asia. Various forces were arising which together would help to form religious Daoism. The scene was set, therefore, for what we have called the classical period, in which the three religions of China came to coalesce with varieties of local religion to produce the system which served China for a long time until its breakdown in the nineteenth century.

Zhuangzi

Zhuangzi (Chuang-Tzu, 369?—286? B.C.E.) was probably the most influential Daoist thinker in ancient China. Laozi has long been regarded as the founder of the tradition, though he may not have existed, and if he did he might have been a contemporary of Zhuangzi. He was a native of Meng, probably in Honan, and was for a while an official in Ch'i-yüan. Not much is known about his life, but he left us the *Book of Zhuangzi*, which was condensed out of a larger mass of writing by Kuo Hsiang (Guoxiang) (died in 312 C.E.) during the Neo-Daoist revival. This is a wonderfully fanciful piece of writing. It includes all sorts of fables, including talking animals and birds and even trees. The aim is to loosen up the reader's intellect, and liberate him from blind adherence to the distinctions and polarizations of language. Zen Buddhism much later was to use a similarly fanciful and paradoxical method to achieve the same goal. The most famous anecdote in the collection is the following story:

> Once Chuang Chou dreamt he was a butterfly, a butterfly which flitted and fluttered around, happy with himself and doing just as he pleased. He didn't know he was Chuang ... Suddenly he woke up and there he was, solid and unmistakably Chuang ... But he didn't know whether he was Chuang who dreamt he was a butterfly or a butterfly who dreamt he was Chou.

The kind of enlightenment achieved by Zhuangzi could cause a person to become a recluse, perhaps in the countryside, where he would live in harmony with the animals and insects inhabiting the area, or he could pass humbly and anonymously for a member of society, secure in his superior vision. This could be an antidote to the formality of Confucian society.

The Classical Period

Confucianism Becomes Official

Despite the espousal of Legalism by the emperor Shi Huangdi (Shih Huang-ti, reigned 221–210 B.C.E.), there were greater attractions for a ruler in taking up Confucian thought—partly its traditionalism, which was important in the legitimation of rule; partly its ritualism, which could be taken up into the practices of the central government; and partly too its moralism (it is, for one thing, unwise to act the Machiavelli if you parade that that is what you are doing; it is better to conceal cynicism behind a mask of morality). And Confucian thought was believable. At any rate, it was under the Han Dynasty, from the first century C.E., that Confucianism came to be an officially sponsored ideology and cult. Offerings were to be made to Kong, and these were linked to state ceremonies in which the emperor made sacrifices to Heaven. Much later, in the seventh century, Confucian temples were established throughout the administrative system of the empire. Tablets inscribed to famous disciples and other prominent figures were included too, so that Confucianism came to be a kind of "civil religion" or national cult honoring those who had served the empire well.

The kind of Confucianism that became a state orthodoxy was the kind of view espoused by the highly influential thinker Dong Zhongshi (Tung Chung-shi, c.179–104 B.C.E.). He expounded the doctrines of Confucian thought in terms of the generally accepted Chinese cosmology of the time, making use therefore of the notions of Yin and Yang, the Five Elements, and Tian or Heaven, which he saw as a personal Lord. He made use too of the idea of the Mandate of Heaven, and evolved a theory of the succession of dynasties. If a ruler does not follow the Mandate by acting morally and wisely, then sooner or later the dynasty will break down. The Yin-Yang theory was applied by him to crucial human relations, especially the three bonds between ruler and ruled, father and son, and husband and wife. In each of these the Yang (ruler, father, husband) is superior. This hierarchical theory of human relationships was pervasive in Confucian China.

In effect, official Confucianism began the process of treating Kong as an honored ancestor, together with other notables and the ancestors of the emperor. This was parallel to the cults which emerged systematically in classical China, especially in the south, of clan lineages. All this was in addition to domestic shrines in which the names of forebears inscribed on tablets came to be the norm.

Daoism Emerges as a Religion

The early Daoist thought which we have looked at became an ingredient, though only one ingredient, of religious Daoism. Another was supplied by the experiences and organizational initiative of the legendary Zhang Dao-ling. In 142 C.E. he received a vision of Laozi, deified, who bestowed on him the title of Tianshi (T'ien-shih) or Heavenly Master. A new scheme of worship was

A priest's robe depicting the Daoist heaven, with the immortals.

ordained, blood sacrifices were banned, and the faithful were to eschew their old gods. The movement became a highly organized sect, to which adherents were supposed to contribute five pecks of rice (so the nickname of the movement became "The Way of Five Pecks of Rice").

A similar movement in eastern China was inspired by a prophetic book which was later included in the Daoist canon, the *Taiping Zhing*, or Classic of the Great Peace. This idea of a future heavenly state in which harmony was to be achieved on earth was the inspiration of a number of messianic uprisings in Chinese history. The Yellow Turban, a religiously motivated rebellion, was eventually violently suppressed, but Zhanglu (Chang Lu), Zhang Daoling's grandson, who was also in conflict with the government, negotiated a surrender, and resided at the court of the Wei Emperor, receiving patronage and protection for the Heavenly Master sect. The organization among other things supplied free food and lodging over a wide area, and in some respects replaced the official government. By now Laozi was treated as the supreme god as Laojun (Lao-chün), Lord Lao; as a human being he was an incarnate manifestation of the Supreme One. This form of Daoism has lasted until the present day, with the chain of Heavenly Masters continuing through the centuries. But other ingredients as well went to make up Daoism as a religion.

One was a consequence of the failure of utopian rebellions. The Taiping or heavenly peace was to be sought within the individual through the practice of a shamanistic type of meditation which might result in a vision of heavenly beings, and even of Laojun. Meanwhile the traditional concern with longevity got combined with the techniques of alchemy, a kind of magical chemistry which sought to find some substance which would prolong life. Also important was the process of healing, it being thought that sickness was due to some moral fault or other. Some of the more practical concerns of Daoism were incorporated into a book by the important writer Gohong (Ko Hung, 283–343), the *Baopuzi* (*Pao-p'u-tzu*) or "The Master who Embraces Simplicity": by the pursuit of good deeds, breathing exercises, care not to lose sperm, and taking a sufficient amount of the elixir of immortality, one might aspire to become an immortal.

As a final main ingredient of religious Daoism we might mention the movement associated with Mount Mao or Maoshan (Mao Shan) in Jiangsu (Kiangsu), and based on revelations to Yangxi (Yang Hsi) in the latter part of the fourth century: he was visited by supreme immortals. This visionary material was incorporated into further scriptures.

So what we have in the Daoist movements, increasingly coalescing into a single definable religion, is a combination of ancient quietism; a strong and fervent devotion to a heavenly Lord, believed to be incarnate in Laozi himself, and to a lesser extent to other immortals; and the belief that the essence of divinity also resides in each individual where it can be cultivated by meditation, breathing, diet, and alchemical experiments. Eventually the

The ritual dimension: inside a Chinese temple in Taiwan.

contemplative practices of Daoism became highly complex and bore some resemblances to high Tantra in Buddhism.

Indeed, in a sense Buddhism became a fifth ingredient in Daoism; its coming into China was a challenge to Daoism in particular. One of the ways the Daoists hit back was by describing how Laozi went west and actually taught a kind of Buddhism to the Indians. But also to some degree Daoism created a kind of counterpart of Buddhism: by arranging its scriptures into three parts like the Tripitaka; by composing scriptures too from the late fourth century onward which are very much Buddhist in spirit, and which a writer on Daoism (John Lagerwey) has described as "pure Mahāyāna Daoism"; and by founding monasteries with Daoist nuns and monks. Their meditation methods and esoteric sexual practices, more ancient than Tantra, had great resemblances to some Buddhist practices.

Naturally there was rivalry for imperial patronage, and during the Tang (T'ang) Dynasty (618–907) the issue swayed. But it was the emperor Gaozong (Kao-tsung) (649–83) who decreed that there should be state-sponsored Daoist and Buddhist monasteries in each prefecture of the empire. This system of protection—and control—of the religions lasted until 1911. It did not interfere with the important role of *ju* or Confucian scholars as administrators. Thus a pattern was born of mutual support and toleration, even if many of the Confucians rather rationalistically treated the monks, nuns, and priests as presiding over superstitions fit for the ignorant masses.

Buddhism Comes to China

Buddhism infiltrated into China along the trade routes that ran north of Tibet; its spread was more by presence than by proselytization. Its earliest movement into China dates from the first century C.E., and by 166 C.E. we find a record of the emperor Huan (Huan) installing statues of Huanglao (Huang-Lao) (a god synthesized from the Yellow Emperor Huangdi (Huang-ti), a prehistoric immortal, and Laozi) and of the Buddha within his palace.

The task of translation was great, and often because of its suitability Daoist language was used, or otherwise some rather unintelligible phonetic attempts to render Sanskrit words. But Buddhism described itself as a path or *dao*; it had its immortal, the Buddha; it practiced acting by not-acting. It is perhaps not surprising that Chinese Daoists, prejudiced somewhat against what was after all a foreign religion (and foreign-looking, as in the garb of monks and the lineaments of the Buddha statues made before the religion was thoroughly sinified or made Chinese), should see it as a garbled version of the ancient teachings of the famed Laozi, who had after all journeyed to the Western Pass and beyond, no doubt to spread the truth there.

Also foreign were the key ideas of *karma* and reincarnation. But these could be turned to fruitful use in China as time went on. The cosmology allowed of many heavens, and the Pure Land school in India had pioneered the attractive idea of a paradise whither those who call on Amitābha with faith would go.

The notion was further developed in the Chinese scene. But the most original of the schools as developed in the Chinese context were the Tientai (T'ien-t'ai), the Huayan (Hua-yen) and the Qān.

The Tiantai School

By now we are reaching forward five centuries since Buddhism first came to China. It had experienced both lavish patronage and some persecution (the main periods were 446–452 and 574–579 in north China and 842–845 throughout the empire). The Tiantai school was named after the mountain where Zhii (Chih-i, 538–97) founded his most important monastery. His was a masterly work of synthesis. The diversity of the texts and schools that came out of India was always something troubling to Chinese who were trying to understand the essence of Buddhism; Zhii resolved the problem by assigning differing teachings of the Buddha Śākyamuni to different periods, because humans had to be introduced gradually to the grand teaching which is found most clearly and magnificently in the Lotus Sūtra.

In his developmental view of the Buddha's teachings he made use of the crucial idea of *upāya* or skill in means—the idea that the Buddha adapts his teachings to the psychological and spiritual condition of the hearer. Thus for instance in the Deer Park at Benares he preached the Theravādin doctrines and practices; but once people had listened and had advanced to the state of saints or *arhants*, he could then teach them that sainthood was not the final or the highest aim. This was when the charm of the high Mahāyāna *sūtras* would beguile them and make them long for the Mahāyāna and realize the partial character of the Hīnayāna. As he lay dying the Buddha recited the Sūtra of the Great Decease, which was equivalent to the Lotus.

All this scheme was designed to unite the whole array of major Buddhist scriptures. Not only that but it was part of Zhii's method of expounding scriptures to ask not just about the theory or the philosophy but what method of meditation a text laid down or implied. The school later was important in Japan, and certainly was influential during the classical period in China.

Huayan and the Interconnectedness of Events

The Huayan school is another school with a very Chinese flavor, though it only restates in another form a basic tenet of all of Buddhism. The school seems to have started before 600 C.E., but its great systematizer, sometimes counted as its third patriarch, was Fazang (Fa-tsang, 643–712). It is based on a vast and syncretic text which was probably put together in Central Asia, maybe in the fourth century, called the *Mahāvaipulya Buddhāvataṃsaka Sūtra*, or *Huayan Ching*, or Flower Garland Sūtra. It represents in a very rich, prolix, and colorful way the thought of the Buddha immediately following his Enlightenment, when he was seeing things "as they really are." It ends with a long chapter, sometimes counted a separate *sūtra*, "On Entering the Realm of Truth," in which a young hero and seeker takes instruction from many teachers during his pilgrimage through life and completes the path of the Bodhisattva.

The Huayan teachings envisage that all phenomena and all the principles which underlie them are interconnected, and are seen to be without mutual obstruction: they interpenetrate perfectly without losing their individual identity. This is a restatement in positive form of the notion of *pratityasamutpada*, or codependent origination, which was part of the message of Buddhism from its earliest days. But while some Indian writers like Nāgārjuna, in taking this idea to its limits, had expressed their conclusions negatively ("Everything is empty"), the Huayan is positive. It likens the world to the famous mythic jewel-net of Indra, a net of jewels in which each one reflects all the others. Those who see this vision with clarity will see the essential Buddhahood of each living being and the presence of the Buddha Mind everywhere. The image highlights the purity deep down in defilements, the eternality of each moment, the sudden nature of enlightenment, and the supreme potential of all beings. It thus presents an optimistic and beautiful picture of cosmic interrelatedness, and represents a Chinese flavoring of central Buddhist doctrines.

For Huayan, other schools were incomplete. Hināyāna noted the emptiness and egolessness of living beings but not of all phenomena. Early Mahāyāna stressed the unreality of things but not the equally important reality of them. Mature Mahāyāna saw the general truth but failed to stress the particularity of individual phenomena. Those who stressed sudden enlightenment failed to note sufficiently the need for effort, and neglected the importance of language (once we have seen through its pretensions) in guiding practice.

Qān as a Chinese Way

The shape of Huayan thinking had some influence on those who developed a uniquely Chinese (and later Korean and Japanese) form of religion, namely the Meditation School, called in Chinese Qān. This was a transcription into Chinese of the Sanskrit *dhyāna*—and nearly all of Buddhism is after all *dhyāna* Buddhism. But it was the style and boldness of Qān thinking which is impressive. In theory it was brought to China, maybe in 520 C.E., via Canton by the legendary monk Bodhidharma. At any rate he was retrospectively adopted as the first patriarch of the new movement, and also came to play a wider role in Chinese folklore, getting in the process assimilated to a Daoist immortal. To him was ascribed the brief statement of the nature of Qān teaching:

> A special transmission outside the scriptures;
> No basis in words or writing;
> Direct pointing to the mind of people;
> Insight into one's nature and attainment of Buddhahood.

At first, Qān was a movement confined to wandering monks, but by the seventh century it established itself in settled monasteries. It was the Sixth Patriarch, Huineng (Hui-neng, 638–713), whose influence was the most

A Tibetan representation of the Buddha-to-be who looks down with compassion, the Lord Avalokiteśvara.

profound. His teachings, and a little about his life, are found in the Sūtra of the Sixth Patriarch, otherwise known as the Platform Sūtra. The debate between Hui-neng and Shi-hsiu, both outstanding pupils of the previous patriarch, partly foreshadowed the drifting apart of the northern and southern schools of Qān, the former emphasizing the gradualism of the approach to enlightenment or insight (*prajñā*), and the latter insistent on the sudden character of insight. Later both these schools came to be important in Japan, and we shall deal with them fully there.

Huineng's Qān developed into a system with certain major features: first the need for master-pupil transmission, rather than learning from scriptures (though of course the scriptures were valued too, especially the Diamond Sūtra, which sums up in short compass the whole teachings of the Perfection of Wisdom school); second, the use of the so-called "public document" or *kung-an*, namely riddles of a seemingly nonsensical sort which the pupil had to try to solve; third, the organization of monastic life around a meditation hall with fairly rigorous training under a master; and fourth, the creation of a vigorous tradition of Qān art.

Lying behind these practices and ideas was the taking of the Buddhist critique of language and concepts very radically. Since concepts are misleading and contradictory they have to be wiped away. We must learn to see things "as they are." A tree is not a tree: it is just that we categorize it as a tree. In itself it is—well, at this point words fail and we need direct experience. Such direct experience of nature reflected early Daoist thinking, and in Qān there is a fine fusion of Buddhist and Daoist thought (or nonthought). This is one of the powerful syntheses between the two cultures in Chinese history. But its danger is anarchy: if we cannot even rely on scriptural authority we have to strengthen the authority of the community—and thus Qān discipline came, paradoxically, to be rigorous. The authoritarianism implicit in the idea that transmission is from master to pupil was emphatic. In order to attain the spontaneity of enlightenment, people had to practice hard at it. You need artifice in order to be natural.

Pure Land and Guanyin

The high Mahāyāna provided plenty of opportunities for piety. According to a traditional scheme the Buddha has three bodies. One is the transformation-aspect, in which he appears on earth to teach living beings. Another is the celestial aspect, in which he appears as a Heavenly Lord, such as Amitābha; in conjunction with such god-like beings there are divine Bodhisattvas, such as, in India, Avalokiteśvara. Third, there is the truth-aspect of the Buddhas, their ultimate reality (or unreality): the Absolute, Emptiness, *nirvana*, the Buddha-nature. The intermediate body or aspect, the celestial, provided a strong focus for piety. This was specially true of the Pure Land or Qingdu (Ch'ing-t'u) movement, which was highly popular by the seventh century C.E. The great Bodhisattva Avalokiteśvara underwent a change, appearing in China as a feminine deity—Guanyin (Kuan-yin), a kind of Chinese Madonna (p. 118).

These tendencies toward piety and faith, and concentration on the numinous, glorious, and worshipful aspects of the Buddhist tradition, provided a supplement to the Daoist pietism directed toward the immortals. It was a highly personalized and in many ways "easy" form of religion, suitable for a degenerating age, when adherence to the severities of original Buddhism was weakening. The Buddhist theory of decline as time went on thus served the purpose of justifying easier and more pietistic forms of the faith. Meanwhile, similar devotional types of belief and practice were growing among Daoists. Thus the so-called Jade Emperor, Yuhuang Shangdi (Yü Huang Shang Ti), Supreme Being, was elevated to rule over lesser spirits, including Buddhas (according to the Daoists; the Buddhists argued the other way, subordinating the Jade Emperor and other spirits to the supreme Buddhas). But despite the rivalry of the differing traditions—culminating in the severe persecution of Buddhism from 843 to 845, resulting in the return of over a quarter of a million nuns and monks to civilian life, the closure of over forty thousand temples and shrines, and the destruction of 4600 temples—they nevertheless over most of the rest of the Chinese history managed to form a symbiosis.

The Medieval Period

The Neo-Confucian Revival

The religions of Daoism and Buddhism, were sufficiently successful to present a serious threat to traditional Confucian thought. Its pragmatism and primary concern with political and ethical issues were oblique to the more intense spiritual interests of people, whether the devotionalism of Pure Land Buddhists and of Daoists (such religion the *ru* (*ju*) tended to despise as ignorant) or the quests for enlightenment and personal immortality of more mystically inclined followers of the faiths. It was to fill this gap in Confucian thought and practice that there arose the movement the West knows as Neo-Confucianism. In Chinese it is known as *Lixue* (*Li-hsüeh*) or "learning of principle."

With this movement we are reaching out into the medieval period, after 1000 C.E., when Chinese religion took its final premodern form. Part of the revival was straightforwardly educational: for instance, Hu Yüan (933–?1059) set up two curricula for the vast academy he founded—one had to do with matters of substance (*ti* or *t'i*), i.e. the study of the classics, and the other with matters of function (*yong* or *yung*), covering practical and scientific subjects including mathematics. Maybe a better translation of "substance" from a modern perspective is "values." Later, in the nineteenth century, the question was raised as to whether it was possible to borrow Western ideas for *yong* while retaining Chinese traditional *ti*. But as well as a reinvigoration of education there was speculation about the nature of reality and the way to knowledge that gave Confucian thought a stronger metaphysical basis. The new thinkers were aware of the subtlety of Buddhist analyses of the world, and of epistemology or the theory of how it is that we know things. The first moves in the direction of a systematic worldview came in the writings of the so-called Five Northern Masters, during the Song (Sung) Dynasty (960–1126). Their thought was summed up and used as the basis for a creative synthesis by the great scholar Zhuxi (Chu Hsi, 1130–1200). Behind phenomena are *li* or dynamic principles. These flow from the Taizhi (T'ai Chi) or Great Ultimate, which we might also translate as "First Principle." It is beyond time and space, and yet it contains within itself the potentiality of all the principles which define the particular patterns in the created order. It is not like the Daoist Ultimate, Nothing, nor is it mere Emptiness; if we use negatives about it, it is because it transcends the language which is adapted to life in space and time.

Everything is composed of *li* and of material force (*qi* or *ch'i*), but the former is logically prior. The mind of humanity shares the creative power of Heaven or the Great Ultimate; and so our spiritual and moral practice should be to recover the original heavenly human nature in us and fight against those impingements of material force which conduce to egoism and lack of concern for other people. Zhuxi also advocated meditation or "quiet sitting," and in this we see a practical effect of Buddhist methods on the Confucian tradition. He made much of what he called "the investigation of things": the probing of principle, both external and internal.

Whether he could be called a theist has been much debated; sometimes he hinted at the personal nature of Heaven. Much of his life was spent in administrative service, and he was strongly activist. He also objected in strong terms both to the Buddhist theory of reincarnation and to the Daoist pursuit of longevity.

Wang Yangming – a Moral Idealism

Much later, during the Ming Dynasty, the other towering figure in the rich tradition of Neo-Confucian thought, Wang Yangming (Wang Yang-ming) (1472–1529), was less concerned than was Chu Hsi with external learning in the investigation of things. For him, knowledge was an inner matter, though it could not be prized apart from action. He was interested above all in the "existential" nature of knowing (so one cannot know suffering without actually suffering). As he wrote: "Knowledge is the beginning of action; action is the completion of knowledge." Wang was very keen to defend the notion of the primordial goodness of human nature, and its identity with the Principle of all things. The sage by his self-cultivation extends his knowledge and his action in such a way that the whole world in effect becomes his body. The seeds of this universalism are there empirically to be observed. When we see a child about to fall into a well, we are immediately impelled to try to save it (this was Mencius' primary example to show the innate goodness of human nature); so we have analogous sympathetic feelings when we encounter frightened birds and animals, or see plants destroyed and crushed, or even when we see tiles or stones broken.

Such somewhat refined notions in the Neo-Confucian tradition were a response in their own way to Buddhism. They set the scene for debates about the right interpretation of the Classics and of the Four Books—the *Analects*, the *Great Learning*, the *Doctrine of the Mean*, and the *Mengzi*—which formed the main substance of the educated person's basis for a worldview during the medieval period of Chinese culture.

The Dimensions of Medieval Chinese Religion

We may now sum up some of the movements and phenomena I have outlined by looking to some of the manifestations of the dimensions of religion by the medieval period in China.

As to *ritual*, this occurred in varying ways at differing social levels. Local temples were the locus of particular gods with their own festival rhythms. At a higher level there were the official temples for the state cult, and notable Daoist and Buddhist shrines and monastic complexes, which were places for various ritual activities. But, as we have seen, a powerful impulse was devotional worship which would ensure a favorable afterlife. Funeral ceremonies, involving both Daoist and Buddhist practitioners, would involve the symbolic transfer of goods, fashioned of paper, and petitions, to the next world. There was also a pan-Chinese festival rhythm, with such special days as the New Year (according to the Chinese calendar), the Dragon-Boat Festival and Harvest-Home; for the dead the Qingmeng (Ch'ing Meng), in which graves are visited and cleaned and repaired; the feast of Hungry Ghosts, etc. Another feature of ritual life was the prevalence of pilgrimages, especially to sacred mountains, which are often associated with important religious figures and events. All this was supplemented by household rites in which offerings were made to gods, whether Daoist or Buddhist, and to ancestors.

In the *experiential* dimension, not only were warm feelings developed in devotional religion, and so a sense of loyalty and gratitude to great Buddhas and the like; but also there were the various higher states of meditation cultivated both in a Buddhist and a Daoist context. Visions and shamanistic experiences were always taken seriously in traditional China. The pioneering of Qān Buddhism gave a new urgency to enlightenment and blended with the sense of harmony with Nature which was always an ingredient of the Daoist tradition.

As to *myth*, the Chinese tradition is not as rich as the Indian in this; but the stories of the Duke of Zhou and of Huangdi, the histories and legends of Kong, Laozi, and other sages, all contributed to a sense of a sacred reality which found rich and complex manifestation in the decoration of temples. Because the Chinese had a strong historical sense, history itself loomed large in the narrative dimension.

Doctrinally the themes of Heaven developed into belief in the Great Ultimate, which had its more negative echoes in such notions as Emptiness and the ineffable Dao. The Yin–Yang polarity and the Five Elements were integrated into a metaphysics of the universe controlled by the rhythms of the Ultimate. There were rich views of the afterlife, but there was disagreement about the truth of reincarnation. To some extent, worry about the afterlife was transmuted in the Daoist strand into concern for longevity, achieved by a whole apparatus of personal discipline mingled with magical alchemy.

Ethically, there was a very lively debate through most of Chinese history, revived during the medieval period through the resurgence of moral speculation in the Neo-Confucian movement. The varied strands of Confucian, Buddhist, and Daoist ethics were not easily to be brought together; but in a rough-and-ready way they served to underpin a loose ideology and worldview that embraced the whole of Chinese society. There was a dialectic in it. The underlying menace and turbulence of the Daoist tradition, fueled sometimes by messianic expectations of a new order, strove against the orderly and elitist teachings of the Confucians; the otherworldly tendencies in Buddhism drew away from both the other traditions. But the whole gloriously eclectic pastiche of Chinese religion had much to offer people of different temperaments, and its medieval pluralism served to keep the wider society stable.

Institutionally the three traditions could exist side by side; Buddhist and Daoist orders were independently organized, and in effect the civil service was the institutional embodiment of the Confucian tradition.

Other Religions in China

Some faiths penetrated into China, especially in the early classical period, and then eventually died out, such as Nestorian Christianity, Manichaeism and Zoroastrianism. Judaism also had a foothold, but by the twentieth century was mainly extinct. The most important foreign presence until modern times was that of Islam. Its adherents were descendants of Muslim traders in the northwest and along the coast, and of soldiers settled in the west, particularly during the eighth century and then during the Mongol period. With the Ming Dynasty, after 1368, the Muslims in China were effectively cut off from the wider Muslim world and became thoroughly Chinese. They maintained Muslim worship and law, and the assumptions of their life were very diverse from those of the majority of the culture in which they were immersed.

One must also remember that China included in its interior and periphery many minority peoples—tribes, for instance—who only gradually became assimilated to the greater Chinese culture. They were a source of strength to the Daoist traditions, which were relatively egalitarian and treated the tribal groups as entitled to religious recognition. This may account for some of the varieties of Daoist practice, as other groups became involved, with their own mythic preconceptions and rites. Important among outlying peoples were the Mongols, partly because under the rule of Genghis Khan (1162–1222) they carved out a vast empire, and because they ruled China from 1280 to 1368. They were religiously tolerant, from a basis of theistic shamanism, and were gradually converted to Islam, Nestorianism, and Buddhism, of which the last turned out to be the most effective. By the sixteenth century Mongolia itself came to be dominated by a system imported from Tibet—a Vajrayāna with Buddhocratic institutions.

The Korean Contribution

China too affected its neighbors. Chinese culture proved to be of wonderful attraction to Korea, Japan (see Chapter 4), and Vietnam. So many of the major features of Chinese religion and philosophy – as well as writing and technology, including printing – were exported and in due course transformed.

From very early times Korea was, naturally enough, under strong Chinese cultural influence, and occasionally it was directly under Chinese rule, for instance during the period from 193 to 37 B.C.E. For the next seven hundred years the peninsula was largely divided between the three kingdoms of Silla, Koryo, and Chosun.

The most important Buddhist thinkers of the Silla period were Wonhyo (617–86) and Uisang (625–702) The former was keen to harmonize the various *sūtras* and schools. He also introduced the canon in some measure to the aristocracy of Korea. Uisang, his friend, visited China, where he studied the Huayan system under Chin-yen (602–68). Uisang became a notable leader of the Huayan school and influenced Fazang who also came under the influence of Wonhyo. These early philosophers helped to consolidate

Buddhism in Korea, and give it wide prestige. A characteristic view of religions and values was expressed by the founder of the Koryo Dynasty (935–1392) in 918, Wang Kon, in holding that Buddhism was to govern spiritual matters, geomancy matters of prognostication, and Confucian thought social and political affairs. Various Buddhist schools were brought in during the Silla period (668–935); the most influential proved to be Qān or (in Korean) Son Buddhism. During the era of the Yi Dynasty (founded in 1392 and lasting till modern times), Korean Neo-Confucian thought flourished considerably.

Buddhist and Confucian teachings effected a merger with traditional Korean religion, with its emphasis on shamanistic priests, both hereditary and chosen by vocation. Its various gods—such as the mountain god, or household spirits—are somewhat like the Roman *numina*, deities to be encountered and dealt with in all kinds of daily encounters; but they were not traditionally arranged in a hierarchy. They predate the unification of the country and often have very particular local status. In some degree, too, this ancient set of religious practices merged with elements of Daoism imported from China.

Of the creations of Korean religious thought and practice, perhaps the most original is the merger effected, in a highly imaginative way, between Huayan and Qān (Son) Buddhism by Chinul (1158–1210). He had become dissatisfied with the rather degenerate form of Son which he experienced on entering the monastic order at a young age. There had over many years been a somewhat bitter bifurcation between Son and the more scholastic forms of Buddhism, and it was partly to bridge this gap that Chinul worked out his synthesis. He is regarded as the founder of a distinctively Korean school of Son, the Chogye school. He incorporated into his techniques the use of the *kung-an*, and sketched a version of the Bodhisattva path in which the adept starts with a sudden awakening at the intellectual level, and progressively advances through the ten stages of the Bodhisattva path to the final direct experience of the truth. He was able by this account to see Son methods as fully in accord with scripture; and the high value placed in Qān on harmony with nature made the more positive metaphysics of Huayan a good ally.

Korean thinkers also made important contributions to the debates of the Neo-Confucian tradition, especially in the sixteenth century, through the writings of Yi T'oegye and Yi Yulgok. The former developed the thinking of Zhuxi, arguing that the priority of principle to material force was ethical rather than ontological. Yi Yulgok argued for the determining character of material force, and he objected to the notion that *li* is always unchanging and pure, since it and material force are correlatives.

These writers were active during the Yi Dynasty, which was itself committed to the Neo-Confucian ideology. This was rather rigidly imposed, but it meant that all officials were heavily infused with Confucian values. It was in this frame of mind that the government of Korea had to face the problems of the modern era, including invasion by Japan and the interpolation of vigorous Western Protestant missionary enterprise.

CHAPTER 4

Japan

The Main Lines of Japanese Religion

The Japanese are remarkably homogeneous culturally. But Japan's religious heritage shows some remarkable variegation. Over many centuries, and living in islands without too much foreign influx (the chief minority is Korean) and without too extensive a group of tribal people (mainly the Ainus in the northern island of Hokkaido), the Japanese people has welded itself together and acquired a strong consciousness of identity. Their language is radically different from that of its neighbors; it has taken over the Chinese writing system, but has developed two syllabary systems of writing in addition, since Japanese unlike Chinese is a polysyllabic language. The complexities of language, and the insular character of their habitat, have allowed the Japanese to retain independence culturally, though they have also been very adept at absorbing elements from other civilizations, in ancient times notably from China and to some degree Korea (see Map 2, p. 107).

The most significant event in early Japanese civilization was the importation of Chinese and in particular Buddhist ideas and practices before and during the regency of Prince Shotoku (fifth—sixth century C.E.). The preceding era we may name the early period. The time from Shotoku till the rise of the Kamakura Shogunate (late twelfth century), we may call the preclassical period; then during the Kamakura and Ashikaga regimes there is the classical flowering of Japanese religious creativity, up to the late sixteenth century, and the intrusion too of Catholicism in the south; then during the Tokugawa Shogunate, until the Meiji Restoration in the mid-nineteenth century, there is what may be called the premodern period, during which for the most part Japan was shut off from the outside world. From 1858 onward, Japan responded to the impact of the modern and colonial era, and this part of Japanese religious history is described in Part II.

It is common for writers in the West to nominate as Japan's two major religions Buddhism and Shinto, with Confucianism and Daoism playing subsidiary parts. It is often thought that Shinto is something which goes right back to prehistoric times. It is true that there is a continuity in the gods, the *kami*, of Japan, and to some degree a continuity of myth. But it is misleading to speak of Shinto as if it were some organized tradition going way back. It is only gradually that Shinto as a self-conscious force emerges. So we shall here speak of the *kami* religion of Japan, which lived symbiotically with organized Buddhism, and only later was institutionalized as Shinto.

The peculiar genius of Japanese civilization found expression in a number of movements—the fervid devotional forms of Pure Land Buddhism, which so emphasized grace that St. Francis Xavier, the Catholic missionary, is reported to have said on his arrival in Japan that Luther had preceded him; the novel forms of Zen (Ch'an) and especially the integration of Zen training into

The practical dimension: the austerity of Buddhist monastic life, seen here at Mount Koyosan, headquarters of the Shingon branch of Japanese Buddhism.

135

Amaterasu, Sun Goddess and greatest divinity of the Shinto tradition. Disturbed that the Storm God had destroyed her crops, she withdrew into a cave, thus depriving the world of sunlight, and was lured out only by the clamor of many *kamis* outside the cave. This print is by Kunisada (1786–1864). V&A Museum, London.

secular pursuits such as martial skills and flower-arrangement; and the blending of Neo-Confucian and Zen motifs. In the modern period there were other novelties, which we shall come to later. The strength of Japanese aestheticism, the deliberate and highly committed following of artistic endeavors, was also expressed in a religious way, so that the boundaries between religious and other activities are peculiarly hard to define.

The Early Period: *Kami* and Foreign Influences

The main center of Japanese power in the misty early centuries of the Common Era was the central region occupied by differing clans in a loose confederation under a Yamato kingship. Differing clans had differing *kami*, but gradually a central core of myths of origin came to play a role in the centralizing ideology of the Yamato emperors. This group of myths in part

136

focused on the great goddess of the Sun, Amaterasu, divine ancestress of the royal family. The complex myths drew their sources from differing cultures, from Polynesia, China, and elsewhere, and were in due course codified in the books *Kojiki* and *Nihonshoki* in the latter part of the seventh century. They helped to justify imperial rule, granted absolutely to her descendants through the goddess. There was no Japanese theory of the "Mandate of Heaven" in relation to the royal family, and the fact that for many centuries actual rule was exercised by shoguns, while in theory deferring to the emperor, is a significant comment on the ultimate sanctity of the imperial lineage. In the early period there was also a gradual penetration of cultural elements from Korea and China. The Japanese fought and settled in southern Korea in the fourth century, though disastrously defeated by the northern state of Koguryo. The

Japanese Religion some key terms

Bosatsu Bodhisattva: a Buddha-to-be, often appearing god-like as a celestial being.

Butsudan An altar with a Buddha image in the household, parallel to a *kamidan* or Shinto shrine (Butsu is Japanese for Buddha).

Daimoku The title of the Lotus Sūtra, which in Nichiren Buddhism is invoked under the formula *Namu Myōhō renge-kyō* ("Homage to the Lotus Sūtra").

Jōdō The Pure Land, a paradise for the faithful: the focus therefore of pietistic hope in faith-oriented Amida Buddhism.

Kami Traditional nature god or spirit.

Kannon The bodhisattva Avalokiteśvara in female form (Chinese Guanyin).

Kokutai The national essence: so the Shinto of the pre-World War II period is sometimes referred to as Kokutai Shinto.

Matsuri Shinto festival or ceremonies.

Miko Shinto shamans or priestesses, brought up strictly as virgins and dedicated to the cult of the local *kami*.

Nembutsu The formula of calling on the Buddha which brings salvation to the faithful according to Shin Buddhism.

Shinto The way of the *kami*, a strong element in Japanese religion and for a while in modern times expressing the mandatory ethos of the Japanese nation.

Tendai A sacramental and esoteric movement within Japanese Buddhism, originally based on the Lotus Sūtra.

Zen Literally "meditation." The name of Japanese forms of yogic Buddhism, exploiting fresh techniques of contemplation.

Shinto: Kojiki, *Preface*

Now when chaos had begun to condense, but force and form were not yet manifest, and there was nought named, nought done, who could know its shape? Nevertheless Heaven and Earth first parted, and the Three Deities performed the commencement of creation; the Passive and Active Essences then developed, and the Two Spirits became the ancestors of all things. Therefore did he enter obscurity and emerge into light, and the Sun and Moon were revealed by the washing of his eyes; he floated on and on plunged into the sea-water, and Heavenly and Earthly Deities appeared through the ablutions of his person. So in the dimness of the great commencement, we, by relying on the original teaching, learn the time of the conception of the earth and of the birth of islands; in the remoteness of the original beginning, we, by trusting the former sages, perceive the era of the genesis of Deities and of the establishment of men.

---

foundations, however, were laid for the decisive entry of official Buddhism into Japan in the mid part of the sixth century.

The multitudinous *kami* of mountains, streams, rocks, and the sea blended with ancestral and tutelary *kami* who were integrated into the life of particular clans. Broadly, the *kami* occupied differing planes of existence: Takamanohara or "high heaven"; Nakatsukuni or "middle land," i.e. roughly the earth; and Yomi, the underworld. Though the heavenly *kami* were important, the *kami* of the middle region often had more immediate interest in human and clan affairs. There were shrines to various spirits, which later in the early imperial period multiplied significantly as a result of state patronage.

The *kami* were important for agriculture and hunting, and ancient practices of shamanism, both male and female, persist right through Japanese religion. Later commonplaces, such as the use of clapping in worship, and purification with water, seem to date from prehistoric times.

The Preclassical Period

Prince Shotoku and the Buddhist Revolution

Traditionally Buddhism is held to have been brought into Japan in either 538 or 552 C.E.; but it was primarily during the regency of Prince Shotoku Taishi (574–622) that Buddhism took root as part of the fabric of Japanese official life. In the second year of his regency, while still a young man (he was nineteen when he became regent), he issued an edict which commended the Three Jewels of Buddhism—the Buddha, the Dharma, and the Sangha, which were to be seen as indissolubly united. Later, in the Seventeen Article Constitution which he promulgated, he stated that these three treasures were to be revered by all beings. So he regarded Buddhism as the spiritual message which gave moral shape to the country. He sent to China for *sūtras* and other documents and himself wrote commentaries on three important Mahāyāna texts, including the Lotus Sūtra. This last work is preserved in the imperial archives,

The experiential dimension: a Zen teacher draws a circle, symbolizing the emptiness and completion of ultimate realization —the experience of *satori*.

and it is claimed to be in Shotoku's own writing. Shotoku is credited with founding one or two important temples, notably the Horyuji Temple in Nara, later the imperial capital. But he also made use of the Confucian tradition, in establishing various ranks of officials at the court; and he did not see any incompatibility between his favoring of Buddhism and support for the cult of the *kami*.

After his death a brief period of chaos and bloodshed preceded the consolidation of his reforms, and a more centralized empire somewhat on the Chinese model was established. Law was proclaimed by imperial rescript—in other words, written law, rather than immemorial custom was what counted, and the emperor himself was treated as a living *kami*. The emperor Temmu, who reigned from 672 to 686, ordered the writing of the *Kojiki* and

The Lotus Sūtra

The World-Honored One, in his tactfulness, told of the Tathāgata-wisdom; but we, though following the Buddha and receiving a day's wage of *nirvāṇa*, deemed this a sufficient gain, never having a mind to seek after the Great Vehicle. We also have declared and expounded the Tathāgata-wisdom to Bodhisattvas, but in regard to this Great Vehicle we have never had a longing for it. Wherefore? The Buddha, knowing that our minds delighted in inferior things, by his tactfulness taught according to our capacity, but still we did not perceive that we were really Buddha-sons.

Now we have just realized that the World-Honored One does not grudge even the Buddha-wisdom. Wherefore? From of old we are really sons of Buddha, but have only taken pleasure in minor matters; if we had had a mind to take pleasure in the Great, the Buddha would have preached the Great Vehicle Law to us. At length, in this *sūtra*, he preaches only the One Vehicle; and though formerly, in the presence of Bodhisattvas, he spoke disparagingly of *śrāvakas* who were pleased with minor matters, yet the Buddha had in reality been instructing them in the Great Vehicle. Therefore we say that though we had no mind to hope or expect it, yet now the Great Treasure of the King of the Law has of itself come to us, and such things which Buddha-sons should obtain we have all obtained.

Nihonshoki, and this helped to give a traditional justification for the new set-up. He is supposed also to have made Amaterasu's shrine at Ise the sacred focus of the cult of the imperial house.

The favoring of religion also meant its control. A law governed the activities of monks and nuns, and a ministry of *kami* was organized, which registered *kami* shrines and priests. Temmu also ordered the compilation of collections of traditional poetry. In 710 the court was established at Nara, which blended the glories of Buddhist faith and the pomp of imperial governance. In 741 the emperor Shōmu ordered the building of a state-financed system of provincial temples, and in 749 he had a vast statue in bronze of the Buddha Vairocana installed in the great Todaiji Temple in Nara. Vairocana is especially associated with the Hua-yen (or in Japanese, Kegon) tradition, being the personalized form both of the universe and of what lies beyond it.

Saichō and Kūkai

The close identification of religion and government, and the lavish subsidizing of monastic life, had cloying effects. As a radical move at reform, the emperor Kammu (reigned 781–806 C.E.) moved the capital from Nara to Heian (Kyoto). The bonds between politics and religion were cut, and government by legal edict was revived. Various economic and military reforms gave the Heian period an energetic start. The severance of Buddhism from the affairs of state was healthy, and led to the creation of two new forms of Buddhism through the activity of the two most famous monks of the Heian period, Saichō and Kūkai.

Saichō, also known by his posthumous title Dengyo Daishi (767–822), was sent as a student to China, after having studied at the Todaiji in Nara. He brought back to Japan the teachings of the T'ien-t'ai, somewhat amplified, and known in Japanese as Tendai. Saichō established the headquarters of the denomination on Mount Hiei, not far from the new imperial capital, and eventually after his death it was recognized as a place for the training of monks (the monopoly for this had been held by one of the Nara centers). His Tendai teachings were more syncretic than the Chinese, as he wove into them important Tantric motifs and the use of sacramental acts.

There was a place in the Tendai scheme of things for *kami*; and there was also a nationalistic flavor—Saichō believed that the Japanese were fully mature in their spiritual life and therefore ready for the consummate teachings of the Lotus Sūtra. He also elaborated his world-affirming theory of *hongaku* or "original enlightenment," which stressed the nondifference between the Buddha's enlightenment and that in ordinary men and women, and the identity between liberation and living in the world. Various new patterns of meditation were worked out, such as sitting ninety days in front of a statue of Amida (Amitābha), circumambulating a sacred statue for ninety days, and so on. These practices were introduced from China by Saichō's disciple Ennin.

Tendai, because it found a place for all stages of religious development, was popular; but its emphasis upon the magical and spiritual effects of ritual were sometimes to be a weakness. This ritualism was even more marked in the other new movement, Shingon, or Mantra Sect. Kūkai, known posthumously as Kōbo Daishi, had initially sought government service and studied Confucian classics, but switched as a young man to Buddhist studies; he had the opportunity moreover to go on a delegation to China and there spent three years studying Shingon in the then capital of Chang'an. He introduced this form of Buddhism into Japan, on his return. He set up at Kongobuji, south of Nara, and also at Toji in Kyoto, as a springboard for propagating his message. He was influential in various directions: he founded the Imperial Academy of Arts and Knowledge, and was a senior religious adviser at the court. He had a warm attitude toward the way of the *kamis*. His teachings prepared the way for later syncretism between Shinto and esoteric Buddhism. He established the headquarters of the new denomination at Mount Koya, and after his death he was thought by his followers still to abide at Mount Koya, awaiting revived manifestation at the time of the coming of the future Buddha Maitreya.

The scheme which he evolved is a complex one. At its apex is the figure of the Buddha Mahāvairocana, conceived as identical with the Truth-body of the Buddha. That Ultimate Reality is described in typical Buddhist terms as emptiness and as the "Suchness" of the Buddha as Tathagata. But his emptiness is, so to speak, a full one. The truth-body is the creative force which is behind phenomena, and which embraces phenomena. In this, Kūkai takes up the thought of Hua-yen. But because inner and outer are correlated (phenomena and ultimate Suchness; mind and body; and esoteric and exoteric Buddhism), the approach to attaining realization of one's essential Buddhahood is sacramental in character. Realization therefore occurs not just through mental meditation but through the use of mysterious powers—the *mudrā* or bodily gestures which also play a vital role in Tantric thinking in India; the sacred *maṇḍalas* or diagrams which he brought back from China with him; and the sacred syllables or formulae, *mantrás*. For Kūkai, exoteric Shingon Buddhism was the highest form because it reflected the eternal Truth of the Body of Mahāvairocana and not the provisional and introductory teaching of the time-bound Buddha Śākyamuni.

The schools of Saichō and Kūkai represent the most solid achievements in the Buddhism of the preclassical period. They involved some adaptation of ideas and practices prevalent in the great Tang capital of Chang'an, which the two sages had the opportunity of visiting together. But it was basically at a later stage, after the coming of the Kamakura period, that Japanese originality in Buddhist religion really flowered, stretching Buddhism in the directions of fervid piety in the Pure Land interpretations, back toward the centrality of meditation in the Zen schools, and in a powerful nationalist direction in the teachings of Nichiren.

The Classical Period

The Pure Land Movements and the Mappō

Fundamental to the revolutions which took place from the twelfth century onward was the idea that we have reached the days of the final Dharma, the *mappō*. The present could be viewed from the standpoint of Buddhist orthodoxy as being a degenerate age in which the more rigorous path could not be trodden effectively, so poor had people's commitment and merit become; but according to the new viewpoint it was a period of optimism and a more democratic way of looking at the Buddha's path. For the tradition had of its nature tended to exclude certain people whose occupations grated against the Buddhist ethic—fishermen, warriors, hunters, peasants, prostitutes, and so on. But in the new age the faith was open to all. The success of the Pure Land movements in Japan was in great part due to their social widening of ultimate hope. The same, but in a rather different way, could be said of Zen.

The greatest figures in the Pure Land movements were undoubtedly Honen (??–1212) and Shinran (1173–1262). Honen involved himself in extensive studies within the Tendai tradition, but was especially drawn to meditation on the Buddha of Infinite Light, Amida. He followed the sacramental method of meditation in which by visualizing Amida he would become unified with him; but through much arduous meditation, in the years he spent in the retreat of the saintly monk Eiku on Mount Hiei, he nevertheless felt dissatisfied: he could not attain a sense of utter liberation. Honen turned to the idea that those who cannot be freed by strenuous meditation can nevertheless gain Amida's favor and assure themselves of rebirth in the Pure Land simply through the repetition of his name in the formula *Namu Amida Butsu*, or "Homage to the Buddha Amida." This simple formula was for those who had to rely, as Honen came to put it, on *tariki* or "the power of the other," rather than upon *jiriki*, "one's own power." Salvation

The mythic dimension: the great Buddha (Daibutsu) Amida in Kamakura in southern Japan, whose size signifies his spiritual stature, which can help to save the faithful if they call upon his name.

had to come from another if one could not in this degenerate age rely on one's own strenuous efforts.

All this was in accord with the great vow of Amida Buddha to help all living beings in the world of suffering. His compassionate nature led to his projection of the Pure Land, where individuals could be reborn in conditions which were particularly suitable for the attainment of final liberation. Insofar as this doctrine undercut the rationale for the extensive monastic training of the Tendai and other influential forms of Buddhism, Honen's rivals saw his new teaching as a threat. While they did not deny his own saintliness, they sought to suppress the new movement in 1204 and then again in 1205. Eventually the indiscretion of two of Honen's monks, in leading court ladies in an all-night worship service, enraged the emperor: they were executed, and Honen was banished for four years from the capital, from 1207. He returned in 1211 and died in early 1212, proclaiming his faith in Amida.

Honen's devotional pietism contained some possible inconsistencies which were the reason for the even more radical transformation of Buddhism that was to be attempted by Shinran. For one thing, Honen taught that *Namu Amida Butsu* should be continuously repeated by the faithful: but why so? Surely it was enough simply to turn once to Amida in faith. Repetition was no doubt creating a new form of practice, easier than traditional *jiriki*, but still a kind of *jiriki*. Second, Honen the monk had adhered to the forms of traditional Buddhism. His knowledge of the scriptures was intense. His adherence to the monastic rules had been severe. But such practice was a hangover from the *jiriki* mentality. Pure Land Buddhism, or Jodoshu, ought to go in an even more radical direction. The man who imparted this new thrust was Shinran, founder of what much later came to be called the Jodoshinshu—the True Pure Land school.

After many years as a Tendai monk, Shinran had been moved by a vision to follow Honen, and he was involved in the crackdown on the new movement, being exiled to Niigata province. There he had another vision, of the female Bodhisattva, Kannon (the Chinese Kuan-yin); and this implied to him that he should have a female helper. He married and had a number of children over the next few years. He lived the life of a poor householder and ordinary person. Since Amida did not require good works, but longed for the salvation of all beings, there was no point in such "good works" as becoming a monk or nun. By a similar logic to that of Luther, Shinran pioneered the move away from monasticism. Even calling on the name of the Buddha was not strictly speaking a condition of being saved, but rather the expression of a faith which after all had been implanted in a person by Amida himself. If the good were saved, how much more so the evil, said Shinran. The utterance of the Nembutsu, the formula, was an outflow of gratitude for the compassionate saving work of Amida.

Though Shinran's view is very similar to Protestant notions of the grace of God, there is a difference arising from the structure of Buddhist myth. In the Christian case there is always maintained a differentiation between God and the human being, however tender the relationship and sense of communion on both sides. But in the case of True Pure Land, the destiny of those who go on to the Pure Land is to attain Buddhahood and indeed return to the world to help to save others.

Something of the spirit of Shinran's faith can be gathered from the following verses:

Too strong for me is the evil of my heart. I cannot overcome it.
Therefore is my soul like unto the poison of serpents.
Even my righteous deeds, being mingled with this poison,
Must be named the deeds of deceitfulness.
Shameless though I be and having no truth in my soul,
Yet the virtue of the Holy Name, the gift of Him that is enlightened,
Is spread throughout the world by my words,
Although I am as I am.

Shinran

Shinran (1173–1262), founder of the True Pure Land School or Jodoshinshu, developed devotional Buddhist piety to its logical conclusion. He was born into a period of acute social disruption which convinced him that Japan had entered into the *mappō* or Period of the End of the Law. In such a time it is impossible to meditate successfully and achieve enlightenment on one's own. Only by relying on Amida Buddha can one be saved, by the power of the Other (*jiriki*). From the age of nine he was a Tendai monk (practicing a synthesis of traditional rituals and teachings). In 1201 he experienced a vision which caused him to become a disciple of Honen, founder of the Pure Land denomination. In 1207 he was sent into exile to what is now Niigata province. There he married Eshin-ni, by whom he had several children. This was an extension of the principle of not relying upon good deeds or one's own effort in the process of salvation during the *mappō* age. In any case he was moved to this by a vision of Kannon (Kuan-yin), who told him she would take a woman's form to be his mate.

Shinran, thus, came to dissolve monastic vows. In all this he was considerably influenced by the rural populace, who had been left without an appealing religion by the more traditional denominations of Japanese Buddhism. While Shinran considered himself a loyal disciple of Honen, there is no doubt he was original in his own teachings. After his exile was rescinded he moved to the region of Kantō, where he worked among the common people, for whom he wrote vernacular hymns and teachings. At the age of sixty he returned to Kyoto, where he lived quietly, revising his writings. His last years were somewhat disturbed. His eldest son claimed that he had a special teaching from Shinran: but Shinran denied it and was compelled to disown his son.

Amida was considered the only final reality, and the sole object of devotion. The formula *Namu Amida Butsu* ('Homage to Amida Buddha'), the Nembutsu, was not a means to salvation but a response in faith to Amida. Similarly, the acts of compassion undertaken by the faithful are themselves a response to Amida's compassion. The likenesses of these ideas to those of Luther led St. Francis Xavier to quip that Luther had beaten Shinran to Japan.

In his teachings Śankara holds to the identity of the Self within and the Divine Reality, the illusoriness of the world and of its Creator, and the need for mystical knowledge (*jñāna* or *vidyā*) in attaining ultimate liberation. In the last resort God, rituals, and so on are unreal, though they have a secondary reality for those who have not been liberated. His devotional hymns testify to his wish to combine popular religion with the pursuit of the ultimate goal.

The humility of Shinran is the obverse side of the coin of the Buddha's goodness and tender love.

Shinran's teaching was to experience a second growth under the leadership of Rennyo (1415–99), who reshaped the community of the Jodoshinshu by developing new pastoral methods, including epistles in colloquial Japanese.

This period of Shinran's life was a turbulent one, with struggles over land

and political power between the older aristocracy and the rising military class; some monastic foundations took part in the fighting, a sign of the decadence of the times. But the new rule of the Kamakura shogunate involved a simpler legal system than the complex *ritsuryo* system which it replaced, and this gave greater freedom to religion, which is one reason why the thirteenth and following centuries were so creative a period in Japanese religious history. Among the innovators of these times was Nichiren, who was unusual in having a school named after him.

Nichiren and Japanese Nationalism

Nichiren (1222–82) was a colorful figure, whose stormy life was in accord with his desire to stir up government to reconsider its attitudes to religion. It was a period of floods and natural disasters, and there was the threat of Mongol invasion (fortunately a typhoon crippled the Mongol fleet, a "miracle" attributed to Nichiren's stand by his followers). Though he studied—as did most other prominent leaders of the period—within the Tendai tradition, he came to condemn it as hollow and false to the true message of the Buddha. He was even more strongly critical of the Pure Land and of Zen. His heart was bound to the Lotus Sūtra, which he saw as the very incarnation of Buddhist truth. He rejected other accounts of Buddhism as false and dangerous, and coupled this fundamental stance on behalf of the Lotus with a strong sense of Japanese national identity. He was a prophetic figure and denounced the then ruling family, the Hōjo, for their toleration of

The ritual dimension: sitting meditation needs discipline, and here a monk chastises a girl for deviant posture.

wrong views, acceptance of pluralism in Buddhism, and devotion to Pure Land teachings. For his pains he was banished in 1261 for two years to Izu Province and in 1271 for nearly three years to Sado Island.

His devotion to the Lotus Sūtra led him to replace the Nembutsu with the formula *Namu Myōhorengekyō*: in other words "Homage to the Lotus of the Perfect Law." He claimed to be a Bodhisattva to whom the Buddha Śākyamuni had entrusted the scripture, and whose reappearance was foretold. Zen Buddhists he denounced because they supposed that the transmission of truth occurs outside of scripture: scripture is needed if the truth of the Buddha's teaching is to be carried down to us. He attacked the Pure Land schools because by concentrating upon the next life they in effect turned people away from harmonizing their present lives. His attacks on the various other schools, including the Tendai that had nurtured him, were bitter and hurtful. He believed that by making people angry and pressuring them through evangelical insistence or *shakubuku* he could bring them to reflect more deeply about their own faith. This fierceness of the Nichiren tradition, and its sometimes militant patriotism, have raised questions in some minds as to whether it really is to be counted as Buddhist. But it came to play an important role at various stages of Japanese history, and it has always claimed to have the true interpretation of the Buddha's message.

The Formation of Zen

The classical forms of Japanese Buddhism emphasize in one way or another a this-worldly attitude. This is especially true of the kinds of Ch'an Buddhism which came into Japan and were developed well beyond the models that had dominated in China. Eisai (1141–1215) was the father of Zen Buddhism in Japan, though he met with quite a lot of resistance; in some measure he compromised, thinking of Zen as an extra ingredient which could be added to the establishment Tendai mix. But he set the tone of the movement.

Very important in the rooting of Zen was the settlement of Chinese teachers in Japan under the patronage of the ruling shogunate. Among them, four major figures in the thirteenth century established a pure form of Ch'an. Subsequently Japanese leadership gave special directions to the Rinzai movement of sudden enlightenment, to which most Zen exponents were loyal.

The monk Dogen (1200–53) brought Ts'ao-tung or Soto methods and teachings over from China. He experienced liberation in working with his Chinese Master and so gained access to the line of transmission of the truth going back to the Buddha Śākyamuni—or so he saw it. The Soto Zen tradition restored the essential contemplative core to Buddhism, which could easily be overlooked in the ritual formalism of establishment Buddhism in Japan.

Dogen's writings were massive. Most important was a ninety-five-volume work called *Shōbogenzō*, or "Treasury of the Right Dharma Eye." This brought him much influence in the capital, Kyoto, and round about. But the latter part of his life he spent in the rugged mountain monastery of Eiheiji. There he inculcated what he took to be the true Zen monastic ideal—a life given to meditation, under fairly strict discipline, and in close contact with Nature.

Dogen's thought was original and basic. He saw that attainment and practice are inseparable. By practicing meditation in the right way, that is, *zazen*, "sitting meditation," a person is brought into direct contact with reality. The most important Buddhist truth is that of impermanence. All beings, both living and nonliving, are ever in flux, and it is not as if beyond the impermanence there were an unchanging Truth or Reality which could be attained independently of the world of impermanence. Rather it is that the impermanence of things is their true nature, and by the same token is Buddha Nature. In sitting meditation, we experience the flux directly and in doing so attain Buddha Nature. This attainment, it needs to be repeated, is not something extra, but is to be seen in the very particularity of the flow of things. So the substance of things lies in time: life is time, a series of "nows" flowingly linked together, yet each now there in its own particularity.

Both Soto and Rinzai Zen are keen to sweep away preconceived ideas. They emphasize the misleading nature of the concepts which we bring to bear in trying to classify and understand the world. A main reason for the strange riddles (*koan*, Chinese *kung-an*) which the Rinzai masters use is to bring our mental processes to a dead halt, so that we can disentangle ourselves from the language which serves as a fog to obscure our clear vision of the way things are in themselves. Consider for a moment. I am looking out of the window while writing this, and see among other things a large fir tree. But does the tree itself ask to be classified in this way? It is only human convenience that breaks up the scene stretched in front of me into discrete parts, such as trees and a lake. As for its being "large," does the tree ask to be compared, e.g. with other fir trees? So although our language is indeed useful for communicating, it gives a particular sort of slant to what I experience. It stands in the way of that visionary unitary kind of experience, sometimes known as "panenhenic" or "one-in-all-ish," which comes before all attempts to break things up into a subject-object kind of dichotomy, me here and the tree over there. Language casts, then, a screen over the flow of things, and so from a Zen point of view it needs to be scraped away. The riddle is one means of doing this.

Originally the *koans* or riddles posed to adepts were drawn from accounts of questions and answers with the masters of the past. This *mondo* or question-and-answer genre often incorporated paradoxes. A good instance is this: a Chinese master was sitting absorbed in meditation, and a monk asked him what he was thinking about. The Master answered: "I am thinking of the absolutely unthinkable." "But," asked the monk, "how can one think what is absolutely unthinkable?" The answer was: "By not-thinking." In other words, you have to get beyond ordinary ideas of thinking.

The aim of using the riddles and of sitting meditation is to attain to *satori* or realization in experience. Because of the doctrine of direct transmission by master to pupil it is usually thought of as something which has in a sense to be certified by a master. It is the master who can tell somehow that the pupil sees things as they really are. Because of the fusion of certain Daoist ideas and those of Ch'an in China, and because of the strong sense of Nature in the Japanese tradition, stemming in part from attitudes to the *kami, satori* often came to be expressed indirectly by reference to natural events. Japanese art and literature became strongly integrated into the practice of Zen. As one brief poem in the Japanese style puts it:

> Last year in a lovely temple in Hirosawa;
> This year among the rocks of Nikko;
> All's the same to me:
> Clapping hands, the peaks roar at the blue!

Zen and the Arts, Martial and Otherwise

One of the main attractions of Zen during the classical period of the shogunates was its double virtue in reforming monasticism and in its appeal to the ordinary person engaged in lay life. It did the former by simplifying monastic life and insisting on both hard labor and the practice of meditation— both of which could be lost sight of in establishment circles. The movement appealed to the laity because it took seriously and in a practical way the Mahāyāna dictum of the identity between the empirical world or *saṃsāra* and the transcendental world or *nirvāṇa*. It took the idea expressed in the Latin tag *laborare est orare*, "to work is to pray," important for Western monasticism, in new directions, for it integrated the meditative task and the skills of ordinary life. In particular, it wove together meditation and the martial arts: archery and swordplay could be developed in a Zen way, hitting the target without aiming (highlighting spontaneity and the equation of means and ends in Zen training). Feminine arts such as flower arrangement and tea-making were also given a Zen mode and flavor. Zen ideals—sparseness, cleanness, control, and spontaneity—came to be influential in all the main arts, such as painting, arranging gardens, and calligraphy.

During the Ashikaga period (1338–1573) Zen's political influence greatly increased, and in effect it became the official religion. This position was enhanced by the fact that Neo-Confucian thought was often blended with the Zen outlook, and Confucian ethics were commended for the laity. Confucian values harmonized with those of a feudal society presided over by a military aristocracy. The idea of the five relationships (father–son, husband–wife, ruler–subject, elder brother–younger brother, and friend– friend) provided a structure of thinking for a hierarchical society in which the system of subordinations is compensated for by the need for a paternal benevolence in the senior partner of any of the relationships.

Shinto and Popular Religion

Buddhism, in Japan as elsewhere, was not a particularly jealous religion. There was no reason why Japanese Buddhists should not continue to reverence

The ethical dimension: reverence for ancestors is part of the ethic of respect for those who have preceded you in life— seniority is important in Japanese society.

Shinto deities, provided that they gave the place of honor to the Buddha, and prime place to Buddhist values. Often, as we find during the classical period in Japan, Shinto and Buddhist holy places merged. Sometimes a Buddhist monk might marry a Shinto shamaness, and the couple could jointly run a temple. Sometimes traditional *kami* places in the mountains would become imbued with Buddhist significance, and so sacred pilgrimages could combine. The increase in the numbers of *yamabushi*, or Buddhist mountain ascetics, helped to blend *kami* and Buddhist values. As for the emperors, they continued to perform regular ceremonies related to their myth of divine descent, without much tension with their personal faith as Buddhists. At the domestic level it was quite natural to have a *kamidana* and a *Butsudan*, that is, a god-shelf and a Buddha–altar. These could happily exist side by side. The Buddhist control of funeral rites and cemeteries gave the religion much impact in ordinary life; but as Japanese typically had their marriages blessed by a *kami* ceremony, there was a synthesis in the treatment of rites of passage. Confucian values would inspire everyday ethics; while diviners and sorcerers of Daoist origin would also play their part in society.

The Coming of Christianity
The period at the end of the Ashikaga regime was marked with violence, above all the devastating civil war known as the Onin War (1467–78), and by relative disintegration of central rule. When Oda Nobunaga succeeded in controlling the capital in 1568 he took revenge on Tendai and Pure Land Buddhists who had put up armed resistance to his regime, and favored Catholicism, which had made its presence felt especially after the arrival of the famous missionary St. Francis Xavier in Hyushu in 1549. Catholicism was initially quite successful. It seemed to many Japanese to be rather like a Jodo or Pure Land sect, only calling on the name of Jesus Christ. The ceremonies had some affinity to the ritualism of Tendai. In a period of much flux and uncertainty, it offered a strong combination of myth, experience, and ethics.

However, the next strongman, Toyotomi Hideyoshi (1536–98), not only broke the power of Buddhist armies, but had twenty-six Christians crucified. After his death the Tokugawa Shogunate was established, and succeeded in creating a new order in Japan. There was fear that the Portuguese and other European powers might destabilize Japan, and the country was sealed off from the rest of the world. Eventually, Catholicism was banned with severity, following a partly Catholic uprising in 1637. All Japanese were, under Tokugawa edicts, required to become Buddhists, at least officially, and a system of Buddhist parishes nationwide was formed which greatly increased the number of Buddhist temples. But the ethos of the regime also was heavily Confucian, and there was a revival of interest in Shinto. We shall return later to the Tokugawa or premodern period when we come to evaluate the Japanese response to colonialism and the depredations of Western mercantile expansion.

Japanese Classical and Premodern Religion

The picture which has emerged is of a vigorous and plural religious system. Its *ritual* dimension existed in different layers and varieties. There was the fervent use of devotional formulae, as in the Pure Land schools and Nichiren Buddhism. There was the return to orthodox meditation, but with a Chinese-Japanese twist, among the Zen schools. There remained the older ritualism of Tendai and Shingon. There were the ceremonies to the gods of Shinto, both associated with Buddhist temples and in disjunction from them. There were the domestic rituals combining Confucian, Shinto, and Buddhist motifs. There were pilgrimages such as the tour of the Thirty-Three Holy Places of Kannon, or that of the Eighty-Eight Temples of Shikoku (of over 700 miles [1100 kilometers], no mean feat in the old days). There were pilgrimages to the Shinto shrine of Amaterasu at Ise, and to many others. Such rituals enhanced and formed religious experiences of various kinds.

The most prominent creation of the classical period was the opening up of the two basic *experiences* of religion—the numinous and the mystical. The devotion to Amida opened up the numinous sense of the glory of God and the unworthiness or humility of the individual in the face of the Ultimate. Zen restored to Buddhism a vigorous concentration on the mystical quest. But here, as well as finding the blank and blinding light within, the adept could directly experience unity with Nature, in a panenhenic type of experience. At the same time Shinto ritual reinforced the desire to experience purity and to remove impurity.

The classical period reinforced traditional *ethics* in particular by drawing on the Confucian ethic. This helped to frame the values of the Way of the Warrior or Bushidō, combining Confucian directions and the spare Stoicism of the Zen tradition. *Socially* and *institutionally*, the classical period saw the spread and popularization of Buddhism and then eventually the reassertion of control by the shogunate. The imperial family and its Shinto connections also remained

Art and religion fuse in the orderliness of this raked garden with natural rocks and trees in Kyoto.

Opposite A statue from the famous Buddhist complex at Borobodur, near Magelang in central Java, which reflects cosmologically the structure of the world. Borobodur combines the idea of the *stūpa*, the *maṇḍala* or ritual diagram, and the cosmic mountain. As you ascend, you pass scenes illustrating *karma* and its effects, to the life of the Buddha, and ultimately *nirvāṇa*.

important, and there was a strong symbiosis between Buddhas and *kami*. The Confucian academic life was dominated by Zen monks, and though there were tensions between the old establishment of Tendai and Shingon on the one hand and the Pure Land and Zen forms of Buddhism on the other, by the Tokugawa period they were welded into a loyal collaboration.

In *doctrine* two outstanding developments of the Japanese tradition were the teachings of Dogen, giving fresh vigor to the *nirvāṇa-saṃsāra* equation, and the extreme but logical conclusions about salvation expressed by Shinran. From the point of view of the *narrative* dimension the most significant concept was Nichiren's view of his own prophetic mission and the fusing of the destiny of Japan and Buddhism effected in his teachings. In fact the myth of a truly Buddhist Japan, taken in a rather strong and exclusive way, gives Japanese Buddhism some analogies with that of Sri Lanka.

But above all, Japanese creativity was seen in the seventh dimension—that of *artistic* creation. The Japanese were wonderful in their spiritual aestheticism: their subtle blend of religion and beauty. No other culture has gone to such lengths as to imbue mundane skills with transcendental meaning. And above all it was Zen with its most original style which suffused so much of Japanese artistic creation with its spirit. Perhaps it is above all in the raked gravel, shaped bushes and rocks, the waterfalls, groomed trees, and cunning vistas of the Japanese temple garden that you can feel the grip of religion upon Japanese culture most profoundly, and the converse too. The cultivation of beauty is itself a kind of religious imperative.

Much of this of course was to be upset in the aftermath of the colonial period. But that is another story, and to that we come in Chapter 19.

Southeast Asia

CHAPTER 5

Regional Patterns

Southeast Asia comprises the states known today as Burma, Thailand, Malaysia, Brunei, Singapore, Indonesia, the Philippines, Kampuchea, Laos, and Vietnam. All of these areas except for the Philippines came heavily under Indian influence—or, in the case of Vietnam, Chinese influence which itself contained Indic elements in the shape of Buddhism. The patterns of the past, which included Hindu kingdoms, as in Kampuchea, have been largely overlaid by Theravāda Buddhism and Islam: the former is the predominant religion of Burma, Thailand, Kampuchea, and Laos, while Islam is predominant in Malaysia, Brunei, and Indonesia. Singapore is basically Chinese in culture, and the Vietnamese tradition has been greatly under Chinese influence and has similar religious characteristics. The Philippines are largely Catholic. The Chinese populations of Southeast Asia postdate the colonial era, having resulted from the importation of Chinese labor into Malaysia and Singapore under the British, and into Indonesia under the Dutch.

Indian influences began to penetrate into Southeast Asia from the second and third centuries C.E.; and because roughly speaking India had a mixed Buddhist and Hindu culture, there was a Hindu-Buddhist mix of ideas and institutions ready to take root in Southeast Asian soil. The main period of the importation of Indian influences was from the seventh century C.E. onward, and the next six centuries saw the establishment of, and interplay between, a number of important cultures. From the thirteenth century, over much of mainland Southeast Asia, there was a consolidation of Theravāda Buddhism after the Sinhalese model. This was also the period when there was penetration of the area by Muslim power. The empire of Malacca, strong in the Malay peninsula and Sumatra, adopted Islam as its religion, and became a center for the spread of Islam into many of the Indonesian islands and into the southern

Opposite The ritual dimension: the vast Buddhist shrine of the Shwedagon temple in Rangoon, Burma. There is one immense *stūpa* surrounded by many small ones. The shrine was actually built around a pagoda, built of solid brick in the sixth century, which has been covered with more than 8500 thin sheets of gold.

155

Map 3 Southeast Asia and Indonesia.

Philippines. Meanwhile the north Vietnamese state of Dai Viet had fought off Chinese invasions, designed to reannex it to the Chinese empire to which it had at one time belonged, and expanded southward to take over the kingdom of Champa, forming an empire roughly the same as modern Vietnam. In addition to the major faiths to be found in the area, various smaller-scale religions belong to the various tribal groups existing right across the region.

It must be emphasized that despite Indian influences and the fact that some Indian Brahmins, merchants, and Buddhist monks must have migrated and settled in the region, the cultural importation of Indian and Chinese elements was just that: it was convenient to borrow the Indian ideology of kingship, for instance, or to use Buddhist ideas in justifying political rule. The substratum of peoples upon which such a culture was grafted was a mixture, but neither Indian nor Chinese in the proper sense. So the imported great religions lived in symbiosis with home-grown popular religions.

It is convenient to look upon the period up to the seventh century C.E. as the early period; the time from the seventh century C.E. to the shaping of Theravāda orthodoxy and the coming substantially of Islam—i.e. to the thirteenth century—as the preclassical period; and the thirteenth through sixteenth centuries as the classical period. Thereafter we are in the modern period and witnessing the varied responses of the region to the impact of the colonial times.

The Origins of Indian Influence

There have been differing theories as to why Indian cultural influences, both Buddhist and Hindu, crossed the Bay of Bengal and established themselves in Burma and other regions of the area. Whence ultimately came those vast monuments at Angkor Wat in Kampuchea and Borobodur in Java? Was it a matter of trade, or conquest, or religion, or what? There might have been elements of all three. But the evidence seems to have moved against what may be called the *vaiśya* and *kṣatriya* theories, that is, those views which look to the merchant and warrior castes, respectively, as the most important in the transmission of Indian cultural forms. The fact is that already there were kingdoms forming themselves in Southeast Asia, of an indigenous kind. But contact with south India (which must have involved some measure of trade, and to this extent the merchant theory has force) presented these smaller kingdoms, on their way to the creation of empires, with a model of ideology and theory of rule which was greatly attractive. The agents of Indianization were similar to those which saw the spread of north Indian ideas and practices into south India: basically we are back with that old formula so common in the Pali texts and elsewhere, the Brahmins and the *śramanas*—Brahmins and recluses, many of the latter being organized into the Buddhist and Jain orders. Holy persons were the bearers of a new civilization and theory of government. Not only that, but Brahmins, who had long acted as skilled advisers, could transmit the theories of government and of architecture. It seems then most likely that the "conversion" of much of Southeast Asia was a religious and ideological one, in which a new theory of rule was deliberately imported to consolidate the power of local princes and empires. All this was superimposed on a basis of the mingled agricultural religious practices of the varied indigenous peoples, who were now being organized by political means into more formidable wealth-producing units through the creation of irrigation schemes to enhance wet rice cultivation on a grander scale.

Kingdoms and Empires

An early empire mentioned by the Chinese was that of Fu-nan, which is probably a representation of the Khmer (Kampuchean) word Phnom, meaning "mountain." No doubt, even as early as the second century C.E., its rulers adopted the title (reflecting practice in south India) of "king of the mountain." This was part of a mythic theory. The capital was built in the shape of a *maṇḍala*, in which the central feature was a stone representation of the sacred mountain at the center of the world on which dwelt the God. So the king's palace was a representation of the sacred center, and he was seen as divine representative on earth. It was he who through his organizational power did the earthly work of creation, bringing order out of chaos and ensuring the fertility of the realm. So in a way, as far as the people were concerned, there was a fair exchange. In exchange for the rice and other agricultural products and artifacts which served as taxes on the population they were given civil order and richness of harvests. A similar ideology was

Apsaras or singers, whose heavenly music and dance give pleasure to men and gods, carved on a main building of the Angkor Thom complex at Angkor in Cambodia, built by King Jayavarman VII about 1200 C.E.

probably used in the kingdom to the east of Fu-nan, namely the state of Champa in the southern part of what is now Vietnam. The northern part of Vietnam was ruled as a Chinese province down to about 900 C.E. In distinction from the rest of Southeast Asia this part was subject to Chinese, rather than mostly Indian, cultural influences.

Eventually, in place of the old state of Fu-nan, a Khmer empire was established, especially under the ruler King Jayavarman II in the ninth century. Their capital, Angkor, came to be a wonderful repository of great buildings; the most important was the Viṣṇu sanctuary of King Suryavarman II (1113–50), known as Angkor Wat. It later was overgrown by the jungle, to be discovered and restored in modern times. The chief sacred focus of the Khmer kingly cult was Śiva: the *stūpa* or sacred mountain is in many cases surmounted by the *lingam*. In such a setting it was important to have Brahmins to perform the essential rites.

Meanwhile, with the decline of Fu-nan, there rose the power of the extensive maritime kingdom of Srivijaya, which probably developed from Indian trading settlements in southern Sumatra, and flourished because of its control of the convenient sea routes between India and China. Its capital was at Palembang, and it ruled over much of Sumatra, parts of Borneo, and the Malay peninsula. There were also Buddhist states to the east, in Java, especially remembered through the vast and beautiful temple complex at Borobodur (p. 153), a *stūpa* complex fashioned like a *maṇḍala*. Up to the thirteenth century, Srivijaya, united to the Sailendra kingdom of Java, was undoubtedly the dominant power in Southeast Asia, and showed the effectiveness of a sea-based empire. It was long an important center of Mahāyāna Buddhist Sanskrit learning.

During the eleventh and twelfth centuries there arose a powerful state in Burma, based on the holy city of Pagan. Its power was destroyed by Mongol invasions, but to some degree it profited from the Islamic conquest of north India, which led many learned refugee monks from the Buddhist university city of Nalanda to flee to Pagan.

The Significance of Islam

The advent of Islam in north India had a profound impact on Southeast Asian culture. The reason was that India under the Mughals cut the region off from the holy places of Buddhism and the traditional heartlands of the Buddhist faith. As Mughal rule extended south, it made some of the older Hindu models of kingship less attractive, and indeed opened up the question of the viability of a Muslim model for the region. At the same time it helped to turn the kingdoms of Southeast Asia in the direction of Sri Lankan Theravāda as a model ideology for rule. The consequence is that basically the region is now divided between Islam and the Theravāda, with the Philippines divided between Islam and Catholicism, and Java still retaining some Hindu elements.

At the beginning of the fifteenth century the state of Malacca was founded as an Islamic entity, and because of its strategic position it took over the earlier mantle of Srivijaya. Though at the beginning of the next century it was itself taken over by the Portuguese, it had a profound influence on the establishment of the Malay sultanates and served as a center of influence which helped the Islamization of parts of the southern Philippines and much of Borneo and Sulawesi.

The Theravāda and the Classical Period

What I have termed the "classical period" of Southeast Asian culture overlaps with colonialism. But though toward the end of the period, in the sixteenth century, Portuguese and other powers from Europe were making their presence felt in the region, this was also the time of the flowering of a Theravādin civilization which has left its imprint on modern societies in the region. Burma, Thailand, Kampuchea, and Laos became predominantly Theravādin, and maintained a continuity of trade and scholarly exchange with Sri Lanka.

In Burma the way to a thoroughly Theravādin model of monarchy and civilization had been prepared by the conversion of King Anawrahta (Pali: Aniruddha), who came to the throne in 1044. His conversion to Theravāda by a famous monk, Shin Arahan, led to the wide influence of the religion, especially under his successor Kyanzittha, who caused the erection of the vast Schwezigon Pagoda in the city of Pagan. Anawrahta had sent for a Buddha relic from Sri Lanka, which was installed there, and a copy of the scriptures, the Tripitaka, to check out against scriptures that had been gained from the conquered Mon people. These contacts with Sri Lanka are significant and heralded much closer ties later on. Hitherto a prevalent variety of Buddhism was Tantra, which Anawrahta set out to replace.

The theory of kingship which the Burmese and others in Southeast Asia acquired partly from the Sinhalese, whose Buddhist civilization had its heyday in the twelfth century under King Parakramabahu and after, was that the king follows the myth of Aśoka Maurya, the ideal Buddhist emperor. A monarch might have to use evil means in coming to the throne or in expanding his empire, as did Aśoka, but ultimately he is a good king and pious Buddhist, who promotes vegetarianism, brings about justice, and encourages the spread of good religion. Such an ideal also sees the king as *cakkavattin*, the "Wheel-turner" (Sanskrit: *cakravartin*), the worldly counterpart to the spiritual role assumed by the Buddha Śākyamuni. He is seen too as a Bodhisatta (Bodhisattva) or Buddha-to-be, and this links up with the myth of the future Buddha, Metteyya (Maitreya). The king incarnates the future Buddha, and thus links past to future, as well as the spiritual to the worldly life. This ideology was a useful one: it assigned parallel roles to political power and to the spiritual force wielded by the Sangha, in a new synthesis which tried to ensure both material prosperity and moral virtue in the state.

This model was perhaps at its most successful in the Southeast Asian mainland nations. In the fifteenth century Burma was ruled from Pegu, in the lower part of the country, by King Dhammaceti (reigned 1472–92), who sought to unify the Sangha; monks from Burma itself and surrounding countries such as Kampuchea and Thailand came to receive ordination. There were missions to Sri Lanka, and Sinhalese monks visited the center at Pegu. This period was represented as being the golden age of the Theravāda political system in the Burmese context.

Thai culture owed something to Kublai Khan's extension of Chinese boundaries and the forcing of many Thai-speakers southward to conquer areas that had been under Mon and Khmer dominance. They learned from these cultures and, under able monarchs, established Theravādin polities in differing parts of what is now Thailand, at Chiangmai in the north and at Ayuthia in the south, which dominated much of central Thailand. Buddhism continued to flourish, and to maintain links with the Sinhalese.

Widespread Thai influence in Laos and Kampuchea was one factor in ensuring that the "Theravādin revolution" spread to these kingdoms. In the case of Kampuchea, the older Hindu polity was undermined both politically and spiritually. The Theravāda monastic ideal kept the monks and nuns in close relationship with the people, and their life of relative poverty was impressive. Moreover it was possible, as throughout the region, to blend local cults of spirits relevant to the agricultural life with orthodox Theravāda, so that a happy symbiosis could be effected.

In these various Theravādin countries there is a similar worldview, but with some divergences of atmosphere and the contents of local religion where it is integrated into the Buddhist structure (there are also tribal cultures which lie partly outside the patterns of Theravāda influence). In the cosmology, the king is seen as a central figure, whose task is to protect the Dhamma (Dharma), assure the prosperity of his people, and encourage the ethical life. The round of rebirth is a generous one, for it includes heavenly possibilities of existence for the faithful layperson who gives generously to the Sangha. The monks and nuns are kept to their role of meditation and learning, as well as preaching to the people and assisting at ceremonies to ward off evil and the like. The capital city itself may become an important

The Buddha reflected in a pool at Maha That in Thailand.

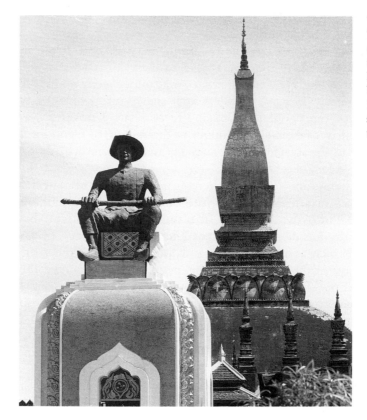

The That Luang Temple in Vientiane, capital of Laos, with the monument of King Setthathirat, who built the temple in 1566. The temple is said to contain relics of the Buddha.

center of pilgrimage due to the building of splendid temples and the importation of prestigious relics from Sri Lanka and elsewhere. The local area will have its temples too, and they will incorporate shrines to local spirits, such as the *nats* in Burma.

It may be noted that throughout the Theravādin region, whether it be in Sri Lanka or mainland Southeast Asia, various forms of somewhat similar folk religion have been incorporated into Buddhism. From the earliest times the Buddha and his followers did not exactly deny the gods. Agricultural life was pervaded by the idea that there was a whole range of spirits with whom people needed to deal. Sometimes Buddhist rituals were brought into play to cope with such beings. There were also various methods of healing and manifestations of shamanism. While Buddhism did not (notably in its Theravādin form) put great reliance on magic, it certainly tolerated it and was happy to maintain an interface with the gods and spirits. It provided an integrated cosmology with which folk beliefs could be accommodated. The strictly rationalist version of Buddhism affirmed by some Westerners was never quite the Buddhism of reality, though it is coming to be held more clearly by some modern Buddhist intellectuals. The gods and spirits are a kind of jungle sown beside the Eightfold Path, and noone prohibits you from entering there (though it does not get you nearer to *nirvāṇa*).

In addition to such folk beliefs there are various indigenous peoples embedded within this Buddhist civilization, such as the Hmong, the Kachin, and so on. They have been witnesses of the Theravāda rather than participants, until fairly recently, when they have moved down into Buddhist areas and begun practicing the religion. But in the traditional practice of their cultures they have not been absorbed. Theirs represents a different kind of indigenous being from that which we have noted as being the typical agricultural ritual of the generally Theravādin culture.

Religion in Vietnam: the Chinese Influence

Unlike the other regions of mainland Southeast Asia, Vietnam was mostly under the influence of China, having indeed been part of the Chinese empire for a thousand years after its annexation in 111 B.C.E. by the Han Dynasty. Subsequently, except for a short time in the early fifteenth century C.E., when it was again under Chinese control, it had its own independent existence; but as the kingdom of Dai Viet it mirrored the Chinese system. Confucianism was the ideology of the court and the basis of the examination system; Taoism and Mahāyāna Buddhism were woven into the triple worldview. It was probably the Daoist element in this mix which was most closely integrated into indigenous folk motifs, partly through mediums, both male and female, who exercised shamanistic powers of healing, and partly through local and national tutelary deities who would preside over the affairs of each village or larger community. But Mahāyāna Buddhism, too, was firmly rooted in the soil of Vietnam, and though there remained some Theravādin monasteries, it was chiefly Chinese-affiliated Mahāyāna that predominated in the country. Thus we have a marked divergence in official religion between the Vietnamese and the rest of mainland Southeast Asia, especially in the classical period, just before the advent of the West.

Islam's Spread into the Region

Though Islam was a relative latecomer to the region it spread with great effectiveness. From the time that Islam had come to dominate the Arab world it also had a grip upon the trade across the Indian Ocean. It was indeed partly for this reason that the Portuguese and others were impelled to seek a way to the East through voyaging around Africa (and Columbus was to take his momentous short cut by going west). This brought Muslim merchants and sailors to the region, and it was doubtless mainly through their efforts that the religion was first planted there. In the thirteenth century the state of Pasai on the Malay peninsula already had an Islamic ruler. Around 1400 there was the foundation of Malacca, to which I have already referred, and from this time on Islam made strong progress. It is clear from a number of sources that Sufi orders took a prominent part in spreading the religion, as they had on the mainland of India, from whence a number of such itinerants came.

In Java and elsewhere in the region, two forms of Islam emerged: one being regular and orthodox, the other being syncretic, blending with older local and

Indian motifs. Moreover, there remain places where a version of medieval Indian religion, combining both Hindu and Buddhist motifs, persists, most notably in the island of Bali. So Islam in the region has strong South Asian infusions, both from these forces, welling up as it were from below, and in the provenance of many of the mystics who helped Islam to spread in the islands. As we shall see later, the great mix of different religious motifs made the encounter between Indonesian religion and the Westerners during the colonial period a rich one.

Beyond the International Religions
As well as the various forces which we have been concerned with here—Confucianism from China, the Theravāda from Sri Lanka, the various forms of Mahāyāna from India and China, Hinduism from India, Islam from the Middle East—there have of course been numerous smaller-scale religions among the various peoples, from the hunters and gatherers of central Borneo to the rice-growers of Sulawesi and from the minorities of Burma to the hill peoples of Laos. Sometimes they have assimilated or succumbed to the larger culture-bearers; but sometimes they have retained their own identity. They too have a part to play in the richness of Southeast Asian life, and they too had to contend with the enormous impact of the colonial period.

The Contribution of Southeast Asia to Religious History

It is worth reflecting briefly on how this cultural complex which we have been surveying imparts any new directions to religious history. The first point that it makes to us, especially if we think that the Brahmin theory of the transplantation of Indian cultural forms to Southeast Asia is right (or at least the theory that the coupled Brahmins and monks were the primary transmitters), is that Hindu culture has or had great mobility. It did not need the substructure of the Hindu caste system to uphold it. It contained an ideology of kingship which was in its day useful and important. Second, the ultimate use of the Indic base in the region to build on it a succession of Sinhala-influenced Theravāda states helps us to redress a certain balance in our perspective. Because Buddhism largely vanished from India proper, and with it forms of the "Lesser Vehicle" of Theravāda, which is also weakly represented in East Asian culture and in the religion of Tibet, it is easy to overlook the Theravāda as a force, save of course that it became a notable one in Southeast Asia. It too had a theory of kingship which was relatively benign and could replace the more florid Hindu and Sanskritic models.

Southeast Asian Islam is interesting not merely for its relative openness to cultural forces of a non-Islamic origin but because its importation seems so much to have been at the grassroots level. Basically Islam spread here in a way quite differently from its mode of outreach in much of the rest of Asia, which was always initially by political conquest. Here was a more intense form of its appeal of piety which had proved vital in the Indian subcontinent, beneath the palladium of Mughal rule.

In the colonial period there came the establishment of the only over-whelmingly Christian country in the East: the Philippines. Perhaps it is no coincidence that this was the one country in Asia which had failed to feel the influence of Buddhism.

Finally, in relation to the dimensions of religion, we see two of them as having an especially prominent role in Southeast Asia. First there is the central *institutional* idea of the divine or to-be-enlightened king, who preserves the Dharma of the realm, and who cooperates (in the case of Buddhism) with the Sangha, and so incarnates the myth of the great Aśoka. And second we can look to the amazing translation of such ideas into *artistic* form in the Angkor complexes, at Pagan, in Borobodur, and elsewhere. Architecture here speaks much louder than texts.

CHAPTER 6

The Pacific

The Pacific Experience

The vast reaches of the Pacific Ocean were the scene of some of the most ambitious navigational feats in human history, especially in the settlement by Polynesians on islands as far apart as Hawaii and Easter Island, and Tahiti and New Zealand. The Polynesians, though vastly scattered, have a certain consistency in their culture which makes generalization possible. It is however not absolutely easy to delineate it, because for the most part the culture which was in being before the advent of Europeans during the eighteenth and nineteenth centuries has vanished. It seems clear that they originated ultimately on the Asian mainland, in Southeast Asia and south China, before embarking on their great voyages.

To the southwest of the large triangle which roughly bounds the Polynesian Pacific, with its corners in Hawaii, New Zealand, and Easter Island, there is that region which is known as Melanesia. Sometimes Papua and New Guinea are included in this area and sometimes not: our habit will be to include it here. It contains various groups of islands, such as the Solomons, Vanuatu, and New Caledonia, as well as Fiji (though the Fijians are marginal in that they share characteristics too with the Polynesians). Roughly, Melanesia comprises a crescent of islands north and northeast of Australia. North of Melanesia and west of Polynesia are the clouds of tiny islands which comprise Micronesia: they cover the area of the continental United States and contain in all about one thousand square miles of territory and about 150,000 inhabitants.

Finally, the Pacific area includes, of course, the island continent of Australia: there exist the various groups of so-called Aborigines. Their religion has been the focus of intense interest and has attracted much writing, but it has also been under heavy pressure from Western culture, as indeed have all the religions of the Pacific region.

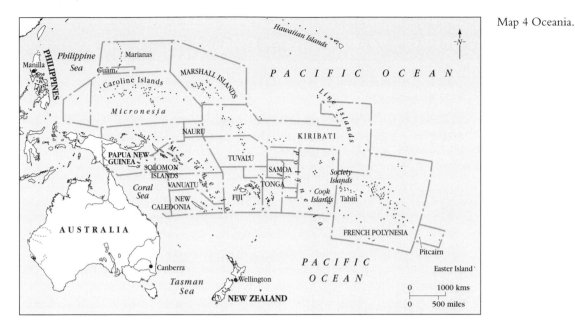

Map 4 Oceania.

The geography of the Pacific—the breaking of the world into islands, the high mountains and deep valleys of New Guinea, and the very great distances in Australia (again, it is about the size of the continental United States)—have conspired to break folk up into small cultural units, and small groups have notoriously found it hard to stand up to the impact of larger cultures. The problem for us then is to penetrate beyond modern conditions in order to present some picture of these Oceanian cultures before the menacing dawn of the European day.

As to the cultures themselves, we shall look at them in the order laid out above: first, the Polynesians, next the Melanesians, then the Micronesians, and finally the Australian Aborigines, or what I shall call "classical Australians." In a way, it is of course artificial to group the four main cultures together (even internally they are largely groupings of convenience without a necessary basis in cultural homogeneity of any extent). Their sisterhood lies in their occupying the Pacific region. In any case my way of describing them will necessarily have to be greatly selective and indeed impressionistic. But they represent important branches of human experience, as they emerge today into the postcolonial light.

Tabu and Mana

Before we embark on a description of some features of Pacific religion, it is worth noting that it is from its vocabulary that have been drawn two highly important words which have been prominent in the comparative study of religion—*mana* and *tabu* (or taboo). The latter indeed has passed into the stock of ordinary English usage. The term *mana* came to prominence through one of the major theories of the origin of religion formulated by the anthropologist

167

Smallscale Religions some key terms

Atua (Polynesian) a god or supernatural being, from the creator Tangaroa to local deities.

Calumet French term now applied to all smoking instruments of Native and South American peoples. Smoking is a ceremonial act, and the pipe is a microcosmic model of the universe.

Corroboree Aboriginal festive occasion with ceremonial rituals and dances, often reenacting myths.

Kachina Masks and other representations of mythic beings used among the Pueblo Indians of the American Southwest.

Mana Sacred and numinous power associated with gods, breach of *tabu*, holy forces in nature, etc.; used by anthropologists and others as a key notion in religions.

Marae (Polynesian) sacred area with shrine.

Masalai (Melanesian word from Papua New Guinea) animal spirits and demons liable to haunt human beings.

Mizimu (Bantu) the spirits of the dead: ancestors.

Nganga Specialist in dealing with illnesses and various evils: a so-called witch-doctor (Southern and Central African traditions).

Shaman (Tungus word from Siberia) a visionary who can, in sharing experimentally in the vicissitudes of the sick, help to cure them and who can locate resources (such as fish and game) in a hunting society; often experiences death and rebirth.

Tabu or *Tapu* (Polynesian) that which is forbidden and dangerous; great mana creates tapu.

Totem (Algonquin word from North America) a natural species of animal or plant life connected especially with a clan, who do not hunt or gather that species: key concept in many anthropological and psychological theories about the nature of religion.

R. R. Marett (1866–1943) in a book published in 1909, *The Threshold of Religion*. He drew upon the reported finding by a fellow anthropologist in a book on the Melanesians published in 1891 that the fundamental concept of their religion was *mana* or power: for instance the power residing in a chief, or a rock, or in some sacred object. It came to be noticed that similar ideas were to be found in a variety of small-scale cultures across the world; and the idea was taken up by some major theorists, notably Gerardus van der Leeuw (1890–1950), who in his famous *Religion in Essence and Manifestation* made power the central notion in his account of religion.

Dimensions of Polynesian Religion

The most important distinction in Polynesian religion is that between the spiritual or invisible world and the world which we can see and experience. The two are interwoven: the gods are the various forces which lie behind visible events, such as thunder or menstruation, and by their nature they are frequent visitors to the habitations of human beings. There is a distinction often drawn between the heavenly world, the place where the gods are when they are not with us, and the underworld whither the spirits of the dead pass.

Mostly, *rituals* are concerned with attempting some control of the gods. If they are to visit us, then it is best that they do so where and when we want, so it is important to prepare dwellings for them and form incantations to bring them hither, please them, and then (quite as important) send them back to where they came from. Anything that has to do with the gods must be done with great care. The taboos involved are simply a reflection of the fact that gods are dangerous. So indeed is any person with great *mana* or inherent power. Thus in Hawaii the fact that chiefs exuded tremendous power, and the fear of weakening that power by having lower-class spouses mate with them, meant that there was sanction for brother—sister marriage. (This has been the case in a number of other societies, notably in ancient Egypt.)

Naturally there were rituals for all propitious occasions, such as the planting of crops, the start of a voyage or hunting expedition. Witchcraft—in the sense of using ritual means to bring about bad results for others, rather than (like most rites) good results for us—was widely practiced also.

The concept of *tabu* pervaded the whole realm of ritual in that it was a general theory of possession and how to encourage and avoid it. For instance, it was thought that gods might be attracted by resemblance, so that the making of statues for them to take up temporary residence in was often thought to be effective. Women were ambivalent: often gods were scared of them, so they could dispel *tabu*, as also could water. But in some cases gods might be attracted by women.

The propitiation of the gods could take various forms, from human sacrifices, which were effective for war and building, to incantations. The effectiveness of a ritual depended on the perfection of its operation, so that there were strict rules: people should keep quiet, etc., during a ritual act. Importance was also attached to the dismissal of the gods, as well as their invitation and propitiation—and in this too the whole concept of *tabu* was important. If humans could control this volatile substance, then it was as important to be able to stop its operation as to start it.

At the *mythic* level, there are various accounts of the creation of the world, often by a great God. A rather moving instance of this is in the following poem from Hawaii about the God Ta'aroa:

He existed, Ta'aroa was his name
In the immensity
   There was no earth, no sky

There was no sea, there was no human:
Above, Ta'aroa calls.
Existing alone, he became the universe.
Ta'aroa is the origin, the rocks.
Ta'aroa is the sands,
It is thus that he is named.
Ta'aroa is the light;
Ta'aroa is within;
Ta'aroa is the germ.
Ta'aroa is beneath.
  Ta'aroa is form;
  Ta'aroa is wise.
He created the land of Hawaii,
  Hawaii the great and sacred,
  As a body or shell for Ta'aroa…

The mythic dimension: Tangaroa (or Ta'aroa), the god of the ocean, was regarded widely in Polynesia as the great Creator, and here lesser deities are seen coming out of his body, symbolizing their dependence on him. The wooden statue, from the Austral Islands, is hollow, and the back can be removed.

Sometimes the creation story is a good deal more complicated. In the Society Islands the same God lived in a kind of contemplative self-sufficiency: but meantime a great octopus held sea and sky together in a firm grip. Ta'aroa called other gods into existence. He also shook himself and feathers fell (he was evidently pictured as a great bird), and they turned into trees and other green plants. Though the Abyss, Rua, killed the octopus by witchcraft, his arms still retained their grip. After various adventures an anarchic being, Maui, the great Trickster of the Pacific, propped up the sky with wedges and got the help of Tane who lived in the topmost heaven, and used a shell to open the sky to light. Tane then decorated the heaven with stars and set the sun and the moon on their courses.

Maui was often thought of as half god and half human. This half-and-half condition is often the characteristic of crafty people in myth, who thereby confound human categories: it is the hallmark of the recurrent figure known as the Trickster. Some figures dealt with elsewhere, such as Enki and Prometheus, fall into this category of Trickster. Maui represents an important motif in Polynesian myth, for though he does not create—which is the prerogative of the gods—he nevertheless may turn what the gods have made into something useful for humans. This is indeed the whole point of ritual, which is not to create power but to canalize it and not to make order but to modify it. Maui for instance stole fire from the gods, so that humans could cook and use it in other useful ways. He fished up various islands with his fishhook, including the North Island of New Zealand, according to Maori myth. He is supposed to have slowed down the sun so that humans could have a day of decent length to prepare food and make things, including nice images for the gods. He is credited with being the ancestor of the human race. He was not worshiped as such, but the stories of his tricky humiliation of pompous gods (who *were* worshiped) were told with relish.

Humans preexist in the "other world," and each enters this world through her or his mother. A woman, likewise, is the conduit of death. The tale is told that Maui intended to kill off Hine-nui-te-po, Great Hine of the Underworld,

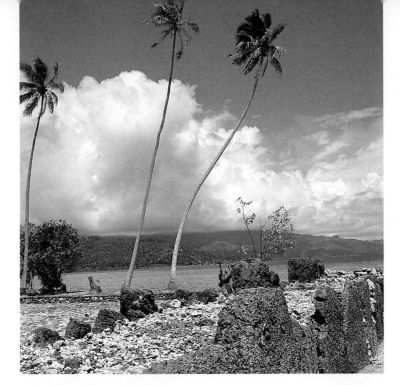

Left: A *marae* or sacred enclosure in French Polynesia, where priests recite chants and make offerings.

Below: Paul Gauguin's *Manao Tupapau (The Spirit of the Dead Watches)* in the Albright Knox Art Gallery in Buffalo, New York, painted in 1892 during his first visit to Tahiti. The work is strongly evocative of the belief amongst the Polynesians that the spirit world and the earthly world are closely interwoven.

the personification of Death, by entering into her through her vagina and eventually coming out of her mouth. He slipped off his clothes, bound his strong club to his right wrist, and told his bird companions to stay absolutely quiet for fear of waking Hine: and so he started to climb into her vagina. The birds naturally thought this a scream and laughed raucously, all of which commotion woke Hine. She saw Maui climbing into her and crushed him to death between her thighs.

Naturally there are vast resources of myth available in the Polynesian world, and these few examples will suffice for a glimpse into this world. The stories of the gods help as metaphors of society and social norms, and it is within the ethos of Polynesian religion that morality has its meaning. But in the nature of the case the pattern of values is heroic and greatly male-dominated. The battles which often engaged the peoples of the Pacific, the great deeds of navigation and fishing, and so on, led to a system of ethics which prized manliness and courage, and the kind of success which was exhibited in *mana*.

As for *experience*: the very pattern of belief about the gods prevalent across the Pacific, seeing everywhere the hands of hidden forces, meant that ordinary life had to be read all the time for omens, hints as to what the gods were up to. As you looked out to the deep blue Pacific waters you could almost see the gods of wind and water and storm; and as you scanned the white beach you could wonder whether the gods were secretly crossing it toward the abodes of human beings. And there around the village, in the curling smoke and in the shadows, were the hints of gods of disease, of the village, of carpentry, of all kinds of secret forces in human affairs. They were like the *numina* of ancient Rome. They lent an air of awe, of the numinous, to the wondrous environment in which human beings had their beautiful and dangerous existence. The murmurings of *tabu* reinforced fear. As the thunder might mutter in the distance, so might the unseen forces of the gods be mobilizing themselves for their own purposes, which yet would bring sorrow or joy to humans. So it was needful to read the sky and the plants and the animals, birds, and fish.

Some people were especially deep in their dreaming and in visions, and they might become specialist diviners and healers. Dreams in particular were significant events. But the whole world of Nature was after all part of the behavior of the gods: their bodies were thunder and rain and pigs and earth. Strange behavior in anything might provide a clue to the gods' intentions, and reinforced the sense of the numinous and of awe-inspiring *mana* which drenched the world of the Polynesian.

In the *material* dimension, masks, dances, carvings, and *maraes* or sacred enclosures were artifacts which helped to attract the gods and so canalize their powers in contact with the human race. The carvings of Polynesian art represented likenesses of the gods, or things congenial to them, so that they might be induced to come, regaled with song and chant and immemorial rituals, and then in due course sent on their way.

Opposite The ritual dimension: aboriginal body-painting. Membership of an aboriginal clan is achieved through an elaborate initiation ritual.

As far as the *organizational* dimension of religion went, although the preparation of *maraes* or sacred enclosures was a communal activity, Polynesian cultures had specialists in ritual, and also those especially skilled in healing, divination, and other arts. There were those also who used sorcery, and there was a dark underside of religion, in which the wrong uses of ritual were greatly to be feared.

Melanesian Religions: Some Patterns

If there are variations in the Polynesian world, there are even more so in the whole range of Melanesia. The island of New Guinea, comprising what are now Papua New Guinea, an independent state, and Irian Jaya which is part of Indonesia, contains more than 1000 languages, some spoken by less than 200 people. The islands have diverse cultures, some heavily influenced by Polynesian motifs, as in Fiji. But if one can generalize, then one might say that the Melanesian religions have more confidence in the manipulative power of ritual, and they feel less dependent on the gods. Gods there are, and all kinds of spirits; but they are closer to the earthly realm and not too difficult in many cases to control. The importance of primary power or *mana* can be seen from this perspective, for it is this energy that humans would like to manipulate, and it is the ritual system which manages to do this that is important to Melanesian culture.

Were there a clear distinction to be made between magic and religion, then Melanesia exhibits more of magic than of religion. But it is not a distinction which bears much fruit. Suffice it to say that for many Melanesian societies ritual is at the heart of things, and the unseen forces with which ritual deals, and which it may create, are the most vital part of the fabric of events. Thus no major calamity and virtually no death fails to be explained either as a result of sorcery or the action of spirits, or as the result of the breaking of some taboo. It follows that disease itself has similar causes, and it is the job of specialists to be able to direct counter-ritual to act against the dangerous forces at work against the afflicted individual.

The range of unseen forces is great. Particular deities are often associated with activities such as fishing or warfare; they often seem remote from human activity, though they may play a role in myth. But even remote culture heroes and gods may be important in another way, as the ultimate sources of various spells and incantations, and knowledge of this will have been handed down secretly from generation to generation of ritual specialists. There are other spirits, or at any rate mythic beings, who are not gods but nevertheless attract fear: demon monsters who inhabit the wild parts of the bush which lie outside the relative order of human settlements, with their vegetable gardens and places for rearing pigs. Closer to the settlements are the hungry ghosts: the newly departed may still have nostalgia for those whom they knew, although they eventually drift away to their own world where they do much the same sort of thing that humans do, but in a rather pleasanter way, probably.

Belief in ghosts ties in with the general Melanesian belief in souls. Souls can be disturbed and even captured by sorcery. Human leftovers, such as cut hair or the remains of what you have been eating, can be used to control a soul. Where this happens the only recourse is counter-magic. In some places, for instance in the highlands of New Guinea, the souls of ancestors play an important role in religion in that they are thought to be able to promote the welfare of the community—through the fertility of crops, for instance. They exist as part of a wider society in which the visible community is embedded.

On the whole, then, Melanesian religion thinks of the spirit world, both divine and human (in the form of ghosts and the souls of ancestors), as being rather close to the visible community in which humans have their primary being. Some features of religion, while not unique to Melanesia, are nevertheless emphasized there. For instance, sometimes complex taboos surround men's dealings with women, who are generally thought to be

The ritual dimension: in Papua-New Guinea and New Ireland masks and headdresses are ceremonial means of assuming the identity of gods and spirits.

inferior. Thus, often a man is not supposed to be below a woman: he should not drink from water in a stream downstream from women; and in some societies villages are built in such a way that men's quarters are built on ridges to ensure physical superiority. Since contact with women is regarded in many places as itself polluting, boys' puberty rites involve vomiting and the letting of blood in order to rid them of the polluting contacts with food cooked by women, menstrual blood, and so on. Sometimes initiation takes the form of entry into a men's secret society, where adepts are eventually shown how to make sacred masks and conduct séances with spirits.

The Meaning of Death

Very strong in the Melanesian context is the regard paid to the proper treatment of the dead. Elaborate feasts and burial ceremonies are the norm, and the corpse is sometimes cross-questioned to check on the cause of death. The extent of a widow's austere seclusion and expression of loss is held as an index of how she was not involved in poisoning her mate. The ceremonial may extend over a long period: first the ritual disposal of a corpse by burial or on a platform, then the collection of the bones, once the flesh has decayed away, and further rites. During this stretch of time it may be that the kin and in particular the widow remain in utter seclusion.

There are indications in the mourning of a deeper layer of ritual in the past when widows were killed, as in New Britain, and sent on with their deceased husbands to the afterlife. The possessions of the departed may also be destroyed, or ultimately consumed as part of a ritual of reintegration of the kin into society.

Even after the round of mortuary observances has been completed, the dead are not necessarily utterly gone: their ghosts may be summoned and consulted in future times, and shrines where their bones are kept may come to function like ancestral temples.

Art and Religion

Especially in lowland New Guinea, but also elsewhere, Melanesian art, and in particular the making of masks for ceremonial purposes, is spectacular. Very often the construction—made out of barkcloth, say, and decorated with colored leaves and feathers, or painted with traditional designs—is short-lived, being made just for some ceremony, such as a funeral. Usually the making of such masks is a highly secret matter, to be kept secret in particular from women. There are other statues or masks of a more permanent kind, representing spirits. There are rites for the introduction of spirits into the masks and for dismissing them. Sometimes the painting of the eyes has special significance. The creation of such art would not of course be classified as such, since the aesthetic as a separate category is itself largely a Western phenomenon: but nevertheless is a testimony to the brilliant imagination of Melanesian societies and the intuitive realization of wonderful ways of representing and expressing the sense of the numinous.

We do not come across much, in the wide spectrum of Melanesian religion, which points to belief in a single Supreme Creator or High God. The *myths* of beginnings tend to deal with the bringing of some order out of a chaos of calamities. The small scale of most societies, and their being surrounded by a space which was largely unknown or fearful (ocean or bush), gave Melanesians a sense of contrast between man-made order and a rather spooky periphery, relevant to human affairs but somewhat threatening. The main feature of religions in the area is the highly developed sense of the practical efficacy of ritual, both for good and ill. Thus of all the dimensions of religion, ritual is here the most highly worked out and prized, and with it the physical manifestation of ritual, namely the body-painting, masks, and icons constructed for the ceremonial life.

Micronesia

The worlds of the Micronesians are varied too; but they have somewhat more concern than the Melanesians with the creation, and the emphasis on female deities is greater. This may be in part because, while males are involved in fishing, navigation, housebuilding, the martial arts, etc., women are in charge of the gardens and agricultural work. Nevertheless, typically women are thought of as inferior and polluting, because of menstrual blood and giving birth. Sometimes, even so, the High God and Creator is thought of as female, and goddesses are frequently credited with the creation of differing food plants. In the Carolines the Great Goddess, Ligoupup, always existed, and made the world. She is conceived as lying beneath the islands, and when she stirs then there are earthquakes. Her son became god of the underworld and the sea and all that pertains to it; her daughter rose to heaven and wed a deity, by whom she had a son, Aluelap, who is the source of all knowledge. Elsewhere the High God is nominated as Anulap, who is ancient and white-haired, and so very weak that two servitors raise his eyelids so that he can see and raise his upper lip so that he can eat. He is a very colorful representation of what historians know as the *Deus otiosus* or "Superfluous God," who is inactive in regard to human affairs (often being so high and numinous that humans cannot think of how he could come to be concerned with the trivial worries of the human race), and is thus no longer worshiped. Still, he is creator, knows all, and is Supreme Being.

In many ways the Micronesian religious world is like that of the Polynesians, and there has been some Polynesian cultural influence in some of the islands. They are a part of the great mosaic of religions of Oceania, opened up eventually to Westerners from the sixteenth century onward, as navigators from an alien world discovered the often idyllic-seeming islands.

Australia: the Land of the Dreaming

Finally, in our survey of the Pacific religions, we come to the classical culture of Australia before the Whites came to settle the land, some two hundred years ago. The societies which inhabit the vast reaches of Australia, from the snowy mountains of the southeast to the red plains of the west, are varied, but they display some traits in common, which we can look on as classical features of Australian religion and society. The two most striking of these are totemism and the concept of the Dreaming.

The Dreaming (or Dream Time) is that period long ago (yet still somehow present to us in everyday life) when the deities moved about on the earth, giving shape and substance to the land, generating human beings, and arranging the rules of society. It was in its own way a creative epoch, but it is much more than some generalized period of cosmogony. The Dreaming helps to explain the most particular items in the environment. That environment is—for the most part—a rather harsh one, in which ingenuity is needed to live successfully. It is a hot land, with red deserts and glittering eucalyptus trees, half dried watercourses and dry gullies, sparse rains and elusive high clouds, grand rounded rocks and strangely contoured hills: a land populated sparsely with ingenious animals—the kangaroo and the wallaby, the ant-eating echidna, the lizard goanna—and bright birds, from the small kookaburra to the flamboyant galahs and bright-colored parrots, and many insects, notably the creators of great anthills and the ever-present flies. It is this environment that received its particularities in the phase of the Dreaming.

Important in the cycles of Australian myth are the routes which the protagonists took across the countryside in the Dreaming. These tales indicate places which are sacred, either because of events described in the myths or more intensely because they relate to the fertility of some relevant species. For instance there is the story of Ngurunderi, in the Murray river region of south Australia. He went down the river in a canoe, after the great Murray Cod, which swished its huge tail to and fro and splashed the water around. Thereby it formed the many bends in the river and the swamps which line it here and there. Eventually Cod was caught by his brother-in-law, and he strewed the chopped up bits into the lower Murray and the lakes at its mouth, to make many species of fish for later humans to gather. Or again, there is a myth from the far north which concerns a famous and widespread mythic figure, the Rainbow Snake. She came from the sea, but at first only found dry—very dry—land. She traveled underneath the earth and came to a waterfall. She went downstream, and when the water disappeared she dug out a large billabong (a pool in a river which is cut off from the flow) and produced an egg, which she set out to harden in the sun, and then slept in a cave. An old man came along and cooked the egg. She grabbed him and dragged him under the water, vomiting up his bones, which hardened. She made two more eggs which hardened there in the pool. She looks after them from the cave above the billabong. This is a highly particular myth, relating to a highly particular sacred site, with its spirit presences, the Rainbow Snake and the old man, frozen as it were into immortality by the tale.

The desert is the great area of mythic tracks where the gods and spirits went on their travels. You cannot know all the stories, and differing tribes characteristically knew different parts of the meaning of the overlapping sacred geography. In such ways the whole land was haunted by divine presences, projected into the Now from the time of the Dreaming. But the Dreaming of course does much more than present us with a sacred cartography: it accounts for social custom, for clan organization, for inventions—in short for the whole of arrangements for living. It explains rituals which in turn are designed to canalize the Dreaming to us so that we can benefit from its powers.

Creation and Fertility

There are various stories of creation and sky gods, who nevertheless tend to fade into insignificance compared to the sacred events of the Dream Time. There is a story in central Australia, among those who speak Aranda, that there was a great emu-footed Father who lived in a paradisal place with many wives and children. These beings were not worried about the earth. Beneath the earth slept many other supernatural beings, who eventually awakened and started their wanderings. Human beings were created by them and taught the various arts which they would need to live in the region. The stories of this Dreaming period became much more vital for the Aranda than any high and "otiose" God. Their existential religion was a matter of communication not with the great Father but with the supernaturals of the Dreaming, and so rituals had to be used, themselves prescribed by the supernaturals, for recreating the ancestors in the present.

Some myths of origin concern fertility, and a famous one of these is the cycle of stories of Djangawwul, who landed on the coast from the hazy island of Bralgu with a male companion and his own two sisters, whom he kept in a state of perpetual pregnancy with his very long and potent penis. There was no question of incest here, as marriage customs had not yet been invented. The offspring of the sisters were the ancestors of the present-day Australian Aborigines. They also created various fertility rituals, in which women are often engaged. The sisters brought with them a cult object or *rangga*, symbolizing the penis. The men stole it and started their own cultic activities.

Fertility is often connected, too, with the system of totemism, which is widespread in Australia. The supernaturals of the Dreaming become linked to clans, a clan being a group which is constituted by patrilineal descendants of a supernatural hero. These ideas can be illustrated from the case of the northern tribe of Walbiris, now some 1400 in number. They are divided into about forty clans, each connected with a totem or personified version of some natural species or object—Kangaroo, Opossum, Yam, Rain, Fire, and so on. These heroes had their stories which told of the localities associated with them—sometimes marking enormously long tracks (one going as far as South Australia) and sometimes quite localized. These sacred places were infused with sacred particles which were the relatively dormant supernaturals. They had to be activated by human rituals, performed by the men's lodge of the relevant clan. Without the carrying on of such rituals the land and the people

An Australian aboriginal bark painting depicting an episode in a story from Western Arnhem Land, with fragile spirits enticing a hunter.

would not stay prosperous. The land, the heroes of the Dreaming, the former ancestors, and the present-day people thus formed an organic web, easy to rupture but happy in its wellbeing if all went well.

Ecopsychism

That organic web was indeed ruptured by the coming to Australia of people who had very different views of the relation of land to people and of supernaturals to society. But we must first make the imaginative leap to that world which has lasted some 30,000 years or more. We know little of its ancient styles when it first came to the Australian mainland. But we can reach back to view Aboriginal culture before the coming of the Europeans. We see a remarkable experiment in living in which diverse social groups crisscrossed the same land, managed between them in a segmented way the sacred places and tracks of a unitary landscape, and saw with the inward eye beyond the rocks and trees and leaping animals to the spirits that infused the creation around them and gave sanction and meaning to their customs. From the outside: dusty humans. From the inside: complicated social divisions and initiations and rites which meshed in with the hunting and gathering, across a changing daily scene. They pioneered a form of ecopsychism, a kind of gently effective way of living in a Nature which was itself conceived as infused with spirits.

It is rather different, this Australian world, from that of Melanesia, Micronesia, and Polynesia, where the sea is often dominant, and the land rich. Here there is a different, drier scene, and one where, more than elsewhere, the diverse social groups are more open to one another, for they share an interwoven system of sacred tracks and places. The Rainbow Snake's eggs have hardened in the sun, and there are unseen persons hovering around, and in, the billabong.

The Americas

CHAPTER 7

A Wide Scene

It seems probable that all or virtually all the ancestors of the Native Americans in both North and South America migrated there from the Asian landmass by a northerly route, via what is now the Bering Strait. There may be some slight influence of Polynesian settlement, and it could be that in the period before Columbus there were Chinese landings; and we know of a small Viking presence. But, given the relative homogeneity of a largely Asian immigrant population (and even there, as today, there may have been great variations), the patterns of culture which were created in the regions of the Americas are extremely diverse. Among other achievements was the creation of some great urban civilizations in Central and South America.

There are five cultural areas which we shall consider here: first, the Andes; second, the rest of South America, comprising differing regions, such as Patagonia, the Pampas, the Gran Chaco, the Amazon Basin, Eastern Brazil, and the Caribbean coast; third, the islands of the Caribbean; fourth, Central America; and fifth, North America. In most of these we deal with very varied phenomena in the pre-Columbian period, and the best we can do here is to be selective in relation to differing types of religions and social values.

In terms of urban culture we can count 1000 C.E. as a watershed, in that it was in the tenth century that the Toltec empire in Mexico, a powerful predecessor of the Aztecs, collapsed, and at a somewhat similar time the Tiahuanaco empire in the Central Andes also disappeared. It was after this time that we see the rise of the great states which were so unsuccessful against the Spaniards. The Maya civilization also disappeared as a viable system in the tenth century. In many ways we might look upon the period before the tenth century as exhibiting classical forms of urban culture in Central America, especially because of the delicacy of Maya art. But on the whole we know too little, even about the Maya, to decipher their religions clearly. With the subsequent period, and the Aztecs and the Incas, we are on somewhat firmer ground. As to cultures outside of Central America and the Inca region, we know relatively little about their forms before 1000. In many cases we have to describe classical religions in small-scale groups as they exist now, for lack of sufficient historical or archaeological knowledge.

The Religion of the Incas

The empires which preceded the Incas in Peru were various—from the Chavín (eighth century C.E. onward) through to the Chimú (1200–1400 C.E.). Unfortunately, we do not know too much of their religious ideas, because, like the Incas, they lacked a written language. The temples seem to have been used for sacrifices, including human sacrifice, and there is good evidence of complex rites related to calendars describing the movements of various heavenly bodies. The Sun and Moon seem to have been important deities, and there are images of gods in the form of animals, such as the puma.

The Inca religious system of the fifteenth century was an amalgamation of preceding cults, and in a way that emphasized and organized imperial rule. Roughly, the empire was a centralized federation in which local chiefs were summoned periodically to the capital Cuzco (or "Navel," that is, center of the earth). The central Temple of the Sun at the junction of the rivers may also

Map 5
Latin America.

have been linked to the Milky Way, also seen as a river. At any rate here was the center of empire. From here radiated theoretical lines along each of which was placed 428 shrines. There were reciprocal relations between Cuzco and the approved sanctuaries of the provinces (but many local cults were suppressed, no doubt through having supported resistance to the greatly expanding Inca empire). The imperial ideology represented the emperor (the Inca) as responsible for the welfare of the empire, and so he was the chief point of intersection of his subjects and the great gods. He had to preside over earthly affairs during the present cosmic cycle; so he was himself a god, the offspring of the Sun, which was the great deity at the heart of the ritual complex at the temple of Cuzco.

The Sun at Cuzco had to share his temple with the Thunder God, whose sphere of operations was lower than the heavens; the Moon Goddess, who was especially important to women; and the Stars. Together they regulated time and the change of seasons. The Father of the Sun, and the Supreme Being (though not the only god), was Viracocha. He it was who formed and arranged things at the beginning of the era, and he was the recipient of prayers, especially from the aristocracy. One such prayer has survived and goes as follows:

> You who are without equal, and span the ends of the earth: you who gave life and force to human beings, saying to one, "Let this be a man," and to the other, "Let this be a woman," you gave them being: Let them live without danger, in peace and health. You who are in the heavens and in the thunderstorm, grant them long life, and accept this our sacrifice.

Beneath the great gods were a cloud of other numinous beings, the *huaca*, and the hierarchical imperial system was also reflected in a hierarchy of gods, down to the village level.

Doctrinally, some great store seems to have been set by the binary oppositions of the cosmos: male—female, Sun—Moon, and so on. Likewise, villages were divided into two halves, and the whole earthly and cosmic system was seen as both in conflict and capable of being harmonized. It was the Inca's chief function to contribute to this harmony, by relevant offerings and by the maintenance of the cycle of public rituals. There are echoes of the Chinese search for harmony amid the polarities of Yin and Yang.

The glories and complexities of the ritual year must have been great. The ceremonies at Cuzco were dazzling, with the Inca on a gold throne presiding over sacrifices in the gold-plated halls of the temple. The ability to control so large an empire in part depended on these rites; but it must be remembered too that everywhere in the villages and homesteads of the vast region men and women celebrated their divine ancestors and had relations to lesser *huacas* to help them with their gardens and food-growing, and in the fight against illness and death. But the weakness of the system was its intense centralization, which is why in 1532 a few adventurers under Francisco Pizarro could strike in such a deadly way at the heart of the system.

Small-Scale Societies in South America

The conditions of existence in South America outside of the Andean region are of course very varied. Many of the groups in the tropical forest regions of the Amazon and Orinoco basins (sadly depleted, by the way, in population since the first culture contact with Europeans, so that also there may have thereby been great socioreligious changes) do not seem to have anything but occasional belief in a High God or Supreme Being. However, such a belief is very widespread in the regions of the Pampas and Patagonia. The rituals related to ancestral cults and the preservation of the dead are much more common in the Andes than elsewhere—perhaps because climatically such practices as mummification become feasible, whereas in steaming forests the dead decompose alarmingly fast. Fertility cults and vegetation deities are important in the northwest Amazon region and elsewhere, but not in the Grand Chaco. So we can point to considerable variety, reinforced of course once one begins to look at the content of the varied mythologies.

One element, however, is almost universal outside the Andes: shamanism. In many areas, the shaman identifies with the jaguar, which can act as his or her *alter ego*. This is probably for a number of reasons. First, the jaguar can swim and hunt in water and so has access to the (generally watery) underworld. Likewise the shaman can visit this region, in the course of saving spirits of humans from death. Second, a jaguar can climb and, like the shaman, has access to upper regions, the heavenly world. It is in any case a numinous creature, and full of ambiguities.

The shaman testifies to the importance of religious experience, for it is by visions, ecstasies, and dreams that he or she receives a vocation. It may be that in many such societies the actual training with an expert is arduous: but at root there is the capacity for vision. This can be, and is, aided by hallucinogens. It appears as if the use of the San Pedro plant is attested for nearly three thousand years, from ancient pottery of the Chavín culture in Peru, where it is depicted. Such hallucinogens were often also combined with tobacco.

The shaman was important because by his experience and ritual powers he could project himself into the invisible worlds. He could thus effect cures in the case of those who might in a sense have died. But he could also enter the worlds of the spirits whose manifestations were in this world—as fish, animals, birds, and so on—and thus he could give guidance to hunters and gatherers (as many of these smaller-scale societies were).

The Caribbean

The major peoples of the Caribbean islands were the Arawaks and the Caribs. After the settlement of the islands by Europeans, the aboriginal inhabitants were wiped out by imported diseases and the hardships of slave labor; they survive only in the descendants of interbreeding with Europeans or with the hardier slaves brought in from Africa. With them went the pre-Columbian

A mushroom-shaped stone from Central America. This may have represented a shaman who was influenced by hallucinogenic mushrooms.

religions of the islands. Traces of their beliefs and rituals are, however, to be found in Afro-Caribbean religion, and we shall see something of these developments in the second part of this book.

Both the Arawaks, who migrated about the beginning of the Common Era, and the Caribs, came from the mainland. As with the South American peoples we have just considered, shamanism was an important phenomenon. There were beliefs in High Gods, and among the Arawak importance was attached to the cult of ancestors. The Caribs were said by Columbus to have been cannibals (the English word derives from the word "Carib"), but this may well have been an unjustified accusation.

Civilizations of Central America

The Maya

The classical civilization of the Maya in southeastern Mexico and in Guatemala and Belize still survives in a fragmentary way, not only in the great

The ethical dimension: a Mayan relief from Yaxchilan in Guatemala, showing a penitent mutilating his tongue before a priest. British Museum, London.

ruins of the area, such as at Chichén Itzá and Mayapán, but also in the cultures of people who still speak Mayan languages. Their cultural achievements in art, writing, and mathematics were considerable; and they invented an ingenious calendrical system which was used to calculate and foretell auspicious days. It was based on units of 20, and so on a 360-day year, being the closest multiple of 20 to the real length of the year. Years were calculated according to a Short Count of 256-year cycles or a Long Count which started at the year 3114 B.C.E. The use of the Short Count persisted among the Maya until the eighteenth century, one of a number of long survivals of the culture after the Spanish conquest.

Time became the fundamental preoccupation of Maya culture, and this was tied of course to the revolutions of the Sun. The Sun God became the main focus of religion: he was also the creator and the first priestly figure who invented writing. The cosmos was arranged vertically in seven layers of heavens and below the earth were the five layers of the underworld, which was the realm of the dead. At the center of the cosmos stood the First Tree, the *axis mundi*. This is reminiscent of many other cultures, and may reflect some shamanistic motifs as having entered into early Maya thought. But it seems that the sacred character of time which could be calculated by an esoteric arithmetic was the chief occupation of the priestly class.

The Aztecs

For the Aztecs their wonderful capital, Tenochtitlán, was the chief marvel of civilization. In its immense size and beautiful architecture it was modeled on the older Toltec city of Teotihuacán, the "Abode of the Gods," some thirty miles to the north, and in its division into four quarters it reflected the Aztec understanding of the cosmos. These four directions together with the center are the typical five directions of Central American (as of Chinese) cosmology. The cosmos had its axis or invisible center in the vertical line which ran through the City, with thirteen heavenly levels arranged above and nine layers in the underworld. The number five was also important for time as well as space. The universe has five major periods, each ending with various calamities. In modern time, we are now embarked on the period of the Fifth Sun, when the sun rises in the East.

But the universe is gravely unstable, for the continuation of order requires continuous sacrifices. Indeed, before the start of the Fifth Sun the gods had to combine to energize the Sun, which did not rise above the horizon, by sacrificing themselves collectively. This myth provided justification for the continuing sacrificial cult which was centered in Tenochtitlán. The Aztec emperor was also the highest priest, and there fell to him the task of maintaining not only the order of the empire but the order of the whole cosmos as well. So the Aztecs had this rather haunting and terrifying thought that indeed the Sun might not rise tomorrow, that the onward harmony of the world was something which was forever in jeopardy. There was therefore a deep resonance between the cosmic and human worlds. The Sun required

Right The Temple of Warriors encloses a shrine to the spirit of the rain-clouds. Reclining figures such as this, known as *chacmools*, are found at both Chichén Itzá and at Tula. The flat stomach formed an altar on which offerings, perhaps the still-beating hearts of sacrificial victims, were placed. Chichén Itzá in central Yucatán, Mexico, is one of the best-known Mayan sites.

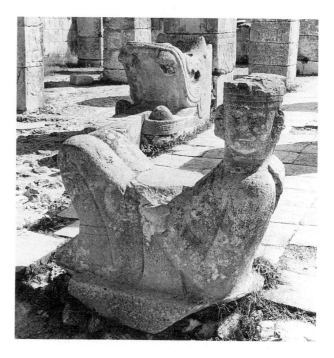

Below, right Quetzalcóatl, a principal deity in central Mexico, whose name means "Precious Feather Serpent," and a standard bearer on the Temple of the Warriors at Chichén Itzá , which encloses a shrine of Chac, the Maya-Toltec rain-cloud spirit.

Below The mythic dimension: Tzazolteotl, a fertility goddess of rather fierce expression, here gives birth; she dealt with sexual transgressions.

The Tasks of the Wise Man (Aztec): Bernardino de Sahagún

The wise man: a light, a torch, a stout torch that does not smoke.

A perforated mirror, a mirror pierced on both sides.

His are the black and red ink, his are the illustrated manuscripts, he studies the illustrated manuscripts.

He himself is writing and wisdom.

He is the path, the true way for others.

He directs people and things; he is a guide in human affairs.

The wise man is careful [like a physician] and preserves tradition.

His is the handed-down wisdom; he teaches it; he follows the path of truth.

Teacher of the truth, he never ceases to admonish.

He makes wise the countenances of others; to them he gives a face [a personality]; he leads them to develop it.

He opens their ears; he enlightens them.

He is the teacher of guides; he shows them their path.

One depends upon him.

He puts a mirror before others; he makes them prudent, cautious; he causes a face [a personality] to appear in them.

He attends to things; he regulates their path, he arranges and commands.

He applies his light to the world.

He knows what is above us [and] in the region of the dead.

He is a serious man.

Everyone is comforted by him, corrected, taught.

Thanks to him people humanize their will and receive a strict education.

He comforts the heart, he comforts the people, he helps, gives remedies, heals everyone.

human blood: this was the ideology of human sacrifice, itself a great stimulus to warfare, which was waged to capture fodder for the gods.

But the mythic cosmology was more than a depiction of the directions and epochs. It was filled in with pictures of the various gods and spiritual beings who animated and controlled the universe, beginning with the ultimate creator, Ometéotl, all-powerful, and a blend of male and female, who fused oppositions in her/his own person. There was Tezcatlipoca, Smoking Mirror, vigorous and frightening in his powers of transformation, identified with the Knife, a divinity vital (or one might say fatal) in sacrifice. There was Xiuhtecuhtli, the fire deity, important too in the priestly cult, where fires had to be maintained at all times and ritually renewed: every fifty-two years, at the end of a calendar cycle, a new fire was kindled in the hole in a sacrificial victim's chest, whence his palpitating heart had been plucked. He was also, as in other cultures, the god of the hearth, basic to domestic daily rites. There was the female Coatlícue (Snake Skirt), powerful in fertility, fierce, decorated with skulls, sacrificial hearts, and other appurtenances of monstrosity.

A god with a special importance was the skillful Quetzalcóatl (Precious Feathered Serpent), important also in pre-Aztec civilization and among the Maya, where his name was Kukulcán. He was the re-creator of the world, inventing agriculture and the various human arts, and diving to the underworld to regain the bones of death; himself dying, he was resurrected, and saved the dead whose bones he reanimated. Around him there developed a

Opposite The city of Machu Picchu, high in the Peruvian Andes and overshadowed by Mount Huayana, is one of the most startling remains of Inca civilization. The site, which was abandoned at the time of the Spanish conquest, included agricultural terraces, habitation structures, religious buildings, and tombs.

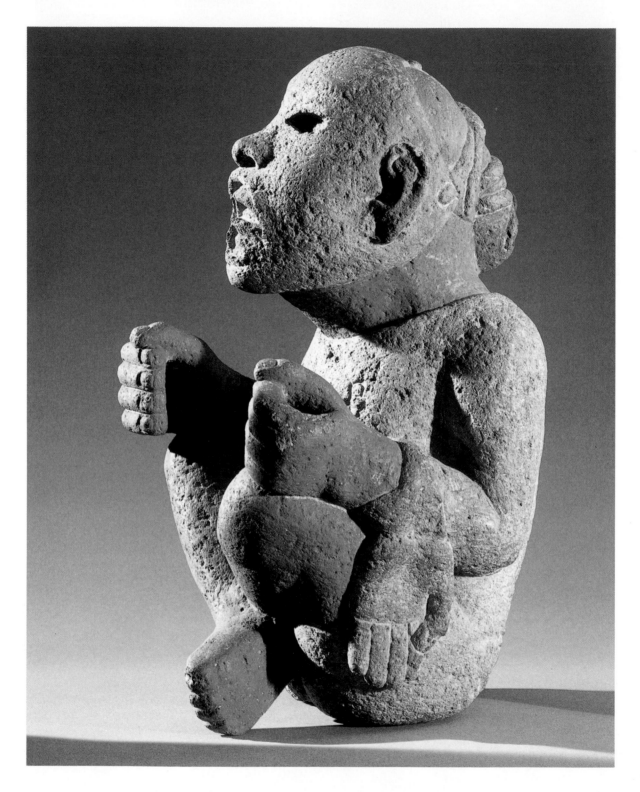

dramatic myth, concerning his miraculous birth, his avenging of his father's death, his training for the priesthood, his rule as sacred king, the fall of his empire, his flight, and his promise to return one day from the east to restore his rule and universal prosperity. It was this narrative which reportedly made Moctezuma II, the Aztec emperor, think that Hernán Cortés, coming in his feathered ships, was Quetzalcóatl returning to reclaim his kingdom. But that of course is a later story.

Then there was the fierce warrior god Huitzilopochtli, Humming Bird of the South, who together with Tláloc—the Rain God and source of fertility for the Aztec empire and the whole earth—was enshrined on top of the great temple pyramid, the Templo Mayor, in the capital. He was recipient of numerous sacrifices. He was the son, mysteriously conceived, of the goddess Coatlícue. All this indicates the close relation that war and fertility had in the Aztec worldview, where the pursuit of prisoners for human sacrifice was itself a force for political expansion.

As we have indicated, the central rites of the empire, presided over by the emperor himself, were human sacrifices in which a victim's chest would be opened and the still quivering heart torn out and presented to the gods. It was a grim rite, and may blind us to the beauty of the city itself, in its fertile valley amid lakes, with towering mountains in view (where Tláloc generated rain), its hanging gardens and intense cultivation of vegetables and fruits, its geometric layout, its white houses and great pyramidal temples, and its ready sunshine. Its weakness lay in its centralization and its commitment to warfare, which was bound to bring countervailing military forces to bear sooner or later.

Here then was a remarkable civilization, with a rather pessimistic worldview, which rested in part on the achievements of preceding cultures—the Toltec and others—and had relations with that now decayed civilization of the Maya. It is clear that mastery of the art of growing maize, which became the most vital staple of the Americas, gave the chance to use agricultural surpluses to create great urban centers, beautiful and elaborate artworks, and extravagant religious cults.

North America

As we move north from the scenes of the great urban civilizations we encounter cultures which are also based on sedentary agriculture, with maize being the central product: notably there are the Pueblo peoples of the Southwestern U.S.A., who used irrigation techniques to shape their intensive agriculture. There are other groups, such as the Apache and Navajo, who blend agriculture and hunting; and some peoples who are still very much hunters and gatherers. To the West, in California and in the Pacific Northwest, there is a variety of cultures, some very much oriented toward the sea and the catching of the abundant sea life of the area. In the Southeast there is rich agricultural land lining the alluvial rivers, and the region was broken into chiefdoms, some sizeable. Life in the Northeast had a predominantly hunting

Opposite The ritual dimension: the figure of Xipe Totec, the flayed god of springtime, clad in the flayed skin of a sacrificial victim. Gladiatorial combat signified his warrior status and his insignia constituted the regalia of the Aztec emperor. The feast, in the spring, also related to fertility and the garb symbolized the breaking forth of the maize cob from its skin.

191

character, where the area was rich with life in luxuriant woodlands, but there too was the cultivation of the "three sisters"—maize, beans, and squash.

In the Plains, reaching up into what is now Canada as well as the great central part of the United States, the introduction of the horse by the Spaniards considerably altered the economy as it facilitated a new and effective way of rounding up and hunting the buffalo. Before that there was a mix of horticulture and nomadism, involving hunting and gathering. The various groups in the area were somewhat more cooperative than elsewhere, insofar as they developed extensive trade and a sign language which enabled interlinguistic communication. Finally there are the varied groups of the Far North including the ingenious Inuit of the Arctic, who had mastered a highly problematic environment.

Now it is obvious that with so varied an economic spread, and so many different language groups, the cultural variation is immense. But it might be useful just to consider four of the groups as a sample: the Hopi of the Southwest; the Iroquois of the Northeast; the Lakota of the Plains; and the Inuit of the North. In the Hopi I shall emphasize the *social* organization of religion and the *material* dimension, in the Iroquois the *experiential, doctrinal,* and *ethical* dimensions, in the Lakota the *ritual* dimension, and in the Inuit the *mythic* dimension.

Hopi Society

In this exposition the Hopi can stand as an example of the wider group of people settled in small towns and villages (*pueblos*) and known as the Pueblo peoples. It is interesting that they are organized, for ritual purposes, in a rather domestic manner, through the existence of a number of different societies each of which has to realize a particular type of ritual. In each of these groups there are priests and lay folk, and because their presentations are integrated into an annual cycle it means that a certain degree of cheerful competition ensures a high level of ceremonial. The ritual societies themselves are at different levels, so that a young person may graduate through them to senior status. At sixteen, males are initiated into the four main male groups, and the women into the women's society. There is a more exclusive male society which organizes the highly complicated and important ceremonies at the time of the winter solstice, when the direction of the sun needs to be changed, and plants, animals, and human life need to be renewed and reintegrated in the general cosmic harmony.

Central in Hopi concerns is of course maize. Corn is the substance of life, and corn meal is sprinkled as a santifying force, much as water is used in Christian ceremonial. Prayer is accompanied by the sprinkling of corn. When a child is born it is presented with two perfect ears of corn. And so on.

One of the most important features of Hopi ritual life is the *kachina* or mask, with accompanying clothes and body paint, through which a Hopi "performer" mediates the spirit inherent in the mask. It is a kind of ikon animated by a dancer. The *kachinas* embody a whole range of supernatural

Kachina masks in operation among the Hopi of the American Southwest. The ceremony shown here, in the Plaza at the Walpi Pueblo, is known as the Powamu and commences in January or February. Here, the *kachinas* are dressed as ogres and go from house to house during the ceremony to scare children into obedience to their parents.

spirits, the dead, and clouds (seen in their own way as spiritual beings); and in this way it is possible to enact the sacred narratives of the people, make social comment, celebrate the gods, and bring blessings on the people. There is a special period, from the winter solstice onward, which is the *kachina* period, at the end of which the sacred masks and other paraphernalia are returned to their home in the mountains until the next season comes around. In this way the material and iconic side of religion is given a living form, since the masks themselves become operative only when they are worn by individuals who are during the ritual possessed by the spirits assigned to them. It is a kind of sacred ballet, and requires material manifestation through the masks.

Iroquois Cosmogony, Experience, and Ethics

For the Iroquois the world was the creation of twins, one good and one evil. The Good Twin not only made that which is beneficent in the cosmos, but he also laid down human customs, which were modeled after the excellences of the sky world. The Bad Twin created what is distorted and horrid and against life. He is like ice, hard and cold. Both Twins made spirit forces which exist, both good and bad, in the world. It is the thrust of Iroquois religion, therefore, to fend off the effects of the Bad Twin and to promote the good forces which the Good Twin has made.

These spirit forces can be experienced directly, and for this reason great attention is paid to visions and dreams. Dreams especially are regarded with great seriousness and attention, for they may reveal some of the good and bad things that are in store for the individual or for the group. In this connection, as elsewhere in North and South America, shamanism is important: the shaman is simply a person with extra insight and dream-capacity. Through dreams an individual will come to be related to some spirit who will act as his friend or guardian. It is important to maintain a good relationship with such a force. Very often, illness is the consequence of a disruption of the friendship. It may also be the consequence of alienation within the individual between his body and his spirit. Dreams could be a clue to the secret desires of one's soul, and these have to be fulfilled. So their diagnosis is important, and is the subject of dream-guessing rituals.

Iroquois lived in longhouses shared by a group of families. This made for a strong emphasis on cooperative enterprises. It is perhaps not surprising that on the larger scale there was the formation in the eighteenth century of the League of Six Nations among the Iroquois (Mohawk, Oneida, Onondaga, Cayuga, Seneca, and Tuscarora). The dualistic cosmogony also emphasized the importance of moral values, as being on the side of life, and evil and bad intentions, on the side of death. There was, as with many other Native Americans, a sense of the harmony of Nature and humans as something which needs to be promoted and enhanced. Something of the ethical feeling underlying this is revealed by the fact that most of the Northeast woodlands people made apology to Nature for killing animals or cutting plants. Apologies would be directed at the animal killed, or rather to the collective spirit which the individual animal manifested, and similarly to the tree-spirit when one cut down a tree.

The ethical outlook of the Iroquois is further revealed by the fact that their most basic form of worship centrally involves thanksgiving directed to a spirit or force. The good manifestations of the Sacred Power which pervades the world must be thanked for the fact that they bring blessings on human beings. By contrast the evil use of ritual through sorcery is to be opposed.

The sense of community is enhanced by rituals for the dead. For instance, at the annual Feast for the Dead food is shared with the ghosts, and song and dance are put on to entertain them. There is a sense of the sacramental character of sharing food. Apart from such a high feast there are numerous family meals for the dead.

Ritual among the Lakota

The Lakota originally dwelt in western Minnesota, but moved further west to the Plains in the first part of the eighteenth century C.E. This was a period of great movement and disruption among North American groups, especially in the Northeast and Plains regions. As a result of their move their economic life changed: they were now mainly concerned with hunting buffalo on horseback. The transition from a settled lakeside existence to this nomadic life led to alterations in their cosmology and values. However, they retained their seven great rituals, some of which are importantly representative of kinds found much more widely in the North American scene. I shall describe three in particular.

The first of these is the Sweat Lodge ceremony. The Sweat Lodge is a small domed structure built of saplings and covered with skins, which also represents

> ### Sacred Songs of the Shaman (Kwakiutl Indians)
>
> "I was taken away far inland to the edge of the world by the magical power of heaven, the treasure, ha, wo, ho.
> Only then was I cured by it, when it was really thrown into me, the past life bringer of Naualakume, the treasure, ha, wo, ho.
> I come to cure with this means of healing of Naualakume, the treasure. Therefore I shall be a life bringer, ha, wo, ho.
> I come with the water of life given into my hand by Naualakume, the means of bringing to life, the treasures, ha, wo, ho."
>
> Then Lebid sang his other sacred song:
> "He turns to the right side, poor one, this supernatural one, so as to obtain the supernatural one, ha, wo, ho.
> Let the supernatural one be the life bringer, the supernatural one, ha, wo, ho.
> That the poor one may come to life with the lifebringer of Naualakume, ha, wo, ho.
> The poor one comes, this supernatural one, to give protection with the means of giving protection of Naualakume, ha, wo, ho."

the shape of the Lakota universe. Heated stones are placed in it, and the water poured on them turns to steam. The person who sits in the structure is greatly heated up, and so he sweats: but also this revitalizes his spirit and he is visited by supernaturals and given visions which provide clues to communal or individual concerns. So a medicine man may gain the understanding which can lead to cures of the sick individuals in his or her care.

Not unrelated to the Sweat Lodge ceremony is the concept of the Vision Quest, the second of the Lakota main rites. A person sets forth and stays on a hillside in a shallow hole for a few days, without food or water. He is typically given a vision which is then interpreted for him by a medicine man.

The third ceremony is the Sun Dance, which is the most significant of the Lakota rites. A tree is ceremonially cut and used as the central pole of a lodge which represents the universe. During a whole day the dancers move around the periphery of the lodge gazing at the Sun as continuously as possible. Some of them are given hooks which are tied to the central tree and planted in their chests. They are encouraged in their sacrificial act by the martial songs and drumbeats of musicians. The families and groups from various tribes are seated

A participant in a Lakota Sun Dance in 1929. The man is blowing on an eagle wing bone whistle to which are attached feathers and buckskin thongs. He is looking towards the central Sun Dance pole, with his right hand raised to honor its power.

A shaman's mask from
the Tlingit of Alaska.

around the lodge to participate in the sacred spectacle. The symbolism of the
affair is important, and connects to fertility, for which the Sun is a source,
while the central axis of the lodge (the *axis mundi*) has phallic meanings. The
dancers bind themselves to the heart of the cosmic mystery, in preparation for
the great midsummer hunts which will replenish the food and life of the
whole group. The ceremony is also a great coming together of nomadic
groups—or was in the old days—and so has a cheerful social significance.

These ritual themes of Sweat Lodge, Vision Quest, and Sun Dance have a
much more general manifestation among Native Americans. They have a
shamanic substratum, a pervasive theme in the Americas.

Myth among the Inuit

The life of the Inuit of the Arctic regions was traditionally a difficult one,
which had to be closely interwoven with the seals and other sea animals on
whom their living depended. So it is not surprising that among at least the
Eastern Inuit there is the widespread story of the Mistress of Sea Animals, or
the Sea Woman. There are a number of cultures in which the figure of the
Master or Mistress of Animals is important (consider Śiva [p. 89] and Orpheus
[p. 234]). Here there is a strange tale of how the sea animals, such as seals,
whales, and walruses, originated. The Sea Woman when still a girl had been
tricked into marrying a Petrel who took her to his land, where she was
miserable. Her father went to rescue her and, bringing her back in a canoe,
was threatened by the Petrel who stirred up a storm. To quieten the Petrel the
father threw his daughter overboard, but she clung to the boat, and he began
cutting off her fingers: first the tips, then when she clung again at the next joint
and so on. The bits of finger became the various species, small seals, bearded
seals, and so forth. The Sea Woman sank to the sea bed, where she still lives.

The moral of the story is that if you do anything offensive to the Sea
Woman she will withhold your catch of animals. Sometimes it was thought
that the transgressions of humans would create dirt which would lodge in the
Woman's hair, and because she had no fingers she was unable to comb it, and
it would become uncomfortable. A shaman would be needed to go beneath
the sea to her abode. After a struggle with her he would comb her hair and she
would release the animals. In some Inuit cultures there were also symbolic
sacrifices to the Sea Woman every year to ensure a good harvest.

Such a myth as that of the Sea Woman attests to the idea that behind a
species or a set of species (the animals which the Inuit hunted) lies a Spirit, so
that we have to enter into propitious relations with that Spirit if we are to have
success in the anxious business of getting food through the year. Here as
elsewhere, the shaman is important.

If anything is close to being a universal theme in the Americas it is that of
shamanism. The sacred center of Tenochtitlán and the pole erected in the Sun
Dance both attest to the symbolism of the *axis mundi*. The Sweat Lodge and
the drugs of ancient Peru both attest to the Vision Quest. The figure of the
priest and healer who also has the secret of fertility is one of the great symbols
of the archaic world.

196

The Ancient Near East

CHAPTER 8

An Overview

Both Mesopotamia—roughly the region of modern Iraq—and ancient Egypt produced dazzling urban civilizations. In the former region the pioneer was Sumer, but the glory belonged first to Babylon, and then to its successor Persia. To the west the Canaanites and Phoenicia flourished, and from Phoenicia were planted the North African colonies which became the Carthaginian state. There were other actors on the scene: the Assyrian empire, some Indo-Europeans such as the Hittites to the north, and, folded in between the great powers, the Israelites.

Sumer, Babylon, and Assyria belong to the same sequence, since the latter two empires borrowed their religious forms from Sumer. Basically, too, Canaanite and Phoenician religions were the same. To simplify our story we can imagine little Israel as a center surrounded by Canaanites, Mesopotamian religions, and Egypt. Israel is important to us because its religion proved to be significant for both Judaism and Christianity, and to some degree Islam too. So, whereas the religion of Phoenicia and that of Carthage are buried under the sands of time, and Egyptian culture of the ancient period is to be seen in museums and as great stone monuments in the desert, and much of ancient Mesopotamia has disappeared, there remains a living stream which runs down to us today from the Jordan Valley.

But dead religions deserve respect also: for that reason we shall at least sketch briefly some of the features of ancient Near Eastern religions outside of that of Israel. We have some literary records and to some degree we can travel into these ancient minds; but this survey will necessarily be highly selective.

Some of the basic dates to keep in mind are these. First, it was around 3000 B.C.E. that urban culture was formed in Sumeria, at the lower part of the Tigris and Euphrates rivers and on the tip of the Persian Gulf. By 1700 B.C.E. there

Map 6 The Ancient Near East.

was a significant dynasty in Babylon, ruling over the provinces of Akkad and Sumer. This First Dynasty of Babylon was overrun by Hittites in 1595. From around 1300 B.C.E., Assyria, with its main capital in Nineveh, was the dominant power in the region and in fact conquered Babylon; it lasted until 612 B.C.E., when Nineveh fell. Shortly thereafter Babylon was taken by the Persians, who came to dominate the whole region until the coming of Alexander the Great (ruled 336–323 B.C.E.). Meanwhile Egyptian civilization had been established from about 3100 B.C.E. with the start of the First Dynasty. For periods Egypt's Asiatic empire, reaching up into Assyria, was formidable. From shortly before 500 B.C.E. the country's history was chequered, being under Persian domination for a while, then Greek—with Alexander the Great and his successors—and then Roman. In the years that followed 1000 B.C.E., the Phoenicians founded Carthage and Utica in North Africa and other settlements as far as southern Spain.

Mesopotamian Religion

Some Figures from the Pantheon

In the nature of the case we do not have full information about ancient Mesopotamian religion, but we do have various hymns and *myths* which give us an insight into some of the gods in the rich pantheon, headed by the God An, which was the focus of priestly *ritual*. Though An was nominally the first god, Enlil, the Lord of the Wind, came to play that role; though with the establishment of the First Dynasty in Babylon, Marduk (the local favorite) was promoted to that status.

Enlil is the god of the religious center of the ancient Sumerians, Nippur. As the wind he guides the rains from the high mountains so that they fall upon the plains; without him no grain will grow, and no wealth can be created to provide the splendid urban culture of which his worshipers are so proud. Wind and Rain can be destructive, so his benevolence cannot be taken for granted. Yet generally the hymns portray him as beneficent and fatherly. Moreover, he holds the tablets which decree the fates of human beings. Many gods come to his city to pay respects to him. His consort is Ninlil, the Lady Wind, and different versions of his wooing of her are told. In one he seduces her while posing as ferryman of the river to be crossed to the underworld.

If Enlil is fatherly and benign, Enki (in the Akkadian version he is Ea) is crafty and good fun. He is the god of the underground waters which, welling up, give fertility. (In Sumerian cosmology there was the idea that underground was a great freshwater sea. Their agriculture, of course, depended on irrigation, and this notion accounted both for freshwater springs and the efficacy of digging wells.) In the myths, Enki is ingenious. For instance, the primordial man Adapa has offended the god Anu by breaking the wing of the South Wind; Enki advises him to get the two gods who act as doorkeepers at Anu's palace to intercede on his behalf. But on no account should he eat or drink when he is with Anu. The doorkeepers do their bit, Adapa is forgiven, and he refuses to eat or drink. When asked why, he tells of Enki's advice. There is much amusement for Anu in this. He knows that the food and drink would not have brought death, as Enki had pretended, but immortality, which Enki did not wish.

Another powerful being who had much influence in the Near East and later in the Roman world is Inanna, known in Akkadian as Ishtar and in Assyria as Astarte. She is a fertility goddess, associated with showers and thunderclouds, and goddess too of war. She is also a harlot and served by harlots. She is supposed even to have become queen of heaven, as consort to An, though she is usually depicted as wed to her Tammuz, a beautiful young male. In a famous narrative she wishes to become queen of the underworld, but the goddess there defeats her and kills her. She is transformed into a slice of meat gone bad. When she does not return her maid seeks aid: eventually it is the ingenious Enki who has a solution. He sends two creatures to the nether world, and the queen there grants them a wish. They ask for the meat, and sprinkle it with grass and water—which restores Inanna to her pristine form. In the tale, further complicated adventures follow, which result in Tammuz's banishment to the underworld to take her place there for half of each year.

Finally, let us glance at the great Marduk. He is something like Indra in the Indian pantheon: god of thunderstorms, and like a young bull. The gods were threatened by the dangerous chaos represented by the female deity Tiamat. The chief gods, Ea and Anu, fail to stave off the challenge, and it is suggested

---

Marduk Creates the World: The Enuma Elisha Tablets

When they had granted him the exercise of
    kingship of the gods,
      They confirmed him in dominion over the gods
      of heaven and earth.
Anshar pronounced supreme his name Asaruluhi:
"Let us make humble obeisance at the mention of
    his name;
      When he speaks, the gods shall pay heed to him.
Let his utterance be supreme above and below!"
Most exalted be the Son, our avenger;

Let his sovereignty be surpassing, having
    no rival.
May he shepherd the black-headed ones, his
    creatures.
To the end of days, without forgetting; let
    them acclaim his ways.
May he establish for his fathers the great
    food-offerings;
      Their support they shall furnish, shall tend
    their sanctuaries.

---

that only Marduk will be successful in combat against her. He demands full authority, which they grant him. In a great combat she opens her huge jaws to destroy him, but he drives in the winds and slays her with his arrow. The wind gods capture her in a huge net, and he uses her corpse to create the present universe, slitting her in two like a fish, one part being heaven and the other the earth. Then he organizes the calendar and various other matters and is hailed by the other gods as supreme.

The myth celebrates Babylon, Marduk's city, and its supremacy. But it also reflects the idea that the creation is the bringing of order, the world formed out of chaos, Tiamat. The epic of creation called the *Enuma Elish* celebrates Marduk's victory and is a kind of script for the ritual and dramatic reenactment of the narrative in great spring celebrations in Babylon every year. It is often cited by scholars of the "myth and ritual" school, influential at the beginning of the twentieth century, to show how we can best understand myth in relation to ritual.

Worship and the Temple

Some of the myths which we have sampled can be seen in connection with the ritual process in the great temples, or ziggurats, erected to celebrate official religion in Mesopotamia. The ziggurats were built on high ground but were also towering structures in themselves, links between earth and heaven. The god resided at the summit. The Biblical story of the Tower of Babel (Genesis 11) reflects knowledge of the Ziggurat of Babylon (for Babel is Babylon). The god residing there shows himself to be present to the community and so concerned with its welfare. It is likely that the daily rituals resembled those later prevalent in India, where the god and his goddess were dressed, washed, and so on. At great festivals there was probably the enactment of a glorious drama based upon the myths which have come down to us. The rites would also involve the king, who would become the relevant god for a sacred marriage festival, ensuring fertility in the kingdom.

But some of the myths are more in the nature of free literary creations and are not necessarily linked directly to ritual. Such is the famous *Epic of*

The mythic dimension: a cylinder seal showing scenes from the *Epic of Gilgamesh* showing Gilgamesh and Ea struggling with a lion, and Arad-Ea crossing the waters of Death. Such cylinder seals are similar to examples found in the Indus Valley civilization. This one dates from the late 3rd millennium, B.C.E.

Gilgamesh, which tells how Gilgamesh is overcome with great grief at the death of his dear friend Enkidu and sets out to conquer death, traveling to visit the wise Utnapishtim, an ancestor of his. But Utnapishtim has no joy to give: he invites Gilgamesh to try to conquer Sleep, which is the younger brother of Death. But Gilgamesh fails and realizes the fateful truth: Death awaits every person. The epic thus addresses one of the great questions of religion, the fate of human beings in the face of death. (The epic also has an account of the Flood, which partly influenced the Biblical story.)

At this point it is worth turning to the Egyptian experience, which is so much concerned with the nature of death and the quest for immortality.

Ancient Egypt

Our imagination is haunted by the silent great pyramids, from the earliest at Saqqara, south of Cairo, to the great Pyramid of Cheops at Giza, built about 200 years later. They stand with an air of enigma, quite as much as the framed statue of the Sphinx. The enigma is that such huge effort and precise workmanship should have been directed to the building of a tomb—and a tomb of that particular geometrical configuration. When we couple this with the fact that the Egyptians became very skilled in the technology of mummification, we recognize a civilization that was much worried by the nature of death and of the hoped-for survival after death. We note, too, the wonderful sculptured portraits which testify to a desire for remembrance.

The most formative time in ancient Egypt was that of the First Dynasty, which was founded when Menes, about 3000 B.C.E., united Upper and Lower Egypt and built a new capital at Memphis. By the Fourth Dynasty, around 2600 B.C.E., there were resources to build the Giza pyramids (just outside modern Cairo). Between about 1750 and 1580 B.C.E., Egypt was harassed and partly occupied by the Asian invaders known as the Hyksos, and this helped to stimulate Egyptian ambitions in Asia, on the other side of Sinai, to provide a buffer against further incursions. A later Pharaoh, Akhenaten (reigned 1356–1339 B.C.E.), tried the experiment of a new, monotheistic religion and moved his capital to El-Amarna, suppressing the old religion of Amun. But his move was unsuccessful. In 946–712 B.C.E., Egypt was ruled by Pharaohs of Libyan descent, and in 664–525 by Ethiopians; and in the two centuries that followed she was twice dominated by Persia. But even after Greek and Roman occupation there was a remarkable continuity in Egyptian culture; and some of the patterns set in the First Dynasty lasted through.

Probably the greatest text of the Egyptians was what has come to be called the *Book of the Dead*, but more correctly is called *The Book of Going Forth by Day*. It is based substantially on much earlier so-called Coffin Texts, so it is partly very ancient; and at the same time it represents the standard Egyptian view of the nature of death and the way to survive it. It was a book to be placed with the dead at their entombment, to help them in their passing through judgment to the afterlife. The mythic scene which underlay the process was the life, death, and resurrection of the god Osiris. Next to Re the great Sun God, who often combined with city deities in the form of Amon Re and so on, Osiris was undoubtedly the most important deity in the Egyptian tradition. By the Middle Kingdom period (about 2050–1750 B.C.E.), when *The Book of Going Forth by Day* was assembled, a sacred drama at Abydos, where he was buried, was the focus of much piety, and this devotional concern in which participants identified with Osiris was still popular in the Roman period. The living Pharaoh was identified with Osiris' son Horus, as the "living Horus," and a dead Pharaoh was identified with Osiris himself.

The influential legend of Osiris, which in some ways prepared the ancient world for the acceptance of the Christian story, was as follows. Seth, brother of Osiris, had a beautifully shaped coffin made. He prepared a banquet and promised the coffin to the guest who would fit it. Only Osiris fitted it precisely, and as soon as he was lying inside Seth had the coffin fixed shut. He sealed the coffin with lead and had it thrown into the Nile. It eventually washed up on the other shore, where it was found by the distraught Isis, Osiris' wife. She had the body returned, but Seth got it and chopped it into pieces and scattered them throughout Egypt. Isis recovered all the bits—save the penis, for which she made a substitute—and reconstituted Osiris. Before embalming him she gave him new life—so much so that Osiris had intercourse with her, and their son Horus was thus conceived. Eventually Horus fought and overcame Seth, but injured his eye in the process. His good eye came to be identified with the Sun and the bad eye with the Moon. The relationship to the Sun meshed in with the cult of the great god Re. Horus was often seen as a falcon, perhaps stretching his wings and invisibly, save to the mind's eye, hooding the whole sky.

Osiris, having overcome death, is the presiding deity of death and patron of the process of mummifying the dead. Osiris is there in the afterlife for the judging of the dead, which is described in some detail in *The Book of Going Forth by Day*. The soul of the deceased is weighed against the feather of Truth:

The ethical dimension: the heart of a person weighed against truth in the realm of Osiris. Ancient Egyptians believed that the dead person's soul journeyed to the Underworld where Anubis (the jackal-headed god) weighed it against the feather of Truth. The result was recorded by Thoth, the ibis-headed god.

this notion of the scales of judgment became a widely used metaphor. In Chapter 125 of the book there is a formulaic protestation of innocence addressed to the forty-two judges, which gives a good insight into the ethics of ancient Egypt. The person protests that he has not stolen, or been covetous, or killed a human being, or damaged a grain-measure, or told lies, or trespassed, or practiced usury, or gossiped, or committed adultery, or had sex with a boy, or been abusive of a king, and so on. The aim of the formula is to ensure that the judges will let the deceased through and he will be able to live in the presence of Osiris and Re. There are other pieces of ritual with which to assist the dead: scarab brooches to stop the heart from speaking against its owner, and figurines of servants, and so on.

Osiris also appears in Egyptian myth as a god of fertility, and his resurrection is associated with the sprouting of grain in the spring and summer, after the "death" of winter. His connection with the Sun, Re, helps to underline this fructifying capacity, since it is the Sun which triggers off and nourishes the growth of the crops.

The dry climate of Egypt and the technology of well-sealed coffins (one of which was, as we have seen, the undoing of Osiris) and embalming meant that the preservation of the dead was an advanced achievement in Egypt. It was an expensive process, but gradually down the centuries the Osiris cult became more accessible.

In Egyptian thought there were in effect two souls. One is the *ba*, which is depicted hieroglyphically as a little bird that flutters up to the sky at death; the other is the *akh* or spirit which survives in the afterlife. An individual ought to be equipped with spells and other precautions so that his *akh* can be perfected. The *akh* in effect is the glorified state of the individual. Such bright ancestors came to be the focus too of a cult of the dead, as in some other societies.

We see in all this the confluence of various factors in the Egyptian experience: a notion of divine kingship, and with it an ideology which favored the preservation of dead Pharaohs; the technology of mummification and other processes for the literal preservation of the dead; the resources for huge mortuary tombs and above all the pyramids (it may be that the cult of the Sun is relevant here, since the pyramidal shape may represent the pouring down of the Sun's rays); the idea of a semispiritual afterlife; the cult of a dying and rising god, Osiris; and the notion that ethical worth should determine immortality, even if blemishes in life can be got around by spells and other good advice in the mortuary literature. The confidence of Egypt in dealing with the dead contrasts with the relative pessimism of Utnapishtim in the *Epic of Gilgamesh*.

Canaanite Religion

Since the Canaanites occupied part of Syria and what is today's Palestine for a long period, overlapping with the Israelites, and fathered the religion of the coast which was referred to by the Greeks as Phoenician, it is important to understand it in relation to Mediterranean culture as a whole, and as a kind of counterpoint to Israelite religion. On the other hand, it has not left significant traces in the modern world, save through the great semitic religions.

Much of our best knowledge of Canaanite religion comes from texts found in the excavated city of Ugarit, at Ras Shamra on the Syrian coast. The pantheon, as elsewhere in the ancient Near East, is complex. It is headed by El or God; but the more vital force is the Lord, Baal, who is associated with the weather and rain, and so brings fertility to the people. Among female deities is Athirat the consort of El, jealous on behalf of her divine offspring; and Anat, the rough goddess of love and war, who is Baal's sister and possibly also his mate. Baal has three great adversaries: Yamm, accompanied by great sea monsters; Litan, the Leviathan in the Bible, another great sea monster; and Tunnan, as in Tannin in the Bible.

In the stories there is a sequence about Baal which is suggestive of one great motif in Canaanite religion, which reminds us too of the Osiris myth. Baal fights against the Sea and with a magical club strikes him dead. But this victory over the Sea, no doubt representing chaos and an uncontrollable element, is not enough. There remains a final enemy, Death, who, like the other gods, is the son of El. Baal sends messengers to Death, but the latter answers that Baal must die like other beings, and Baal submits, taking with him his tools—clouds, lightning bolts, rain, and the like. The news of his death rouses Anat to do something about it. She buries him and then fiercely attacks Death, slices him with a sword, riddles him with a sieve, burns him with fire, grinds him with a mill, and sows him in the fields. Baal is restored to power. This whole story is of course replete with the idea of the dying and rising God whose death and resurrection correspond to the facts of the agricultural year. It is a myth, like its Egyptian counterpart, which is about both death and fertility, and about both human life and the supply of plants.

It is obvious from this and other sources that in some degree Canaanite ritual also concerned seasonal fertility. But the texts show there is much more beside. There are rites where the king purifies himself and makes offering to various gods. Another ritual described offers a bull to Baal for help with fighting off enemies. And there is a third sort of event in which the whole population of Ugarit gather to make public expiation for their wrongdoings, in order to win safety from their enemies. It may be that some of the myths—possibly the myth of Baal and Death—also had dramatic enactment at sacred ceremonies. Another ceremony concerned the moving of images from one place to another.

Some Phoenician Variations

In general, Phoenician religion develops similar themes. There is an extra importance to the chief Lord or Baal, since as well as making fields fecund he guides Phoenician sailors, who venture further and further from their home in the Levant. The chief female goddess is Astarte, both a war goddess and a fertility figure. She draws on many sources, from the Mesopotamian Ishtar, the Canaanite Anat, and others besides. She is often simply addressed as "Lady." She was venerated at Tyre and Sidon and in the great new city of Carthage. She was found in Malta, Sicily, and Cyprus (whence originated her Greek sister with whom she was naturally identified, Aphrodite). There were diverse dying and rising gods, of whom the best known perhaps was Adonis, whose rituals dominated the city of Byblos. His name means simply "Lord," and the same title was used in Israelite religion, as *adonai*.

Although the rites of Adonis and other such gods had an agricultural origin, it is clear also that they came to take on a more personal and individual significance, so that the sacrificer who participated in the sad events of the death of the god and the orgiastic rites accompanying the celebration of his revival could share in the numinous event and so in the renewed life of the deity.

I have put some emphasis, in these glimpses of the rich religious heritage of the ancient Near East, on the attitudes to death displayed. This is partly because death is at the intersection of public and private life; and I have meant to indicate that even the most gloriously collective aspects of ancient religion in the Semitic world had, or developed, significance for individuals—at least those with the wealth to be able to take part in the rituals. It may also be that this theme of the dying and rising god may have prepared the way for the acceptance of Christianity in the area. But there is another theme, which seems to have come into conflict with Israelite custom and thinking; namely the idea of the fertility goddess, and in general the cult of fertility. It is something resisted by the prophets of Israel, but it was clearly important in the ideology of states which relied on agriculture and sought the extra wealth from rich harvests to pay for their increasingly splendid urban temples and palaces.

Israelite Religion

The Beginnings

It is now time to turn to Israelite history, which provided materials, especially as written up in the various books of the Bible, that continued to have religious significance long after the societies they reflected had ceased to exist. It is worth noting, too, that though Judaism, Christianity, and Islam project themselves back in time to Abraham and to the religion of the Israelites—so that it is tempting to think, for instance, of Moses as the founder of Judaism— strictly speaking what we know as Judaism did not yet exist. There is some historic or other connection between Jews and their predecessors the

Jewelry from the fourteenth to fifteenth centuries B.C.E. showing the figure of the goddess Astarte. In Sumerian mythology Astarte was Inanna; in Babylonian and Assyrian myths she was Ishtar; and in Phrygian myth she was Cybele.

Opposite The death of Mani. The Persian Mani (216–76) established a religion that claimed to be a final, universal revelation. His doctrines, known as Manichaeism, were widely influential, having an impact on Gnosticism and, indeed, reflecting some Gnostic ideas.

Israelites, of course: but in the period we are talking about, from 1200 B.C.E. or so down to the time of Alexander (say) around 330 B.C.E., what existed was a stream of religious development which swelled into Judaism much later, at about the time that Christianity took its first classical form, three or four centuries after Jesus.

Most of our sources for the story of Israel come from the Bible, supplemented by fairly extensive archaeology. From the perspective of the history of religions we can use the Biblical narrative to establish a fairly clear account of the evolution of beliefs among the Israelites; but we have to use it judiciously as a source, the way we have used other scriptural traditions in this book.

The earliest period of the religion of the Israelites is a kind of prehistory: the period of the Patriarchs, beginning with the narrative of Avraham (Abraham), who came from Ur of the Chaldees in Sumeria. His God is described as El (also the name, as we have seen, of the highest god of the Canaanites). His son Yitshaq (Isaac) was father of Ya'akov (Jacob), who had various adventures: during one he had a dream of a ladder leading up to Heaven, and named the place where he had it Bethel or House of God, which became the cult center, before Jerusalem, in northern Israel. On his return from a visit to Mesopotamia he had a wrestling contest with a mysterious being and his name was changed to Yisra'el. His twelve sons bore the names of the twelve tribes of Israel, and these became a confederacy which struggled successfully to dominate both northern and southern Palestine.

Many of the stories of this shadowy earlier period have become vital in the living faith of those who look back—the story of Avraham's willingness, in obedience to God, to sacrifice his only son; how Lot's wife turned into a pillar of salt; the destruction of the evil cities of Sodom and Gomorrah. But we know very little really about the religious shape of the period before the revolution that, it appears, was effected by the leader of those Israelites who were working as slaves for the Egyptians before they escaped through the Sinai peninsula. They conquered the land of Canaan in the name of a new religious ideology of commitment to one God, whom they called YHVH or Yahweh (and who, in the West, is often named Jehovah, a partially Latinized rendering of the Hebrew name). Scholars are not certain at all when Mosheh or Moses lived, but it was perhaps soon after 1300 B.C.E.

The Mosheh Revolution and the Entry into Canaan

The whole story of Mosheh seems to be a composite one, with differing traditions and ideas being woven together in the narrative as we have it, which derives from four or maybe three sources: the Book of Deuteronomy; the source which scholars call "J" (for Jehovah) because it stresses the concept of Yahweh; the closely related "E" (which uses the name Elohim for God rather than Yahweh); and the so-called Priestly source or "P." These were probably composed between about 700 and 400 B.C.E. Much is speculative in these discussions of origins and the composition of texts. But it may well be that

Mosheh was indeed the revolutionary leader who did in fact cause the strict adoption of loyalty to Yahweh which became the hallmark of the official religion of the Israelites, and won out as a clear form of monotheistic faith, and so left a great mark on the whole historical process.

Mosheh is depicted as having escaped death as a baby by being put in a boat of reeds, which was found by the Pharaoh's daughter, so that though he was an Israelite he was brought up at court as a prince. But, because he struck and killed an Egyptian for oppressing an Israelite worker, he had to flee into the region beyond Egypt, in the deserts to the east. He there dwelt with a priest of Midian and worked as a shepherd. During this period he seems to have adopted in some modified form the religion of Midian, focusing on the God Yahweh. When later he led the Israelites out of Egypt, in that great event which Jews would come to know as the Exodus (Greek for "departure"), he took them to Mount Sinai. Moreover, during his period in Sinai he had experienced the numinous vision of a bush which was burning and yet was not consumed by the fire, and he heard the voice of Yahweh, calling him to a leading role in the life of his people and the service of God. It was like a number of the prophetic visions of a much later period.

It was under his chief leadership, though in conjunction with his elder brother Aharon (Aaron), that he led the Israelites out of Egypt in a miraculous fashion according to the Biblical narrative, with events such as the plagues on

Mosheh teaching the people of Israel the Ten Commandments, from an early medieval Bible.

Exodus

And the Lord said to Moses, "Say to the people of Israel, You shall keep my sabbaths, for this is a sign between me and you throughout your generations, that you may know that I, the Lord, sanctify you. You shall keep the sabbath, because it is holy for you; every one who profanes it shall be put to death; whoever does any work on it, that soul shall be cut off from among his people. Six days shall work be done, but the seventh day is a sabbath of solemn rest, holy to the Lord; whoever does any work on the sabbath day shall be put to death. Therefore the people of Israel shall keep the sabbath, observing the sabbath throughout their generations, as a perpetual covenant. It is a sign for ever between me and the people of Israel that in six days the Lord made heaven and earth, and on the seventh day he rested, and was refreshed."

Egypt, the Passover and the parting of the sea, saving the Israelites and then swamping the Egyptians. These events are commemorated of course at the great Jewish family feast, the Passover.

Most important were the events on Mount Sinai, when Mosheh ascended the mountain to have converse with the numinous Divine Being and to receive the agreement or covenant, including the Ten Commandments which were to become the basis of the Torah, or Law. (I translate Torah by "Law," though some Jews prefer some other appropriate translation such as "Teaching": they wish to avoid a translation which might reflect what is to their minds an unfortunate Christian stigmatizing of Law as opposed to Grace, in the New Testament.) It was henceforth the loyalty of official Israelite religion to the idea of One God, with no other gods, which brought it into conflict with Canaanite religion.

The Temple

The process begun by Mosheh led to the domination of Canaan by the Twelve Tribes, so that a substantial part of the land was under their rule by as early as 1200 B.C.E. Eventually the pattern of leadership changed to kingship. The second king and great hero, David, captured Jerusalem and created the capital there. He had the ambition of building there a central temple, but it was left to his son Shelomoh (Solomon, 965–925 B.C.E.) to do this. His wonderful construction, known as the First Temple, lasted till its destruction in 586 B.C.E.

Its building was a means of centralizing all the cults of Israel in one focus. The advantage was both political and spiritual. It meant that the monarchs had greater control (though on Shelomoh's death political power was split and the Northern and Southern Kingdoms of Israel and Judah emerged: Israel did not survive the destruction of its capital Sumeria in 721 B.C.E., the overrunning of the region by Nebuchadnezzar of Babylon, and the subsequent period of Persian rule). The spiritual effect of having the central rites at Jerusalem was that it was easier to wipe out unacceptable forms of practice at the shrines scattered through the land. The Temple came to be a monopoly. It is of course true that, by the lavish care that Shelomoh bestowed on the Temple and by his desire for a glorious cult, there were elements in the worship which went beyond the more austere requirements of Yahwistic worship.

The building consisted of a large high hall, with cedar beams and cedar doors decorated with gold. At the west end was a windowless shrine inside of which was lodged the most holy object of ancient Israel, the Ark which contained the stone tablets on which the Ten Commandments were inscribed. Above were two gold cherubs. In front of the building was the altar used for sacrifices. Gradually around about it various outbuildings were erected, housing priestly implements and clothes and the like. It was ultimately enclosed in two great courtyards, approached by three sets of gatehouses and three flights of stairs.

After its destruction in 568 B.C.E., fifteen hundred of the elite of Judah, the Southern Kingdom, were taken in exile to Babylon. When some of these exiles returned in 538 B.C.E., they began to rebuild the Temple on the same site. It was dedicated more than twenty years later. Much later still, after many modifications and additions, King Herod the Great in 20 B.C.E. began the reconstruction of the entire complex, creating a beautiful building partially on Roman lines. Such rebuilding in fact continued more or less throughout the period, culminating in the destruction of the Second Temple in 70 C.E.

The altars of sacrifice in front of the Temple must have presented a busy sight, not altogether in harmony with modern feelings. Many animals and birds would be killed, and their blood drained, many functioning as burnt offerings in which the whole of the animal would be burnt. There would be offerings of grain and other foods too. Since the Temple came perforce to be a place of pilgrimage, in times of prosperity when many people could afford to pay for sacrifices, the daily killing must have been great. Many of the sacrifices were expiatory in character, where a person gave up something of worth, for instance a goat or a sheep, in a concrete manifestation of his feeling of sin or guilt at something he had done. So the sacrificial aspect of the Israelite religion, like its general worship, was focused on an ethical God.

The Prophetic Tradition

In many religions we can contrast prophetic and priestly types. If the Temple was the heart of priestly religion, something else was the heart of prophetic faith. It was a mixture of vision, vocation, and ethical values. The true sacrifices to God should be, as one prophet remarked, a broken spirit and a humble heart. The inwardness of religion is the vital essence of it. Later Judaism always had something of this polarity: the very complexity of the Law meant that there were many, many externals in the Jewish religion, but like ancient Chinese *li* they were useless without the sincerity of inwardness.

There were "official" prophets in Israel and Judah, whose job it was to make predictions before military campaigns and the like. There were others attached to cult centers. But the great Prophets, who came to be rendered orthodox by the incorporation of their teachings into the sacred writings of the tradition, were detached from such organizational ties and were more individualistic in their utterances. Because their proclamations and criticisms were on the side of what became the official religion, their turbulence tended to be vindicated after their deaths. Their critical awareness, based upon personal religious experience, provided an indispensable element of renewal in a tradition which had its heavy investment in the expensive rites of the Temple and a detailed understanding of the provisions of the Law.

There are many prophets to choose from, but let us just briefly mention three or four: Amos, the two (or three) Isaiahs, and Jeremiah.

The Book of Amos dates from around 750 B.C.E. and incorporates an account of the prophet's inaugural vision. He saw the Lord at the altar, and so his criticisms of ritual do not stem from a rejection of the sacrificial cultus. But he is highly critical of those who think in a period of prosperity that these riches are the result of the rituals, and are a sign of God's blessing. It is too simple a view in an age of social injustice. God's relationship to Israel is founded on Israel's social and moral duty. The ruling class had better beware. The day of the Lord is not sweetness and light, but darkness. In such ways the prophet attacks the smugness of his time and demands that the externals of worship be tied to inner worthiness of aim and compassion for the poor.

The prophet Yesha'yahu or Isaiah lived not very long after Amos. But the Book of Isaiah is a composite work, which includes a major second part or Deutero-Isaiah (Second Isaiah), and maybe a third bit tagged on at the end. The first part belongs to the eighth century B.C., the time of the Assyrian invasions, while the second refers to the Persian period. I shall refer to the two prophets as Yesha'yahu and Deutero-Isaiah respectively.

Yesha'yahu reports his inaugural vision as having happened while he was in the Temple, and it is a majestic and numinous experience:

> In the year King Uzzi'ah died I saw the Lord sitting upon a throne high and lifted up; and his train filled the temple. Above him stood the seraphim: each had six wings—with two he covered his face, and with two he covered his feet, and with two he flew. And one called to another and said: "Holy, holy, holy is the Lord of hosts; the whole earth is full of his glory." And the foundations of the thresholds shook at the voice of him who called, and the house was filled with smoke. And I said "Woe is me! For I am lost; for I am a man of unclean lips, and I dwell in the midst of a people of unclean lips; for my eyes have seen the King, the Lord of hosts!"
>
> Then flew one of the seraphim to me, having in his hand a burning coal which he had taken with tongs from the altar. And he touched my mouth and said "Behold, this has touched your lips; your guilt is taken away and your sin forgiven." And I heard the voice of the Lord saying "Whom shall I send, and who will go for us?" Then I said "Here am I! Send me." And he said "Go and say this to the people..."

There are various themes here. First, the vision which inaugurates the prophet's career is numinous and colorful. This is not that still inward light that illuminates the mystic or the Buddha but rather the exterior and dualistic vision of an Other. The very vision makes the prophet feel his unworthiness, and the guilt of the people to whom he belongs. But the vision is also a calling: the mysterious seraph comes and burns the uncleanness away from his mouth. And Isaiah responds willingly to the call after this: "Here am I!"

Yesha'yahu is concerned particularly with two political developments of his day: the attempt by the Northern Kingdom to replace the Southern monarch Ahaz with a favorite who would conform his policy to the strategy of the North (which involved an alliance with Syria or Aram against Assyria); and the Assyrian war against Jerusalem. For Yesha'yahu, historical and political developments are never merely so, but they have to do with the designs and will of God. For him also, Ahaz and the Davidic succession are important. The present troubles of Israel are the result of ethical misconduct. Assyria is God's means of punishing his people, but there is no need for ultimate worry. At the last moment Jerusalem will be purified and a remnant will return.

The unknown prophet known at Deutero-Isaiah had a tremendous influence on later religion, through his idea of the Suffering Servant of the Lord ('*eved YHWH*)—probably a metaphor for the people of Israel, but Christians read it as a reference to Jesus—who is rejected by his fellow men, yet bears God's message and has a mission to restore justice. The '*eved YHWH* represents an ideal which places value on faithfulness rather than prosperity. Yet in the end all will be well: Deutero-Isaiah looks forward in Chapter 11 to the time of the Anointed One, the *Mashiah* (Messiah), destined to restore Israel and to usher in a period of cosmic peace, when the wolf will lie down with the lamb, and the leopard with the kid, and the lion with the fatling. And then the earth will be full of the knowledge of the Lord.

Third Isaiah—the last section—presupposes the restoration of the Temple. It affirms the importance of the Sabbath, it criticizes foreign cults rather harshly, and it opposes the Temple rituals. In this it is somewhat different in emphasis from other prophets' writings.

In the stormy days which led up to the taking of Jerusalem by the Babylonians under Nebuchadnezzar, Yirmeyah (Jeremiah) called on the people to submit rather than resist. He naturally got into trouble as a traitor; but as he saw it neither the Northern Kingdom of Israel nor the Southern Kingdom of Judah had been able to live up to the covenant with God. He did not point his finger at any one class, but at all. Once Israel had entered into the Promised Land, the nation had become unfaithful. Yirmeyah called the people to repentance; but if his call remained unanswered then inevitably the destruction of the land was assured.

As a person Yirmeyah seems to have been depressive. He was unmarried, lonely, a person of strife who stirred things up, at the call of God. He wished, indeed, he had never been born. But he felt the prompting of the Lord to speak the gloomy truth to the populace. There was hope, even so; and Yirmeyah predicted that God would make another covenant which would be so written into the hearts of people that they would stay loyal.

In being so convinced that the old Israel would in effect be destroyed,

Yirmeyah paved the way for a more individualistic understanding of relationship to God. This was already implicit in the Torah at Sinai, in that its ethical requirements are placed in a personal framework. Much of the religion of the Israelites is based on the idea of a chosen people: but it also relates to individual acts and choices.

In the latter part of the sixth century B.C.E., following a decree of the Persian king, Cyrus the Great, in 538, the restoration of the Temple in Jerusalem was permitted and the exiles returned from Babylon. Under the leadership of Ezra, a large group set out from Babylon, with great financial resources, and arrived in the holy city. Amid the devastation they found that many Jews had married Gentiles and had given up their strict adherence to the lifestyle that had sustained the people before. All mixed marriages were dissolved, and, at the feast of Sukkot, Ezra read out the Torah from a great book at the ceremony in which the notion of a scriptural basis for the religion became an official doctrine. After a period of fasting and the confession of sins, the people undertook at another ceremony some months later to renew the covenant by supporting the Temple and observing the *Shabbat* (Sabbath) and the various laws of the Torah.

Maybe the book which Ezra read out was the Pentateuch or First Five Books of the Bible, which thus at this early date became the sacred scriptures. Or maybe it was something less. But in due course it was these Five Books that became regarded as the Written Torah. The so-called "Oral Torah," handed down verbally since Mosheh, was looked on by later orthodox Jews as authoritative also. It was an important buttress of Rabbinic Judaism, which we shall come to later.

The Dimensions of Israelite Religion

This brief highlighting of some events in the Israelite experience, down to the Second Temple and the jelling of Jewish culture which took place before the coming of the Greeks and Romans and the absorption of the Jewish people into the Graeco-Roman experience, may enable us to understand some of the main features of the varied dimensions of this religion.

First; regarding *doctrine*: God is seen as supreme and then as alone. It became a monotheistic religion, and so apart from neighboring faiths and rituals. This development was doubtless due to the revolution in practice associated with the name of Mosheh. Second, as far as the *narrative* dimension goes, ancient Israel had the memory of the Exodus, the hopelessness of the desert, and the conquest of Canaan. This narrative held a major place for the idea of the covenant with God. Third, in regard to *ritual*, there was a ban on graven images, which helped to separate Israel from many of the fertility and other cults of the area, though this separation seems to have been a constant struggle. The foundation of the kingship, leading to the centralization of worship at the Temple, was an important factor in maintaining the separateness and imageless character of Israelite worship. But the experience of exile also meant that an important elite became committed to maintaining the rituals even without the Temple. For this and other reasons, the restoration of the Temple also saw the beginnings of the idea of synagogue worship, in which congregations could take part.

As to the *experiential* dimension, the call of the Prophets became an important counterpart to the conservatism of the priestly tradition, intent on the niceties of sacrifice. The call blended with a sense of ethical destiny, which gave the Prophets their special edge as critics of the kingly and priestly establishment. The visions, too, reinforced the sense of the numinous presence of God.

In *ethics*, the law code which is already encapsulated in the Ten Commandments gave Israelites a clear vision of the conduct expected of those in a treaty relationship with God. Organizationally, the fact that by the end of our period there was the conception of written scriptures prepared the way for the rise of a scribal class whose job was to interpret the written texts. These were in parallel with the hereditary priests, whose main tasks related to the Temple liturgy.

The *institution* of kingship was important politically, even if finally not successful; but it came to be even more important in the mythic imagination of the people, who might look forward to an Anointed One who would restore the kingship and usher in a time of great peace and solemn prosperity. This vision was in part the result of the realization of the fragility of the Temple in political terms.

Finally, as to the *material* dimension, the Temple of course was the great big artifact on which Israel spiritually depended. Its glory under Shelomoh was great, and its restoration with the return of the exiles from Babylon was a reassurance. But there were other artifacts, such as the scriptures. They could—and eventually did—replace the tablets in the Ark of the Covenant. Perhaps the greatest material thing for the people in the end was the land of Israel. But the land was very much at the crossroads of great powers—the Assyrians, the Egyptians, the Babylonians, the Persians, the Greeks, the Romans.

Israelite religion was not altogether unaffected by the religions of the area. In particular it blended with Canaanite religion as well as separating itself out. The surrounding cultures could easily understand the slaughter of sheep and pigeons on the altars before the Temple; the glories of kingly power expressed by the pillars in front of the Temple; the importance of sacred writings; and the visions of the Prophets. But Israel's blend was very specific, and it had a great capacity for survival; for many of its customs, and many of its great ideas, were taken up by later peoples.

CHAPTER 9

Persia and Central Asia

The Unification of Medes and Persians

The military genius of Cyrus the Great, king of the Persians, resulted in the defeat of the Medes in 550 B.C.E., and the bringing together of the Iranian peoples into the single most important power in the Near and Middle East. The dynasty which he founded, the Achaemenids, lasted until it was defeated and taken over by Alexander the Great and his successors the Seleucids, two centuries later. The period from the second century B.C.E. until 24 C.E. was dominated by the Parthians. After a period of disorganization Persia was, from 224 until 637, again a major power under the Sasanid dynasty, which finally collapsed under the onslaught of the Muslims from Arabia.

Iran was importantly the source of various major religions which have influenced world culture. First there is Zoroastrianism, which can be held to exist in six phases. Its early period lasted until the sixth century B.C.E., when it entered its second phase as the official religion of the Achaemenid dynasty. Then there is a period of flux until the third century C.E., when it was reconstructed as the official religion of the Sassanid dynasty. Next, there is the persecution under the Muslims, and its migration in part to India. Finally there is the modern period when it has flourished within a modest population.

Also there was an important current within Zoroastrianism which some count as a separate religion; but it is perhaps better considered as the main stream of reconstructed Sassanid religion. This current is known in the modern West as Zurvanism.

Then again there was a dynamic and marvelously syncretic religion which was founded by Mani (early third century C.E.) and is usually known as Manichaeism (sometimes as Manichaeanism); it remained widespread and influential until the ninth century in China, Central Asia, Persia, and the West.

Also with a Persian background was the mystery religion called Mithraism, which was active throughout the Roman Empire, but which we shall discuss in Chapter 10.

Zoroastrianism

The Life of Zarathustra

The name Zoroaster is derived from a Greek mangling of the name Zarathustra. This great prophetic figure lived at some time before 600 B.C.E. Late Zoroastrian sources say that he lived three hundred years (or less) before

---

Zoroastrianism some key terms

Adur or *Atar* Sacred fire. All fire is considered purified and is ritually tended in temples and holy places.

Ahura Mazdā The Wise Lord, the creator God: later Ohrmazd.

Amesha Spentas The seven (later six, since Ohrmazd is identified with one of them) Holy Immortals, regarded as offshoots or emanations of God.

Angra Mainyu The Hostile Spirit, source of all evil, destined eventually to be overcome by Ahura Mazda: later Ahriman.

Bundahishn Creation of the world arising out of war between the Good and Evil Spirits.

Chinvat The bridge of separation and judgment: if the good in a soul predominates, it is led across the bridge by a beautiful maiden. Otherwise, an old hag leads the soul across the bridge, which is like a razor-blade, and the soul slides into hell.

Frashokereti The act of creation, the occasion of resurrection, and of the final judgment.

Fravashi The eternal spirits of human beings, which exist in heaven rather like angels: the implication is that humans have freely chosen to assume material form.

Manthras Words of power: prayers drawn mainly from the earliest scriptures attributed to Zarathustra.

Yasasna Temple rite, or worship generally.

Yazatas Heavenly beings or angels thought worthy of worship. The most popular is Mithra.

Zurvān Time, the focus of a deviant but important movement in later Zoroastrianism, known as Zurvanism: both Ohrmazd and Ahriman are supposed to derive from this one Being, who is beyond good and evil.

Map 7 Central Asia, including the Silk Route.

Alexander the Great, which might place him around 630 B.C.E. But most scholars think that he was older than that, and there is a rough consensus that he probably was of the tenth century B.C.E. He probably came from the region of what is now Afghanistan, or maybe from just inside the modern Iranian border. It was a region of East Iranian culture.

About his life we have few reasonably hard facts, though later legend was to fill in the spaces and see his career as that of an ideal human being, wise and good. Five songs or *Gāthās* in the scriptures are ascribed to him, and in these he mentions that he belonged to a priestly class. The East Iranian or Indo-Iranian culture had many affinities with the Aryan culture of the Vedic period in India, and so his position was analogous to that of a Brahmin. According to tradition he left home—possibly having already experienced the arduous training necessary to the priesthood—at the age of twenty, and at thirty had a powerful inspiration and vision which led him to begin to preach his new and highly original message.

The main component of this was his monotheism, seeing Ahura Mazdā as the One God: the Wise Lord, as his name says. He fathered twin spirits, Spenta Mainyu and Angra Mainyu (Beneficent Spirit and Hostile Spirit). They each make a primordial choice, the one for *asha*, goodness (which corresponds to the *ṛta* of the Veda) and the other for *druj*, the lie—in a word between good and evil. That primordial choice faces each person in her or his life. Zarathustra also seems to have taught the existence of six semi-independent

220

abstractly named entities, the beneficent Immortals: Good Thought, Best Truth, Desirable Power, Great Devotion, Wholeness, and Immortality. Were they a kind of concession to the prevailing polytheism? Perhaps not enough: for opposition from other priests led Zarathustra to leave his native area and advise at the court of King Vishtaspa, a convert to the new religion. This was supposedly at the age of forty-two. He was married twice and had a number of children: one of the *Gāthās* celebrates his third daughter's wedding. He died at the age of seventy-seven, assassinated by a priest.

His religion also protested against some features of the prevailing warrior religion of his time, which involved the sacrifice of bulls and the use of the hallucinogenic *haoma* (the same doubtless as the Vedic *soma*). In various ways, then, he was a threat to established ways. The question which is unclear is how this distant and somewhat hazy tradition came to be adopted as the imperial faith of the Achaemenids. In this the Magi seem to have played an important part.

The Role of the Magi

The Magi are of course most famous as having come to Jesus' manger in Bethlehem, wise men from the East. Possibly they were a priestly tribe or caste originating in the west of Persia, among the Medes. They practiced marriage between close relatives, a custom which later spread to Zoroastrians; and they were responsible for dealing with the dead: their characteristic mode of disposing of them was by exposure of the corpses to animals and birds—a method which has become standard in Zoroastrianism, involving *dkhmas* or Towers of Silence where the vultures can pick the flesh off the bones. As priests who were thought necessary to ritual functions, the Magi played a role analogous to the Brahmin class in India, and with the unification of the empire in 550 B.C.E. they assumed an important role. In any event it seems that they came to adopt Zoroastrian beliefs, though not without embroidering and modifying them, in the service of the imperial state. Their learning enabled the corpus of ancient Zoroastrian texts to be handed down to us, as assembled by them from the fifth century B.C.E. onward. In the Sassanid period they were responsible, it seems, for the reformulation of the religion and its doctrines.

The scriptures divide roughly into three phases: the original poems of Zarathustra, the *Gāthās*; then the rest of the *Avesta*, compiled around the sixth century C.E. but based on collections made about a thousand years earlier; and then the texts in the Pahlavi language, written in the ninth century C.E., during the Islamic period, when the Zoroastrian community was under threat. These last are of a commentarial nature, with summaries of knowledge, replies to Christian, Islamic, and other doctrines, and so on.

The Drama of the World in Zarathustra's Teaching

In the original teaching of Zarathustra, so far as we can make out, the history of the cosmos is conceived as a drama. If Ahura Mazdā is perfectly good, then

Angra Mainyu, the spirit of Evil, in his struggle against Ahura Mazdā, decides to tempt the ancestors of the human race. This fourteenth-century illustration shows a late Zoroastrian view of the fall of the human race, doubtless influenced by Christian ideas. Angra Mainyu here speaks with the primordial couple, offering them two fruits.

evil must come from some source which is both dependent on him (as Ahura Mazdā is the Creator of all things) and yet independent of him (for he is absolutely good). The idea that Angra Mainyu, the adversary, is evil because of a wrong choice, is a fine solution to the problem, though the source of the idea of evil still remains mysterious. The evil in the world struggles against the good, and humanity, which is capable of choices, must side with the good in the drama which will culminate in a third age when good and evil will be separated and the good will be rewarded with judgment and immortality. All this picture provided a monotheistic frame, but at the same time it was realistic to the experience of human beings, which sees the world as a mixed place.

This threefold drama, and especially the concept of the future age when human beings will have pure bodies in a state of resurrection, has been very influential in the history of religions. The idea spread to Judaism, to Christianity, and to Islam. There will at the end of time be a wonderful refreshing of existence, making it splendid again. The Lie will be defeated and humbled: the Hostile Spirit will be driven away and finally annihilated. And in the process human beings will be made immortal. These ideas were already there in the beginning of Zoroastrian religion, but they became considerably elaborated as time went on.

High Zoroastrianism of the Achaemenid Period

As Zoroastrianism developed into a state cult under the priestly guidance of the Magi, it began to reabsorb features of surrounding religions. Thus, the gods began to reappear within the fabric of the faith, though not the evil *daevas* or demonic gods denounced by Zarathustra. First of all the shadowy and abstract Immortals (Amesha Spentas) became personalized. Perhaps for the Prophet they were unseen forces which could possess the good person, but later they were as gods. In the *Yashts*, a section of the Avesta, we find various divinities being nominated as being "worthy of worship" or *yazata*. Among these are the Sun and the Moon; a rain god, Tishtrya; Anāhitā and Mithra (to them I shall return in a moment); Vayu the wind, the personified Haoma, and various other beings, including the angel-like figures which guard individuals, the *fravashi*. There are also Saosha and Rashnu, who with Mithra judge the souls of the dead. If we define a god as a being whom people worship, then we have in the *yazatas* the reintroduction of a kind of polytheism, even if the many gods are subordinated to the One God. It is a little like the situation in the Indian tradition.

In the first state of creation Gavaēvōdāta and Gayamaretan are the prototypes of animals and men; and the latter forms with Zarathustra and Saoshyant a triad of great figures relevant to the times. Eventually three Saoshyants were postulated, one each for the beginning of a new millennium (incidentally, this imagery of a thousand-year cycle gained a strong grip on Western imagination, and it reappears, for instance, in Hitler's notion of a Thousand-Year Reich). The last Saoshyant will bring immortality to humans and fight a last battle with the forces of evil, who will be destroyed.

This idea of a future summation of history had to be combined with a somewhat different piece of imagery, that of the Chinvat Bridge, which stretches from the great cosmic mountain at the center of the universe to Paradise and becomes as narrow as a razor's edge. When the individual soul reaches the Bridge it is judged by Mithra and the other judges, and is confronted by its image: if good, this image is like a beautiful young girl; if not, like a hag. The bad souls slip off the razor's edge into the fires of everlasting torment, and the righteous proceed onward to Paradise. Eventually this imagery was combined with the other, when Saoshyant looks on the world and restores it to imperishable glory, the souls of the just are united to glorious bodies, and the sacrifice of a cow drink made of blended *haoma* and fat from the cow will confer immortal life upon them.

But despite the reinsertion of gods and goddesses into the religion, on the whole Zoroastrianism retained its imageless state and did not erect statues or have temples for individual deities. There were some exceptions: King Artaxerxes II (reigned 404–358 B.C.E.) put up temples of Anāhitā in the chief cities of the empire. But on the whole the battle against anthropomorphism was successful. The Zoroastrians in effect combined the ancient Indo-Iranian, nomadic, imageless type of religion with the rejection of "pagan" gods in the name of monotheism: they arrived at the same conclusion but from another direction as the official religion of the ancient Israelites.

Many of these ideas, and their accompanying practices, were a good deal more elaborated during the Sassanid period, from the third to the seventh century C.E., which also saw the growth of the Zurvanite myth and theology. To that I now come.

Divine Time: Zurvān

Already during the Achaemenid and Greek periods there had evolved a series of ideas which were later elaborated in the Pahlavi literature which looks back to the glorious days of Sassanid times. It was an idea which in some ways reversed the thrust of the original dualism of Zarathustra. He had postulated a personal Supreme God and twins below him, one good and one evil. In Zurvanism the dualism was between Ohrmazd (Ahura Mazdā) and Ahriman (Angra Mainyu). These were twin offspring of a higher force, namely Time or Zurvān.

The reason for this way of modifying the original pattern was doubtless that, both in the late Achaemenid period and during Greek rule under the Seleucids, the notion of Time had an attraction, partly because of the influence of Babylonian astronomy on Persian culture and the derived astrological means of forecasting good and evil futures, and partly because of Greek notions of Fate. At any rate Zurvanism arrived at a new metaphysical interpretation of the world by sacrificing the ultimacy of the ethical good. Zarathustra had elevated the perfectly good God to the supreme place but sacrificed his power, setting up an evil principle from primordial times who would struggle against him, even if destined ultimately to be defeated. In Zurvanism, a morally neutral Time was elevated to the governing position, with both combatants on an equal footing in the cosmic struggle. Although the good God, Ohrmazd, ultimately wins, metaphysically he is not ultimate.

Sassanid Zoroastrianism in its Dimensions

Zoroastrianism was refounded in the third century C.E. under various leaders, most importantly Kerder. Some of the *narrative* elements to which we have referred become more elaborate. Thus the Saoshyant or Savior who was to come in the final age was supposed to have been born of a virgin who was impregnated while bathing in a lake where the seed of Zarathustra was preserved—and where it had indeed been guarded by no less than 99,999 *fravashi* over the ages. Time, an increased preoccupation, was divided into segments. The age of the cosmos was supposed to be 12,000 years. This was in four stretches of 3000 years. During the first age, the mental age, Ohrmazd starts his creative activity and begins the war with Ahriman. They do a deal and agree to mingle for 9000 years. The next stage sees a shift from the mental to the material state. The third sees Ahriman's assault on the creation of Ohrmazd. At the end of that period the good God prepares for the coming of the Prophet, whose revelations begin the fourth age. There are three thousand years left; at the end of each thousand years a savior appears, and the last savior ushers in the revitalized cosmos. All this combined history and myth in an interesting and influential way.

In the *doctrinal* dimension, as we have seen, we have the experiment of Zurvanism as a counterpoint to the monotheism of the more orthodox tradition, which had however made compromises with polytheism. As for *ethics*: this dimension was integral to the fabric of Zoroastrian thinking, which focused on the struggle between good and evil. On the whole, Zoroastrian ethics were highly world-affirming, even if the figure of Ahriman was influential in later world-denying creeds such as forms of Gnosticism and Manichaeism.

Regarding the *ritual* dimension, the main feature was the very complex fire ceremony, with the sacrifice of *haoma*. Fire was thought of as purifying in essence, and the rites attached to it required considerable time and knowledge. The calendar was also dense with festivals, such as celebrating the *fravashi* on the day of Nō Rūz, or New Year's Day, and at five other great festivals: at the middle of spring, at midsummer, at the corn harvest, in the fall, and at midwinter. Vital, too, were the feasts of Mithra and of the star god Sirius.

The *institutional* dimension in post-Sassanid times of course no longer involved state participation; but over the periods when the religion flowered,

For the Sassanids Zoroastrianism was a powerful state religion, and the emperor combined religious and political functions. Here Shapur I (reigned 241–72) receives the submission of the Roman emperor Valerian, after the emperor had been defeated by Shapur at Edessa in 260.

the priesthood was tied to the imperial system. The Magi, as we have seen, made up an hereditary caste, and they assisted with social affairs, such as the initiation of the young, marriages, and funerals. Whether any among the Magi were religious specialists in some further sense, as prophets or ecstatics, is open to some question. Although Zarathustra himself was a visionary, we do not have much evidence on the *experiential* dimension of the religion.

Finally the main *artifacts* of Zoroastrianism were the fire temples and the *dakhmas* where the dead were exposed. In art the winged disc came to represent Ahura Mazdā; but as an aniconic or imageless religion Zoroastrianism had less to offer in art and statuary than most other faiths.

The mental imagery, however, was most powerful. The imagination of other traditions was haunted by the Chinvat Bridge, and the resurrection of glorified bodies, and the coming of a Savior, and the thought of life as a struggle between good and evil. Though Zoroastrianism was only to survive in small numbers—maybe 150,000 people today—the religion has had vast influence and is a noble mode of organizing belief in one God.

Mani and Another Use of Dualism

The prophet Mani was born near the city of Ctesiphon in Mesopotamia around 217 C.E., just before the establishment of the Sassanid dynasty. He had a visionary experience when he was twelve, and a few years later, when he was twenty-four, he received an angelic order to preach the truth in public. He spent his life in energetic missionary work, committing his teachings to writing and to painting. He had a high regard for pictorial art and thought it ought to be part of religious communication; he compiled a book of *Images* to illustrate the doctrines. His missions took him to Baluchistan, and he was granted permission by King Shapur to preach throughout the Persian empire. But after Shapur's death Mani fell from favor: the Magi were intent on reconstructing Zoroastrianism after the Parthian period. He was arrested and died after interrogation and being kept in chains, probably in 277 C.E. when he was sixty.

It seems that Mani thought of his religion as a suitable new state religion for the Sassanid dynasty, and this explains some of the hatred between the Magi and him. He genuinely seems to have seen his doctrines as universalistic, for he held that in part they made up the essence of the teachings of the three great founders, Zarathustra, the Buddha, and Jesus. He himself was raised as a Christian, in a Baptist denomination influential in his region, and so it became common for Christians to think of Manichaeism as a Christian heresy. But its dominant doctrine, of the separation of good and evil, light and darkness, seems to have owed much more to the Zoroastrian tradition.

Despite the persecution of the new religion for a while in the Persian Empire, it persisted there right into Islamic times. It had great success in going west, spreading through much of the Roman Empire in the century after Mani's death. Its most famous adherent, who then however converted to

Christianity, was St. Augustine. It was also persecuted by Roman emperors, both before and after the Christianization of the Empire. In 527 C.E. an edict threatened death to followers of Mani, so it must have still had some vigor then.

The basic doctrines of Manichaeism were that the soul has fallen into the material world; that unless something happens it will remain trapped in the round of reincarnation; that God, the Father of Greatness, sends a savior who will rouse those asleep in darkness; and that the way to salvation is by knowledge—direct experience of the Light.

The war which exists between the Father of Greatness and the Prince of Darkness has much to do with sex, for the latter wants to produce as many bodies as possible to house and trap the light. Light lives in the seed, and Mani seems to have woven some Tantric ideas into his religion, about the importance of the retention of sperm. Those who were adepts were expected to refrain altogether from sex; the married laity should observe strict monogamy. The Manichaean Church was built along somewhat Buddhist lines, with the clergy living in monasteries and being supported by the lay folk. The clergy were supposed to practice truth-telling, nonviolence, celibacy, abstinence from meat and other impure foods, and poverty.

The myths of origin in the Manichaean scheme are somewhat lurid. As a result of the first clashes between the Father of Light and the Prince of Darkness the world is created, the lower regions being caused by the Prince of Darkness and the sun and stars by the offspring of light. These contests also generate some monsters. Primordial matter causes the demons Ashaglun and Namrael to eat the monsters and then to mate, and they bring Adam and Eve into being. But the Savior is sent from above, who arouses Adam from his ignorant sleep and shows him the light within, which ultimately has heavenly origins.

Manichaeism's ethics were strict and humane, abjuring all kinds of violence for lay and clergy alike. People were expected to give to the church either a tenth or a seventh part of their earnings. They were to fast on Sundays and during a month before the annual Bema celebration. They were to confess their sins weekly and annually at a collective ceremony. They had to pray four times a day. The Bema festival was a remembrance of Mani's suffering and death. The Bema itself was an empty throne, and this was a little like the early Buddhist practice of not showing the Buddha.

No doubt the Manichaeans encouraged meditative practices which would bring out the light within. At any rate it is through such a direct knowledge of the Light that the adept could finish the round of rebirth and ascend back to the Light which was the soul's source.

This was a vigorous but pessimistic religion, which may have spread in part because of its claims to universalism in bringing together themes from Christian, Buddhist, Zoroastrian, and other sources. In part it may have appealed because of its gentleness. Alongside its pessimism there was also hope, for the faith in a Savior pointed to a way out. With its austerity it may have looked good at a period when State religions were showing their corrupt side and harshness.

We have followed the story of Persia until the close of the Sassanid period. Persia was destined to be overcome by the forces of Islam, and entered on a quite different period of its civilization. Meanwhile let us glance briefly at Central Asia, from the edges of which the Prophet Zarathustra had come.

The Geographic Significance of Central Asia

The region to the northwest of India, reaching up into what is now Afghanistan and Soviet Central Asia, for long had a special meaning for the world cultures, since it was through there, north of Tibet, that the trade routes ran which joined the West to China and to India (see Map 7, p. 220). Because this area lies open to invasion from the great northern plains that stretch from Europe to Eastern Siberia, it has also been a channel for the entry of relatively untamed peoples into the lives of the various major areas. In early days it was the place through which the Aryans migrated into India. Later, it was the area where Buddhism spread outward from the north Indian plains. From there Buddhism was to have special influence to the east. Oddly, it never had much impact in a western direction.

It may be noted, too, that it was Buddhism which spread, rather than Brahmin culture and religion. Here was a contrast with developments in Southeast Asia. By about 650 C.E., when Islam had begun to explode out of the Arabian peninsula, various religions were living together in great tolerance in Central Asia: Zoroastrianism, Buddhism, Nestorian Christianity, Judaism, and Manichaeism.

In the seventh and eighth centuries Islam became lodged in the region, and in the end it was to become dominant. A crucial victory was the defeat of the T'ang emperor of China at the battle of Talas in 751 C.E. The rulers of the different Turkestani areas in the region were converted to Islam, and in consequence other religions came under pressure: the Buddhists, seen as idolaters, were especially condemned.

In the early part of the thirteenth century the region was conquered and its cities sacked by the Mongols under Genghis (Jinggis) Khan, and for more than a century the rulers were tolerant shamanists or had a leaning to Nestorian Christianity and Buddhism. But, as it happened, the Mongol rulers eventually converted to Islam, especially under Timur (1336–1405). We shall return to these events in dealing with Islam.

Shamanism from North Asia

Central Asia has also been a conduit for shamanistic ideas and practices. In early times it may be that the śramanic tradition in India was affected by the shamanism of northern and central Siberia. Again, the Mongol religion incorporated strong shamanistic ingredients.

Till modern times shamanism has been a main feature of the great area stretching from European Russia to Kamchatka. The shaman is a spiritual specialist who has to undergo initiation; but prior to that he may have to undergo a great sickness. He will emerge from this experience, and from initiation, a vigorous and creative person, who will be able to help others, and who possesses visionary powers.

Often his ordeal is imagined as the extraction of his bones from his body and their reassembly—a kind of death and resurrection—brought about through the agency of shamanic ancestors or other hidden and spiritual forces. His vision may mean that he is able to discern where it is best to hunt or fish, and this is a valuable characteristic for his group. He may be repository of the tribe's poetical tradition and be an enactor of myth and legend. But above all he will be a healer, who helps others to go through death and resurrection like himself. He will be able to go into trance, where he is possessed by some powerful god or spirit. He can fly up to heaven and descend into the underworld, both to conduct souls to their final home and to rescue those who are so sick they have already entered into the realm of death. The shaman will often wear special dress and carry a drum, which helps to create through its beating and rhythm an altered state of consciousness, important during the public seances conducted by the shaman.

The type of cosmology associated with shamanism is of a cosmos which has as its center a sacred axis, what Mircea Eliade has called the *axis mundi*. This sometimes is a high mountain where the gods live, which reaches down into the underworld. There will be many gods and spirits, including those of ancestral shamans (who often take the aspiring shaman through the pains of his visionary death and resurrection). In the case of the Mongols, there was a supreme god called Tengri presiding over the sky; and shamanistic rites were adapted to the ideology of imperial rule, in a combination of ancestral rites with a seance—such a rite still continues in Inner Mongolia, addressed to the spirit of Genghis Khan.

In the circumpolar regions of the Eurasian landmass and North America, the religions of the Same (pronounced "Samay") or Lapp people, those of Siberia, and the Inuit and others in Alaska and Canada, all have vital manifestations of shamanism. Since also in Korea and among North and South American Indians and in parts of Central Asia the same can be seen, maybe it implies a diffusion from Siberia. But equally it may be a common human practice in some kinds of society, notably those involved in hunting and gathering. Since such a mode of subsistence is increasingly difficult in the modern world, shamanism may be on the wane, though we may also note the continuing popularity of shamanic themes in all sorts of contexts, from psychoanalysis to literature and New Age spirituality.

Since the shamans of North Asia seem to have pioneered techniques of ecstasy, they may thereby have laid the foundations for two different directions in which religious experience has developed: in the one direction there is the inner, nonvisionary but highly technical attainment of higher states of consciousness, as in Buddhism; in the other direction, there are the numinous and visionary experiences of prophets and others, where the Other appears, apparently spontaneously, to the subject.

CHAPTER 10

The Greek and Roman World

Various cultural currents mingled together in the Mediterranean world to form Graeco-Roman civilization. But the two broadest streams were those of Greece, with its splendid but politically fragmented civilization, and of Rome, with its genius for conquest, law, and synthesis. A stepping-stone to the unification of the Mediterranean was the unification of the Greek East and various Levantine cultures through the conquests of Alexander the Great in 336–323 B.C.E. Another was the Roman defeat of the major rival power of Carthage in the three Punic wars of the next two centuries. With the Roman conquest of the East and the final stabilization of the empire under Augustus Caesar after 30 B.C.E., there came into firm existence a new Graeco-Roman civilization of great power, beauty, and spiritual vigor.

Certain dead civilizations also contributed obscurely to the later creativity of Rome and Greece, such as the Etruscans in Italy, absorbed by Rome in early days, and the Minoan civilization of Crete and its mainland offshoot, Mycenean culture, which was overtaken by conquest by Greek-speakers. The Roman Empire later synthesized and absorbed many streams of thought and practice from the subjugated peoples, and nowhere was this more obvious than in the case of religion: the cults of Isis from Egypt, Mithras from Persia, Cybele from Asia Minor, and Astarte from Syria; Jewish religion from Palestine; Manichaeism from Persia; and Christianity, also from Palestine, are prime examples, to set alongside such homegrown religiosities as the older paganism of Greece and Rome, the mysteries of Eleusis, Orphism, the intellectual faith of Platonism and its daughter Neoplatonism, Stoicism, and Epicureanism (see Map 8, p. 232). The empire was a great melting-pot of spiritual notions. In this chapter we shall sample some of these riches.

First there are the traditional religions of Greece and Rome, up till the flowering within these societies of wider ideas and philosophical movements.

So we are dealing with Greece up to the fifth century B.C.E., and Rome virtually till the first century B.C.E. Next we shall look at the philosophies and new religious movements of Greece and the Hellenistic world down to the first century C.E. We shall then do the same for Rome before looking at the ebb and flow of religions in the early Roman empire, including Jewish religion and Christianity but in the wider context of other movements, such as Gnosticism, Mithraism, and other philosophies and mystery religions. We shall leave later developments to Chapter 11, which will see the emergence of classical forms of Christianity and Judaism.

Greek Religion

The Pattern of Gods

The system of classical Greek religion is, in terms of belief and worship, polytheistic. There are many gods, and much later this idea was itself castigated by the monotheistic Christians and Jews. It is true that there was a supreme god, a first among other immortals, a chief. And impressive he was too: the

---

Graeco-Roman Religion some key terms

Cosmos The universe as an orderly whole.

Holocaust A whole burnt sacrificial offering.

Hubris Overweening pride and the desire to gain equality with the gods, which typically proves disatrous.

Logos Reason within humankind, sometimes treated as the principle governing the cosmos, as in Stoicism and in Philo and Christianity (where Logos is also creator and mediator).

Manes The spirits of the dead: the collective ancestors.

Mysteria Mysteries or mystery religions, such as those of Isis, Eleusis, and Mithras, involving the revelation of truth in dramatic form by initiation.

Mythos A story and in particular an authoritative story about the gods.

Numen Spirit, e.g. in a stream, copse, mountain, or other sacred spot or force.

Philosophia Love of wisdom, or a system of ideas which helps us to understand and cope with life, such as Stoicism or Neoplatonism.

Religio That which binds us to the gods, religion.

Temenos A sanctuary or sacred area often including a temple.

Theos God, or God as supreme being, as in Aristotle's philosophy.

mighty Zeus, ruler of the sky, sometimes joined in a triad with Poseidon, god of the sea, and Hades, god of the underworld. Zeus had destroyed a previous group of deities, the mighty Titans, and their leader Kronos. He was not just god of heavenly light, but also a just and kingly god, who was concerned with justice for human beings, and who supported good rulers. He was father of gods and men, the final ruler; but like a chief, he had his advisers and friends around him, and he could not fully control them. Various of his wives and consorts indicate some of the powers and ideals that he had gathered round his person. His great wife, Hera, helps him to sanctify the institution of marriage. When coupled with the earth goddess he represents the male fecundation of the world. In his mating with Themis, goddess of order, he brings regularity into human and cosmic affairs. They engender the Fates which rule over human destiny. And so on. If Zeus's frequent espousals and couplings were sometimes criticized later on as giving a bad example to men, they were from one perspective merely a sign of his various powers. And gods were different from us: they were the immortals, and it was *hubris*, or overweening presumption, even to compare ourselves to them.

Another deity we can sample among the clouds of spirits in the Greek world came from Cyprus, where she may have been stimulated by the example of the Semitic goddess Astarte. Aphrodite is the spirit of fertility and love, wed to the beautiful Adonis. In Homer she turns out to be the daughter of Zeus and Dione. She was to inspire the great sculptor Praxiteles (active c.370–330 B.C.E.) to produce the greatest portrayal of her nude. She was a

Map 8 The Greek and Roman World, showing the boundary and provinces of the Roman Empire, c.100 C.E.

serious goddess, but she could have her wild side, for in the city of Corinth she was served by sacred prostitutes.

A god of uncertain origin but great influence was Apollo, an ideal young man in appearance and the patron of music, healing, prophecy, and the safekeeping of cattle; he was also, and most importantly, the god of the Panhellenic (all-Greece) shrine of Delphi. He may have been non-Greek in origin, in that he was supposedly the offspring of a Titan, which may reflect some old struggle between the Hellenic gods under Zeus and their predecessors. On the whole Apollo stands for orderly inspiration and creative prediction. He can be contrasted with the much more disorderly Dionysos. The main gods of Greece lived on Mount Olympus, the great mountain of central Greece and once considered to be an *axis mundi*. But Dionysos was not an Olympian, although it came to be said that he was the offspring of Zeus and Semele. He was the god of wine and the leader of orgiastic feasts and revels. Dionysos was associated with the religious origins of drama, in ritual performances in which sacred narratives were enacted. His cult forms the centerpiece of what is in many ways the most powerful play by the dramatist Euripides (480–406 B.C.E.), *The Bacchae*.

The many gods had a national meaning, but each was also rooted in the individual city-state or *polis*. In the heyday of Greek culture, around 600–400 B.C.E., the *polis* was the typical unit, even if Athens, for example, gathered around it an empire of subordinate cities and their territories. Each little region had its own shrines and gods, so Greek religion was an interplay between the localized cults and the Panhellenic religion which most of the culture shared: not only the Olympians, but central holy places like Delphi, where Apollo's oracle was; not only the great poets, above all Homer, who became the foundation of Greek education (and to a lesser extent Hesiod, about 700 B.C.E.), but also the Panhellenic games such as the Olympiad.

The Importance of Sacrifice

The central ritual activity of Greek religion was the making of sacrifice to the gods. For the most part it involved the slaughter of animals. It is said that the first sacrifice was brought about by Prometheus. He was a primordial hero and trickster. He tried to deceive Zeus by making the portion he set aside for the gods look good: actually it was the animals' bones covered in fat; the good meat was concealed by rather revolting entrails and the like. He thought this would be good for the human race; but Zeus, who saw through the deception, cunningly took the bones and failed to reveal to Prometheus that a carnivorous life is one of death. So Prometheus unknowingly chose death for the human race. The institution of sacrifice thus drew the line between the gods, who were the immortals, and the mortal humans.

Animal sacrifices were well integrated into ordinary living, for they were the times when Greeks ate meat; so enjoyment and pious duty were thus harnessed together. Similarly, the priesthood for civic purposes were the magistrates, so again there was no divide between religion and the life of the *polis*.

Sacrifices to the earthly gods, the chthonian deities who belonged to the soil and the underworld, were holocausts, burnt whole. The blood, instead of spurting up toward heaven, as the sacrificer slit the animal's throat, poured downward through a hole in the ground. Instead of a high altar, there was a low altar.

Heroes

Though the Greeks distinguished sharply between gods and humans, there was nevertheless a kind of transitional being or demigod who was important for cities, for families, and sometimes for all Greeks: the hero, who was celebrated after his death with a shrine, and who had attained legendary status. Perhaps he was the father of a colony, or a great ancient hero like Achilles or Heracles. He might be associated with the civic past, or with a profession (as was the legendary doctor, Asclepius). To a limited extent their existence formed an ancestor cult. At any rate the heroes, though not divine, were nearer to the gods than other humans; many were thought to be the offspring of gods, and some attained immortality.

Religions Within Religion

In the complexity of the melange of cults which existed in the Greek world, certain movements had a more personal meaning, and these formed religions within the greater religion. (In some degree this description applies also to movements started by philosophers such as Pythagoras and Plato.) They included the Dionysian movement, turbulent and orgiastic; Orphism, purificatory and in search of release from rebirth; and the Eleusinian mysteries, sacramental and dramatic.

Let us begin with this last. It centered on the sacred complex of Eleusis, some distance outside Athens. The annual celebration of the rites or mysteries (from *mustai* meaning initiates, based on a verb meaning to keep silent, for the initiates were sworn to secrecy) involved a public procession from Athens, bathing of the initiates in the sea on the way, and the secret goings-on in the cave and temple of Eleusis. The drama there, the rites, the spoken words, the presentation of sacred images by the light of flaring torches, were said to be profoundly moving. As Aristotle said, you went there not to learn anything but to have an experience (a rhyming jingle in Greek: *ou mathein alla pathein*). The sacred drama concerned the descent of the distraught corn-goddess Demeter into the underworld, to which her daughter Kore or Persephone has been abducted to marry the infernal god Hades; eventually Zeus imposes a solution: Kore is to spend half the year in the world and half below. This agricultural myth was transmuted into a higher meaning, to do with the changing of the life of the initiate. Those who were initiated were then able to feel extra depth to their religious life amid the daily routines of the *polis*.

Orphism was a loosely defined movement named after the primordial singer, whose voice can enchant the beasts and the plants and rocks. Orphism

Some of the most powerful rituals were those of initiation, especially at Eleusis, the site of an important Greek sanctuary in Attica, which was dedicated to the goddess Demeter. The relief shows Demeter with her daughter Persephone, whose myth was an integral part of the Eleusinian rites or mysteries.

had its own priesthood, who traveled about advocating a pure way of life, involving vegetarianism and other means of self-purification. The Orphics saw the cosmos as having started perfectly, as a Cosmic Egg (according to one version), and then progressively becoming more chaotic. The soul is entombed in the body, the Orphics said, and is doomed to transmigration if salvation is not sought. The whole movement was something of a quietist rebellion, in that the ban on meat meant a ban on partaking in sacrifices and therefore in civic life. In a culture in which nothing of importance was ever decided without a sacrifice, the Orphic message must have seemed disturbing and revolutionary.

In some degree there was an overlap between it and Dionysian religion, which encouraged rather the opposite behavior. The myths were connected, and in Orphism there was the conception that Dionysos had been eaten by the Titans, who were burned up by Zeus and whose ashes provided the material for creating the human race—so each person contains within himself the divine spark of Dionysos. Dionysianism encouraged women's orgies in the wild places, and frenzied dancing, and the consumption of the raw flesh of animals torn apart—an accepted breach of its own taboo. Or, in its tamer, civic form, it provided for a sort of Mardi Gras as a counterpoint to the solemnity of many other civic religious occasions.

Next, there is the movement, periodically revived, of Pythagoreanism. Here we begin to make the bridge between religious and philosophical visions. Pythagoras (570?–500 B.C.E.) came from Samos in the Aegean, but his main work was conducted in Croton, a Greek colony in southern Italy. There he founded a religious order which also took political control of the city. Pythagoras died in Metapontum, in Asia Minor, exiled from Croton for some reason. His order proliferated and was influential for more than fifty years in the area. This order looked on Pythagoras as a holy man, perhaps divine, who taught various spiritual, practical, and philosophical things. According to his view the ultimate constituents of the world were numbers—an idea which was ultimately to have a profound impact on Western thought. The discovery of the mathematical ratio involved in musical harmony had a large effect on Pythagorean thinking. The world somehow flows from the relationship between the bounded, symbolized by numbers, and the unbounded. The soul was held to be involved in reincarnation; and by a process of purification, by following the precepts of Pythagoras, including food taboos—for instance on the eating of beans—the adepts could free an individual from this round of rebirth. So the Pythagorean message was a blend of theoretical, mathematical learning and practical spirituality: and all this was related to political action. As we shall see, all these three motifs were important for Plato.

The Love of Wisdom and Religious Goals

Already there were connections between what we would call religion and that activity which was known as the love of wisdom (the literal translation of the term *philosophia*). In modern times, in the West, philosophy has become increasingly technical and theoretical. It is true that sometimes it incorporates a worldview—often that of scientific humanism, in the English-speaking world in particular—but it tends often to define itself in opposition to religion and indeed to the idea of wisdom. But this was not so in ancient Greece.

Apart from Pythagoras, some thinkers, known now as the Presocratics—Thales, Anaximander, and Anaxagoras among them—pioneered speculative thought. Heraclitus (c.540–c.480 B.C.E.) said that everything is in flux, and that you cannot step into the same river twice (a doctrine reminiscent of those of his contemporary, Buddha Śākyamuni). Parmenides saw reality as unchanging Being. Socrates (c.470–399 B.C.E.) concentrated on seeking the definition or essence of things, asking questions like "What is courage?" and generally stirring his contemporaries to reflect about moral issues—for which he was condemned to death for corrupting the young. The teachings and methods of these men prepared the way for Plato, and thence for Platonism and later Neoplatonism, which often took a highly religious form.

Plato (429?–347 B.C.E.) was influenced somewhat by Orphic and Pythagorean thought and argued, in his delightful dialogue, the *Phaedo*, for the doctrine of reincarnation. He held that human souls were unable to retain their splendid original state of immortality and so sank down into bodies, to wander through life from existence to existence. But knowledge enables them to rise again to a state of liberation. Knowledge involves knowing essences, which for Plato are defined by the Forms which earthly things imitate and participate in. The World of Forms is where the soul came from, so acquiring knowledge is really remembering. And this, according to Plato, is how Socrates' method of arousing thought managed to work: as Socrates himself said, he was a midwife of knowledge.

An engraving of the Greek philosopher and mathematician Pythagoras (?570–500 B.C.E.). The founder of a religious order, he believed numbers were the underlying elements of the universe.

The World of Forms is a great hierarchy, with at the top the Form of the Good which informs all other Forms because each is ideal. So the soul through knowledge can climb up to the Form of the Good and perceive it in a vision. Plato's intuition was thus both mystical and intellectual, and part of the rigorous training of the disciple had to be in mathematics. In his school in the grove known as Akademos (hence the words "academic" and "academy") he had written over the entrance the words *Mēdeis ageōmetros eisitō*—"Let no one ignorant of geometry enter here."

Plato was not only concerned with theory and vision but also with politics. He made some fruitless visits to Sicily at the behest of the dictator Dion of Syracuse. But most of his life was devoted to education, and it was one of his pupils, Aristotle (384–322 B.C.E.), who took Plato's philosophy in a different direction, bringing the essences down to earth, and developing marvelous analytical treatments of biology, psychology, physics, metaphysics, ethics, politics, and logic which were to have a profound effect on European thought.

Platonism provided a noble and unified vision which could be set alongside the religion of the mysteries and the new movements, and, up to a point, alongside traditional religion and civic cults. But Plato was very critical of the poetic tradition of Homer and Hesiod and the low morals ascribed to the gods. In Greek religion, around 350 B.C.E., there was a mixture of differing levels of public and private religion, with certain high philosophical speculations woven into the fabric of life. In a way Greek religion was like that of the Indian tradition of the same period—not yet synthesized in a cohesive system, but full of potentialities which were to be realized later.

Alexander and After: Some New Philosophical Movements

Greece was unified, and the city-states tamed, by Philip II, king of Macedon (382–326 B.C.E.) and his genius son Alexander the Great (356–323 B.C.E.)—a pupil, by the way, of Aristotle. In a series of brilliant campaigns, Alexander swept aside the Persian empire, Greece's vast neighbor, which had long been its polar opposite in politics, thought, and religion. He laid the foundations of Greek-influenced regimes in Egypt, Syria (including Palestine), Persia, and Bactria in Central Asia. In Greece itself he brought to a close a turbulent but wonderfully creative period and ushered in the age which we know as "Hellenistic." During this time some new philosophies were pioneered which became influential both in the Greek East and the Roman West of the Mediterranean world.

Epicurus (342–271 B.C.E.) taught most of his life in Athens, and made use of the atomic theory of his predecessor Democritus: he argued that everything in the world is composed of atoms in emptiness. The soul too is a composite, and so when a person dies his atoms are dispersed and that is that. The gods are made of refined atoms but exist outside of our world, and they are not concerned at all with what we do or do not do. The best thing is to cultivate moderation in the pursuit of reasonable pleasure and to cultivate the virtue of *ataraxia* or equanimity. Later this worldview was put into poetic form by the Roman poet Lucretius (c.96-c. 55 B.C.E.), who in his *De rerum natura*, "On the Nature of Things," sought to dispel fear of the *numina*, gods and spirits.

About 300 B.C.E., Zeno of Citium founded the school which was known, after the cloisters or *stoa* where he taught, as Stoicism. He demythologized the gods, treating them as natural forces. The universe was controlled by mind (itself a material entity, though of a superior, refined nature—and poetically this could be called Zeus). On death we exist no more: but we are superior to animals because we possess reason. The wise person steels himself in the face of ultimate extinction, and bears himself with courage, self-control and realism in the face of evil and death, which are unavoidable ingredients of the way things are. This austere doctrine had an appeal to Roman nobility, and was taught in Rome by the Greek slave Epictetus in the first century C.E. and in the famous *Meditations* of the emperor Marcus Aurelius (121–180 C.E.), who became emperor in 161.

The latter part of what is called the Hellenistic age saw the conquest of the Greek East by the Romans and the fusion of the Mediterranean world into a single multicultural empire. In order to see the religious character of this new age, we need to retrace our steps to look at early Roman religion.

Roman Religion

The Numina and Civic Virtue

Roman religion was focused on deities and spirits who can collectively be called *numina*—mysterious spirits who roused reverential fear. Its gods ranged from the great Jupiter, with his consort Juno, through Mars or War, Venus or Love, and Ceres of the grain harvest, to such specialist deities as Sarrator, the god of weeding, and Januarius, the god of the threshold. The whole of reality and of human activity was punctuated and pervaded by the *numina*.

The aim of public worship in the early Roman system was to ensure that the gods remained or became benevolent. The calendar was a mosaic of feast days for worshiping varied gods. March, for instance, started off with a sacrifice to Mars, after whom it was named; and there were days for the blessing of horses, arms, trumpets, and so on. In addition the various games had religious significance—chariot races, wrestling, boxing, and later on (borrowed from the Etruscans) gladiatorial combats. To administer all these public events there

The numinous figure of the great Greek god Zeus is tempered by the increasing realism and humanity with which the Greeks depicted their gods.

were different classes of priests, headed by the supreme priest, the *pontifex maximus* (a title later to be taken over by the Popes), and including the Vestal Virgins, appointed each for thirty years and enjoying great prestige, who had to maintain the sacred fire in the court of the goddess Vesta. There were also differing kinds of diviners, such as the augurs, who predicted the future on the basis of the flights of birds—a custom which has a vestigial hangover in European countries where people may be superstitious about seeing an odd number, but not an even number, of magpies.

The public rites had their complement in household ceremonies, addressed to the *lares* or household gods, and to the ancestors, honored as *di manes* or divine shades. All this system made the Romans a very religiously observant people. As they grew outward, absorbing other cultures, the pantheon expanded. Since, too, the Romans were increasingly exposed to Greek culture, both because of the overrunning of Greek cities in the south of Italy and through the importation of educated Greek slaves as tutors and so on, the tendency was to identify Greek and Roman gods freely—Jupiter and Zeus, Venus and Aphrodite, Juno and Hera, and so on. This prepared the way for a blended Graeco–Roman civilization when ultimately the Romans overran Greece and the Hellenic East. This they did effectively from the mid-second century B.C.E., when they annexed Greece, having shortly before razed Carthage; and in 66 B.C.E. Pompey organized the whole of the East, as far as the Persian border, into provinces subsidiary to Rome. Not long after that, Julius Caesar conquered Gaul and started the subjugation of Britain. By the time he died, in 44 B.C.E., the Roman empire was more or less in place. It was taken over, after wracking civil wars, by Caesar's adopted son, Octavian, who assumed the title of emperor (*princeps*) and, in 27 B.C.E., took the solemn, rather religious name of Augustus.

The Spread of Mysteries and Philosophies

Perhaps because of the pluralism of the new empire, and because of the abatement of civic concern in the states which it had absorbed, religion became more individualized and was seen more and more as a matter of choice. The imperial ideology, it is true, required sacrifice to the emperor, as a means of expressing loyalty. But within that limit there was a remarkable flux of beliefs and practices. Among these movements were many mystery religions, which, like the cult of Eleusis, gave dramatic shape to the initiation of those who wish to pursue purity or immortality and to take part in the power of the god or goddess.

The mythic dimension: the god of light, Mithras, who killed and ate a sacred bull, was especially popular among Roman soldiers. This offshoot of the Iranian religion related to the myth of Mithras as the unconquerable Sun.

Already some of the Oriental deities had taken root in Rome, such as Isis of Egypt who had had a temple on the Aventine hill since the second century B.C.E. She brought feminine powers to bear on faith. Isis, of course, restores Osiris to life, and likewise the initiate is given new and restored existence by the goddess. She was regarded as the supreme deity; and the initiate's vision of her is movingly depicted by the writer Apuleius (second century C.E.) in *The Golden Ass*. The hero, who has unfortunately been turned into an ass, is ultimately redeemed from his brutish existence by the goddess.

A mystery cult that had special appeal to the Roman soldiery was that of Mithras. Mithras was credited with slaying the bull which would renew life, in alliance with the Sun: this myth was celebrated with the sacrifice of a bull in the half-underground temple which was characteristic of the cult. The worshipers present at the action partook of a subsequent feast. (Or, at least, this is a prevailing interpretation of our archaeological evidence.) Mithraism became a kind of initiatory club, its rites engendering the feeling of renewed life and comradeship.

At a higher level educationally there came the development of the Neoplatonic movement, especially through the writings and teaching of Plotinus (205?–269 C.E.) and his successors Porphyry (232?–303) and

Plotinus

Plotinus (who probably lived from 205 to 269 C.E.) probably influenced the religious worlds of Christianity, Judaism, and Islam more than anyone else. His Neoplatonism became a particularly strong ingredient in the Christian faith and constituted the beginning of a tradition which formed another stream, together with the Biblical tradition, in the intellectual and practical formation of Christianity. He was raised (probably) in Egypt, where he studied with Ammonius Saccas. He appears to have been interested in Eastern thought. Some knowledge of Indian philosophy of the period could have been available in Egypt, because of trade contacts. He joined an unsuccessful military expedition to Persia. He got to Antioch, and from there settled in Rome. During the last part of his life he taught and wrote his massive work, the *Enneads*, edited by his pupil Porphyry.

Plotinus was a mystic in the sense that he had an inner experience of the divine; and he saw the world as being a reflection of the One. This One is the same as Plato's Good. A person can reunite with the One through contemplation. But the one is beyond all words. This was the source of the negative way, where you define God through what he is not, which became influential in medieval Christian thought. Plotinus' language in pointing to this vision is beautiful and powerful. His gentle authority brought him excellent disciples who carried on his message, which is perhaps best summed up in his final words, on his deathbed: "I am trying to bring the divine in myself to the divine in the All."

Neoplatonism: Iamblichus on the Mysteries

No sacral act can be effective without the supplication of prayer. Steady continuance in prayer nourishes our mind, enlarges the soul for the reception of the gods, opens up to men the realm of the gods, accustoms us to the splendor of the divine light, and gradually perfects in us [our] union with the gods, until at last it leads us back to the supreme heights. Our mode of thinking is drawn gently aloft and implants in us the spirit of the gods; it awakens confidence, fellowship, and undying friendship [with them]; it increases the longing for God; it inflames in us whatever is divine within the soul; it banishes all opposition from the soul, and strips away from the radiant, light-formed spirit everything that leads to generation; it creates good hope and trust in the light. In brief, it gives to those who engage in it intercourse with the gods.

Iamblichus (250?–330). Plotinus was from Upper Egypt and studied with the teacher Ammonius Saccas in Alexandria before setting off on an expedition to eastern Persia in the hope of learning something of Eastern thought. Later he started teaching in Rome, gathering about him some influential disciples. He greatly modified the teachings of Plato.

At the summit of Plotinus' system is the One—known simply as the One, without any further way of talking about it except that it is the supreme God and emanates in the form of the Intellect or Nous. This contains within it the intelligible Forms of Plato's system. Beyond that, Intellect has a further emanation, the Soul, in which the Forms are seen in space and time. The Soul is on the brink of becoming the material world, into which the human soul descends. The world has many beauties, though it is a kind of prison that entraps the human soul. The One spreads love or passion (*eros*) for itself to the souls of human beings who begin the ascent back, through intellectual, ethical, and mystical endeavor, to the One. As he lay dying, Plotinus is supposed to have said: "I am trying to bring the divine in myself to the divine in the All."

Such teachings ultimately had a lot of appeal to Christians who were trying to make a blend between their monotheistic Jewish tradition and the classical culture of their environment in the Roman empire. Neoplatonism could be detached from paganism and its ideas could be made use of in formulating a deep Christian theology. Their emphasis too on con-templation gave Neoplatonic writers an edge at a time when monasticism was growing, after the Christian takeover of the Roman empire in 330 C.E. and the consequent need to reaffirm commitment and purity of life in a world gone easy.

So we find in the Hellenistic world and the early centuries of Rome a variety of mystery religions, some from the East, and of philosophies which could make special appeal to the literate elite. There was something else brewing too, and that was a challenging religion which also had some appeal across the whole empire: the religion of the Jews. To understand this we need once more to retrace our steps a little.

Religion in Palestine

The Vicissitudes of the Jews

The period from the reconstitution of the Israelite tradition under Ezra to the period of the Roman empire saw Palestine under Greek rule, that of the Seleucids. It also saw some Persian influences, through the notion of the resurrection, and an increased emphasis upon apocalyptic prophecies, with concomitantly the elevation of the figure of the *Mashiah*, Anointed One of the House of David, who would come to restore the kingdom of Israel. All this emerges in the Book of Daniel, replete with dazzling imagery. After many attacks on the people of Israel by foreign adversaries, God sends a great leader to lead them in defeating their foes and establishes an everlasting kingdom. The wicked are condemned to perish, and the good live on.

Various parties emerged before the time of Jesus, and it was in this plural and chaotic time that he started his own movement. There were the Pharisees, who were looked on as innovators because they introduced ideas like the resurrection of the body which scribal conservatives rejected. The latter belonged to the party of the Sadducees, who preserved the Torah, and had chief control of the Temple rituals. There were Jews who were Hellenizers, won over to the excitements and lifestyle of Greek civilization. There were Zealots, who were involved with plotting armed resistance to the Roman occupation. There were the Essenes and the Qumran community, who withdrew to a secluded life in the desert, in order to preserve the Torah intact and create a counterpoint to the Temple rites. There were in Alexandria the group known as the Therapeutai, who pursued the contemplative life in a spirit of asceticism. There were men like Philo of Alexandria, who took Greek learning seriously and sought to express the higher truths of Jewish belief and practice in Greek terms. These currents of belief flourished in Palestine and more widely in the Roman empire, for there was an extensive diaspora of Jews even before the fall of the Temple in 70 C.E.

Jesus' Movement as a Jewish Sect

Yehoshu'a, or Jesus, (of Nazareth) lived at a stormy time, with political tensions high. The Jews had already shown themselves stubborn in the early years of the new Roman emperor cult, and this was to be a continued source of friction. Their exclusive monotheism may have been noble, but it also appeared, to the imperial administrators, to be strange. Jews were divided religiously, as we have seen, but these divisions also signified political ones. There was a stormy edge of revolt in Jewish society, and it was eventually such a revolt that led to the destruction of the Temple.

Yehoshu'a's movement ended up by being strikingly successful. He came from an obscure part even of the Jewish world, namely Galilee; he had a very brief and fairly turbulent public career of two or three years, after his baptism by his cousin Yohanan (John), another strong preacher, who like Yehoshu'a considered that the time was at hand when the kingdom of God would be ushered in. Yohanan was a wild man but a prophet, deliberately courting the empty places and the landscape beyond urban civilization. Yehoshu'a on the contrary mixed much with men and women of all walks of life, pure and impure, high and low, and worked in cities. He preached a message resting on the conviction that a new age had come with his coming, and that he had a specially intimate relation with God, whom he called Abba, Dad. He often referred to himself with the mysterious title "Son of Man," found in Daniel and elsewhere. But he also saw himself firmly embedded within the Jewish world. He would expound the Torah (or First Five Books of the Bible), the then scripture, which was to be expanded into the so-called Tanakh, or "Law, Prophets, and Writings," which make up the full Hebrew Bible (and which

In the catacombs, which were rediscovered only in the sixteenth century, the Roman piety toward the dead was formalized in niches such as these, where urns containing the mortal remains of the dead were stored. The catacombs were a model for later Christian crypts.

became, with slight variations, the Old Testament of the Christian community as it grew away from the Jewish mainstream). Yehoshu'a also frequented that important institution, the synagogue. Synagogue worship, congregational in style, was an important facet of orthodox Jewish life already, in cities such as Capernaum where Yehoshu'a himself taught.

He gathered about himself a group of men disciples and women followers, and began healing and teaching in a striking way: his parables and stories sometimes seemed esoteric but they were vivid. It was chiefly through such stories, and through colorful and lively epigrams and sayings, that he taught, judging from the style of what has come down to us. He may well have claimed to be *Mashiah* or Anointed One, and his family had some claim to be linked to the House of David. If he did use the idea, he used it in a novel way: not meaning a warrior king, come to restore Jewish rule, but as a Suffering Servant, a new sort of king with a crown of thorns. Many of his teachings used old concepts in new ways, and this maybe was a source of misunderstanding. At any rate he came into sharp collision with the ruling council or Sanhedrin, and was handed over to Pilate, the Roman administrator, for execution by crucifixion, with a notice on the cross to the effect that he was "King of the Jews." The transformation which overcame his group a few days later, according to the accounts in the New Testament, when they came to believe in his resurrection from the dead, was the source of the vigor with which they carried on the movement.

So, apart from all the other currents in Jewish religion of the time, we have the continuation of Yohanan's group and, more significantly in the Graeco-Roman world, the Yehoshu'a movement. This came to be transmitted by Paul, teaching especially in Greek and traveling to the various Jewish centers—that is, the main cities—of Greece and Asia Minor and then to Rome itself. And there was not only Paul but other vigorous disciples also. By not requiring circumcision of Gentile converts, Paul turned the movement into an easy access into some of the nobler features of the Jewish tradition, whose monotheism had an appeal to reflective Gentiles, and whose ethics were inspiring in many ways to people in the empire. This new offshoot of Jewish religion, full of verve and some apparent secrecy, had the appearance of a new mystery religion.

Also around this period there grew up other religions with Jewish connections which are collectively known as Gnosticism. Precisely what form they took on the ground is obscure; but in content, though not in organization, they resembled Manichaeism. It was a Gnostic teacher, Marcion, whose doctrine was that the God of the Old Testament was evil, and who edited and in effect censored Paul's letters, who forced the growing Christian community, in the second century C.E., to set about the job of deciding which writings they used were canonical, or approved by the community as containing God's truth. The formation of the Christian Bible in the second and third centuries C.E. was one of the signs that the religion was crystalizing into that full-fledged form which we know as Christianity.

Jews and Christians in the Hellenistic World

In all this rich interplay of religious movements, rituals, belief systems, and customs, and amid shifting allegiances within the overall stable framework of the empire, why did the Christians win out?

The new mystery religion had some inherent advantages. First, because of its Jewish monotheism it was universal in scope. Second, in looking to a God-human in Jesus it presented a theme very familiar to the Graeco-Roman world. Third, it was able, from the third century onward in particular, to pick up themes from the Platonic tradition which would make the faith appealing to the educated person. Fourth, the nature of its "mystery," a sacred meal, was coupled to a scheme of initiation which meant much more in the way of commitment to beliefs than the other mystery cults. Fifth, periodic persecution, which Jews also experienced, reinforced the solidarity of the group. Sixth, the empty formalism of the emperor cult and the marked pluralism of belief among the imperial elite pointed to the lack of a coherent state ideology. It was the Christian's good fortune that Constantine I (d. 337)

The emperor Constantine, who symbolizes the triumph of Christianity over ancient paganism, is here portrayed as a Christian, bearing the cross in his hand. Wall painting by Manuel Panselinos from the Protaton, Mount Athos, Greece, thirteenth century.

saw in Christian teachings such an ideology, and reorganized the Empire with it as official teaching; it was at his command that the first great Council of the Church was called. Seventh, the new religion had consistent organization, with its system of overseers or bishops; it was only matched in this by the Manichaeans. Eighth, it was able to fight off its pessimistic Gnostic rivals and the Manichaeans with its relatively positive attitudes to the world.

The Dimensions of Early Christian Religion

By the second century, Christianity was beginning to settle down. In *doctrine* it affirmed that there was but one God, who had created the world without any hindrance, so that it was basically good. Its *mythic* dimension affirmed, however, that the primordial humans had disobeyed God and had been driven from Paradise. Yet God wished to save the human race, and the people of Israel had been chosen as the instruments of this. By keeping faith in one God going, till the time when the Savior came to earth, they were crucial to the whole salvation-history. Christ on earth had died for human sins and had made available God's grace to the faithful. Those faithful basically were the churchly community; and the grace came in particular through the ritual participation in Christ through the thanksgiving service, held typically in wealthier members' houses.

In *ritual* there were the sacraments, like baptism, by which after a course of instruction a believer was admitted to the group. There was the eucharist, typically followed by a communal meal, in which the followers of Christ showed their mutual love and solidarity. Love was the root of the *ethical* dimension; and Christians got a good reputation for raising the status of women in marriage, for faithfulness, and for that general probity summed up in the Ten Commandments. The *institutional* dimension, with areas looked after by bishops and with a priest, as far as possible, for every community, was

Christ the Creator: John's Gospel

In the beginning was the Word, and the Word was with God, and the Word was God. The same was in the beginning with God. All things were made by him, and without him was not any thing made that was made. In him was life, and the life was the light of men. And the light shineth in darkness; and the darkness comprehended it not.

There was a man sent from God whose name was John. The same came for a witness, to bear witness of the Light, that all men through him might believe. He was not that Light, but was sent to bear witness of that Light. That was the true Light, which lighteth every man that cometh into the world. He was in the world and the world was made by him, and the world knew him not. He came unto his own, and his own received him not. But as many as received him, to them gave he power to become the sons of God, even to them that believe on his name, which were born not of blood, nor of the will of the flesh, nor of the will of man, but of God. And the Word was made flesh, and dwelt among us (and we beheld his glory, the glory as of the only begotten of the Father), full of grace and truth.

"The Breaking of Bread," one of the frescoes found in the catacomb of Priscilla, Rome, and dating from the second or early third century. In addition to communal meals, frescoes depicted miracles of healing and Christ as the shepherd of his flock.

flexible in times of strife. Certain big bishops, those of Rome, Antioch, and Alexandria, had special prestige; and so, later, had the bishop of the new imperial capital, Constantinople. They were also beginning experiments with monasticism, and this was later to be a vital stream of organized meditation and illumination in the Church. In religious *experience*, there was stress on the vision of Christ, in line with Gnostic practice; but also, and perhaps above all, the feeling of the Love of God which was manifested in the gatherings of Christians, inspired by the Spirit. It was early in the life of the community for there to be much *art*, especially in the context of Jewish imagelessness. But as a material object they did have the Greek text of the Hebrew Bible and of the new scriptures of the rising community.

The Christians had a human parallel to the Gospels and the other writings: they had the source of truth seen in the lives of the martyrs and the saints. It was the Christian holy men and women above all who showed the power of God and the grace of the new community—as they saw it—in the proliferating congregations of the empire.

Roman Imperial Religion as a Total System

The Christians and Jews were of course somewhat hostile to the imperial religious milieu. What others saw as meaningful stories they saw as deceptions. They did not acknowledge that their own narratives might look like sacred myth to others. But they did exist for two or three centuries as a subtheme in that wider configuration which saw Zeus or Jupiter as supreme god from a popular point of view, but to be reinterpreted if you wished philosophically as the supreme Mind. The various deities represented so many powers and above all forces for the renewal of life. There was a strong air in the empire of the need for propriety, so that the proper imperial and civic rites should be

A mosaic of Christ the Pantocrator or Ruler of the Universe, fills the dome of the Church of the Virgin within the monastery at Dafni (Daphni), near Athens. The eleventh-century Byzantine church contains some of the finest mosaics in Greece.

Left The ritual dimension: Jews, dressed in Moorish style, worship in a synagogue. Although they had some disadvantages under Islam (and, on the whole, even more stringent ones in Christian countries), their ritual life was basically unimpeded.

Above The institutional dimension: the monastic center at Cluny in central France was a significant powerhouse of reform. Pope Urban II (reigned 1088–99) consecrates the third abbey church (1095). The pope stands on the left of the altar, with Abbot Hugh on the right. Until the rebuilding of St. Peter's, Rome, this was the largest church in Western Christendom

Right The narrative dimension: the Angel replenishes the four rivers in Eden, while Adam and Eve are cast out into the desert, from a twelfth-century manuscript.

Li tur fapuruunt
que nie gent eftoient
ens; et auoient leuee
la baniere au duc four

les dont il yauoit plente.
Li dus metoit afoce fes
gens es tours a tous les.
our fe hastoit d'auoir

Baudium de tour. Gal
fes de wars. Galfes de broers
Thomas de la fere. Guiars de

performed, to keep things going and to cement the good relations between the Beyond and ourselves. Within the total loosely bound system there were alternative mysteries which pious folk might wish to take part in. Those which did not respect the emperor were subversive and deserving of persecution. The central gods of Rome were meanwhile being integrated with local deities throughout the empire, from Britain to Cyrenaica, and this process helped to bring a sense of solemn loyalty to the far-flung parts of the empire. In its own way it was a satisfactory system, for it functioned to a great extent pluralistically.

Judaism Defines Itself

Several crises assaulted the Jewish tradition. There was the tragic and tormenting sack of the Temple after an unsuccessful revolt against Rome in 70 C.E. There was the later razing of the city of Jerusalem itself and the building of a Roman city there, Aelia Capitolana, in 130 (occasioning the revolt, ending disastrously, of Shimon Bar-Kochba, hailed by the famed Rabbi Akiba as *Mashiah*). There was also the problem posed by the growing Christian movement, getting farther and farther as Jews saw it from the orthodox scriptural tradition. When Christian ideals triumphed and Judaism found itself having to adjust to the new reality, it had somehow to define itself.

Already Judaism had been preparing itself. Notable sages such as Hillel and Shammai (first century B.C.) were seen as leaders of the community, and were prized for their legal learning. After the destruction of the Temple and the development of Judaism side by side with Christianity, the role of the rabbi or teacher became preeminent. The worship of the synagogue had preceded his era, but became much more important following the demise of the sacrificial cult. Also the rabbis kept alive the expectation of a *mashiah* or messiah. We can say that from the fourth century, when classical Christianity took its Roman and Greek forms, we see the formation too of Judaism as the religion which is still recognizable today. The long series of experiences leading through Israelite religion, its restoration by Ezra, the confusions of the Greek period, and the need to face up to the destruction of the heart of the ritual cult, now

Among Christians cremation was replaced by burial awaiting resurrection. The carving on the mid-fourth-century sarcophagus depicts Jesus' passion in the form of a Roman triumph, with a laurel wreath being offered (left) in place of a crown of thorns. In the center depicted by the symbols for Chi Rho, are the first letters of the name Christos in Greek. Museo Pio Cristiano, Vatican Museums, Rome.

Opposite The ethical dimension: it was considered a duty to fight to regain the holy places of the faith from the infidel Muslims. This depiction of the taking of Jerusalem in 1099 during the First Crusade was included in a French, mid-fourteenth century edition of William of Tyre's *History*.

culminated in a fully formed Judaism. Like twins, Christianity and Judaism grew up together. It was not of course destined to be a happy relationship. The two religions differed markedly on how they saw the Hebrew Bible, and on most other things.

During the first centuries C.E. the position of rabbis in Jewish life was greatly strengthened: these were men of power and knowledge, charismatic leaders, but above all experts in the Torah. The reason for their prominence had in part to do with the fall of the Temple. There were to be no more sacrifices to God. The glories of the renovated building were gone, and Jerusalem itself was devastated. The religious Jews who wished to perpetuate tradition had to find it in records: in books. Study came to replace sacrifice as the most central Jewish ritual, for it was by intensive study of the Torah that the whole of the rest of the ritual life of the Torah-following Jew was defined. Once life had been easier: you could go to Jerusalem. Also, the Jewish religion of the period was already heavily oriented toward the synagogue, and there scripture was preserved.

Christians could take what to Jews was an unkind line: Jesus had foreseen the destruction of the Temple. Jews had been disobedient because they had rejected the Messiah, and indeed had been caught up in the killing of him. A powerful anti-Jewish myth was brewing up in the mind of the Church. Also, Christianity was built on the assumption that the new king had already come. A new age had dawned; there was no great significance left in the Temple. So somehow Jews, by contrast, had to defend their Temple though it was gone. It was preserved in the memory of people, and the study of the rules and meaning of sacrifice became a substitute for sacrifice itself in the literal sense. There are, by the way, analogies here to the Upanishads, when sages asked for the meaning of the sacrifice and found it in an inner quest.

In certain respects the triumph of the new Judaism, in which the daily life of the Jew was in accord with the rules as minutely analyzed and interpreted for the changed conditions, was a victory for the Pharisee party. They already had begun to apply laws of purity, essentially devised for priests, to the community as a whole. It was also a victory for the notion of the dual Torah. There was the written Torah, the first part of the Hebrew Bible, but there was also the oral Torah, which flowed from Sinai (said the rabbis of the new age). This oral Torah, by an irony, became written down, as the Mishnah and its commentary the Tosefta. This collection already existed by about 200 C.E. The two versions of the Talmud—the Jerusalem or Yerushalmi and the Babylonian or Bavli—represent an extensive commentary upon these materials. The Babylonian Talmud was of course based on long experience in exile, in a foreign land, so authoritative expression could there be given to the oral Torah.

The development of a great mass of rabbinic interpretations in effect made rabbis the carriers on of revelation for the community. It brought them a central position, and learning became a central ideal of the Jewish way of life. So what we have emerging is a religion which is based, not just on the

Hillel

Hillel (flourished about 40 B.C.E.) was a rabbinic leader of the period of the Second Temple. He was held in great affection and came to be treated as leader of the community. This was despite the fact that he came from Babylon and was sometimes treated with hostility as a foreigner. He migrated to Palestine after being educated in Babylon, so that he could study in Jerusalem. He acquired a considerable reputation, and together with his colleague and rival, Shammai, founded a school of legal interpretation. He represented the growing status and centrality of the rabbi as a figure in Judaism, which was then beginning to take on the form which is familiar to us today, where the synagogue and the oral Torah and its interpretation became dominant (perhaps after the destruction of the Temple in 70 C.E.).

Hillel was softer in his rulings. He defended the poor: one of his typical rulings provided an ingenious way of ensuring that those in need could get a loan during a sabbatical year (when normal rules are suspended). Hillel's position was egalitarian: even ordinary folk should have the opportunity to study. Indeed study was becoming a mode of worshiping God.

He was elected patriarch of the community in Palestine, and his successors likewise till the fifth century C.E. He was regarded as not merely learned, but as a paragon of patience and humility. His brief definition of Judaism was: "What you find hateful, do not do to others; the rest is commentary." But of course that commentarial expertise and insight was vital, and Hillel represents an ideal, of the person who is a sage, but a sage dependent on Torah, of active engagement with God's message as derived from Sinai.

Hebrew Bible, but on the two legs of the written and oral Torah. It laid much responsibility on those with learning; and it centered on communities united in synagogue worship. The Jewish family unit was basic, and it was there that some of the most vital of ritual activities were performed in the unfolding cycle of Jewish feasts through the year, which enlivened and enriched the daily performance of all those duties related to ordinary living which the Law prescribed.

All this was very different from the interpretation of life in the Christian community. Christians had no oral Torah. In many ways, for them the Torah was abrogated. The Messiah had already come. The Jewish adherence to ritual observances and rules of purity from a bygone age seemed like perversity. For the Christian the right interpretation of the Bible was obvious, and those who did not see it were willful. Thus was born an unfortunate epistemology which was to fuel later anti-Semitism.

The End of Graeco-Roman Religion

Naturally the victory of Christianity was not absolute and immediate with the favor of Constantine and the subsequent Council in 325 C.E. Yet it was in many ways very rapid. In 391 the emperor Theodosius ordered the end of pagan sacrifices. In 399 the destruction or in some cases conversion of pagan sanctuaries was effected. Though the philosophical religions might hang on, they too were taken up into the emerging doctrinal synthesis achieved by the heirs of the Greek and Roman world, men such as St. Augustine (354–430) and the Eastern Fathers.

The result was a blend of two ways of life, for Christianity did weave into its fabric many of the values of the Hellenistic world and the Roman empire. It was thus able to transmit across a rather chaotic period, from the fourth century onward, a whole complex of Graeco-Roman values which were not entirely buried by Christian orthodoxy. But the Churches did get rather preoccupied henceforth with right doctrine. Christians saw themselves as the true believers, but Judaism had never put that much stress on belief *per se*.

Classical and Medieval Christianity and Judaism

CHAPTER 11

The Trinity Doctrine

The Council of Nicaea was summoned by the emperor Constantine, as we have seen. It was the culmination of a process in which the Christians had been increasingly defining themselves in terms of what they believed. Doctrinal orthodoxy was important to establish from an imperial point of view, given that the faith was destined to become the ideology of the imperial state; but why was it so important too for the Christian leadership? In part at least the reason was that Christianity was not like Judaism, a mainly ethnic religion in the sense that you became a Jew by being born into the tradition. Yet it defined itself as a new Israel. How was that Israel to be defined in practice? To a greater and greater extent the definition had to be by belief.

Already in the years leading up to its dramatic success, in the hard days of martyrdom and underground proselytization, the Christian community had had to fight off reinterpretations of its message which were considered to be dangerously wrong. It had fought off in particular various Gnostic groups who had often, in their pessimism about the world and the flesh, seen Yahweh the Creator God of the Old Testament as being evil. Christians had insisted on the underlying goodness of the world despite the Fall of the primordial human beings, Adam and Eve. The Christians had had, too, to react to the synthesis offered by the Manichaeans, who saw the teachings of Jesus, the Buddha, and Zarathustra as converging in the worldview of Mani.

Also Christians had—while respecting Greek philosophy—resisted the seductions of Graeco-Roman paganism: they drew a line between Jewish or Christian stories and pagan ones. The latter were just stories, while Christian narratives, based on real facts, were indeed historical. It was from this negative

The doctrinal dimension: at councils, such as the Council of Nicaea in 324, the more abstract doctrinal formulae of Christian orthodoxy were formulated and affirmed. Here, under the supervision of Constantine and Pope Sylvester, the heretical books of Arius, Victorinus and others are consigned to the flames. The clothing and other details are anachronistic and belong to the sixteenth century C.E.

appraisal of myth that the modern colloquial sense of myth being a false story has come.

Christians had already debated some of the issues concerning the relation between their faith and the glittering culture in which they found themselves, and through which they were making their way. The Latin-writing "Father" (a title Christians gave later to the most vital theological figures of the period), Tertullian (160?–?225) belonged to the literary circles of Carthage in North Africa, and used his literary and rhetorical training through many influential writings. But he was very rigorous in drawing the line between pagan ideas and practices and Christian ones. He is credited with the famous question, "What has Athens to do with Jerusalem?" Yet ultimately it was the synthesizers who won out. It became, if not necessary, at least helpful, to define some of the central doctrines of the community through Greek philosophical terminology. This essentially is what happened at Nicaea in regard to that most characteristic and yet also baffling teaching of Christianity, the Trinity doctrine.

Constantine in particular was worried by a serious rift in the Christian Church over the status of Christ. There was a group under the leadership of a priest called Arius (250?–?336), of Alexandria in Egypt, which made Christ noneternal, being himself created by God; but on him the Father bestowed divinity. The slogan of the movement was "There was [a time] when he was not." Part of its motivation lay in the desire to preserve monotheism more clearly.

The Christian faith had found itself in a strange position in regard to Jesus. From both the practical and the theoretical point of view it wanted to affirm the divinity of Christ; but it was, after all, a movement which had come out of the Jewish tradition. It had suffered persecution because of its unwillingness to compromise with pagan polytheism. It was firmly committed to belief in one God.

From the practical angle, it was involved in a central ritual, the Eucharist, which involved the worship of Christ. It was blasphemous to worship anyone

Christianity some key terms

Atonement At-one-ment, that is, the bringing together of humankind and God through the death and resurrection of Christ.

Baptism The sacrament of immersion in water, or being sprinkled with water, whereby a person is initiated into the Christian Church.

Bible The collection of books which are treated by Christians as the record of God's revelation.

Christ The anointed one or Messiah who is the agent of salvation.

Church The community of Christians on earth and in heaven.

Communion Known also as the Eucharist in Anglicanism, the Mass in Roman Catholicism, and the Liturgy in Eastern Orthodoxy: the primary sacrament of sharing Christ's life by partaking of the bread and wine as his body and blood.

Grace The power of God entering into humans to empower them to good deeds and salvation.

Ikon A picture used in Orthodoxy as a window on heaven, and an object of devotion to the faithful.

Love Greek *agapē*, the reverential affection for other human beings which is the primary Christian virtue.

Sin The estrangement of humans from God, thought to be due to the actions of Adam and Eve in the first instance.

Theosis Process of becoming divinized or like God: the goal of Eastern Orthodox spiritual effort.

Trinity God as Three in One, as Father, Son, and Holy Spirit: being three persons or centers of consciousness in one being.

Map 9 Western Europe showing some of the key places of the early Middle Ages.

except God; so Christ must be God. This was the practical part of their affirmation of Jesus' divinity. But theoretically too they needed the idea. Christ died for our sins, in a state of solidarity with humanity, with human beings. He expiated our sins. So he must be one of us. But as Savior he must be divine, because it was blasphemous to hold that anyone but God could put away sins. So from the perspective of the doctrine of salvation, too, Christ had to be divine, though human at the same time. All this generated the search for formulae which would deal with these problems: a formula which would make it plain that the Christian was not committed to worshiping two or more gods, but only one God; and a formula which would make sense of the two natures (divine and human) of the selfsame person. The threefold-ness, by the way, of God was arrived at since the Spirit of God which guided the Church from within was also regarded as divine; so any formula that applied to Christ should also apply to the Holy Spirit.

These issues came to be debated at various Ecumenical (or all-Church) Councils, of which seven are recognized usually as canonical Councils, stretching from Nicaea in 325 to Constantinople in the ninth century C.E. The resulting formulations did not always work, for they occasioned splits in the Church often enough, and led sometimes to mutual charges of heresy. The history of doctrinal definition has not been a very happy one; and yet the Christians felt themselves impelled toward it as a means of saying what the New Israel was.

The eventual outcome of Nicaea was a highly important pronouncement on the nature of the Trinity. In Greek terms it was declared to consist in three *hupostaseis* in one *ousia* or three entities in one being. In the Latin somewhat different language was used, with a rather different effect. God was said to be *tres personae in una substantia* or three persons in one substance. These became classical ways of defining the Trinity, and constituted the achievement of St. Athanasius (296?–373). But Arianism, though banished from orthodoxy, continued and made great inroads in the conversion of Northern Europe in subsequent centuries.

Roman Versus Greek Forms of the Faith

The decision to divide the Empire in the sense of having two capitals, one located in Byzantium or Constantinople and the other in Rome, reinforced the cultural divisions within Christianity. The ritual of the Eastern Church became more complex as it took over some of the features of Byzantine court ritual. There was especially in the East the veneration of paintings of Christ and the saints—the holy ikons. The style of churches which was gradually evolved took on a domed appearance, with the interior of the dome representing heaven. The mysteries of the Liturgy or Eucharist took on a heavenly aspect.

Affecting both East and West was the evolution of the monastic life. It was especially attractive to Christians to have an alternative way of life in celibacy and austerity, when the Church, because of its political success, was encountering the corruptions which were attendant on that. The Church took the line that a priest's efficacy in conducting a Eucharistic service is not impaired by his personal unworthiness; but there was also recognition that there needed to be new outlets for the heroic ideals which had carried the Church forward. These were to some degree fulfilled in the monastic movement. The great symbolic figure in the Christian imagination was the legendary St. Antony of Egypt, close associate of St. Athanasius. He wrestled with temptations in the desert and helped found a group of hermits whose way of life later, through rules developed by St. John Cassian (360?–435) and others, formed the basis of monasticism both in the East and in the West. Henceforth until the Reformation nuns and monks were an integral and vital part of the organization of all Christianity and nurtured within their establishments both the practice of meditation (and the pursuance of mysticism) and the main elements of study and scholarship.

Northern Europe and the East-West Split

The drifting apart of the two main wings of the Church was assisted by the differing political fates of the two parts of the empire. The East was stabilized around the Byzantine monarchy. This empire might make concessions to the Huns along the Danube and the like, but basically it was not till the coming of the Muslims in the seventh century that it really lost great tracts of territory, and even there it retained its heartlands. On the other hand the West was badly overrun by barbarian peoples from the latter part of the fourth century onward. The Goths had been mainly converted to Christianity before they broke into the imperial domains, but it was an Arian form of Christianity that had been preached by the great missionary Ulfilas. The destiny of Northern Christianity was in part determined by the baptism in 496 of Clovis, king of the Franks, who helped tame the Goths on behalf of orthodox Roman Christianity. It was to deal with the Arian heresy that the Western Church, at a Council at Toledo in Spain, inserted the clause *filioque* into the Creed. The implications of this we shall return to. Meanwhile the alliance between the Franks and the Church led to the ultimate foundation of the so-called Holy Roman Empire with the coronation of Charlemagne as emperor in 800 C.E. The bases of medieval Christianity, with its North-South axis in the West, were being laid.

The question of the small clause, *Filioque*, meaning "And from the Son," was more serious than at first sight might appear, and for two reasons. The purport of the insertion was that the Holy Spirit proceeded from the Father and *from the Son*. According to Orthodox theologians in the East this upsets the balance of the Trinity, which according to them consists in a perfect unity of Persons in which the Father eternally generates the Son and from whom the Holy Spirit eternally proceeds. The Father so to speak enhances a balanced unity. But secondly, and worse from the point of view of the Greeks, the formula was added by the West without consultation with the East and was indeed the usurpation of authority by the Bishop of Rome, that is to say, the Pope. He was arrogating to himself a role in the formation of new doctrines. Only a Council recognized by the whole Church could do this. These questions, first of doctrine and secondly of the authority of the Pope, have plagued relations between the two great wings of the Church ever since. They helped to confirm the mode in which these parts of Christendom were drifting apart.

As both parts were projected forward into the medieval world, the one as spiritual heir of an empire that effectively had broken up, and the other as the official religion of an empire which was also subjected to increasing external pressures, they differed somewhat in doctrine, organization, and practice, and we can see something of these divergences by looking at the dimensions of the religions.

The Dimensions of Christianity East and West

First, let us look at the *organizational* dimension of the two. In the West we have a gradually more centralized organization under the Bishop of Rome, the Pope. But it was a monarchy of a spiritual or religious nature, and the increasingly fragmented nature of Western Christendom maybe made it the more imperative that Rome should be seen as an authoritative center. In the East, so long as the empire lasted, there was a form of what came to be called "Caesaropapism," where the emperor considered himself one with the apostles and played an active role in the determination of Christian doctrine and discipline. In fact, however, the Patriarch of Constantinople and the other leading bishops of the Eastern Church often stood out against the emperor: so it was a dual system of rule by the secular and religious heads. But obviously the power of the emperor was great, and some emperors played a vital role in controversies, such as the debate about ikons. But from the seventh century great regions of Eastern Christianity came under Muslim rule, and in such conditions the Christians were considered a separate community and administered through the leading bishop or patriarch of each area, which gave the Church a limited secular function.

In the West the priesthood came to be secular; but in the East an ingenious relationship between monasticism and parish clergy was worked out. If, after training, a priest did not marry, he became a monk. It was from the ranks of the monks that bishops were elected.

As for the *material* dimension of the faith, the early Church had used decorations, for instance in the catacombs. With the coming of official recognition worship moved out of houses and villas which were used or donated for worship. Pagan shrines were suppressed, and their sites or buildings taken over. The basilica form became dominant in the West. This was originally a long building with high windows and aisles which was used for secular purposes. Now it was used religiously, with the end portion being screened off and used for the altar and the seating of the clergy, the central part for the faithful, and the forecourt for postulants (those who wanted to become Christians). Those who were undergoing instruction had to withdraw from the nave to the forecourt or the aisles during the Mass or liturgy proper. The Eastern tradition favored the domelike structure whether on the base of a Greek cross or on a longitudinal base in the manner of the basilica, as in the famous Hagia Sophia in Constantinople built under Justinian in the sixth century. Its great domes and vaults were covered with gold mosaic; its columns gleamed with polished marble and porphyry. It exuded golden light from within, seemingly weightless, a glorious example of the Byzantine style.

The tombs of rich Roman Christians had long displayed sculptures, but the East retained a ban on three-dimensional representations, as offending against the commandment forbidding graven images. But the ikon or picture of Christ or Mary or a saint became increasingly popular. It came to be customary to screen the wall between the nave and sanctuary with such holy pictures. But from 723 to 842 the Eastern Church was riven with a swaying struggle over ikons. The iconoclastic (ikon-smashing) party was dominant over much of this period. In the Western Church this notion that there was something heathen and heretical about the use of holy pictures and sculptures did not appear until the sixteenth-century Reformation. The excommunication by the Pope of the Easterners on this score deepened the rift, and had its expression in the crowning of the Frankish King, Charlemagne, as Holy Roman Emperor in Rome in 800, he taking the significant title of Augustus. The ideologies of the Western empire and of Christianity were here fused. In the East the pro-ikon party won in due

The experiential dimension: a sixteenth-century ikon of Christ seeks to combine the majesty of the numinous feeling of the worshiper and the sense of serenity arising in the contemplative life.

263

Augustine

Augustine (354–430) was a major thinker in the Western Church and also an important spiritual leader. He was born and raised in Tagaste and later became bishop of Hippo (both places are in present-day Algeria). His main education was undertaken in Madaurus and Carthage (in present-day Tunisia). His mother, Monica, was a fervent Christian, though his father, Patricius, only converted to Christianity when nearing death. Augustine was, on his own account, profligate as a student. At any rate he had a longstanding affair, and fathered a son Adeodatus ("given from God"). After his studies he returned to Tagaste, where he taught rhetoric.

During these years he had become a Manichaean, and was consequently estranged from his pious mother. But he also became enthusiastic about pursuing philosophy, as a result of reading Cicero. He gradually became disillusioned with the Manichaean faith, though he also found the Bible inferior as literature to philosophy. Eventually he migrated to Rome, and on finding an opening as public orator in Milan, which he obtained, he migrated there, where he came under the influence of Ambrose. The latter's interpretation of the Bible tended to be allegorical and not literal, and this softened and eventually eliminated Augustine's previous harsh criticism of Christian scripture. Ambrose also introduced Augustine to a deep understanding of Plotinus, the well-known mystic and Neoplatonic philosopher. In all this he was drawing closer to the Christian faith.

He was joined in Italy by a group of his family—his mother Monica, his brother, his companion and Adeodatus, cousins and sundry students. Monica's pleadings, Ambrose's philosophical teachings, and his readings in the Bible combined to exert pressure on him. One day, he had a dramatic experience: in the garden he heard a child's voice chanting "Take and read" (*tolle lege* in Latin); he took up the Bible and his eye fell upon a passage from Paul. It said, "Not in reveling and drunkenness, not in lust and wantonness, not in quarrels and rivalries, arm yourselves with the Lord, Jesus Christ." His conversion led to his being baptized by Ambrose at Easter, 387. He decided to return to Africa, but before embarking at Ostia, Monica died.

After a sojourn in Rome, he set forth again for Africa. Eventually in 391 he was consecrated a priest at Hippo (now Annaba in Algeria), where he also became bishop. His writings were numerous and influential, above all his *Confessions*, *On the Trinity*, and *The City of God*. In the first he pioneered a new form of writing, in the second he gave a Neoplatonic view of Christianity's central doctrine, and in the third he sketched a new philosophy of history. In 410 Alaric, the Visigoth leader, sacked Rome—a traumatic event, and it was in response to this that *The City of God* was written. Augustine had founded a monastery and it was after a life of simplicity and celibacy that he died in 430, while Hippo was under siege from the Vandals.

course, and since that time the reverence of ikons has been a central element in Eastern piety: much more important in fact than the corresponding use of pictures in the West.

As for *doctrine*, there were differences in emphasis, though not very great. The dominant theologian of the Western Church, until the medieval period, undoubtedly was St. Augustine of Hippo in North Africa. Converted from Manichaeanism under dramatic circumstances, he was a pioneer of different literary forms—of autobiography in his *Confessions* and of historical interpretation in his *The City of God*. In this latter book he contrasts the City of God with the City of Earth, of which Rome is the prototype. He does not strictly speaking identify the City of God with the Church, but he did come to accept that the earthly power might be used to ensure conformity of doctrine—a license for the state, under the Church's guidance, to persecute heretics. But more importantly, he laid great stress on original sin, the sin of Adam and Eve which was transmitted down the generations. It was God's incarnation, and his gift of grace, that overcame sin and brought salvation.

Augustine attacked the Celtic monk Pelagius (died 418) for affirming human free will. He laid the groundwork for the doctrine of predestination—that the individual from the beginning is chosen by God and predestined to salvation (or alternatively *not* chosen and predetermined to damnation). This somewhat negative emphasis was carried on in the Western Church, which tended to underline Christ's death as an atoning sacrifice for sin, thus putting us right with God. By contrast St. Athanasius emphasized how God became human in Christ so that humans might become divine; and the Eastern Church tended to stress this idea of *theosis* or divinization. These are only diversities of emphasis.

Doctrinally, also, the two sides split, as we have seen, over the *Filioque* clause. Eastern theologians have always stressed the important spiritual message of a correct view of the Trinity, more intensely than their Western colleagues.

As to the *narrative* of the New Testament and beyond, the Western Church put a great emphasis of course on the role of St. Peter, first Bishop of Rome. The commission to Peter by the risen Christ, "Feed my sheep," and other texts, were used to back up the Pope's primacy. Also Rome was seen as center of the world, after Jerusalem. The death of both Peter and Paul in Rome was an important ingredient in the whole story of the faith. But whereas in the West the secular Rome was decadent, in the East it had fused very easily with the Church, and the golden glories of Byzantine art added a new dimension to the Graeco-Roman experience.

Regarding the *ritual* dimension, a vital divergence was in language, since Latin was the Western vehicle of worship (so that later in the Middle Ages, as vernacular languages diverged from the Church's language, a certain alienation was bound to occur). In the East the liturgy was in Greek, and in a number of other languages that, like Greek itself, remained in secular use. More importantly, the atmosphere of the Eucharist in the two traditions began to pull apart, especially with the Eastern use of ikons, and the fact that the main

The institutional dimension: here the decretals of Boniface VIII (reigned 1294–1303), seen in council, signify the increase in papal power, which grew throughout the Middle Ages, until the Reformation.

ritual action was more concealed, since the altar area was thoroughly screened off by the wall holding the ikons, the iconostasis. The light is there behind the screen, and the priests make forays into the congregation, with the Little Entrance bringing the Gospel to be read, and with the Great Entrance bearing the bread and wine. The church is a representation of heaven, and the movement is from God to humans. The Roman churches, which were longer buildings, were more a movement up toward God.

The Western Church came to list seven sacraments as being recognized—the Eucharist, Baptism, Marriage, Confirmation, Absolution, Ordination to the Priesthood, Extreme Unction (for the dying). But the Orthodox had a wider view, including other rites such as blessing the house, burial, blessing water at Epiphany, etc. Both Churches celebrated Good Friday, when Christ died, and Easter, when he rose from the dead. But the Eastern celebrations of Easter are more dramatic, replete with the spreading light of candles in the early hours of Easter Day and the proclamation "Christ is risen."

As to *experience*, both East and West were committed to the monastic ideal, and within that the practice of contemplation and the notion of an inner, mystical union with the divine grew. Later, as we shall see, the Eastern Orthodox experimented with breathing techniques and the like, and the use of the Jesus Prayer, "Lord Jesus Christ have mercy on me a sinner," said in connection with breathing in and out. The importance of numinous visions of God and the Virgin remained in both wings of Christendom. These were expressed in diverse ways in the art of East and West. Especially striking is the deep and overwhelming majesty of the Eastern ikon of Christ Pantokrator or Ruler of All (p. 249).

The *ethical* injunctions of the two Churches were very similar. If anything the Western Church—in part because of St. Augustine—had the gloomier view of sexuality, which was the cause of the transmission of original sin. The increased spread of the ideal of priestly celibacy also had its effects on preaching. Celibacy and virginity were both held up as high ideals, the more so as the other great way of bearing testimony to faith, martyrdom, faded somewhat in the more relaxed days after Christianity became the official religion.

Other Eastern Churches and Eastern Missions

We have so far been concentrating on the Greek Church of the Eastern part of the Roman Empire. But the Church from early days could be said to have an even more Eastern presence. There were the Aramaic-speaking Christians of Jerusalem, dispersed after the destruction of the Temple in 70 C.E. and the subsequent forcible expulsion of the Jews. Their successors were the Syriac Nestorian Church, based initially in Antioch, and spreading outward. It was led by Nestorius (381?–?451), who was identified with the heresy known as Nestorianism, affirming that Christ has two natures, one human and one divine. The Nestorians came to control the diocese of Seleucia-Ctesiphon in Mesopotamia, and through that had an immense missionary activity to China, Central Asia, and India. Syriac Churches were an important part of the Eastern Christian world, even if formally in schism with the Orthodox.

The ritual dimension: an Ethiopian Coptic priest in his vestments.

In Armenia, Christianity became the official religion of the court even before it did in the Roman Empire, in 314 C.E. under Tiridates III. The country had previously been largely Zoroastrian. The Armenian Church, using an Eastern-type liturgy, accepted the first three Councils of the Church, namely those of Nicaea in 325, Constantinople in 381, and Ephesus in 431.

In Egypt and Ethiopia, Coptic Churches became established, so called from the language which they used, being an ancient Egyptian tongue written in a variation of the Greek alphabet. Ethiopia became especially important in later Africa because it symbolized an ancient black kind of Christian faith, important to remember in the colonial era when the dominant structures of Western religion were in the hands of Whites.

Meanwhile, Byzantine Christianity was reaching north toward the peoples of Eastern Europe and Russia. From early days it had made some inroads into what is now Romania; but it was not until the early Middle Ages that the great mission work of St. Cyril and St. Methodius was to be effective. But it is best for us first to see some of the work of the Latin missions which had a bearing on the area of Eastern Europe also.

Outreaches of the Western Church

Probably the most important Church on the fringes of the West was that of the Celts in Britain and in Ireland. The British-born St. Patrick (390?–?460) was kidnapped and enslaved by the Irish in his youth, learned their language, and later returned to Ireland where he had a substantial role in the evangelization of the island. The Romano-British Church also played a part in the Christianization of Southwest Scotland through St. Ninian, who set up a center of study and monasticism in the Wigton peninsula. Later St. Columba from Ireland set up a monastery further north in the island of Iona.

The Celtic Church had a characteristic form of monasticism with monks and nuns together, and held to some customs not shared by the Roman Church, toward which it had some antipathy. But in 664 the Synod of Whitby led to a rapprochement between the Celtic Church and the Roman, dominated in Britain by the Anglo-Saxons who had been converted as a result of the mission of another St. Augustine to Canterbury in 597.

The British Church made its contribution later on to the task of converting the Germans and others in Northern Europe who had mostly lain outside the old Roman Empire. It was crucial for Christianity to move north, for in the seventh century it was hit by an obliterating storm from the south. The followers of Islam conquered the southern part of the Mediterranean and the Near East, thus slicing off a large part of both the Western and Byzantine Empires. They came into Spain and overran most of it and Portugal. Northern Europe was brought in to redress the balance.

The dynamism of Christianity in Britain and the strength of the Franks combined in the missionizing of Germany, most notably by St. Boniface (a native of Devon in the west of England) who worked in central Germany, in Hesse and Thuringia. In 716 he cut down the sacred oak at Geismar, a signal that paganism was being replaced by the Christian faith. In the tenth century two Norwegian kings brought the faith to Norway: Olaf Haraldsson, who became a martyr by dying in battle, and Olaf Tryggvesson, who among other things pressured Iceland into voting for Christianity as its public (although not private) religion in the significant year of 1000 C.E. Poland, Hungary, and Bohemia were also proselytized from the West, as was Croatia.

And so by the eleventh century Europe from Sicily to northern Norway was effectively Christian. In the eastern part of Europe the Orthodox mission was also fairly successful. There were parts of the Baltic still to convert, but the main work was done.

It was sometimes done from the grassroots, by lonely missionaries, and, more importantly, by the planting of monasteries. These could train local vernacular clergy, provide learning, help with agricultural development, and supply a good example of Christian living. Sometimes, however, the acceptance of Christianity came from the top. Kings, emerging stronger in a period of chaos, could use Christianity as an ideology of rule: it supplied learning, which could be used in administration; it possessed a body of law; it was universal in its values; and it could be harnessed to a military worldview, despite the peaceful monks. It could promise greater consistency than the old pagan cults, which it was not afraid to attack, even physically.

Eastern Mission—the Conversion of Russia

The achievements of missionaries out of Byzantium were equally important, and especially those of the brothers St. Cyril (826?–869) and St. Methodius (815?–884). Both were in good positions, the one as professor at the imperial university and the other as a provincial governor. But they withdrew from these occupations and began mission work together, first among the Khazars, who lived northeast of the Black Sea, then in the Balkans. Their most lasting achievements were the devising of an alphabet (the so-called Cyrillic script) for the Slavic languages, and the encouragement of worship in the vernacular languages. Christianity infiltrated into Russia from various directions, and in 988 Vladimir, Prince of Kiev, was baptized. He was married to a sister of the Byzantine emperor, and it was Eastern Christianity that took root in Russia. Again, the Christian religion, losing ground in the south and east of the Byzantine empire, made substantial advances in the north.

So far we have extended the story of Christianity beyond its chief formative period, which was in the fourth and fifth centuries C.E. We have seen it evolve into its main classical forms. We shall later look at it in its greatest premodern period, that is to say, the so-called Middle Ages—both in East and West. This was a time of glory and achievement for a Christian-dominated civilization, faced, however, with a perhaps more glittering culture, that of Islam. Within its fabric it contained—as did Islam—another important faith, also emerging in its classical form in the fourth and fifth centuries C.E.; this was Judaism. We turn to see something of what happened to this religion in the early circumstances of its existence under official Christianity and then Islam.

The New Life of Judaism

In the Roman Empire, before the conversion of Constantine, conversion to Judaism was not uncommon, but by edict Constantine made it punishable by death. Later, Islam made a similar provision regarding both Christians and Jews within the territory of Islam. This was a factor in the consolidation of Jewish identity. Nevertheless the Jewish people lived in remarkably diverse circumstances. There were the Jews in Yemen and in the Khazar Empire, both countries which for relatively short periods became officially Jewish; there was the great community of Babylon, so influential throughout the Jewish world; the Jews of Palestine, Egypt, North Africa; the Sephardic Jews of the Iberian peninsula; the Jews of Italy, France, Britain; the Ashkenazic Jews of Germany and Central Europe; and later those of Eastern Europe. There was no single circumstance of being Jewish. But there remained, even in these divisions, a reasonable amount of communications, facilitated by the fact that Jews played an important role in trade: because of the Christian and Muslim bans on usury, money business was largely left to them.

Amid the disadvantages of being Jewish, there were some bonuses. In Islamic countries there was a reasonable place for the Jewish community, and Jews were able to benefit from the cultural and philosophical achievements of Arabic civilization, through which they had renewed access to the Greek classics. Especially in Spain there was a great period of Jewish culture, culminating in new forms of poetry, such as the *Crown of Royalty*, by Ibn

Gabirol (1021–69), still recited by Sephardic Jews on the eve of Yom Kippur, new commentaries on the Torah, and the like. Yehuda Halevi (1086–1143), as well as writing poems about the love of God and Zion, composed a dialogue and polemic about why the Khazars had chosen Judaism over Christianity and Islam. The greatest philosopher in this creative milieu was undoubtedly Mosheh ibn Maimon, commonly known as Maimonides (1135–1204) who wrote a great commentarial work, the *Mishneh Torah*, and a famous philosophical treatise, *More Nevukim* or "Guide of the Perplexed." In this he employed the method of the negative way in theology—you can say what God is not, but not what he is. Maimonides thought, with Aristotle, that the notion that God created the world is compatible with the everlasting character of the world (a view much disputed by other philosophers). He had great influence among Christian thinkers, including St. Thomas Aquinas. Maimonides also formulated the famous Thirteen Articles or principles of belief which have remained the most used summary of the Jewish creed since that time. They fall into three groups. The first concerns God—his existence, unity, incorporeality, and eternity. The second is about Torah—prophecy's validity, the uniqueness of Mosheh's message, the divine origin of the written and oral Torah, the eternity and changelessness of the law. The third group relates to reward and punishment—the omniscience of God, divine compensation for good and evil, the coming of the Messiah, and the resurrection of the dead.

The Jewish Year

It was during this early medieval period that the practice of the Jewish calendar reached its full form. Judaism had always emphasized the sacredness of certain times. Indeed with the taking away of the Temple and, effectively, of the land of Israel, Jews found their sacredness more in time than space.

The weekly rhythm underlined the holiness of the Shabbat (Sabbath) for practicing Jews. At sundown of a Friday—for Jews consider that the day begins with sunset rather than dawn—the woman of the house lights the special candles and says a prayer over them, and there follows a meal which is made holy by being the Shabbat meal. The day of course lasts till the following sunset, and is the occasion for prayers in the meetinghouses or synagogue. Jewish law prescribes the refraining from work on this day.

As well as the weekly rhythm there is also the yearly rhythm, beginning with the Jewish New Year, Rosh Hashanah, and followed ten days on with Yom Kippur, the Day of Atonement, the most holy day in the year. There is the family festival of Passover, and there are such other originally harvest festivals as Shavu'ot (Weeks) and Sukkot (Booths). In the winter there is Hanukkah, recalling the Maccabees' rededication of the Temple in 164 B.C.E., and there are various other less sacred days. This rhythm of the year helps Jews to reenact the vital points in their history and their relationship to God.

As well as the ritual year there were the 613 commandments which the pious Jew was supposed to observe, and the net of obligations and customs which the rabbis had woven to cast over life as a perpetual reminder of the Jew's special place in the world which God had made. By following the obligations of both written and oral Torah, the Jew not only followed an ethical path but in effect also a religious path. What counted above all was his or her inner realization of the meaning and dedication implied by the outer acts of conformity.

Jewish Mysticism—the Qabbalah

The inner meaning of Jewish piety was no doubt reinforced by the outer problems of the community. The Crusades, beginning with the first in 1095, were occasions for pogroms against the Jews in many parts of Northern Europe. Such anti-Jewish hostility was in most countrysides not far below the surface. Both because they were religious nonconformists in an age when faith was increasingly enforced by a nervous yet powerful Church, and because they were much identified with commerce and lending money, the Jews attracted stereotypes which in turn stimulated oppression. They were expelled from England in 1290 and Spain in 1492, for instance.

It was in Provence and Spain, in the twelfth and thirteenth centuries, that there arose the movement known as the Qabbalah or Tradition, which revived the mystical strand in the Jewish tradition. This had been evident in the so-called Merkavah (Chariot) mysticism of a much earlier time, that of Rabbi Aqiba in the first and second centuries C.E. The "chariot" refers to the chariot of fire in which the prophet Eliyyahu (Elijah) ascended to heaven, and which is used as a symbol of the inner ascent of the mystic to the higher realms of experience.

Doctrinally the Qabbalists saw God as the Ein Sof, the endless, ineffable, somewhat like the Neoplatonic One; but from the Ein Sof there emanate ten powers or entities, referred to as the Sefirot. Symbolically they are arranged in a diagram which represents the human form, like a great person. Different lists use different names, but they are as follows: Crown or Thought; Wisdom; Understanding; Greatness or Mercy; Power or Judgment; Grandeur; Eternity; Splendor; Foundation; Kingdom. These emanations from God are supposed to have played a part in the creation of the world. Most importantly the Qabbalists explored the techniques of meditation and ecstasy, especially Avraham Abulafia (1240–?1291), who may have been influenced by Sufism or Islamic mysticism.

One strand in Qabbalistic thought was that human acts can have divine effects. It means that somehow God needs human beings as they in turn need God. This could give Jews a more profound way of looking at the process of keeping the commandments of the Torah: such acts had their reverberations on high.

Maybe such ideas were especially satisfying during a time of increasing oppression in Christian Europe. Eventually the norm in the Middle Ages was for the Jews to be heavily segregated, less so in Eastern Europe and Russia where they could begin to open up new agricultural lands; but especially in

Germany and Central Europe, where existence in the ghetto became the norm.

The Dimensions of Judaism

We can sum up Jewish life by looking at its dimensions in the medieval period. The *ritual* life was much more fully elaborated as a result of the victory, from the fourth and fifth centuries in particular, of the religion of the rabbis. The various injunctions of both written and oral Torah controlled the various acts of daily life, serving as a constant reminder of being God's special people. The ritual dimension was in part enacted in the meetinghouse or synagogue but also very substantially in the home. *Ethically*, Jews were expected to keep to the high standard of the Ten Commandments and other injunctions promulgated by rabbis (for instance in the early Middle Ages an edict from a

---

Judaism some key terms

Hasidim (or *Chasidim*) A movement founded in Eastern Europe (Ukraine and southern Poland) in the late eighteenth century, with an emphasis on mysticism.

Haskalah Nineteenth-century Jewish enlightenment, following on the opening up of Judaism to European thought and culture.

Israel The land which is the focus of Jewish aspiration.

Kabbalah The "received tradition" of Jewish mysticism expressed in such texts as the *Zohar* (thirteenth-century Spain).

Kashrut Jewish dietary requirements, i.e. what is "kosher" or unpolluted, pure.

Mashiah The "Anointed One" or future king who will establish a new age in Israel.

Mitzvah (plural *Mitzvot*) Commandment: there are ten main ones and traditionally 613 in all.

Rabbi A teacher of the traditional Torah, and learned teacher and spiritual counselor of a community.

Shabbat The "rest" day, from Friday sundown to sundown on Saturday.

Talmud A major text of the Jewish tradition, in Aramaic, being in two forms, the Babylonian and Palestinian. The former is in principle binding, as to its legal and ethical or halakhic provisions, on all orthodox Jews.

Torah The teaching or law, handed down in both written and oral form to Moses on Sinai: identified in written form with the first five books of the Hebrew Bible.

Yahweh The chief name of God in Hebrew.

rabbinical court forbade polygamy, being married to more than one woman, even though such a practice was well attested in the Hebrew Bible and had some currency among Jews within the Islamic civilization).

In *doctrine* the insistence on strict monotheism was vital and remained so: but Jews retained a different view of revelation from the surrounding Christian culture. They looked forward to the coming of the *Mashiaḥ*, and their whole myth of history was different from that of Christians, for whom the Anointed One had already come. The sufferings of the Jewish people were still a necessary continuation of the special dedication of this community to God. The surrounding Christian culture did not take kindly to this *myth* of history: they thought that Jews were frustratingly willful in their refusal to see the true meaning of the Old Testament (which of course they did not even see as an *Old* Testament). The vast interpretations of the Talmud and the whole idea of Oral Torah were still understood by Christians.

Experientially the Jews appreciated the experiences of light and fellowship in the round of the calendar year and the rhythms of the Shabbat. They also explored the whole experience of the mystical union with the Divine, through Qabbalistic techniques. *Organizationally* they were able to retain some cohesion between parts of the Jewish world through travel in pursuit of trade. Rabbinical courts were not uniform in judgment, but the vast accumulation of interpretation of the Law gave a structural resemblance between diverse parts of Judaism. In the Islamic world there was greater opening to the lovely civilization about them, which gave them some room for maneuver. Christendom glittered less and was more oppressive, so that Ashkenazim (German and North European Jews) were more driven in on themselves and so more conservative and withdrawn than the Sephardim (Jews of Spain and Portugal) and other "southern" Jews.

The ritual and the narrative dimensions: the Western or "Wailing" Wall of the Temple destroyed in 70 C.E. is the most sacred spot for Jews; praying there unites them with their ancient sufferings and dedication to God. The above scene was taken in 1867.

An Hasidic Jew pictured in Jerusalem: his face reflects the desire to experience God, but through obedience to the Torah, which has a cosmic significance and provides the outer discipline for the inner quest.

Artistically, the chief places for ornamentation and the use of material forces for religious purposes lay in the decoration of synagogues and religious manuscripts. Early synagogues contained various mosaics, depicting the Ark of the Covenant; the *menorah* or seven-branched candlestick; branches of palm trees and lemons; even signs of the zodiac. The Ark containing the scrolls of the Torah was the chief liturgical focus in the Synagogue, and the containing material came to be increasingly decorated. In early synagogue buildings there seems to have been no special place for the women, but later they came to be segregated in galleries.

As Judaism entered the Middle Ages it had to live with what appeared to be a more and more monolithic Christianity in the West. It existed among Eastern Christians also; but much of its life was passed within the Islamic world. Yet any security that they had there was threatened by reconquest. The position of the Jews in Spain became problematic as the Catholics slowly drove the Muslims from the peninsula, during the centuries up to 1492, when they were finally eliminated; and that was the signal too for the expulsion of the Jews.

Medieval Christianity

Eastern Christianity: Outer Retreat, Inner Advance

The Seljuk Turks took Jerusalem in 1071, and this heralded disturbing times for the Byzantine empire. Their advance into Asia Minor was marked by the capture of the emperor in the same year, and soon they were at the walls of

Constantinople. Their victory at Manzikert, when the emperor was taken, was a decisive affair in European history. Henceforth Asia Minor or Anatolia would become the heartland of the Turks, and the boundary between Islamic East and Christian West would lie culturally between that region and the Greek islands. Constantinople held out.

The Turks also triggered the new movements known as the Crusades. The holy places of Palestine were now closed to Christian pilgrims; so the Papacy instigated the Crusades in 1095. The First was quite successful: Jerusalem was taken and remained in Christian hands for nearly a hundred years. But the

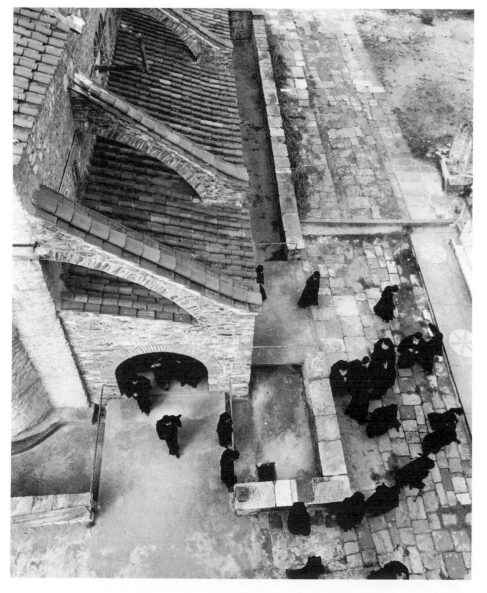

The material dimension: monks gather at the Protaton, Karyes, which is supposed to be the oldest church in the monastic republic of Mount Athos in Greece. It is said to be a tenth-century replica of an original built by Constantine.

Gregory Palamas

Gregory Palamas (1296–1359) was a mystic and theologian of the Orthodox faith—probably indeed the greatest during the whole medieval period. He was only seven when his father died, but he stayed on at the imperial court in Constantinople. He was deeply educated in philosophy and Christian theology and was gradually drawn into a life of asceticism and contemplation. When he was twenty he left for Mount Athos, and at his first monastery there he was instructed by a Hesychast (and was adept therefore at breathing techniques which were part of this spiritual tradition). He moved on to the great monastery of Lavra, and then to a hermitage, that of Glossia. But the threat of a Turkish invasion led him to leave Mount Athos, and he became a priest, and lived outside the city of Thessaloniki at a hermitage. But in 1331 Serbian incursions sent him back to Athos.

There he engaged in debates with various opponents, notably one Barlaam, a South Italian Greek, who attacked the Hesychasts as *omphalopsychoi* ("those with their souls in their navels"). In response Palamas composed *Triads in Defence of the Holy Hesychasts*. In this he was backed by the Church. However, the death of the emperor at this point led to confusion. Palamas was imprisoned, because of the hostility of the Patriarch. But later a Hesychast was appointed to the patriarchal throne, and Palamas was made bishop of Thessaloniki. In 1354 he was, however, captured by the Turks while traveling to Constantinople and only released a year later. He died in 1359. Though God, according to his theology, is in his essence unknowable, through his uncreated energy or grace he can be discerned. And if a person practices Hesychasm he can be united with this uncreated light. Thus he is made divine (a process known as *theosis*—divinization). This was the interpretation of the Orthodox teaching that God became man so man could become divine.

Fourth Crusade was diverted, and Constantinople was sacked. A Latin kingdom was set up there; this trauma undoubtedly weakened a restored Byzantium. A new empire, that of the Ottomans, out of Anatolia, threatened the empire and made its way deep into the Balkans. So in many ways the Greek East was on the defensive during the medieval period. The ultimate fall of Constantinople in 1453 signaled a new great captivity for the Greeks, and the center of Eastern Orthodox power shifted to Moscow, perceived now as a Third Rome, the other two (Rome itself and Constantinople) having failed in their destinies.

But during this troubled period some remarkable developments took place in Eastern piety. Monasticism was renewed, especially on Mount Athos in northern Greece, which became in 1052 a kind of self-governing monastic republic, concentrating on the male celibate life of contemplation and the performance of the liturgy. One of its inhabitants for a time was St. Gregory of Sinai, a famous mystic, who had so strong a bent for the solitary life that he had judged the liturgy irrelevant, and had had to leave Sinai for a wandering life. He settled in Bulgaria, where he became the prototype of the later Russian *starets* or wandering holy man. More orthodox in his mysticism, and perhaps the greatest Eastern Orthodox theologian, was St. Gregory Palamas (1296–1359). Highly educated at the court in Constantinople, he became an ascetic at the age of twenty, residing on Mount Athos for a while, practicing the methods known as Hesychasm (literally Quietism). Here the adept used physical means, including control of the breathing, in order to gain higher states of consciousness, culminating in a vision of the divine light. One fierce critic castigated the Hesychasts as being *omphalopsychoi*—people with their souls in their navels. Gregory argued that though God in himself is inaccessible and indescribable, he possesses uncreated energies: the human being can participate in the light which was displayed on Mount Tabor at the transfiguration of Christ. This uncreated light appears within the human being, and can be perceived if the human being can concentrate his intellect or *nous*, which is usually distracted, since the Fall, by the things of this world. The training in Hesychasm in effect is a method for ascending to the light within.

Monks painting ikons at Mount Athos, Greece. These are mostly replicas of Byzantine originals. The ikons serve as "windows on heaven," of which the most glorious was Christ himself.

In attaining to God's uncreated light the human in effect becomes a god: he undergoes *theosis* (a great theme in the Orthodox tradition which we saw being expressed in the fourth century by St. Athanasius). St. Gregory Palamas, in setting forth this scheme of salvation, repeated and summed up some of the central motifs of the Orthodox tradition, while his defence of Hesychasm ensured the important place of the contemplative quest in the life of the Church.

Although the Church had to experience the rule of the Ottomans throughout Greece and the Balkans, from the fall of Constantinople in 1453, its renewed vigor in the preceding period made possible its survival. Also the religion was making headway in Russia, and the ideal of the Third Rome helped to give Russian Orthodoxy a messianic flavor.

Western Medieval Culture—a New Civilization

In the West the Middle Ages saw the creation of a relatively homogenous civilization, with its center of gravity in Northern Europe, where great monastic foundations had helped with the spread of agriculture and the creation of new wealth. Monastic reform, indeed, was one of the main bases of the medieval culture. Thus the Abbey of Cluny, founded in Burgundy in 910, provided a leading powerhouse of influence and reform. Under Abbot Hugh in the eleventh century, it underwent great expansion, and established many daughter houses. Many of these were well endowed, as rich lay folk saw a division of labor in society and paid the monks to pray intensely on their behalf. The monastery of Cîteaux, also in Burgundy, took reform further, and simplified the monks' life, going back to the rule of St. Benedict; and it too had enormous outreach. It was founded at the end of the eleventh century and fifty years later had over three hundred daughter houses, partly because of the effective preaching of St. Bernard of Clairvaux (1115–53). There was also reform among the nonmonastic clergy, especially through the Augustinian canons, who lived together in dormitories and thought of themselves as reviving the ideals for the clergy voiced by St. Augustine of Hippo. The hierarchical character of the Church was reinforced by the increase in bureaucratization and legalism at the Papal court, modeled after a lay court. The greater pretensions of the Papacy led to a bitter struggle between secular and ecclesiastical authorities, with the Church beginning to gain the status of a parallel power-system.

Two new orders in particular were to have profound influence. First, there were the Dominicans who were brought into being by St. Dominic (1170–1221), who wanted to create a band of preachers who would live the good life of poverty. Initially he had in mind the conversion of the so-called Albigensian heretics in the South of France. But his order had a wider role in education, and then in the exercise of the Inquisition. Second, the Franciscans, created by St. Francis of Assisi (1181/2–1226), whose strict ideal of poverty later caused some dissension among his own followers, were an influence on ordinary people through their preaching and hearing confessions in the context of a modest way of life very different from that of the princes of the Church.

The Middle Ages also saw a new mobilization of the ideals of knighthood on behalf of the Church. The Crusades created a new channel for the energy of often violent and turbulent princes and warriors. The Orders of militant monks, above all the Templars and the Teutonic Knights, who pushed the bounds of Christendom northeastward along the Baltic coast, captured some of the ascetic values of Christianity on behalf of military action: very much on the assumption that battling on behalf of Christendom was a way of fulfilling the Gospel.

It was also an age of revived learning. Through the Arabic translations and then the Latin translations of Arabic, scholars had some access to Aristotle and other Greek writers. They proved to be a stimulus to new reflections, and above all to the synthesis achieved by the Dominican St. Thomas Aquinas (1224–74), whose many and magisterial writings, especially his *Summa Theologiae* and *Summa contra Gentiles*, left a lasting stamp on Catholic thought.

Hildegard of Bingen

Hildegard (1098–1179), possibly the greatest woman operative in the medieval Church, was a mystic, nun, writer, musician, artist, and preacher. She also insistently affirmed the equality of men and women in the service of God. She was the tenth child of an aristocratic family, dedicated by her parents to God, and sent to an anchoress, Jutta, for her upbringing. From early childhood she had visions of what she called the reflection of the living Light. The hermitage where she was taught (mainly to read Latin) became a convent adhering to the Benedictine rule; when Jutta died, Hildegard was elected her successor in 1136. She received a call to write and began to compose *Scivias* ("Know the ways"), her greatest work. Meanwhile she was becoming a celebrity, and the convent, St. Disibod, was flooded with postulants. One reason for her fame was that she wrote to Bernard of Clairvaux, who authorized her visions; and partly because the Archbishop of Mainz had heard of them and of her *Scivias*. While at a synod at Trier over which he presided, the Pope sent legates to fetch a copy and read from it to the synod, which was much impressed. Hildegard, in view of the numbers wishing to join St. Disibod, decided to set up a new community on the other side of the Rhine at Rupertsberg. After a struggle, she won against the reluctant monks and in 1150 she moved. In 1165 she founded a daughter house at Eibingen. She entered into a widespread correspondence with popes, emperors, prelates, abbesses, abbots, nuns, monks, and lay people. She preached in various parts of Germany, including Trier and Cologne, and in Lorraine. After *Scivias* she wrote a kind of medical encyclopedia. She also wrote fairly extensive church music, and paintings which illustrated her works. Her last years were marred by controversy over the alleged burial of a heretic in the Rupertsberg churchyard, and over her music. She was strong-minded, though frail in body, and responded vigorously. Sixth months after the lifting of the ban on her community, she died.

Aquinas' whole system was based on a distinction between what can be known naturally by reason and what has to be derived by revelation from God. The former domain is extensive, for by Five Ways, as they were called, that is five main arguments, you could establish the existence of God. God also, by these proofs, was good, intelligent, incorporeal, and so on. So a pretty large edifice of philosophy was built by Aquinas on this essentially intellectual foundation. Supplemented by revelation, it provided a great system of ideas which defined the mental basis of the Christian life. Much of his work looked to Aristotle, but Aquinas made use of many other sources, such as St. Augustine and the writings attributed to Dionysius the Areopagite, the convert of St. Paul.

The distinction thus established between reason and faith gave a definite role to the philosopher, as governed hopefully by reason, in the illumination of the Christian faith. At first Aquinas' dependence on Aristotle, then not popular, made the authorities suspicious of his doctrines, but their rigor and clarity gave them great power in later thinking.

Popular piety was far removed from such speculations: it concentrated on relics, on hearing the Mass, on pilgrimage. Holy journeys to Canterbury, Rome, Compostela, and Jerusalem created much merit for the faithful and wiped away many sins. The whole system of Crusades also was a kind of pilgrimage: great enthusiasm was generated in a newly selfconscious Christendom ready to flex its muscles against the infidel. Alas, that included the infidel

The ritual dimension: Canterbury, in southern England, was a major pilgrimage center in the Middle Ages after the archbishop, Thomas Becket (1118–70), was murdered there. The pilgrimages were the inspiration for Geoffrey Chaucer's masterpiece, *The Canterbury Tales* (begun 1387). This scene depicts a group from London arriving at the cathedral.

at home: Jews and heretics were often persecuted. Thus, in the thirteenth century a full-scale Crusade was undertaken in southern France against the Albigensian heresy—so called after the city of Albi, a main center—which professed a kind of Manichaean doctrine, affirming the world evil and the Church corrupt. In 1233 the Dominicans were charged with the job of rooting out the heresy. Much cruelty was involved in putting down the movement, which had a threatening effect on the Church, partly because the ethical standards of the *perfecti*, or those committed to the higher life of Albigensian religion, were notably higher than those of many of the contemporary clergy.

Also important in medieval Christianity was a flowering of mysticism. In some ways the most powerful figure was that of Johannes Eckhart (1260?–?1327), whose philosophical account of the inner experience of God was daring and exciting. For him the creature gets his very being from God: God indeed is the only being, truly speaking. The mystical life consists then in striving to be conscious of the divine being within oneself. This chimes with what Bernard of Clairvaux had said—that to reduce yourself to nothing is a divine experience. But Eckhart's theology met opposition, and some of the propositions he affirmed were condemned.

A more personalistic way of expressing the ultimate experience of union with the divine was adopted by the Flemish priest Jan van Ruusbroec (1293–1381): "In this darkness … is born an incomprehensible light, which is the Son of God …" It was also an age of women mystics of great power, above all St. Catherine of Siena (1347–80), who saw God's being as consisting in truth and love, through which he reaches out to the human beings who have cut themselves off from him by the Fall.

There were tensions in this civilization, however, heralding the split which followed from the Reformation. There was the gap between the growing vernacular languages and the official Latin of the Church—hence the suspicion with which translations of the Bible were viewed by church officials. There was the persistent question of the supposed poverty of the clergy and its contrast with the magnificence of the Papacy and many of the princes of the Church. There was the cost of many of the huge and wonderful edifices that the Church was building across Europe. There were the political tensions between the kings and princes north of the Alps and the Papacy in Rome. There were the discomforts of ecclesiastical power in many spheres.

But the culture of Western Europe was nevertheless vigorous, as shown by the way it expanded northeast and southwest. The Muslims were being driven back out of Spain. New wealth was being created in Italy. The infidels were at bay in the Mediterranean. New techniques were being pioneered for exploration, and by the fifteenth century Portuguese ships were edging their way around Africa and making landfall in the East. In 1453 the fall of Constantinople brought classical learning flooding into Europe as scholars escaped the Turks.

How should we sum up Western Christendom at this time, during its medieval dominance? It was proud, conformist, increasingly confident against the infidel, complex in doctrine and philosophy, and catering to the masses in the richness of its kinds of piety. Masses, pilgrimages, the condemnation of heretics, beautiful frescoes on church walls, stained glass windows, statues of the saints, illuminated books, vast cathedrals, soaring spires, the pomp of prelates and the vestments of priests, candles, holy water, the veneration of relics, the hope of glory and horror of hell, the time-slices of purgatory, the feast days and fasts, the processions, the preachings of Crusades and other ventures, the lives of saints, the austerities of hermits, the composure of nuns, the great abbeys of monks, the grace of the Virgin, the prayers in Latin, the solemn chants—all these contributed to a mosaic of religious practices which channeled piety toward the sacred Trinity. For the intellectual, credible; for the pious, rich in devotion; for the mystic, deep in theology; for the woman, ideal in the Virgin; for the man, a vigorous and militant faith: the Church was involved in a memorable synthesis.

It was a synthesis which would split—partly because of the Renaissance, partly because of the great voyages and the new colonial ventures, and most of all because of the religious revolution known now as the Reformation.

Worlds that Disappeared

The Celts

The medieval Christian world submerged the paganisms of the north and west and east. The Celtic, Germanic and Slavic religions would become a romantic memory. Yet their spirit somehow lingered on. Let us end our account of medieval Europe by sampling these religions—so far, that is, as we can get at them from our somewhat varied and partly fragmentary sources.

Caesar remarked that the god the Celts worshiped more than anyone was Mercury: he was probably identifying that god with Lugh, who occurs across the Celtic world. He was the young one who vanquished the demons. As a David type, he killed with his slingshot the giant Balar. He was the deity of the harvest who associated with fertility goddesses. Above all he was a symbol of sacred kingship, and presided over the other world. Later he was to merge with one or two Christian saints. In all this we have echoes of other Indo-European ideas.

Likewise with the Druids, supposedly extirpated from Britain by the Roman general Paulinus in 62 C.E. Roman accounts of the Druids are melodramatic, yet there can be little doubt that such a priestly class existed—it was part of the deep structure of Indo-European societies. Their chief function was to preside over the sacrificial life of the people. A record of the twelfth century C.E. from Ulster tells of a horse sacrifice still being performed. The king had to mate with a white mare, and then bathe in the soup made of it, eat some of its meat and lap up some of the broth. There are echoes of the Indian horse-sacrifice here, from the other end of the Indo-European world. The priests had access to sacred knowledge and could exclude a person from the sacrificial cult, thus ostracizing him from society.

As for fertility cults, these no doubt lie behind the legend that St. Patrick drove the snakes from Ireland, serpents being above all symbols of fertility. And eventually no doubt the Irish, like other Celts, could find some solace and substitutions in the new Christian order. Christ, like Lugh, as a young man defeated the hosts of Satan. And Celtic saints could easily reincarnate the goddesses. The Irish goddess of learning, a figure like the Roman Minerva, who delighted in knowledge of nature and the fruits of the earth, and commanded poetry, in effect became St. Brigid of Kildare, whose monastery of Cell Dara was on the site of a holy oak. She and her nuns, according to a later account, guarded a perpetual fire (like Vestal Virgins, no less) surrounded by a hedge, to which no male had access.

Celtic religion was close to the other world, so that there were many points of access: caves, streams, numinous places, sacred trees of varying kinds—oaks, beeches, and holly trees. The Christian world took over many of these sacred spots to build churches, and saints were associated with healing springs and the like. The magic of the Celtic world was transformed for the sober purposes of Christian living, and to win the hearts of those whose poetry was always bubbling to the surface.

The Vikings

The Scandinavian seafarers were remarkably effective, and sometimes destructive, in their foraging into foreign lands to settle. They dominated, the east coast of Ireland and the Isle of Man, southern and western Scotland, England, Normandy, the Baltic coasts, the rivers of Russia, Iceland, and parts of Greenland. Their impact upon monasteries in the Christian West was often severe. But eventually they too succumbed to the seductions of Christian ideology. In this they were helped by some of the figures of the Scandinavian pantheon.

In the great religious center at Uppsala there were images of the three great deities Odin, Thor, and Frey. Odin is the father of all, master magician, knower of great runes (or *mantras* as we might say, looking to India), dealer in law, ruler of the underworld. Thor is lord of the air and thunder, and is a great warrior deity, given to taking great drafts of intoxicating drinks, and so somewhat like Indra. If Odin is master of the priestly power, Thor incarnates the warrior power; while Frey deals in fertility. His mount is a swift boar, which was in this ancient world a fine edible creature. His sister Freya is the most powerful of the female divinities, very promiscuous, who has sex with all the gods, thus giving them vital power.

This quartet is far removed in spirit from the Trinity and the Virgin. But the hero Balder, son of Odin, is of a different cast: young and beautiful, he has nightmares. His mother Frigg makes all things swear never to harm her son, but forgets the mistletoe. One of the gods, blind Loki, throws a branch of it at him; it pierces him, and he dies. He is buried with his grieving and dying wife in a ship. The goddess of the nether world will not release him unless all things weep for him—and they all do, save one giantess. He will not return till after history finishes in the great storm of Ragnarök. This end-of-the-world motif is very vivid, and came to be reinforced in Christian times. It is the twilight of the gods, *Götterdämmerung*.

Some scholars think that the myth of Balder owes something to Christian influence. It may be so; but in the form I have just set forth it is of course thoroughly "paganized," and the new Christian message coming from missionaries would still sound fresh and call forth echoes. But in the dark and stormy world of Germanic myth the atmosphere is very different from the medieval Christian myth, wrapped in its clothing of learning and reason which lay far beyond what counted for knowledge on old runic shores.

Slavic Themes

Again in the Slavic lands we find the dominating force of the Indo-European gods. And yet below them we can also see the lineaments of an ancient pre-Indo-European goddess, who deals in death and fertility, who is both a hag and a virgin, a sign of matrilineal society, a moist Earth Mother, pregnant before the spring. The white god Belobog is ruler of the day and year, and contends against darkness and death. In the Slavic world the bipolar oppositions are powerful: light and dark, day and night, life and death. There is almost a Zoroastrian feel to pre-Christian Slav religion. Among the gods Perun, god of thunder and associated with the oak, was powerful in dispensing justice and in fighting against enemies. And as elsewhere the ancestors were strong to protect folk. When a rich person died he was dressed up in his finery and seated in a boat, to take him to the other shore. His weapons were placed around him. His wife was stabbed and seated beside him, to share in his life beyond life. The boat and all the finery and goods were burnt in a great blaze, and feasting would continue for days; and then people would be careful in maintaining the cult of the dead for the days and months and years to come.

The round Slav temples on hilltops, with images of the gods within (images which have virtually all perished), might give kings and chiefs power here and there. But with the building up of Kiev as a city, new knowledge and new values had to be taken up. Islam had its advantages as an ideology; and Judaism had been taken up by the Khazars. But as it happened it was the Orthodoxy of the Byzantine empire which had the greatest appeal, and so Christ had to be identified with the god of light, and Satan with death and darkness. The light had to be found within, in the mysticism of the Church.

It was these and other forms of culture across the North European plain which were absorbed and submerged in the new Christianity. It turned out that the poetry of the Celts, the story-telling of the Scandinavians, and the religious intuitions of the Slavic peoples, took new forms in Christian civilization. The Cross was pictured like a world-tree, Yggdrasil, with the judgment seat of the new God beneath it, and Christ not Odin hanging from it. Thus the fusion of North and Christian South sets the seal on European medieval civilization.

Classical and Medieval Islam

CHAPTER 12

Islam—an Overview of its Spread

Islam, the religion of Submission (as its name indicates) to the one God, took off from the northwest part of Arabia in the seventh century and rapidly spread north and west. It went north into Palestine and Syria, Iraq and Iran, and into Central Asia. It went west into Egypt, Libya, Tunisia, Algeria, Morocco, Spain, and Portugal. Beginning with Muhammad's migration from Mecca to Medina in 622, the political rule of Islam expanded with amazing rapidity. By 664 the new empire had taken Kabul in Afghanistan and by 670 Kairouan in Tunisia. By 732 it was beyond Bukhara and Samarkand in Central Asia, and fighting at Poitiers in France (where however it was defeated). This first phase, till the establishment of the Abbasid dynasty and the shift of the capital to Mesopotamia, may be called the early period. From 750 to 1258, the time of the Abbasid rule over all or part of Islamic territories, was what may be termed the classical period. Then from the mid-thirteenth century C.E. until the impact of Western powers in the colonial experience—until roughly the eighteenth century—we have what may be called the medieval or premodern period.

Altogether Islam became the dominant religion over the whole of the Arab Middle East, along the shores of North Africa, across the Sahara in northern West Africa, through much of East Africa down to Kenya, through Iran, Afghanistan, and what is now Soviet Central Asia, in north and northeast India, in Malaysia and Indonesia, in Turkey and a part of the Balkans. It is a significant minority religion in the Indian subcontinent as a whole, and in Thailand, the Philippines, China, Madagascar, Yugoslavia, and Tanzania. Broadly, it stretches in a crescent from the eastern tip of Indonesia to West Africa. Though the religion has strong Arab cultural ingredients, above all in the use of Arabic for the Qur'an, the majority of Muslims come from other

Map 10 The expansion of Islam to 750 C.E.

cultures. The most populous Islamic countries are in South and Southeast Asia: Indonesia, Pakistan, Bangladesh, and the Republic of India.

Islam established its main outline very rapidly, partly because it had a single founder, namely Muhammad, partly because it had a foundation document, namely the Qur'an, and partly because in having a political aspect it had to take rapid decisions on organization in view of its great success. The story of the religion turns of course very considerably on the life of the Prophet, and with that we begin.

The Life of the Messenger of Allah

The Prophet Muhammad was born in Mecca, which at that time, probably in 570 C.E., was a highly prosperous place. This was because of its strategic position across the routes from the eastern Mediterranean, and from such rich cities as Damascus, to the ports which served the trade to India and Sri Lanka. It was also even then a sacred city, for it contained the sacred building, the Ka'bah. Accordingly it was the scene of annual pilgrimage from the tribes around about; and the area around the Ka'bah was a sanctuary during certain months, thus moderating the impact of tribal warfare. The dominant tribe in Mecca, to which Muhammad belonged, was the Quraysh. His father and mother died when he was young, and he was raised by relatives. As a young man he found himself without the capital necessary to engage in trading; but a wealthy widow, Khadijah, employed him and subsequently married him. Though he became active in trade, he had had opportunities for reflection: he is said to have spent a month each year meditating in a cave near Mecca.

It was in 610 that he began to have some striking religious experiences

Map 11 The expansion of Islam to 1500 C.E.

which set him off in his career as a messenger of Allah. To begin with he mentioned his revelations only to his family and close associates; but after about three years he began his public career. His message was not altogether welcome for at least two reasons. First, in attacking polytheism, which he came to do with increasing clarity, he threatened the livelihood of those who depended on Meccan shrines: and in any case in such matters people tend to be conservative. Second, the ethic he pronounced was not fully in accord with the money-making policy of the rich merchants of the city: everyone would have to appear in the end before the judgment seat of the mighty God. Later, too, Muhammad would be involved in conveying revelations which altered the legal shape of society, especially in regard to marriage.

His message made little headway at first in Mecca, though he accumulated some fifty loyal followers. In 620 and 621 he received feelers from the city of Medina to the north, and in due course, in 622, he was invited to migrate there and take up the leadership. The city and area had been in a state of faction for a number of years, and the hope was that Muhammad with his diplomatic skills and unifying message would be able to bring harmony to Medina. This he did and came to control its political affairs. Then began an armed struggle against the Quraysh and the people of Mecca; and in 624 he defeated them in battle at Badr. After a few years of intermittent struggle Muhammad entered Mecca and became its leader. A battle shortly thereafter, at Hunayn, disposed of some of the outlying tribes, and Muhammad was master of a large slice of Arabia. Already he had plans for conquests in Syria and Iraq. But in June 632 he died.

He was a considerable military and political leader, magnanimous and decisive, and had behind him the assurance of faith, as a result of his prophetic experiences. To Muslims he is an ideal figure, someone to be admired and followed, and seen as virtually perfect—the finest of human beings, to whom Allah entrusted his final revelation. Though Muslims are of course much opposed to any attempt to deify Muhammad—for that would be to set up another god beside God, which is the deadliest sin—in practice he is the supreme ethical ideal and more closely followed than Christ, partly because of the accumulation of biographical stories about him. These traditions, or *hadith*, are carefully sifted according to traditional methods, and constitute in effect a secondary source of revelation to that which is contained in the holy Qur'an.

The Prophet and His Experiences of Revelation

Muhammad seems to have started his religious career as Prophet in part because of his first experiences, which were of a numinous character. There was a mighty being, on the horizon, whom he thought of as God but later concluded must have been the archangel Gabriel. The archangel made him read from a book (though Muhammad is said to have been illiterate). He was commanded, according to surah (section) 96 of the Qur'an, "Recite in the name of the Lord …". This was probably the first surah to be revealed. At other times the Prophet felt certain words in his heart, which he took to be revealed by God. All these utterances were brought together in the Qur'an, a collection which is of very great power and beauty, in resonant and compelling Arabic. How, say Muslims, could an illiterate person create such a masterpiece? At any rate, the numinous experiences of the Prophet are reflected in the tremendous and mysterious tone of the Qur'anic words.

There was also the famous night journey of Muhammad to the Temple Mount in Jerusalem, now marked by a mosque, from whence he ascended to the seventh heaven. On his way he saw Moses, Abraham, and Jesus. Among other things the five daily prayers were supposed to have been revealed on this occasion. This experience was no doubt a visionary episode, but later piety often makes it into a literal journey astride Muhammad's winged horse Buraq. This interpretation was part of the tendency to surround Muhammad with miracles and to make him even more than a Prophet: he was supposedly prevented by God from sinning, for instance. But the orthodox theologians insist that one miracle was enough: the creation of the Qur'an. Or rather, not its creation—for it was with God forever—but its presentation to the human race.

From a human point of view the Qur'an looks like a miraculous achievement of sublime artistry. In any event, being written down so rapidly during the lifetime of Muhammad, and being pretty much consistent in its teachings and prescriptions, it has not created the problems encountered in

The Transcendence and Immanence of God: Qur'an

God is the Light of the heavens and earth;
  the likeness of His Light is a niche
     wherein is a lamp
     (the lamp in a glass,
  the glass as it were a glittering star)
  kindled from a Blessed Tree,
  an olive that is neither of the East nor of
    the West,
  Whose oil wellnigh would shine, even if
    no fire touched it;
  Light upon light;
  God guides to His Light whom He will.
And God strikes similitudes for men,
  and God has knowledge of everything.
In temples God has allowed to be raised up,
  and His Name to be commemorated
    therein;
  therein glorifying Him, in the mornings and
    the evenings,
  are men whom neither commerce nor
    trafficking diverts from the remembrance
    of God and to perform the prayer, and to
    pay the alms,
  fearing a day when hearts and eyes shall be
    turned about,
  that God may recompense them for their
    fairest works and give them increase of His
    bounty;

and God provides whomsoever He
  will, without reckoning.

And as for the unbelievers,
  their works are as a mirage in a spacious
    plain which the man athirst supposes to
    be water,
  till, when he comes to it, he finds it is
    nothing;
  there indeed he finds God,
  and He pays him his account in full;
  (and God is swift at the reckoning)
  or they are as shadows upon a sea obscure
    covered by a billow
    above which is a billow
    above which are clouds,
    shadows piled one upon another;
  when he puts forth his hand, wellnigh he
    cannot see it.
And to whomsoever God assigns no light, no
  light has he.

Hast thou not seen how that whatsoever is in
    the heavens and in the earth extols God,
  and the birds spreading their wings?
Each—He knows its prayer and its extolling;
  and God knows the things they do.

looking at the New Testament, which came into being through different hands over a much longer period, and has undergone great editing.

It is easy to think of the Qur'an simply as a book and to say that the Muslims have faith in the words of a holy book. But this does not convey the centrality and power of the Qur'an in Muslim eyes. If you were to look for a rough equivalent to the Christian Incarnation (the divine nature of Jesus) in Muslim piety, it would be the Qur'an. It is divine thought and divine law incarnated in words: it is mysterious sound which has everlasting life and existence, an examination from the one Divine Being. One of the attributes of God is speech, and the Qur'an is God's eternal speech. Of course, recitations or written copies of the Qur'an are all created; but as divine speech what lies behind and within the Qur'an is eternal. All this gives it a much deeper meaning and a much higher status than that of the Bible.

Also, the Qur'an must be seen alongside the claims made by the faithful on behalf of Muhammad. He was not just the greatest of the Prophets, in a line stretching from Abraham and Moses through Jesus to himself—he was also the final Prophet, the "Seal of the Prophets," the *khatm al-anbiyā*. It was he who delivered the definitive expression of Allah's speech.

All this implies a divine plan. Abraham and the rest are God's means of communicating with the human race, and are part of his education of human beings in the process of *islam* or submission to his will. But it should be noted that the very process of looking back at previous religious heroes as being in the line of prophets made them exemplary figures also, so that Islam could claim to have ancient roots, though it was the last of the great religions to be revealed. It gave Islam a positive view of Judaism and Christianity, though this could also seem to adherents of those faiths to be somewhat patronizing. Muslims considered of course that Jews and Christians had tampered with the messages of the Prophets, for instance by looking on Jesus as divine, which was blasphemous. This retroactive acceptance of elements of the other two traditions could be concretized in very particular claims, for instance that the Ka'bah was built by Adam and then rebuilt by Abraham and Ishmael (Isma'il). Whatever others may feel about the validity of such a claim, Muslims will see in this something which is part of the warp and woof of their faith, and so undeniably certain.

The revealed and everlasting nature of the Qur'an gives Islamic faith a great strength, especially because the book is not to be translated. It is only in Arabic: there can be no non-Arabic Qur'an, for it is primarily sound. The writing is like the score from which you perform. The non-Arab may use paraphrases as a kind of commentary to help her or him. But the true Qur'an remains the Arabic Qur'an. In this sense, God thinks in Arabic.

The Dimensions of the Faith Muhammad Founded

Thus, built on the rock of Muhammad's career and the revelations of the Qur'an, there arose the great edifice of a new faith which itself helped to define a new civilization, for long a glittering challenge to its neighbor Christendom. What were the dimensions of this faith?

First, let us start with *ritual*. Above all, the Muslim has the duty of praying five times daily, facing toward the Ka'bah, according to certain formulae of words and bodily postures: before sunrise, early afternoon, late afternoon, straight after sunset, and before retiring. One should also keep the fast during the holy month of Ramadan, which is the ninth month of the lunar year: between dawn and sunset there should be no eating, drinking, smoking, or sex. And one should try to perform the pilgrimage to the Ka'bah at least once during one's life. These three rules constitute the second, third, and fifth of the so-called Pillars of Islam. The first is a duty to commitment: one should recite the credo in public: "There is no god but Allah and Muhammad is his messenger." The fourth is to pay the alms tax, or *zakat*. Thus the community should look after the welfare of the poor. Friday is a special day of prayer, with congregational worship and preaching in the mosque.

The fact that Muslims have to orient themselves toward the Ka'bah and are urged if at all possible to go there on the great annual pilgrimage (the *hajj al-akbar*) means that there are continual reminders of the unity of the whole community, however much from time to time it may be riven by political or religious conflict.

As to the *experiential* dimension of early Islam, obviously the Prophet's own visions and the numinous power of Allah left its stamp not only on the Qur'an but also on the community's sense of the tremendous nature of God. The deepest sin known to Islam chimes with this sense: it is *shirk*, setting up some other god beside God. So we have a sense of the overwhelming presence of God, who yet in his mercy communicates with human beings to lead them on the right path. Later on, as we shall see, a different, mystical sort of experience appears: the sense of that which lies within, gained through the practice of contemplation. This was due to the Sufi movement.

As for the *ethical* dimension, we have to see that morality for the early Muslim was thoroughly woven into the political task of founding a good and just society under the guidance of God. Throughout the history of Islam there

Left The doctrinal dimension: "There is no god but Allah and Muhammad is his messenger," inscribed on a sixteenth or seventeenth century Turkish tile.

Right The ritual dimension: a plan of Mecca rendered on a seventeenth-century Turkish tile.

Opposite The narrative dimension: Muslims swearing allegiance to the Imam 'Ali (c.600–661) at Kufa after the murder of the *khalifa*, 'Uthman ibn 'Affan, in 656, a vital part of the narrative of the beginnings of the Shi'a.

is recognition of the central place held by the law or *shari'a*. The obedience due to God should lead to the recognition of human equality. Rights may vary, as with men and women. But in principle all are equal before God. Social legislation and the payment of *zakat* stress our religious duty to the poor. Kindness should be cultivated, especially by husbands toward wives. Polygamy is allowed, but only four wives per man; and the rights of women are protected by the dowry system and legislation regarding divorce. The Prophet himself can be followed as an example, and the *hadith* are a vital source of moral inspiration.

Institutionally, Islam organized itself as a state to start with, and only gradually did the total community—the *umma*—break up. In theory this should be unified under a leader, or successor to Muhammad, known as the *khalifa* or Caliph. From time to time in later Islam the Caliphate was revived. As for religious institutions more narrowly conceived, there were prayer leaders from early days, and later professional exponents of theology and law.

Islam some key terms

Allah The one true God.

Hajj Pilgrimage to Mecca, urged on all Muslims.

Imam Prayer leader, and in Shi'a Islam one of the twelve great leaders of the community, the last having gone into hiding or occultation, to return at the end of history.

Jihad The struggle for Islam, interpreted either as righteous war or as a spiritual striving.

Nabi A prophet, among whom are some of the great figures of the Jewish tradition, and Jesus; the final one is Muhammad.

Qur'an The sacred revelation or word of God, being eternal, and revealed to the Prophet.

Salat Worship or prayer, enjoined on Muslims five times daily.

Saum Fasting, especially during the month of Ramadan between sunrise and sunset, enjoined on all Muslims.

Shari'a Islamic law.

Sufi A mystic within Islam, typically belonging to one of the various *tariqas* or orders.

Umma The whole Muslim community.

Zakat Giving alms to the poor. One of the pillars of Islam, with the profession of faith, prayer, pilgrimage, and fasting.

Doctrinally, the single most important strand in Islam is the unity of God, who is creator of the universe. He has human beings as his regents over the earth, which was made for their ultimate benefit. Though varying emphasis in the Qur'an can be found, the trend is to think of God as determining each person's destiny. As we have seen, the Qur'an was believed to be the eternal speech of God. The Muslims were strong in condemning what they saw as the tritheism, or three-God-doctrine, of Christianity; but God can be addressed through the rich notion of his Ninety-Nine Names, beginning with *al-Rahman*, "the Compassionate." Among other popular names are *al-Hafiz*, the Preserver; *al-Haqq*, the Real; *al-Qadir*, the Powerful; and *al-Rashid*, the Director.

As to the *narrative* dimension, we have seen that the Islamic story implies a chain of Prophets from Abraham, and indeed before that from Adam, down to Muhammad. The coming of the last Prophet is of course central to the whole narrative understanding by Muslims of human history. The amazing success of the community in its early days, and the mighty conquests, were a sign of Allah's grace and mercy. Eventually the final hour of the world will come with various signs, the descent of Jesus, and a fire which will drive people to the place of judgment.

Materially, Islam soon enough began to have its houses of prayer; it was only later that they became a glory of Islamic architecture. Since the ban on any concrete representation of God was extended to cover God's image in the human face and form, much came to be made of calligraphy as an art. But in the early days the chief material aspects of Islam were the cities of Medina and Mecca, and above all the pilgrimage sites in and around the latter. There was, for instance, the valley of Mina to the east of Mecca, where pilgrims spend a night, and the mount of 'Arafat, where Muhammad had his first visions.

Beyond the Early Period: the Formation of Classical Islam

The early decades after the death of the Prophet were marked with dissension over the leadership. Muhammad's father-in-law Abu Bakr was first appointed. He lasted two years and was succeeded by 'Umar, who organized the growing Arab empire along fairly simple lines: the Arabs looked after war and religion, and non-Arabs—and these were for the most part non-Muslims—paid taxes but rather lighter ones than they had been used to. 'Umar was followed by 'Uthman. His assassination led to the first civil war within Islam, when Muhammad's cousin and son-in-law 'Ali's succession was opposed. 'Ali was assassinated in 661, and in 680 his surviving son Husayn was ambushed at Karbala in Iraq; he was to become the prime martyr figure for the Shi'a movement, which we shall come back to later. Under Mu'awiyah and his successors (661–750), the Umayyad dynasty, centered in Syria, carried on the giddily successful policy of military expansion.

Opposite The material dimension: the great glory of Islamic civilization is revealed in its wonderful and graceful architecture – seen here in a mosque in Isfahan in Iran.

'Ali

'Ali (?600–661 C.E.) was the cousin and son-in-law of the Prophet Muhammad and became the fourth *khalīfa* or Caliph of the Islamic tradition. He is regarded by the Shi'a as the legitimate successor of the Prophet and married Muhammad's last daughter, Fatima. During the Prophet's lifetime he showed vast courage in defending him, subsequent to his having been as a ten-year-old one of the very first to acknowledge Muhammad's divine mission. At the death of the Prophet 'Abu Bakr took over as Caliph, and 'Ali withdrew somewhat from public life. But after nearly a quarter of a century there was civil war and on the assassination of 'Uthman, the third Caliph, 'Ali was chosen to lead the community. 'Ali made Kufa (in modern Iraq) his capital. Civil strife continued. First 'Ā'ishah, one of the widows of the Prophet, led an expedition against him, unsuccessfully; then Mu'awiyah, governor of Syria, launched an army at him. After an inconclusive arbitration, a body of rebels, the so-called Khārijites, broke away from 'Ali's party. One of these killed him at Kufa in 661. His body was secretly buried at nearby Najaf, which became a major place of Shi'ite pilgrimage.

'Ali was venerated for his various qualities: for his wisdom—he became the epitome of sagacity; for his generosity, for his worldly poverty, for the intensity of his prayer life, for his formidable courage, for his humility, and for possession of his sword, which in the poetic tradition was personified. His wife too was elevated in subsequent imagination: she was the perfect woman, and was referred to as the Lady of Paradise.

In the end, a revolution in 750 brought the Abbasid dynasty to power at Dar-es-Salam, a new capital constructed at Baghdad in Mesopotamia. A glorious new cultural phase of Islam was thus entered, though disintegration occurred later through the establishment of rival Caliphates, in North Africa—where Cairo was conquered in 969, and became a brilliant capital under the Fatimid dynasty—and in Córdoba in Spain, ruled by the second 'Umayyad dynasty from 929. The Islamic community was divided, but it was a fine period of Islamic civilization. There were stresses, one of them being the disaffection of the Shi'a party, who were loyal to the descendants of 'Ali and who opposed the traditionalists of Sunni.

New religious forces were entering the body of Islam. One was the effect of Greek learning, and in particular philosophy, upon Islamic theology. Another was the mystical movement, the Sufis, who brought contemplative methods into the practice of Islam. Meanwhile the law or *shari'a* had to be interpreted, and diverse schools had been growing up.

The Development of Islamic Theology

One of the major movements in the second and third centuries of Islam (c.700–900 C.E.) was that of the Mu'tazilah, great systematizers of *kalam* or dogmatic theology. In their pursuit of a rational worldview they took over atomism, but gave it an extension beyond that of Greek philosophy. They saw the world as a succession of instantaneous and atomic (separate and indivisible) events, including human actions. God gives a person strength through an instantaneous empowerment before a person acts; but the choice is later and is still that of the individual. The Mu'tazilah also did not want to make God's attributes something other than God, so it was no use saying that the Qur'an was God's speech as something eternal. It was produced by God and was not everlasting.

Their doctrine of free will was founded in the thought that God is just. So it is inappropriate to believe in any form of predestination. In such ways the Mu'tazilah defended a rationalist position, and they were for a time patronized by the court in Baghdad and adopted as the official line. But there were elements in their thought which were not popular, notably the denial of the eternal character of the Qur'an. Moreover they were intensely against anthropomorphism, and saw the statements in the Qur'an as being metaphors, when God is said to have hands, or sit on a throne.

It was al-Ash'ari (873–975) who most decisively formulated the Sunni or mainstream tradition. He argued that anthropomorphic expressions apply to God literally but in a manner which we do not understand. The Qur'an he defended as eternal, being an attribute of God, who has attributes in a mode different from created beings. And he held that God is all-powerful and determines human actions, but individuals acquire responsibility for their actions. In effect this left as the mainstream Islamic position a form of predestinationism. Men and women are predestined to good or to bad actions, and to heaven or hell (including purgatory, the fate of true believers who sin).

The Spread of Sufism

The movement which is known as Sufism (from *suf* meaning the coarse wool worn by ascetics) was an attempt to introduce into personal life a kind of spirituality which would compensate for the excesses of Islamic culture after its notable successes. Sufism was involved with ascetic training, but it issued ultimately in mystical contemplation. Sufis aspired toward that purification of consciousness which leads to the feeling that ordinary consciousness, with its dualism (the distinction between me as subject and God or the world as object), disappears. They therefore often came to speak of union with God, and even being merged with or becoming God. Now this was not at all to the taste of mainstream orthodoxy. In Islam there has always been a very strong emphasis on the radical difference between God and human beings. Some Sufi claims could be thought blasphemous. The Sufis seemed to think that by the annihilation of their egos they could make a place for God and so in some sense become God. It was not surprising that the orthodox should resist such ideas.

The Sufi movement started with groups who would cooperate in the cultivation of piety. There grew up the custom of having a leader or *shaykh* who would act as a spiritual teacher and master. The groups not only pledged themselves to simplicity of life, but engaged in forms of meditation—very similarly to the contemplative orders in Christianity and to much in Indian mysticism. Perhaps the most famous of all Sufis was al-Hallaj, who illustrated some of the tensions in the situation. An admirer and follower of Jesus (also of course an Islamic Prophet), he reportedly said, "I am the Real—*al-Haqq*," which was taken as tantamount to saying that he was God. In his teachings he spoke most of the love of God, and he openly referred to his divine experiences. As a result he was accused of blasphemy and executed on the cross, in 922 C.E.

But the strong piety and zealous teaching of the Sufis, "friends of God" as they called themselves, were too valuable to be sacrificed by Islam. Sufism was given a powerful defence, but in a moderate form, by the great philosopher al-Ghazali, from northeast Persia (1058–1111). He gave up his post as professor at the university in Baghdad to take up the life of a Sufi, and thus had both intellectual and spiritual preparation for the task to which he was called, which was to give an account of Sufism which would show its deep compatibility with orthodox tradition.

He argued that the language of Sufis, sometimes extravagant, need not be taken literally. The Sufi when he reached his high state of union was like a person drunk—and they themselves often used this metaphor. What they say during this state comes from their unawareness of any context: but once they are out of the state they can acknowledge that however close they might have been to God, nevertheless a distinction between the Divine Being and the human soul remains.

Sufism was important in the spread of Islam. The holy person commands respect in many societies. In North Africa the *baraka* or mysterious power of the saint, in Central Asia features of shamanism, in India the prestige of the yogin—such manifestations were taken over by the Sufis. They had much, too, to do with the spread of Islam into Malaya and Indonesia.

The Development of Islamic Law

As the Islamic community expanded, and as times and cultures changed, it was necessary to expand the interpretation of the law. In general it was important to have criteria for deciding. Four main roots of the law were evolved. The first is the Qur'an itself. If a law is clearly stated there then it is indeed obligatory. The next root is the tradition or *sunna*. This is where the collection of *hadith* about the life and sayings of the Prophet is important to the system. Third, there is analogy, to be thought out by relevant reasoning or *ijtihad*. Fourth, there is *ijma'* or consensus.

By the tenth and eleventh centuries the main structure of Islamic legal thinking had been put in place. The effect ultimately was somewhat deadening, and it was said that the "door of *ijtihad* is closed." The main schools had been established, and it became customary to use a system called patchwork to arrive at legal changes—by taking a ruling from one school when that of another proved too severe or not severe enough, etc. The various

Rabi'ah

Rābi'ah (731/7–801) was a notable woman mystic in Islam. She was born of a poor family and was a slave in Basra, having been sold to a wealthy citizen. Her master, however, gave her her liberty, recognizing her evident piety. She lived as a recluse thereafter, for a time in the desert, and then in Basra. She was celibate (which in the Arab world of the time was very unusual), and devoted herself to communing with God. Reputedly, she was the first in the Sufi tradition to preach the notion of the pure love of God. Because of her reputation for austerity and sanctity, she gathered disciples around her when she moved to Basra. Her life is overlaid by legends, including that of her having been seen with a flaming torch and a pail of water. This signified her desire to set Paradise alight and pour water into Hell, to equalize them, so that no person could love God out of the hope of Paradise or the fear of Hell. Another story has it that when she went on the pilgrimage to Mecca, the Ka'bah moved forward to greet her arrival. The story about the torch and the pail undoubtedly reflects her sentiments. The theme of the selfless love of God came, through her, to suffuse much of the Sufi tradition. She remains the foremost example of piety in the tradition, and her feminine gender never seems to have affected her as a saint and mystic. 'Attār, who composed the famous compendium called *Biographies of the Saints*, accords her a prominent place. While she wrote nothing, her prayers and sayings were gathered together and attained great popularity. Her life was seen as a model both for ordinary folk and for later mystics and ascetics, and she is probably the foremost woman in Islam, after some of those in the first generation.

schools prevail in different parts of the world: the Hanafi in the Indian subcontinent, Central Asia, Egypt, Syria, Jordan, and Iraq; the Maliki in North Africa; the Shafi'i in Southeast Asia; the Hanbali in Saudi Arabia; the Ja'fari (Shi'a) in Iran; and the Kariji in Oman and East Africa.

The law covers all topics, from morality to civil law and from criminal law to courtesy. It is interesting that five classes of action are recognized: those which are obligatory, those which are recommended, those which are prohibited, those which are disapproved, and those which are indifferent. This fivefold distinction helps to give Islamic law a great deal of subtlety.

Jihad or Struggle

An aspect of Muslim law which is important historically is the notion of the duty to struggle on behalf of the faith, and indeed to fight on its behalf to expand the territories over which the faith dominates. It became customary in the classical period to divide the world into two spheres, the *Dar al-Islam* or Abode of Islam and the *Dar al-Harb* or Abode of War. The Qur'an looks on it as a duty to fight against polytheists, and against Christians and Jews till they pay the *jizya* or tax as an acknowledgment of the supremacy of Muslim rule.

This in turn guaranteed protection to the People of the Book. Non-Muslims were exempted from serving in the army, though they could as volunteers. The duty of struggle, Jihad, is sometimes counted as the Sixth Pillar of Islam. The doctrine of a duty literally to fight has been softened in many ways. It can be argued that early wars as mentioned in the Qur'an were conducted in self-defence; it is held that there is a greater struggle than that of literal warfare, and that is the inner war on behalf of faith, to eliminate temptations and obstacles to true obedience to God. This is a particularly Sufi teaching.

The Rise of the Shi'a and the Concept of the Imam

While Sunni teachings and interpretations of the law remain dominant in Islam, some areas, especially Iran and Iraq, have prevailing Shi'a cultures. In origin the division derives from the clashes between the family of 'Ali, cousin and son-in-law of the Prophet, and the 'Umayyad dynasty. The followers of 'Ali considered that he should rightly have been Muhammad's successor. His grandson Husayn, who according to Shi'as is the Third Imam or Spiritual Leader of Islam, was lured to Iraq in 680 and slain at Karbala with a band of followers. This martyrdom is celebrated each year during the festival of the tenth day of the lunar month of Muharram. It climaxes ten days of processions and signs of mourning for the death of Husayn, when his horse, covered with representations of his blood and arrows, is led in procession, and models of his tomb are carried through the streets. This kind of demonstration appeals to those who wish to stress the theme of suffering and martyrdom in Islam. It may owe some of its influence in the Middle East to the similarity of the Husayn motif to the death of Christ.

But as the Shi'a movement came to solidify itself during the classical period, even more important than the martyrdom theme was the theory of the religious leadership, the Imamate. The term *imam* in Islam can mean the ordinary prayer leader in the mosque. But it can also be used more pregnantly for the religious Leader of Islam. Theoretically the Caliph and the Imam should be the same. But in practice, because the Caliphate became immediately corrupted through the wrong succession, the vital line is that of the Imams. The dominant Shi'a group holds to a succession of twelve Imams, and for this reason they are sometimes referred to as the Twelvers, as distinguished primarily from the Isma'ilis, who stop the count at the seventh Imam Isma'il, who died just before 765. According to the Twelvers, the last Imam, whose name was Muhammad, disappeared as a child and will eventually return. He is a kind of Messianic figure, and is referred to as al-Muntazar, the expected one.

The conception was then that this Imam was in concealment (*ghaybah*). At first this was with a succession of agents who did his will; but when these had died out, that is, from 941 onward, there began the "major" concealment (or occultation as it is often called in English). The thought that the Hidden Imam still exists in a state like that of paradise in the unseen sphere of God has proved a powerful inspiration within Shi'a Islam. Through dreams and visions it is possible for earthly leaders to be in contact with him. But the fact that the great hero of Shi'a is Husayn, who died a bloody martyr's death and that the leadership of the community is hidden, means that there has been a tendency for the movement to be quietist, and to accept the political rule of others, though a Shi'a dynasty did come to power in Iran.

So the Shi'a tell a very different story about the history and outcome of Islam from that believed by traditionalist Sunnis. Shi'a *doctrines* point to the light which guides the succession of Imams as something which was handed on from the Prophet. In *ritual* there grew to be a cult of the Prophet's daughter Fatima, somewhat like that of the Virgin Mary; and the celebrations of the death of Husayn mark a strong emphasis on identifying with suffering (in some parts of the Shi'a world, self-mutilation at Muharram is normal, scarifying the body with cuts). *Experientially*, Sufism, cutting across the two main communities, was strongly entrenched in Shi'a, although its effects were to help Sunnis resist further Shi'a spread. For the gnostic (secret knowledge) motif was very prominent in the Shi'a, as were esoteric practices. The Sufi movement helped to make this a normal feature of the *sunna* too, though the religious imagination could be externally much more orthodox because of the depth of Sufi inner experience. As to *institutions*, the Shi'a had its own circle of learned authorities who represented a different strand from mainstream Islam. *Ethically* and legally they had a similar position on most matters to the mainstream, except for the concept of *mu'ta* or temporary marriage, for a fixed term.

The Isma'ili Variant of the Shi'a

Isma'iliya has as its most famous achievement the establishment of the Fatimid Caliphate in North Africa and Egypt, from 909 to 1171. It was a glittering period and saw among other things the establishment of the great university of al-Azhar, whose judgments on law and theology were to become normative in the Muslim world. The Isma'ilis stopped the clock at the Seventh Imam. According to their cosmology the world was created by the supreme Absolute through a series of emanations from the godhead, and in this they wove in Neoplatonic elements in their later philosophical expositions of the metaphysics of creation. Then the world went through differing ages, beginning with six Prophets culminating in Muhammad, and then seven Imams ending with Isma'il. He on his return would become the seventh Prophet. He would then abrogate Islamic law.

Very important was the notion that Prophets who spoke forth had to be interpreted, as to the inner meaning of their utterances, by special "silent ones." In other words the whole Isma'ili system was based on secret knowledge. It also contained a hierarchical series of ranks of adepts, with an initiatory path upward. Their opponents accused them of various faults, including the secret teaching of atheism at the highest level and ultimate disrespect for the law. For a time some Isma'ilis used the killing of individual enemies as a method of warfare, and were accused of topping up the dedicated killers with hashish. This word lay behind the term "assassin," which passed into Western languages at the time of the Crusades.

Offshoots of Islam: Druze and Alawi

Another derivative of the Shi'a tradition is that of the Druze, named after a founder, al-Darazi. The other two founders were Hamzah, a Persian, and the Fatimid *khalifa* al-Hakim (985–1021). Both these were killed in 1021, and al-Darazi about a year earlier. These three leaders went into occultation. Druze belief centers on the supposed divinity of al-Hakim, who indeed regarded himself as divine and persecuted Sunnis, Jews, and Christians; he demolished the Church of the Holy Sepulcher in Jerusalem. His enemies regarded him as insane; but the Druze regard him as the incarnation of the One, who is destined to return to earth at the last to rule over the world. The Druze, prominent in Lebanon, Syria, and Palestine, later evolved into a two-tier society. The elite are the knowledgeable ones who have had the full initiation into the secret doctrines: they are supposed to lead impeccable lives and abstain from violence. The masses have a more relaxed ethic. Intermarriage within the society, and the closure of their ranks to outsiders, has made the Druze a tightly knit society.

The Alawi of northwest Syria are another relatively small group; they profess the Shi'a tradition and were somewhat influenced by Christian ideas and practices during the Crusader period. To some degree they represent a folk tradition which is much laxer about strict Islamic practice than the scribal Shi'a tradition. They have long been regarded, with the Druzes, as unbelievers.

These traditions are interesting illustrations of the merging of Islam with other strands of religion; but, though they have had some importance over the centuries in Levantine politics, they are unimportant in relation to the main sweep of Islam, which in the classical period was divided broadly between Sunni and Shi'a variations.

Medieval Islam

Islam in Spain: Ibn Rushd and Ibn al-'Arabi

Two of the most widely known Islamic writers, one a philosopher and the other a Sufi, came from Spain. This itself is testimony to the riches of the blended Hispanic and Islamic civilization which flourished in Spain especially in the twelfth and thirteenth centuries. Ibn Rushd (1126–98) was educated in Córdoba, chief intellectual center of western Islam, and much of his life was spent as a judge there and in Seville. He was commissioned by his Sultan to write summaries and commentaries on the works of Aristotle. He brought to the attention of scholars elsewhere, including Aquinas, features of the Aristotelian position which were highly controversial from a Christian point of view, and indeed also from the point of view of usual interpretations of the Qur'an—these were doctrines such as that of the everlasting or eternal nature of matter, and the blending of individual souls in the one Active Intellect upon death. This seemed to deny individual immortality. He wrote a famous reply to Ghazali's distinguished book *The Incoherence of the Philosophers* which he entitled *The Incoherence of "The Incoherence."* Though by all accounts a good Muslim, Rushd and some fellow students of Aristotle were indicted for irreligion in his last years, and he was sent into exile.

Ibn al-'Arabi (1165–1240) studied extensively in Seville, and also came into contact with Sufi teachers living there, to whose style of life he was attracted. During a visit to Córdoba he is said to have had an encounter with Ibn Rushd, whom supposedly he bested in debate. But the climate was not too good for someone of his mystical inclinations, and intolerance, as the case of Ibn Rushd has shown, might have restricted his writings and reflections, so he left Spain in his thirties for the Middle East. He visited Mecca and the Ka'bah and ultimately settled down in Damascus. During his years in Spain he had met Fatima, a famous, and by then old, Sufi woman, whose visage he had seen as if bathed in light. In Mecca he had a like experience, but in relation to a young beauty, Nizam, daughter of a Sufi master from Persia who had befriended him. He wrote a wonderful poem about her, called "The Interpreter of Warm Longings," which attracted criticism as being libertine. But the poem had a deeper meaning, for she was a symbol of the divine *Sophia* or Wisdom. Throughout his later writings he insisted on the importance of what are called depth hermeneutics, so that we do not just interpret texts, including the Qur'an, by their surface sense.

As a result of his experience he formulated a philosophy of the One which was both radical and controversial, in, among other writings, two particular books, *The Meccan Revelations* and *The Jewels of Wisdom*. In the experience of the One, the soul of the individual experiences complete disappearance, *fana'*. There is only the One, and all subject-object consciousness disappears. When he returns to the world the mystic experiences *baqa'* or "survival," in which he sees the Many in the light of the One. The One manifests itself as a determinate God and as the world of creation. There are resemblances between Ibn al-'Arabi's system and that of Advaita Vedānta in the Indian tradition, and he was to have an influence on Dante Alighieri.

As well as the poetical, philosophical, legal, and other riches of the Spanish Muslim tradition, there were great architectural achievements, such as the Great Mosque in Córdoba and the wonderful Alhambra palace in Granada.

Developments after the Mongol Incursion

The thirteenth century was a terrible era of devastation, because of the irruption of the Mongols, initially under the leadership of Genghis Khan. In the first years of the century the Muslim centers of Central Asia were destroyed, along with much of the Persian empire. In 1256 Hülegü Khan, Genghis's grandson, sacked Baghdad and slaughtered large numbers of Muslims. The Mongol successor state in Persia, the II-Khan principality, was eventually won over to Islam, so that the Mongol rulers began to favor the faith. Later, Turkish power under Timur caused devastation across Central Asia and into India, where the Muslim capital of Delhi was sacked. But a descendant of Timur, Babur, established his rule in Delhi and founded the Mughal Empire, which turned out to be a great patron of both Islam and the arts.

Meanwhile, though the Mongols had struck at the rising Ottoman regime, the latter was to make its way in Asia Minor. Turkish in texture, it ultimately conquered the Byzantine empire and established rule over most of the territories formerly ruled by it, in a kind of alliance between Muslims and Christians. In the fifteenth century, although Islam was driven out of Spain, in much of the rest of the world it underwent a renaissance. It was penetrating deeply into Indonesia and Malaya. It made its way through the patronage of the Mughals in India. It was busy crossing the Sahara and moving into Black Africa. Though the Middle Ages of Islam brought it into conflict with rising European power, it was nevertheless a constructive period. In Central Asia, in India, and in Ottoman territories, rich varieties of architectural style, calligraphy, and painting flourished.

Islam in Central and South Asia

During the reign of Timur, who was a pious Muslim, virtually all non-Muslim practice in Central Asia was wiped out. But a great part of the consolidation of Islam in the region was due to the work of the Sufi orders. As elsewhere in the Muslim world, the tombs of mystics became more potent often than mosques in the popular imagination, and the houses where adepts met and were to be seen in prayer became symbols of the new piety. It was in Bukhara that the influential Naqshbandi order was founded in the fourteenth century; it penetrated both intellectual and unlettered circles. The tomb of its founder, outside of the city of Bukhara, became a famous place of pilgrimage in the region. Other orders, by introducing shamanistic practices, also helped to bridge the worlds of Islam and indigenous religion.

The Mughals in India created a fine syncretic civilization, incorporating Central Asian and Indian motifs. Admittedly the emperor Akbar failed in his attempt to found a pluralistic ideology for his rule, and there were also severe Hindu-Islamic tensions, especially during the reign of his successor Aurungzeb. Perhaps the most creative of all the Mughals was Shah Jahan, who came to the throne in 1627, and was the ultimate creator of the Red Fort and the Taj Mahal, blending Persian and Indian themes in a great new architectural synthesis. Also wonderful was Akbar's city of Fatehpur Sikri, which was eventually left empty because it had no assured water supply.

In India, as in Central Asia, a great part of the missionary activity on behalf of the faith was done by Sufi orders. The figure of the Sufi master was a familiar one, with echoes of guru, *sadhu*, and yogin. The Sufi orders were willing to move away into peripheral places, and not stick to the centers of power. They made use of vernacular languages, from Bengali to Tamil, and they also participated in the widespread *bhakti* style of religion of the period.

They involved themselves in social rites to provide a counterpoint to Hindu society. Sometimes the Muslim wandering ascetics looked very much like Hindu ones, and were scarcely respectable by ordinary Muslim standards, e.g. in their relative nakedness, use of smeared ashes, and so forth. For some, becoming Muslim was socially advantageous, and the Hindu world had to pay penalties for untouchability.

At a more intellectual level, the influence of Ibn al-'Arabi was great, since he presented a point of view congenial to the Hindu mystical tradition. Also important later on, from the time of Aurungzeb, was the spread of well-endowed teaching institutions or *madrasahs* which could create a class of indigenous scholars of Islamic teaching and law.

Dimensions of Medieval Islam

In reflecting upon the achievements of medieval Islam, we can see something of its varieties in the different dimensions of religion.

Ritually, it had its unity because of the *hajj* and the patterns of daily prayer, virtually universal throughout the length and breadth of Islam, from Indonesia to West Africa and from Bukhara to Zanzibar. But in many areas folk religion had gradually decreed the sacredness of the tombs of saints, thus blending popular piety and the inner pursuit of union with Allah. The cycles of the Muslim year were not the same for Sunnis and Shi'a, especially because of the mourning of the death of Husayn.

Experientially there remained tensions between those who saw Islam in terms of orthodox prayer, and the sense of the numinous majesty of Allah, and those who saw the central experience as lying in and beyond *fana'*. Such tensions also involved diverse ways of interpreting texts and the role of the Prophet.

Legally and *ethically*, Islam had its medieval variations, and the need to adapt to very different societies had its effects. But the world of the *madrasahs* was relatively uniform, and prestige was attached to great centers of learning and law such as al-Azhar. There were similar centers in the Shi'i world, for instance the holy city of Qum in Iran, with its academies and leading scholars. At the edge of Islam there were sects with a reputation for flouting the law, such as the Isma'ilis.

In *doctrine*, we have great riches of philosophical diversity, from the somewhat assertive positivism of al-'Ashari to the problematic ideas of the Aristotelian, Ibn Rushd (who as Averroes was so influential in the discussions of the Latin-speaking world), and from the rationalistic (but fading) Mu'tazila to the luxuriant thought of Ibn al-'Arabi. In *myth*, the chief divergences were about the Imams and the nature of the hidden Imam. Ibn Khaldun (1332–1406), the famous Islamic historian, could give a balanced view on the nature of the Caliphate and the question of the end of the world, both recurrent themes in political and popular speculation.

Institutionally, Islam had no priesthood and no central hierarchy: even political power was thoroughly fragmented by the medieval period, though the Ottomans could claim a wide sway over many of the heartlands of the faith and so could have claims to the Caliphate. Establishments were informal and depended much on reputation. There were scarcely any controls, other than consensus, on Islam as a system: and the surprising thing is not its diversity—which was great—but its degree of homogeneity.

In the arts and the *material* side of religion, medieval Islam saw a vast flowering of the poetical heritages, the architectural achievements, the literary creations, the calligraphic varieties and painting schools of the diverse empires, from the Ottomans to the Mughals, and from Morocco to Indonesia. But it was an uncertain civilization, for it was already coming into conflict and contact with new forces from the West which heralded catastrophes and unexpected conquests. Why should it be that the great faith which the Prophet had conveyed to the Arabs, and the Arabs to the world, was destined for trouble, worse than that brought by Genghis Khan?

Classical African Religions

CHAPTER 13

The Configurations of Africa

The traditional religions of Africa before the colonial period divide roughly into four groups. Firstly, there is old Christianity, which in its Coptic form is present in Ethiopia and has had a long history, from at least the fourth century C.E. There has also, secondly, been a community of Jews there. Thirdly, there is Islam, which occupies most of North Africa, though traditionally there are some Christians, including the Coptic Church in Egypt, scattered in among the Muslim majority. Islam has also come south, across the Sahara to much of West Africa, and into the Horn of Africa, the Sudan, and beyond. Then, finally, there are what may be called the classical (traditional) religions of Black Africa. It is with these latter that we are concerned in this chapter.

During the period up to 1500 C.E., trans-Saharan trade from the Muslim countries of North Africa stimulated the creation of larger kingdoms to the south—for instance the empire of Ghana in the interior of West Africa, from the eighth to the eleventh centuries, and its successor Mali, at its peak in the fourteenth century. There was also the state of Songhay and important Hausa trading cities in what is now northern Nigeria. In Nigeria and to the west were the forest kingdoms of Oyo, Benin, and Akan. Further east, in the fifteenth century, there was the Funj empire in the Sudan. Various nomadic peoples were filtering south through Africa, among them Bantu-speaking groups. In Zimbabwe, between 1200 and 1500, and in the lower Zaire, in the region of Kongo, were other concentrations of culture and power. Some of these developments were affected by the incoming European influence which had become more marked with Portuguese settlements and expeditions from the fifteenth century. But the dearth of written records means that it is hard to penetrate clearly into the early period.

It is also, of course, hard to say that there is anything precisely common

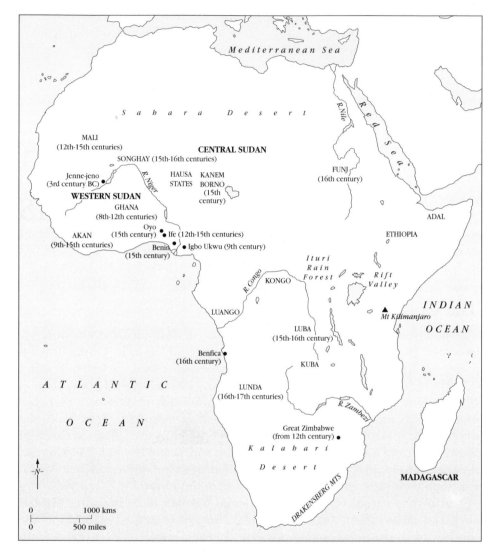

Map 12 Africa before European colonization, showing some of the major empires and kingdoms.

which we can label as African religion: it is only in recent times that African self-consciousness has arisen. Yet there are themes which recur. What we shall do is survey what we can know about religion as it existed when European contacts began. Classical religion of course was to be deeply affected by the colonial experience, and that is the theme of later discussion. So also is the emergence of Afro-American religions in the Caribbean, Brazil, and North America as a consequence of the slave trade.

The creation of kingdoms in the medieval period involved the formation of an ideology of divine kingship, which can still be found in the classical religions of West Africa in particular. This was a natural change, but not of course without conflict, and so we find some traces in ritual of the fight which local cults put up in face of imperial pretensions. As elsewhere in human culture, kings were often associated with the fertility of the land. Generally speaking we are looking at a period after the introduction of settled agricultural practice (often necessary to create the wealth to sustain a widespread monarchy), and this itself tended to breed cults related to the production of riches from the land. These could be grafted onto the kingly ideology. It seems to be the case that the ideal of the sacred king was arrived at in several places in Africa independently, a testimony to the human force of certain ideas with new economic and political developments.

Changes in the practice of agriculture spread south from the Sahara from about 1500 C.E. onward, with shrines emerging related to the promotion of the fertility of crops. Other changes occurred with the introduction of new technology, notably ironworking. It is therefore worth bearing in mind that much of our evidence relates to a period which is the result of a variety of changes in religious as well as social organization and ideas.

Dimensions of African Religion

Some Doctrinal Themes

Mostly, the *doctrinal* content of African religion is anthropomorphic: that is, gods and spirits, those unseen forces which explain and affect human life, are

A Bushman or San woman, belonging to the diminishing group of hunters and gatherers around the Kalahari desert, who represent an ancient non-Bantu population of small, yellow-skinned peoples; her face-paint is designed to ward off threatening spirits.

thought of and related to in human terms. Moreover, much of religion, naturally enough, has to do with human life. This means that personal and this-worldly models predominate in myth. Nevertheless, there is in Africa south of the Sahara a common belief in a Supreme Being, who ultimately controls human destinies. But such a being may be so remote, and unseen to the inward eye, that he plays little part in daily cults or in the mythic imagination of the people. Many myths convey a sense of an original order which became disturbed somewhere during the creative process, which explains how it is that death and disorder have come into the world. Though death is a notable theme in African thinking, individual survival does not rate as an important doctrine, though ancestors are vital to the onward welfare and existence of the community.

While there may be a Supreme Being, the daily concerns of people relate more to the many and more immediate gods. These can act as agents of the One but they also have their own independence. So the general pattern in Africa could be said to be a kind of refracted theism, in which divine power is broken down into the actions of the gods.

Mythic Themes

There are many *myths* of death and disorder. One theme concerns messengers of life and death. God sends a slow animal to deliver the news that humans will have everlasting life. It is often thought to be the chameleon, which has the joyous colors of the rainbow in its makeup. But it is sluggish, and God sends another animal, impatiently, like the swift-running hare, to deliver the news of death. So it turns out that humans are subject to death. God may have wished us eternal life; but it is the result of natural events that we have to die. On another mythic view, death came into the world because of sleep. We (or rather our primordial ancestors) were told to stay awake till God came back from some trip; but we were overcome by sleep and so missed what would have been God's declaration that humans are immortal. The message failed. This myth suggests that sleep is the foretaste of ultimate death. It seems that we cannot escape the inevitable consequences of our finitude.

A number of myths relate death more directly to the very difference between God and human beings. At one time, according to a myth from Zaire, God and humans lived together in the same village. But the humans quarreled so that in disgust God exiled them to a place below. There they experienced hunger, chills, sickness, and death, and so they wanted to regain their earlier paradisal place. They began to build a great wooden tower, which rose up, up, and up. In due course it seemed to have reached heaven, and the builders at the top were overjoyed and celebrated with flutes and drums. God did not like the noise, and angrily flattened the tower. Another tower motif is this: in the early days, by their beastliness, arrogance, killing passions, and lack of obedience, human beings made God wish to drive them away; but they kept coming after him, till a spider spun a wonderful thread, and God and his entourage were able to climb on it into heaven. The humans tried to pile up a

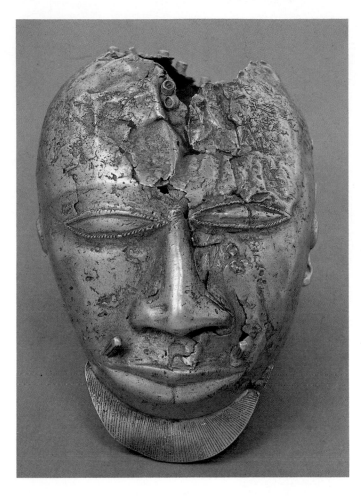

Above The social dimension: in a number of West African contexts kingship is integral to social organization, and the king may play a role as intermediary between heaven and earth; shown here is a beautiful burial mask from the Ashante in Ghana.

Right A fine bronze sculpture, dating from the fourteenth or fifteenth century, of a Yoruba king from Ife, Nigeria, wearing a crown of feathers and pearls. It is thought that the line of holes was added so that a beard could be attached. Yoruba culture survived, although in a somewhat fragmented form, in some of the Afro-American groups transported to the Western hemisphere by slavery. British Museum, London.

The Gabon Pygmies on Exile

The night is black, the sky is blotted out,
   We have left the village of our Fathers,
   The Maker is angry with us…
The light becomes dark,
     the night and again night,
The day with hunger tomorrow –
The Maker is angry with us.

The Old Ones have passed away,
   Their homes are far off, below,
   Their spirits are wandering –

Where are their spirits wandering?
Perhaps the passing wind knows.
Their bones are far off below.

Are they below, the spirits?
Are they here?
Do they see the offerings set out?
Tomorrow is naked and empty,
   For the Maker is no longer with us – there,
   He is no longer the host seated with us at
    our fire.

---

huge tower made of the branches of trees, and this ended disastrously, for the tower crashed down.

Sometimes God is annoyed when an old woman batters the underside of heaven with a pestle, so he withdraws heaven from earth to establish once and for all the difference between him as an immortal and the mortals below. This may have something to do with the connection between human culture and death. The most basic act of human culture is cooking, and stories may connect this with alienation from God and the arising of death. It is as if the desire for independence from one God is what makes human beings subject to death: independence is inseparable from finitude.

Another theme, apart from death, is the figure of the trickster, sometimes seen as a spider (which is an ambiguous creature, between earth and sky). In a Pygmy story, the spiderman Tore gave humans water by stealing it from an old dame. He also stole fire for them when, on visiting a smithy, his loincloth caught fire. He ran agonizingly through the forest, begging the fire to leave him and enter the trees instead; which it did, and that is how it is that fire is made by the friction of sticks. The smith is often a vital person in Africa, a prototype of creator and intermediary between order and disorder. Often the primordial ancestor is conceived of as a smith. It was of course above all through the use of iron that effective agriculture could spread, and much of human culture besides.

Some Ethical Themes

A person is thought of as having various psychic aspects, some of which go on after death in a kind of half-existence. Many groups cultivate the deceased as individuals, until such time as they merge into the generality of group predecessors. Sometimes an ancestor is reborn in part in the individual and functions as a kind of guardian spirit. At any rate, mostly, the dead are to be treated with respect. The procedures of the funeral and mourning become vital social obligations to heal the wound caused in a group by the separation of one of its members.

Opposite top The ritual dimension: masked dancers among the Dogon, from east Mali and northwest Burkina Faso, whose subtle and complex cosmological doctrines are reflected both in the material layout of their villages and in the organization of ceremonial life.

Opposite bottom The ritual dimension: among the Dinka of the Sudan the leadership role is played by priestly persons known as Spearmasters. Here a funeral ritual is followed by relatives crawling over and around the grave. In the background is an ox that has been sacrificed.

As the stories of death have hinted, human perverseness is displeasing to God. Human beings are given to quarreling and greed, and to other socially unfortunate dispositions. Often these tendencies are symbolized in the figure of the sorcerer who plots against the group, acting by night in the bush, naked and incestuous, cannibalistic and living with wild beasts. The opposite of such characteristics define a general *ethic*: actions must be harmonious; open and in the light of day; decorous (genitals should generally speaking be covered) and sexually orderly; cultured and corresponding to the rules of society.

Some Ritual Themes

The most potent *ritual* in sub-Saharan Africa is sacrifice. This may take the form of the offering of plant life, but more characteristically it involves taking life, of sheep, goats, cattle, or chickens. The blood of the animal often is thought to represent its life force, and so it has power, for instance to ward off evil forces. Sacrifice is, as elsewhere in the world, a gesture of communication with the god. Human desires are made known to the divine being, and it is hoped that the sacrificial act will promote such good things as may be desired. Sometimes sacrifices are used as a form of healing, by transferring disease to the animal. Sometimes a sacrifice is a way of expiating the bad deeds of human beings. Since there are ruptures between the seen and the unseen worlds, sacrifices represent a conduit of life and power between the worlds.

There are seasonal festivals making the transitions to new times, as in New Year and harvest times; and rituals for transitions to new positions in the social order, such as the coronation of kings and the installation of chiefs, the passing of the dead into the world beyond, the marriage ceremonies of individuals (which also often cement family alliances), and so on. Among the rites of passage especially significant are the initiations of boys and girls. Widely practiced are the rites of the circumcision of boys and the cutting of the clitoris (clitoridectomy) of girls. Other scars and bodily marks are a sign of death to the old childish condition and the taking on of new responsibilities as an adult.

Music is, as elsewhere, a vital ingredient of worship and ritual. It is generally thought that the spirit world is especially responsive to human music, which may at the same time be divine, because ultimately derived from divine sources. Typically some distinction is made between sacred and other music, and usually there will be a wide repertoire of hymns and songs connected with the gods and ancestral spirits of the group. Music can be used for healing, for fertility purposes, and of course for celebration.

Some Experiential Themes

The awareness of the gods in the rivers and the rains, in the forests and in the sky, in lightning and wild animals, is given by a sense of numinous and uncanny power. There are also dreams to consider: they may sometimes signal the presence of a spirit to the individual which may herald some sin or misdeed for which there is need of expiation. Very common throughout Africa are those occasions, which can be spontaneous, of the possession of a person by a spirit. This may be frightening, and it may call for rituals to cause the spirit to depart; but it also may be benign, for the person gets thus as close as possible to her god. Priests who are closely identified with particular deities may speak in their name, and so acquire a prophetic function. Some curative practices which involve those who are skilled in questioning and diagnosis may be aided by shamanistic methods, in which the healer takes on the sickness and visits the other world in other to rescue the sick person from the dead.

In a real way, then, the deities of Africa are really present in society and are commonly *experienced*. They are not theoretical entities but living presences, as also are the ancestors. The mountains and rivers and prairies and jungles are laced with presences, and they are the scene in which the drama of human existence takes place, and Fate weaves its patterns.

Religious Specialists and Social Patterns

There is a spectrum of religious specialists in the societies of Africa which range from priests, associated with cults and rituals, through prophets and diviners, to healers. African traditional ways of curing sickness have developed considerably over the last four centuries or more, and healing cults have during this period taken a more prominent part in the total fabric of African religion. Sickness is tied into religion because a god may make himself known to an individual through the very fact of sickness. A medium is often a person who has been sick, but overcome it. So cured sick people often attach themselves to a shrine to act as a mouthpiece of the god. They may then attract attention, and people may bring the sick to them for professional treatment. Divination is another social service performed by classical religion, for instance among the Yoruba in West Africa, who have an especially sophisticated form of divination. This tells something of the future and forces the client to confront the realities of choice.

As we have seen, kingship is typically regarded as a sacred institution, and in societies which are united under the rule of a king he will himself have priestly functions in representing the divine order in the world over which he rules: so the maintenance of political order is not separate from the processes of making the land and the people fruitful. Sometimes the ruler of a region may have the earth as his spirit wife, and fertility themes are here prominent; but the spirits that underlie and control cultivation are different from those that underlie and control wild life. The Ashanti in Ghana, for instance, make a sharp divide between the mother of the fields and her dangerous sister who lives in the underworld. The mother of civilization is somehow closer to humankind.

Sacred Shrines and Religious Art

Many shrines are simply places where spirits reside: a grove in the forest or a fancy-shaped rock in a river. If you look across a landscape in Africa there will

The Oba (ruler) of Benin in his elaborate armor, which is fashioned from thousands of coral beads. Although the kingdom of Benin is now part of Nigeria, the Oba continues to rule his people as a divine monarch.

be places especially charged with power, where the presence of a spirit is more eminent. But some shrines are human, or at least involve buildings or markers, such as the palace-like buildings of gods in parts of East Africa. Such buildings may contain images of the god, and in any case a section in which the god resides and another section for the people, linked by an altar across which the sacrificial offerings are made.

In southern Nigeria, among the Edo people, there is a marvelous tradition of making carved bronze heads of the Obas or kings. Such bronzes are representative of individuals but they are not individualized portraits. Indeed, much of African art is symbolic rather than representational, so you can know from the bits and pieces of a mask what it is (who it is, really) that it represents. Masks and body painting are prominent ways of displaying temporary and ritual possession. It is in such visible forms and through the dance that the gods make themselves manifest to human beings. Headdresses and masks can also manifest the dead and the creative powers, such as that of the female, in the dialectic of rites which celebrate the complementary roles of the sexes in the universe. Some sculptures, for instance those of kneeling women among the Yoruba, reflect the devotees themselves; this is the human response to divine power rather than a direct representation of divine power itself.

It is common in Black Africa to believe in the continued presence of ancestors in society. Here, a previous ruler escorted by his servants is represented at the shrine of the living Oba or ruler of Benin, in West Africa.

Some Representative Patterns

Having looked briefly at some of the classical dimensions of African religion, let us now look at some instances from the mosaic of African societies that make up the culture of the Continent. We shall visit West Africa, East Africa, Central Africa, and Southern Africa, and glimpse different styles of societies.

Yoruba Religion

The Yoruba are quite a large people, of between twelve and fifteen million, occupying portions of southwest Nigeria, Benin, and Togo. Their mythic stories tell of a founder, Oduduwa, and this probably reflects some historic memory of the usurpation of power and the foundation of the people. One of the most vital feasts of the sacred year is the annual celebration of male ancestors, which takes the form of a stately procession and masquerade in which the participants are clothed in swathes of material which whirl outward in constantly changing forms, making the ancestors manifest. Another festival, the feast of the mothers, celebrates female power. Other celebrations deal with the founders of towns, and with the dialectical relations between chief and priest, king and sacred expert.

At the head of the extensive pantheon of *oriṣa* (gods, conceived of typically as having originally been humans, who through their great achievements

A shrine to Ogun, God of Iron and War, at Ife in Nigeria: characteristically this spirit has no covered shrine, but lives by the roadside.

attain high status in the afterlife) is Olorun. The other gods are thought of as his children. They are reckoned to be 401 in number. Olorun is not worshiped directly, though in recent times some shrines dedicated to him have been founded: the assumption is made that offerings to the lesser gods make their way to Olorun, so that many rituals end with the formula: "May Olorun accept it." Again, he did not create the world directly but deputed this task to Obatala, though it was Oduduwa who actually finished off the job. There was a great battle between him and Obatala, which is ritually reenacted. The banishment of Obatala is followed by his being invited back again amid great rejoicing.

The many gods in fact represent the greatly fragmented character of Yoruba society, and so the various gods are favorites in different places. To some extent the breaking up of Yoruba society is a modern phenomenon, dating primarily from nineteenth-century struggles for power. Olorun therefore also expresses a sense of ultimate unity. Moreover, he is the determiner of individual destinies. Before birth a person's guardian soul kneels before the great God and a destiny and time of life are fixed. Some variations may be possible later, but the span of life remains inflexibly destined. If you have followed a good life, Olorun will judge you worthy after death, and after a short while you will be reincarnated. Those who lead a bad life are consigned to a hot place of destruction and punishment.

Of all the gods of Yoruba religion the most widely found and effective is Ogun, deity of iron and war and hunters, a kind of celestial Bismarck. To him is sacrificed the dog, who can help in hunting and war. His fierce character betrays the human fact that we live off the destruction of others, and a people safeguards its identity by making war on others: for otherwise they would swallow your people up. And eating necessitates such activities as the hunt, the primordial activity of the human race before even the plants were tamed, still less the animals.

The rituals of sacrifice have power to bring the spirits into the presence of the worshiper, and to channel the numinous power which pervades the cosmos. Despite the many spirits in the Yoruba pantheon, the conception of the world both seen and unseen is a unified one.

Nuer Religion

The Nuer, like their close relations the Dinka, herd cattle amid the great savannas and marshes of the southern Sudan. Their life centers on cattle, so that alliances and rifts reflect themselves in gifts and thefts of beasts. They traditionally looked upon themselves as the only true humans, assigning to other groups only a shadowy existence. So their world was sky and grassland and cattle and constant wandering migrations—in many ways a beautiful and easy life, yet marred by human strife from time to time. The great spiritual being or force is Kwoth, who dwells in the sky but also pervades life, either through his own energy or in the form of lesser spirits of the sky and of the earth. These beings are sometimes threatening and difficult, bringing sickness and misfortunes; but Kwoth himself is benevolent. Sometimes the problems besetting people are caused by sins they have committed, and sacrifices will restore the situation.

We see here something of a simplified pattern of relation between the many gods and the one Spirit. It reflects a comparatively simple society, which has priests but no elaboration of kingship and the like. It was the British anthropologist E. E. Evans-Pritchard whose *Nuer Religion*, published in 1956, helped to change many attitudes to African religion: first, because he took religion seriously as an independent variable at a time when others often saw it as a mere side effect of social relationships; and second, more importantly, because his account of Kwoth made the deity sound much closer in idea and feeling to God as understood in the known theistic traditions than had other accounts of African divinity. And rightly so: though Kwoth is especially associated with the sky, and the rainbow is imagined as the necklace of God, so it was too with Yahweh, and Jesus' prayer does start "Our Father who art in heaven…"

Mbuti Religion

If we now move southwest from the Sudan into the rain forest of the Ituri in Central Zaire, we come upon one of the Pygmy peoples who live their lives in a difficult environment in which every expedition for game is fraught with danger. For most of their history, such Pygmies have lived in their own secluded way, and it is only recently that they have been in communication with the wider world. Theirs is no doubt a vanishing mode of life.

Their world is a dense tropical rain forest, full of haunting calls, the screeches of birds, and the chatter of wild animals. Their life is hunting and gathering, and hunting is a vital part of their fight for existence. There is in their religion the sense that the world was created by a God who retired to the sky: a *deus otiosus*. More important is the divine culture hero, Tore, who is responsible for endowing the Mbuti with fire and other arts, for instance skills in hunting and the collection of honey, an important part of their diet. The forest itself is replete with divine forces, which must be dealt with, and the dead are merged into the forest to take their place among such spirits.

The Mbuti have fairly extensive initiations, for instance for girls. The ceremonial known as Elima occurs when a girl first menstruates. She and others in similar condition are secluded in a special hut in the forest for several weeks and receive instructions from the older women about what they need to know. This includes the music which women sing. Indeed, music forms an important ingredient in the invocations of the forest spirits, and in order to revive the life of the forest after some calamity, such as the death of a member of the village. Ceremonials here are postulated on the thought that the divinity behind the forest has caused it to sleep and not to look after human beings, and it is for such a reason that death has come into the life of the group: the forest needs to be roused if it is to resume its beneficent aspect. Pygmy groups also celebrate a ritual of apology to the spirit of the animals that they have killed—something which is reminiscent of bear rituals in northern Siberia. One cannot fail to be impressed by the echoes sounding from one hunting society to another.

Zulu Religion

It is only a little over 150 years since the Zulu were welded together as a people, in the beautiful rolling hills of Natal, beneath the great ranges of the Drakensberg Mountains. Since then great changes have occurred, including the conversion of most Zulus to various forms of Christianity, including Zulu Zionism. That is something we shall have to look at in Part II.

Zulu religion as such blends together some old themes, including the story of death recounted earlier, in this case how the lizard outstripped the chameleon, both of these creatures being despatched by uMvelinqangi, the first being to come into existence. He is also credited with bestowing on humanity their ancestors and the customs for dealing with them. These ancestors, known as *amadlozi*, are important in Zulu thought, which sees the world as having a large invisible community stretching beyond the human. Ancestors more than three generations back are settled and not threatening, but later than that they need to be appeased—so that they may settle—with the offering of sacrifices such as goats. After death, rituals are performed to

Mbuti pygmy women of the Ituri rain forest in Zaire. They are hunter-gatherers without much degree of internal social differentiation and live in symbiosis with the Divinity surrounding them and permeating the forest.

bring the shade of the departed into the community of the ancestors. The senior males are involved in managing such rituals, which gives them authority in settling disputes, since the *amadlozi* are involved in the processes of harmonizing the community. The king's ancestors are traditionally called on before battle, and were important for the welfare of the whole nation.

An important deity is a great fertility deity, iNkosazana, the Princess of Heaven, who is invoked before agricultural activities, many undertaken by women. They may plant a special small field for her beside a river if possible, and such an offering may generate fertility. She also plays a vital role in the initiatory ceremonies for girls as they enter upon puberty. The role of women is ambiguous in Zulu society, since they form a bridge between different patrilineages, and have an outsider status in their husband's group, but nevertheless form a vital part of the transmission of lineages. The diviners are predominantly women and have central roles in the cure of sicknesses and other disharmonies. Women are specially subject to possession by spirits, and when this occurs it gives them shamanic powers.

But the traditional cosmology is fading under the impact of wars, land seizure, and other ills which have befallen the Zulu people in the last hundred years or more. That, as I have said, is a later story.

Reflections on African Religion

We have had glimpses of diverse societies—the urban kingship of the Yoruba, the pastoral simplicity of life among the Nuer, the green menace of Pygmy forest life, the great cattle-rearing society of the Zulu—which provide a sample of thousands of societies and religions. We have noted some themes from the dimensions of classical religion. Though there is some talk of revival of these ancient ways today, it is likely that their future lies within some larger synthesis, not only between differing African societies and conceptions, but also between them and the forces which have been crowding into Africa from outside. African religion is a deeply important facet of human history up to the modern period. It will remain a resource for Black Africans, and more widely for humans. But it has never been a single system, or even approximated to the sense of a single tradition which has marked some of the historical world religions.

If there is now a sense of African unity, it is due to the reaction against a threatening colonialism. It is to the history of this colonialist epoch in the world's affairs that we now turn.

Part II

	GENERAL	TRADITIONAL, AMERICAN, AFRICAN, SHAMANISTIC ETC	HINDUISM AND JAINISM	SIKHISM
1500	Hernan Cortes defeats Aztecs (1519–21) Babur, first Mughal Emperor of India (1526–30) Francisco Pizarro defeats Incas ((1531–5) Ivan IV, the Terrible, of Russia (r.1533–84)	Nubians destroy Christian kingdom of Meroe (1504) Songhay destroy Mali empire (1546)		Guru Nanak (1469–1539) bases religion (c.1519) on teachings of Kabir (1440–1518) Angad (1504–52), 2nd Guru
1550	Idris Alooma, king of Kanem-Bornu (1570–1619) Dutch revolt against Spanish (1572) Toyotimi Hideyoshi (1537–98) unifies Japan (1582–98) Dutch Settlement of Java (1595)	Idris Alooma becomes king of Kanemn-Bornu (1570–1619) Songhay destroyed by Morocco (1591)	Akbar defeats Hindus at battle of Panipat (1556) Mughal Empire (1556–1707)	Amar Das (1479–1574), 3rd Guru Ram Das (1534–81), 4th Guru Amritsar founded (1577)
1600	Shogunate in Japan (1603–1867) Thirty Years' War in Europe (1618–48) Taj Mahal built, India (1632) Qing Dynasty, China (1644–1911)	Oyo empire (Nigeria) at height (c.1600) Portuguese destroy Mwenemutapa empire (1628)		Arjun Mal (1563–1606), 5th guru; compiled Adi Granth (1604) Hargobind Das (1595–1644), 6th guru, raised army to defend religion against Muslim rule of Shah Jahan (r.1628–58)
1650	Great Fire of London (1665) "Glorious" Revolution in England (1688) Peter I, the Great, Tsar of Russia (1682–1725)	Bambara kingdoms (upper Nigeria) rise (1660) Portuguese defeat Kongo (1662)	Maratha kingdom founded (1674)	Hari Krishen (1656–64), 8th guru Tegh Bahadur (c.1621–75), 9th guru; becomes Sikh martyr for refusing to convert to Islam Gobind Singh (1666–1708), last guru, creates Khalsa (1699)
1700	Rise of Bantu kingdom in east Africa (c.1700) War of Spanish Succession (1701–13) Afghan rising against Persians (1709) Nader Shah of Persia sacks Delhi (1739)			On death of Gobind Singh the scripture, Adi Granth, becomes the guru (1708)
1750	Seven Years' War (1756–63) James Cook charts east coast of Australia (1769) Declaration of Independence (1776) in USA French Revolution (1789)		Ram Mohan Roy (1772–1833) reformer of Hinduism	
1800	Enlightenment in Europe Napoleonic Wars (1803–15) Simón Bolivar secures independence of Colombia, Venezuela, Peru and Bolivia (1819–25) Maori chiefs in New Zealand accept British rule (1840)	Defeat of Zulus by Boers at Blood River (1838)	Christian missionary activity on India (from 1820s) Dayananda Sarasvati (1824–83) founder of Arya Samaj Brahmo Samaj revitalization (1828) Ramakrishna Paramahamsa (1834–86) promotes the idea that "all religions are one"	Ranjit Singh (1780–1839) founds Sikh kingdom Shiv Dayal (1818–78) founder of Radhasoamis Sikh Wars (1845–6, 1848–9)
1850	Charles Darwin's The Origin of Species (1859) Civil War in US (1861–5) USA buys Alaska from Russia (1867) Sigmund Freud (1856–1939) Liberation of serfs in Russia (1861) World's Parliament of Religions, Chicago (1893)	Ringatu (1860s) and Ritana movements founded amongst Maoris Emergence of Cargo cults in Melanesia (1860s) Peyote cult amongst Native Americans (1890s) Simon Kimbangu (1889–1951)	Narendranath Datta (Vivekenanda; 1863–1902) acclaimed in West Vijaya Dharma Suri (1868–1922): fostered Jain renewal Arya Samaj founded (1875) British rule in India (1857–1947)	
1900	World War I (1914–18) Russian Revolution (1917) Rudolf Otto: The Idea of the Holy (1917) Wall Street Crash (1929) World War II (1939–45)	Aladura movement in Nigeria (1920s) La philosophie bantoue (1945) by Placide Tempels Beginnings of apartheid in South Africa (1948)	Hindu Mahasabha begins in the Punjab (1907) Dr K.B. Hedgewar (1889-1940) founds the R.S.S. Partition of India (1947)	
1950	Korean War (1950–53) Vietnam War (1954–75) Fall of Berlin Wall (1989)	Resurgence of Aboriginal religion in Australia (1970s-80s)	Jain monks become established outside India Hindus' increasing spread into West	Sant Fateh Sing (c.1911–72) advocates creation of Punjab as separate Sikh state within India Sant Jarnail Singh Bhindranwale (1947–84) advocates independence of Khalistan 1000 Sikhs killed in siege of Golden Temple, Amritsar (1984)

BUDDHISM, CONFUCIANISM, DAOISM AND SHINTO	JUDAISM	CHRISTIANITY	ISLAM	NEW RELIGIONS
Francis Xavier arrives in Hyushu in Japan 1549	Revival of Kabbalism	Diet of Worms; Martin Luther excommunicated (1521) Jesuits founded (1534) John Calvin at Geneva (1541) Council of Trent (1545–63); start of Counter–Reformation Francis Xavier to Japan (1549)	Ottoman Turks capture Palestine (1517), Egypt (1517), Algeria (1529), Tunis (1535) and Hungary (1541)	
The Jesuit priest Matteo Ricci (1552–1610) visits the Chinese court Christian missionaries banned in Japan (1596)		French wars of religion (1562–98) Doctrine of Anglican church established (1563) St Bartholomew Day massacre (1572) in France St Vincent de Paul (c.1580–1660) Edict of Nantes (1598) grants religious toleration in France	The Turks conquer north coast of Africa (1554) Akbar (1542–1605) becomes Mughal emperor in India (1556) Ottoman attack on Malta fails (1565) A Christian fleet defeats the Ottomans at the Battle of Lepanto (1571)	
	Shabbetai Tzevi (1626–76), false messiah Barukh Spinoza (1632–77), philosopher	Baptist movement begins in Netherlands and England (early 1600s) King James's Bible (1611) Japan suppresses Christianity (1616) Pilgrim Fathers to N. America (1620) George Fox (1624–91) founds Society of Friends Capuchin monks go to Congo (1645)	Spain expels Moriscoes (1609) Blue Mosque at Constantinople (1609)	
		First Roman Catholic church in Beijing (1650) Revocation of Edict of Nantes (1685)	Ottoman Turks occupy Hungary (1664) Aurangzeb begins to impose Muslim orthodoxy on India (1680) Turks fail to take Vienna (1683) Battle of Mohács (1687) Venice captures Athens (1687)	
	Baal Shem Tov (1700–60) Moses Mendelssohn (1729–86), philosopher	John Wesley (1703–91) founds Methodists (1739) James and Jane Wardley found Shaker movement (1747)	Ibn 'Abd al-Wahhab (1703–92), founder of Wahhabism	
China overruns Tibet (1751) Nakayama Miki (1798–1887), founder of Tenrikyo in Japan	Ya'akov Frank (1726–91) 1791. Jews defined as full citizens in France	Ann Lee (1736–84) takes Shaker movement to US (1774) Methodists become separate body (1795)	Indian *khilifat* movement (1818–1924)	
Opium War (1839–42): Britain at war with China Treaty of Nanking opens up China to trade with the West (1842)		Joseph Smith (1805–44) founds Mormons (1830) Brigham Young (1801–77) leads Mormons to Salt Lake City (1846) Ellen Gould White (1826–1915): creator of Adventists	Muslim areas fall under European influence (1800–1900s) Mirza Ghulam Ahmad (1835–1908) founder of Ahmadiya movement Muhammad 'Abduh (1849–1905): Islamic modernist	3000–4000 adherents of Sayyid Ali Muhammad (1819–50), known as the Bab, executed (1848–51) (Baha'i) Annie Besant (1847–1933): notable Theosophist
Taiping Rebellion in China (1850–65) Self Strengthening movement in China (1860s) Meiji Restoration in Japan (1867–1912) Shinto becomes state religion of Japan (1878–1945) Anagarika Dharmapala (1864–1933) founds Mahabodhi Society (1891) Reform Movement in China (1898)	American Reform Judaism established (1869) Dreyfus Affair (1894–1906) Theodor Herzl (1860–1904) founds World Zionist Organization (1897) Pogroms in Russia following assassination of tsar (1881–2) Aliyah (migrations to Palestine) begin (1882)	Missionaries to Africa Vatican Council (1870); Papal infallibility declared Charles Taze Russell (1852–1916) founds Jehovah's Witnesses (1872) Mary Baker Eddy (1821–1910) founds Christian Science Movement (1876) William Booth (1829–1912) founds Salvation Army (1865)		Baha'Allah (as Nuri is known) refines Baha'i faith, stressing obedience to the state Baha'Allah exiled to Baghdad then to Acre (1863), Theosophy founded (1875) by Mme Blavatsky and H.S. Olcott Marcus Garvey (1887–1940) advocates Black nationalism Kardecism in Brazil (1870s/80s)
Abbot Taixi (1899–1947): Chinese Buddhist thinker Confucianism becomes state religion in China (1913) Communists win Civil war in China (1949)	Second wave of Aliyah (1904–14) Balfour Declaration (1917) Nuremberg laws strip Jews of rights (1935) in Germany Holocaust (1940–45) Israel declared an independent state (1948)	Papal clampdown on Catholic Modernism (1907) Karl Barth: *Church Dogmatics* (1920s) Discovery of Nag Hammadi manuscripts (1945) World Council of Churches founded (1948)	Establishment of Muhammadiya movement in Indonesia (1912) Caliphate abolished by Turkey (1924) Muslim Brotherhood founded (1928) Partition of Muslim Pakistan from Hindu India (1947)	Shoghi Effendi Rabbani (1897–1957), first Guardian (1921) (Baha'i) Garvey founds Universal Negro Improvement Association (1914) Haile Selassie of Ethiopia regarded as messiah by Rastafarians Umbanda religion in Brazil (1920s) Wallace D. Fard disappears 1934 (Nation of Islam)
Great Council of Buddhism held in Burma (1956) China invades Tibet; Dalai Lama flees (1959) Cultural Revolution attacks all religions in China (1966–76) Chinese government limits religious freedom (1989)	Rabbinate given jurisdiction over family and personal law in Israel (1953) Six-Day War (1967) Yom Kippur War (1973)	Second Vatican Council (1962–5) Gustav Gutierrez initiates Liberation Theology (1969) United Reformed Church: union of Presbyterian Church in England and Congregational Church in US (1972) Barbara Harris ordained as first woman bishop in US (1989) Anglican General Synod votes in favour of women priests (1992)	Muslim states join OPEC; Muslim resurgence begins (1970s) *Fatwa* against Salman Rushdie (1989) Civil war in Afghanistan between Taliban and forces of General Massood (from 1989)	Unification Church (Moonies) founded in Korea (1954) Malcolm X killed (1965)

CHAPTER 14

The Explosion of Europe and the Re-forming of Christianity

The Unleashing of New Forces from Europe

World history changed around 1500. Europe had been a rather peripheral civilization before then, often struggling not to be overrun by Muslims and Mongols. After 1500 it unified the oceans by great sea voyages; it radically altered the shape of its primary religion, Christianity; it began processes culminating in the development of modern science, capitalism, nationalism, liberalism, and industrialization. These were powerful and sometimes fascinating, often devastating forces. They bred among other things colonialism, and with it great alterations to other continents and ways of life. North America came to be dominated by White men. Hispanic culture permeated the rest of the Americas. The African slave trade shifted large numbers of Blacks to Brazil, the Caribbean, and North America. Later on, Australia and New Zealand were overrun by Whites, and White settlements at the Cape bred a new area of conflict. Colonial empires were established in India and later most of Southeast Asia, in Indonesia, in the Caribbean, in Africa, and in North and Central Asia. Only with difficulty could China and Japan fight off European empires. Oceania too was dominated by the West. By the end of the nineteenth century there was scarcely a part of the world which did not feel the impact of colonialism. It was as if in 1500 Europe was just a branch of world history, and thereafter the world was part of European history. So this was a new turn in the story of the human race.

The experiential dimension: the divine love pierces St. Teresa in Gianlorenzo Bernini's sculpture *The Ecstasy of St. Teresa* (1645–52), in the Sta Maria della Vittoria, Rome. It is one of the best-known of Baroque sculptures.

The new European civilization, very different in many ways from that of the Middle Ages, was glittering, dynamic, rich with ideals, and often cruel. The Renaissance marked a new explosion of literary and artistic creativity. The Reformation marked a new reshaping of Christianity in the West. Science and capitalism released new forces of material creativity. The Enlightenment generated new hopes of political freedom and liberal thought. The eighteenth century saw inventions like the steam engine; new economic theories, as in the seminal work of Adam Smith (1723–90); lovely architecture and music; new philosophies and methods of agriculture; and two basic revolutions, one in America and the other in France.

Christianity and the New Dynamic

Christianity's position in all this was ambiguous. In some degree the idea of a rational universe created by a God with a mind analogous to the human mind prepared the way for the confident exploration of the physical world which marked the work of such key figures as Galileo Galilei (1564–1642) and Isaac Newton (1642–1727). The events which came to be known as the Reform-ation undoubtedly helped to spread new thinking and a speculative cast of mind. But there were reactions *against* freedom of ideas by the Churches too. Christianity felt challenged by the new forces released in Europe and America, and it had to make accommodations to them in a way similar to those later made by other religious traditions through the impact of Western trade and colonialism. Christianity had to cope with the effects of the new science on its traditional picture of the universe: the trial of Galileo for heresy and the intellectual debates over Evolution in the nineteenth century were two main instances of this. It had to cope with the industrial revolution which created new classes of urban people, alienated often from the traditional rural values of much Christianity. It had to cope with the state in the era of nationalism and new systems of education. It had to cope with liberal ideas which often eroded traditional modes of authority. In all this it was also divided, because of the fragmentation brought on by the rise of Protestantism. But it had new sources of dynamism—revival in the New World, powerful missionary activity in the colonial era, and the exploration of new forms of belief and practice.

The nineteenth century also saw other ideologies than those of the prevailing liberalism: most notably the creation of Marxism, which was to have an enormous impact on the twentieth century. There were ideas too of the corporate national state, which were to be one of the sources of Nazism and Fascism. All these in their different ways provided a challenge, and indeed alternatives, to traditional religion. Judaism, which had been carried forward under great restrictions and sometimes oppressive stresses within European civilization, found a new destiny after emancipation in Europe, great new opportunities in the United States of America, and hopes of a reestablishment of Israel. The shattering darkness of the Holocaust nearly drowned out the new light; and the foundation of the state of Israel in 1948 provided a new concreteness to the religion and the tradition.

IMAGO·ERASMI·ROTERODA·
MI·AB·ALBERTO·DVRERO·AD·
VIVAM·EFFIGIEM·DELINIATA·

ΤΗΝ·ΚΡΕΙΤΤΩ·ΤΑ·ΣΥΓΓΡΑΜ
ΜΑΤΑ·ΔΙΞΕΙ

·MDXXVI·

Desiderius Erasmus (?1469–1536), the renowned classical scholar of Rotterdam, whose humanistic learning was one of the roots of the new attitudes leading to the Reformation. The engraving (1526) is by Albrecht Dürer

In the ensuing sections we shall first look at the religious meaning of the Renaissance, then at the beginnings of the Reformation—Lutheran, Calvinist, and radical; then at the Counter-Reformation, the reshaping of Catholicism in Europe; then at the relations between religion and the new nationalisms; then at Jewish emancipation; then at Eastern Orthodoxy and the Russian move eastward; then at varieties of Christian response to the new knowledge and liberalism in the nineteenth-century context; then at new ideologies like Marxism; then at the imperial expansions and mission movements out of Europe; and finally at Christianity and Judaism in Europe during the twentieth century. In the next chapter we shall see some of the same themes, but in the very different context of North America.

The Renaissance and Its Religious Meaning

That broad movement of culture, especially in the visual arts and in philosophy, which we know as the Renaissance, had its high point in Italy in the years around 1500, when Leonardo da Vinci and Michelangelo were at the height of their powers, and the Papacy was a brilliant patron of the new arts. It was a period when, under the stimulus of a rediscovered classical civilization, the artists and sculptors transcended their Roman and Greek heroes. It was a time of a brilliant and colorful depiction of reality in painting, which glorified this world even more than the next. It was a period too of freer thought and humanistic scholarship. Desiderius Erasmus (1469?–1536) used the new Greek and Latin scholarship to rediscover Christian origins, and was critical of dogmatic theologians who by their disputes overlaid the morality of Christ and his human face with the crust of stale speculation. Examples of the freer thought were a succession of Italian Neoplatonists: Marsilio Ficino (1433–99), Pico della Mirandola (1463–94), and Giordano Bruno (1548–1600). Ficino propounded a version of Neoplatonism, with a Christian clothing put upon it. But he believed in a kind of perennial philosophy which had been taught by various teachers in various traditions. Pico showed that the Aristotelian and Platonic philosophies can be blended and are compatible: he was also

Map 13 Reformation Europe c.1600 C.E.

influenced by Ibn Rushd and the Qabbalah. He was on the edge of heresy. Bruno had a vision of an infinite universe, both in time and space, whose atoms are universally interrelated. He saw God and the universe as like two sides of the same piece of paper. But his doctrines were denounced as heretical and he was burnt at the stake.

All these figures had a fresh vision derived from the Hellenistic world, which had been opened up by contemporary scholarship: ancient civilization was perceived as oriented toward humanity and replete therefore with humanistic values. Moreover, the new learning and the new art were substantially patronized by the Papacy, and the values of the Florentine Renaissance were carried over into the Vatican. As a triumphant expression of these values, St. Peter's in Rome was being rebuilt at huge expense.

The Reformation: Theology and Political Power

Luther

The sale of so-called indulgences (permits, so to speak, to escape so many years of purgatory, a sort of halfway house to heaven where the soul is purged of sins not deadly enough to consign it to hell) was a factor stirring unease in Germany and helping to fuel the fire started by Martin Luther (1483–1546). Some of the proceeds from the indulgences sold in Germany were destined for St. Peter's. Some were being set aside to pay for the election expenses of the Archbishop of Mainz, unbeknown to Luther, who sent the Archbishop a copy of the 95 Theses or propositions for debate which he presented on October 31, 1517. The Archbishop's move to investigate Luther's orthodoxy helped to give publicity to the whole affair.

Luther was the son of a copper miner and was born in Eisleben in Thuringia. He went to university at Erfurt and after his first degree went on to study law. But in the fall of 1505 a vow which he made to St. Anne during a shattering thunderstorm caused him to abandon law and become an Augustinian monk. Eventually he received a doctorate and taught at the new university of Wittenberg from 1513 onward. Before that he had had a trip to Rome, which he thought would be a fine spiritual experience—but he found the holy city reprehensibly worldly. This was one of the seeds of doubt which were sown in his mind over the years. It was in 1517 that his momentous Theses came out. Some time before then, probably (for dates are uncertain) he had had a profound evangelical experience which altered his attitudes and led him into the main claims of his theology. Basically the claims he made were two. First, in theology we should rely on scripture alone; and second, our salvation depends not at all on works but on faith alone—or to put it another way, it depends solely on the grace of God.

This rejection of the idea that good works or other human means can make a difference led him to denounce a whole slew of Catholic practices: indulgences, which rested on the absurdity of buying God's favor; celibacy in the priesthood and among monks and nuns; pilgrimages; Masses for the dead;

and so on. A great deal of Catholic popular piety was swept away. Also the pretensions—as he saw it—of the Church to exclusive knowledge and understanding were pushed aside, and Luther himself translated the Bible and wrote and composed many hymns, thus helping to forge the German language. The struggle for Reform was also the struggle for vernacular languages against the dead hand of Latin. There was already restlessness in Germany over the power of the Papacy. As it turned out, Luther's at first purely theological dispute with the Church made a good pretext for princes to seek some degree of extra independence. Luther received protection, very important for his cause, from Frederick, Elector of Saxony, and as the revolt against Rome spread, various princes adopted forms of Lutheran practice, which gave them a large ecclesiastical as well as political control over their lands.

The Reformation movement was much assisted by the printing press. The Reformers used the pamphlet as a powerful genre of writing, and they brought theological controversy into the market place. The preacher also helped to give wide dissemination to the new ideas. So the movement spread, partly for political reasons; but its inner basis was piety, love of God, the sense that salvation can come only from God, and a disrespect for the bureaucratic apparatus of the Church at large.

There was military and political conflict. At the Peace of Augsburg in 1555, the principle was admitted (a concession to realities) that *cuius regio eius religio* "Of whom the rule, of him the religion": in other words, the prince or king determined the religion of his subjects. Germany and other parts of Northern Europe came to be divided between Catholics and Protestants, and, fatefully, Lutheranism inculcated obedience to the State.

The abolition of monasteries with their rich lands was also a temptation for rulers. It provided means for consolidating their influence, by granting lands to those who helped them. It resolved here and there some pressing financial problems.

Luther was a formidable writer. Pamphlets, theological treatises, translations, hymns poured forth from his pen. Much owing to his activity, the services of the Lutheran Church took on their rolling and numinous form, and their tender sense of the loving mercy of the Divine Being. The sonorous sounds of Luther's German could give the congregations a new sense of the vitality of their faith.

Calvin

With Luther the cork was out of the bottle. It is fine no doubt to be able to use the Bible as one's authority, but it is a book, or rather set of books, of many meanings. Interpretations could vary very easily. So there followed other Reformers who took a rather different line from Luther's. The most notable of these on the more orthodox or "magisterial" end of Protestantism was John Calvin (1509–63). By "magisterial" here is meant those Reformation movements which sought alliance one way or another with the State. The

The revolutionized authority: all the paraphernalia of Roman Catholicism, such as the monastic life, the papal tiara, and the keys of the kingdom supposedly entrusted by Christ to his Church are outweighed by the Bible in this Calvinist picture. The person organizing the weighing is Calvin himself.

"radical" Reformers detached religion from politics in this sense—though such a move was itself perceived as intensely political.

Calvin was a French lawyer, who had written what was originally a slender book, *The Institutes of the Christian Religion*, later greatly expanded, and who took part in the Reform in the city of Geneva. Though he left for a while, he was invited back and put into practice his notion of a political society which was committed to true religion and morals. His form of Church government, known as presbyterianism, became a characteristic of Reform churches of his tradition elsewhere, as in Holland and Scotland. But his most characteristic teaching was his doctrine of predestination. If salvation is by God alone, then he has already chosen who is to be saved and who is not. What you do does not affect this divine destiny. So good works are merely symptoms of salvation and cannot affect the outcome. Such predestinationism took a strong hold on the intellectual imagination of one wing of the Reformation. It was a rather philosophical variant on the theme of "by faith alone," of the Lutherans.

Also, for the Calvinists the most vital thing was the preaching of the Word. Thus, Calvin altered the plan of the cathedral in Geneva. The altar was taken away, and halfway along the church is the pulpit, with pews gathered so that they face the pulpit not the altar. The very rearrangement of the furniture of the church signaled a large change in ideas. The Bible as preached became the norm. Good conduct was something that happened in this world, not something that had to be specially cultivated in nunneries and monasteries. Virtue was democratized, and a somewhat puritan acceptance of the work ethic was a consequence. Some, notably Max Weber (1864–1920), have seen in

Quakers in a meeting house in London, taken from an engraving of 1737. A woman preaches – and this indicates the freedom from social preconceptions which was found in the Society of Friends.

this worldly asceticism a clue to the creation of capitalism. Much creation of wealth by hard work and little spending through puritanical abstention add up to savings which can supply the capital for building up enterprises.

The Radical Reformers: Anabaptists and Others

But the most radical of the Reformers were those who began to see religion as a matter of individual faith. In going back to the Bible and trying to re-create the ethos of the early Church, some Reformers rejected infant baptism. Only adults could gauge their faith and have the experience of conversion. They were dubbed Anabaptists or "Rebaptizers," and later, more simply, Baptists. They were radicals because their emphasis on personal and individual faith meant a break with the idea that some collective body such as the State could decide what its citizens' religion ought to be. This simple but revolutionary idea caused great unease among Catholics and Reformers alike, and the Anabaptists were often persecuted by both sides, one favorite way of disposing of them being by drowning in a river—an ironic and cruel comment on the rite of baptism.

334

Among early rebels of the Anabaptist tradition was Thomas Müntzer (1488?–1525) who believed in a new socioeconomic order and the imminent coming of a new age. A well-educated person, he became a Lutheran pastor, but wound up being chaplain to a large-scale peasants' revolt suppressed with cruelty at the battle of Frankenhausen, where Müntzer was taken, tortured, and killed (1525). Another violent uprising was the setting up of a revolutionary kingdom of the Saints at Münster in 1534, also suppressed. The major leader turned out to be Menno Simons (1496–1561), originally a Catholic priest, who was much harried by authority, but was finally able to settle with his followers on the German coast: later this expanding group was able to get land in Eastern Europe and Russia, many being skilled at drainage and the opening up of new farmlands. Their successors, known as Mennonites, became an important strand in North American piety.

From these Anabaptist beginnings came various nonconforming groups—Baptists, Congregationalists, or Independents, later the Quakers and others who argued for the separation of true religion and the State. They also were some of the spiritual ancestors of North American religion.

But initially the Reformers who favored alliance with the State prevailed amid a wide struggle for power with Catholicism. In England, Henry VIII (reigned 1509–47) for political reasons broke away from Rome and closed the monasteries. Elizabeth I (reigned 1558–1603) reversed the effects of the short reign of the Catholic Mary I (reigned 1553–58) and established the Anglican Church in its present form, with the Queen as governor of the Church and able to decree rites and ceremonies, religion being controlled by submission to the credal statement known as the 39 Articles. The later English Civil War led to various compromises between the more Catholic and Lutheran parts of the Church and the more puritanical and Calvinist. So the Church of England became another variant on the Reformation. Scotland, however, became Calvinist, and Ireland persisted in largely Catholic practice.

The Shape of Europe after the Reformation

As a result of various armed and propaganda struggles Europe divided on the principle of *cuius regio eius religio* (p. 332). Much of northern Germany, which was still of course divided into many states, was mainly Protestant; the south and Austria were Catholic. Poland and Hungary, and Italy, Croatia, Spain, Portugal, and most of France were Catholic. Parts of Switzerland and the Netherlands and Scotland were Calvinist. Lutheranism predominated in Scandinavia. In Eastern Europe Orthodoxy was powerful, as in Russia and elsewhere; but the Islam of the Ottoman Turks was encroaching on the Balkans, eventually threatening Vienna. In Spain, not long before the Reformation, the last Muslim power had fallen to the militant Catholic Crown, and it was this form of the faith that went with the Conquistadores to the New World.

At this point it is useful to pause and consider the great transformations that had been effected in Christianity as a result of the Reformation. It was in effect a new founding of the faith, and one which the Catholics themselves had to recognize in a measure, for they themselves underwent that reshaping of their own institutions in the movement known as the Counter-Reformation.

The Dimensions of Reformed Christianity

In the *ritual* dimension, the Reformers effected both major and minor changes. The changes all, however, involved the use of vernacular languages: Latin was got rid of—although it remained the language of theology. Lutherans and Anglicans kept to a ritually simplified version of the Eucharist as their most frequent service. But Presbyterians and the radicals tended toward treating the Eucharist as a solemn occasion to be conducted on special occasions or monthly. Their staple diet was the worship service, with the preaching of the sermon as the centerpiece. The new churches which were to be built reflected this, as we shall see (p. 342).

Many aspects of ritual piety were swept away, even among Lutherans and Anglicans, such as pilgrimages, the use of the relics of saints, and statues of the Virgin Mary. Indeed the latter was considered by most Reformers as having attained quite inappropriate status in Catholicism, and devotion to her became, until the Anglo-Catholic revival in the nineteenth century, strictly a badge of Roman faith. In general a great simplification of rituals took place. There was a change in the doctrine too: the central Catholic notion that the bread and wine are converted into the body and blood of Christ at the Eucharist was greatly modified, and so there were banned practices such as the actual veneration of the consecrated bread (or Host, as it was called), which itself became a notable feature of Catholic piety in the period after the Counter-Reformation.

In *ethics*, there was a revival of the ideals of the ascetic life, but in quite a different context. Temperance and self-discipline were for everyone. No distinction should be made between laypeople and monks and nuns, or between persons from the Church's history given the title of saints and the ordinary members of a Christian community. Nor was there a radical difference between pastors on the one hand and their congregations. The pastor might be specially trained for his office, but the priesthood belongs to all believers. And so there was a renewal of ethics in the Reformation and a more serious and challenging call (so the Reformers would think) to the life of justice and righteousness. Christianity should permeate every part of life. This was also Catholic doctrine. But the Reformers argued that the practice was otherwise: Catholicism had made too many concessions to human weakness.

In *doctrine* it was above all the thought of God's grace which held the center. Partly this was going back to St. Augustine: more, it was going back to the reading of St. Paul's Epistles. Salvation was in the gift of God. The Protestants often reemphasized the numinous holiness and terrifying wrath of God, the more to underline his sweetness and mercy in stooping to lift up humankind. And though the mood of the Reformation was often highly intellectual, especially among the Calvinists—and though, indeed, the movement helped

Opposite Martin Luther and the Wittenberg reformers with Elector John Frederick of Saxony, the Magnanimous (1503–54). Luther is on the far left, and his friend Philip Melanchthon is in the front row on the far right. Painted c.1543 by Lucas Cranach the Younger (1515–86). Toledo Museum of Art, Ohio.

Overleaf Map 14 showing the distribution of the majority religious groups in each country at the end of the twentieth century.

KEY
Majority groups
- Chinese
- Protestant Christianity
- Catholic Christianity
- Orthodox Christianity
- Shi'a Islam
- Sunni Islam
- Hinduism
- Judaism
- Theravāda Buddhism
- Mahāyāna Buddhism
- Tibetan Buddhism
- Secular
- Other

STONIA
LATVIA
BELORUSSIA
UKRAINE
OMANIA
BULGARIA
GEORGIA
ARMENIA
Turkey
CYPRUS
LEBANON
ISRAEL
JORDAN
EGYPT
KUWAIT
BAHRAIN
QATAR
SAUDI
ARABIA
UTD. ARAB
EMIRATES
OMAN
SUDAN
ERITREA
YEMEN
DJIBOUTI
ETHIOPIA
AIRE
UGANDA
SOMALIA
KENYA
RWANDA
BURUNDI
TANZANIA
SEYCHELLES
COMOROS
AMBIA
MALAWI
MOZAMBIQUE
ZIMBABWE
MAURITIUS
TS-
NA
MADAGASCAR
WAZILAND
LESOTHO
SOUTH
AFRICA

RUSSIAN FEDERATION

KAZAKHSTAN
MONGOLIA
A
UZBEKISTAN
KYRGYZSTAN
AZERBAIJAN
TURKMENISTAN
TAJIKISTAN
S
I
A
NORTH
KOREA
JAPAN
SOUTH
KOREA
SYRIA
IRAQ
IRAN
AFGHANISTAN
CHINA
PAKISTAN
NEPAL
BHUTAN
TAIWAN
BANGLADESH
INDIA
BURMA
LAOS
THAILAND
VIETNAM
CAMBODIA
PHILIPPINES
SRI LANKA
MALDIVES
BRUNEI
MALAYSIA
SINGAPORE
INDONESIA
PAPUA
NEW GUINEA
O
c
e
a
n
i
a
AUSTRALASIA
NEW CALEDONIA
AUSTRALIA
NEW ZEALAND

In contrast to the Reformation simplicity a new ornateness pervaded the revived Roman Catholic Church. This Jesuit church in Antwerp signified the vigor of the new Order which was a powerful instrument of the Papacy in the struggle for converts.

to give an impetus to the reordering of European universities and the unleashing of great energies of philosophy—nevertheless the main trend was against the use of reasoning to find out about God. That is, the Reformers stressed above all the centrality of revelation, and by that they meant the Bible. So Aquinas' great edifice of an alliance between faith and reason, between revealed and natural theology, was dismantled.

The Bible, no longer screened by a learned language, now spoke directly to people's feelings; it became the great fount of *narrative*. Printing brought it into many households. You could judge about matters of truth by referring to it, without relying on learned commentary or priestly exposition. It became a series of dramas against which men and women could measure their lives: they could relieve the wanderings of the Israelites in the desert, the bad times of Jeremiah, the visionary life of Daniel, the ministry of Christ, the hardships and heroisms of the Apostles. The Old Testament, which on the whole had been kept away from the laity by the Catholics, was a rich source of ideas and stories. Something of Jewish life could be relived in a new key: especially the keeping of the Sabbath, according to new puritanical rules, and especially in the Calvinist domains.

Sometimes the Protestants took the narrative imagery with deadly seriousness in interpreting their own times (hence the messianic expectations of Thomas Müntzer, which we have glanced at). The Roman Church and the Papacy came in for most negative treatment: the Pope was the Antichrist, and his Church was not the bride of Christ but a harlot. Bitterness became commonplace in the strife which succeeded the Reformation.

As to the *experiential* dimension, the emphasis which existed in the Roman Catholic Church on mysticism, the training of the self in the contemplative life, which was very much the ideal of the monasteries and convents, diminished. There were one or two notable Protestant mystics, such as Jakob Boehme (1575–1624), who had a great influence on the formation of the Quakers, and on later German philosophical thought, above all G. W. F. Hegel (1770–1831). But the disappearance of the cloister in favor of the hearth led to a greater emphasis on personal devotion and family prayer. It led to a warm pietism, rather than the exploration of the depths of the soul. The reemphasis on the Old Testament also led to a perception of the wrathful and numinous character of Deity, a feeling of utter dependence on the Holy One, and a sense that we are all unworthy: only from the Holy can holiness flow, and only by grace are we saved from sin.

As to the *institutional* dimension, the Calvinists ruled by a democratic method, having local committees, general assemblies, and elected leaders. Each congregation called a minister to serve it. The Lutherans and Anglicans were much less radical in reshaping their systems. They kept to the use of bishops, priests, and deacons—the threefold order of the early Church as they saw it. The monarch had a regulative say in the affairs of the Church, and the Church-State alliance was solid: hence it was necessary to regulate those who did not conform.

The Reformers used methods of persecution as did Catholics. In their countries, nonconformists and Catholics did not have civil rights, or had only restricted ones. It was not until the nineteenth century that all of these disabilities were removed. In England, Catholicism was for a time the virtual equivalent of treason, because the war between Spain and England, culminating in the defeat of the Spanish Armada in 1588, was also an ideological or religious war. Loyalty to Queen Elizabeth meant loyalty to the religion which she headed. The Virgin Queen replaced the Virgin Mary.

It was religious regulation which led some of the more radical puritans and reformers to emigrate, either to the ill-defined lands of Eastern Europe and the Baltic or to the New World. But ideals of toleration made headway in Europe after the Thirty Years' War (1618–48) sickened and exhausted those who had engaged in religious struggle. John Locke (1632–1704) was one of the notable theoreticians of toleration.

The deepest crisis for Reformers lay in the removal of Papal authority, in the sense that they rapidly found how interpretations of the Bible could vary

The institutional dimension: in Lutheran countries the king or prince controlled the Church, and likewise among Anglicans. Elizabeth I (reigned 1558–1603), here seen praying, was Head of the English Church.

and form the basis of conflicting systems. The Bible was a paper Pope, but who was to ensure conformity of belief and practice? This was one argument for the alliance of Church and State: the State could enforce unanimity of doctrine. Hence it was that Anglicanism had the 39 Articles by Act of Parliament; and hence it was that Protestants were expelled from Austria in 1597 and eventually from France in 1685. Other groups sought a different mode of inner conformity by having rather democratic procedures and agreement on teachings. But the crisis of authority has remained with Protestantism, which is why it is divided into so many denominations and sects.

In terms of the *material* dimension, Catholic Churches which were taken over had their more outstandingly un-Protestant features removed, and the interior was sometimes reshaped, as at Geneva. New buildings were much plainer, especially in Calvinist countries—plain white walls, no stained glass, no ornamentation, but a great pulpit, plus a communion table. In Calvinism singing of hymns was discouraged: only the singing of the Psalms was allowed, for they were truly Biblical. Even in the Church of England, under Puritan influence, it was illegal to sing hymns until 1820, though the practice had come in earlier with the influence of Methodism. Often a form of iconoclasm occurred, as when Oliver Cromwell's English troops smashed up a number of Scottish churches and cathedrals.

The effects on painting were to secularize it: no longer was there a demand for altarpieces and holy pictures in Protestant parts of Europe. The Dutch took to interiors, portraits, seascapes, landscapes; the English to landscapes and portraits. A tradition arose which helped to stimulate the great eighteenth-century Scottish portrait artists. All this was part of a new and more objective vision of people and Nature which had vast effects in the formation of modern scientific thinking.

These, then, were some of the revolutionary effects of the Protestant Reformation. It led to a new creation of Christianity: sober, rhetorical, book-bound, devotional, dogmatic, national, plain, but endowed with energies which stimulated trade, exploration, science, nationalism, democracy, and conflict.

This Dutch interior shows the simplification of the ritual dimension brought about by the Reformation.

The Counter-Reformation and the Formation of Modern Catholicism

The dreadful crumbling of the Roman edifice in the first stormy years of the Reformation called for some remedy. It was only, however, in 1545 that the Papacy succeeded in calling a general Council, at Trent, which lasted intermittently until 1563. This had profound effects in clearing up abuses within the system and in providing for a revitalized Church with greater centralization. Its chief effect was to reject reconciliation with the Protestants. But the appointment of bishops and priests was reformed; training for the clergy was reorganized and made more intellectual; the Vulgate or Latin Bible was revised; the administration of the Church was reshaped; doctrines of the seven Sacraments and of justification by faith were reformulated; and loose ways of dealing with indulgences, the cult of saints, and so forth were tightened up. The strength of the central government of the Church was enhanced. All those things of which the Protestants were most critical— including the devotion to the Virgin Mary, the cult of saints, pilgrimages, the adoration of the Host, the central place of the priesthood, and the ecclesiastical hierarchy—were reaffirmed in practice.

At about the same time there was forged a most powerful weapon for mission activity and the reassertion of Catholic values: the Society of Jesus, founded by St. Ignatius Loyola (1491?–1556). He had been raised mainly at the court of Spain and had embarked on a knightly and military career. The bad wounds he received at the battle of Pamplona led to a long convalescence when his reading stimulated conversion to the religious life: he went to the Holy Land and on his return to Spain founded a small order of priests—not monks—which was to become the Society of Jesus, its members being known as Jesuits. He gave a military flavor to the rigorous training he devised: his *Spiritual Exercises* was a powerful manual for those who would serve Christ in the world. He put his new order at the disposal of the Papacy. With its iron discipline and highly intellectual training it became a significant factor in the reconquest of parts of Europe for the Catholic Church, working in France, southern Germany, Austria, Poland, and elsewhere. It was also very effective in the mission field in India, China, Japan, and Latin America.

The Council of Trent, a little ominously for the future of the Church, also created the Index of Forbidden Books, and so for four centuries and more it was involved in censoring the reading done by Catholics. It was all part of the discipline necessary to hedge around papal authority. But within the limits of doctrinal orthodoxy the Church took on renewed vigor. In 1622 it set up a missionary department, the Congregation for the Propagation of the Faith (*de propaganda Fide*—from this word came the modern "propaganda"). In the welter of new voyages, discoveries, and colonies there were vast gains for Roman Catholicism to offset the European losses. The Baroque style of the seventeenth century gave new magnificence to churches—with lush post-Renaissance holy pictures, highly decorated ceilings, marble altars and twisting candleholders, golden monstrances wherein the Host was held up for devotion, elaborate side chapels, statues of the Virgin in blue with stars about her head, and the new forms of liturgical music which were to culminate in the Masses written by Joseph Haydn (1732–1809) and W. A. Mozart (1756–91). New orders also grew, and there was a revival in mysticism, with St. Teresa of Avila (1515–82) and St. John of the Cross (1542–91), among others, forming a famous school of Spanish mystics.

As a result of these and other factors the Roman Catholic Church was revitalized in its religious life. It managed to fuse a new intellectual discipline with the piety of ordinary people and so to cater for traditional populations. But it bought some of its advantages at a great cost, which was to become apparent with the period of the Enlightenment and the rise of European nationalism.

Enlightenment, Capitalism, and Nationalism

The breakdown in authority which the Reformation and its aftermath displayed had its philosophical effects. The Reformation had elevated reason above authority; and for some thinkers, reason rather than faith should reign. The terrible struggles of religion stimulated the desire for toleration, and with it rationality. There arose a rationalist current in European life and thought which cultural historians call the Enlightenment. Part of the new movement enthroning reason had its origins in France, with such writers as Voltaire (1694–1778), fiercely anticlerical, wishing to crush the Catholic Church, and Montesquieu (1689–1755), social theorist and urbane moralist. Its French climax was in the work of Denis Diderot (1713–84), who edited the massive *Encyclopédie*.

In Germany perhaps the most vital figures were Gotthold Lessing (1729–81), dramatist and theologian, whose *Nathan the Wise* was a drama devoted to pleading for toleration, with its central figure of the fine Jew; and Immanuel Kant (1724–1804), who combined two great themes of the Enlightenment, the importance of reason and the essential need to be critical. He had been roused, as he said, from his dogmatic slumber by reading the skeptical writings of the Scotsman, David Hume (1711–76), who was both a philosopher and a noted historian. Already the advance of a more scientific approach to history was beginning to cause rumblings over the truth of scripture, or at least over its inerrancy. This was to bring acute troubles to the maintaining of Biblical authority. If the Pope of Rome had been rebuffed, and the paper Pope was weakened, then where would authority be found? That was to be one of the great themes of religious debate in the nineteenth and twentieth centuries.

It was another product of the Scottish Enlightenment, Adam Smith (1723–90), who laid the foundations for capitalist economics, which was one strand in the great changes that were overtaking the world. Consider the inventions of the era: in 1775 came the manufacture of steam engines; in 1793

Eli Whitney revolutionized the cotton industry with his new cotton gin; in 1814 the first practical steam locomotive was built; in 1831 Faraday demonstrated the principle of the electric dynamo; in 1846 ether was first used as an anesthetic in an operation and so on. It was a marvelously inventive age, in which the sciences really began to show their practical utility. In agriculture, too, there were great changes, with the use of rotation of crops and later the varied reaping and other machines which made the opening up of the North American prairies so advantageous. In short, we come rapidly on the period of industrial revolution and the high age of early capitalism. It was a period when the middle classes asserted themselves: this was one of the meanings of the French Revolution in 1789. Another meaning was nationalism.

Already, of course, the national idea had shown its muscle during the Reformation. But the Industrial Revolution and the Enlightenment together gave it new impetus, for in the nineteenth and twentieth centuries nationalism and modernization were associated. Larger units of operation were needed, and the nation-state could provide these. Liberalism was thought to be the politically dynamic mode of conducting the new creation of wealth. A new literature sowed the idea of national cultures.

From the time of the French Revolution onward the fight for national identity became irresistible: national aggrandisement became natural. Empires were a corollary. The very nations which fought for unification and freedom were also involved in the acquisition of colonial empires—Holland, France, Germany, Italy, Great Britain, Denmark, and others. So we see, entering the stage of world history, this explosive force of nationalism, which by its very aggrandizement stimulates nationalism and resistance in others, and which has become the general principle by which we are all governed. We have a United Nations, not United Persons.

All this paved the way for the making of new ideologies which had something of a religious flavor, even when strongly antireligious in belief, such as Marxism. Because the idea of the nation-state is a bit weak on doctrine, it has tended to blend with wider ideologies and religions. Italian nationalism blended with liberalism, as in its own way did French; British imperialism dedicated itself to what it saw as Christian civilization; Irish nationalism had as its doctrinal guarantor Catholicism.

In other ways, too, nationalism functioned like a religion. Its myth was the national story, to be taught in schools, once modernization had produced universal education. Its rituals were the flag, the national anthem, the military marchpast—all pioneered in France with the tricolor, the *Marseillaise*, and the citizen army. Its ethics were those of the good citizen, law-abiding, taxpaying, ready to fight—or, if a woman, ready to help produce the babies of the nation. Its priesthood was the teachers, and its saints were the heroes and poets of the past; its organization was that of the State itself. Its emotions were those of patriotism and nostalgia for the homeland. It was, in short, a powerful religious force with which all traditional religions had to make some sort of accommodation.

In the new Europe of the nineteenth century the relations between religion and nationalism were varied. There was the pervasive idea of the national religion in such countries as England and Sweden; but now citizens who were not of the majority faith had to be accommodated too. There was overt hostility between the Church, eager to retain its territorial foothold in the Papal States of Central Italy, which were thought of as a guarantee of its independence, and the largely liberal nationalist *Risorgimento* (resurgence). There were new compromises when Germany became united, with divisions of the educational system, but the general thought was that Christianity is for personal life and the State is for public duty. Folk now died for their country, for the most part, not for religion as such. Where religion or ideology and nationalism combined, then you got a very powerful force. Incidentally, the multinational empires were destined for trouble by the very fact of nationalism, and all of them in Europe—the Russian, the Austro-Hungarian, and the Ottoman—collapsed.

Jewish Emancipation and the New Europe

From the late Middle Ages onward, persecution and other factors shifted the center of Jewish life eastward in Europe. It is true that in Britain, France, and Germany a Jewish elite managed in the eighteenth century to obtain status, in the German principalities especially, through good posts in court circles as fiscal administrators, physicians, and so on. But the large population density was in Poland and Russia. In the late eighteenth century over 800,000 Jews were absorbed into Russia, and were allowed to settle within the so-called Pale, comprising Lithuania, Belorussia, the Ukraine, and the shores of the Black Sea. Poland was also an area of settlement, though not actually within the Pale. It was in Eastern Europe that the great awakening known as Hasidism occurred.

In some ways the path had been prepared by the Sabbatean movement, focused on the person and claims of Shabbetai Tsevi (1626–76), of Smyrna in Turkey, who had been proclaimed by a follower (Rabbi Natan of Gaza) as *Mashiaḥ* or Messiah. It seemed a suitable time, for the sufferings of the Jews were extreme at this time. Not only had they been expelled from Spain and Portugal, but they were subjected to a great wave of killings during the Cossack uprising of 1648–58. Shabbetai Tsevi was a charismatic, if somewhat eccentric, figure: and Messianic expectations were aroused throughout Jewry. When in 1666 he was confronted with the choice of death by torture or conversion to Islam, he chose the latter. There were those who followed him still, and the movement was to go underground and reemerge in Poland under the leadership of Ya'akov Frank (1726–91), who eventually converted to Catholicism. But the fact that many Jews throughout Europe and the East had been fooled by Shabbetai Tsevi left its mark: a more patient and at any rate a different solution to the problems of the Jews had to be found.

One movement which did have a long-term effect was Hasidism, associated

Jews in Samarkand: within the Russian empire Jews were subject to pogroms, notably in 1881–2, following the assassination of the tsar, Alexander II, for which the Jews were widely blamed. Samarkand, a city in Uzbekistan, was, in fact, a center of Muslim culture and remained so until the Russian Revolution.

with the Ba'al Shem Tov (or Besht for short), the "Master of the Good Name," which was the title given to Yisra'el ben Eli'ezer (1700–60). The Besht, in his area of the southern Ukraine and the Carpathian Mountains, revived the ideals of Jewish Qabbalah, but in a popular way. He was a charismatic healer, a mystic, and an inspiring teacher who emphasized the need to practice *devequt*, the constant communion with an ever-present God. It was a pious movement, and not unorthodox save perhaps in organization. It stressed warmth of feeling as well as training oneself in communion; but this was all within the structure of strict obedience to the law. In the fifty years after the Besht, the Hasidim tended to form their own communities and came up against the Gaon of Vilna, who was the supreme Jewish legal figure in Eastern Europe, and who came to oppose the Hasidim with some alarm and bitterness. But in many ways it was a revitalizing force, giving inner meaning to the outer performance of the Torah; and it had a special role to play as one of the main strands of Jewish Orthodoxy in the United States.

In contrast to the inward-looking strain of Hasidism, the central Jewish experience of the eighteenth and nineteenth centuries was the wider spread of emancipation, and with it the fuller entry of Jews onto the scene of the dazzling culture of the times: it was for many stepping into the world of Beethoven, Kant, Goethe, and Gainsborough. In the year (1791) when Jews were defined as full citizens of France—the first European country to do this—Boswell's *Life of Johnson* was published, and Mozart's *Magic Flute* was performed.

In some degree the two greatest Jewish philosophers had prepared paths that emancipated Jews could take. Barukh Spinoza (1632–77) had left Judaism behind but not betrayed it by embracing some alternative faith. He was an urbane humanist: so, later, did many Jews retain their Jewishness but without the religion. Spinoza, by the way, pioneered Biblical criticism from an

Mendelssohn

Moses Mendelssohn (1729–86) was a German philosopher and Jewish leader, who was the principal figure in the transition of Jews from the ghetto into European society. Thus he was a father of Reform Judaism. He was the first Jew to publish in German. He was born in Dessau (in eastern Germany) and at the age of 14 after a traditional education, including the study of the philosophy of Maimonides, he moved with his rabbi instructor to Berlin. There he was exposed to the sciences and the mood of the European Enlightenment, as well as modern European languages. He became the model for the dramatist Lessing's famous play *Nathan the Wise* (1779). As a result of his literary successes Mendelssohn became a "protected Jew" with a right of residence in the capital. His soirées at his home were a source of intellectual influence. His book *Phädon* came out in 1767. It was a defence of the notion of the immortality of the soul, and enhanced his reputation among the literati.

But in 1769 he was asked why he did not, as an enlightened person, become a Christian: his challenger was a Swiss pastor. He soon became immersed again in his Jewish roots: he protected Jews not only in Alsace from anti-Jewish legislation, but also in Switzerland itself, through his Christian friends. He also published a German translation of the first five books of the Hebrew Bible, printed, by the way, in Hebrew characters. In 1783 he published *Jerusalem, order Über religiose Macht und Judenthum*, in which he argued for freedom of conscience in religion and a separation of Church and State. In it he obliquely argued for Jewish rights. He also argued that Jewish law (revealed) is binding only on Jews. But Jewish adherence in principle to the law should not prevent them becoming full and loyal citizens of the State. His associates were, incidentally, prominent in the Jewish enlightenment (the *haskalah*). He was therefore important to the liberalizing trends which made it possible for Jews to live both in the modern world and in the faithful tradition of the past.

historical point of view. The other philosopher was Moses Mendelssohn (1729–86), who espoused deism, or the Enlightenment belief in the God of Reason, but defended Judaism as a system of revealed legislation in which the ceremonial side of life was laid down as a constant reminder of the truth and as a hedge against the idolatry of false ideas. In effect he proclaimed the feasibility of being German in culture and Jewish in personal practice. He foreshadowed later forms of both Orthodox and Reform Judaism.

Varieties of Judaism and Jewishness

As more and more countries achieved emancipation and religious toleration, Jews were faced with various new choices. These choices were to become clearer in the United States, which emigration from pogrom- and poverty-laden Eastern and Central Europe rendered the prime center of Jewish life. But basically they were as follows: there was complete assimilation into the new nationalities, usually not possible because of consciousness among the population that you were Jewish; there was cultural assimilation, while remaining Jewish in faith, particularly through the new kind of Judaism that emancipation helped to create, Reform Judaism; there was Orthodox Judaism, now somewhat modernized by carrying on the precepts of the religion as far as possible within the new national environment; and later, at the end of the nineteenth century, there were the prospects opened up by the ideology of Zionism which sought a national homeland for Jews themselves. Zionism, like other nationalisms, went with a modernizing program; and because of this, and its attempt to force the Mashiah's hand, so to speak, it came to be largely opposed by the Orthodox.

The transformation of Jewish religion into a private rather than a community matter was heralded by the response which prominent Jewish figures gave to Napoleon when he convened them into what came to be called the Sanhedrin (after the Jewish Council in Jerusalem). The point at issue was whether they were truly French citizens; or were they a nation within the nation? They answered that Israel was no longer a nation, and that those aspects of the Torah which applied to those days were inoperative. Nor were the arrangements for partial autonomy made in some parts of Europe any more relevant. So in effect they were fully French in citizenship and Jewish in religion.

This response was a foretaste of a general view current in the rest of the nineteenth century in Europe: Judaism was a universal faith, an ethical monotheism, and did not need the clothing of ethnicity. Nor did it need the symbols which once were relevant: the return to Zion, the rebuilding of the Temple, and the restoration of Israel. These pictures of the future were played down by the Reform Jews, and they were not quite realistic to the Orthodox; their concrete content ironically was affirmed by the Zionists, many of whom were not religious Jews.

Napoleon's enlightened views, such as they were, did not spare France from anti-Semitism, which broke out in 1894 in the affair of Alfred Dreyfus

Despite the liberal pretensions of late nineteenth-century France, the Dreyfus affair showed the strength of anti-Jewish sentiment throughout the country. Alfred Dreyfus (1859–1935) was court-martialed on spurious charges of espionage in 1894 and sent to the penal colony of Devil's Island, French Guiana. His case was championed by Emile Zola and Georges Clemenceau, but he was not exonerated until 1906. He is shown here on trial in 1899.

(1859–1935): here was a Jewish officer charged wrongly with selling secrets to the Germans and only cleared in 1906, after he had spent years on Devil's Island, a French penal settlement in the Caribbean. It was in part because of continued anti-Semitism, especially in Austria-Hungary and Russia, that the idea of Jewish nationalism flourished from the time of the first Zionist Congress held in 1897 under the architect of modern secular Zionism, Theodor Herzl (1860–1904).

We shall return to the religious issues in describing Judaism in America. For Judaism, European civilization was attractive, but possibly corrosive, sometimes welcoming, often hostile. The religious possibilities were limited, and they were all realized in the ensuing drama of the way Judaism and Jewishness figured in the modern world. In nationalism, it turned out there lay a deadly enemy: for it was a form of nationalism that fueled the Nazi party, and with it the Holocaust.

Russia and the New Learning; the Drive East

Because the Muslims in the shape of the Ottoman empire had more or less occupied the territories of the old Byzantine empire, this whole swath of Eastern Orthodoxy was cramped for living and breathing space. It continued to survive under the Ottomans, but its possibilities as part of the so-called Millet system (which allowed for subcommunities such as Christians and Jews to follow their own laws and to be administered through their own leaders) were limited. However, Russia, already vast and destined to acquire an even vaster empire to the east, was there to represent the Faith. Moscow was to be the Third Rome, destined in hope to lead the forces of the faith in the restoration of a purified and true Christianity, now that the second Rome was conquered and the first Rome was corrupted and weakened by Protestantism. Although Christianity was established first at Kiev, this center of power was shattered by the Mongols, and though there were important other Christian centers at Novgorod and Pskov these fought a hard battle for self-preservation against the Teutonic Knights pushing forward from Prussia. It was Moscow, therefore, which succeeded in becoming the new capital, and in the late sixteenth century its archbishop was dignified with the title of Patriarch and became the major Orthodox religious leader outside of Islamic captivity.

After the defeat of the Mongols of the Khanate of Kazan in eastern Russia in 1552, the way was open for the annexation of lands to the east. By 1689 virtually all of Siberia was taken over, mainly because of the lucrative fur trade. Under Peter the Great (reigned 1682–1725) and Catherine the Great (reigned 1762–96), Russia conquered areas of the northwest and of the Black Sea coastal region which enabled it to open up new seaports at St. Petersburg and Odessa, greatly enhancing trade. But Peter's modernization also involved controlling the Church: the Patriarchate was abolished, not to be restored till 1918, and the Church was ruled by a synod. Already there had been schism: in the seventeenth century Patriarch Nikon (1605–81) had tried to bring in reforms of the ritual, including the use of three fingers rather than two for making the sign of the Cross, and this was seen as impugning the special calling of Moscow to be the Third Rome. What Nikon was trying to do was to bring Russian practice in line with that of Byzantium. A large breakaway group known as Old Ritualists or Old Believers continued in the old ways, despite persecution. The majority of Ukrainians, for separate—largely nationalist—reasons, constituted themselves the Uniate Ukrainian Church, in communion with Rome but using Eastern rituals and customs.

The new lands to the east, which extended into Alaska in North America, were subject to considerable missionary activity in the eighteenth and nineteenth centuries. This was also a time of revived spiritual life. The practice of Hesychasm was brought in from Mount Athos, and texts of Greek spirituality were translated. The figure of the holy elder (the *starets*) became a regular feature of Church life: a person who by his charismatic personality and saintliness was reckoned to have treasures to teach—somewhat like the Hindu guru, but in the very different religious and cultural milieu of Russia. The most famous of all such holy men was St. Serafim of Sarov (1759–1833), who entered the monastery of Sarov as a young man on the advice of a *starets*. From 1793 till 1815 he lived as a hermit near the monastery; in the years 1815–25, retiring to a cell, he was inspired by divine revelation to counsel people and speak with them. For him the heart of the Christian life was experiencing the grace of the Holy Spirit; and the light of the Spirit reportedly shone from his countenance for those who approached him for healing, advice, and prophecy.

Such figures had profound influence on some of the great writers of Russia, including Fyodor Dostoyevsky (1821–81) and Leo Tolstoy (1828–1910). They in turn formulated profound religious ideas in their writings. Dostoyevsky, in his famous novel *The Brothers Karamazov*, portrayed a *starets*, Father Zosima, who presented anew the ancient Christian faith, but purified in a way by the scarifying critique of God produced by Ivan in the novel, and his story of the Grand Inquisitor of Spain who gives short shrift to a returning Jesus. Tolstoy in his later years preached a simple love and pacifism which were to earn him excommunication from Orthodoxy but the gratitude of M. K. Gandhi, whose mind he helped to form.

But despite the Orthodox Church's strength, clouds around it were forming. The Russia of the late nineteenth century was divided between modernizing Westerners—often armed with strange new revolutionary theories, from liberalism to anarchism—and Russophiles who put their faith in the old Russia, the wisdom of the peasant, the holy mission of Russia in a suffering world, and so forth. In 1861 the serfs were liberated, and Russia embarked on a new wave of modernization. But its effects were vitiated by poor leadership. In 1905 Russia was humiliated by the Japanese at the land battle of Mukden and the sea battle of Tsushima. Unrest gave a foretaste of revolution, as workers demonstrated in the streets and troops shot them down. The doom of the monarchy and of the old order was sealed by defeat in World War I: with that collapse there came revolution.

Meanwhile it should be noted that Tsarist expansion had continued as the frontier of the Empire was driven south through Central Asia, so that now it contained a substantial Muslim population on the borders of Afghanistan and Iran.

Modern Europe

Developments in Christianity in Western Europe

The new knowledge and the new methods of inquiry stimulated by the Enlightenment involved elements which were to prove a threat to Biblically based Christianity. The use of history in a modern manner to probe the past rather than just to tell a story inevitably began to raise questions about the historicity of the Bible; while the formation of Evolutionary Theory was among the factors in greatly shaking confidence in traditional cosmology (which already had had to be modified in view of Newtonian physics).

The first of these strands in the intellectual challenge to tradition was in part sparked by the highly influential philosophy of Georg Wilhelm Friedrich Hegel (1770–1831). In his view the processes of existence are manifestations of one Absolute Spirit (*Geist*). One of his reasons for this was the breakdown of Kant's compromise. Kant thought that we project categories on the world of experience, but that experience itself is the product, in some sense, of "things in themselves" beyond the phenomena. Critics saw this as a weak point: in Kant's own view categories could not be applied to that which lies beyond experience, and so one should use neither singular nor plural nor the notion of cause or existence in speaking of the "things in themselves." So Idealists like Hegel, having scraped away objective reality from behind the world of experience, saw the world as experience.

Hegel's originality lay in seeing the Absolute as dynamic—as working, for instance, through the processes of history. And he saw these as following a logic, which he called the dialectic: a notion of profound influence on Karl Marx and so on the world. In history, according to Hegel's view, one movement (the thesis) is faced with its opposite (the antithesis); in the conflict between the two a synthesis is formed. This synthesis then becomes the thesis, which stimulates its own antithesis and a new synthesis; and so on.

Different religions are popular, imaginative, and intuitive ways in which human beings have tried to grasp the Absolute; in Christianity the Absolute is thought of as achieving self-consciousness. Ferdinand Baur (1792–1860) took up Hegel's dialectical view and saw Jesus as thesis, Paul as antithesis, and Catholicism as synthesis. All this was a speculative trend, but stimulated much historical inquiry into the actualities of what we could know about Jesus. From this arose the great industry of modern critical scholarship directed at the New Testament and at the earliest Christianity. Such an industry flourished especially in the nineteenth century, in the Protestant faculties in German universities, and from there spread to Britain, the United States, and elsewhere.

Once the Bible was treated not as authority but as evidence, not as holy writ but as historical material, not as evidently true but as often woven together from theological desires and oral traditions, it lost its old authoritative force. This presented a clear crisis for the Churches.

This crisis was deepened by the publication of the Evolutionary Theory of Charles Darwin (1809–82), published in 1859 in his book *The Origin of Species*. If Christians had before accepted physics, it was only because a sharp line was drawn between it and the study of living things. It seemed a great shock to Victorians (both to many scientists and to many but by no means all Church people) to think of humanity as descending from apes, as being so closely kin to the animals—which were often seen in a poor moral light, as witness the use of such words as "brutish," "beastly," and so on. Besides, Holy Scripture spoke of the direct creation by God of the species, not their slow evolution as Darwin proposed. Moreover it seemed that some of the strongest arguments people had had for belief in a good Creator—such things as the cunning anatomy of the eye, the beautiful design of an eagle's wings, the

The doctrinal dimension: the British magazine *Punch* laughs at Charles Darwin's Evolutionary Theory, which was often seen to be in conflict with Christian and biblical orthodoxy. The cartoon, which was drawn by Linley Sambourne, suggested that Darwin had been led astray by the serpent, representing Satan.

"Scripture Reader in a Night Refuge," an engraving by Gustave Doré (1832–83) for *London* (published by Blanchard Jerrold), shows a preacher in a Victorian workhouse reading the Bible to the homeless. Doré's drawings, on which the engravings were based, were done in 1869–71. Throughout the nineteenth century groups of parishes throughout Britain built work-houses for the elderly, disabled, orphaned – all those who could not find work – who were forced to live in often extremely harsh conditions.

delicate artistry of the lyre bird and the spider—were undercut by the theory that these wonders had arisen as a result of the survival of the fittest.

History and Evolution—these ideas and much else besides called into question the literal accuracy and truth of the Bible. Adam and Eve would disappear among the monkeys. Jesus' sharp outline would melt behind the hot uncertainties of historical scholarship. Little could be depended upon absolutely, and much of what was orthodox belief might have to be hedged with maybes. Was science becoming a cuckoo in the nest of theism? Was scholarship taking the backbones out of believers?

Another, quite different, challenge was the uprooting of society which the new industrial revolution presented. Men and women flocked into sordid cities, where they were enslaved to great machines and tyrannized by clocks. If some turned to gin and prostitution it was not surprising. Meanwhile the country parish system crumbled, designed for a different age and another kind of life. So the established Churches everywhere felt themselves weakened, even though in England, for instance, Methodism was very active in the industrial era and there were gallant attempts to reshape religious organization toward the needs of the new society.

These three examples stand for all those forces of scholarship and philosophy, of scientific inquiry, and of social challenge that met Christianity in the Europe of the nineteenth century.

One response to all this was to embrace it. The quest for the historical Jesus and the new discoveries of science might weaken confidence in the literal truth of the Bible: but so what? It did not need to be either a textbook of history or a manual of biology. Science has to do with this world: religion deals with this world seen in the light of the next world. Religion sees tigers and planets lit by the light of God and seen in the eye of faith. And the Bible is about the actions of God but is not itself a guaranteed recording of them. Moreover, Evolution is good news: it hints at how we have risen from earlier stalkings and screams in the undergrowth to our present moral stature: and in that elevation of humankind religion—above all, so the argument goes, the Christian religion—has played a crucial part. As for the sorrows of capitalism, yes, they should be mitigated: but human invention and energy are already fashioning a brighter world. We should be optimistic at rising toward the Kingdom.

In many ways the greatest of all exponents of this nineteenth-century liberal Protestantism was Adolf von Harnack (1851–1930), who saw Luther as having only partially reformed Christianity, freeing it of ritualism, hierarchy, and so on, but keeping the dogma uncritically in place. We need, in Harnack's view, a historically anchored faith which looks to the Gospel of Christ, which stresses the love of God the Father, which we can experience, and the love of one's neighbor by the help of God's grace, but which takes a critical view of Christian tradition.

Another response, which I shall describe more in detail when dealing with North American religion, is to deny the force of liberalism and to go on affirming the literal truth of the Bible in the teeth of scientific skepticism. This fundamentalism often combined with a fervent evangelical zeal, and remained a dynamic force in the Christian tradition. Yet another response was to bolster the strength of faith by emphasizing the importance of the organization of the Church. Within Protestantism this kind of move occurred in effect as the Oxford Movement, which underlined the vitality of Catholic ritual within the Church of England, and revived high theories of the sacred authority of the Church—but some of its adherents, most notably John Henry Newman (1801–90), crossed over into the Church of Rome. This revival had its effects very much in the ritual dimension and material aspect of Anglicanism, being a stimulus to the revival of Gothic architecture in the large church building and rebuilding program undertaken for the expanding population of Victorian England. The Pre-Raphaelite movement in art helped, too, to present a revitalized late medieval style of religious painting.

But more important than all this was the reaffirmation of Roman Catholic Church authority, partly through the Council known as Vatican I, held in Rome in 1870, which asserted the doctrine of the infallibility of the Pope in matters of doctrine and ethics when he speaks *ex cathedra*, literally "from the throne," that is, in his sacred and official capacity. It was also reaffirmed through the crackdown in 1907 on what was called Catholic Modernism: a number of writers and theologians were exploring the liberal approaches which had had such impact in Protestantism. Biblical scholarship in the Catholic tradition, and certain philosophical lines of reasoning, were greatly restricted. This attempt to trammel the members of the Church was in the long run bound to end in failure, but it held the line until the Council known as Vatican II (1962–65), summoned by Pope John XXIII (1881–1963).

As to the challenge of the new social world, some Christians in Europe responded by adopting a version of Christian Socialism. In Britain the Labour movement, with its trade union affiliations and leanings toward a Socialist solution to economic problems, was greatly permeated by the spirit of the nonconformist Protestant denominations, such as Methodists and Baptists. Indeed, Methodism had been in the vanguard of social action from the early part of the nineteenth century. In the United States the movement known as the Social Gospel was important, and we shall come to that later (p. 376).

New Ideologies as Alternatives to Religion

Of all the new thoughts which were produced in the nineteenth century the set which had the greatest impact on the world was Marxism. It became the ideology of revolutionary groups who identified the troubles of the world with the capitalist system itself. Karl Marx (1818–83) had early in his career fallen under the influence of Hegel, but he took key Hegelian categories in very different directions. He edited radical journals in Germany and Paris; eventually in a year of great revolutionary activity in Europe, 1848, he settled in the more tolerant atmosphere of London. There in great poverty he wrote prolifically, helped financially by his rich friend Friedrich Engels (1820–95), and engaged in revolutionary organization.

His, and Engels's, philosophy was materialist, as distinguished from the

The iconography of the Russian Revolution and its aftermath: Karl Marx, Friedrich Engels, Vladimir Ilyich Lenin, and Joseph Stalin.

idealism of Hegel. The dialectic of history was to be seen in differing economic systems in collision and contradiction. Capitalism itself contained contradictions, because the interests of the bourgeoisie who owned the means of production demanded that they exploit the workers: their profits came out of the extra value imparted to materials by labor. Class conflict was bound to intensify, held Marx, and would lead to a revolution, then to the so-called dictatorship of the proletariat, and then to the establishment of a classless society. It was a fine vision; it was backed with impressive economic evidence and theory; it gave confidence, since revolutionaries were on the side of history; it was itself a secular eschatology, having some of the flavor of Messianism.

As to religion, that, to Marx, was a byproduct of the socioeconomic situation and a symptom of alienation. It was the cry of the oppressed and the opium of the people. The exposure of religion was the first intellectual task of all, and in his famous *Theses on Feuerbach* Marx showed his indebtedness to Ludwig Feuerbach (1804–72), another follower and critic of Hegel. Feuerbach saw God as being a projection, by us, of essential human attributes such as reason and love. Marx took this "projectionist" strand and gave it an economic interpretation. It may be noted that projectionism—that is, the theory that God and other supernatural entities are projected onto reality by human beings—is a powerful ingredient in modern thought, appearing in a different form, for instance, in the thought of Sigmund Freud (1856–1939).

In many ways, Marxism itself was a worldview with a religious flavor, not directed toward a higher world but toward the transformation of this. For *doctrines* it had the writings of Marx, Engels, V. I. Lenin (1870–1924), and others. For *myth* it had the pulsating rhythm of history culminating in the earthly paradise of a classless society. For *ethics* it had the ceaseless pursuit of social justice and the maintenance of class struggle. For *practice* it had the need to realize theories concretely, in revolutionary activity. For *experience* it had the nurturing of ardor and of hatred toward class enemies. For *organization* it had the various Communist parties. When it became the official doctrine of various countries, these religious features were to be much accentuated.

Not all Marxists were Communists: there was also a more moderate strand of Marxian Socialism which became important in Europe and elsewhere, and tried to combine Marxism with a liberal-democratic idea of the State. For Marx himself had been skeptical of the importance of law and other means of preserving political rights. He despised some of the creations of the bourgeoisie as shams, and so the ideal of individual freedom did not, in a political sense at least, figure largely in his thinking, and as it transpired, virtually all the Communist parties turned out to be totalitarian in outlook. Democratic Socialism with Marxist ingredients was, however, an alternative option.

The rise of Marxism in the late nineteenth century stimulated some responses from Christians, probably the most notable being the Encyclical letter to the Church entitled *Rerum novarum* ("Of new things"), issued by Pope

Leo XIII (1810–1903) in 1891. Leo had earlier condemned Socialism as a plague, but he recognized that in the industrial age new forms of organization were necessary, and in the Encyclical he laid the theoretical basis for the formation of Catholic labor unions and ultimately of Catholic political parties committed to democratic forms. He had also been prominent in the reform of Catholic education, and in his *Aeterni Patris* (1879) had made a revived form of Aquinas' thought, called Neo-Thomism, virtually mandatory for Catholic thinkers. As it happened, this was not a strong enough system to challenge easily the growing power of Marxist and secular thought on European intellectuals. Indeed, among European intellectuals in the early twentieth century, Christianity was no longer a predominant belief.

Various forms of secular ideology were influential. For those who thought that Marxism was not based enough in realities and was too speculative, and who favored a more liberal and democratic way of thinking, a kind of empiricism with humanist ethical values was attractive, such as the thought of Bertrand Russell (1872–1970). He was a notable representative of scientific humanism, which sees humanity as the highest value, love of fellow humans as the highest ethic, and science as the best way of relating to the cosmos. Humanism was an alternative to religion in the West: it was and is atheistic, though some humanists prefer to use the word "agnosticism" to characterize their position, meaning the lack of knowledge and evidence one way or another to assert or deny the existence of God (the word was invented in 1869 by the biologist and philosopher T. H. Huxley (1825–95). Later, humanism was given a more personalist tone and a grounding in dramatic human choice in the atheistic Existentialism of Jean-Paul Sartre (1905–80) and others. A form of scientific humanism came to dominate English-speaking philosophy under the influence of scientific empiricism and language analysis.

Partly under the influence of Hegel, who saw the State as a kind of incarnation of the Absolute Mind, right-wing ideologies appeared, which were hostile both to the liberal ideals of the Center and the revolutionary impulses of the Left. In Italy there was Fascism, espousing a corporate State which organized professional, union, and industrial life in the service of nationalist expansion and a return to the glories of the Roman Empire, under Benito Mussolini (1883–1945). More serious and more devastating still was the Nazi ideology, which presented a hypernationalist ethos, an assertion of German and "Aryan" superiority, and a program for conquest and the elimination of inferiors, notably Jews. Though Fascism in Italy could live on reasonable terms with Catholicism, in Germany the Nazi ideology had a religious (and anti-Christian) character of its own. The parades, the Hitler salute, the uniforms, the flags, all gave it a strong *ritual* element. The *emotions* of being saved through the Leader in the restoration of a fallen Germany were strong. Though its *doctrinal* and theoretical bases were weak, the *myth* of Aryan Germany was a powerful one. And the idea of the Thousand-Year Reich was a beguiling eschatology. The role of the Führer was religious too: the plain German who had fought in World War I, now ready to transcend aristocrats and generals and lead the nation on the warpath (never mind that he was an Austrian!) Though Fascism and Nazism scarcely survived the death of their leaders, much the same tendencies can coalesce into the modern right-wing dictatorship, often military, and sometimes in alliance with and sometimes in conflict with the churches.

Imperial Expansion and Missions Outside Europe

Nineteenth-century European history is greatly incomplete without the story of European expansion. Apart from Russia's vast land empire, there was the formation of formidable empires by Britain, France, Holland, and Germany, and lesser empires by Belgium, Italy, and Denmark. By contrast, the older empires of Spain and Portugal were substantially diminished through the independence movements in Central and South America, and at the end of the century by the detachment of Cuba and the Philippines from Spanish rule by the United States. But Britain consolidated its rule over nearly all the subcontinent of India and was probing north and northwest into Afghanistan and Tibet. It held part of Southeast Asia and great parts of the Pacific. It controlled the Cape and was poised to take part in the scramble for Africa. It was dominant culturally in Canada and the Caribbean. France had much of Indochina and was moving into North Africa. Holland held Indonesia and some other island possessions. Germany took part in the African carve-up, acquiring large tracts of Southwest and Southeast Africa and parts of the West. Britain dominated in East Africa and Southern Africa, but also was substantially present in the West. France had huge swathes of West and North and Central Africa. Belgium took the Congo, later Zaire; Italy was later to move into Libya, Somalia, and eventually Ethiopia.

All this gave great opportunities for mission work. The Christian Churches moved in under the aegis of the empires. Protestant missions predominated in Protestant empires, and Catholic in Catholic ones; but over much of the globe rival missions, either from differing denominations or differing nations, were in competition. The scandal of this from a Christian point of view led to one of the first major events in the so-called Ecumenical Movement or movement for Christian unity, namely a mission conference in Edinburgh to promote Christian cooperation. The results of the missions we shall see in other chapters: but their existence reinforced the European idea that the British (or French, or whoever) represented a Christian civilization which would bring both rational and spiritual enlightenment to the unfortunate masses of the non-European world. Christian missionaries, however, also became involved in nationalist movements which sought the same liberty and rights for the conquered as were enjoyed by the conquering nation.

Christianity and Judaism in Twentieth-Century Europe

The destiny of the religions was considerably affected by the secular ideologies which functioned as alternatives. In Russia, the Revolution brought the Church into a new captivity. World War I, with its devastating power to kill mass armies, saw the collapse of that optimism which had been one ingredient of liberal Protestantism. The rise of Fascism in Italy in due course tempted the Catholic Church into a new deal or concordat with the Italian State in 1929 which gave the Catholics certain rights over education and marriage law and the like. The rise of Nazism posed dilemmas for the German Churches, and brought agony to the Jews. Secular humanism came to be the prevailing ethos in most parts of Scandinavia and was strong in Britain. World War II, often thought of by the Western Allies as a struggle between good and evil, mobilized Christians on both sides, as usual, and ended with the extension of Stalin's Communist empire into Central Europe. The Spanish Civil War of 1936–39 saw bitter anticlericalism at work. Altogether the period up to and indeed beyond World War II was an unhappy one for the major religions, and for Judaism it was catastrophic.

Two significant books were published in 1917 and left their imprint on the European religious scene. One was by Karl Barth (1886–1968), and was his commentary on the Epistle of Paul to the Romans. It heralded the production of his major work, *Church Dogmatics*. It was a statement of Protestant theology which cut against the optimistic liberalism dying along the Western Front. It kept to modern canons of scholarship but from a conservative angle. For him the "Christ-event," rather than the words of scripture as such, constituted the revelation. But he kept strongly to Paul's notion of grace, and restated this in a way which rejected all forms of natural theology. Only by revelation do we know anything of God. It was a hard-line position which made Christian revelation discontinuous with all other religious ideas and teachings. These were, just as Feuerbach had said, a mere projection of human concerns. Christianity has value only as the response of people to the revelation in Christ. This dogmatic position, narrow and nonrational, had great influence between the Wars both among Christians of the liberal wing and in the mission field. Its prestige was enhanced because Barth stood up against the Nazis and, with other members of the so-called Confessing Church which resisted Hitler (1889–1945), signed the so-called Barmen Declaration of 1934.

The other book was Rudolf Otto's *The Idea of the Holy*. Otto (1869–1937) saw in the Holy the key category of religion and analyzed the experience of the Holy as numinous, a mystery that both awes and fascinates. In thus basing his philosophy of religion on a kind of experience, Otto revitalized an older tradition, but he did so very much in the context of the comparative study of religions. By the 1970s and 1980s, Christian theologians had at last begun to see with clarity that other religious traditions in the world represent a genuine challenge to old-fashioned theology and need to be taken seriously. The imperial age had not been without its fine Christian scholars who studied other religions, but the main tenor was of European and Christian cultural superiority. Otto as one of the revitalizers of the comparative study of religion was an important figure. It turns out that his emphasis on the numinous is good in characterizing the feel of various kinds of theism, where God is the

Other; but it does not work so well in characterizing non-theistic mystical experience, especially Buddhist. So we need to think of more than one basic type of religious experience. But that does not invalidate the approach which Otto was pioneering.

In Europe, over much of the twentieth century, the huge questions have been very immediate because of the rise of dictatorships. Neither Protestantism nor Catholicism had an altogether honorable encounter with Hitler, but there were martyrs to the faith, notably Dietrich Bonhoeffer (1906–45). The largest question has been reaction to the Holocaust or *Sho'ah*—the killing of about six million Jews in Europe in the concentration camps and gas ovens of the Nazis. Other groups were also terribly treated, such as Gypsies, Russian prisoners, and many others: but anti-Semitism was a vital ingredient in Hitler's thinking, and a central part of the Nazi ideology, which was drenched in thoughts of pure Aryan blood and so forth. Christianity had a role in the creation of anti-Semitism: partly because of old charges, from the New Testament time onward, that the Jews "killed God"; partly because of a naïve epistemology which held that the Jews culpably failed to recognize that the Old Testament foretold Christ; partly because of the xenophobic Crusading spirit; and in various other ways. Christianity is only now coming to terms with this past.

But the Holocaust has been of course even more of a trauma for Jews. Many a German Jew was proud to be German until Hitler, and so in a number of other countries. So there was the initial shock of rejection. But when the full awfulness of the Holocaust unfolded, there was a deep question shockingly posed to believing Jews: How could a good God have produced such a calamity? Some have turned away from the faith. Others have seen it as just an extreme case of the free will with which the Creator has endowed people. Others have seen it as opening up a new period of Jewish history, when faith in God and adherence to the Covenant become absolutely voluntary, since the monstrous event of the Holocaust releases Jews from their obligations (this position is found in the writings of Irving Greenberg). Some Orthodox Jews have seen it as a punishment for sins, maybe for Zionism. But such an interpretation scarcely rings true: for so devastating a punishment the sin would have to be disproportionately monstrous. Meanwhile hope continues, for it was partly out of the ashes of Europe's madness that the State of Israel was built, achieving independence in 1948 and surviving miraculously through several wars.

The effect on the Jewish people of the Holocaust and the founding of Israel was to concentrate them densely in North America and in Israel—for many Jews from Arab and Muslim countries also migrated there. There are, of course, other centers of Jewish life, such as those in South Africa and Britain, but the center of gravity has shifted to the United States, while modern Israel has come to occupy a more vital place in the thinking of most Jews than even the old Zion had. "Next year in Jerusalem" has a concrete meaning now.

The Updating of Catholicism

Among the Christian Churches of Europe probably the most vital events since World War II have been those connected with the Ecumenical Movement— the founding of the World Council of Churches in 1948 – and the reforming Council, Vatican II (1962–5), which led to radical changes in Roman Catholic thinking and practice.

In *doctrine*, Vatican II saw the melting away of Neo-Thomism. In matters of *narrative* the winds of Protestant scholarship were allowed to riffle the pages of the Bible. In *ritual* the Latin tradition was abandoned and the Mass was simplified and translated into the vernacular languages of the world. In *ethics* a more open attitude prevailed, and renewed concern for the poor. In *experience* new experiments with devotion and charismatic ecstasies were initiated. In *organization* the Church was somewhat democratized. In architecture and the *arts* new forces of modernity were released. Ecumenically, the Roman Catholics became much less reserved, and now play a vital role in initiatives of Christian cooperation.

In short, Vatican II represented a vast source of change. For John XXIII it was an act of *aggiornamento* or "updating" the Church. Large numbers of priests and monks and nuns, however, about this time began to leave their vocations, though most remained loyal Catholics. New forces of rebellion were released in the Church, which consequently became highly dynamic and not always obedient to the dictates from the Vatican (notably in matters such as birth control, where many Catholics simply disregarded papal pronouncements against the use of artificial methods).

In postwar Europe there has been another force affecting the practice of Christianity. The fact that Church authority is largely unenforceable in pluralistic communities has led to a wide proliferation of new religious movements, while Christianity and Judaism have come face to face with other world religions on what they had come to regard as home territory. Many adherents of Islam, for instance, have come to work in Western countries, so that it is the third largest denomination in Britain; and young people have found much in Buddhism, in Hindu movements, and in new experiments in living. With the added fact that the majority in many Western European countries are non-practicing and many of them reject traditional Christianity, there now exists a much more fluid picture of belief in Europe. Things were not quite the same in the Communist East.

Reflections on Modern Europe

It many be noted that in Europe, more or less continuously from the reign of Constantine the Great until this modern period, Christianity in one form or another has had official status. It is now, for the European populations, more or less a voluntary matter. There is thus a new weakness and a new vitality in religion. The weakness is that the Churches appear statistically in decline; the strength is that voluntary religion is deeper than conforming religion. Further, we note that since the various postwar economic revivals – German, Italian,

British, and so on – Western Europe is a consumerist entity. Choices have rarely been so abundant. And something similar is beginning to happen in religion; a kind of consumerism, with many new varieties being added as cultures cross and merge. Poverty remains, but more at the margin in the West. Hence Christianity looks increasingly to the global village to fulfill its role of serving the poor.

Oddly, though, despite the multiplications of new sects and religious movements, the currents of mainstream Christianity have greatly converged. The differences of *ritual*, for instance, have been greatly moderated since Vatican II and among the Protestant denominations. Nor are there quite such acute divergences of *doctrine*. Only perhaps on the *mythic* side is there acute division: those who take the Bible more or less literally form a conservative movement cutting across denominations; and there is a corresponding movement of more liberal Christians who likewise have similar interpretations of the Bible. There are differences in *ethical* stance, e.g. over abortion; but somewhat at the margin. Martin Luther King, John Paul II, Mother Teresa, Bishop Tutu, Robert Runcie (former Archbishop of Canterbury), although of quite different historic pasts, gained wide Christian recognition in this ecumenical age. But the center of Christianity has already moved southward from Europe, into Africa and Latin America and in general the so-called Third World. No doubt Europe will be open to new influences.

North America

CHAPTER 15

A New Pluralism

The Christianities and Judaisms of North America, and particularly of the United States, have pioneered a number of new forms and circumstances. For instance, the division of Church and State in the American constitution was a novelty in its day, largely unprecedented at least among European nations. Again, it was in North America that some of the most vigorous revivalist movements of modern Christianity occurred. There are also religions born in North America, like the Mormons and Christian Science. Roman Catholicism and Eastern Orthodox Christianity had to take on rather a different flavor in the New World. And it was in America that the modern forms of Judaism were most extensively developed and in some cases created. Side by side with all this, there is the fate of the Native Americans to contemplate, their populations greatly diminished by European diseases and bullets, their cultures greatly subverted, and developing new varieties of religion to cope with such disasters.

North America is also vital for the history of modern religion because it demonstrates the ways in which great immigrations and a melting-pot of cultures affect traditions. All these facets of American religion give it great vigor. Very often the migrants became much more committed to their faith than they would have been had they stayed at home, and this sometimes makes it difficult for Americans to appreciate the degree of religious secularization which has occurred in parts of Europe, especially the North.

In the twentieth century, too, North America has seen experiments in living, mainly from the late 1960s on, which have multiplied options and incorporated some Eastern religions into Western patterns of life. It has also had the vigor of Black religion to vivify it, and this has incorporated Islamic elements, as well as the strongly emotional faith of evangelical Protestantism.

In addition there has been migration, especially from the Far East, which has brought Chinese and Japanese, later Korean and Vietnamese, Buddhism (and other concomitant religious forms such as Daoism and Confucianism) into the North American picture, especially in California.

There are differing periods for us to look at. First there is the colonial period up to Independence; then there is the initial period of United States religion up to the mid part of the nineteenth century; then the period of rapid immigration, the opening up of the frontier, and the Civil War; then there is the twentieth century. In Canada, roughly the same framework will work, since similar conditions prevailed, though without slavery.

The Religious Affairs of the Colonies

In the settlement of North America, Britain predominated along the eastern seaboard, especially after the fall of New Amsterdam to Britain, as New York, in 1664. The more southern colonies, Virginia, Maryland, the Carolinas, were settled in principle by members of the Church of England; while the more northern colonies, Massachusetts, Connecticut, Rhode Island, Pennsylvania, and west New Jersey, had a predominantly dissenting character.

The most famous landfall was that of the *Mayflower* at Plymouth Rock in Massachusetts in 1620. The New England colonies provided a refuge from persecution and social disadvantage in England and a focus for new religious aspirations to found a "City upon a Hill," a new Zion. The Puritans of New England did not necessarily extend to their members the rights of religious toleration: a new conformism became apparent in the colonies, which were substantially self-governing. New theocracies were built. However, some notable exceptions to this were not long in appearing.

One was the Rhode Island colony founded primarily by Roger Williams (1603–83). He was in his beliefs a Calvinist; but he was most vigorous for the separation of Church and State. He joined the Baptists, as conforming best to what he expected of a Christian group, and founded the first Baptist church in America, in Providence. He secured eventually a permanent charter for the new colony, of which he was president for three years, and there freedom of religion was assured. In retrospect he has been seen as a great pioneer of separatism and a forerunner of the later First Amendment of the United States Constitution, passed in 1791: "Congress shall make no law respecting an establishment of religion or prohibiting the free exercise thereof."

The Quaker colonies of west New Jersey and Pennsylvania also incorporated religious toleration. William Penn (1644–1718) played a leading part in efforts to secure the passing of the English Act of Toleration Act after the so-called Glorious Revolution of 1688. In Pennsylvania there were ethical restrictions imposed, such as the rejection of forts and armaments, since the Quakers were pacifists, and the outlawing of slavery. Incidentally, full rights were accorded the Delaware Indians. So religious dissent had an important political message. This stemmed from the thinking of George Fox (1624–91).

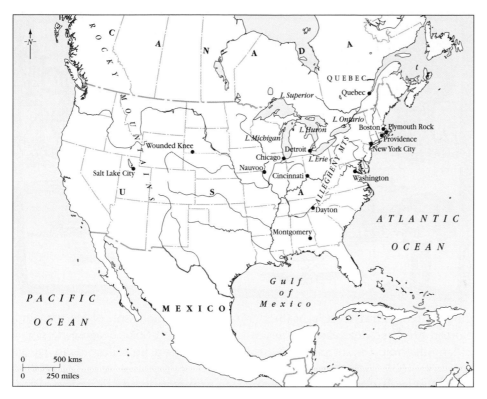

Map 15 North
America.

The movement which he founded, the Society of Friends, nicknamed
Quakers, looked to inner experience and the "light that lights every person" as
the source of true religion, and conscience as the source of true morality. They
simplified worship to the meeting in which people awaited inspiration before
speaking or leading the group in prayers. Their meetinghouses were of the
simplest. They were pacifists, and accorded each person equal dignity. It was
the recognition of Christ in every person that took them on the path to a fine
egalitarianism, which of course extended to slaves and native Americans. They
became an important strand in Puritan thinking in America, but only in the
very earliest days of the Pennsylvania colony did they have a majority role, and
for the most part they have been a relatively minor group, though influential
beyond their numbers. Both Quakers and Roger Williams made a point of
friendship with the "Indians," in often bleak contrast to other White—Native
American relationships.

Many of the New England Puritans were Congregationalists in their
organization. Someone has referred to Congregationalists as decentralized
Calvinists. Their government was through independent congregations, as the
name implies, and they rejected the more complex and centralized
Presbyterian system, for the most part (Presbyterianism was stronger to the
south in the Middle Atlantic States). In their thinking they were often
millenarian, and they saw a special destiny in the New England dream of a

The narrative dimension: the Puritan migration to New England has entered powerfully into the story of America's history. Puritans are seen here illustrating a ballad celebrating the Independents' voyage to New England, a journey from persecution, shown on the left, to a new life, shown on the right.

purified faith. Thus, Cotton Mather (1663–1728), famous son of Harvard and Boston preacher, defended the fusion of Church and State because he saw a redemptive role for society in New England. In this he followed his father Increase (1629–1723)—wonderful, these Puritan names!—who thought of New England as a place for the final consummation of the work of the Reformation. Cotton Mather thought that the Second Coming of Christ might take place in his time and in New England. Such shining hope and the feeling of a special destiny for the American colonies was to carry over into the optimism and sense of chosenness in the Republic.

Early on, the Congregationalists had paid good attention to education, founding Harvard in 1637 and Yale and other colleges a bit later. Thus America had more investment in higher education than England, which till the early nineteenth century had only the two universities of Oxford and Cambridge. But though intellect was important in colonial American religion, the heart was too.

The Great Awakening of the eighteenth century was a formidable revival, the first in a cycle to influence and stimulate American piety. Its onset in 1734 was experienced in the church of Jonathan Edwards (1703–58), perhaps America's greatest theologian, in Northampton, Massachusetts. The movement was passionate and charismatic, and was further spurred by the preaching of George Whitefield (1714–70), English preacher and itinerant revivalist. His sermons were marked by great enthusiasm up and down the Atlantic Coast. He was looked at askance by the Anglican Establishment, though ordained a priest, but got a good reception from Congregationalists, Presbyterians, Reformed, and Baptists. Among other causes which he espoused was the opening of Dartmouth College in New Hampshire to Native Americans.

The Baptists benefited from the Great Awakening, for it made some of their doctrines and practices more relevant. Their separatism (that is, their rejection of an established Church) was meaningful in an enthusiasm which saw true Christianity in the fruits of religious experience rather than conformity to orthodoxy; and their itinerant mode of preaching was something which now became normal. They began to make great advances, and from that base were to be very effective as the frontier moved over the Alleghenies and into the wide beyond. More complex, established Churches found it hard to follow the shifting populations.

Moreover, the Baptists, with their warm and charismatic appeal and favoring of conversion-experiences, had a special appeal to the Blacks. For by the mid-eighteenth century there were already over 100,000 slaves in the South. The Baptists were on their way to becoming the largest religious denomination in America. In advocating adult baptism they followed the Anabaptist principle.

Another important strand in American Protestantism was beginning to grow just before and during the period of the Revolution. It was Methodism, so

A Mennonite assembly in America. Note the simplicity of the meeting house and the prominence of the pulpit. The Protestant sect originated in Zurich in 1523 and spread throughout Germany and the Netherlands, but when the members of the sect began to be persecuted, many migrated to North America and settled in Germantown, Pennsylvania.

called from the notion that one should live according to a "method" laid down in the Bible. This movement had started, through the work of John Wesley (1703–91), as a means of revitalizing the Church of England. But Wesley was much influenced by the Moravians, a mainly German group stemming both from the work of John Hus (1369?–1415), the Czech reformer before the Reformation, and from eighteenth-century Pietism, a warm devotionalism associated with the leader Count Zinzendorf of (1700–60). Their warm feeling for Christ and devotion to him was appealing to Wesley. The Methodist movement was enhanced by the great hymns composed by Charles Wesley (1708–88), and was to make important strides in postcolonial America.

Mingled with emotionally oriented religion and the Puritan ethos were ideas derived from the Enlightenment—anticlerical Freemasonry, deism, feeling for the rights of man, commitment to toleration—and all these found their fulfillment, as far as religious organization went, in the First Amendment, which made a vital statement about the meaning of the American Revolution. So it was that Anglicanism reformed itself, no longer as an Established Church, but as the Protestant Episcopal Church of the United States. In Virginia its endowments were lost, and many clergy left for Canada.

Nevertheless a vigorous Anglican tradition survived. The first American bishop, Samuel Seabury of Connecticut (1729–97) was consecrated by Scottish Episcopal bishops, who had no established status and indeed were regarded at the time as being in schism with the Church of England.

Roman Catholics in Colonial North America

The most important area for Catholicism was not in the British colonies but in Quebec. There the Church became in part a sign of ethnic identity, especially after the fall of Quebec to the British in 1759 during the Seven Years' War, a disaster for the French. The Quebec Act of 1774 however granted full citizenship to Catholics and allowed the Church to maintain its tithing system. The Province was brought into the colony of Canada.

The position of Catholics in the British colonies to the south was much less favorable. Maryland had in principle been a colony for English Catholics, but a Puritan majority in the colony repealed the Act of Toleration in 1664, and Catholics were deprived of voting rights.

It was during the nineteenth century that American Catholicism made vast progress, because of the large numbers of migrants from Ireland, Italy, Poland, and other European countries with strong Catholic populations. We shall come to that shortly.

From the American Revolution to the Middle of the Nineteenth Century

The opening up of the frontier into Kentucky, Ohio, and elsewhere beyond the Alleghenies had begun in earnest, and in the new optimism of the young Republic a Second Great Awakening occurred at the turn of the century, with revival meetings in tents along the areas of new occupation. The mobile folk who were opening up American farmland were susceptible to evangelical fervor, and so it was that the warmest type of preaching and religion—Baptists, Methodists, Congregationalists—made the greatest impression.

Meanwhile, in New England, there was a shift among many Congregationalists towards Unitarianism, which took over many of the beautiful churches of the area. This move into the Unitarian persuasion was in no small part due to the influence of William Ellery Channing (1780–1842), of Boston, whose sermon on Unitarian Christianity in 1819 summed up what many already thought—that Christ, though morally perfect, was nevertheless subordinate to God. It was like the old Arian position (see p. 258), which made Christ noneternal, being himself created by God. It rejected the full-blown version of the Trinity doctrine which had been the hallmark of Christian orthodoxy. Unitarianism was to make strong advances among the educated elite of the period and the area.

It also had a frontier with the movement known as Transcendentalism, associated above all with Ralph Waldo Emerson (1803–82) and Henry David Thoreau (1817–62). Transcendentalism as a view emphasizes the presence of the divine in Nature, and the need of the individual to be true to himself and

Brigham Young (1801–77) was born in Vermont and joined the Mormon Church in 1832. He led the migration to Utah in 1846 and founded Salt Lake City in 1847.

371

to work in harmony with Nature. It has affinities to Daoism and some aspects of the Hindu tradition, by which Emerson was somewhat influenced. Transcendentalism helped to stimulate interest in the comparative study of religions, and was one of the factors lying behind the famous World's Parliament of Religions in Chicago, 1893. It also had an influence on Christian Science.

It was in the first part of the nineteenth century that the first important homegrown American religion was created, by the prophet Joseph Smith II (1805–44), from upper New York State. Stimulated by visionary experiences and guided, he said, by an angel, he discovered at the Hill Cumorah some gold plates which he translated as *The Book of Mormon*. This claims to give the story of some of the peoples of North America before Columbus, some of whom were ancestors of the Native Americans, and who were migrants from the Lost Tribes of Israel. In 1830 the Church of Jesus Christ of the Latter-Day Saints was formed (the full name dates from 1838). The story of this new movement was tremendous. Smith and his followers moved to Kirtland, Ohio, and then further west, eventually setting up a fine city with its own temple in Nauvoo, Illinois. Near there, at Carthage, Joseph Smith and his brother Hiram were murdered in 1844. Their new theocracy was becoming too powerful, and some of the new teachings and practices (including polygamy) were scandalous to outsiders. Brigham Young (1801–77) led the main body of the Mormons, as they were nicknamed, to Salt Lake City in Utah. He set about establishing an empire there, the State of Deseret; but Congressional unease and pressure led eventually to the incorporation of Utah into the United States, with theocracy and polygamy abandoned. Many converts, especially from Britain, went out on the hard trail to Utah. Mormon cohesiveness, puritanism, and family values had a strong appeal. Some of the doctrines—that God is material, that there are many Gods, and that human beings may become Gods—have been modified, and in many ways Mormonism is now a conforming evangelical kind of Protestantism, with the colorful additions of the *Book of Mormon* and the charismatic memory of the genial and masterful Joseph Smith.

The Effects of Mass Immigration

In the second half of the nineteenth century the processes of settlement and industrialization speeded up. This sucked into America large numbers of immigrants, many of whom were Catholic or Jewish, foreign to the prevailing Protestant ethos. Both groups were regarded with some suspicion. But up to the period of World War I these groups made their fundamental adjustments to the New World.

For Catholics the question was a double one of integration. On the one hand, how were the masses of immigrants of different nations to live together in one Church? There were Irish and Poles, Hungarians and Italians, Germans and Mexicans, to be blended together. On the other hand, how was

Catholicism to be woven into the fabric of American life? The key to both of these operations was education, and Catholicism paid a great deal of attention to it. There evolved a system of parish schools and Catholic colleges and universities which made the transition into American life feasible without the loss of religious tradition. Part of the task, too, was showing others that Catholicism was in no way disloyal to the American heritage: by prominence in games, such as American football, in cultural life, and appropriately in politics, Catholics could demonstrate their all-American character. The Church devoted most of its energies to social affairs, to building (most extensively and floridly), and to education. Catholic Orders were prominent, many engaged in these social and educational tasks.

For Protestantism the immigration brought North Europeans, especially Swedes, other Scandinavians, and Germans. All this added up to Lutheranism, which became especially strong in the Midwest and often provided a bridge between the national culture and the New World. In Canada a similar process of migration brought in many Scots and Northern Irish Protestants, as well as Germans and others, and this gave its own flavor to the Protestant heritage in Canada, which became very strongly Presbyterian.

The period saw new chances for Black religion to flourish, for the Civil War ensured that Blacks would gain emancipation, and Churches which had existed before now blossomed out. Already in 1816 there had been formed an African Methodist Episcopal Church, following the lead of Richard Allen (1760–1831), who had formed the first Black Methodist congregation. With emancipation there was a great exodus of Blacks from White-controlled denominations to create new organizations for Black Baptists and so on. The Reconstruction period saw the foundation of various important Black colleges and universities. But it was followed in turn by a darker period of renewed oppression.

One option was to look to migration back to Africa. Freed slaves were settled in Liberia, which became independent in 1847. Africa remained a symbol for Black Americans. Bishop Turner (1834–1915), a Methodist, said that it was necessary for Black people to have a Black God, and that only in Africa could Black people exercise their full powers. The ideal of a restoration of Africa's past glories by the action of those who had gone through the suffering of slavery was a not uncommon theme. In fact rather few Blacks actually returned to Africa. But there was much dynamism in Black Christianity, and even more from the time of World War I onward.

The Development of African-American Religion

Another factor in the development of African American religion was the migration of many people from the rural South to the Industrial North and Midwest—to Indiana, Chicago, Buffalo, New York, Philadelphia, and so on. This was most marked after the Civil War and during and after the World Wars, which saw a new thirst for labor. This projected the struggle for freedom into a new awareness of social and political injustices. Gradually African

American Christianity became wholly suffused with the fight for justice, but at the same time it cultivated some features which had begun to shape themselves in the days of slavery.

First there grew up a strong emphasis on *experiential* religion. In any case the nineteenth and twentieth centuries in the United States had seen a strong evangelical emphasis, which encouraged the same expression of religion. The strong feeling of being gripped and guided by the Spirit of God was a forceful feature of African faith, which also sought fuller expression through ecstatic utterance and dance.

This led, secondly, to characteristic patterns of *ritual*: more flowing and expressive than many of the traditions of the Whites. There developed characteristic patterns of music—such as Gospel and the Blues. Contributing to this dynamism was the distinctive style of the Black preacher, whose chanting rhythms interacted with the emotions of the congregation. Many powerful preachers, by the way, were women.

As to the *institutional* dimension, that was to some degree affected by migration. It was often in storefront churches that religion took root, and through much of the community the attitude of protest and compassion for the poor and underprivileged was part of the daily life of congregations. Ministers found it natural to blend into secular organizations, such as the National Association for the Advancement of Colored People, and in general to take part in politics.

The *ethical* dimension saw a similar blending of private and public virtues. The tendency for Africans to have to live in urban ghettoes brought its own challenges. The churches had to take part in the struggles to combat the ravages of poor education, drugs, and demoralization; and it was important to give people hope. While some leaders wanted to create a separate identity for African Americans, this should not be at the expense of cutting themselves off from their neighbors. A shining example was found in the struggle for civil rights.

As for the *mythic* dimension, naturally the story of Black Americans is dominated by the wrenching history of coming from Africa cruelly to a new land. The novel *Roots* is still bewitching. The American myth of the settlers who came to the new land was not at all appealing to the Blacks. Their heaven, if anywhere, was beyond the Jordan, in another future than this earth, where so much suffering had been endured. Some hoped for some saving return to Africa; and some for a future where God's justice will have been given to all peoples, including Black.

Regarding the *doctrinal* dimension, much of the writing on African–American theology links up with the social struggle, and it builds on the myth of the Exodus in a new way. It is a critique of a European and White American theology which sees God as tolerant of slavery in the past. It also shows how true Christianity identifies with the poor and the oppressed. Some, of course, go further and move over into Islam as a way of rejecting the official Christian faith.

Finally, in the material dimension a new African art is being fashioned, in which Jesus and Mary are depicted in new and original ways.

Native American Religious Movements

The spread of White settlement across the Plains to the far West was an unmitigated calamity for the Native Americans. From early on, the Native American experience of the Whites had not been happy. Thus, in 1622 the Pamunkey Algonquins rebelled against their treatment at the hands of the Jamestown settlers in Virginia, and were defeated. With the coming of the Whites across the plains and the diminishment of the buffalo, various new religious movements emerged, which tried to deal with the problems of the Indians. The Ghost Dance religion of Wodziwob foresaw a time, imminently, when dead Indians would be raised up, the Whites would go away, and a new life would begin again. A second wave in 1889 started from Nevada, under Wovoka, and spread across the Plains, sadly culminating in the massacre of Wounded Knee, when Sioux thought their sacred shirts rendered them immune to bullets (a belief found in various parts of the world during the period of colonialism). The Native Americans were put into reservations, and reduced to a miserable condition, ravaged by loss of morale, alcohol, and impotence in the face of White control. Nevertheless revival was on its way, during the twentieth century, with a reassertion of Native American values. To this we shall return.

Varieties of Judaism in the Formative Period

The destiny of Judaism and of the Jewish people was bright in America. But it was not without pain that the solutions to living in the modern world were worked out there. The price of toleration was that religion had to become substantially a private matter, and though Jews could assemble in living areas in the big cities, they did not have the relative legal independence that they had sometimes achieved in Europe and the Middle East.

The first main wave of migrants to America, often German in origin, were ready for modernization. By the end of the Civil War a reasonable affluence had been achieved in the community, and the formal organization of American Reform Judaism was appropriate. In 1869 a group of rabbis formulated a statement of belief which rejected the notion of a personal *Mashiah* and of the restoration of Zion, in any literal sense. In brief, Jewish expectations were demythologized. A few years later Rabbi Isaac Wise (1819–1900) formed the Union of American Hebrew Congregations and through that organization started Hebrew Union College in Cincinnati, which remains the premier instructional center for Reform Judaism. Reform Judaism was supreme in America: it sought to present Judaism as a universal religion, working for the establishment of God's kingdom in which human beings would be united and sanctified, and not as the structure of a divisive community. Worship was remodeled, anglicized, and (from the Reform perspective) purified. It corresponded much more to Protestant norms, and the buildings tended to be called temples rather than synagogues. It was liberal and modernist in theology and combined up-to-date literary and historical scholarship with traditional Jewish learning.

At the time when Reform Judaism was taking shape there were new waves of migrants from Eastern Europe—many of them Hasidim, and most of them concerned not with German-style Reform but with Polish- or Ukrainian-style Orthodoxy. The Orthodox became self-conscious in this Orthodoxy as a reaction to the shape of Reform. The first attempts to deal with the problem of new immigrants (half a million up to 1900, and more than a million more between 1900 and 1914), for instance the founding of the Jewish Theological Seminary of America in 1885, were not successful, but after a second try the new form of organization proved more effective. The Jewish Theological Synagogue was reshaped in 1901, and Solomon Schechter (1847?–1915) was brought over to head it up. But the direction in which it developed was toward a third force in Judaism, namely Conservative Judaism, which combined a high degree of liberal scholarship with a conservative view of the practice of Judaism.

Orthodox Judaism created the Yeshiva University for the training of rabbis and others. Since this included secular studies it was fairly adaptive. Indeed, American Orthodoxy has tended to live successfully within the economic and social institutions of the United States, while keeping to the practice of the Torah. The beliefs of the Orthodox tend to be conservative, considering the Torah as Pentateuch to have been revealed by God at Sinai, and conforming closely to traditional laws or *halakhah*. For the Orthodox the Conservatives have moved too far and the Reform Jews have abandoned the substance of the faith. But after World War I times there were further developments, with the increased influence of Hasidism and the variation on Conservatism known as Reconstructionism.

Meanwhile in all this was the complication of Zionism. Generally speaking, the Orthodox and many Conservatives were anti-Zionist. The secular aspirations of the Zionists were unacceptable. Even so, there were some religious Zionists, who later were to become more important in the state of Israel itself.

There was also a fifth movement in regard to Judaism—away from it: Jews who left the Jewish religion and sought their destiny in the wider delights and challenges of American society.

Christianity and the Social Gospel

In looking at the latter part of the nineteenth century and the early twentieth century, we need to take account of the movement often labeled the Social Gospel. This was one of the major ways in which Protestantism addressed itself to the consequences of capitalism and the problems of modern urban life. It was stimulated chiefly by the work and thought of Walter Rauschenbusch (1861–1918), who worked in the Second German Baptist Church in New York for over a decade and was able to experience the sufferings of those who toiled at the bottom of the urban heap. The Churches were less fitted for the large modern city than for the easier integration of small town life.

More New Religions

In the latter half of the nineteenth century the creation of new forms of religion continued. Three characteristic and important ones are the Seventh-Day Adventists, the Jehovah's Witnesses, and Christian Science. In the first and last of these, women played a crucial role. The Adventists were built up by Ellen Gould White (1826–1915) and her husband James. They arose from the disappointment of a prediction made by the Adventist group founded by William Miller (1781–1849), that Christ would come on October 22, 1844. Some time later, Ellen White, who had been injured by a rock thrown at her head when a child, and had been unconscious for weeks—so that by consequence she was subject to much sickness during her long life—had a vision. This taught her that the Sabbath, as the Bible says, is on the seventh day, namely Saturday; and that indeed a new era of judgment had started on October 22, 1844. As a result, she and her husband became the central figures in the creation of the Seventh-Day Adventist Church, which steadily grew. It also adopted health methods dictated by Ellen White's visions. After his death she became matriarch of the group, and her theology shifted more toward an emphasis on grace, thus bringing the Adventists closer to mainstream evangelical Christianity. Her life, with its initiatory vision and its near-death experience, exhibited, in very modern form, themes of shamanism.

The Jehovah's Witnesses stem from the teachings of Charles Taze Russell (1852–1916) and of his dynamic successor Joseph Franklin Rutherford (1870–1942). Their name springs from the conviction that Jehovah is the proper Biblical name for God. They look forward to a wondrous restoration of the earth and the salvation of 144,000 souls who will reign with Christ in heaven. They pray to Jehovah through Christ; but their chief activity is publication and preaching. They consider that since 1914 Satan has been ruling over the world, and so they should not take part in State activities or fighting, and for this reason are much persecuted for pacifism and insubordination. They forbid priesthood and the like, and refuse blood transfusions, being contrary to Jehovah's laws (Leviticus 17). They have remained very energetic in mission work, and there is scarcely anyone in the West who has not been approached by them.

Mary Baker Eddy (1821–1900) was a product of New England Puritanism, but rebelled against Calvinist predestinationism. In her search for the truth the most decisive experience occurred to her in 1866 when she miraculously recovered from the consequences of a severe accident while reading an account of one of Christ's healings. She then set about trying to understand the world and the New Testament in the light of this, and nine years later she brought out her *Science and Health with Key to the Scriptures*. For her God is All, and so matter, considered in itself, is unreal: we can be healed first of sin and then secondarily of sickness by yielding to God's grace or influence, and by seeing the all-pervasiveness of Mind or Spirit. There are echoes of Transcendentalism in her thought. But when she came to preach this message she found a lot of hostility from orthodox Christians. In due course she founded her own Church, and later recognized it as the First Church of Christ Scientist in Boston, in 1892, which serves organizationally as the mother church to all the churches around the world. Again, as with Ellen White, we meet the confluence of healing and the Gospel: in many ways it is a religion which has rediscovered a major aspect of original Christianity. In 1908 she founded *The Christian Science Monitor*, indicating her commitment to education.

These three are, with Mormonism, samples of the new American religions. They reverberate with differing parts of American religious dreams. Mormonism has the sense of moving west to the chosen land, the sense too of being the instruments of God's will, and seeking for a theocracy, alas in a land committed to the First Amendment. The Jehovah's Witnesses testify to the dream that Satan rules—there has often been a feeling of the great struggle between good and evil in the American heart. The Seventh-Day Adventists seek to figure out the end of history. The Christian Scientists look to salvation here and now.

Evangelicals and Fundamentalists

The Rise of Fundamentalism

We have noted already how liberal Protestantism played a dominant role in Europe. Such liberalism of scholarship could not be far away from the American scene, with its high commitment to education. And yet so much of American religion was tied to the Bible. It was in America, therefore, above all, that the conservative reaction to liberalism took place. This was to be known as fundamentalism, a term derived from a series of pamphlets called *The Fundamentals: A Testimony to the Truth* which appeared before World War I, attacking modernist or liberal views of the Bible and defending "fundamental" doctrines, namely the literal infallibility of the Bible, the Virgin Birth of Christ, the Substitutionary Atonement (Christ's death atones by way of substituting for sinful human beings), the Resurrection of the Body, and the Second Coming. More loosely, fundamentalism means taking the Bible as literally inerrant or as "literal where possible" (for obviously the Bible itself contains metaphors). More loosely still, the term is applied to a strong antimodernist reaffirmation of any faith, for instance Islam. In the Christian context it is associated with evangelicalism—that is, the belief in the authority of the Bible, the claim that salvation can only come through close personal faith in Christ, the regeneration of spiritual life, typically through some conversion experience, and a transformation of moral life, including typically Bible-reading, prayer, abstention from specified wickedness (such as smoking, drinking, and promiscuity). Fundamentalism tends to be a branch of evangelicalism: not all evangelicals are fundamentalists. But since they all tend toward an authoritative and inerrant Bible, the lines are hard to draw.

In the nineteenth century the emphasis of fundamentalism in America became oriented toward a gloomier view of human nature and destiny through the doctrine of premillennialism. This is the view that Christ will come again after a dark period of strife and war in order to institute the millennium. The alternative, postmillennialism, is more optimistic: human affairs are improving, and we shall establish the millennium on earth before the Second Coming. A powerful figure in the premillennial movement was the great revivalist Dwight L. Moody (1837–99). Most fundamentalist and evangelical revival was involved in promoting personal, individual holiness, but not all. The Salvation Army, founded in 1865, was at the forefront of social work in the big cities of Britain and the United States, organized as a military group, and hoping to save the derelict by setting a caring example to induce them to reform.

The evangelical movement comprised large denominations or parts thereof, such as the Southern Baptists and Missouri Synod Lutheranism, and much Black Protestantism. So there were wide sympathies for the more strident affirmations of Biblical inerrancy by tough-minded fundamentalists.

The latter were also influenced by the method of interpreting the Bible called dispensationalism, associated with Dwight L. Moody, and expressed in a relatively scholarly way by C. I. Scofield (1843–1921), who published his *Scofield Reference Bible* in 1909. According to this way of reading the Bible, it refers to a succession of different eras or dispensations—e.g. the age of innocence at the start of the human story in the Garden of Eden, the

The ritual dimension: an important ingredient in the proselytizing of the frontier was the evangelical meeting, here seen in modern form.

dispensation of the Law from Moses to Christ, and so on. Human history nears its end, which will be marked by the Second Coming of Christ, the "rapture" of believers who will be taken up into the sky to meet him, a vast war, the conversion of the Jews, a thousand-year kingdom ruled over by Jesus from Jerusalem, and finally the Last Judgment. This theme is a powerful one for modern fundamentalists.

Twentieth-Century Evangelicalism

For many evangelicals in America, the aftermath of World War I was disturbing. Already there was a sense that the older evangelical values which they thought were intrinsic to American nationhood were being submerged or swamped. Already the immigration before the War had deeply marked America with the Catholic (not to mention the Jewish) influx. Old bastions of New England Protestantism, such as Massachusetts and Connecticut, now found Catholic majorities in the major cities. The same went for some sizeable Midwest towns, notably Chicago. Then, the immediate ethos of the 1920s was culturally frivolous, or so it seemed. A new pluralism seemed to undermine mainstream values. It was partly in this mood that the nation had decreed Prohibition in 1919. As it turned out, this produced the speakeasy and the Mafia, and it was done away with by President Franklin D. Roosevelt (1882–1945) after he came to power in 1933. But it was a powerful expression of evangelical values in American society.

Less effective, however, was the challenge to science mounted by the politician William Jennings Bryan (1860–1925), who acted as prosecutor in the famous Scopes trial in Dayton, Tennessee, when a teacher of that name was indicted for teaching Evolutionary Theory. Bryan's position attracted much ridicule in the world press, and shortly after the trial, as it happened, he died. Periodically, to this day, there are similar legal challenges to the teaching of biology and of pluralist values in the public schools. Part of the problem lies in the dogmatic epistemology (or theory of knowledge) of the fundamentalists, who cannot think that there might be legitimate alternatives to the interpretations that they place on the Bible; or indeed genuine alternatives to the Bible itself. This leaves a tension between their Christianity and the essentially pluralistic character of the American Constitution and way of doing things.

Fundamentalism withdrew into a period of regroupment in the 1930s. But evangelical religion remained a great dynamic, especially among Blacks. It was out of this milieu that there came the most important Christian leader in the United States in the twentieth century. This was Martin Luther King (1929–68). Raised in Atlanta, and educated at Morehouse College and Boston University, he was influenced by Walter Rauschenbusch and sociological reading, by Thoreau and his line on civil disobedience, and by Gandhi. In Montgomery, Alabama, he led a bus boycott and in other ways campaigned nonviolently for civil rights, helping to alleviate the condition of Southern Blacks, especially in education. He was assassinated in 1968. His was a liberal evangelical position, influenced by a touch of the Hindu tradition.

Above: Women priests wait in a square to be ordained into the Church of England by Bishop Barry Rogerson in Bristol, England, 1994.

Far left: The evangelist Billy Graham speaks during a service at the Robert F. Kennedy Memorial Stadium in Washington in 1986.

Near left: Louis Farrakhan, leader of the Nation of Islam, addressing the Million Man March on Capitol Hill, 17 October 1995.

The more ecumenical wing of evangelical revivalism was represented by Billy Graham, a highly successful preacher and crusader, who opened out his campaigns to cooperation with all the mainstream Churches. But it was to be the arrival of television which created the most prominent type of preaching—the TV evangelism of such as Jerry Falwell, Oral Roberts, and Robert Schuller of the Crystal Cathedral in Anaheim. The last of these is really rather removed from mainstream evangelical preaching, stressing the credo of the power of positive thinking in a vaguely Presbyterian setting. The others, though, have a fundamentalist background, and it was in part the resources of TV ministry which powered the revival of the religious Right in the late 1970s. It was in 1979 that Falwell formed the movement known as the Moral Majority, and in this and other ways evangelicals entered strongly into the political process. President Jimmy Carter helped give evangelicalism in general fashionability. But whereas he and other liberal evangelicals were not opposed to some fundamentalist legislation in the 1970s, the Moral Majority saw the times as decadent. Old American values were being attacked. There were Equal Rights, whittling away at the traditional family role of women; legalization of homosexuality; legalized abortion; new religious movements and cults; defeat in the Vietnam War (1965–73 for the United States); and Watergate. Since the new campaigning appealed to conservative ethical values, it combined easily with patriotism and attracted alliances with the Roman Catholics—which would have been anathema in the 1920s.

Dimensions of Evangelical and Fundamentalist Christianity

It is useful to look back on the evangelical experience and its fundamentalist variant to reflect on its dimensions. As to the *narrative* dimension, the stress is of course on the Bible—the story of Eden, Israel, Christ, and the coming of the Spirit. This vivid narrative can be arranged for interpretive purposes as a series of dispensations. There is division about the future story between those who look to Christ's coming as before or after the great harmonious and victorious period, the thousand years or millennium. The threat to their story posed by liberal or modernist readings of the Bible, and by such theories as Evolution, leads them to take a strong stance on revelation.

The *doctrinal* dimension affirms unequivocally the existence of God and the Trinity; and it also seeks a philosophical position which will allow a literal interpretation of the Bible to live with most of science. The Evolutionary thesis is attacked (often not without some reason) as itself being overdogmatic and having difficulty over the methods of evolution (random gene shuffling plus natural selection do not seem adequately to account for quantum leaps in animal evolution). The fundamentalist wing of evangelical Christianity has lately espoused a seemingly scientific alternative theory (that is, one using the jargon of science), known as Creationism.

The *experiential* dimension is of great importance, not only because of the general evangelical espousal of conversion and being "born again," as the

Opposite: The Mormon Temple in Salt Lake City, Utah, as seen just after sunset. The Mormons settled in Salt Lake City in the mid-nineteenth century, brought there by their leader Brigham Young.

modern fashion has it, but also because there have been fed into evangelical Christianity streams of Pentecostalism, among both Blacks and Whites. This encourages speaking with tongues and ecstatic experiences of the Spirit, in line with the accounts of Pentecost and the coming of the Spirit in the early Church. There was, for instance, the Azusa Street revival started in 1906 in Los Angeles by William J. Seymour, a Black preacher. At first the various forms of Pentecostalism tended to be rejected by mainstream Christianity, but they gradually made their way in. Some of these motifs combined with faith-healing, which also was used in television religion in the 1960s and on. In any event, one way or another both White and Black evangelicalism is fervid in its emphasis on personal experience of Christ.

As to the *ritual* dimension, there is a strong emphasis on personal prayer, and preaching is probably the prime form of rite, with hymn singing and Bible readings. The revivalists did much to stimulate hymn-writing, usually to Victorian tunes. The pastor or preacher has to develop his skills as a rhetorician, and this gives evangelical Protestantism a very fluid nature. People switch congregations because A is a superior preacher to B, and gathering a congregation is a vital task: its size being an index of evangelical success.

As to the *social* and institutional dimension, there is a tendency for the hardline fundamentalists to separate themselves off from evangelicals who are in their view too soft, or who cooperate with the wrong people, such as liberal Christians, Roman Catholics, and Jews. So there are networks of fundamentalist congregations. But, as we have seen, there is a wider cooperation on the political front, through the so-called Moral Majority. Evangelicalism is heavily entrenched and possesses some notable seminaries, such as Fuller Theological Seminary in Pasadena, California.

As to *ethics*, there is a strong affirmation of what may be called conservative individualism. Society is made up of individuals, and its quality will reflect the life of individuals—who should be sober, hardworking, sexually faithful, patriotic, keeping the Sabbath, and so on. Some fundamentalists particularly dislike certain fashions which they identify with permissiveness—long hair, beards, and women's slacks, for instance. They are unsympathetic to liberal political causes, on the whole; though among evangelicals there are widespread social concerns.

Finally, in *material* terms, evangelicals are not much committed to the visual side of religion, being somewhat heirs to the old iconoclastic tradition. But it is characteristic for them to be keen on up-to-date methods of disseminating their message. The new-style television preachers are a case in point: all the most recent technology is used. It was reported for instance in the Los Angeles Times of March 11, 1978, that the Christian Broadcasting Network in Virginia Beach, Virginia, had acquired the use of the RCA Satcom II satellite and had ordered 12 million dollars' worth of earth stations. In an earlier age, Aimee Semple McPherson (1890–1944), the Pentecostal evangelist and founder of the Foursquare Gospel Temples, had used radio dramatically (not to mention great choirs and theatrical techniques). This modernity of means is summed up too in the fact that Robert Schuller began his successful preaching career in southern California by holding meetings in parking lots (he considered most churches limited their membership in an automobile age by not having extensive enough parking lots).

In many ways, then, evangelical Christianity can be nontraditional, but at the same time it claims to stand for older values that it feels may have been betrayed by the liberals. It represents one way of coping with the crisis in authority posed by the relation of modern knowledge to the Bible. But it flourishes because it represents a concrete way of life that it can identify as Christian and involves great intensity of experience and ritual.

Developments since World War II

The Religious Revolution of the 1960s and 1970s

After World War II there was a variant on the loss of satisfaction experienced by many Americans after World War I. This time the threat to the American way of life was perceived externally as the Communist menace. A somewhat Zoroastrian myth underlay foreign policy, of a cosmic struggle between good and evil. McCarthyism came in as an internal force to root out dissent. By the 1950s, during the Eisenhower years, America was comfortable and conformist. This was the heyday of the mainstream liberal Protestant Churches and of unreconstructed Roman Catholicism. It was followed by the hopeful Kennedy administration, which itself betokened a new living together between Protestants and Catholics. It was also the period when the United States was concerned most with supporting the new state of Israel, and a genuine confluence of what were perceived as Christian and Jewish interests emerged. The new religious establishment was Protestant, Catholic, and Jew. But it was a period of relative harmony due for a big shake-up. The late 1960s saw the rebellion of many young people and the birth of the Counterculture. It was a rich and fruitful period, but a disturbing one. Ominous events were at hand: the assassination of President John F. Kennedy (1917–63) and the opening of the Vietnam War (1965); while for Catholics there was the exhilarating but disturbing second Vatican Council (1962–5). For Blacks the 1960s were a period of new opportunities, though the killing of Martin Luther King in 1968 was a reminder of the violence and prejudice still there in American society.

The revolt, partly against mainstream American religion, took various forms. One was a search beyond Western religion—a complex voyage into Eastern religions. Above all, this search concerned inner consciousness and the pursuit of mysticism. These features of religion of course existed within the Catholic and Orthodox traditions, but the latter was little known, while American Catholicism tended to be activist and in that epoch was in any case digesting the reforms of Vatican II. Monks and nuns were leaving orders, while the young sought mysticism in foreign traditions. It was an irony. Under the guidance of gurus such as Alan W. Watts (1915–73), who expounded Zen, and of writings such as those of Aldous Huxley (1894–1963), whose *The Perennial Philosophy* put mysticism at the heart of universal religion, and whose *The Doors of Perception* commended depth experiences created by mind-altering drugs, young folk took off into Eastern religious experiences. The Beatles sat at the feet of the Maharishi Mahesh Yogi in Rishikesh, India; and others experimented with LSD and other substances. The ethos was against the Protestant ethic and in some measure against the capitalist and technological world. Paradoxically the young sometimes used the technology of drugs to overcome the technology of the outer world.

The Counterculture also had its violent strand, especially in those circles where Marxist-style revolution was adopted as the ideal. That Marxism could ever be fashionable in America after the McCarthy era was surprising. But the writings especially of Herbert Marcuse (1898–1979) became fashionable. Some of this revolutionary feeling was triggered by the Vietnam War, with its inequities and burnings. The pacifists increased, partly under Eastern influence: hippies came to be seen as against war, holding up flowers and chanting the slogan "Make love not war." A new antiwar activism stirred the mainstream churches. Mingled into these movements was a new concern for the environment. There was a large move toward sexual liberation too, and from that epoch stemmed the now customary cohabitation of people without marriage and the "coming out" of homosexuals. All this remains shocking still to many Americans, but it became widespread social fact.

Of the more permanent consequences of that era we can point to the rooting of Eastern religions, especially Buddhism, from Tibetan to Zen and from Mahāyāna to Theravāda, on American soil; the stronger presence of the Hindu tradition, partly through the Hare Krishna movement; the survival of smaller so-called cults, such as the Unification Church of the Reverend Sun Myung Moon and the Children of God movement; the wider use of yogic and other meditation techniques among the wider population; the increased recognition by Christian and other mainstream religious groups that they need to take the challenging existence of world religions more seriously; the environmental movement, and increased interest in vegetarianism and animal liberation; and greater sexual permissiveness. Also given a boost during this period, because of the advent of Black Power, was Islam among Blacks, as we shall see.

The perhaps inevitable backlash against many of these movements and ideas came in the late 1970s and early 1980s. The Moral Majority was a symptom of this. But the trends listed are here to stay. The Eastern emphasis among Whites was reinforced by immigration from East Asia especially, so that in California, for instance, Anglo Buddhists mingle with Asians of various nationalities, who enrich their experience of Buddhism. All this has brought into relief the great extent of American pluralism, and this makes it hard for those who wish to put the clock back to a more monistic Protestant era.

Meanwhile the radicalism of the 1960s and early 1970s encouraged new patterns of identity among Blacks, Native Americans, those of Mexican descent, and others; and helped to give great vigor to the women's movement, which had some strong effects in relation to religion.

Women in Christianity and Judaism

It was in the 1960s and 1970s that women most prominently began to conduct a critique of the Christian—and to some degree the Jewish—traditions. An example is Mary Daly's *Beyond God the Father*, which drew attention to the persistent gender discrimination in the Christian tradition, and the assumption that the male gender is primary. The language of the Bible is largely sexist. It does not take much reflection for us to see that gender as applied to God cannot be literal, except on some very strange assumptions about the material character of the Divine Being, which virtually all religions reject (for God is held to be a spiritual Being). God does not literally have hair on his (or her) chest, so any literal ascription of gender is nonsense. But when we see that gender is metaphorical, then it becomes important to use "she" of God as well as "he." Strictly God is neither male nor female, nor both, nor neither. The women's protest movement in Christianity drew attention to male supremacy as expressed not only in so much of the language of religion but—perhaps more importantly, and certainly more concretely—in the organizations of religion. Maleness has been largely entrenched in the hierarchies of episcopal religions, from the Orthodox to the Anglicans, and has been there too in the other denominations. The struggle for greater women's rights in these matters is far from over. In her *In Memory of Her* (1983), the writer and Biblical interpreter, Elizabeth Schüssler-Fiorenza, draws attention to the centrality of women's experience in the founding of Christianity; and here and elsewhere, the new discipline of women's studies gives a new and stirring perspective on the development of religions. Similar critiques and new slants have emerged in the Jewish tradition, and while the women's movement is strongest among liberal Protestants it has a sizeable presence in Roman Catholicism.

The feminist critique of religion has generally accompanied an increased role for women in most denominations. The Unitarians were early in this: they inducted two women into their ministry as early as 1871, though this was followed by a masculine backlash in the first decade of the twentieth century. In 1977, the Unitarian Universalist church abolished sexist assumptions and language. Among African Americans there was a larger place afforded to women preachers, and in 1948 women were recognized for ordination in the African Methodist Episcopal Church. The various Protestant denominations followed suit, with the Anglicans in England waiting until 1995 to allow women priests (though elsewhere in the communion, in America, New Zealand, Australia, and elsewhere it was already common practice). Though in the Catholic Church there is a vigorous espousal of women's rights, the opposition by many men and above all the Pope has prevented the ordination of women as priests, and similarly the Eastern Orthodox have remained conservative in this respect. In Reform Judaism women rabbis have been recognized since 1972, though they have sometimes been assigned to smaller congregations and been paid less. Conservative Judaism has moved toward equality of women in the community. But Orthodox Judaism has rejected such innovations. The general situation is that women, while increasing in importance, are still lagging in status in the chief Western religions. Of the world's religions Buddhism seems to show the most equality from the earliest times, in regard at least to a sacred role as priests or nuns. The situation in the West reflects, but does not quite mirror, the women's movement. As another issue in gender matters there is also the question of the recognition of homosexuality, with varying degrees of openness on this issue.

Black Experience: Turning One's Back on Christianity

Black Christianity had been powerful in the 1960s and it achieved much. But at the same time there were attractions in seeking identity by an alternative route, and the chief of these was Islam. The story of Black Islam is a fascinating one, as we shall see, because of its move from unorthodoxy to orthodoxy. Blacks in America, generally speaking, did not have much contact with worldwide Islam, though of course quite a number of slaves had originally been Muslim. In the 1920s some Ahmadiyah missionaries from India came to America, and a number of Black converts were made. But much more significant in the next forty years was the so-called Nation of Islam.

A peddler called Wallace D. Fard came to Detroit in 1930 and began preaching and organizing, but disappeared in 1934. His chief minister was Elijah Poole (1897–1975), renamed Elijah Muhammad. He declared that

A crowd raises its hands in response to the preaching of Malcolm X, the assumed name of Malcolm Little (1925–65). A campaigner for Black separatism and for pride in racial achievement, Malcolm X founded the Islamic-Socialist Organization of Afro-American Unity in 1964. He was assassinated in Harlem by Black Muslim opponents.

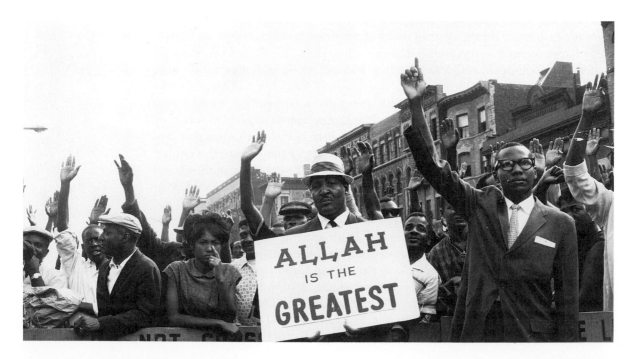

Black Elk

Black Elk (1863–1950) was a Native American shaman and medicine man, who also had a good knowledge of the White man's ways. He wanted the power of his visions to reach people, and was therefore happy with the book of John G. Neihardt called *Black Elk Speaks* and would have approved of that of Joseph Epes Brown called *The Sacred Pipe*. The latter was posthumous. One writer argues that these books will become the core of the canon of Native American theology. He was born in Wyoming, a member of the Lakota nation. When he was only nine years of age he was afforded a vision of the divine powers known as the Thunder Beings, the first in a sequence which expressed his shamanic powers. With the adoption of the horse, his people hunted to the west of the Black Hills; but they were later forced into a reservation in South Dakota. In 1877 he saw in a vision the nature of the Horse Dance and was persuaded to reenact it in 1881. This was in pursuit of his wider vision of the unity of the Lakota and of recreating the sacred flowering tree within the sacred hoop. It was partly in the hope of restoring his people by learning more about the ways of the White man that he joined Buffalo Bill's Wild West show, traveling to the East Coast, and thereafter London (where he met Queen Victoria) and other European countries. On his return he became a Christian. He was present at the dramatic and sad ending to the Ghost Dance movement through the battle of Wounded Knee in 1890 (he was also present, by the way, at Custer's Last Stand). As a consequence he returned to his commitment as a medicine man and shaman; he did not see a conflict between the Lakota vision that possessed him and his Christian faith. But his great dream of a united people living harmoniously together and in peace with Nature was important in inspiring the Pan-Indian revival of the 1960s. Out of defeat could arise resurgent hope.

Wallace D. Fard was Allah, and that he was his messenger. He taught that human beings were originally black, but a bad scientist created an evil race of Whites who were allowed by Allah to rule for six thousand years, after which civilization would collapse in chaos, to be replaced by a new world ruled over by Blacks. The moral was that Blacks should segregate themselves. Purity of life was to be followed—no alcohol, no smoking, no drugs, no pork, no movies, no cosmetics.

Eventually the most articulate spokesperson for the movement came to be Malcolm X (1925–65), who rejected Martin Luther King's nonviolent approach. However, he went on a pilgrimage to Mecca in 1964 and saw that in fact the teachings of Elijah Muhammad were incompatible with those of true Islam. When he returned, he broke with his erstwhile mentor and founded the Islamic-Socialist Organization of Afro-American Unity. He was killed in 1965; and ten years later Wraithuddin Muhammad, son of Elijah Muhammad, took over the movement on his father's death and moved in the direction prefigured by Malcolm X. He became Orthodox, opened the community to Whites, changed the name to the American Muslim Mission, and stimulated the membership to take part in political life and social action and not cut themselves off from the mainstream of American life. Some of the Nation of Islam predictably stayed faithful to the older vision, under the militant leadership of Louis Farrakhan. Meanwhile Muslim communities from other parts of the world have settled in the States and have been joined by American Blacks. The Muslim population of greater Los Angeles is rapidly overtaking the Jewish population, for instance. It is obvious that Black experience of Christianity has often been negative, in times of slavery and segregation and persisting racial prejudice, and this constitutes a main reason for seeking brotherhood in Islam.

The Revival of Native American Religion

Meanwhile the twentieth century has seen some success in the Native Americans' struggle for recognition of their rights. In some degree this has furthered and been furthered by a pan-Indian ideology. To start with there has been the spread of practices and ideas across cultural and national boundaries. Notable among such is the peyote cult, focusing on the sacramental use of the peyote cactus. This had been in use in Mexico before the present century, but it gathered force in the 1890s, spreading through the Plains. The rituals are conducted under the loose canopy of the Native American Church, which has had a powerful struggle to gain recognition (the combination of missionary prejudice and the fact that they used a mind-altering drug placed special obstacles in their path). The central ceremonial, to commemorate birthdays, for funerals, at prayer meetings, and so on, takes place in a *tipi*, and is conducted according to a fairly complex pattern culminating in singing under the influence of the peyote, which brings a feeling of nearness to God (often conceived in Christian terms, with the Virgin and so forth: some adherents of the tradition use the Bible in the ceremonial, so it is in a sense a partly Christian movement, but with strong Native American grounding). All this has helped to give a sense of—if not pan-Indian—at least cross-Indian solidarity.

Further in this direction of Native American unity is the use of a combination of traditional rituals, from peyote to the Sweat Lodge (see p.194) and from the Sun Dance to the Ghost Dance, in order to promote health and well-being; and this loose pan-Indian religiousness is fast becoming a primary underpinning of struggles to regain sacred places. In this the activist American Indian Movement has been a major force. At the same time, in higher education, increasing attention has been paid to Native American religions, a consequence of the great growth of Religious Studies as part of the new flow of ideas in the 1960s and the 1970s. To some extent this revival links with the struggle of Americans of Mexican descent to establish their rights and dignity, since there is a like concern with some of the ancient religious traditions of Mexico and Central America.

Eastern Christianity in the United States

Although a much lesser group than the dominating Protestants and Catholics in America, the Eastern Orthodox Churches have a presence through the migration from countries such as Greece, Romania, Bulgaria, Yugoslavia, and Russia, as well as from the Arab Christian Levant. While Greek Churches depend upon the Greek Ecumenical Patriarch, the trend in other nationally organized groups in North America is to join the so-called Orthodox Church in America, which was constituted under that name in 1970. There is also an independent Russian Church known as the Orthodox Church Outside Russia, which is based in New York. Arab Orthodox Christians look to the Patriarchate of Antioch. The swing toward cooperation and unity is assisted by the replacement of the vernacular languages by English. Orthodoxy has a significant if numerically small role to play in the total life of American religion.

Liberal Christian Theology in the Twentieth Century

Meanwhile amid the complexities of some of the developments we have noted, the dominant Protestant thought remained in essence liberal—in the scholarly though not always the political sense. The most important figure during the 1930s and on into the early 1950s was Reinhold Niebuhr (1892–1971), who served for a short time in a parish amid the car workers of Detroit and taught at Union Theological Seminary in New York, which was the most vital center of Protestant theology until the 1970s. Niebuhr's Detroit experience engaged him with political and moral issues. His stance was somewhat like Barth's, and he was often called neo-orthodox, although he disliked the term. In politics, for long, he was thought left-wing and for a time was a socialist. But with his Old Testament emphasis on linear history, his strong sense of the sin and frailty of human beings, and his emphasis on God's grace and love, he was far from holding any utopian views; and he was far from thinking that there were easy solutions to human social problems, as the title of his most famous book indicated: *Moral Man in Immoral Society* (1932).

Another Union teacher was the second overshadowing figure in Protestant theology, Paul Tillich (1886–1965). He was removed from a teaching position in Frankfurt am Main, Germany, in 1933, and was at Union from then until 1955. His position was a twentieth-century reshaping of natural theology, but in the mould of Existentialism, that is, a philosophy which takes seriously human experiences of the world. For him, religion was a pervasive aspect of all life: it was humanity's ultimate concern, that of the individual. We have to interpret religious symbols in this light. For instance, the story of Adam and Eve is ultimately about human finitude (and so about our sense of the infinite—which is symbolized as God). A person grasps the inner meaning of the story through his or her own experience of facing up to finitude and living in the presence of death. By his symbolic, emotionally anchored account of the Christian faith, Tillich managed to present it in a form which many found refreshingly modern and credible, especially in his *Systematic Theology* (1951–63). In his last days, part of which were spent in Japan and in

California at Santa Barbara, he came to appreciate the vital importance of Christian dialogue with other religions.

But if Tillich was popular in the 1960s, new skeptical forces left him somewhat behind. New secularist emphases took a grip of much Protestant theology, in the thought of writers such as Paul van Buren and T. J. J. Altizer, known as the "death of God" school. In many ways the most influential of these writings was *The Secular City* (1965), by Harvey Cox (who later substantially changed his position at least twice). The death of Jesus was seen as a negation of the very notion of the transcendent God "out there," and these thinkers experimented with a kind of Christian atheism. This was the ultimate in the liberal attempt to keep Christian faith believable in an age of empiricism and science: it abandoned belief in favor of feeling and action.

This phase of theology did not—could not—last long, for now the tide of the 1960s, romantic, credulous, pluralistic, religious, washed across the nation. Partly because it was a revolt against the Vietnam War, it was transmitted rapidly into Canada where many young people migrated in order to avoid the draft. This development did not at first affect Christian theology much, though methods of Yoga and Eastern spirituality were often incorporated into Christian and especially into Roman Catholic faith. But both the work of Martin Luther King and the antiwar struggle by many Christians, including the Catholic Daniel Berrigan and the Protestant William Sloane Coffin, revitalized Christian pacifism.

By the 1970s the women's movement and other growing concerns stimulated a new view of the Christian and Jewish traditions; and there were influential attempts at minority theologies—Black and Red, for instance. Toward the end of the decade there was greater interest and concern with so-called Liberation Theology from Latin America, which combined Marxist and Catholic (plus a few Protestant) motifs. To that we shall return in looking at the Hispanic American situation in Chapter 24.

Among Roman Catholics, probably the most influential figure in these times was the Jesuit Karl Rahner (1904–84) who combined traditional and existential strands in his thinking, somewhat like Tillich. Also widely received in the United States was the Tübingen dissident Catholic theologian Hans Küng, whose questioning of Papal doctrines and willingness to translate tradition into modern forms has a wide appeal. Increasingly Roman Catholics in the United States since Vatican II have converged in their style and substance of thought with Protestants. So there is a broad stem of relatively liberal theology which has maintained its vigor, though probably it reached its greatest solidity during the 1950s and 1960s.

Some Secular Forces

Meanwhile the context of religion in the United States was of a pluralism in which for many people it was not traditional religion nor even new religious developments which catered for their spiritual needs. Some were humanists, and others sought a solution to religious problems in some new therapeutic trends based on meditation techniques—such as *est* (Erhard Seminars Training; they spell "est" without a capital)—and in other movements concerned with human potential. These exist alongside older institutionalized mental health movements, such as Freudian, Jungian, and other types of psychotherapy. On the whole, organized political ideologies which often have functioned like religions, like Marxism and Fascism, have had little importance in the United States, save insofar as Marxism has sometimes blended in with other worldviews, as in Liberation Theology and Black Power.

The Modern Period in Judaism

The Conservative and Orthodox movements were strengthened in the period before World War II—the Conservative by the thought of Mordecai Kaplan (1881–1983), who started the Reconstructionist Movement in 1935, and the Orthodox by the arrival of important teachers of the European tradition. Kaplan emphasized the holistic concept of the Jewish people and their continuing religious culture as something which had to be preserved and adapted. His loss of faith in the Orthodox idea of revelation led him to stress the positive character of Jewish life, as responsive to divinity; but he effectively abandoned belief in an anthropomorphic God. He sought to counterbalance the effects of Gentile culture in eroding Jewish life by building up strong cultural organizations in which Jews could experience their tradition. His revision of the prayer book occasioned an Orthodox demonstration in 1945 in New York City, in which copies were burned.

Important was the strengthening of Hasidism, through the settlement of Lubavitcher Hasidim (from Lubavitch in Belorussia, their center; more correctly called Habad Hasidim) in New York from 1941. Their leader is a member of the Schneersohn family, whose *rebe* or leader during the early Soviet period, Joseph Isaac Schneersohn (1880–1950), struggled powerfully for religious Jewry till his exile in 1927. Since the 1960s the Hasidim have attracted a large number of previously unaffiliated young Jews into their ranks. Their uncompromising Orthodoxy is attractive for the formation of Jewish identity in a period of religious flux (especially as many young Jews entered new religious movements and took up Buddhism, etc., in the 1970s). Other Hasidim in the United States include the Satmar variety, out of Hungary and Romania. A leading figure among them, Yo'el Teitelbaum (1888–1982), argued that the terrors of the Holocaust were divine retributions for Jewish unfaithfulness—for becoming secular and for joining Zionism. This is an extreme instance of Orthodox resistance to the Zionists.

The other way in which Judaism developed powerfully in the time since World War II was in its links with Israel, founded in 1948. As we have seen, some religious Jews were against such a state. But otherwise loyalty to Israel could attract secular Jews, Reform and Conservative, together with some Orthodox, to the cause. It gave Jews a much greater sense of solidarity, following as it did on the Holocaust which itself did not discriminate among Jews.

Orthodox Jews praying in gratitude for the foundation of the State of Israel, won May 14, 1948. Twenty minutes after the proclamation of the State, it was recognized by president Harry S. Truman.

Judaism experienced a revival, then, especially in the 1950s and 1960s. In the 1970s there was a new movement for the formation of study and worship groups, called *havurot*, for highly committed Jews. There were more Jews who were converted back into the faith, somewhat similar in spirit to "born again" Christians. Division among the Conservatives over the ordination of women was a negative factor: but on the whole Judaism became highly vigorous by the 1980s, despite a decline in the overall number of practicing, especially Orthodox, Jews. This decline is in part because of legal requirements for marriage; for throughout the modern period intermarriage between Jews and

Gentiles has been widespread, and it has favored groups like the Unitarians rather than the Jewish community.

Reflections on American Religion

Several patterns emerge from the foregoing account. First, liberalism, industrialization, capitalism, pluralistic democracy, individualism, and modern science and technology have arisen from within Western civilization, and indeed partly under the stimulus of Christianity and especially Protestantism itself; but Christianity has still had to cope with them as if they were external forces. The questions have been: How much of beloved tradition could one persist in maintaining? How far was a revolution forced on the various denominations?

Second, the dominant Protestant ethos in America, while of course favorable to democracy, was eventually faced with the dilemma that pluralism was in conflict with its civil religion of trust in God, manifest destiny, and a working ethos. The 1960s and 1970s underlined the pluralism—both moral and religious—within American society. The contradiction was not so evident in slower-moving Canada, with its establishmentarian leanings. But the United States Constitution built into itself a pluralism which was at odds with maintaining the traditional Protestant dominance, at least ideologically.

Third, the reaction against the attempt to synthesize liberalism and science on the one hand and Christian belief on the other—an attempt that was characteristic of mainstream Protestant Churches—became hard-edged in the fundamentalist movements, which in some respect were actually more revolutionary and radical than the mainstream synthesis. The mainstream made adjustments to doctrine and reshaped myth, but left much of the ritual and organization in place. Increasingly, revivalist Christianity took individualism, capitalism, and technology seriously: the preaching was and is set squarely in the marketplace, and it uses up-to-date technological methods, it often discards established Churches and denominations, and it concentrates on the experience of the individual. Instead of rooting faith in a Bible that most Christians could agree was revelation, the fundamentalists turned the very ground of faith itself into an article of faith. Commitment had to be to both Jesus and Bible, often more to the Bible, and interpreted as literally as feasible. The cost lay with the doctrinal dimension, for the question of whether you did not really have to sacrifice science and humanistic history in all this could be acute. Also, the epistemology or model of knowledge, based in faith and authoritarian in tone, was at odds with pluralism; so that fundamentalism tended to cling to a form of civil religion and patriotism, especially after the traumatic blow to national pride consequent on the Vietnam War.

Fundamentalism is usually called conservative, which it may be politically; but in fact it takes the Bible out of its ancient milieu and uses it today as if it were a contemporary newspaper. It is what may be called neofoundationalist, taking the foundation epoch of Christianity (its own version of Biblical Christianity) and using that as the exclusive norm.

Meanwhile, and fourthly, the Catholics have undergone their overdue attempt to update the faith, which means to synthesize with modern historical and scientific knowledge, to make the liturgy more immediate and simple, and so on. The Roman Catholics have changed through all the dimensions, but have retained the basic characteristics of organization. For it is through the framework of the *organization*, relatively stable, that they have been able to achieve great experimentation. In *experience* there have been experiments with Pentecostalism and a revival of the mystical tradition. In *ritual* there has been the move into the vernacular language. This has welded together Catholics with differing ethnic identities. In *ethics* there have been divisions, with generally speaking a loosening up: in fact most American Catholics do not heed Papal pronouncements on birth control, though on the other hand anti-abortion sentiment has led to an alliance on this and some other issues with conservative Protestants. In *doctrine* there have been new attempts at updating, especially through the lowering of resistance to Evolutionary thought. In the *narrative* dimension the Bible has come fully under modern scrutiny among Catholic scholars, since modernism is no longer condemned as it was at the beginning of the century. In *organization* there has been stability as I have said; but house meetings and other ways of intensifying study and devotion are not without significance.

Meanwhile Black Christianity has greatly come in from the cold. Women's rights have made their impact on many religious groups. Native Americans are synthesizing a pan-Indian religion with which to deal with the oppressions and incursions of the beefier civilization.

Altogether, with analogous Jewish reactions playing their part, modern America has a much more pluralistic and diverse aspect today than heretofore. It foreshadows a world situation of intermingling and experimentation, of consumerism and searching in religion, of individual choice. It is an exciting and creative period, doubtless, but one which leaves many people naturally perplexed. Maybe this is why the appearance of certainty in preaching and in tradition is attractive.

Are there discernible patterns in American moves into modernity? Surely. Where the social and organizational dimension was strong enough, as in the Catholic tradition, it was possible to resist liberalism, to moderate individualism, to mount social programs to cope with industrialization, and to make necessary but perhaps not excessive concessions to nationalism. But in the long run most groups have made powerful accommodation to modern life.

South Asia and Reactions to Colonial Intervention

The Varieties of Indian Life

Our concern in this chapter is with the South Asian scene, and with the consequences of the conquest by Britain of the subcontinent (including what is now the Republic of India, Pakistan, Bangladesh, and Sri Lanka, with operational control of Nepal, and a political interest in Tibet). This major conquest was foreshadowed by earlier operations of the Portuguese, Dutch, and French. It was the aftermath of the Seven Years' War (1756–63)—when the British, largely by their superior naval power, defeated France—that brought British domination of Ceylon (Sri Lanka: since "Ceylon" was the name most used during the colonial period, and until 1972, I shall use it in discussing the developments of this period) and India (again, at this time the term covered the whole subcontinent, and this is how we shall use it for events up to 1947). It was a novel experience, historically speaking, for India, which had hitherto always been invaded from the northwest. It was also novel because the nation that came to conquer was already undergoing various industrial, social, and political changes which were to have their echoes in India and Ceylon. How could these old civilizations respond to the challenges of an emerging modern world? The matter was complicated by the very heterogeneous character of India and Ceylon themselves at this time.

The Islamic impact on India had been great, but by the time of the major British advances it was in severe decline. It was said that the power of the great Mughal, whose seat was in Delhi, only reached as far as Palam, where Delhi airport now stands. In the latter part of the eighteenth century there were

397

various powers in India—the Maratha Confederacy dominating central India, the state of Mysore and a number of smaller kingdoms in the south, the remains of the Mughal Empire, the rising Sikhs in the Punjab, and many other principalities. It was not yet a unified land. Differences of language, religion, and interest left it largely divided as the British extended their control. By 1805 the Mughal emperor had come formally under the control and protection of the conquering power. Much of the Ganges river area was under the British, who ruled out of Calcutta. The east coast was conquered, and so was a large part of the south. The British had taken the island of Ceylon from the Dutch, except for the kingdom of Kandy in the central mountains (it fell in 1815). The various pieces of the area controlled, however, still displayed great variety. In many areas Islam was the dominant religion; in most of the rest, that undeveloped federation of rituals and beliefs which we now know as Hinduism, and in Ceylon Buddhism predominated. Christianity was beginning to capitalize on colonial rule. The Sikhs were breaking away to form a new political power and, in effect, a separate religion.

The Formation of Sikhism

As a preliminary to the story of the interaction of the British and the traditions of India, it is useful to trace the story of Sikhism, which represents the result of the collision of Hindu and Islamic power. We have already seen some of the first developments: but these belong to the early times, before the Sikh clash with Mughal dominance led to the fashioning of a new community cemented together by the turban and other external marks of male belongingness, and by loyalty to the religion of the Guru Granth. This community was fashioned, too, by an alliance of different Punjabi castes, notably the cultivators known as the *jāts* and the merchants who were strong patrons of *bhakti* or devotional religion, which the Sikh tradition embodied. The evolution of Sikhism from a syncretic and peaceful way of combining Hindu and Muslim motifs—the religion of Kabīr and Nānak—to the militant organization which was finally fashioned by the Tenth Guru, Gobind Singh (1666–1708), has puzzled observers. But it is only the tendency of religions to represent themselves as unchanging, as though the religion of Kabīr were the religion of Gobind Singh, which causes this puzzlement. It was basically in the time of Gobind Singh that Sikhism as we know it was formed. It makes use of a past tradition and leadership, of course, going back to Nānak.

Already before the time of Gobind Singh the community was in process of forming itself into a military organization; but it was his reforms which set Sikhism on the path of becoming both a military and a religious power. He is represented as being the very ideal of chivalry and loyalty and is an example held up to the male Sikh. This quality of chivalry combines both martial and spiritual dedication.

His father, Tegh Bahadur, the Ninth Guru, was executed on the orders of the Mughal emperor in 1675, and before his death proclaimed Gobind as his successor. After some successful warfare against both the Hindu Rajputs and

Opposite The material dimension: the ritual center of Sikhism is the Golden Temple in Amritsar, which is also a beautiful material expression of the Sikh religion. The temple takes the form of a large complex of buildings built around a large, central lake. Armed demonstrators were evicted from the temple by the Indian army in 1984 and 325 were killed. Indira Gandhi was assassinated later that year by resentful members of her Sikh bodyguard.

Gobind Singh

Gobind Singh (1666–1708), the last Guru or leader and teacher of the Sikhs, who finalized the transformation of the Sikh community. He was a paradigm of courage, loyalty to God, pride, and chivalry. He was a master of Sanskrit and Persian as well as Punjabi, and was an accomplished poet. His father was executed by the Mughal emperor when he was nine, but in due course he became a powerful general himself. In 1686 he defeated the neighboring Rajputs in battle and a year later he won a victory over the Mughal governor of the Punjab. He had a respite from warfare at his capital of Anandpur, which he fortified formidably. Later, however, he was forced to evacuate it. He was on his way to the Mughal capital, possibly to complain against the governor for murdering two of his sons, when the news came of the death of the emperor. Gobind decided to back Prince Moazzim, and together they won a decisive battle. Gobind then went to visit the new emperor at Agra. Accompanying him on an expedition thereafter he was assassinated, but before he died he proclaimed himself the last Guru. Henceforth, the *Adi Granth*, the scripture, was to be the Teacher.

His most dramatic act in reforming the Sikh community was in 1699, when after the morning service he addressed the throng of Sikhs from in front of a tent. He invited someone to come forward who would be a sacrifice, by the cutting off of his head. Eventually he drew five men forward and took them behind the tent. Gobind reappeared with a dripping sword: later it was revealed that he had slaughtered five goats. The five men were honored for their bravery and loyalty.

Gobind prepared a definitive edition of the scripture, and assembled his own compositions in the *Dasam Granth*, which are also revered in the Sikh community. He is referred to as the "tenth emperor" or *padshah*.

the Mughals, Gobind established his capital at Anandpur, and summoned his followers there for a ceremony on April 13, 1699. After the morning devotions he called for five men to offer their lives in sacrifice, and took them behind a tent, to reappear with a sword dripping with blood. However, he had killed five goats, and the men reappeared, to be nominated by him as founding members of the new community or *Khalsa* (literally "Community of the Pure"). He caused them to drink out of a common bowl, from a drink he had made called *amrit* or nectar, conferring immortality. Importantly, this sacramental act was designed to break down caste barriers within the new community. They were to change their names to Singh or Lion. So in theory every Sikh is called Singh. In practice, as we shall see, there are complications to the story.

Each Sikh man has to wear five badges of his belonging, the five K's as they are called: to keep his hair and beard uncut (*kais*); to carry a comb (*kangha*) to keep his hair tidy; to wear *kacchā* or knee-length breeches, then used by soldiers; to wear a bangle (*karā*) on his wrist as a sign of loyalty to the Guru;

Opposite The great Hindu goddess Kālī, showing her power. Kālī, the wife of Śiva, is the goddess of death and destruction.

A nineteenth-century lithograph from Amritsar showing Nānak reciting poems to various Sikhs, ascetics and others. Nānak (1469–c.1539), the founder of Sikhism, was strongly opposed to the caste system.

and to carry a short sword (*kirpan*). Sikhs are forbidden alcohol, tobacco (then being introduced into India), and meat slaughtered in the Muslim manner, that is, by being bled to death.

The final great reform of Gobind was to proclaim that after his death they were to have the Adi Granth, or sacred book, as their Guru. It is therefore referred to as the Guru Granth (Teacher Book), and is a central object of veneration in the typical Sikh temple or "Guru House," *gurudwara* or Gurdwara. The Granth is a collection of writings going back in part to Nānak, including saints from before him, such as Namdev, Kabīr, and Ravidas. Its final recension was done by Gobind Singh. The original collection in this form was put into the Golden Temple at Amritsar in the Punjab, which became the spiritual center and focus of pilgrimage for the Sikhs.

With its great variety of languages from north India and its styles of poetry, the Granth gives a broad sense of the devotional life of the region. At the social level it has a lot of emphasis on the irrelevance of caste and race. It condemns distinctions. It also underlines the vital role of purity of motives. One does not win God's grace by the performance of external acts but through the devotion of the heart. It emphasizes the performance of truth, sincerity, and the attainment of equipoise (*sahj*) and knowledge of the Divine.

Despite these teachings, Sikhism developed, as we have seen, its own battery of external practices. Maybe this was inevitable. But it creates a lively dialectic between loyalty to a particular, transcaste community and the realization of universal humanity.

The new community eventually established dominance in the Punjab under the leadership of Ranjit Singh (1780–1839), but shortly after were defeated by the British and incorporated into British India. The British harnessed the military expertise and spirit of the Sikhs by using them prominently in the Indian Army which they created. But not all Sikhs were actually oriented toward full incorporation in the Sikh community. As well as the "unshorn" ones who carry on the externals, there are many other followers known as *sahajdhāris*, who are regarded as taking longer to attain full membership. After all, the tradition of Nānak was a general *bhakti* form of religion, and so a cloud of devotional Hindus form a penumbra of the Sikh movement.

There are also other movements which have relationships to Sikhism. On the one side are the followers of Kabīr, known as Kabīrpanthis (those who follow the path of Kabīr); on the other hand, more directly indebted to Sikhism through the Adi Granth, are the Radhasoamis, founded in Agra by a banker, Shiv Dayal (1818–78), who carry on the Guru tradition and stress the vital importance in God's communication to the world of the essence of sound, *shabd*, the Word. In this form of faith, which itself is split into differing groups, there is stress on the union of the disciple with the Teacher and the unity of the Teacher with the Divine. It is a kind of incarnational Hinduism, but it owes a lot to the Sikh connection. The name signifies the unity between the soul, symbolized by Rādhā, the lover of Krishna, and the Master or *somai*. The Khalsa idea (p.401) has remained strong, and in fact during the latter days of the British became more militant in a blend of Punjabi and all-Indian

Map 16 The partition of India as decreed in 1947.

nationalism. Later still, in the 1980s, Sikh militants have gone further, agitating for an independent state which would be predominantly Sikh, in the Indian Punjab.

In a way the history of the Sikhs illustrates in sharp form a general point, that when religion A meets religion B it may turn out that a blend, AB, occurs, which becomes by the force of circumstances a third force—in effect a new religion. In the Sikh case this move also led to a marked transformation, of a sharp kind. In the circumstances Sikhism could easily have been counted just as a variant on Hinduism, as the Kabīr movement was; for Hindu religions have fluid boundaries. It could simply have learned from Islam and incorporated Islamic elements into its fabric. But by forming a political community its role has become less ambiguous. By and large, Sikhs now feel themselves as belonging to a separate religion: and a modern complaint about the Indian Constitution is that it does not recognize separate status for the Sikhs in terms of the law and the like.

The Rāj: Challenge and Response

British Influences

With the defeat of the Sikhs in 1849 and the occupation of Sind, the mosaic of British rule in India was complete. However, in 1857 a rebellion by Indian soldiers, disturbed at rumors that the grease used for gun cartridges contained beef and pork fat, offending religious susceptibilities, spread into a wider revolt. This in a sense was an early war of liberation, though rather blind, since there were no clear ideological goals. It was fiercely crushed, and in 1858 the old administration by the East India Company—originally a purely commercial enterprise—ended. In 1871 the empire of India, with the Queen as Empress, was instituted. This British rule, or Rāj, was complex, since many states, some quite large such as Hyderabad in the center south, were left, in a kind of internal patchwork embedded within the areas of direct rule. The princes recognized the supremacy of the Queen, but had a fair amount of leeway as to how they might rule, under the advice in each case of a British Resident.

But the system was a kind of unity, and it brought the whole of India under one aegis, and one moreover that was interested in modernizing and unifying the country. Under the East India Company, missionaries were long excluded from Company territory, since commercial interests did not like the prospect of upsetting the inhabitants. But from 1820 onward, mission activity in British territories began. Before that—apart from the old Catholic missions under such workers as the highly original Roberto de Nobili (1606–56 in India), who adopted Brahmin ways and Indian philosophical concepts in expounding the Christian religion—there had been the highly successful work of establishing a college and missionary center in Serampore, which was a Danish enclave, and in one or two other places.

In the early British mission period the evangelical Christian critique of Hindu customs was strong, and led to the government's suppressing suttee, namely the practice wherein a widow followed her husband on the funeral pyre. It was partly because of such incursions on tradition, and out of a desire to restore the old order, that the Indian Mutiny, so called by the British, occurred. But after 1858 there were plenty of modernizations and critiques of tradition—railways, a whole system of higher education, new commerce, agricultural changes, English as the language of government, and so on. It was these changes which led to various responses on the part of the Indian religious traditions; the same could be said of Ceylon also.

The forces which the British Rāj brought with it can be systematized as follows, particularly as they bore upon the developing Indian middle class which was at the interface between the cultures.

First, there was mainly evangelical Christianity, confident in the superiority of Western culture, and often believing that modernization and Christianity would go together. It was critical of Islam's social backwardness (in the eyes of Christians from abroad) and of Hindu idolatry and harmful customs (e.g. child marriage, caste, and temple prostitution).

Second, there was the more secular ethos of imperial administrators, heavily influenced by the utilitarianism of Jeremy Bentham (1748–1832) and John Stuart Mill (1806–73), which held that the rational basis of ethics and law is the maximizing of happiness and the minimizing of suffering. Such administrators did not shrink from social and administrative reform.

Third, there was the force of capitalism, which demanded a railway network (a major creation), but also ruined indigenous industries such as cloth-making in favor of the cotton mills of Lancashire: but it was a force which, with imperialism, was creating a global system of economics, and from that no country could escape.

Fourth, there was the force of nationalism, which in Britain's case held to the superiority of Western Christian civilization and in particular that of Britain: it was self-righteous and confident, and was epitomized in the attitude of the historian Lord Macaulay (1800–59), who advised higher education for India because then the follies of Asian thinking would be left behind. But of course nationalism spreads by generating its opposing nationalism, and for the first time, from the 1860s onward, India began to experience a sense of India as a people.

Fifth, there was the force through which many of these others were to be conveyed and implemented: education and in particular higher education, whereby a new English-speaking elite was fashioned which was to be the main impetus toward change. Colleges and universities were set up in various centers: Bombay, Madras, Calcutta, Delhi, and the princely states. Education was encouraged by missionaries, many of whom devoted their lives to it, feeling that by some osmosis Christianity would rub off on the new elite.

Sixth, lying behind education was the force and prestige of science. It could be seen that a new scientific worldview had contributed to the technical powers of British and Western civilization, which had such important economic and military effects.

First Stirrings of Hindu Response: the Brahmo Samāj

Bengal was the center of the East India Company's power, and it was there that the first consciously reforming movement within the Hindu framework started, led by Ram Mohan Roy (1772–1833). He had been educated in the Muslim center at Patna on the Ganges, and had then undertaken Sanskrit studies. His linguistic aptitude led to his learning English, and he gained a job with the Company in 1803. He published in 1804 a book in Persian, which criticized the polytheistic aspects of the Hindu tradition. His exposure to Islam here allied itself to his attraction to eighteenth-century rationalism. His translations of five main Upanishads into English were designed to show that the Hindu tradition had as its true focus the one Reality, Brahman. He published, too, in 1820 a book called *The Precepts of Jesus* which argued that Jesus taught a vigorous ethical way of life, which need not be overlaid by the complexities of myth and doctrine which the Christians had added to the original message. In brief, he expounded a Hindu unitarianism, espousing belief in one God, and was iconoclastic about the many images and rites presided over by the priesthood.

Roy founded the Brahmo Samāj or Divine Society, which carried forward, through other leaders such as Debendranath Tagore (1817–1905) and Keshab Chandra Sen (1838–84), the message of social reform from a Hindu perspective. Roy was also influential in the agitation which led to the abolition of suttee in 1829. He was influenced by Unitarian missionaries in Calcutta, but was keen to express what he himself could take to be an essentially Hindu worldview. This he found in his Unitarian interpretation of the Upanishads. Smitten by a disease when visiting England, he died in Bristol in 1833.

His movement was of profound importance in pioneering a new view of the Hindu tradition from the perspective of a class of upwardly mobile caste Hindus. These were not of the upper echelons of the Brahmins, whose concern was too much with ritual purity, but lower-class Brahmins, merchants, landowners, and others, who stood to benefit by the replacement of Muslim power and culture by British. The ultimate problem for the Brahmo Samāj was that its "rationality" and purism in belief would cut it off from the mass of Hindus.

There is of course more than a hint in Ram Mohan Roy of the transcendent unity of universalist traditions (Muslim, Hindu, and Christian), and this cross-religious unity was ultimately destined to be a most vital factor in the formation of a modern Hindu ideology. As far as the forces sketched above are concerned, the Brahmo worldview could cope well. It was able to make a reply to evangelical Christianity of its purity and even faithfulness to the original message of Jesus (naturally such a "reduction" of Christianity greatly infuriated the missionaries in Calcutta). It was adapted to social reform and a new economics. It was compatible with the new English education. It had not yet developed a nationalism, which was to come: it was early days for Indians to think of themselves as unified. But it appealed to Bengalis, who had their own national sentiments.

Dayānanda Sarasvatī and Hindu Fundamentalism

Brahmo Samāj also had some influence on a Gujerati guru whose movement was to have wider influence; Dayānanda Sarasvatī (1824–83), founder of the Arya Samāj ("The Noble Society" or "Aryan Society"). His reform ideas went even further back than the Upanishads, to the rishis (*ṛsis*) of the Vedic hymns.

Born in Kathiawar in western India, Dayānanda left home to become a wandering recluse: into this mode of life as a *sannyāsin* he was ordained in 1847. For a while he studied with a famous grammarian of the old style in Mathura in north India. The pundit held that the only true texts were the ancient ones of the seers, and that much later Hindu philosophy and theology was false and sectarian. Dayānanda came to attack Hindu image worship: but it was not until he visited the Brahmo Samāj that he saw the value of modern methods of propagating his message. Debating in Sanskrit was not the way.

In 1875 he founded the Ārya Samāj, and two years later the movement took off when he gained the support of merchants and others who wanted arguments to stave off Christian attacks on the Hindu tradition. The message was radical, in that so much of the Hindu tradition, including the rights of Brahmins, was renounced. Dayānanda held that the only true scriptures were the Vedic hymns: even the Brahmanas and Upanishads were to be abandoned as later accretions. The germ of modern science was to be found in the Vedic hymns (such items as atomic theory), and their main teaching was pure monotheism.

The rituals of the Ārya Samāj—their worship of the one God—were open to all, and could be conducted by anyone; women and outcastes could study the scriptures. It was thus a radically egalitarian movement, with some feeling of nationalism, not yet however fully developed. It happens that the Ārya Samāj made great headway among overseas Hindus of the Indian diaspora, in such places as South Africa, or Fiji, whither Indian laborers had been transported on contracts known as indentures, so that they were called "indentured laborers," after the abolition of the slave trade, to work in the plantations of (mainly) sugar.

But because the Ārya Samāj is so strong a reforming movement it has become rather cut off from the mainstream of the Hindu tradition. It has become, if you like, a sect within the wider confederacy of Hindu religions. In response to Christianity and to the dominance of Western civilization, something more forceful was needed, which would mobilize and reform the Hindu way of life. It would have to make sense of the mass of Hindu practice and at the same time provide new growing points in the intellectual and nationalistic life. For one thing, the Ārya Samāj's extreme scriptural fundamentalism excised too much of Hindu learning; for another its iconoclasm was unacceptable to many, many Hindus, fond of their myths and festivals, and in revolt less against the Brahmins than against too much foreign influence.

It may, however, be useful to pause here to consider the strategies of response to foreign criticism and reform. If you want to remain somehow true to your tradition, and yet you wish to or need to effect reforms within it, you can base your reform on some element in the past; for instance, you can reach back right to what you conceive the very beginning of your tradition. Such a reaching back to foundations is better called "neofoundationalism" than "fundamentalism," and can, while appearing to be very conservative, be remarkably radical. In the case of the Ārya Samāj, virtually everything was changed—ritual, ethics, doctrine, myth, social organization, material focus.

There can, though, be other models. You may wish to repudiate some features of your tradition in the name of establishing some golden past that may be later than the scriptures. If it be the classical age of your culture, you could call such a reforming move "neoclassicism." It was this reaching into the classical past, and then interpreting it in modern terms, that turned out to be the most successful way of coping with the challenge of the West, both in India and Sri Lanka. In these various ways to hold onto tradition while making the adaptations necessary to survive vigorously in the modern world, part of the question was as to how much of the existing tradition it is necessary to sacrifice. The more one can retain, the more satisfactory the adjustment will seem.

In fact the Ārya Samāj, though using more up-to-date methods of missionizing, still did not come to terms fully with modern science and education. Modern scholarship had already turned its attention, of course, to India's past, including its scriptures. The neofoundationalism of the Ārya Samāj had less appeal to those who knew something of liberal scholarship. Its position about the Vedic hymns was not easy to sustain. Moreover, Dayānanda Sarasvatī, through no fault of his own, did not understand well the nature of modern scientific method. To hold that the scriptures contain the gist of modern scientific knowledge is to miss the point of the dialectical, critical character of the development of science. Nevertheless, his movement was able to continue and to expand because he devolved responsibility to branches, and gave expression to practical democracy.

There was another factor at work, which militated rather against the hard line of the Ārya Samāj. That factor was the coexistence of different religions in India. From the perspective of Indian nationalism, now growing with greater self-consciousness, some view of Hinduism which could make sense of the other religious traditions could be important and attractive.

Ramakrishna, Vivekānanda, and the Modern Hindu Ideology

It was indeed such a pluralist perspective which made itself felt through the life of Ramakrishna (1834–86) and the missionizing work of Swami Vivekānanda (1863–1902). Vivekānanda can be said to be the chief spokesperson for the modern Hindu ideology. This drew on the resources of the classical age in the shape of the Vedāntin philosopher and religious reformer Śankara, and through a modern interpretation of his thought presented a picture of the Hindu tradition that seemed to make marvelous sense of it, but of the other religions too. It also made wonderful sense of the

A statue of Ramakrishna in a Ramakrishna Vedānta temple. A sage, teacher, and mystic, Ramakrishna (1834–86) claimed that the mystical experience was the ultimate aim of religion.

great sweep of Indian culture, and could become a framework for expressing Indian nationalism. It was, moreover, an ideology well able to cope with the various forces mentioned earlier. It could also help to resolve a question of the times: whether the only way forward was violent revolution, as some held; or whether there could be some evolution which would allow India to develop its own form of democracy. The issue of violence was taken up, of course, by Gandhi, and the democratic impulse was developed further by his great political ally, Jawaharlal Nehru. To these figures we shall of course return.

The alliance between the sainthood of Ramakrishna and the sophisticated teachings of Vivekānanda gave a kind of dual status to the new ideology—it could appeal both to the masses, for whom the figure of the Kālī-worshiping guru was familiar, and to the middle classes, to whom the English-educated Vivekānanda could write appealingly. It paralleled the later alliance of the archetypal Gandhi and the sophisticated Nehru.

Ramakrishna (his religious name: he was born Gadadhar Chatterji) came from a Brahmin Vaiṣṇava family in rural Bengal. After the death of his father, he went to Calcutta to assist his brother who was running a new temple to Kālī, which also had shrines to Śiva and to Rādhā and Kṛṣṇa: it thus effectively contained the main strands of Bengali and Indian *bhakti*. After his brother's death, Ramakrishna became priest of the Mother (Kālī) and became absorbed in ecstasies relating to her. He felt himself mad with Kālī, but a wandering ascetic woman, skilled in Tantra, came to the temple and put him through a long course of Tantra which moderated his *bhakti* and turned his ecstatic experiences into more playful and manageable forms. Still later an Advaita Vedāntin ascetic came there, one Totapuri. Ramakrishna took up the practice of nondual meditation and achieved the highest state, regarded as liberating, in which even the Mother and God as personal entities disappeared. Ramakrishna also experimented with meditating on Allah and Christ, and claimed that his intense visions of God in following these paths were of like character to his Hindu experiences. This convinced him of the ultimate unity of all religions.

Despite all this inwardness, Ramakrishna was a teacher of some popular appeal, speaking in vivid images and stories and parables. He attracted attention among the middle classes of Calcutta too, and among those who were toying with Western religion in order to "modernize." Ramakrishna recalled some of the strength of the Hindu heritage, especially its experiential dimension. Among these folk coming to the half-mad religious genius of the Kālī temple in Dakshineshvar was young Narendranath Datta, of the *kāyastha* caste (originally *sudra*, but upwardly mobile and part of the gentle-folk, or *bhadraloka*, of Bengal). This young man was impressed enough himself to become a renunciant, under the name of Vivekānanda, but only after completing college and after his father's death. Ramakrishna saw in him a person of great power and destiny.

It happened that Vivekānanda was a member of the Brahmo Samāj, and he found Ramakrishna's image-laden earthiness a problem, but he held him as his guru and prepared himself spiritually up to the time of Ramakrishna's death, after which he helped to continue Ramakrishna's message. During an extensive pilgrimage which he made through the length and breadth of India he came to evolve the main tenor of his philosophy. This was to have profound impact because he was able to visit Chicago for the World Parliament of Religions in 1893, where he made his reputation and eventually returned to India a famous man. In 1895 he founded the Vedānta Society in New York, now seeing his mission as worldwide, and in India in 1897 he started the Ramakrishna Mission, with an order of monks as a modern group to teach social reform, perform works of education and social service, and preach a universal Hinduism.

Basically Vivekānanda's views were as follows. The Divine exists at two levels. At the higher level it is without qualities; it is not to be described. But in the nondual meditative experience it can be known: indeed, one knows the Divine from within, for one is divine. This realization dispels any illusions we may have about the world. But at a lower level God has qualities and takes on form: she is Kālī or he is Śiva or Viṣṇu ... or Ramakrishna. Humans experience God in these various images, and she or he becomes the recipient of devotion or *bhakti*. All the religions have the divine at the core, but they image God in differing ways. The Hindu heritage is the one which has seen most clearly that the various names of the Real are just that, different labels. World religions could work together if only they took this positive path of seeing the different myths and doctrines as providing the guidelines for paths which all lead to the One. Within each one of us there resides the divine, since we can achieve nondual union with it. So humanity is itself divine. Once we see the divine in one another, it will promote an ethic of love and social concern.

This ideology presented Hinduism not as a backward religion but at the forefront. It was the rather benighted Christians who tended to ascribe absolute truth to their own faith and complete error to alternatives. It was the forward-looking Hindu who saw his own pluralistic faith as a foreshadowing of the emerging World Religion. Vivekānanda's neo-Vedānta also made sense of Hinduism for perhaps the first time. Now Hindus could explain the unity of their own baffling, diverse religion or religions. It could be said that now Hinduism truly came into existence, or at least into self-conscious integrity. This was why Vivekānanda's message became so immediately popular with the English-speaking elite. And it did so without taking a superior line about the imagery and ikons of village and popular Hinduism. It might be that the person who venerates a snake has a rather limited view of the Divine, but he is on his way, and may in due course rise to the heights of nondual awareness where all differences are put on one side. So Vivekānanda first of all dealt effectively with the Christian challenge.

Next, as to utilitarianism and social reform, he could claim, too, to be a humanist concerned about human happiness: but happiness has to be seen in depth. It is not enough to equate it with fun and pleasure. You must be true to human nature, and human nature is divine. And of course we need to take seriously the needs of individuals, and it is for this reason that the Ramakrishna Mission engaged itself in social action. As for the new global awareness brought on by the capitalist system, he, Vivekānanda, was living testimony to this by going to the World Fair in Chicago; and what he there preached was a religion for the whole of humanity, a new global religion but at the same time a very ancient one. From the gleaming insights of the rishis you could draw light for the modern and future world. As for nationalism, Vivekānanda's ideology was perfect for India: it could unite all Indians, Muslims, Jains, Parsees, Christians, as well as Hindus. It expressed pride in India, for its vast cultural achievements, and it could do all this in ways that were not necessarily chauvinist. With Vivekānanda, Indian national self-consciousness came of age.

The ideology also fitted higher education. The philosophy which was taught in colleges in his day was neo-Hegelianism, following some of the British developments of Hegel's ideas. It was very similar to the philosophy of Śankara, and so it was easy to combine the two. The Logical Positivist and empiricist revolution was yet to come. So it was not difficult to harmonize the thought of East and West. Moreover it was clear to those who went into these matters that Indian philosophy itself was highly sophisticated, and had much to offer those who wished to have greater understanding of the relation of science and religion. As for science: the scientifically educated person should have no great problem with Vivekānanda's philosophy. There could not be any clash between physics and biology on the one hand and belief in God on the other, since the Divine in itself was inexpressible, utterly transcending thought but not experience. As experienced, too, religion was empirical. It was not just uncritically accepted dogma. Moreover, the Hindu tradition was not plagued, as was Biblical Christianity, with the problem of Evolution: in Sāṃkhya philosophy (p. 75) it indeed laid out an evolutionary scheme. Not only this, but historical inquiries into the sacred texts did not invalidate their central meaning. They were like fingers pointing to the moon, and the moon is the nondual experience of the Divine Being.

Though Śankara's philosophy provided the underpinning, it was in fact adapted by Vivekānanda, and also by later exponents of the modern Hindu ideology. The main problem with the original Advaita Vedānta philosophy was that it stated that this world—indeed everything other than Brahman, the indescribable Absolute—is an illusion (*māyā*). This doctrine was scarcely designed to stimulate social and political action. The teaching about *māyā* was therefore played down—with some justification, in the sense that Śankara's reason for taking this world as illusion was that it was noneternal. Nothing which is not eternal is fully real, from a spiritual point of view. But it is not of course literally the case that what is impermanent is unreal. Anyway, the new prophets of Indian nationalism and of the unity of religions took a positive view of this world. For this they could indeed turn to the teachings of the *Gītā*, and the notion that one should serve the divine through the path or discipline of works or action (*karmayoga*). This stress on *karmayoga* was something which Gandhi would also draw from his beloved scripture.

Although Vivekānanda's own message and mission were channeled through the Ramakrishna movement which he founded, his appeal was much wider, and the general kind of position which he expressed became the regular middle-class view about Hinduism and religions. The dividing line between piety and patriotism could easily be blurred. The national hymn became *Bande Mataram*, a Bengali hymn addressed to the Mother (Kālī); and India itself was figured as a Mother. The geographical limits of India were more consciously too in people's minds. Vivekānanda, among other things, had stimulated the building of a temple on a tiny island just off the coast at Cape Comorin (Kanyakumārin) at the tip of India. It was a recognition of the unity of India: this was not—as earlier Bengali pilgrims might have thought—a foreign country (Kerala, speaking Malayalam). Others before had made similar journeys; but the temple expresses national sentiment, not just piety. So later leaders, while not accepting all or part of Vivekānanda's teachings—men such as Nehru who was an agnostic—were still impressed with his position. And modern ideas of Hinduism flow as much from him as from any other interpreter in relatively recent times.

Hinduism as a single all-India system had been invented: and not just the Hinduism of the sacred books and philosophies (for the Upanishads were fairly far removed from ordinary practice), but a Hinduism that embraced all its florid aspects—images, processions, pilgrimages, temples, fasts, holy men, bathing, ashes, caste, and all: for Vivekānanda had struck upon a fine way of justifying the whole ritual dimension of Hinduism, save perhaps some which tied in with social discriminations. All rituals were imperfect responses to an only fragmentarily seen divine Reality.

Dimensions of Modern Hinduism

If we look to the middle-class expression of the Hindu tradition in this century, what does it look like from the perspective of the various dimensions?

First, in *doctrine*, we have noted that a predominant place has been given to Śankara's philosophy: equally important ones such as that of Rāmānuja have been comparatively neglected, at least in public rhetoric. They were supposed to have been taken care of under the synthesizing umbrella of nondualism. The doctrines of rebirth and *karma* as the working out of the effects of your actions in other lives were still affirmed; but small problems were beginning to arise about how such a belief blended with modern biology, e.g. genetics. If I owe my characteristics to my two parents, how is there a place for a third force (the effects of previous actions)? The most canvased response was: my soul homes in on my parents in order to have the proper effect of previous lives. A good soul will home in on holy and prosperous parents, a bad one on disaster-prone parents. So it turns out in India that, though there is little problem about belief in God, there may be growing doubts about rebirth.

In regard to the *mythic* or narrative dimension, much that was there simply stays in place in the modern ideology. Stories of the gods, especially of the great incarnations of Viṣṇu, are edifying. It was noted that the importance of sexual themes contrasts with the very inhibited views of nineteenth- and twentieth-century Britons. However, a new puritanism had spread among the educated elite. Stricter emotional controls on sex were more important as higher education stretched beyond youth into early womanhood and early manhood, particularly in a country where marriages tended to be dictated by families and within the framework of the caste system. Indians tend to defend such a system as producing better relationships than the unstable Western ethos of love-marriages.

As Indian contributions to civilization and modern thought became more openly expressed on the world scene, so there was a recognition of some kind of destiny in history which India had: perhaps to teach the materialist West some of the spiritual ideas and techniques and values which she could draw from her long history. Among the heroes of this new destiny was Vivekānanda, but there were to be others, notably Mahātma Gandhi.

As to *ethics* and social life, Vivekānanda appreciated the need for change and modernization of attitudes. Caste was a sensitive issue: mostly it was defended as a division of labor system which had, alas, been turned into a hereditary affair, and hedged around by unnecessary religious scruples. It was Gandhi who was to do most on this front. Already some changes had come about socially. The most pure castes, who worried most about contamination and pollution from others, did not do so well as others under the new system, where contact with the British and with other castes in offices and on railways became closer. But the hardest aspect to change was in regard to intermarriage.

Regarding *ritual* life, the modern era has produced changes, but largely through nonideological forces. The railway and then the bus network has greatly increased pilgrimages and mounted heavy pressure on centers such as Benares. But the general principle of the modern Hindu ideology was to leave as much in place as possible.

Regarding emotion and *experience*, the modern period saw the growth of national sentiment, as we have seen. Sometimes such feelings found outlets in extreme political pro-Hindu organizations which interpreted the Hindu tradition in a much less pacifist sense than Vivekānanda, Gandhi, and others: for instance the R.S.S. (Rastriya Svayamsevak Sangh), founded in Maharashtra by Dr. K. B. Hedgewar (1889–1940), which combines revived Hinduism with military exercises (Sanskrit and arms drill) and has a dedicated celibate leadership with wide influence in youth organizations.

However, Vivekānanda and others have stressed the importance of inner spiritual experience, which has always been more important ultimately than patriotic feelings, and which realizes a person's true divinity. This aspect of modern universalist Hinduism was taken up by a number of Western writers, notably Aldous Huxley. The wide diffusion of Śankara's ideas in the West tends to cause more emphasis to be placed on this liberating experience than the actualities of Hindu life would dictate, for in India *bhakti* and the adoration of a personal God mythologized in various ways are much more dominant. Still, Hindu Yoga was new to the West, and it was something which India could offer as central to its culture, on which the Indians, both Hindus and Buddhists, had spent much effort in the past, and which might be illuminating for the West. This sometimes reinforced an often expressed opinion among modern Hindus that India has an essentially spiritual culture, while the West has slipped into a crass materialism.

From the point of view of *social* organization, the modern period has seen some erosion of the position of Brahmins. This was partly because it became common to translate Hindu scriptures and to congeal them in books rather than to rely on the sacred memory of trained Brahmins and the haunting tones of chanted sounds. The new middle class might itself importantly contain Brahmins, but many others besides, and the new knowledge was from a foreign source and different from the traditional authoritative sources of Hindu sacred knowledge. Also, some of the revivalist movements were anti-Brahmin. In the old days it was maybe the Brahmins with their Sanskrit knowledge who had formed a net of cultural unity on the subcontinent; but now there were stronger bonds—the railways, the British Rāj, the English language. Indeed, the whole status of Sanskrit was in doubt. What part would it play in a modern India? The fact was that the influential books written in India in the late nineteenth and early twentieth centuries were all in English. For these reasons there was some disturbance of the social hierarchy. But caste has remained a powerful force hard to deal with, for any revolt against caste still simply produces a new one.

As to the *material* side of Hindu life, there is not much to say in regard to the modern Hindu revival. Craftsmanship of the old kind in fashioning temples and statues is doubtless on the decline. But there has been no absence of pious people to put up temples and monuments that help to celebrate the new India. We have noted for instance Vivekānanda's temple at Cape Comorin. After his time we would have to note developments such as the mythological movie—long translations into film form of the great epics—and new styles of the printing of holy pictures and so on. But the material things that the new ideology celebrated were the great shrines and carvings of the past, which testified to the grandeur and strength of Indian society.

Muslim Modernism in India

Because the British defeated Mughal power in the North and a number of powerful Muslim rulers such as Tipu Sultan in Mysore, and because the old Mughal emperor had let himself be drawn into the rebellion of 1857, the Muslims initially were less adapted to the values of British rule, and less favored by the British, than the Hindus. The first major Islamic thinker to adapt publicly to the new conditions was Sir Sayyid Ahmad Khan (1817–98), who had a traditional Delhi education in Arabic and Persian sources, and who was employed by the East India Company for over thirty years. He was profoundly impressed by the events of 1857 and 1858. He saw in them the inevitability of British rule, and indeed in some sense a justification. He saw the new scientific knowledge as good and ultimately proceeding from God: drawing on old Islamic philosophical principles, he saw reason and revelation as functioning in parallel. But he thought that Islam had been overgrown with foreign life, much of it unfortunately embodied in the *shari'a*, the Law. He took in this matter a neofoundationalist view: that is, he distinguished between the teachings of the Holy Qur'an and the mass of *hadith*, which he considered to be very unreliable, having been orally transmitted over long times. So he was a modernist in the sense that he urged legal and social reform, and in seeing the harmony between Western science and Islamic religion. Besides, Western science owed its initial impetus to Islamic sources, through the transmission of Greek ideas and Islamic scientific developments to the medieval West. After a visit to England in 1878–80 he established the Mohammedan Anglo-Oriental College in Aligarh, thus beginning the process of opening up to young Muslims the possibilities of English-language higher education. He urged Muslims not to join the Hindu-dominated Indian National Congress, fearing that Muslim minority status in a nationalist movement would be perpetuated.

But though Khan's modernism pointed one way forward, it did not of course eliminate the causes of friction between Hindus and Muslims. In a revived Hinduism there was a call for protection of the cow: yet Muslims traditionally slaughtered cows at certain festivals. The Hindus agitated for Hindi, written in Devanagari script, to have equal status with Urdu (much the same language but peppered with more Arabic and Persian words), written in Arabic script. Such causes of conflict, in north India especially, must be seen as a constant background noise in the history of modern India. The drums of violence may at times have been muffled, but their beat was still to be heard.

Some Indians have blamed the British for a "divide and rule" policy, and there were undoubtedly some British actions which helped to fuel the conflict, notably the partition of the province of Bengal in 1905. It sparked off terrorist bombing and some degree of communal violence. But the religions were at the ritual level remarkably incompatible. Muslims considered *shirk* or idolatry as the most heinous sin, and they were surrounded by Śiva statues and Ganesh and heaven knows what among the impenitent Hindus. Every statue was an offense, especially when it was carried in procession in front of the mosque. For the Hindu, Muslim cow-slaughter was an offense against their very deeply felt veneration, from time immemorial, for the cow. And if Muslims should think it their duty to smash an idol, or if Hindus were to stop Muslim sacrifices, then mayhem would break loose. So there was a constant problem of the peaceful coexistence of these two great religions.

Insofar as the tensions could be resolved by intellectuals, then Sir Sayyid Ahmad Khan's position, influenced by Sufism, could help in a better understanding with Hindus. But he himself was strongly attacked by many of the *'ulama* (the learned men of Islam), and his modernism was out of tune with the feelings, under threat, of many of his coreligionists. We shall take up the story of Islamic responses, later: but we may note Sir Sayyid as being a forward-looking thinker who made the move to modernism with self-conscious confidence and strong educational interests.

The Early Twentieth Century

Gandhi: A New Force in Hindu Response

If there was a criticism that could be made of the modern Hindu ideology it was that it could be left at the theoretical level. But with M. K. (Mahātma) Gandhi (1869–1948) we meet someone who solidly combined practical and theoretical ideas. He was raised in Kathiawar, and had close contacts both with Hindus and non-Hindus. His mother's religion was a kind of evangelical devotionalism, within the *bhakti* tradition, somewhat influenced by Islam. The area he came from was one of the main Jain regions, and he was influenced by the Jain ideal of nonviolence.

At the age of nineteen he went to London to study law, and there came into contact with the Theosophical movement, which combined Eastern motifs with a concern for comparative religion. Annie Besant (1847–1933), a leading Theosophist, was to play a notable part in Indian nationalist politics. He also was in touch with followers of Tolstoy. After his return to India he practiced law unsuccessfully in Bombay before being offered a job in Durban, Natal, South Africa. He went there in 1893 (a significant year, since it was also the date of Vivekānanda's trip to Chicago).

He worked twenty-one years in South Africa, until 1915. It was in South Africa that he worked out the methods of nonviolent political resistance which he was to use to good effect against the British in India. Here, too, was

Gandhi

Mohandas Gandhi (1869–1948) was in many ways the major political and religious leader of India in the twentieth century. He was born in Kathiawar in Gujarat, a fairly mixed religious area. He was influenced as a boy and as a youth by Muslim friends, by Jains, and by his family, which belonged to a Hindu devotional movement that eschewed images of God and insisted that the devotee had direct access to the divine, without depending on a priesthood or sacramental rituals. In later years he was influenced by Christianity through his correspondence with Tolstoy and his friendship with C.F. Andrews, an Anglican missionary. From Jainism he derived a deep regard for *ahiṃsā* or non-injury to living beings. He eventually gave this a political meaning through the use of non-violence in the struggle for independence and social justice.

In 1888 he went to England to study law and met various socialists and others: from them he derived his conviction that a social ethic should be an integral part of religion. In 1893 he took a job with a firm in South Africa and it was there that he developed his philosophy of non-violence, which he put into practice on behalf of the Indian community. He stayed twenty-one years. On his return to India in 1915 he was already something of a hero and came to lead the Indian Congress in its struggle for independence. He added to his key appeal to *ahiṃsā*, the notion of truth (*satyam*) as God, and the notion of renunciation. These ideas were concentrated on the idea of *satyagraham* or holding to truth. He extensively employed these principles in "fighting" for national independence. He and Nehru, a very different character with a very different agenda, joined together in the struggle.

After 1947, when India gained independence, but with the terrible price of partition in the subcontinent, he used the weapon of fasting to still communal rioting in Calcutta in 1947 and in Delhi in early 1948. But a Hindu, incensed by his positive attitude to Muslims, killed him on July 30, 1948. India subsequently treated him as "Father of the Nation" but his pacifist ideas and advocacy of a simple village-based economy were deemed, on the whole, impractical.

where he took on the garb and mien of a saintly holy man. But he was not a recluse: he was always in the thick of events. What he did in effect was to give the old Jain and Indian idea of *ahiṃsā* (non-violence) a political context and meaning. He also gave the notion of renunciation a new social context. The main point of his practices of austerity and simplification of life was to prepare himself spiritually for the struggle against oppression and injustice. The most important single thing that he taught was that our motives in such struggle must be pure. It is no use being outwardly nonviolent if you hate your enemy in your heart. In this he was influenced by the Christianity of the Gospels: "Love your enemies" became for him a prime precept.

In general principle the line which he took on religion and religions was very like that of Vivekānanda, but it was stated imprecisely. He made much use

The ethical dimension: Mahātma Gandhi (1869-1948) gave a new ethical and political value to the principle of non-violence, characteristic of the Jain, the Buddhist, and, to some extent, the Hindu traditions.

of the word Truth (*satyam* in Sanskrit), and for him Truth was God and God was Truth. His method of passive resistance he called *satyagraham*, or holding fast to truth.

In his prayer meetings, Gandhi used devotional prayers and hymns, including Christian ones. Thus in *practice* he held to some view about the unity of religions; but he did not wish to spell out a highly systemized philosophy or set of *doctrines*. Nor did he make much of the *narrative* and *ritual* dimensions of religion. Yet he was very observant of his own rules of abstinence, in order to train himself better. The main locus of his action was at the *ethical* and *social* level, and he was less interested in the formalities of religion. But he was undoubtedly influenced by the monastic ideal, both Indian and Christian (in South Africa he was in touch with Trappists). His ashrams or communities were a creative adaptation of the Indian model to the purposes of the modern struggle. Around him he gathered dedicated followers who helped him organize his boycotts and strikes and other forms of action.

He struggled initially for the rights of Indian workers in South Africa. These had been brought mainly to work the sugar plantations, being reckoned more amenable to that kind of work than the local Africans. Gandhi set up two ashrams, one called Phoenix near Durban, the other Tolstoy Farm near Johannesburg.

Because of the publicity from his leadership of the Indians in South Africa he was already famous when he got back to India after over twenty years, in 1915, where he joined the nationalist movement, now burgeoning during

World War I. It was in 1919, after the war in which Indian troops had loyally fought, that a most disillusioning event occurred, for those who counted on British gratitude. In the Jallianwalla Bagh in Amritsar, in the Punjab, a British general fired on a crowd with great bloodshed. An official inquiry was held, but General Dyer went unpunished. The Rāj was nervous. This helped to spark Gandhi's first great noncooperation campaign, a year later. At this time Gandhi was cooperating with the Islamic *khilafat* movement, arguing that Muslims should get autonomy because they owed allegiance to the Caliph in Istanbul. However, the Caliphate was abolished by the Turks in 1924. The Muslims of India were to follow a different vision.

Gandhi, in and out of jail between the Wars, conducting fasts, marching to the sea against the Salt Tax, meeting with Viceroys, managing to be the leading voice in the Congress movement, was a major factor in the struggle for independence, which ended—successfully in one way, and unsuccessfully in another—in 1947. A Socialist government in London had decreed the end of the Indian empire. But the Muslim alternative vision had meant that India was to be divided, and it was a division that sparked massacres by Muslims of Hindus and by Hindus of Muslims, along the troubled borderlands of the new states and far beyond. The population, the heat, the poverty, the multiplication of rumors—these things make India volatile at the best of times.

This end to the national struggle deeply upset Gandhi, who, however, immediately set about trying to bring peace to the troubled areas. It was his concern that Hindus should respect Muslims that attracted criticism from fiercer nationalists, one of whom gunned him down at a prayer meeting in Delhi in 1948. But Gandhi with his spiritual power, his wiliness, his humor, his kindliness, and the creativity of his life, was to influence many others, including Martin Luther King. There are many Christians who look to his example (maybe asking themselves the question of how it came to be that the best Christian in this century, as some think, had to be a Hindu). He represents the practical poise of the new Hindu ideology.

Muhammad Iqbal and the Idea of Pakistan

It would have been surprising perhaps if no one had sketched out an alternative to a united India, because of the strong Mughal heritage in the north and northwest. Also, for Muslims there was always the nagging question of how to arrange the law when under foreign or non-Muslim domination. Sir Muhammad Iqbal (1877–1938) was a noted poet who had been knighted by the British government for his works in Urdu and Persian. His philosophy was one which looked to a true, morally dynamic Islam, toward which Islam as it is must reach. He saw history and life in terms of an evolutionary process toward the higher ethical life. He also, significantly, in his presidential address to the Muslim League in Allahabad in 1930, urged the creation of a Muslim state in the northwestern parts of India. Only where Muslims were free to put the law into operation could a true Islam be realized.

His ideas on this front were a bit vague. It was Rahmat Ali, living in

Iqbal

Muhammad Iqbal (1877–1938) was a poet, philosopher and Muslim reformer, who influenced the creation of Pakistan as a separate Muslim state. He was born in Sialkot (now in Pakistan) and educated first in Lahore. Thereafter he went to Europe, where he took an undergraduate degree at Cambridge, a doctorate in Munich, and a legal qualification in London. He was already writing poetry and before he went to Europe he expressed an interest in Indian nationalism, but his sojourn there altered his perspective, and on his return he espoused a pan-Islamic viewpoint. He wrote in Persian, to influence people beyond the Indian subcontinent. Though he was deeply influenced by the writings of Rūmī and therefore belonged importantly to the Sufi tradition, he shaped his outlook to a new activism. He gloried in the Islamic past, but was struck by its modern state of decay and depression. With the fall of the Ottoman empire after World War I, the whole of the Islamic world was under Western domination. His call to action first led him to a repudiation of quietism in favor of a creative affirmation of the self, and then to a call to self-sacrifice in the service of justice and brotherhood. His masterpiece is considered the *Song of Eternity* (1932) describing the ascent of the poet under the guidance of Rūmī and reminiscent of Dante and Virgil. He is judged to be the greatest Urdu poet of this century. But his most influential philosophical work was contained in *The Reconstruction of Religious Thought in Islam*, delivered as lectures in 1928–9. In 1930 he put forward the idea of a separate Muslim state in India: consequently he is honored as the Father of Pakistan. Though he criticized nationalism, the notion of a Muslim state in northwest India derived from his pan-Islamism. His call for a new moral energy among Muslims was extended to others too, and could in principle revitalize the West, which, though it could create wealth, was bankrupt morally.

Cambridge, England, who gave them more precision. He invented a name for the new country, Pakistan, which consists of the first letters of some of the key provinces: Punjab, Afghan Province (or Northwest Frontier Province), Kashmir, and Sind, plus the last portion of Baluchistan. Later Rahmat Ali added the idea of another Muslim state in Bengal, far away to the east, which he called "Bangistan." Actually Pakistan at first included East Bengal, but after a civil war this did evolve into a new state, that of Bangladesh. Rahmat Ali's ideas at first put off the Muslim leader, Muhammad Ali Jinnah (1876–1948), but after 1936 he was won round, and it was his intransigence in fighting for this new state which meant that in 1947 Partition was inevitable.

Pakistan turned out not to be a very stable country, even after the civil war in 1971 which led to the separation of Bangladesh. A succession of military regimes replaced the early civilian administrations, save for a period after the Bangladesh war. It has introduced Islamic law into its system, but is rather far from the vision of a revived Islam which was what Iqbal had looked to.

Although not an especially pious Muslim, Muhammad Ali Jinnah (1876–1948) was concerned, as President of the All-India Muslim League, to protect the interests, and he took a large number of them out of India to form the new state of Pakistan, of which he became the first Governor General in 1947.

Some Other Religious Movements in India

Though Vivekānanda represents the mainstream of Indian modernism, there were other movements of some interest and importance in the modern period. There were those like the R. S. S., which took a much harder line in promoting Hindu values. There were also movements which involved trying to improve the lot of the less favored groups. Gandhi himself, from 1935 onward, devoted much effort to helping the untouchables, whom he dubbed the Harijans (literally Sons of Hari, i.e. God; this name, once favorable, is more recently less approved by Harijans themselves, who find it somewhat patronizing). But for some the future did not lie within Hinduism at all: this is in evidence in the life and work of Dr. B. R. Ambedkar (1891–1956). He made impressive educational and academic progress as a young person, aided by caste Hindus among others, ending up with a doctorate from Columbia University in New York and another from the University of London. From the 1930s onward, most of his energies went into mobilizing the untouchables of his region, Maharashtra. Shortly before he died he converted formally to Buddhism, though he had written about the Buddha in a book published five years earlier and he had long seen in it a faith which was a fine alternative to the Hindu tradition. Four million of his followers also converted at that time, so that now there is a whole scattering of Buddhist temples across Maharashtra.

Very different in import and style was the attempt to synthesize East and West very radically in the life and writings of Aurobindo Ghose (1872–1950). He had been educated in England from the age of seven till he was twenty-one, and only on his return to India did he discover his native land. But he had come into contact with the evolutionary philosophy of Henri Bergson (1859–1941) and in India he made a synthesis between this and Upanishadic thought. But this was only after a phase of nationalistic activity, including a spell in prison. In 1910 he moved to Pondicherry, French India, and did not further engage in politics but set himself to write and meditate. After a few years he was joined by a French woman who helped to organize his ashram and to realize his ideal of Integral Yoga. His theory was that Spirit first descends into the material world and then conversely begins its evolution upward. This evolutionary process begins with what looks like inert matter, but this secretly contains consciousness. Integral Yoga is a means by which human beings can, at this crucial stage of history, assist the evolutionary process and be drawn upward to a higher level of spiritual existence. This movement has drawn many Europeans to it, and is mellifluously expressed in Sri Aurobindo's many writings and above all in his masterwork, *The Life Divine*. His views have an uncanny resemblance to those of the Catholic writer Pierre Teilhard de Chardin (1881–1955).

These were movements of the rich period in Indian life between the 1920s and the 1950s, when the main struggle took place for the reassertion of Hindu and Indian values. Something different has to be said in regard to a later period, when new Hindu movements tended to become global in scope, because of the opening up of international communication after World War II and the increased interest in Eastern thought among Westerners.

Buddhism in Ceylon: A New Modernism

Meanwhile a somewhat differing evolution of events had occurred to the south, in the administratively separate island of Ceylon. The British had taken the central kingdom of Kandy in 1815, and for a while, in terms of the treaty settling the war, were obliged to support the Buddhist establishment of the Sangha. But the interpolation of Christian missions led to other pressures, and for a while Buddhist morale was depressed. In the latter half of the century a number of public debates between Christian missionaries and Buddhist monks revived interest in the defense of the faith, and Buddhists were satisfied of the greater rationality of their traditional religion.

Also important from the angle of reinvigorating Ceylonese self-esteem was the visit by an American, Colonel Henry S. Olcott (1832–1907). He had been involved originally in the formation of the Theosophical Society in 1875, with the charismatic Russian woman, Madame H. P. Blavatsky (1831–91), in New York. Olcott became a Buddhist, and the Theosophical Society always had Buddhist leanings, though its headquarters were established in Adyar, Madras. His support of Westerners who saw deep value in Eastern spirituality was of incalculable encouragement to Sinhalese Buddhists. And Olcott himself was very vigorous. He and the Theosophical Society helped to found Ananda College, the leading Buddhist school in Ceylon, and he prepared the way for the renewal of Buddhist scholarship, though himself not a scholar.

There is some analogy to Olcott's effect in Ceylon with that of Annie Besant (1847–1933), another Theosophist, and feminist – a brilliant speaker and organizer, whose work in India included being so involved with the Indian Congress movement that she was elected its first woman President in 1917, and the foundation of the institution which grew into Benares Hindu University, one of India's foremost universities and enshrining Hindu values. Interestingly, she adopted a gifted Hindu boy, Krishnamurti (1895–1986), who was expected to be a Theosophical World Teacher. After Besant's death he struck out very much on his own, and in fact taught ideas very similar to those of Mādhyamika and Zen Buddhism, on the inability of concepts to capture the real world.

At the turn of the century, Westerners like Olcott and Besant did great service in helping the people of South Asia to see, in a period of great cultural arrogance on the part of the British and other Westerners, the vital meaning and importance of the indigenous religious traditions. Also important was the work of editing and publishing the Pali texts. This was greatly due to the impetus of the British scholar T. W. Rhys Davids (1843–1922), who founded the Pali Text Society. This helped to give Ceylon Buddhists a clear view of their own basic heritage.

The introduction of Western-style education into Ceylon had similar effects to those we have noted in India. But the transition to independence was much gentler in Ceylon than in India. The cosmopolitanism of the Ceylonese found Western democracy congenial, and a great deal of home rule was already established before World War II.

Two major forms of Buddhist modernism arose in this context. One was neofoundationalist, treating the Buddhism of the Pali canon as the norm—or rather seeing the Pali canon when suitably censored as being the norm. It was thought that rather a lot of the matter in the canon, about gods and spirits and so on, was the result of mythologizing the Buddha's original message, which had been purely rational and spiritual. Shorn of these supposed accretions, the canon was seen philosophically as much in line with modern science (which sees the world as evanescent atoms in motion) and philosophy (for was the Buddha's teaching not empirical?). The difference from some Western forms of rationalism was that Buddhism admitted the importance of paranormal, illuminating experiences. If there was room for doubt it might be over the doctrine of rebirth, but that too could be accommodated with modern thinking, provided we did not think about it naively. Naturally, this highly slimmed-down Buddhism was not the religion of the masses: for them color and myth were more important than philosophy. But Buddhism had the merit of teaching an ethical path, which could be conveyed to the masses. Such a Buddhism of course was quite attractive to an English-speaking elite: and for Europeans this Buddhism gave one the possibility of spirituality without having to believe in God (a belief which many Westerners had come to find incredible and even tiresome, with its tendency to childish anthropo-morphism, as they saw it).

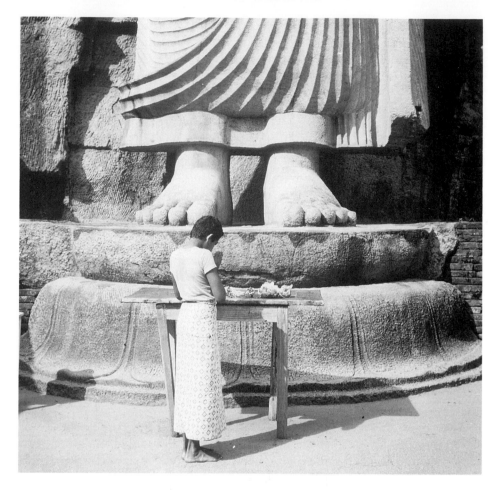

The pious layman: here a Sinhalese does homage at the feet of a vast Buddha statue in Sri Lanka.

Among other signs of revival and modernism was the work of the reformer Anagarika Dharmapāla (1864–1933), who did much in Buddhist education, and worked to restore the Buddhist pilgrimage sites of India, especially Bodh Gaya, the site of the Buddha's enlightenment. To this end, in 1891, he founded the Mahabodhi Society, which received support from Buddhists in other parts of Asia and was a factor in the rise of ecumenical Buddhism, resulting in the creation of organizations such as the World Fellowship of Buddhists.

Though nationalism was a strong ingredient in Buddhist revival in Ceylon, its impact was muted by the relatively easy transition which the country made to independence. It was mostly after independence, achieved in February 1948, that the strongest period of national resurgence came among the Sinhalese. This was expressed in the election campaign of 1946, when many Buddhist monks were involved on the side of the newly formed Sri Lanka Freedom Party. What it wanted was a reestablishment of something like classical Sinhala Buddhism, from the great days of Parakrama Bahu the Great and the high tide of Buddhist civilization. Its aim was now not so much modernist, philosophical Buddhism but a new arrangement in which Sangha and State would once again have a close relationship.

For a major problem in Theravādin countries—not only Ceylon—was how to reconstruct the world once the king had been removed by conquerors. In the old days there had been a reciprocal relationship between king and Sangha, with mutually defined roles. Now that we were in a democratic age with modern institutions (and moving from under a foreign monarchy), what was the system to be? The ideal of Sinhala as the only official language (the main slogan of the 1956 campaign) reinforced the concept of a Sinhala Buddhist culture. Of course there were Sinhalese who were not Buddhists, mainly Christians, and their position was not easy. But the vast majority were Buddhist. Sri Lanka (it changed its name in 1972 with a new constitution) embarked on a period of neoclassical Sinhalese revival, in which the Buddhism of the chronicles was more stressed, and money was poured into reviving the architectural glories of Anuradhapura and Polonnaruwa and fostering Buddhist schools and universities.

All this caused great unrest among the Tamils, mainly Hindus of the Śaiva Siddhanta school, whose ancestors had been brought in as laborers in the nineteenth century. It was a conflict that ultimately led to civil war in the 1980s and 1990s. The Buddhist revival did not generate a clear ideology of toleration, such as that created by modern Hinduism. This was despite the generally tolerant character of the Buddhist tradition and the possibility of calling on such an ideal figure from this point of view as the emperor Aśoka. The majority Sinhalese moreover felt themselves really to be a minority, because of the large number, over fifty million, of mainland Tamils in the Indian state of Tamil Nadu.

Despite these problems, the period after independence was one of great cultural vigor. Buddhist philosophy, especially, flourished through the writings of such vital figures as G. P. Malalasekara (1911–68) and K. N. Jayatilleke. A new parliament building in traditional Sinhalese style near the place of the old capital at Kotte was created, and the general favoring of Buddhist arts saw a considerable revival of the material dimension of the tradition. Buddhist monks traveled abroad, and the influence of Sri Lankan Theravāda on world spirituality has been great, in part because of a vital renewal of the practices of meditation. At the same time Buddhism has involved itself in social work. In this it has been influenced by Christian organizations, which are also reflected in such institutions as the Young Men's Buddhist Association.

After Independence

India since Partition: Some Trends

The principles of pluralism were built into the Republic of India's Constitution. India became a secular state, in the sense that there was a separation between religions and the State (the only exception being a clause about cow-protection among its guiding principles). It was important to achieve some kind of political balance, so a Muslim and a Sikh as well as Hindus have been President (a largely ceremonial office, but important symbolically).

One of the Presidents, in office from 1962 to 1967, was Sarvepalli Rādhakrishnan (1888–1975), who had been at the forefront of popularizing Indian philosophy in the West, and in working out a coherent account of what I have called the modern Hindu ideology. He stressed the importance of work in the world, and criticized the view that an idealist view of life is detached from the processes of this world. In this he modified some versions of Advaita Vedānta. He was also influenced by south Indian Vaiṣṇavism. He was critical of Western scientific materialism insofar as it left no space for the intuitions and experiences of religion.

Independent India reformed women's law in the traditional Hindu context, but was less bold in relating to Muslim law. There were other social changes, including the attempt to moderate the impact of untouchability by using various means of what in the United States came to be called "affirmative action." The impact of rapid modernization in various sectors was to expand the Indian middle classes, and some of the religious movements which began to have an impact in the West had their impact too among Indians. It was, from the 1960s on, a favorable period for the export of Indian gurus, yoga, and objects of devotion. With the spread of a greater prosperity through the Green Revolution, industrialization, and other factors (though poverty was desperate too), access to travel increased the popularity of a whole number of pilgrimage centers and intensified religious worship throughout India.

While the Vivekānanda-Rādhakrishnan style of modern Hindu ideology stayed important, some of the non-Advaitin schools of Vedānta, plus some of the regional schools, such as Śaiva Siddhanta in Tamil Nadu and Sri Lanka, made their public voices heard. Publications drew attention to these various strands in Indian theology and philosophy. A richer perspective on the Hindu tradition could be had. There was also the development in Indian politics of a more conservative kind of Hindu attitude, which looked more to the founding of what was seen as a genuinely Hindu State, rather than the pluralistic version which came to be in 1947. But India is such a tinderbox of ethnic, communal, and linguistic tensions that the pluralistic alternative has so far proved to be necessary. The Republic moreover carved itself up into states built primarily on a linguistic basis, and this helped to stimulate indigenous poetic and religious traditions in the various regions. It also brought a position where it was divided fairly evenly between Sikhs and Hindus, and this led one faction of the Sikhs to agitate in the 1970s and 1980s for a separate State.

Minority Religions and Their Adaptation to Modernity
It is useful at this point to look to the minority religions and see how they have dealt with modernity and life under a Hindu majority: religions such as the Parsis, Jains, Christians, and Sikhs. About the Muslims (to whom we shall

return in Chapter 20), suffice it to say here that they have been very substantially loyal to India in its wars with Pakistan, and indeed India helped Muslim Bangladesh in its struggle for independence. But there have also been sporadic and sometimes intense local communal clashes.

The Jains had of course long integrated into Hindu society and found no special problem in the withdrawal of British rule. They had experienced something of a renaissance in modern times. They were always well represented in the merchant class, and the modern epoch gave them new opportunities. The stimulus of Western Orientalism in reviving traditional Indian studies led to the revival of Jain appreciation of their own scriptural and cultural tradition, through publications and the founding of such institutions as the Lalphai Dalpathbhai Institute of Indology in the western city of Ahmedabad.

During the eighteenth century, Bombay began its rise to become the major port of India and eventually one of its greatest cities. The Parsi community, which was largely to be found on the west coast, began to collect in Bombay, to learn English, and to work with the British. Nevertheless, some of the large figures of the Indian Congress and nationalist movement were Parsis, men such as Dadabhai Naoroji (1828–1917).

After 1947 the community was loosened up somewhat, insofar as non-Parsis were employed more in Parsi businesses. It remains well respected, though not without its crises. One has to do with mixed marriages: do the offspring of non-Parsi wives count as Parsi? Indian law confirmed the community's traditional directive, which was in the negative. But though this has led to a weakening of the group (a crisis not unlike that among Orthodox Jews in the United States), new impulses have come from the overseas Parsis. Many migrated, after World War II especially, to London, Canada, the United States, Hong Kong, and elsewhere. This overseas group is less traditional in outlook and may in due course have a modernizing effect on Indian Parsis themselves.

The traditional Zoroastrian way of dealing with the dead, by exposing the corpses on Towers of Silence or *dakhmas*, is also for practical reasons in decline, and in most areas Parsis are buried. A growing Western scholarly interest in Zoroastrianism has helped to stimulate, partly among the Parsi diaspora, a revival of Parsi studies and the presentation of the religion in a newly sophisticated way.

In some ways the reactions of Christians to the Indian nationalist movement are the most interesting. Obviously Christians were suspect in some quarters because they belonged to the religion of the colonial power, though many Christians associated themselves with the national struggle and were close associates of Gandhi. The pressure was the greater for Christianity to show its indigenous destiny: and both Protestants and Catholics have introduced Indian styles into their ritual, their spiritual training, and their modes of thought. It is common to make use of Indian *bhajans* with *bhakti*-style singing. Catholics have experimented with Indian-style Masses, dispensing with many European practices such as the use of pews. They have been assisted in this by the reforming mission of Vatican II. At Dharmaram College in Bangalore, which is associated with a study center in Rome, much use is made of Indian philosophy in trying to expound Christian faith. One could look to various other such experiments and trends, which have given Indian Christianity a strongly Indian flavor. Dharmaram, as it happens, belongs to the tradition of the Thomas Christians, to whom we can point as showing the antiquity of the religion in India. They, like various other Christian groups and ashrams, make use of Hindu and Buddhist methods of Yoga and meditation in the quest to deepen Christian spiritual life.

The Sikhs had been involved in a struggle in the Punjab in the 1920s and 1930s over the matter of the control of their temples. The danger from a Sikh point of view was that an increasing number of them would drift back into the Hindu environment. In the late nineteenth century the Singh Sabha had been formed for educational and religious purposes, and had in some degree checked that drift. But the Temples remained in the hands of the *udasis* who were not outwardly conforming Sikhs. This had come about in part from conservatism dating right back to the formation of the Khalsa by Gobind Singh: the pre-Gobind type of holy person was still in charge of temples. The struggle was promoted by a militant party, the Akali Dal.

During Partition, the Sikhs found themselves existentially on the same side as the Hindus, and were regarded as such by Muslims. This gave most Sikhs a loyalty to the new Republic of India. However, as time went on there were problems, as the Sikhs saw it, in preserving their distinctive rights in law and elsewhere, and so agitation grew for a Sikh state in the Punjab. This the Indian central government has resisted. It was because of this that Indira Gandhi was assassinated by her own Sikh bodyguards in 1984. A few months previously she had ordered the Indian army to storm the Golden Temple complex in Amritsar, which a rather extreme young leader, Jarnail Singh Bhindranwale, had turned into a stronghold.

The Indian constitution looks on Sikhs as Hindus from a legal point of view, but there are many Sikhs who wish to set forth Sikhism as a separate religion in its own right. In this they are supported by many Sikhs now living overseas, especially in Britain and Canada, where a vocal minority believe in a separate Sikh state, known as Khalistan, independent from the Republic of India.

Tibetan Religion and the Communist Takeover

Up to World War II, Tibet, because of its geographical situation, was remarkably little affected by outside cultural forces. It is true that in 1903 a British expedition under General Francis Younghusband—later, ironically, a founder of the World Congress of Faiths—captured Lhasa and forced on Tibet a treaty opening it up to British diplomatic and commercial access, a protocol which was reluctantly signed by China in 1906. The move was part of the British plan of forestalling Russian moves southward in the region. The Communists, heirs to Chinese nationalism, took over Tibet after their victory in 1949, very firm in the conviction that China had sole rights over Tibet in principle. In 1951 an agreement was made whereby the existing ruler, the Dalai Lama, should continue his theocratic rule; but from 1956 there were increased pressures for social reform and economic restructuring, and preparations to constitute Tibet as an autonomous region of China.

In 1959 a revolt started among the eastern Khambas, which was put down quite easily by the Chinese: but the Dalai Lama and thousands of monks and others fled Tibet into India, and eventually the Dalai Lama, a gifted and charismatic young man called Tenzin Gyatsho, established his headquarters in northern India, at Dharamshala. As time went on, he became an internationally famous and respected figure in world spirituality, and at the same time a symbol for Tibetan national identity. Subsequently, suppression of religion and the destruction of monasteries, manuscripts, and artwork were a result of Chinese rule. An effect of the exile of so many Tibetan monks has been the foundation in many countries in the West, as well as in India, of communities, and the teaching of Tibetan forms of Buddhism throughout the West. It has led to a great revival of Himalayan studies and a deepened knowledge of Mahāyāna Buddhism, insofar as many key Greater Vehicle texts exist in Tibetan translation though lost elsewhere. The consequence has been to add to the forces behind the advance of Buddhism as a viable religion for the West.

Buddhism of a Tibetan kind is of course also extant in such areas of India as Ladakh in the northwest and in parts of Nepal and along the Himalayan

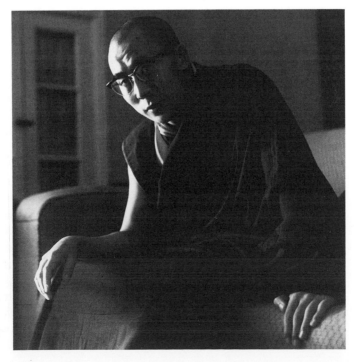

The Dalai Lama, the spiritual and political leader of most Tibetans, driven into exile in 1951, continues to hope for the restoration of autonomy to his people. Most Tibetans are Lamaist, a form of Mahāyāna Buddhism, which is also practised in Mongolia.

foothills. In Nepal there has been considerable change since 1959, when the country was opened to free access from the West, and its old Hindu-Buddhist society in the Kathmandu Valley has been subjected to pressures of tourism (often hippie tourism in the heyday of the 1960s counterculture) and economic development. It is interesting as a society, in giving us some insight into the coexistence of the two religions during the classical and medieval periods of Indian history—in fact the normal state of religion in the subcontinent until the eleventh century.

Reflections on Religion in South Asia in Modern Times

The chief culture and religious change in the last two centuries has been the introduction through most of the area of the English language and British higher education systems, often under missionary control, and accompanied by the idea that modern thought and Christian faith go naturally together. In fact, as Western history in modern times shows, they by no means do naturally combine, and there are tensions between scientific humanism and Christianity. For the inhabitants of India and Ceylon it soon became possible to evolve new ways of uniting Hindu and Buddhist values on the one hand and the need to adapt to modernity on the other. The preference in these societies was for a way of developing nationalism with traditional religion blended in. This called for the formation of ideologies which could do this, while at the same time dealing with the questions of science, liberalism, and the like. This was achieved by the modern Hindu ideology of Vivekānanda and Rādhakrishnan, and by the compatible practice of Gandhi. In the case of the Muslims, the modernism of Iqbal led them along the road to Pakistan, which has yet to evolve a stable system other than military dictatorship and a somewhat superficial Islamization. This is a topic that belongs within the wider context of modern Islam (see Chapter 20).

In the case of Sri Lanka the values of Buddhism and of minority Hinduism were able to adjust to the principles of democratic openness, and Buddhism was easily able to show its compatibility with modern scientific thinking. Socialism had attractions too: old-established Marxist parties have been a feature of the democratic political scene in Sri Lanka since the 1920s. Likewise some of the Indian nationalisms were attracted by Socialist methods. The problem in Sri Lanka was how to realize the nationalist ambitions of the Sinhala Buddhist majority without unsettling the minority Tamils. Unfortunately the vision of a revived Classical Buddhism of the glorious days of Sinhala civilization did not mesh with the need for federal-type institutions in the island. The expectations aroused for the young by the Sinhala education system of high schools and universities could not be fulfilled, and the rising of 1971, under the aegis of an ideology, superficially Marxist, but calling for self-sufficiency and Communism (similar to the ideology of the Khmer Rouge), was a symptom of this frustration. Nevertheless the postwar period has been, as we have seen, a creative period in Sri Lankan history.

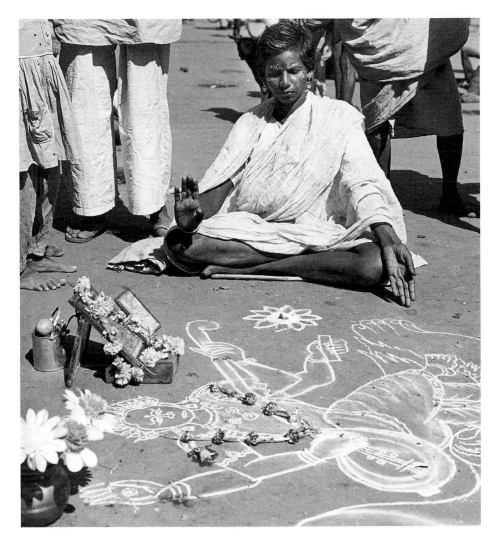

A woman sadhu venerating the goddess Sarasvati at Puri in Orissa, eastern India. The river Sarasvati is one of the sacred rivers of Hinduism, personified as a river goddess, wh was later made the consort of Brahma and is worshipped as the goddess of learning and the creative arts.

The Indians were fortunate in having in their heritage the materials for forming a sophisticated ideology which did not alienate the masses, but was able to harness their religious feelings to political ends (above all through the charismatic figure of Gandhi). They were thus not forced, in the interests of national independence, to change so drastically that many of their traditions had to be jettisoned. They reached back into their tradition, reshaped it, and gave it modern force.

Part of this new Hinduism was the self-confident claim that after all Hindu ideas have universal application, and Hindu practices have much to show the world. In the 1960s and 1970s, particularly, this fact became evident, through ways in which elements of Hinduism were taken up in the West. There were first and foremost the gurus. There was the whole complex of yogic practices, sometimes simplified as in Transcendental Meditation (popularized in part by the Beatles). There were *bhakti* movements, such as ISKCON (International Society for Krishna Consciousness). The general theory of Hinduism in this modern form—that all religions point somehow to the same truth—is attractive to many in the West, and there has certainly been an increase in ecumenism and friendship between liberal religious leaders. So a sort of neo-Hindu ideology may itself become more widely believed in the future. All these developments mean that the Hindu tradition is a universal religion in the world today, with its own positive message. It is not just a religion for those born within the caste structure of the Indian subcontinent.

We may note, too, that in the last century and onward there has grown up an increasing Hindu diaspora beyond India—in East Africa, South Africa, Fiji, Mauritius, the Seychelles, Guyana, the West Indies, Malaysia, Singapore, and elsewhere—largely as a result of the export of labor to plantations. More recently a middle-class wave of doctors, scientists, and other specialists has reached the Western world, as for example in Los Angeles (in Malibu Canyon a lovely re-creation of a south Indian temple has been built by the subscriptions of well-to-do Indians in Southern California). This diaspora Hinduism has tended away from the stricter requirements of caste, and toward a greater concern with such movements as the Ārya Samāj, the Divine Light Movement, and the Rāmakrishna Vedānta Mission. These Hindus have also been prone to move into Pentecostalist and other emotionally charged forms of Protestantism, which supply some of the feel of *bhakti* religion. But they will constitute a more and more important part of the voice of modern Hinduism, and will probably reinforce the message of the Hindu tradition as a universal faith.

In brief, the Republic of India, and Indian culture more widely, has been able to make good use of its resources, selectively of course, in order to create a Hinduism which makes sense both of pluralism and of unity, and to have something which is both ancient and modern. At the same time the smaller religions in India have been able to make their way in the new India, thanks in part to the pluralism implicit in the secular constitution. Hinduism has entered on the world stage. So has Buddhism, which has created an attractive Theravāda modernism, even if Sinhala neoclassicism has not found a theory within itself for the accommodation of minorities: there is as it were no "theory of Hinduism" among Buddhists, but there is a "theory of Buddhism" among Hindu intellectuals.

Buddhism has also benefited on a worldwide basis through the tragic Tibetan events, since its ideas and tradition have become very widely diffused through the work of the Dalai Lama and many other Tibetan monks and refugees. We shall return to some of these issues in discussing diasporas later on. And we shall have a deeper look at the Islamic component of the South Asian scene when we deal with modern Islam and its predicaments and achievements in Chapter 20.

Above A scene from the inauguration of a Śiva temple.

Left Pilgrims arriving for the Kumbh Mela festival at Prayag (Allahabad) in Uttar Pradesh, northeastern India. The city stands on the confluence of the rivers Ganges and Jumna (Yamuna). Every twelve years, participants arrive at the festival to wash away sin and illness by bathing in the river water.

A woman burns incense in one of the smaller incense burners in the courtyard of the Temple of a Thousand Buddhas in Sha Tin, New Territories, Hong Kong. Such practices survive despite attempts in mainland China to root them out during the Cultural Revolution in the 1960s and 1970s.

The Communist leader Mao Zedong (1893–1976) seen here at the Twentieth Anniversary celebrations of the founding of the People's Republic of China.

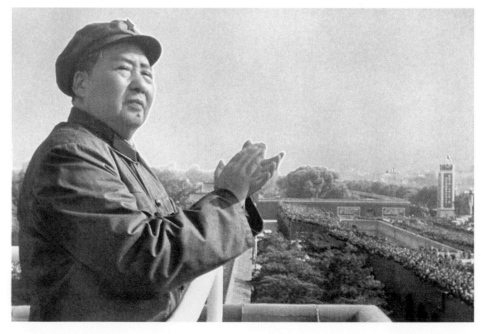

China and Korea in Modern Times

CHAPTER 17

The Chinese Predicament in Colonial Times

It was an irony that the eighteenth century in many ways was one of the most glorious in the history of Chinese civilization, particularly under the rule of the Qianlong (Ch'ien-lung) emperor (1711–99), whose on the whole efficient administration (marred by later corruption) and wide patronage of the arts was the high point of the Qing (Ch'ing) or Manchu dynasty. Contacts with European powers tended not to be of the threatening proportions that the nineteenth century brought. There was widespread admiration among European intellectuals for Chinese culture and the Confucian tradition. Earlier, the famous Jesuit Matteo Ricci (1552–1610) had made a great impression at the Chinese court for his astronomical and other knowledge, though the Jesuit plea that Chinese Christians should be allowed to continue ancestral rites in the Confucian mode was rejected by the Vatican on the pleas of the Franciscans and Dominicans; and this decision weakened Christian influence at the court, owing to the displeasure of the Kangxi (K'ang-hsi) emperor (1654–1722), who had favored the Jesuit view. It was in the nineteenth century, though, that the real conflicts between China and Europe, and then America, were to develop.

The East India Company benefited from the British naval supremacy established in the Seven Years War (1756–63) by dominating the trade with China. China had various goods to offer, including china; but the most important commodity was tea. The demand for it in Britain had taken off. There was no comparable thing which the Chinese wanted from Europe or from India. But in time the opium trade increased, though the sale of opium in China was illegal. When in 1839 an imperial commissioner terminated all trade through Canton (Kwangtung) and confiscated opium held in store, the British decided on war. By the Treaty of Nanking which brought the Opium

War to an end in 1842, various ports were opened to British trade and British consuls permitted there, Hong Kong was ceded to Britain, opening the way to a sequence of unequal treaties, whereby extra territorial concessions were granted to European powers in a whole series of cities along the coast of China. The Chinese gradually lost control over their customs operations, and the Western powers, later joined by resurgent Japan, had China more or less at their mercy.

There were other problems that China had to face: Muslim rebellions in Sinkiang, which was formally incorporated into China as a province; rivalry with an advancing Russia in Central Asia; persistent peasant rebellions; and problems in Manchuria from Russia and Japan. But it was mainly the problem of how to cope with the Western seapowers which exercised the imperial mind, especially after the burning of the Summer Palace in the Anglo-French war with China of 1856–60 and the flight of the emperor from Peking. It was also the time of the beginning of the main missionary era from the West, especially among Protestant missions. The Chinese traditional philosophies and religions were under pressure both from Western technology (through which European naval forces could be so successful) and from Western spiritual ideas. An attempt to resist these forces, but in an intuitive way and with little comprehension of what lay behind them, was the so-called Taiping rebellion (1850–65), a protean upheaval with millions killed in bloody conflict. This movement was itself patterned in some ways on other revolts of the era, but it has many lessons to teach about Chinese response to the West.

Hongxiu Quan and a New Religion

The Taiping movement was both religious and political. It was named after the concept of the Taiping (T'ai P'ing) or Great Peace, which was an old Chinese millenarian ideal, used by Daoist revolutionaries from time to time. In origin the notion of the Great Peace or Great Harmony (as it may also be translated) referred to a past Golden Age, in the Confucian classics. Often new emperors looked on it as their mission to restore this great harmony. But it was also harnessed as an idea to millenarian expectations, especially among Daoists: it figured in the great uprising of the Yellow Turbans, in 184 C.E., which overthrew the Han Empire. It was used by Manichaeans and Daoists in their ideologies of uprising against Confucian order and of the coming of a new society in which harmony would be promoted by minimalist government.

It was now used in a new context by Hongxiu Quan (Hung-hsiu Ch'üan, 1813–64). He was a Hakka, a minority linguistic group in Guangxi (Kwangsi) and Guangdong (Kwangtung) provinces. Feeling oppressed by neighboring groups, they were already being organized in militias, when Hong's revelations gave a direction and ideology to the movement. Hong had tried the national civil service examinations but had failed several times. He had come into contact with Christian missions through some tracts by the convert Liangba (Liang Pa, 1789–1855). The turning point was his visionary experience of the Father (Jehovah) and Jesus—Hong himself being addressed in the experience as the younger brother of Jesus. He was granted a seal, sign of imperial status, a sword to drive out demons, and scriptures. He proclaimed himself to be the new Messiah and took the title of Taiping Tianzi (T'ai-p'ing T'ien-tzu) (Heavenly Emperor of the Great Peace), joining with his cousin Feng Yunshan (Feng Yün-shan, 1822–52) in organizing military congregations with a revolutionary and anti-Manchu slant. They also drew on the thinking of some of the southern Chinese secret societies known as Triads.

Taiping Rebels, as shown in the *Illustrated London News* in 1857.

The Taiping ideology was vigorous and included many elements introduced about a century later by the Communists: equality for women, colloquial language as the literary norm, the banning of the Confucian classics, the smashing of idols and other aspects of the old religions, the State holding of land and its working by groups of families, the fusion of military and political commands at all levels. Not all these programs were realized in the chaos of civil war, but they represented a remarkable ideal of the radical reconstruction of China. In all this there was of course some Protestant influence, especially in the violent campaign against what was seen as idolatry. Some missionaries, when the upheaval began to be successful—and the scope of the revolution was very great: the southern capital of Nanking was captured in 1853, and a northern expedition to take Peking was only with some difficulty repulsed at

Map 17 Modern
China and Korea.

Tientsin—saw in it a force for the Christianization of China. But closer
inspection of its syncretistic character caused disillusion; and, in the eventual
suppression of the movement, Western auxiliary forces under the command of
General C. G. Gordon (later to die in Khartoum during the Mahdist uprising)
took part.

The Chinese government forces operated with great skill, and were
fortified ideologically by Confucian values which they saw to be threatened
by the rampaging Taipings. In 1864 Nanking was retaken. Hong had died of
sickness during the siege. A year later the huge rebellion had been suppressed,
but not before in all some twenty million people had died.

Hong perhaps had an intuitive understanding that, with foreigners defeating
China in the ignoble Opium War, a new dispensation was called for, with the
reshaping of the Chinese political and social order. But his Protestant
shamanism, though it made for powerful new revelations, was not geared to
any intellectual alternative to the Confucian ideology. At the *ethical* and *social*
levels, the Taipings were effective, with their energetic puritanism (banning
opium, tobacco, liquor, and so on), and their emphasis on the equality of the
sexes, etc. They provided, with their system of God Worshiping Societies, an
effective and simplified *ritual* of devotional religion. With their attacks on

tradition and their smashing up of temples they hoped to give a new sense of the future. In their appeal to the myth of a new age of harmony and their assumption of a messianic role in history, they had the *narrative* material which could consolidate a new and optimistic sense of destiny. But *doctrinally* and intellectually the movement was—to say the least—very weak. They did not have any real sense of what lay behind Western power—of the meaning and nature of science and of the necessity for a new education system. Though they substituted for the Confucian examination system an alternative one based on the Christian classics (the Bible), this was not much of a challenge to reflective thinking about China's problems.

In short, the Taiping style was insufficiently analytical and too mythological to attain any permanency. For ultimately revolution, as opposed to peasant rebellions, has to have a defined direction and a sense of how to train people for coping with the modern world. Theirs was a halfway house: it was much more than a peasant rebellion, but it fell short of being a true revolution. It was—as in many societies—a thrashing about of forces which sensed the need for change, but had not the right eventual message or the ultimate means of institutionalizing it. But it was for China, on top of its troubles with foreign powers, a sapping experience; and it made more urgent the search for ideas and a program which could restore Chinese power in a period of rapid disintegration. There were moreover other serious uprisings at the same time—that of the so-called Niens in central China, and a serious outbreak of Islamic rebellion in the northwest because of discrimination against Muslims.

The Self-Strengthening Movement

The penetration of China by Western powers was such that by the early twentieth century there were over fifty treaty ports designated for foreign residence and trade, from Manchuria to Kwangtung and from Tientsin to Yunnan. These places provided a kind of intellectual and commercial stimulus, though they represented an unequal balance of power. They created a beginning of industrialization and of Chinese capitalism, but such that capitalists were often inextricably linked to foreign concerns. The capitalists were what the Communists were to call the *comprador* class, using a Portuguese term (the "buyers"). Missions also played their role: although missionaries were often arrogant in relation to Chinese religion and culture, they did play, as in India, a vital role in the setting up of higher education on the Western model in China. This introduced some of the fruits of Western scientific education.

The basic problem for China was how to combine the insights of Western science and of traditional beliefs. Was it possible, as a famous tag had it, for Chinese learning to provide the basis and Western learning the practical use? There were various attempts to sketch how this could come to be.

A movement known as "Self-Strengthening" was one outcome of China's weakness. It had been started by Feng Guifen (Feng Kuei-fen, 1809–74) in the 1860s, following the words of an earlier scholar who had said "learn the superior barbarian techniques in order to control the barbarian." The movement was responsible for the starting of various programs and projects— the Foreign Ministry's language school, various arsenals, dockyards, sending students for education in America, merchant shipping, and so on. But such a piecemeal program was not enough. In this sense the instinct of the Taipings was right. You cannot bring modernity to an antique society without modernizing the society itself. The Chinese empire remained a centralized bureaucracy, resting on ancient Confucian and other values entrenched in a feudal society; it did not understand the link between science and the critical spirit and a new conception of the nature of human knowledge.

At the least, some reappraisal of the Confucian tradition, some Neo-Neoconfucianism, was called for. This was a necessary preliminary to institutional reform. One may mention the frustrating effects of a more piecemeal approach in the life of China's great general and statesman Li Hongzhang (Li Hung-chang, 1823–1901), who took a leading part in the suppression of the Taipings and lent his influence to the Self-Strengthening Movement. He wanted modernization and helped it, from a rather traditional Confucian base. He could not, for all his skill, stop the defeat of China by a resurgent Japan in 1895. When he died in 1901 he felt that still the state of China was weak, despite his efforts.

Part of the frustration no doubt arose from observing the failure of the Reform Movement of 1898 and the disasters attendant on the Boxer Uprising, an anti-foreign uprising in 1900. The 1898 reforms had much to do with the life and thought of Kang Yuwei (K'ang Yu-wei, 1858–1927). He was born in Guangdong province in the south, and was educated chiefly by his grandfather (his father died when he was a child). As a young man he became disillusioned with Confucianism and made explorations into Mahāyāna Buddhism and Daoism, as well as Western thought and knowledge. Eventually he became convinced that a new formulation of the Confucian tradition held the key to the process of modernization. He emphasized human-heartedness or *ren*, seeing it not only as a central value of Master Kong, but also as the key to a philosophy of liberty, equality, and utilitarian reformism. History was to culminate in a time of selfless harmony, preceded by a time of emerging peace. In the great unity of the future, traditional Confucian values would be submerged in universal harmony, but the key to realization of the ideal was a gradualist and reforming approach. He considered that Confucianism should be the State religion, and indeed this came about under the Republic in a law of 1913.

In 1898 Kang and his associates were admitted into government, and in a hundred days a whole set of reforms was promulgated. But the inept political behavior of the Reformers let in a conservative backlash at court, and the repeal of the legislation. At least, however, an attempt at structural change had been made. In 1911 the collapse of military support for the imperial regime led to the proclamation of a Republic, and in 1912 the last Manchu emperor abdicated (though he lived on, through various vicissitudes, to become a gardener in the imperial palace he had once occupied, under the Communists).

Nationalism and the Various Options

The growth of Chinese nationalism in a modern sense was of course the result of the arrogant and damaging behavior of Western powers and Japan. On all sides China could feel encroached upon. In the west the British were gaining control in Tibet. In Central Asia and in Manchuria the Russians were advancing. In Korea the Japanese were consolidating themselves. In the treaty ports, some of them deep inland on the great waterways, Western powers were exercising control.

However, Chinese civilization did not provide an obvious ideological basis for nationalism. In the old days, China had no foreign ministry and did not expect to have to deal with foreigners as equals. They could come to petition the emperor and to recognize his suzerainty. The world outside China, except across the Wall, did not much engage the Chinese imagination: and only in that case because it was from the north and the northwest that invasions had come. Moreover, the Manchu dynasty itself was still felt to be foreign, so loyalty to it was not so easy to engage.

Kang Yuwei and his followers were in effect trying out a version of Confucian neoclassicism: a reshaping of the Neoconfucian tradition and an attempt to accommodate tradition to modernity. It was however unfortunate for this experiment that Confucianism was tied to the old education and examination system, which was abolished in 1905. Had the imperial family taken the option of modernization much earlier, as did the Japanese, then the outlook for a revived Confucianism would have been much brighter. But this was not something to expect, because the whole imperial system was built on the assumption of Chinese superiority and of the barbarous nature of foreign culture. At the same time, Buddhism was ill adapted to expressing Chinese nationalism, and the most substantial Buddhist thinker of the twentieth century in China, the abbot Taixi (T'ai-hsi, 1899–1947), was more concerned with a revival of meditation and piety, and with raising the level of Buddhist education, than he was with patriotism *per se*. Daoism, for its part, was more tied in to secret societies and inner Chinese revolt than to the problems of reestablishing Chinese dignity in the marauding imperialist politics of the era. Daoism as popular religion, moreover, was not very easily geared into the scientific mentality.

Of the Western ideologies, liberalism was undoubtedly attractive and could be combined, for an elite, with Confucian attitudes: but the basis of liberal politics is a strong middle class, and this was wanting for various reasons in the fabric of China. One reason was that the Chinese bourgeoisie was somewhat entangled in a foreign system. It weakened their opportunities and political powers. Second, power in the first half of the twentieth century was controlled by naked military force, and it was a time when bourgeois politics were not widely feasible. Third, the educated Chinese were divided still between those

The Guomindang leader Sun Yat-sen in traditional dress. His blend of Socialism and democracy with traditional elements was destined to fail, although his three tenets of nationalism, democracy, and social reform are accepted by both Nationalists and the Chinese Communist Party.

traditionally raised and those who benefited from the new strands of Western education.

In some degree the ideology expressed by the Christian nationalist leader, Sun Yat-sen (1866–1925), might supply the answer; but this too had its limitations. He was, like a number of other prominent national leaders, a somewhat marginal figure. Born near Macao in south China, he was educated in Hawaii and at American colleges. Well known internationally through his writings, he was the obvious candidate to be president when the Republic was created in 1911, and was so briefly; but he was outmaneuvered by the warlord Yuan Shikai (Yuan Shih-k'ai, 1859–1916), who took over the post and suppressed Sun's party, the Guomindang (Kuomintang). It was not till the early 1920s that Sun's Guomindang became fully established, and this was with Soviet Russian assistance: Moscow sent advisers, notably Michael Borodin (1884–1951).

The ideology of the Guomindang was based on Sun's Three Principles of the People—namely nationalism, democracy, and popular livelihood—and on his work on "Fundamentals of National Reconstruction for the National Government of China." Sun envisaged three stages: military unification of

China, a time of tutelage, and then full democracy. It was assumed that the Guomindang would become the party entrusted with such tutelage. In this idea he was influenced by the Communists, who joined the Guomindang and became a constituent part of it. A military academy was founded in Guangdong, the commandant of which was the young Chiang Kai-shek (1887–1975), whose later career was to confront China with the problem of having nondemocratic tutelage, even if it is thought of as being on the way to democracy: what happens when you are taken over by a military dictatorship? Sun died in 1925, when the future of his movement was much in doubt.

China was humiliated by foreigners, but it was not a colony. Had it been controlled by a single power, the political struggle would have been clearer. China in 1900 was half-independent and half-ruled by a committee of foreign powers. It was only on some occasions that nationalist passion could be aimed clearly; for instance during the May 4 Movement in 1919, a great wave of chiefly student protest over what was seen as the betrayal of China at the treaty of Versailles. This was so particularly because defeated Germany's rights in Shandong province were not restored to China but were simply assigned to Japan, which was a victor on the Allied side.

The enthusiasm provoked by this demonstration led to greater interest in new political options, among them Marxism. The Russian Revolution of 1917 made a large impression across the world, and, as a kind of counter-capitalism and countercolonialism, had obvious attractions for many of the peoples of Asia. The foundation of the Chinese Communist Party and its growth into a part of the Guomindang were signs of another choice that China might have in its struggle to regain national prestige and independence. As it turned out, it was the thought and strategy of Mao Zedong (Mao Tse-tung, 1893–1976) which proved to be so effective in rebuilding China.

It was ironic that, in order to combat the West, China had to reach out and take up a Western ideology, one which had much greater contempt for traditional Chinese values and religion than the most radical forms of missionary Christianity. Admittedly Mao made changes to Marxism, making it more adapted to Chinese conditions. But the advent of his revolution saw the curbing of Buddhism, the closing of monasteries and temples, the suppression of Daoist practices, assaults on the cult of ancestors, and a strong anti-Confucian campaign—not to mention attacks on minority religions.

Mao and New China

Mao's Rise to Power and the Japanese War

In 1926 Chiang launched a largely successful military campaign from south China to unify the country. In 1927, after the capture of Shanghai, he caused the execution of much of the leadership of the Communist party there. This showed that the struggle would have to be undertaken rather in the countryside than in the centrally controlled urban environment. It was Mao who clearly grasped two facts: one, that the peasants of China were bound to be the backbone of any revolution owing to their great numerical predominance; and the other, that the way forward was through military campaigning. He was to become a great theorist of guerrilla war. In all this he was moving away from Marxist orthodoxy, which saw the urban proletariat as the vanguard of the revolution, and which also saw a bourgeois phase as a necessary preliminary to the workers' revolution (for this and other reasons Joseph Stalin (1879–1953) went on supporting Chiang Kai-shek and the Guomindang through World War II).

From 1927 to 1934, Mao found himself leading a Soviet government in Jiangxi (Kiangsi) province, and engaged in warfare with the Guomindang, through various encirclement campaigns. Then the Communists were forced

Mao

Mao Zedong (1893–1976), though not strictly a religious figure, attracted strong devotion. He became a kind of God. His philosophy, usually known as Maoism, came to be the ruling ideology of China until his death. Mao was raised in Hunan, and was the son of a peasant who had become prosperous. Forced to work on the family farm at 13, he shortly after rebelled and enlisted in a higher primary school and then a secondary school in Changsha. In 1911 he joined the revolution as a soldier: the Manchu dynasty was overthrown. He moved to Beijing, where he worked in a library. He was profoundly influenced by the May 4th Movement in 1919 and by Marxism. In 1920 he became headmaster of a primary school in Changsha. He helped, in 1921, to found the Chinese Communist Party, which was affiliated with the Nationalist Party or Guomindang. In due course, however, the Guomindang leader Chiang Kai-shek turned on the Communists, and partly as a consequence Mao set up a military movement among the peasants in Jiangxi. This did not accord with orthodoxy, since Marxism-Leninism held that the urban proletariat should be in the vanguard. Eventually Chiang's forces broke the defence of the Chinese Soviet in Jiangxi, and Mao and his comrades set forth on the heroic Long March to northwest China, where they arrived in Yenan in 1935 after more than a year's fighting retreat. During the March Mao was confirmed as leader of the party. After they arrived they consolidated their position enough to join the Guomindang in the nationalist struggle against the Japanese. After the latter's collapse the Communists opened up again the civil war, and in 1949 effectively conquered China save for Taiwan. At first China began a phase of development on the Soviet model, but then experimented with Mao's ideas—the Great Leap forward in 1957–8, in many ways a disaster but ushering in a system of communes in the countryside, then the Great Proletarian Cultural Revolution, primarily from 1966 to 1969. This was an anarchist kind of upheaval. It reflected a romantic element in Mao's thinking. In his old age he became increasingly corrupt: but during the Cultural Revolution he also acquired god-like status and some of his writings were anthologized to make the Little Red Book, in effect a scripture for the masses.

to opt for a breakout, and there started the famous Long March, when their Jiangxi army and other groups marched to the Communist enclave in northwest China, in Shensi. It was a march of heroic proportions, with many battles, struggles for food, deprivations, and over 6000 miles covered. Only about one-tenth of those who set out made it to the end of the March: but its effect was to preserve the main Communist leadership (Mao became chairman of the party during the affair), and to allow them to prosecute war against the Japanese, who invaded China in 1937 (by which time the Communists had settled in Yenan). The successful prosecution of guerrilla campaigns during the Sino-Japanese War left the Communists in a strong position in north China at its end, especially as the Soviets took Manchuria from Japan in 1945 and turned it over to Mao's forces. The Communists then took on Chiang Kai-shek and won the civil war in 1949.

Mao's Thought and the Worldview of Red China

We have seen that Mao adapted Marxism in various ways. He was also much more voluntaristic in his thinking than most Marxists: that is, he emphasized the role of human willpower in shaping history. He became also more disillusioned with the intellectual life after the success of the revolution. He was to some extent inspired by Daoist ideals of anarchism and simplicity, and in the 1950s he began to turn his back on the Soviet model of development, which he thought might breed a centralized bureaucracy out of touch with the needs of the people.

Eventually, when he unleashed the movement known as the Great Proletarian Cultural Revolution (harking back to the events of May 1919, to which we have referred, known as the "Cultural Revolution"), much of the educational system simply disintegrated. Books and learning were no longer important. Millions of young people flooded into the streets and into the countryside to drag down much of the State and party apparatus. It was part of Mao's vision of keeping the pot boiling, and never letting revolution settle down. He had a fluid, restless vision of human betterment; and the Chinese, though blank and poor, yet could by their faith and efforts surpass others in building a new classless society in which men and women would join in the struggle to overcome faults.

It is not necessary here to recount the ins and outs of the power struggle during the years from 1965 to 1976, when Mao died and his Cultural Revolution formally came to an end. It had been a new, rather violent, experiment in social reconstruction. It involved, among other things, the intense adulation of Mao; the constant use of a selection of his thoughts in the so-called Little Red Book, compiled by Linbiao (Lin Piao, 1907–71), who became his heir apparent but died after trying to escape to Russia when he allegedly plotted against Mao; and the rejection of traditional learning, both Western and Eastern, in the pursuit of intense commitment.

Particularly this phase of Mao's career, and of the history of China, presses us to ask whether here China had acquired a new religion. It is appropriate to

The ritual dimension: the Little Red Book of excerpts from Mao Zedong's writings served as a sign and repository of faith. Here school children demonstrate their loyalty.

think so. There were distinctively religious characteristics belonging to the Cultural Revolution. In one way, the question of whether Marxism-Leninism-Mao Zedong Thought is a religious worldview is not that vital: it is certainly a system of beliefs and practices which for a crucial period became, and still remains to some degree today, the norm for Chinese belief, and which has been used to try to wipe out rival worldviews which *are* religions, such as the traditional trio of Daoism, Confucianism, and Buddhism. It is useful to think of Maoism here in relation to the dimensions of religion.

First, during the heyday of the Cultural Revolution the Little Red Book was used in a *ritual* manner, like sacred scriptures. The book was carried around, held aloft at rallies, consulted for insight and as a guide to action. Moreover, there were continued rallies, public confessions in which people who had made mistakes were expected to confess to them, and reverence everywhere for the Great Helmsperson, as he was called. (Mao, a very strong feminist from his early days, might have approved of this translation!) Second, *emotionally*, there was large investment in the figure of Mao as a kind of Amitābha figure, and there was repeated talk of conversion experiences in which people came to see their lives purified and renewed by their new commitments. Third, at the *doctrinal* level, there were the principles of Maoism, and in a wider context Marxism, to master, for they not only defined the way the world is but also gave directions for action. Fourth, there was the powerful *narrative* of China's historic weakness and corruption, her prostration before the great powers, the formation of the Communist party, the heroic struggle in Jiangxi, and the even more heroic Long March, the battles against Japan, the Liberation, the making of a new China. So then plenty of myth, not to mention all those stories about people being cured through positive thinking (about Mao's thought), driven to great deeds, and the like. Then, fifth, there was the austere *ethic* of those times—the self-sacrifice which building the new China demands, the need to be alongside the peasants in their hardships, the ethos of the equality of women, the abandonment of hierarchical thinking (and even filial piety, that old Confucian virtue). It was a morality diametrically opposed to the orderly, respectful, traditional modes and etiquette of Confucian behavior. Sixth, there was a new *social* elite: the cadres, the young, those who armed with the Little Red Book would constitute a kind of counterculture and an organization against the big institutions of Party and State, a kind of new this-worldly monasticism roaring through the streets and the countryside. Seventh, there was the *art* of the new era: simple, propagandistic, largely Western in technique but without bourgeois ornament, serving the people, Socialist Realist, showing forth the heroics of the myth.

All this added up to a kind of new religion that harnessed some of the emotions and thoughts of Daoism (the anarchism of Laozi, the alchemy of right commitment) and of Buddhism (the Pure Land, but here and now, and

The social dimension: a collective farm. Chinese society was thoroughly reorganized after 1949.

Mao as a celestial Buddha, but right here in Beijing). It was by passing through the crucible of this religion that modern China was formed, if often by reaction.

The effects on the traditions were devastating. Monasteries were closed and turned into granaries and the like. Many manuscripts and books were destroyed. Much of religious practice was stopped. Images were destroyed. Ancestors were no longer venerated. Graves were not swept, nor holy mountains climbed. Monks and nuns worked the fields. Bibles were confiscated; Muslims were discriminated against. It was, in short, a period of religious and ideological persecution; and even now there are strict limits to the cautious rebuilding of the traditional practices.

The Irony of the New Period in China

With the death of Mao in 1976, power reverted from the more extreme wing of the party, as represented by the group known as the Gang of Four, including Mao's wife, Chiang Ch'ing. The country entered a more pragmatic era. Even so, it was of course still to be guided by the principles of Marxism. This being so, there have been debates as to how far it is possible to combine such orthodoxy with the borrowing of Western methods of scientific education, trade, and technology. The irony is that China has come to the same position it was in one hundred years ago, but in a new form. No longer is it a matter of Confucian values for culture and Western methods for function, but of Marxist ideas for values and Western technology for function. Thousands of young Chinese have been sent abroad to study in the West, and the whole educational policy of the Cultural Revolution has been reversed as China scrambles to make up for past losses and to build a new and more prosperous society. But can it do so without the freedoms which go with Western systems (including here the Japanese)? The contrast, of course, with Japan is remarkable, and for many Chinese it is painful. So now China is plunged once again into its old debate.

Meanwhile the present era is more relaxed, and it is possible for religion to some extent to come out of hiding. There is a slow resumption of some of the older patterns. But undoubtedly the traditional threefold religious system of China has been shattered, and it will never resume its original, prerevolutionary, form. Any new synthesis, we must suppose, will have to incorporate Marxist materialism.

Reflections on Modern China

We have noted that Marxism will have changed the face of Chinese (and Tibetan) religion permanently. During the revival which is slowly beginning in the time since Mao's death the place of religion is bound to be relatively private, in the sense that religious practices will depend largely on private decisions; so it is no longer possible to see the three religions of China as an integrated system, a kind of federation of ideas and practices. The Westernized concept of the three traditions as more or less independent religions is likely to become a reality (just as in the modern period a previously undefined "Hinduism" has actually come to exist in the self-consciousness of Indians).

In all the vicissitudes of Chinese modern history the decisive moment came perhaps during the May 4 Movement, after 1919: Chinese intellectuals turned increasingly to Marxism, there was widespread disillusion with liberalism, and little edge to modernist forms of traditional religion. The Guomindang philosophy might have developed in a more liberal direction had not Chiang seized power, and then been involved in the struggle against the Japanese. It is, however, difficult to see real alternatives to the direction in which China has gone.

The Chinese Diaspora

Meanwhile, China is not just the mainland. For one thing, the defeated Nationalists set up their alternative China in Taiwan, which does to some great degree carry on the traditions of the old China, alongside modern technology. Then there is Hong Kong, dominantly Chinese, and rejoined to China in 1997, but itself also an alternative China. There are important settlements of overseas Chinese—in Malaysia, Indonesia, Singapore, the Caribbean, the United States, and elsewhere. In some areas they have encountered severe problems, especially in Vietnam, where many of the refugees, the so-called "boat people," in the 1970s and 1980s were ethnic Chinese, and in Indonesia, where the coup of 1965 was very severe on Chinese institutions and people. In Singapore, a dominantly Chinese culture has performed brilliantly, creating a marvel of paternalistically controlled capitalist welfare. In the United States and other Western countries, the Chinese have been active and have merged successfully into the dominant cultural ethos.

There has been in the last forty years a revival of Western interest in Chinese religion—in Neoconfucianism especially, in various kinds of Chinese Buddhism, and in Dao as a religion. The new Confucianist emphasis is complemented by official teaching of its ethical values in the State school system in Singapore, and this concern with tradition may herald similar revitalizations elsewhere.

Modern Korean Religion

The Choson dynasty in Korea during the early modern period (seventeenth and eighteenth centuries) had as its official ideology Neoconfucianism. Buddhism was excluded from the capital; and Catholicism, which, through Jesuit missions to China, was beginning to interest some leading Korean intellectuals, was resisted vigorously by the court. Despite persecution, Catholicism went on growing during the nineteenth century. Following the Korean-Japanese treaty of 1876 there was more and more penetration of Korea by Japanese commercial interests, and in their wake missionaries from some of the Pure Land organizations, and later Nichiren Buddhism.

Opposite A Thai dance showing a demon trying to steal a magic jewel, drawn from the classical Hindu epic the *Rāmāyaṇa*. Hindu culture became an important ingredient of Thai civilization (see Chapter 18).

Korean Confucianism: burning incense at the shrine of deceased great scholars.

Meanwhile Zen or Son Buddhism was undergoing something of a revival, primarily through the work of the teacher Kyongho (1857–1912).

The occupation of Korea by Japan in 1910 altered the dynamics of Buddhist leadership, especially when in 1926 the Japanese brought in legislation which made legal the marriage of monks (this had been advocated as part of the process of modernization). The Son organization in particular was split, a more conservative minority fighting to retain its traditional celibate way of life and to maintain the disciplines of meditation. After World War II, in 1954, in South Korea, the administration of Son monasteries was handed over to this conservative group, the Chogye-chong. This gave modern Korean Zen Buddhism a unity and strength which has made it one of the dominant religious traditions of South Korea.

Protestant Christianity has made great progress in Korea. From the 1880s on, American and other missions were very active, and the religion grew at a strong rate during the twentieth century despite the Japanese occupation. Probably there are about six million Protestants today in Korea, and proportionately it has been more successful there than in any other Asian country. The forms are chiefly Methodism and Presbyterianism, and they were left to progress pretty much under Korean leadership; an evangelical, Biblical piety is very manifest. The reasons for the relatively large success of Korean Protestantism are debated, but they arise from the following factors. First,

Japanese sponsorship of Buddhism from 1910 to 1945 deprived that religion of the appeal based on national sentiment that it may have had elsewhere. Second, the processes of modernization and industrialization may have favored the spread of a "rootless" religion: Korea has produced new religions of its own, as we shall see. Third, the missionaries were sympathetic toward Korean nationalism. Fourth, in the 1970s the religion doubled its numbers, and it may be because of the impact of consumerist individualism on traditional Korean society during the economic miracle.

The result has been some tension between the more individualistic religions (of which we can name Son Buddhism and Protestantism, and increasingly Catholicism) and traditional Confucianism: this is reflected too in politics, in the divide between the democratic movement and the military dictatorship. In North Korea, religious echoes are muffled, and it is hard to diagnose what is going on there beneath the surface of the very longstanding dictatorship of Kim Il-sung, who flourishes his own brand of conservative or hardline Communism, written up in his collected works which are published in every national language in the world.

Responses both to the Confucian feudal tradition and to Christianity are represented by various of the new religions of Korea, dating from the nineteenth and twentieth centuries. Two of the most important of these are the Ch'ondogyo and the Unification Church of Sun Myung Moon.

Ch'ondogyo was founded in 1860 by Ch'oe Suun (1824–64) as the Tonghak movement, literally "Eastern Learning" (by contrast with the Western learning represented by Christianity). he claimed to have had a revelation from God, and was shortly after martyred by the government as his teachings were regarded as subversive. The writings of Ch'oe Suun and of his two successors as leaders comprise the scriptures, and the religion came to be known as the Religion of the Heavenly Way (Ch'ondogyo). Though it now plays little overt role in South Korean politics, it was long thought subversive, from different directions: by the Korean dynasty because it led an uprising in 1894, and by the Japanese because it took part in the Korean independence movement of 1919. It is strongly egalitarian and criticizes the whole hierarchical character of traditional Korean Confucianism. It believes in God as pervading the world and as being present in individuals: one of its slogans is that "The human being is God" and gains oneness with God through the sincere practice of faith. Its rituals involve prayers and the calling of the divine down into the self, together with scripture reading and meditation on purity. It combines some traditional Korean motifs and Christian ones: in some ways it is reminiscent of Quakerism.

It is against the background of evangelical Protestantism that we may view the teachings of Sun Myung Moon. He was a child preacher who had an experience in 1936 which he saw as a commission by Jesus to spread a new message. He also claims visions of the Buddha and other religious leaders. In 1954 he founded what is known for simplicity as the Unification Church. Its tenets involve a reinterpretation of the Bible; loyalty to Mr. Moon as possibly—that is, if he fulfills his destiny—the new Messiah; a new system of

Opposite The experiential dimension: a golden Buddha at the Shwedagon Temple in Rangoon calls upon the earth (as indicated by his left hand) to bear witness to his attainment of Enlightenment (see Chapter 18).

The Unification Church combines elements from Korean culture with a blend of Confucian and Christian values. The movement regards itself as a great family, led by Mr. and Mrs. Moon at its head as father and mother. Here, newly weds listen to a blessing given during a mass wedding ceremony held in Seoul in 1995. Interethnic and interracial marriages are the norm and are thought to be a means of combating racism. Sun Myung Moon's book *The Divine Principle* teaches that the purpose of creation was to set up the perfect family in a perfect relationship with God.

marriage designed to unite members in a large Family of which Mr. Moon and his wife are the True Parents; and the hope of unifying the world and the world's religions in a single harmony (in combat however with Communism, which is seen as the present chief manifestation of evil in the world). In practice the religion—which has made converts in the West, though most of its members are Korean and Japanese—favors explorations of the unity of science and religion, the promotion of crosscultural ties through intermarriage of its members across races and nations, and a whole range of modern enterprises, from manufacturing to fishing. It is an interesting synthesis of Korean and Protestant themes. It is Biblically oriented (with the addition of its own scripture, *The Divine Principle*), but its family structure has reminiscences of Confucianism, internationalized. It has a theology which combines Christian themes and those of the Yin-Yang dialectic of the East Asian tradition. For various reasons the Unification Church has attracted a lot of controversy, but it is the first major religious mission out of Korea to the West.

To sum up: in Korea, as in Japan, the concern to modernize combines with elements drawn from varied traditions, including indigenous shamanism. However, because of Korea's conquest by another Asian power, the logic of events took a different path: often Buddhism and Japanese State Shinto were presented as the religions of the rulers, and this gave Christianity a very different role from that which it had elsewhere, where it was identified with the colonial power. This helps to explain its growing success in Korea. But the full story of the evolution of worldviews in Korea cannot yet be told, because of the military and ideological divide between North and South. We may note, too, that in modern times Zen (Son) Buddhism has emerged strengthened by its experiences and represents a resource which other countries are beginning to tap.

Modern Southeast Asia

CHAPTER 18

Southeast Asia and the Colonial Period

The impact of the colonial powers in Southeast Asia was rather piecemeal. Early on, the Dutch and Portuguese, especially, penetrated the Straits of Malacca, and in due course the Dutch created a wide-ranging empire in the East Indies (Indonesia). The British came to be interested also for trading reasons in Singapore, which they virtually founded, and Malaya, with parts of Borneo left for dispute between the two European powers. The British also in the nineteenth century acquired lower and then upper Burma, as an adjunct to their Indian empire. The French, rather late in the colonial scramble, had an interest in Vietnam, and eventually annexed virtually all of Indochina, including North and South Vietnam, Laos and Cambodia (Kampuchea). The United States, after its war with Spain in 1898, rewarded itself with the turbulent Philippines. The only nation not to be administered by foreign powers was Thailand.

Burma and most of mainland Indochina were Theravādin in religion, and Vietnam also had a strong Buddhist presence. To the south, Malaya and Indonesia were predominantly Islamic. We shall deal with their development in Chapter 20. The Philippines is the only predominantly Christian, in this case Catholic, country in Asia.

The effect of colonial rule on the Buddhist countries was partly to sever the bond between the Sangha and the government, by removing the existing monarchies. It also dramatically injected into these societies the educational systems and fruits of Western culture, forcing some reappraisal of the traditions.

The colonial period did not last all that long, however. World War II brought the Japanese into the area, at first hailed as Asian liberators from European rule. Although the Vietnam War (which was a continuation of the anti-French struggle resumed after the expulsion of the Japanese in 1945) did not end till the 1970s, substantially it was the 1950s that marked the main boundary between the colonial and the postcolonial eras.

The region came to evolve, in response to the colonial era, along very different lines. The Philippines' modernization came in effect through its conversion to Catholicism and occupation by Spain and the United States. The restoration of its Constitution after the Japanese occupation was not sufficient to prevent the slide into military dictatorship and the persistence of Marxist and Islamic rebellions. In many ways the country followed the pattern of Latin American countries, since the existence of large landowners has given point to Communistic ideas among the poor peasantry.

In the rest of the region there are some interesting variations. Thus, ultimately, a rather old-fashioned line in Marxism prevailed in Vietnam after many years of anticolonial and civil war. There were other, rejected options: a rather right-wing dictatorship based on Catholic and conservative Confucian support; and a Buddhist neutralism which was a significant factor in the Vietnam War. In Laos and Cambodia there were fruitless attempts to restore the stability of the old-style kingship with Sangha support in the face of revolutionary movements. That movement in Cambodia was the "Red Khmer," or "Khmer Rouge," a movement with its own ideology, which I shall call for the sake of analysis "post-Buddhist quasi-Marxism," which had devastating effects on the country, and has been replaced essentially by orthodox Marxism under the occupation forces of Vietnam.

In Thailand—which managed to escape occupation—a modernized Buddhism stayed on as the ideology of the State, despite some Marxist and Islamic rebellions. Alliance with the United States kept it importantly in the capitalist domain. Burma, on the other hand, had been affected by Socialist values, which it saw as a means of preserving the organic identity of the society, and most of the period of independence after World War II has been devoted to the practice of isolation. It has what may be thought of as a Buddhist autarkism or self-sufficiency as its aim: this ideal has some resemblance to the Khmer Rouge ideology. Finally, in the other predominantly non-Muslim regime of the region, namely Singapore, this island Republic has undertaken a rapid modernization through welfare capitalism under a vaguely Confucian paternalistic regime.

In the whole region some complications follow from the embedding within the larger ethnic groups of smaller nations or tribes, such as the Hmong in Laos and the Kachin and Karen in Burma, who have played an independent part in events—being for instance in perpetual civil war with the Burmese government and under non-Buddhist, mainly Christian, leadership.

Thailand and the Process of Modernization

The survival of Thailand as an independent state in the 1840s and beyond, when European traders were becoming active in the area, was largely the work of two reforming kings. The first, Mongkut (1804–68), had a remarkable career. He happened (somewhat in the Thai fashion) to be in a monastery when he was passed over for succession to the throne in favor of an uncle, and he stayed on as a monk until his accession quite a time later, in 1851. During this period he became a fine Pali scholar and questioned many of the existing practices in Thai monasticism—which led him to accept reordination, together with a number of followers, in the Mon lineage (the Mon being a minority ethnic group), and in effect founded a new branch of the Sangha, which was called the Dhammayuttika Nikāya or "Branch of Those Adhering to the Dhamma"—or, in Thai, Thammayut. It gained great prestige among the Thai elite, both in towns and in the countryside, and attracted the patronage of influential laypersons, both men and women.

Later, when Mongkut became king, he had as such to patronize the whole Order, including of course the majority, the validity of whose ordination and practice he questioned. But it was the Dhammayuttika branch which still attracted his special favor, and it became an arm in his concern for the modernization of his country. His attitudes were not only spiritual and directed to the deepening and reforming of the life of Buddhist monks and nuns, and restoring Pali studies. Doctrinally he was a neofoundationalist, going

Mongkut

Mongkut (1804–68) was a reforming Buddhist ruler of Thailand, who was important in the modernization of Buddhism in Southeast Asia. He had entered the monastic order temporarily in 1823 and then on a longterm basis during the region of his uncle, King Rama III. He was intellectually dissatisfied with the training he received at a forest monastery near Bangkok and transferred to one in the capital, where he could do serious work in Pali. During a later spiritual crisis he met a Mon monk (belonging to a minority group in Thailand and Burma), who persuaded him that the Theravādin tradition was authentic and stayed true to the Buddha's teaching. Mongkut went back to his earlier monastery and inaugurated various reforms, establishing the Dhammayuttika lineage. Among his reforms was the notion that a traditional cosmology incorporating various superstitions should be replaced by a modern one based on empirical evidence. In 1851 he inherited the throne, and introduced various Western teachers and advisers, who helped him to transform the educational and social fabric of Thailand. His actions were most important in creating a modern form of Thai monasticism, which used the scriptural tradition to sweep away various abuses, and used modern knowledge—especially scientific knowledge—to interpret the Pali canon.

Meanwhile Western powers were approaching. The British took over Burma, and the French Vietnam, Laos, and Cambodia. He skillfully negotiated an independent status for Thailand, using his position to mediate between the two powers. His son, Chulalongkorn, continued with his reforms after his death.

back as he saw it to the canonical foundations of the faith. Like others, later, in the West, he saw the Buddhist canon as essentially rationalist and empirical. It was from this point of view that he came to reject the old model of the universe which was used to justify the role of kings in the medieval period.

According to this model the king exists at a focal cosmological point. The universe is conceived here as being at three levels. Above is the ascending scale of heavens, to which you have access through meditation, but which more concretely are the levels where exist different gods of varying bliss and longevity. To be reborn in such a heaven is the reward for greatly meritorious work. Below the earthly realm there is the world of ghosts and demons and purgatories, where those who have sinned greatly are reborn, and where they undergo grisly fates. In the middle realm, which is where Buddhas appear, there are various sorts and conditions of living beings, and one's height in the scale of beings is again determined by merit. At the heart of this earthly realm is the *cakkavattin* or universal monarch (literally "Wheel-turner"—a title for the Buddha who began the turning of the wheel of the Dhamma or Teaching, but assigned also to the figure of the ideal ruler). The ideal is usually identified with the emperor Aśoka, who became a template for Southeast Asian monarchy. The king has a crucial role in the scheme of things, because in maintaining order and the Sangha, and in promoting virtue, he increases merit and gives humans the greater opportunity to ascend in the scale of life and to attain heavenly as well as earthly welfare.

It was a noble picture, but it was presented in an antique way. It involved, as did Christian and other traditional cosmologies, a three-decker universe, infested too in this case with gods and spirits permitting fanciful explanations of natural phenomena. It was this kind of picture which Mongkut demythologized. He saw the universe as essentially moral and the role of Buddhism as promoting ethical and spiritual welfare. He had his foreign minister and close associate write a book setting forth this more empiricist account. In it, heaven and hell became not so much places as states of mind and useful pedagogical devices. Scorn was lavished on the older explanations of things in terms of gods. Religion was thoroughly spiritualized. It was an early and courageous version of Buddhist modernism and was suffused with the spirit of naturalism.

The program of reform was carried on by Mongkut's son, Chulalongkorn (reigned 1868–1910), who centralized further the Sangha under government supervision, and set up Buddhist academies for the better training of the clergy. Buddhists in Thailand, and elsewhere in Southeast Asia, came to see Buddhism as compatible with (some thought prefiguring) modern science, and the law of dependent origination was seen as a way of stating the fundamental principle underlying the universe. It is true that there are many naturalistic elements in the Pali canon, and the rationality and intellectualism of the Buddha are evident in the texts. So the neofoundationalist style of modern Thai education of the clergy lent itself to the interpretation of the faith in a modern manner.

At the same time, however, nationalism was intensified, in accordance (one might say) with the very spirit of the age, but also as a means of unifying the country and bringing outlying areas and cultural groups into the national synthesis. This made Buddhism into the national religion in a more intense way, and led to some formulations of Thai Buddhism in the 1970s which are strongly chauvinist in outlook. But the spiritual improvement of the Sangha has led to a dialectic between official religion and the spirituality of outstanding and saintly men who have attained high states of meditation and to whom are often ascribed miraculous powers by the laity. They often operate at the periphery of political life, but still such saints have their overall role in reminding the laity that the Sangha is a vehicle of spirituality and not just an organization for maintaining social and national values.

The retention of the monarchy in Thailand has given the polity a certain stability through a variety of military coups and changes of regime since World War II. There remain problems here as elsewhere about the status of minority religions, particularly Islam in the south of the country, under a Buddhist establishment. It is a problem not effectively solved, either, in Burma, the other Buddhist state in the area.

One may see the Thai model as an effective realization, primarily through the genius and farsightedness of Mongkut and Chulalongkorn, of a modernist transition without the severe political disruption caused by foreign conquest, and one where the monarchy was retained, so that it could play a modernist role in the emerging national polity. But in other countries, though monarchies were kept on, they were under foreign control, as in Laos, Cambodia, and Vietnam, under the French. In due course these monarchies were swept aside in the establishment of Vietnamese Communist domination in 1975. Though there had been lay movements and Sangha reforms in Laos and Cambodia, they were not at a very developed level, because of the slow emergence of higher education. But Cambodia had benefited from Thai reforms in that the Dhammayuttika branch of the Sangha was brought in there.

The Burmese Solution: Withdrawal from the World

Burma was absorbed into Britain's Indian empire through three nineteenth-century wars. Through the war of 1826 Britain took the coastal states of Arakan and Tenasserim, with Assam (which remained part of India after Burma was administratively separated in 1935). Through the war of 1852 Britain got lower Burma. Through the war of 1885 it gained upper Burma, right up to the Chinese frontier in Yunnan. In 1890, it added the Shan States, wedged between China and Thailand. The country as a whole never fully settled down under British rule, there being a succession of rebellions, some under Buddhist leadership. For instance, in the Saya San rebellion in 1930–31, put down with some hardship by the British army, a former monk was proclaimed king and gained support from members of various nationalist societies formed in the 1920s.

This attempt to go back to the model of kingship was not, as it happened, very attractive to the emerging intelligentsia, who were more attracted by Socialism. The attempt was made to blend Buddhist and Socialist values, especially in the thought and practice of U Nu (1907–95). He sought to establish a Buddhist Socialist regime in Burma, before being eventually removed in a coup by General Ne Win in 1962. Though the new regime did not so explicitly work toward his goals, in effect they followed the same ideology, and until the end of the 1970s Burma was largely cut off from foreign influences, travel being banned or severely restricted. A constant campaign had to be fought against secessionist forces from among the Christianized, non-Buddhist ethnic groups.

Though Ne Win repealed U Nu's ordinance making Buddhism the State religion, Buddhism remains predominant, of course; and there is a strand in Buddhist thinking which favors Burma's isolationism. In 1956 the Burmese Sangha had gained prestige by the holding there of a Great Council of Buddhism to celebrate the 2500th anniversary of the Buddha's decease and attainment of final *nirvāṇa*. Burmese Buddhist methods of meditation also became influential in Sri Lanka and the West in the years after World War II.

The isolationism of Burma can be explained, perhaps, by the collectivist transposition of ancient individual ideals. The notion of the hermit or forest-dwelling monk is vital in the Buddhist tradition: in Burma, it is as if a whole nation has wished to withdraw from the wider world. The ideal is that Burmese values will thus remain pure and uncontaminated, either by the destructive forces of Marxism which have done so much harm to Buddhism over so much of Asia, or by the corroding influences of Western materialism and capitalism. Buddhism in Burma will remain thus free, perhaps a bit mixed up with the religion of the spirits, the *nats*—who here as elsewhere in peasant Asia form an army of forces in the jungle, the field, the sky, and the streams, who have to be dealt with—but within the framework of the Dhamma. We note that not only in Burma but also in Sri Lanka among the J.V.P. (People's Liberation Front) and in Kampuchea there are similar ideas of withdrawal from the capitalist world, but in these cases the ideals are more secularized and politicized.

Cambodia and the Purification of Kampuchea

In 1887 Cambodia became part of the French Union Indochinoise, after the suppression of a major rebellion. Cambodian troops fought for the French during World War I, and as a reward higher education and administrative opportunities for native Cambodians were somewhat expanded. But throughout Indochina the French rather alienated the intelligentsia through their insistence on purely French education, based on the assumption of the great superiority of French culture.

Though Laos and Cambodia became independent under their own monarchies in 1954, after the First Vietnamese War had ended in French defeat

Khieu Sampan (b. 1925) the Vice-President of the Cambodian government during Pol Pot's regime and one of its most most influential ideologists, seen here in 1974.

at Dien Bien Phu, they came to be sucked up in the general armed struggle of the region in the 1960s and 1970s. In 1975 the Cambodian capital, Phnom Penh, fell to insurgents of the Khmer Rouge under the political control of Pol Pot, who ruled till 1979. Then Vietnamese intervention brought in an orthodox Marxist regime under Vietnam's control, but not before there had been great changes and massacres.

These were carried out in the name of an ideology which had been sketched out first by Khieu Sampan (b. 1925) and articulated by him in a doctoral thesis he wrote for the Sorbonne in Paris. In that work he analyzed the condition of Cambodia, which he saw at that time under colonial and neocolonial domination. In order to get true economic independence, he argued that it was necessary to isolate Cambodia completely and to go back to an agricultural and self-sufficient economy. It was a bold vision, which he thought out with clarity to its bitter end. Though he thought in Marxist terms, the direction was un-Marxist, for it looked backward to an agrarian past rather than forward through the smoke of the industrial revolution. As a British academic, sympathetic to the regime, put it wittily after a visit there: "I have seen the past, and it works."

In addition to the strictly economic vision of Khieu Sampan there were notions of national purity at work too. Kampuchea (the name was changed under Pol Pot) was to be rid of the impurities brought by colonialism and capitalism. One of these impurities was education, another urban living. Shortly after taking the swollen capital, the Khmer Rouge ordered everyone out. People went, thinking it a temporary measure, even if they had to rumble along in hospital beds. But it was permanent: the Khmer Rouge simply abolished Phnom Penh as a functioning city. Educated people were everywhere executed: and among these were counted the members of the Sangha. About a third of the population perished, many of them by hunger. A new, intolerant religion had taken over, what I have called a "post-Buddhist quasi-Marxism." It still persists as a minority faction in the continuing civil war that has followed on from the effective take-over by Vietnam, which retains an army of occupation both there and in Laos and has tightly curbed Buddhism.

In the Khmer Rouge ideology, Kampuchea saw the application of a secularist hermitism, a more brutal and greatly less traditional version of Burmese isolationism. And yet the logic of it all was in the last analysis nationalist: it was done in the name of the Khmer people, in the context of Khmer independence and "freedom." Ideology was ultimately at the service of the most powerful secular value of them all—the power of national feeling and the national idea.

Vietnam and the Long Struggle Against Foreign Domination

As I have said, the French did much to alienate the intelligentsia of the region, especially in Vietnam, with its strong infusion of Confucian thought, which was scarcely ready to admit the superiority of French ideas. The diverse tendencies in Vietnam rose to the surface during and after World War II, when Japanese rule gave way first to the proclamation of independence by the most organized of the wartime resistance movements, the Communists under Ho Chi Minh (1890–1969), and then the attempt by the French to regain their former possessions. That struggle led to the French withdrawal and the division of the country into North and South. But this did not prevent the fight from slowly resuming, by guerrilla means in the South; and so eventually, for fear of Communism, the United States got sucked in, sending troops in 1965.

It was during the following decade that the religious tensions in the South were manifest. The population was mixed. Though there was a strong Buddhist Sangha, there were also many Catholics: Vietnam was by far the most Catholic country in Asia, after the Philippines. Many Catholics had fled from the North and swollen the numbers in the South. But the ideology of Catholics tended simply to be negative: anti-Communist. There were also in the South some new religions, like the Buddhist-inspired Hao Hoa and more importantly the syncretistic Cao Dai. There was a growing lobby of Buddhists who took a neutralist stance, wanting neither Marxism nor Western materialism (as it was often perceived: and certainly the Americans fought the war in a materialist way, supposing that military victory could be achieved by firepower, air power, the favorable body count ratio, and so on).

The Cao Dai is a syncretistic Vietnamese church which was founded in 1926, amid great éclat, by a Vietnamese intellectual called Ngo Van Chieu

Ho Chi Minh, the communist leader of North Vietnam. He founded the Indo-Chinese Communist Party in 1930 and, on his return to Vietnam in 1941, after thirty years' exile, formed the Vietnam Independence League, the Vietminh.

(1878–1932). It is highly eclectic, but may be said to be more than anything Daoist in inspiration. The name means "High Tower," which is a Daoist symbolic representation of the Supreme Being. In accord with the old Vietnamese tradition, the threefold religion of the Chinese-Vietnamese culture was incorporated into the beliefs and practices of the new religion, which nevertheless wove in other Western and nationalist strands. Its organization was modeled on the Catholic: having a Pope, cardinals, archbishops, and so forth. It is an interesting feature of Daoism—as of the Bön tradition, too, in Tibet—this tendency to mimic its rivals' organizational structures. In the old days it was Buddhist monasticism that was the model: here it was Catholicism.

In addition to the Supreme Being, the Cao Dai also reverence other spirits, such as the Buddha, Confucius, and Sun Yat-sen, not to mention Jesus and Muhammad, and great figures of the conquering French such as Joan of Arc and Victor Hugo (the task of one official was to continue the latter's writings; there is in the Cao Dai a strong spiritualist element, so communication with Victor Hugo and taking down further works by dictation presented no problem in principle). It sought the unity of religions, as may be gathered from

The ethical dimension: with vast self-control a Buddhist monk burns himself to death in protest against the actions of the South Vietnamese government. Generally Buddhist monks took a middle position between the two sides in the Vietnamese civil war. Though suicide is not commended in Buddhism, it had come to be a sporadic custom in China and was somewhat revived in Vietnam during the war.

this list of honored spirits. But in its nature it was destined to become a separate organization. It was too strongly organized to be an effective umbrella for other groups: until 1955 it even fielded its own army. It was in the North-South struggle emphatically anti-Communist. Its hope was for an independent Vietnam which would follow a middle path between the superpowers. In this it was sympathetic to the growing Buddhist movement in the South.

That movement contributed to the fall of the government of Ngo Dinh Diem, a Catholic, who was better able to organize outside support than to mobilize loyalty within the country; and during the 1960s the United Buddhist Association under the leadership of the monks Thich Tri Quang and Thich Thien Minh was prominent in the political struggle, but from a neutralist perspective. The self-immolations of Buddhist monks and nuns on behalf of their ideals were moving demonstrations of commitment and helped to highlight the essentially divided character of South Vietnamese religious and ideological loyalties. The victory of the Northerners in 1975 led to the elimination of dissent; and it was abroad that the manifestations of indigenous Vietnamese religion were continued—in the United States, especially, whither many Vietnamese fled, and where centers such as those of the Cao Dai and relevant Buddhist associations flourish.

And so, over much of the old Indochina, there reigns in effect the Chinese system: the realization of national independence through Marxism. But in the case of Vietnam, mindful of Chinese domination in the past, it was advantageous to ally closely with the Soviet Union, and to survive through Russian economic and military support, while fighting an occasional border battle with the Chinese. The logic of nationalism dictated this. But the logic of nationalism dictates otherwise in Laos and in Kampuchea, and no doubt anti-Vietnamese nationalist ideologies will surface there.

The Singapore Experiment in Welfare Capitalism

The only other non-Muslim country in Southeast Asia is Singapore, a city-state which was essentially created by the British. It was founded by Sir Stamford Raffles (1781–1826), in 1819, as a trading post. It was for long part of Malaya, and as such had a great influx of ethnic Chinese during the later part of the nineteenth century in connection with rubber plantations and tin mines. These people made their way in commerce, and when Singapore gained independence as part of Malaysia, a wider federation, in 1963, and later in 1965 broke away under the dynamic leadership of Lee Kuan Yew (b. 1923), it had a spectacular success as a hub of capitalism in Southeast Asia.

Singapore is governed by a form of welfare capitalism. Since there are substantial minorities in the small island republic, such as Indians, Malayans, and Sri Lankans, the regime is keen to emphasize its pluralism. Nevertheless a kind of education-oriented elitism is the main ideology, reminiscent of Confucianism. One might call it Economic Post-Confucianism, if one wanted a label, where learning and virtue are seen as the basis for economic success. Within this framework traditional religions such as Buddhism and Daoism have a modest place, plus Christianity and Hinduism.

Of all the Asian states other than Japan, Singapore has been the most successful in pursuing the capitalist path. It has gained immensely from independence, since the British notions of development and education were somewhat old-fashioned. Also, Singapore serves as something of a beacon for the overseas or diaspora Chinese, it being a conspicuous example of their success, while in Vietnam and Indonesia, and in some degree Malaysia, they suffer from a degree of discrimination.

Reflections on the Southeast Asian Scene

It can be seen that varying options have arisen in relation to the religions of the region. In some cases, nationalism has led to the decisive and often bitter rejection of traditional ideas and practices and the substitution of secular ideologies. Of these ideologies the most conventional is the Vietnamese under the leadership of Ho Chi Minh. The least conventional is the alarming nationalist quasi-Marxism of the Khmer Rouge. The Buddhist variations comprise the modernizing conservatism of Thailand, through a forward-

A Buddhist three-day retreat in Laos before the country was taken over by the Communists.

looking monarchy, and the Socialist hermitism of Burma. The most vital syncretism among all these is probably the modernist Thai adaptation, synthesizing canonical Buddhism and Western ideas, but building on a slowly evolving popular Buddhism which prizes the monks and nuns who attain high levels of spirituality, but also appreciates the modernizing spirit (as well as the practical fruits of modern technology, of course). Then there are the unresolved questions of Cambodian and Laotian culture. Meanwhile, Singapore has made a bold dash for post-Confucian capitalist prosperity, blending this with religious pluralism and a welfare state.

One major effect of the terrible history of Southeast Asia, through and after the colonial period, has been the large number of refugees. They have settled mainly in North America, but some, too, in Australia and elsewhere. They have brought their forms of Buddhism with them and so helped to plant that religion more firmly in the West. Since religion has suffered greatly in Marxist lands, and since most of these in Asia are Buddhist lands, it follows that Buddhism has suffered more than any other religion (more than any other save, proportionately and in sick drama, the Jews). It means that the center of gravity of Buddhism has shifted to the South—to the Theravādin countries—and in many ways to the capitalist West, where it flourishes markedly. Among other refugees, one may also mention tribal people such as the Hmong, many of whom have made their place in the United States, about to pioneer a quite different future for their culture.

Japan in Modern Times

CHAPTER 19

Into Seclusion

The Arrival of the Jesuits

By the middle of the sixteenth century the Portuguese had established a whole range of trading ports from East Africa through India to the East Indies. The chance shipwreck of some merchants in 1543 in southern Japan led to more regular visits to Kyushu, including that of the spectacular Jesuit missionary St. Francis Xavier (1506–52), who had already done great things in Goa and southern India. His mission, though fairly brief, allowed Christianity to take root in southern Japan, especially in and around the port of Nagasaki.

Christianity had considerable initial success, in part because the Jesuits were accommodating culturally in their presentation of the faith. Xavier had used the name of the great Buddha Dainichi for "God," and had used Buddhist titles and the like, and the promise of a Pure Land as the heavenly paradise awaiting the faithful. It could all look very much like a form of Pure Land Buddhism (and in a way this perception was the truth—the conceptions of grace were similar between the two religions, even if Xavier could complain that Pure Land doctrines were more like Lutheranism).

Xavier and his successors were helped by the fact that during the power struggle to unify Japan at the time, the main contender, Oda Nobunaga (1534–82), was angry at Buddhist resistance to his plans, burned the great Buddhist center at the Tendai monastery on Mount Hiei, and to counteract Buddhism encouraged Catholic Christianity. His successor, Toyotomi Hideyoshi (1536–98), was equally anti-Buddhist in policy, but was also somewhat anti-Catholic, because he feared that the presence of missionaries might itself begin to thwart his plans for national unity. From 1596 missionaries were banned, and in 1597 he caused twenty-six Christians, including Franciscans and Japanese converts, to be crucified.

Map 18 Modern
Japan.

The advent of Spain, trading between Mexico and the Philippines, was also disturbing, and when the shogunate was established in Edo (Tokyo) under the eventual winner in the struggle, Tokugawa Ieyasu (1542–1616), Christianity and foreign contact were excluded. Buddhism and the *kami* were instituted as the official religion. Persecution of Catholics was especially severe after the uprising in Shimabara, Kyushu, in which many Christians took part in 1637. The regime came to institute a parish system throughout Japan in which every family had to register with a temple. Temples were put in charge of burials and cemeteries, and this strengthened the link between temples and families. Also, with the exception of a controlled Dutch trading post at Nagasaki, foreigners were completely excluded from Japan, and the country underwent a rigorous policy of national seclusion (*sakoku*).

Religion in the Tokugawa Era

The Tokugawa was a system of remarkable consolidation, which gave Japan breathing space until the next crisis, in the middle of the nineteenth century, when it became evident that seclusion would break down. It retained the imperial family as a sacred focus of the nation, but the administration was under the shoguns of the Tokugawa family—as it were, national and hereditary prime ministers—and devolved through a feudal system presided over by local warrior feudatories or *daimyo*. The social order was fairly rigorously defined by law and etiquette. The hierarchy in broad terms was: warrior, farmer, artisan, merchant (with one or two impure groups below). Though merchants were at the bottom, by the end of the Tokugawa period commerce and cities had expanded so that their status had improved with the accumulation of wealth.

As far as religion went, the Tokugawa system not only integrated the population with Buddhism, and Buddhism itself with the *kami*; but it expected the various ranks of society to conform to the proper norms. The warrior class had to follow the Bushido, for example: the Way of the Warrior. As a concept this surfaced at the start of the Tokugawa era, and as it came to be expounded by Confucian scholars it combined the twin ideals of learning and the martial arts. The new warriors of the era had to get involved in administration and the running of society, and so their education became important. In fact as the Tokugawa period went on they came to fulfill many professional goals, as administrators, lawyers, doctors, as well as soldiers. This was one of the ways which Confucianism was blended into the Tokugawa ethic. Another was by the combination of Zen and Confucian thought; and Zen also played its part in giving the martial arts a spiritual meaning and basis.

Theoretically it was a good period for Buddhism, but criticism of the regime was not allowed, and the only new form to emerge was Obaku Zen, brought in from China by Ingen (1592–1673) near the beginning of the Tokugawa period. It combined elements of Pure Land and Zen practice. Ingen's stricter practice was a challenge to the other schools and contributed to their reform and revival. But the Tokugawa period also saw new views of Shinto tradition and Confucianism being developed. The Tokugawa shogun Mitsukuni (1628–1701) caused a great historiographic enterprise to be undertaken, which was the reinterpretation of the history of the imperial family according to Confucian principles. This work, the *Dainihonshi*, played a part later in the ideology of the Meiji restoration.

Also of some significance in the eighteenth century was a revival of nationalism through the so-called *Kokugaku* or National Learning movement, under the leadership of such intellectuals as Motoori Norinaga (1730–1801). This saw the history of Japan as having three periods: a first pristine period, then a period of corruption by foreign influences, and finally a period of restoration and rediscovery of the ancient past. This stream of ideas and feelings helped to reinforce national sentiment during the closing years of the Tokugawa shogunate.

Opening Up and Inner Transformation

The period of isolation, however, could not last forever. The Western powers in the early part of the nineteenth century were already forcing China to make grave concessions. It could not be long before like demands were made of Japan. Severe disquiet caused by the sailing into Edo (Tokyo) Bay of a squadron of American ships under Commodore Matthew Perry (1794–1858) in 1853, and resentment at the imposition of an unequal trade treaty in 1858, contributed in 1867 to the overthrow of the Tokugawa system and the restoration of imperial government known as the Meiji Restoration (Meiji being the name given to the imperial reign). Though in theory a conservative act, this turned out to be a radical event, since the ideologists of the new Meiji era had a good idea of the measures they wanted to adopt.

From 1867 to World War I lay ahead a period of breathtaking change and early success in the processes of modernization and in the political expansion of Japan. The war with China in 1894–5 was followed by the Russo-Japanese War, culminating in the devastating naval victory of Tsushima in 1905; the annexation of Korea in 1910; and the joining of the Allies against Germany in World War I, confirming Japanese status as an "honorary Western nation."

The Japanese were quick to grasp that military power, necessary if they were to be strong enough to keep out the foreigners, depended on modern science and technology; and that the latter required education, which in turn demanded a modernized society. They were therefore determined to change their own society. This they did by various measures: forming a conscript

The 124th Japanese emperor, Hirohito (1902–89), dressed in ceremonial robes for his enthronement in 1926. His reign, known as the Showa era, was marked by militarization and aggressive wars against China, Britain, the United States, and others.

470

army, founding Western-style universities, sending students overseas, creating modern industries, adopting the shape of a Western constitution, abolishing feudalism, and giving new roles to the warrior classes: in a revised military and navy, in the new professions, and in creating new modes of thought.

The foundation, however, of all this was nationalism, and the foundation of nationalism was loyalty to the imperial family and through them to the national essence, the *kokutai*. Because Japan was an island nation and forever living in the shadow of imperial China, it already had a well-formed nationalism; and it did not have to grope around, as China had, to realize that it was a nation among other nations (rather than being simply the central kingdom); or, as India had, to discover its cultural unity over against a foreign power. The very principle of the now discredited Tokugawa regime had been the unification of Japan as a distinct entity and the closing up of Japan for fear of foreign influences. Now the national essence was the same, but the means were different: by a deliberate policy of opening up, the Meiji reformers would be able to control foreign influences and bend them to the task of creating a new and powerful Japan. In this they were amazingly successful.

The first large measure affecting religion was an imperial rescript or edict separating Shinto and Buddhism. This led to a series of events which weakened Buddhism—popular pressures against monasteries, the erosion of the Tokugawa system of parishes, some anti-Buddhist sentiment, the laicization of many monks and nuns. The separation in question was thought necessary in order to create a Shinto ritual system which was on its own and linked up to the imperial family. As it was, many Shinto shrines existed within Buddhist temple complexes. The *kami* were often regarded as forces in the world somewhat inferior to the Buddhas but not to be denied by Buddhists; and, as elsewhere in Asia, there was a continuum between practices that were in the narrow and purest sense Buddhist and others that drew on indigenous deities. However, even in the Tokugawa period there had been a self-conscious notion of Shinto as a system of gods and practices distinctive to the Japanese national essence. And so the way was prepared for this rather violent separation of Shinto and Buddhist shrines and practices; and in the popular enthusiasm Buddhist temples got damaged as a result of the separation edict (*Shin-butsu hanzen rei*).

Shinto as a State Religion

There was more to come under the Constitution. This was based on French and German models (the Parliament was called, for instance, the Diet). In it there was guaranteed freedom of religion. What the Japanese did was to formalize what was implicit in nineteenth- and much of twentieth-century nationalism. They made all Japanese observe the rituals of official Shinto, because these related to the dominant ethic of the constitution, loyalty to the nation. In order to ensure this, however, and at the same time guarantee religious liberty, they hit upon a fine expedient—by declaring Shinto not to be a religion. In a way the situation was not unlike that in Marxist countries, where the constitution declares freedom of religion, and Marxism, which is the compulsory ideology of the State, is not of course a religion.

The original thought had been to make revival Shinto a kind of doctrinal ideology which was to be subscribed to by all citizens; but with the failure of the campaign to proclaim the ideology, fostered briefly among mostly unwilling Buddhist monks, in the early 1870s, State Shinto in effect got slimmed down. Priests were in fact forbidden to preach during ceremonies, so that Shinto could end up as a universal system of ethics and ritual, with of course myth attached, but not as a set of teachings which could divisively challenge other systems of ideas. To clarify matters, various new religious movements, such as Tenrikyo, which had some Shinto overtones, were reclassified by the State as being Sect Shinto. The consequence is that in modern times three or more kinds of Shinto are referred to: Shrine Shinto, which is Shinto as typically to be found in today's Japan, a set of practices rooted in the shrines (now separated from Buddhism); State Shinto, which existed from 1882 till 1945, when it perished as part of the aftermath of World War II; and Sect Shinto, which covers a number of new movements. Reference is also sometimes made to Buddhist and Confucian Shinto, covering syncretic forms of worldview.

In nominating Shinto as a necessary part of the ethos of Japan, the Meiji government was giving formal expression, as I have said, to the overriding importance of the nation over other values. Actually the same tended to apply in Western countries—through, for instance, the rituals surrounding the American flag or the British monarchy—even if in theory the nations in question counted themselves as Christian.

In brief, State Shinto—and the same is largely true of Shrine Shinto in the period since World War II—was a partly truncated religion, since it did not develop a set of doctrines. It did, however, form the emotional heart of a nationalist ideology which saw the expansion and the defence of the nation's power as the sacred duty of all Japanese. Its ethos linked up with a modern reinterpretation of Bushido as the way even of the conscript soldier. The stoicism and valor with which so many fought in successive wars is a testimony to the grip of such ideals.

The Impact of the Modern Era on Buddhism

At first the Meiji restoration seemed disastrous to Buddhism. The support which had been part of the Tokugawa system was withdrawn. The loss of patronage and membership was severe. The campaign of separation of Shinto and Buddhism damaged many temples and institutions. But in the new opening up to Western knowledge there were new opportunities.

Some elegant syntheses of Eastern and Western thought were attempted, the most luminous of which perhaps is that of Nishida Kitaro (1875–1945). His first important book was published in 1911, and set forth a philosophical method influenced by Kant, Bergson, and William James, in which he pioneered a method of examining experience. For him pure experience, that

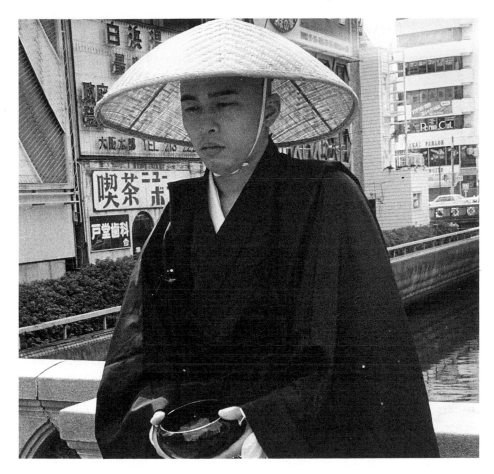

A monk begging in modern Osaka.

is, experience unmixed with concepts and self-consciousness, is without the subject–object dichotomy by which we usually interpret experience. His relation to Zen ideas is obvious here. He gave a new slant on the Mahāyāna notion of nothingness, through his conception of absolute nothingness as the mirror of all individual existence. He was in such ways trying to blend some Western inquiries stemming from Kant's time, and the search for what lies beyond experience, with Buddhist categories of thought.

A not altogether dissimilar attempt was made at a later time by the famous Zen scholar D. T. Suzuki, or more properly Suzuki Daisetz Teitaro (1870–1966). The two men were friends, and from their correspondence can be discovered the closeness of their general thinking. But Suzuki's chief contribution was in editing and translating Zen works and writing about Zen in a way which related it to both science and mysticism, and so sparked a general interest in Zen in the Western world. He was an important figure in making Japanese thought global in character. The fact that Westerners have become interested in aspects of Japanese Buddhism also has stimulated a revival of Japanese concerns with Buddhism.

Japanese New Religions

More dynamic than some of these more philosophical movements between the Meiji restoration and World War II were Japan's new religious movements, some of which have a Buddhist and others a vaguely Shinto background. Actually, some of these had their origins before the end of the Tokugawa regime and are associated with the disturbing social changes of the period: but their heydays were later, and they have flourished during the post-Meiji period. Let us take up three examples from the modern period: Tenrikyo, Omoto, and the Nichiren Shoshu.

Tenrikyo: the Center of the World and a New Community

Tenrikyo has in origin a Shinto ambience; during the reorganization of religion in 1888 it was treated as one of the so-called Sect Shinto movements, and in due course nationalistic values were forced upon it. But after World War II, under the Constitution of 1947 which ensured genuine religious freedom, it purified its teachings and resumed its onward course as a fairly successful missionizing religion both at home and in various areas abroad including the United States.

It was started by a woman, Nakayama Miki (1798–1887), during the stormy years of the collapsing Tokugawa era. She was in early life devoted to Pure Land Buddhism, and wished to become a nun. But in deference to the wishes of her parents she married, and subsequently was dedicated to Shinto deities. It was in her forty-first year that she received a vision which formed the center of the divine revelations to her and later to her close disciple Iburi Izo (1833–1907). Her mission was to prepare the way for a perfect divine kingdom in which human beings will share a life of joy united with God. This messianic element in her teachings led to clashes with the State, both during her lifetime (she was imprisoned on several occasions) and after her death. As a revelatory figure she was thought of as *Kami no Yashiro*, that is, the Living Shrine of God, who descended into her. The revelations were characterized by having three predetermined characteristics—being the right soul, the right place, and the right time.

The place is very important for Tenrikyo religion, since it functions as focus of its most important practices. It is the *jiba* marked by a pole installed in the shrine at what is now Tenri City, near Nara, the old capital of Japan, which is the place that the revelations indicate as being the point of origin of the human race. The large shrine there contains the space necessary for the performance of the dance ritual which sums up and reenacts the story of God's creation.

Miki the foundress showed her humility and chosenness through her compassion for others (her habit of giving landed her family in great poverty) and in healing powers. The teachings she left outlined the essentials of the new faith, while those ascribed to her disciple Iburi contain quite a number of directions about the organization of the movement. The Church is today

Nakayama Miki

Nakayama Miki (1798–1887) was the founder of the Tenrikyo, a new religion in Japan (actually dating from 1838). In her early days she was a devotee of Pure Land Buddhism. She wished to become a nun, but her parents wanted her to marry, which she obediently did. She was restricted by her husband and mother-in-law. At the age of forty she became ill, and was treated by a so-called mountain priest (*yamabushi*), and subsequently was possesed by a *kami* (divine spirit), which she identified as Tenri-O-no-mikoto or Lord of Heaven. He commanded her to devote her family's material wealth to benefit humanity. They resisted, and indeed because of her visions and the like considered her crazy. Eventually they acceded to her wish to devote herself to the God. By this time they were impoverished because of her demands.

She not only had visionary revelations: she also became a faith-healer as well as using shamanistic practices.

Miki considered the present state of the world as corrupt. Greed has ruined us, and we humans have fallen away from the original purity through union with the *kami* which the human race originally displayed. She hoped that a new age was about to dawn. Her theology was monotheistic: Tenri-O-no-mikoto was the supreme creator; and it was at the sacred center or *kanro-dai* (literally "Nectar Platform") in Tenri City that the human race was born. She also designed a form of sacred dance for performance there which reflects the myth of creation. Because of the perceived revolutionary implications of her teachings she was several times imprisoned. On January 26, 1887, she died, having asked her disciples to perform the sacred dance the *Kagura Zutome*. It had been prohibited by the police. She asked whether God's laws or those of the human race were more potent, before passing away. Her disciples saw her as passing into a spiritual state. She remained there at her sanctuary, the *jiba*, to assist her disciples in the world. Many of her verses were collected into a scripture for the church. The succession was carried on through Iburi Izo (1833–1907), her closest follower. The church now numbers more than three million.

grouped under a chief priest, descendant of Miki. It has grown somewhat and has about three million followers, and a very flourishing center at Tenri City, including the *jiba* shrine, a university, a remarkable library with some most valuable first editions and ancient manuscripts from both East and West (including Adam Smith's *Wealth of Nations*), a hospital, a publishing house, a mission headquarters, and a whole series of large dormitories for members returning to visit the *jiba*. Thus a city has grown up around the shrine.

The *narrative* dimension of Tenrikyo centers both on creation and on the life of Miki, who is thought to have remained in a spiritual state at her sanctuary, to help the faithful. Hers is held up as a model life (a contrast, incidentally, to the male warrior virtues which are so much held in esteem in Japanese society). As for the *doctrinal* dimension, God is seen as the true God and divine Parent who pervades his creation but at the same time is specially present to devotees. His desire to create is so that he may see human joy and harmony, but this is prevented because of selfishness, and the revelation is designed to overcome this. Human life is treated as something lent by God (borrowed by the human being), and this provides an ethical motif to Tenri teachings, which we shall come to shortly. Salvation also requires the purification of the heart, and this can be achieved over a period of lives, through reincarnation. This softens the impact of the particularism of the *jiba* as the holy center where one should prepare for final union with God, since good conduct and purification can help one to receive the divine gift of being reborn at the *jiba*.

The *ritual* dimension centers on the sacred dances in the central shrine. Pilgrimage to the center is a vital ingredient in the organization of the faith. As to the *ethical* side, we have noted how regarding one's life as being on loan spurs devotees to be selfless and to use their talents on earth for the divine cause. Using Shinto-like language, where the image of dust obscuring a mirror is prominent, the faults of humans should be wiped away as being the so-called "eight dusts" covering up the human heart, one's true nature. They are such as hatred, anger, greed, arrogance, and so on. The general ethos is this-worldly, concerned with building up the visible life of the community.

On the *material* side we have noted the importance of Tenri City. The actual main shrine is beautifully built with expensive wood, but it is without ikons, unless one counts the *jiba* pole toward which the celebrants face. There are some patterns used on priestly robes which are reminiscent of Shinto modes, but basically the rites are separate from those used in Shinto.

The religion focuses strongly on the notion of parental love: God is a loving parent, and the creation saga of Miki emphasizes this idea. It leaves out of the whole saga of creation the complex of motifs associated with the goddess Amaterasu and the myth of the imperial family. This was one of the causes of friction between Tenrikyo and the State Shinto that the Meiji system put in place. Tenrikyo has a lot to say to those who belong in nuclear families in the post-industrial age, in a Japan which has undergone headlong industrialization and other vital social changes, including the defeat of World War II.

Omoto and Some Other Related Movements

Omoto (Great Source) never recovered from being disbanded on the orders of the government before World War II. However, it had great effects in stimulating other movements. It stemmed originally from the shamanistic visions of Deguchi Nao (1837–1910), a peasant woman. She saw in the talents of Deguchi Onisabiro (1871–1948) proof of his being a messianic messenger from God, whose coming she had predicted, and he was adopted into her family, becoming her son-in-law. The theology promulgated by the new religion was that souls descend from the divine world of spirits into this material world. The coming of Miroku (Maitreya Buddha) was prophesied, with whom Onisabiro identified himself. The movement saw the present state of Japan as evil and in need of divine reconstruction, which would come with the new age. It tended to look on that new age as involving a return to rural harmony: in such a life religion would be lived as art, with an aesthetic beauty and harmonious feelings.

The movement was a reaction against industrialization and the whole modernization of Japan, and though it professed patriotism in accord with the dictates of State Shinto its myth and doctrine were in many ways in continuing opposition to the route which the State was taking. It was right-wing in politics, but with an emphasis on village life and the repair of agriculture. Because of these heretical policies it was suppressed in the 1930s. But it had an influence on other new groups, including Perfect Liberty Kyodan or PL Kyodan as it is known, created by Miki Tokuchika (b. 1900) in 1956. This especially took up the theme of life as art. Thus the first three of its twenty-one principles read as follows: "Life is Art. The whole life of the individual is a continuous succession of self-expressions. The individual is a manifestation of God."

We may see in Omoto a somewhat turbulent attempt to explain the present problems as being due to the withdrawal of the original *kami* from Japan, and the hope of a new age in which many of the evils of our time will be swept away by a messianic figure or under his leadership. The appeal of the message lay in its revolt against the fashions of the times: against capitalism, against the Constitution, and against both World War I and World War II. It argued, too, for the essential unity of all religions and for world harmony. It was thus a strange mixture of peaceful and extreme authoritarian views.

Both Tenrikyo and Omoto have a background of Shinto, but both in effect have fashioned alternative myths. Neither conformed to the State Shinto or the official Shinto of the imperial family. But they went in different directions: Tenrikyo toward a building up in a practical way of a city and a center here on earth, Omoto back to an earlier vision of a rural paradise. They both testify to a period when the Shinto framework in a broad sense was exhibiting strong dynamics, and breaking out from under the newer Shinto which was being shaped both before and during the Meiji era (and then the Showa era, from 1912)—a newer Shinto which, while professing antiquity, nevertheless was self-consciously forming itself into a separate tradition rather than a functional correlative of Buddhism and Confucian values.

Just as China had the three religions which over much of its history served as a loose federation of spirituality and ideology, so Japan traditionally had a working combination of Confucian ideology, Buddhist doctrines and practice, and the *kami*. These forces were becoming separated out in the new Japan. Basically, Western institutions and ideas were taking the place of Confucian values; Buddhism was becoming self-consciously separate from the State; and Shinto was being formed into a separate system. In the nationalist period, up to World War II, State Shinto did not strictly teach any doctrines, as we have seen, in order to retain its power to unify people, but it had its imperial myth.

The disturbing thing about the new religious movements was above all their teaching of alternative myths. This harmonized with their origins in visionary experiences embedded strongly within folk culture. It would be only at a later stage that the need for more abstract and analytic doctrines would appear.

Nichiren Shoshu and the Soka Gakkai

Strictly, we are not here speaking of a new religion, but rather of the revitalization of the older tradition which had been set in motion by Nichiren of the thirteenth century. This revival was due to the work of Makiguchi Tsunesaburo (1871–1944), who wove into his philosophy some elements of Western thought—notably utilitarianism and pragmatism. He dispensed, therefore, with the concept of truth as a separate category but stressed the attainment of benefits by present practice in accord with the general tenor of Nichiren's teaching. The supreme goal of human beings is happiness, and in his reforming of the Nichiren message Makiguchi founded an organization later to be reshaped by his most faithful disciple, Toda Josei (1900–58), as the Soka Gakkai or Value-Creation Society.

This aimed at increasing benefit to members in accordance with beauty and altruistic desires—the foundations of art and morality respectively. This is seen within the framework of a vigorous faith in the benefits of repeating the invocation to the Lotus Sūtra and in other ways following the general life and precepts of the Nichiren Shoshu (followers of Nichiren). Because of the group's deviation from the nationalist norms of the war period, Makiguchi and Toda were imprisoned, and it was in prison that Makiguchi died. The Soka Gakkai is a lay organization, and it came to have considerable success in the period after World War II. It did so partly because of its rather aggressive style of proselytization, called the *shakubuku*, which can be translated as conversion by breaking the person down. Toda's reconstruction of the movement, after its banning and during the time of renewed spiritual hope after the War, was a marked success, and it went on to play an active role in politics through its political wing, the Komeito Party.

The aim of the Soka Gakkai is benefit here and now and the promotion of a worldwide organization which will eventually issue in world peace. Its rituals concentrate on the invocation of the Lotus Sūtra (or *Daimoku*). This should be chanted daily, morning and evening. Replicas of the sacred scroll inscribed by the founder Nichiren and placed in the temple at Taisekiji near Fuji-san are the focus of devotion, and Nichiren is seen as the very embodiment of Buddhahood, even beyond the Buddha Śākyamuni. But the modernization of philosophy undertaken by Makiguchi gives the Soka Gakkai essentially an up-to-date air, different from the more traditional forms of Buddhism.

In its organizational style and philosophical underpinning, the Soka Gakkai has taken Western models. In its myth and ritual it is the successor of the older Nichiren School. It is from this point of view a successful syncretism, to preserve the essence of this older tradition in the changed circumstances of modern Japan.

Nationalism in Japan and its Aftermath

The elevation of State Shinto into a sphere above religion, as it were, involved a blend of religion and the State which was perhaps made inevitable in the Japanese case by the special role which was assigned to the imperial family in the reconstruction of Japan. The shogunate had already prepared the way by keeping the emperor as a sacred monarch, separate from the business of actual administration. The Meiji restoration superficially gave back power to the emperor, but as the polity was evolving toward a Constitution which mirrored some European practices, the status of the emperor was never unambiguous.

For the most part he functioned as a kind of sacred oracle, to be informed and consulted in matters of State but not to be involved directly with particular policies. It was a special mechanism, this, for the conduct of affairs— with the imperial family hitched to the Shinto ritual and the myth of its own descent from Amaterasu—which gave a powerful focus to national loyalty. The emperor became the personalized form of the *kokutai* or national essence. The latter was a kind of Absolute, and the emperor the manifestation of that Absolute in personal form. The various religions of Japan, including Christianity, which had emerged from secrecy and oppression after the Meiji restoration, were necessarily subordinated to the national Absolute. All this might have seemed antique, save that nationalism was the very political arrangement under which nineteenth-century capitalism had chosen to organize itself.

The warpath which took Japan on its various stages to World War II was of course the path of imperialism. This had been fashionable among the White powers. Britain, Russia, France, Germany, Italy, Holland, and in a limited way the United States, had all engaged in it in the Pacific area in recent times, and, earlier, Spain and Portugal had taken a hand. By the late nineteenth century this had come to be justified by more than bare chauvinism. It was supposed to bring the benefits of Western civilization, usually conceived as Christian, to the "natives" of the areas conquered. Japan in her actions up to the time of Versailles had acted in harmony with the overall assumed imperialism, save insofar as she could hardly represent "Christian" civilization. But the ethos changed radically thereafter. In the 1930s her attempts to take over Manchuria and her war with China were severely condemned (as indeed was Italy's attack on Ethiopia). Evidently the nineteenth century was the time to do these things, which became criminal in the twentieth! Moreover, Japan backed the wrong side in the lead-up to World War II, entering into an alliance with Germany and Italy. The penalties she paid were severe: most of her cities burned and blasted out by huge air raids, culminating in August 1945 in the atomic bombs on Hiroshima and Nagasaki (the latter, by an irony, the most Christian city of Japan).

These tragedies did not in fact halt the whole process of modernization. On the contrary they helped, in that the true capital was in the brains and skilled

Priests at the Meiji Shrine in Tokyo, which is dedicated to the emperor Meiji (reigned 1867–1912) and is a reminder of Japan's great period of Westernization.

hands of the Japanese rather than in the factories and shipyards already in place: bombing enforced modernization on the material side. The Western models of life which had been presented to Japan were three in number, at least: there was the liberal democratic option, largely tied to capitalism, though it could be modified with welfare Socialism; the Marxist model, with central State control and a totalitarian system of regulating ideas and behavior; and the Fascist model, which was totalitarian hypernationalism. It was this last model which Japan had slid into following, and it was this that was decisively defeated in 1945. Since America was the chief force of occupation and had a decisive role in shaping the new Constitution, it was the liberal model which was to prevail. At the same time the emperor was left in place as a constitutional monarch (but with undertones of sacrality, nevertheless, which remain in Japanese attitudes).

In October, 1945, the Allied Occupation abolished State Shinto, and on New Year's Day, 1946, the Emperor announced that he was not divine. The result was the dispersal of Shinto into Shrine Shinto. The transition was calm enough. The legislation which abolished counting by families in affiliation to religious organizations, such as the Buddhist parish system, meant a more individualistic stance in relationship to membership, but religious allegiance has grown. Thus, as far as Shinto goes, it is reckoned that the association connected with the great Meiji Shrine in Tokyo is over a quarter million strong. There are about eighty thousand shrines in the country, most of which are joined in the Association of Shinto Shrines, devoted to the training of priests, general education in religion, the development of shrines, and so forth. The associations or clubs of believers concern themselves with general maintenance, the fostering of Shinto music, boy scout activities, etc. So religion has moved onto a voluntary basis. Similar remarks can be made about membership of Buddhist temples.

Does an Overall Japanese Worldview Exist?

The multiplication of new religions, especially in the period after World War II, the separation of religion and the State, the voluntary nature of affiliation with the religions, the onset of extensive Japanese immersion in Western thought, have led to an apparently very fragmented and confused state of affairs. Because of the possibility of belonging to more than one association, and the old tradition of combining different strands of faith and cultus, the total number of registered believers in Japan greatly exceeds the total population. The liberal basis of the Constitution, and of an open society devoted with great dedication to the pursuit of capitalist success, plays a vital place in the Japanese worldview, but how does it fit in with the traditional religions? Indeed, is there a single Japanese worldview at all?

If there is a central conception which prevails, it is probably that of harmony. A number of the new religious movements are keen to stress the unity of the world's religions; and, though the Nichiren Shoshu is aggressive, most Mahāyāna Buddhist groups seek harmony. Shinto, too, has an interest in maintaining its harmony with other religions, partly because it does not possess any rigid system of doctrines which might bring it into conflict with them. From this point of view democracy is a method of defusing rifts, especially between religious groups, insofar as the separation of religion and the State gives a peaceful basis for the voluntary pursuit of values. It also is in consonance with the Japanese ideal of gaining consensus before any serious line of policy is undertaken.

Religion has a role in promoting national harmony, and there is some hankering for the outward displays of royal religion which some other countries, most notably Britain, can still indulge in. But though religion has something of this public role, it is primarily concerned to satisfy the existential or emotional and physical needs of people—through meditation and devotion, and to some extent philosophical insight, in the case of Buddhism; through self-purification and the harmonies of nature in the case of Shinto; through moral improvement, as in the case of Confucian values; and through tolerant attitudes, in the espousal of Western-style humanism.

In contrast to what happened in India and China, Japan's course in the face of colonialism and capitalism has been remarkable. She did not, as did the mainstream Indian nationalists, reach down into her own past for a philosophy from the classical period to adapt to the modern world and to give new shape to the anticolonial struggle. She did not, like China, reach out for a Western ideology to adapt against the West, and to express nationalism in a masked way. She did use elements of her tradition, but with a clear recognition of the role of nationalism in the modern world. By taking the Shinto motif, violently wrenching it from its previous entanglement with Buddhism, and promoting it as a ritual of national solidarity, the Japanese Meiji reformers attempted to give an explicit and sacred basis for the pursuit of the national ideal and conformity with the national essence. At the same time they took up as much in the way of liberal constitutionality as seemed necessary. The fact that there was no doctrinal baggage attached to Shinto left it apt for promoting unity in the nation but not in any way for teaching things which could seriously come into conflict with modern ideas and scientific thinking.

But from two angles the reformers were not able to avoid conflict with religion—first, because some of the new movements offered powerful alternative myths to the stories of Amaterasu that formed the ultimate basis of the authority and sacredness of the imperial family; and, second, because religions have the habit of being universal and so not simply ready to bow to the absolute demands of nationalism. The path to war—both in World War I and more in World War II—led to the absolutizing of the national essence, the *kokutai*, and the clear subordination of religions to patriotism (similar things in practice had occurred elsewhere, in Europe for instance).

Pilgrims ascending Mount Fuji (Fujiyama), the sacred mountain of Japan. In the months of July and August each year more than a million people climb to the Shinto shrine on the summit of the volcano, which has been extinct since 1707.

A Buddhist requiem for broken telephones at the Zojo-ji Temple in Tokyo.

The basis that had been built in the nationalist phase could, however, remain, and Japan took (was virtually forced to take) a move toward liberalism. This has evolved into a different sort of attempt to take over some Western ways and blend them into an overall Japanese synthesis. While this remains largely unexpressed, it centers on a vaguer notion of national harmony, to replace the more concrete feeling for the *kokutai*. Religions can fit within this harmony through a pluralistic framework of thought and practice. In these conditions, Shinto has undergone considerable revival as a focus of yearnings for harmony both within society and with Nature.

Western culture, with its heavy stress upon the arts, has some echoes in Japanese aestheticism. The Japanese have retained a strong affinity for Nature, even despite the creation of a very powerful and often dirty human environment in the course of the headlong economic revival from the time of the Korean War onward. Society remains very crowded and formal; and the shrines and temples remain important outlets which allow human beings to see beyond their immediate milieu, the exigencies of correct social behavior, and the relentless pursuit of a growing Gross National Product.

If we look to India and China as comparisons: the Japanese have not retained as much of tradition as the Indians, but they have modernized more pervasively; they have not sacrificed their cultural traditions to the degree the Chinese have, and, again, they have modernized more pervasively. They have not had the same global influence in religious terms as the Indians, but some of their teachers and practices have migrated: individuals, such as Suzuki; traditions such as Zen and, to some extent, Nichiren Shoshu; and religious ways of treating the arts.

CHAPTER 20

Islam Passes through the Shadows

Setbacks and Responses

The Reversal of Islamic Fortunes

The year 1683 marked the high tide of Ottoman expansion into Europe. The forces of the Turkish empire failed to take Vienna, which was relieved by an alliance headed by the Polish king, John Sobieski (reigned 1674–96). During the next century large parts of the Balkan possessions of the empire were taken by the Austrian Habsburgs—Hungary, a large part of Romania, Serbia, and other lands. Originally a small principality in Anatolia, the Ottoman empire had risen through its conquests of land formerly belonging to the Byzantine empire to a power which stretched from Central Europe to Kurdistan and south to Egypt. It stretched over most of the Arab lands, including the Holy Land, and considered itself to be heir to the great early civilization of Islam. But European techniques of warfare had gotten better, and the Ottomans had stood still.

It was not only in Europe that troubles were besetting the Muslim world. The Mughal empire in India was in complete disarray by the end of the eighteenth century, and by the middle of the nineteenth the subcontinent was dominated by Britain. During the seventeenth century the Dutch were extending their hold over mainly Muslim Indonesia. In the nineteenth century Malaysia was taken over by the British, and Islamic North Africa by the French, save that in the early twentieth century Italy gained Libya. The British dominated Egypt and the Sudan. In Central Asia the Russians were advancing into the mainly Muslim areas. Greece freed itself from Turkish rule, and the rest of the Balkans was liberated from the Ottomans, during the nineteenth century.

After World War I the Ottoman empire was broken up, and the Arab countries came under the rule of Britain and France through a League of

Nations mandated territories scheme: Iraq, Transjordan (later Jordan), and Palestine to the British, and Syria and Lebanon to the French. Britain controlled the small Gulf States. Saudi Arabia was independent under its monarchy and system of Wahhabi Islam (of which more below); but Persia was intermittently under Western dominance. So virtually the whole of the Muslim world found itself occupied by the West. It was a traumatic experience for a once proud and glorious civilization.

Wahhabi Reforms: Back to the Sunna

The eighteenth century was a period of restlessness in Islam, and there were attempts at the social and moral reconstruction of the faith. Such restlessness was in part sparked by the recognition of the weakening of the Islamic world in the face of Europe. But the Wahhabi movement started in one of the least affected areas—Arabia, which was then seen as so poor and barren that it was little regarded by the marauding Western sea powers. Ibn 'Abd al-Wahhab (1703–92) started his studies in Mecca and Medina, where he was inspired with the task of renewal in Islam, and instructed in the Hanbali school of jurisprudence. Later he studied in Basra and began his preaching career calling for the purification of the religion.

After his return to Arabia he formed an alliance with a local ruler, Muhammad ibn Sa'ud, and after his death with his successor. The Saudi State came to control most of Arabia, but the Egyptian governor was ordered to suppress it, which he did in 1818. Later on the Saudis made a comeback and a second State was established, which however fell apart by the 1890s. But, in 1902 a dynamic leader from the Saudi family, one 'Abd al-'Aziz, usually called Ibn Sa'ud (1879–1953), captured Riyadh, and the third, and most important, Saudi State was established, which saw the country develop its fantastic oil riches, and so become a leading power in the region. Wahhabism remained the choice of the royal family and is the official ideology of the State.

The teachings of Wahhab were a call to reform and to go back to the original doctrinal and legal basis of Islam. Wahhab above all preached *tawhid*, or the Unity of God, and condemned those forms of practice which for him signified creeping polytheism, such as the veneration of saints at their tombs, which was common popular practice among Sufi-oriented people. His major writing was called *Kitab al-Tawhid* or the Book on the Unity (of God). He was radical in his interpretation of this, since anything which might come in the way of faith in the one God—anything which ascribes ultimate concern to something other than God—is polytheism in principle and so to be condemned. He rejected many parts of medieval law and custom as being innovation and went back to a more strictly Qur'anic law. He also revived the notion of *ijtihad* or informed reasoning as being a source of guidance. Such reasoning had to be directly based on the Qur'an and the early tradition or *sunna*. He used it as the basis for rejecting many of the opinions of medieval jurists. In short, his renewal movement was more or less what we have described as neofoundationalist, going back to the basics of Islam and sweeping away much in medieval practice. The Wahhabi movement regards itself not as a denomination of Islam but as a call to reform, and yet it has come to accept the name (originally used by opponents) as if it were a denomination. It rejects Sufism, which has come under fire from a number of different directions in the modern Islamic world.

The alliance between Wahhabism and the Saudi royal family is institutionalized in the system by which Wahhab's descendants are made the chief religious advisers: they are the "family of the shaykh." Ibn Sa'ud used religious fervor in forming an organization of soldiers who were bonded together as the Brotherhood or Ikhwan. In 1929 they revolted, because the State had adopted a fairly pragmatic style which offended against their commitment; but the rebellion was put down. It may be said that in subsequent years a rather pragmatic style has continued to blend with the revivalist conservatism of the Wahhabi ideology, especially since World War II, when the Saudi royal family has had to struggle with the thrills and problems of large oil-based riches.

It may also be noted that Saudi Arabia holds a special place in Islam because of its control of the holy places and the *hajj*. Though Wahhabism has a somewhat fundamentalist air, it does represent in its own way a revived mainstream Islam. It stands for a thought: that if Islam is suffering ravages from other civilizations this is because it has not remained true to its tradition. The egregious wealth of Saudi Arabia argues the converse: if a country prospers it is because it has remained faithful to the dictates of God and the spirit of early Islam. But its critics may fault it for having made too many compromises with modernity from the West, and for ruling through a royal family—a concept not welcome to many Muslims of more traditionalist yearnings.

In fact what the Saudis have done in a way largely unparalleled elsewhere, except in Kuwait and some of the Gulf States, is to institutionalize a vast family of three thousand members or more who are as it were the skeleton within the flesh of the nation, and keep control of most of the important functions of the State. So family and national loyalty are fused in this elite. They also have hired many people to work in Saudi Arabia without giving them political rights. So it is a system of layers of elitism: the elite of the family; the wider family; the nation; and the guest-workers. But the fidelity of the family to Islam is not in doubt, for the constitution of the country is the Qur'an.

Ideologically, too, in accord with Wahhabi ideas, the country is strongly opposed to willful ignorance, of which a prime example was the atheism of the Soviet Union. It is strong therefore in its anti-Communism; but from this it does not follow that it is sympathetic to Western values, which furnish many examples of *shirk* or polytheism by putting things other than God before God. We shall later come to look at some other forms of conservative revivalism within Islam, which became one option in the face of the West, and need not preclude technological modernization. Briefly, such a conservatism depends on the feeling that Islam withers because believers have not been faithful enough to its pure form.

Islamic Modernism: Muhammad 'Abduh

Egypt was part of the Ottoman empire, which was nominally at least the main representative of the Muslim community or *umma*. But it was easily detached by the West, and the opening of the Suez Canal in 1869 showed that France and Britain had a continuing stake in the region. Anglo-French joint rule followed, and after a rebellion in 1881–82 under Arabi Pasha, in which the British fleet bombarded Alexandria, Britain took direct control. It was through this period that Muhammad 'Abduh (1849–1905) lived and worked. Probably the greatest modernist of nineteenth-century Islam, he was educated at al-Azhar, the famous medieval university in Cairo.

He also came under the influence of another reformer, Jamal al-Din al-Afghani (1838/9–97), a colorful figure who professed pan-Islamic ideals. Al-Afghani thought that the weakness of Islam was primarily because of its disunity, and during his travels in India he deeply disapproved of those Muslims who accepted British rule. Against them he wrote a powerful tract. His own position was that of the medieval Ibn Sin'a. People have through reason a natural means of the knowledge of God, but such a use of reason is not easy, and for the masses the prophets—and above all the Prophet—have given forth revelations couched in rich symbolic forms. This was a position which could adjust easily to the advance of modern knowledge: as our understanding of the world increases, so will our way of seeing the Qur'anic revelation change. Al-Afghani was a great preacher of pan-Islam, and he hoped to revive the universalist aspirations of the Muslim community in the face of the advancing West, particularly the British.

Muhammad 'Abduh partly agreed with these views. His involvement in the revolt of 1881 led to his exile. In Paris he and al-Afghani published together a radical journal calling for revolution and social reform. Later he was able to return to Egypt, and indeed became a judge and in due course *mufti* of Egypt and chief interpreter of Islamic law, from which position he engaged in the reform of Islamic law and the system of religious endowments.

In his thinking he attacked various elements which in his view had wrongly crept into Islam, such as fatalism, and the blind acceptance of tradition. He was influenced by early Islamic rationalist thinking and underlined the importance of free will in human life. As for science, this was itself developed in the West in part because of Islamic contributions, and there was no incompatibility between faith and modern knowledge. It would be fatal if Muslims for wrong reasons rejected modern knowledge, since it would condemn them to backwardness. So he wished to promote a purified Islam which went back to early days, without such accretions as obsolete medieval knowledge and the cult of saints. He was, however, somewhat influenced in this theoretical work by Sufism: the inwardness of religion showed the spiritual compatibility of faith and science. He saw early Islamic institutions as pointing toward legislative democracy. For him (in response to Christian missions and claims to civilizational superiority) Islam is the perfect religion, which takes up and universalizes what is good in the Jewish and Christian traditions.

It was under the influence of such modernism that many Islamic states, emerging from under colonial domination, including Egypt itself, were able to combine Islamic religion and reforms in the law, e.g. over polygamy and in areas such as banking and charitable trusts. The main planks of modernism were as follows. First, Islam must rid itself of medieval accretions, including Sufi rituals. Second, the Qur'an and the tradition had to be interpreted according to the spirit rather than the letter of the teaching. Modernism was influenced by the Wahhabi example in going back to beginnings, but it was liberal and antiliteralist. Thus law was to be seen under the light of reason, which included arguing by analogy and taking account of the general wellbeing of the community. Such practices as wearing Western dress and eating meat which was not ritually slaughtered were allowed by modernist decisions. Third, Islam was seen as a system which was to be realized in this world: and to build a modern Islam was to do much more than preach heavenly rewards.

Following on from 'Abduh was the work of Muhammad Rashid Rida (1865–1935), from the Lebanon, whose magazine *Al-Manar* (The Lighthouse), which he published out of Cairo, had wide influence. Though he was against what he thought of as innovations in belief and worship brought in since the time of the *salaf*—the first generation of the Prophet's followers— he was for change in regard to social norms. He thought of the Qur'an as laying down general principles rather than legal details of right action and the proper organization of society. Because of his appreciation of the central place of the Arabs in Islam, because of the language, he was somewhat identified with the Arab nationalist movement between the World Wars. Nationalism, as it happened, was a special problem in the Islamic context, which had the theory of a single Islamic community and a central leadership or Caliphate.

Nationalism and the Islamic Anticolonial Struggle

It was clear to intelligent observers that nationalism was one of the ingredients of the Western mix and much involved in the process of modernization, in Europe and abroad. But when applied in the Islamic context it had mixed results. The Indian *khilafat* movement (1818–1924) was based on something wider than nationalism, namely Muslims' loyalty to the Caliphate (*khilafat*). The Caliphate had been maintained in a weak form by the Ottomans, and after their fall was kept on briefly as a religious office in Turkey and then abolished, which caused the collapse of the movement. Still, it did represent one strand in Islamic response to Western imperialism, a pan-Islamic movement. Modernism, however, did move in a nationalist direction, and it was possible to blend national loyalty into the wider framework. Thus the slogan was used in Algerian Muslim schools before World War II: "Islam is my religion; Arabic is my language; and Algeria is my fatherland."

In the run-up to World War I and in its aftermath, Arab nationalism was widespread, but aimed in the first instance at the Ottoman empire. This blended in easily enough with modernism; but there were also some attractions in Arab Socialism, as a concept which battled somewhat against what were seen as the socially disruptive effects of Western ways. Some movements such as Ba'ath Socialism, which achieved power in Iraq and Syria in the 1960s, were explicitly secular movements.

Turkey and the Nonreligious Solution

The most spectacular response to events was in Turkey, which under Mustafa Kemal (1881–1938) went the whole way in dealing with the problem of the West. The revolution in Turkey in 1923 followed the bitter war with Greece, which finished in 1922 and ended with the mass transfer of populations and the abolition of the Sultanate and the Ottoman system. The Ottoman empire had modernized itself in a mild way during the so-called Tanzimat (Reordering) period from 1838 onward, and before World War I briefly under the movement known as the Young Turks. But it was Mustafa Kemal, who renamed himself Kemal Atatürk, who decisively institutionalized a major antireligious and secular revolution from 1923 onward.

First, a Western-style constitution was introduced, in which in theory sovereignty was vested in the people. Second, secular education was introduced, in the Turkish language, and the old religious schools were abolished. Third the *shari'a* (revealed law) was done away with and replaced with civil law. Fourth, the Sufi orders were suppressed, saints' tombs were desacralized, clerical garb was for the most part banned, as was the fez head-dress, Arabic was no longer used, Arabic script was abolished, and the language was romanized. Women were discouraged from using the veil, polygamy was stopped, and other apparent forms of discrimination against women were made illegal. Marriages were secularized.

All this profoundly shocked religious traditionalists; but superficially at least it turned Turkey into a European-style country. Nothing more drastic has happened in the rest of the Muslim world, except in those few Muslim areas which have become Marxist: Albania, the South Yemen, and Soviet Central Asia. The Turkish experiment has not been wholly successful, in part because the promise of constitutionalism has been married with military dictatorships. A revival of religious interests has occurred, and some of the harsher Atatürk measures against religion have been modified.

The Muslim Brotherhood in Egypt and Beyond

Egyptian nationalist hopes were in part pinned on the evolution of democratic government after World War I, but this was hampered by the monarchy and by foreign control of the country. As an alternative to a moderate modernism, the Muslim Brotherhood emerged as another option, also modernizing but not in a modernist way. It was founded by Hasan al-Banna (1906–49), who was a primary school teacher. He wished to have a revival of Islam in a vigorous way and he thought of his outlook as being what was called Salafiyah, that is, rooted in the religion of the first generation of Muslims, the *salaf*. We have seen how Rashid Rida made use of this concept also (and it was a theme which became prominent in North African reform movements). Al-Banna had been attracted to Sufism, and though the Muslim Brotherhood which he formed eschewed much that has accrued to Sufism through the centuries, it did hold to the Sufi stress on individual piety.

The Brotherhood was a society which embraced a variety of activities: it was interested in politics and economics, as well as indulging in athletics. It was a typical modern urbanized religious movement in these ways, not owing much to tradition. But it was radically neofoundationalist in its doctrine and prayer practices, and it worked too for the liberation of Muslims from foreign control. The Muslim Brotherhood (*al-Ikhwan al-Muslimun*) rapidly became a highly effective organization in Egypt, with about a million members by the beginning of World War II. By its conferences, its preaching, its publications, and its general activism it made its mark. It also trained secretly in violent and revolutionary tactics.

The creation of the State of Israel provided the group with both opportunity and tragedy. Many young Muslim Brothers took part in the fighting. But on the armistice the Egyptian police chief was assassinated by a Brother, and a while later the Prime Minister. In 1949 Hasan al-Banna was himself killed, probably with official approval. The movement was proscribed by the government. Many fled to carry the organization into other Arab countries, notably into Syria. In 1951 it was legalized again, and had great expectations when the "Free Officers" under Gamal Abdel Nasser (or Nasr, 1918–70) came to power. But the Brotherhood was suppressed again. Later it was allowed to operate again under Anwar as-Sadat (1918–81); an extremist version of the movement was behind his assassination in 1981. Again, the problem was Israel: Sadat's peacemaking efforts were thought of as a betrayal of the Arab cause.

Colonel Gamal Abdel Nasser (1918–70), a popular Arab nationalist leader, is here mobbed by supporters. As prime minister and later president of Egypt, Nasser was a strong advocate of Arab unity, although toward the end of his presidency he became increasingly dependent on arms and aid from the U.S.S.R.

In Syria in the city of Hama, a center for the Brotherhood, as many as ten thousand are thought to have been killed, and similar events took place in other major cities in Syria, in 1982. They were regarded as a threat to the Alawi regime, based on a small sect, but secular in its ideology. It may have been offshoots of the Brotherhood who seized the main mosque in Mecca in 1979, when much bloodshed followed. So in various parts of the Arab world the group are active, and are regarded as a threat to existing government. They are, as one might expect, as severe on those Muslims whom they consider to have betrayed Islam as they are on the Western threat to Islam (as they see it), often made concrete by the State of Israel.

Though the members of the Brotherhood are modern in their methods of organization and propaganda, they are not modern in their attitude to education and the State. They consider it their duty and their destiny to struggle for the restoration of the *shari'a*. A pluralistic State in a Muslim country is a betrayal. A truly Islamic State would have the Qur'an as its Constitution. This hard line on the law is important and calls into question the very possibility of Islamic modernism. And because they advocate the proper implementation of the law, they would no doubt agree with the dictum of Lord Cromer, who had written in 1908: "Islam reformed is Islam no longer."

Palestine and Israel

The questions of how Muslims should respond to the West has been further complicated by the contradictory promises made by Britain about a Jewish homeland in Palestine and the subsequent foundation of the Jewish State in 1948. This has sharpened Arab nationalism and a sense of solidarity with the Palestinian Arabs. Separate wars in 1948, 1956, 1967, and 1973 have kept up a strong sense of hostility.

Israel itself is the realization of the Zionist program formulated in the first Zionist Congress in 1897. But it contains religious ambiguities. Zionism was a secular nationalism. Many of its better-educated supporters were and are Socialists, and Israel was for them the heralding of a new age. In the communes or *kibbutzim* which were planted in Palestine the ideal of collective living was realized, often with a strong aura of Socialist idealism. Because of the strong connection with nationalism, Zionism sometimes took a right-wing political hue, as in the thought of Vladimir Jabotinsky (1880–1940). As for religious Jews, they were often opposed to the Zionist movement, or indifferent to it; the plans to hold the first Zionist Congress in Munich were called off owing to the objections of German rabbis.

However, there were religious supporters of Zionism, most notably Avraham Yitshaq Kook (1865–1935), a mystic and scholar who became chief rabbi in Jaffa from 1904, and who saw in the Holy Land the promise of a renewal of the faith: in this he was opposed by most of his Orthodox coreligionists. He also argued for goodness in all the major religious traditions and for an openness toward all faiths.

An Egyptian vendor sells tracts and scriptures in a Cairo street. In the last twenty years, Islam has undergone a revival among students and others.

His son Tsevi Yehuda Kook (1912-82) went beyond earlier religious Zionists, who had believed that the task of the Orthodox was to keep the status quo in Israel against the encroachments of the secular way of life. He was involved in the forming of a militant and activist form of Orthodoxy, concerned especially with expansion and the planting of settlements on the occupied West Bank of the Jordan (occupied after the Six-Day War of 1967). This movement is known as the Bloc of the Faithful, or the Gush Emunim.

The ambiguities of religion in Israel are perhaps most poignantly symbolized by the group known as the Neturei Karta (Guardians of the City), nearly all hyper-Orthodox Hasidic Jews, who often stone cars on the Shabbat and otherwise demonstrate strongly against violations of Jewish law in Jerusalem. They are a close community, live in one area of the city, are permitted to govern themselves, pay no taxes, do not go to war, wear traditionalist clothes, and study the Torah. They are anti-Zionists in the new Zion.

The problems lie however more deeply in the logic of the State of Israel. Since it was formed on a national basis, it is a State essentially for Jews. But the identity of Jews has been preserved largely by religion. This leads to necessary tensions when the State hopes to separate itself from religion, as befits a democracy. Moreover, to complicate matters, the new Israel took over what was essentially a hangover from the Ottoman Turks, who gave the Jews of Palestine and elsewhere in the empire, under the *millet* system, a measure of control over their own affairs and the administration of their own law through a chief rabbinate. By a law of 1953, the rabbinate has jurisdiction over family and personal law (so there is no civil marriage in Israel). Since the rabbinate is Orthodox, it means that Reform and Conservative Jews have no status in these matters in Israel. For Jews, citizenship is by the norms of the *halakhah*, the law: but the State professes to be secular. That is one problem. The other relates to the status of non-Jewish citizens. It is obvious that Muslim and Christian Arabs will not be allowed to use voting-rights to overthrow the Jewish State, so in this way the status of these groups is bound to stay somewhat inferior. And yet the institutions of Israel are pluralistic and democratic, for the most part. This tension will no doubt remain unresolved. Meanwhile the Palestinians will see themselves cruelly deprived of their homeland.

An added religious tension comes from the fact that Jerusalem is regarded as a Holy City by all the three great religions, and some pious Muslims vow not to rest till they have got back Jerusalem for the Islamic cause. Moreover, it is traditional in Islam to distinguish between the Dar al-Islam, the "House of Islam," and the Dar al-Harb or "House of War," with the latter being the scene for armed struggle or *jihad*. The State of Israel is like a painful intrusion into

Torah scrolls defiled by Palestinians in Israeli-occupied territory being examined by Chief Rabbi Shlomo Goren, prior to burial.

the territory properly belonging to Islam, and it is the duty of Muslims therefore to struggle against it. From the Islamic angle, then, Zionism is like a dagger thrust at the heart of the faith. It is also a continuation, from the point of view of the Arabs, of Western colonialism, because without United States support the State of Israel, they argue, would collapse. So there remain many sources of bitterness and strife.

The Islam of North Africa

To the west of Egypt the major part of the North African coast and its hinterland is the so-called Maghreb, from Morocco to Tunisia; it is sometimes

Algeria has tried to blend Muslim traditions with modern democracy, although the success of the fundamentalist Islamic Salvation Front in elections in 1990 led to the declaration of a state of emergency and the establishment of military rule.

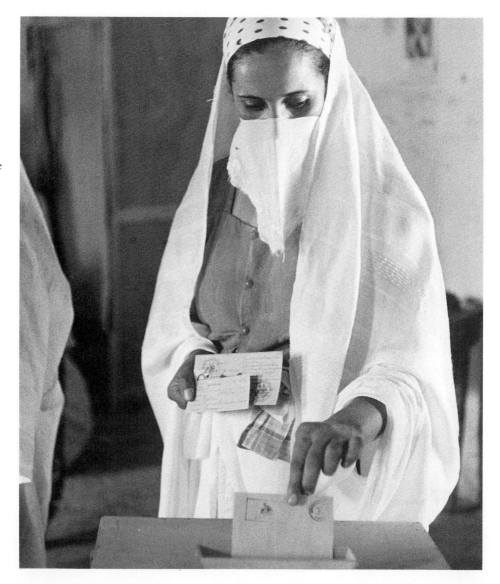

regarded as including Libya (see Map 10, p. 286). The religion of the area came to be dominated by the marabout (*murabit*), a holy person who had wondrous powers as a saint. Such holy men came to be rallying points for centers around which brotherhoods would congregate, and with the brothers the women and children of their families. In many areas the whole population would belong to one center or brotherhood or another, and many people to more than one. All this became very much the standard religion of the Maghreb. The saint's holy power persisted beyond his life, and his tomb would be credited with the same force of *barakah*. It was a North African version of a widespread Sufi phenomenon; and the marabouts were important too in the spread of Islam across the Sahara and into West Africa.

But with the coming of French rule over the region (and, later, Italian rule in Libya), there was less influence of such religion, in that the Salafiyah movement, with its reforming neofoundationalism, came to be the more dominant perspective among the new middle classes, on whom nationalism as an ideology began to take a grip. The Salafiyah's explanation of how the Maghreb had been taken over by foreigners was that the religion had been corrupted and divided by the brotherhoods. The Salafiyah was a general movement in the Maghreb, and combined with anticolonial nationalism. But when the various countries achieved independence, religion came to be subsumed very much under the State, whether in royal Morocco, in Socialist Algeria, or in more capitalist Tunisia. In Libya there was also a neofoundationalist critique of the brotherhoods: in due course Colonel Muammar Qaddafi (b. 1942) introduced his Green Revolution, which was thoroughly modernizing and Socialist in emphasis, and with a strong faith in the Qur'an alone rather than in the traditions which had accumulated in Islam. In all these countries the *'ulama* became subordinated to the State.

Iran and the Backlash Against Modernization

In Persia, under the Safavid dynasty, from the sixteenth century, the Shi'a position was consolidated, and it became the official religion. Under the reign of Shah Abbas (1527?–1628, reigned from 1587) the culture flourished greatly, with the building of beautiful Isfahan (p. 294). Religion however was beginning to be enforced, and his reign marked the start of a period of intolerance, which did have the effect of entrenching Shi'a Islam. Eventually, in the eighteenth century, the Safavid dynasty collapsed, and a period of shifting fortunes began, which by World War I saw Russian, including Bolshevik, and British intervention in the affairs of Persia. In 1921 a coup by Reza Khan (1878–1944), who later took the title of Shah of Shahs, led to a fairly stable regime which lasted until 1979.

Reza's policies followed those of Kemal Atatürk. He abolished religious schools, modernized education, discouraged the veil for women, and set Persia (or Iran as it was called from 1935) on a path of Westernization, at least in the cities. Because of his sympathies with Hitler he was deposed in 1944 by the joint action of the British and Russians, who occupied the country; but his son Mohammad Reza (1919–80) succeeded him and took further steps, especially in the 1960s and 1970s, to aid modernization and the huge building up of the armed forces, paid for by massive oil royalties.

The Iranian Revolution of 1979 in part was a traditionalist backlash against the changes, and in part a reaction to the police repression with which the Shah imposed his regime. The opposition forces were a variety of movements—the Tudeh party which was Communist; liberal Muslims; Islamic Socialists; and the neofoundationalist Shi'a movement headed up by the Ayatollah Khomeini (1900?–1989). He had been arrested and then deported in 1963, living first in Iraq, a major Shi'a center, and then in a suburb of Paris, France. His message was a rather new one: he wanted the establishment of an Islamic Republic.

Khomeini's Islamic Republic would conform to the dictates of Islamic law, and certain constitutional safeguards for this were to be built into the system. It was to be democratic, with a parliament. Though this was in itself a somewhat conservative program, it was also radical in relation to the Iranian past, which had been dominated by kingship. Its purpose was, in the name of

A women's day demonstration, exhibiting loyalty to the revolutionary regime and the Ayatollah Khomeini.

Islam, to remove tyranny and worldly pretensions. It was also radical in demanding an experiment in Islamic living which made the law apply to banking and the processes of capitalism as well as to marriage arrangements and family living. It was to Islamicize the universities and the whole system of education. It was to make public life obviously and consciously pious.

Negatively, the Islamic Republic was to struggle against the twin Satans of Soviet atheism and the irreligious materialism of the West. It was also to struggle against atheist tendencies in the Muslim world, as in Iraq, with its Ba'ath (Renaissance) party regime. Hopefully it would be able to export its revolutionary impetus beyond its borders. And indeed in many countries and circumstances Muslims, though they might disagree with Khomeini's post-revolutionary regime, admired the way it reestablished a kind of Islamic independence from the West.

Baha'i: A New Religion from within Islam

Khomeini's Iran was not a tolerant place. It was natural that with this revivalist ideology certain groups would be hounded, notably the Baha'i. For they were regarded not as a separate religion but as Muslim heretics, on whom there could be little mercy. The Baha'i movement has become a worldwide religion, with its American headquarters in Wilmette, Illinois, and its world administrative center in Häifa; but it can be seen also as a radically modernizing movement from within the ambit of Shi'a Islam.

It follows the teaching of Mirza Husayn Ali Nuri (1817–92), known as the Glory of God or Baha'Allah. He was a follower of the movement known as the Babis, who followed the Bab or "Gate" to the truth. Identified as the Gate was one Sayyid 'Ali Muhammad (1819–50), who was born in Shiraz in Persia. Eventually, when his followers, who looked on him as a link between them and the Hidden Imam of the Shi'a tradition, were involved in rebellion against the regime, he was executed by a firing squad in Tabriz. His teachings involved a symbolic interpretation of the Qur'an, and looked for the coming of a savior figure.

It was with this figure that the Baha'is identify Baha' Allah. When he came to declare his prophetic status, after having a dramatic religious experience when in prison in Tehran, most of the Babis followed him. Exiled to Istanbul, he was later banished with his followers to Palestine by the Ottomans, and settled in Acre. They are another group that looks on the land of Palestine as the Holy Land.

His eldest son, Abbas Effendi (1844–1921), also known as 'Abd al-Baha (Servant of the Glory), carried on with the work of mission and organization, and visited Egypt, Europe, and America. In his will he appointed Shoghi Effendi Rabbani (1899–1957), the eldest son of his eldest daughter, as his successor; since *his* time the movement has been run by a Council.

The *doctrines* of the Baha'i are evolutionary in tone. The various religions of the world, and they were thinking primarily of the Western trio, are not obsolete or wrong but are stages on the way. Thus it is all right to think of

Muhammad as the "Seal of the Prophets," but only in the sense that he had completed the work of his predecessors. Even the Baha'Allah will in due course be superseded. There is much emphasis on the inherent unknowability of God, but his Logos makes itself known. So doctrinally the Baha'is are keen to point to the relativity of religious truth and the underlying unity of all religions.

From a *narrative* point of view the Baha'is see the Baha'Allah as inaugurating a new age in which the community of the human race will become the main arena of action, moving toward world government and stressing the equality of all humans and of men and women. A world language (English) is favored, and nonviolence in human affairs. *Ethically*, therefore, the movement stresses brotherly and sisterly love, abstention from alcohol, and service to humanity.

Ritually, the movement asks for daily private prayers, and certain periods of fasting, but it is not a heavily ritualized tradition. The Baha'is, because of their commitment to the underlying unity of religions, are concerned with different forms of religious *experience*, including the development of meditation. *Organizationally*, they have an elective system which is nevertheless theocratic. As for their *material* expressions, the various great temples, such as the one in Wilmette, are huge and impressive structures which contain in their decorative motifs the symbols of the various world faiths.

In brief, though Baha'i arose from within the matrix of Shi'a Islam and makes uses of its eschatological themes, latching onto the idea of the Hidden Imam, it has evolved into a quite different faith with its own distinctive and modernizing characteristics. It is an example of a spiritual revolution which intuitively recognized the global state of world culture before its time and gave religious preparation for this unified world.

It is thus attractive to people around the world, especially reflective folk who are dissatisfied with the rivalry of the more traditional religions. It experienced great growth in South Asia, and in Africa, where its Islamic coloration but outward-looking message has made it attractive. In Iran it is the largest religious minority, but currently because of the Iranian revolution under a deep cloud. Its world membership may amount to about two million.

Islam Beyond the Middle East

Pakistan: an Islamic State?

One of the severest questions posed to the new State of Pakistan was set by the Jama'at-i Islami, created as a political movement by Mawlana Mawdudi (1903–79) in 1941. Mawdudi was suspicious of the secularizing Jinnah (p. 421), but moved to Pakistan on the partition. He was often in bitter opposition to the government. His movement was devoted to the ideal of an Islamic State in which non-Muslims would not have full rights. He foresaw the use of Islamic law in public life and took a holistic view of the religion, which fused politics, economics, private life, and public worship into a single whole. He was jailed for his part in anti-Ahmadiya (p. 505) riots in 1951–53, and even condemned to death, though the execution was not carried out. His party remained a vital force in Pakistan, although it lost a lot of ground during the civilian rule after the war with Bangladesh; and it never had much support in what is now Bangladesh, especially because it supported the Pakistani State in its war there. But its agitation for an Islamic system did bear some fruit with the adoption by the Zia ul-Haq regime of Islamic law.

On the other hand Bangladesh, founded in 1971, never really has displayed enthusiasm for the idea of an Islamic constitution.

Islam in Central Asia

The Muslims of the former Soviet Union are found in three main areas, in the Caucasus, in the middle Volga region, and in Central Asia. During the time of Russian expansion to the east there were attempts to convert many Muslims, especially in the region of the Volga. And in a sense the Soviet State continued a like policy, save that the religion being preached is Marxist atheism. However, in Turkestan under the Tsars there had been a hands-off policy in relation to Islam; proselytizing by Christian missionaries was forbidden, and so, even, was preaching by Tatar modernists (the Tatars having been much more directly affected by Islamic modernism). Such a policy was designed to foster Islamic backwardness and to make Russian rule easier to impose. The result was that when the Revolution occurred a revolt broke out in Turkestan which was anti-Soviet and to some degree religiously motivated, and which took ten years to suppress.

Thereafter the settlement of Russians in Central Asia and the promotion of atheistic propaganda proceeded apace. Despite this, Islam has survived and indeed in its own way flourished, despite the imposition of strict controls on the mosques and the educational system. Religious education and publication were virtually banned, with the exception of minor training schools run by the government for a limited number of clerics. Yet it is reckoned that about eighty percent of the non-Russian population still are believers. This is out of a Muslim population of some thirty million in Central Asia. It is reckoned that of the population twenty percent are "fanatics" (the Soviet category); that is to say, they are believers by conviction. Others are more traditionally oriented. But even of the twenty percent who are atheists, virtually all practice circumcision and Islamic burial. Yet in the whole region there are less than two hundred mosques, probably, which still function as such.

So on the one hand public Islam is more or less washed out; yet Islamic practice and belief still persist in a more private way. What is the explanation? It is partly of course due to nationalist sentiment—these peoples feel themselves somewhat under threat from what they perceive as Great Russian chauvinism—but the more immediate explanation is that the Sufi *tariqas* or brotherhoods still exist, and they are almost impossible for the regime to control, since they can operate secretly and by word of mouth, and they do not need to come into public conflict with the authorities. They represent a huge religious underground movement (the same applies in other regions such as the Caucasus).

Of the Sufi orders the Naqshbandiyah is the most important. It was founded in Bukhara in the fourteenth century and for long played a highly visible role in the politics of the region. It is moderate in its asceticism and was well suited to playing its missionary role in the Soviet Union. Also important is the Qadirīya, founded in the twelfth century by the saint 'Abd al-Qādir (1088–1166), from the Caspian area, whose tomb in Baghdad is a major center of pilgrimage. (Incidentally, this custom of pilgrimage to saints' tombs is a major complaint of reforming, neofoundationalist Muslims, who regard the practice as a medieval innovation.) In much of the rest of the Muslim world there is a reforming prejudice against Sufism. It is often seen as one of the reasons for the corruption of the faith and its straying from the true way. But in the former Soviet Central Asia it has been a major cause of the persistence of Islam.

The attempt, moreover, of the Soviets to make their influence firm in Afghanistan, when they moved in forces in 1979 to help the beleaguered Marxist regime after the ouster of the king in 1973, generated strong though not very united resistance from mainly Islamic guerrilla groups in that country. It was not always possible for the Soviet government to rely on the loyalty of its Central Asian troops in these circumstances.

Southeast Asian Islam

There were no major Islamic communities in Southeast Asia until the thirteenth century. A major influence thereafter was probably Bengal and more broadly India; but there was also notably trade with Arabia and Persia. Muslim traders were one major factor in the gradual penetration of Islam, and local rulers hired Muslim advisers. But also vital was the effect of holy men and preachers, Sufis in particular, whose mysticism could blend with Hindu and Buddhist motifs, especially in Java. Force was also sometimes important, as coastal rulers took over their regions, establishing independence from inland feudal rulers. By the late fifteenth century Islam was dominant in Java and gradually penetrated the more distant islands of the Indonesian archipelago. The consolidation of Islam in the area occurred well into the colonial period. It also reached the southern Philippines, southern Thailand, and parts of coastal Burma (now Myanmar).

During this time the Malay language became thoroughly impregnated with Arabic and Islamic borrowings and came to be written in the Arabic script. It is basically this language that forms the basis of the national languages of Malaysia and of Indonesia. In the latter case it is also suffused with Sanskrit and Indic expressions deriving from the Hindu culture of Java. These tongues are now written in Roman script.

The Dutch became dominant in the area, though Britain took over much of Malaya from 1795 till 1824, including the settlement of Singapore. Previously the Portuguese had been influential in Malacca and elsewhere. It was partly because of European dominance, which lasted until after World War II, that nationalism burgeoned, and also modernist thought.

Opposite The material dimension: a recent mosque in Brunei, the oil-rich sultanate on the island of Borneo.

Right: The Iranian leader Ayatollah Khomeini (?1900–1989) who came to power after the Revolution of 1979 and turned Iran into an Islamic state, photographed here in 1979.

Below: Interior of the Grand Mosque in Doha, Qatar.

The impact of Islamic modernism in the area was great, as was that of the Wahhabi reform movement. In 1912 there was the foundation of the well-organized movement known as the Muhammadiya, which was designed to purify Islam, and especially that of Central Java, of the folk elements of Javanese religion. In other words it was designed to root out aspects of the typical peasant worldview and some of the persisting aspects of the Hindu-Buddhist tradition of the area. But it came to be a pan-Indonesian movement, and it modeled itself organizationally on the methods of the Dutch Reformed Church in its missionary and publishing activity. It did much in the reforming and modernizing of Islamic religious education, too.

There are also strong moves of a more conservative nature, both in Malaysia and in Indonesia. Thus in the latter country, three or four armed revolts on behalf of an Islamic State in different regions have broken out since independence in 1945. In Malaysia some of the states of the federation apply Islamic law, and there are moves to give it federal status. There is some dissatisfaction also in Indonesia with the ideology under which officially the State is ruled, which is summed up in the so-called Five Principles or *Pancasila*. This is of course originally the name given to the Five Precepts or Virtues of the Buddhist tradition.

Here Javanese influence is paramount, since Java is the hub of Indonesia and its values are often presented as applicable to the entire vast country. This formula seeks to create a pluralistic framework for Indonesia as a whole: the Five Principles are belief in God, nationalism, democracy, humanitarianism, and social justice. With the last four of these the Muslims have in principle no quarrel (though some see nationalism as itself something which has to be subordinated to the Muslim ethos). But belief in God is deliberately interpreted vaguely, so that the religion, say, of the Torajas of central Sulawesi is included under this head, even though from a Muslim point of view it is a polytheistic or animistic system. After all, Indonesia is a great concatenation of islands with people of many different cultures and languages and stages of economic development: for this reason the central government prefers a pluralistic ideology so as not to alienate various regional groups.

Reflections on Modern Islam

We have looked at Islam in the areas of the world where it is dominant. We shall be considering it somewhat in later connections—in Eastern Europe (Chapter 22), in Black Africa (Chapter 23), and elsewhere. We have seen that modernism and neofoundationalism have been the dominant motifs, and in these movements there is some distancing of Islam from the past. Sufism, despite its popularity in some circles in the West, has been heavily criticized, especially by neofoundationalists, though it made a vital contribution to the life of Islam in the Soviet Union. It was of course of great importance in the conversion of large areas of South and Southeast Asia, since it supplied a kind of bridge to preexisting religions and folk cults.

Gradually, Islam is consolidating itself through reform movements and becoming more homogeneous. This is partly due to the fact that modern air transport makes the *Hajj* to Mecca much easier than it was, and this helps to cement Islamic unity. On the other hand, clashes of interest are promoted by nationalism. The break-up of the Islamic world into sometimes conflicting entities can result in bitter conflicts, for example the war which started between Iraq and Iran in 1980, partly based on different ethnicities (Iraq in attacking Iran wished to take over the southwest corner of the country, which has an Arabic-speaking majority), partly on differences of religion (though Shi'a is very strong in Iraq), and more on differences of ideology, between the secular thought of the Iraqi regime and the Iranian revivalism of Khomeini's government.

Despite such obstacles to Islamic unity, at least the infrastructure is being laid, as more areas of the world take up a renewed Islam, going back to the early days, and thinking about or actualizing the rule of Islamic law. But there does remain a gulf between the religious revivalists who want to go back to early foundations and the more radical adaptors of the faith who aspire to some version of Islamic modernism. The signs are conflicting: as Islam spreads

The ritual dimension: pilgrimage to Mecca has vastly increased with the coming of the jumbo jet. The circling of the Ka'bah, or Tawaf is captured by this continued-exposure photograph, with people swirling round the sacred site through the night.

into Europe and America and reaches more places where it is in a minority, the greater is the pressure for modernism. But where it has control of the majority of the population, the greater the pressure for a revivalist imposition of the Law. And we still await some answer to the question posed by Lord Cromer: is a reformed Islam Islam any longer?

Perhaps some of the tangles in Islamic law can be gleaned from the following events in Malaysia. It must be born in mind that Malaya, the heartland of a complex confederation, has a substantial Chinese minority (as well as some others), and they by and large are not Islamic. It happens that Malaya is federal and divided into various princely states. In one of them three young women from another state took part in a beauty competition; but the chief Muslim cleric in the state decreed that it was illegal from the point of view of the *shari'a* or Islamic law to participate in beauty competitions (of course a Western phenomenon offending traditional Islamic values). Worse was to follow, since the senior mufti also alleged that several ministers of the government were guilty of apostasy in that (in another state) they had prevented the Islamic criminal code from taking effect, which mandated amputation and stoning as punishments for theft and adultery. Meanwhile, there has been a tightening up of the dress code for women, based on the Arab custom (not traditional in Malaysia), which was not very popular. However, on a different tack the sultans' authority in the various states is associated with Islam, and this cuts against the modernizing drive of the present government, who want to see a tolerant faith. The prime minister has ordered a review in which all the laws of all the states will be made uniform. But will that benefit minorities? The whole scenario, with Malay tensions between the Chinese and others, the need for modernization, and traditional attitudes churning against each other, is messy.

A Footnote on the Limits of Islam: Ahmadiya

Finally there does remain a question about the self-definition of Islam, which maybe we can illustrate through the Ahmadiya. This is a movement which originated in India, and which has had a fairly good success in proselytizing in certain parts of the world, for instance in West Africa. It has had probably the greatest mission success of any Islamic organization, and has over ten million members in various parts of the world.

The movement rests on the teachings of Mirza Ghulam Ahmad (1835–1908), who came from a village, Qadian, in the Punjab in north India. He was a Muslim revivalist who was drawn into making special claims for his own status. He regarded himself as a *nabī* or prophet, and it was this above all that alienated many orthodox Muslims, since for them there is absolutely no need for further prophecy after the career of Muhammad: this was why he was the Seal of the Prophets. He also saw himself as Messiah in some sense, and as the returning avatar of Viṣṇu, predicted in the Hindu system. He did not think of Messiah-hood as having some kind of transcendent ontological status, since he argued that Jesus did not in fact ascend to heaven, but escaping from the

In Dakar, Senegal, Muslims pray outside the overcrowded main mosque.

cross departed on a journey which took him to Kashmir, where his tomb is to be found in Srinagar. This idea about Jesus of course offended both Muslims and Christians, the former because the usual interpretation of the Qur'an has it that Jesus was never crucified. But in most ways, the life of the Ahmadiya conforms to Islam, though it rejects the idea of military *jihad*.

A split in the movement led to a branch being set up with its headquarters in Lahore (now Pakistan), which denied that Mirza Ghulam Ahmad was a prophet but called him merely a reformer: this branch has stayed close to formal Islam. The more radical branch, the Qadiani, set itself up in Rabwah, in Pakistan, in 1947. Its successes in the mission area were due not only to the sincerity of its exponents, who emphasized the vital part of sincerity and not just outward observances in religion, but also because of the adoption of modern Christian methods of mission—street preaching, pamphlets and other forms of publishing, good organization, and sometimes aggressive propaganda. But it has attracted enmity from the orthodox, and in 1954 it was ruled in Pakistan that it was not a form of Islam and should not use claims which suggest that it is.

It will be observed from this that the tendency in modern Islam is to place a close definition on the religion in terms of doctrinal orthodoxy: a non-practicing orthodox Muslim is much better placed than a practicing non-Orthodox person. By an irony the Ahmadiya movement is now much worse off legally in Islamic Pakistan than it would have been if it had stayed in Hindu-dominated India.

Dimensions of Revived Islam

Despite the importance of the Iranian revolution, it may well be that the future lies more with the revival movements within Sunni Islam, such as the Brotherhood. At any rate in a number of countries, such as the Sudan, Pakistan, and Malaysia, there is the pattern of Islamic law being required: and there are calls in a whole range of countries for similar legislation. This spirit of revivalism seeks to restore practice to what it was; but often its mission is conducted in most up-to-date terms. We can discern some of the dimensions of this Islam as follows.

Doctrinally it has a tendency toward more rather than less literal interpretations of the Qur'an. It is not hostile to science, but it rejects some of the philosophies of medieval and premodern Islam. As far as its *narrative* dimension goes, it of course accepts and focuses on the career of the Prophet: but it also sees Islamic culture as having betrayed the spirit of true Islam through various innovations, and it is because of all this that Islam has fallen into its relatively sorry current state. *Ethically* and legally it calls for the revived application of the *shari'a*. It is strict about such matters as alcohol and the conduct of women: it usually favors the use of the veil. Since it is traditionalist but not quite traditional (for it arises from the very situation in which tradition is being challenged and overridden), its espousal of tradition is a matter of self-conscious commitment, so that there is a great emphasis on being "converted" to true Islam. It has a much more notable evangelical fervor than would be typical of simply traditional Muslims. *Experientially*, therefore, it is vigorous: but it is not much oriented toward the mystical meditation of the Sufis, since Sufi practices are often what has brought Islam (in its eyes) into disrepute. *Organizationally*, revivalist Islam is much indebted to the methods of Christian missionaries, while it also lays stress on Islamic education. *Ritually*, it is pious in reaffirming the importance of regular public prayer worship. *Materially*, it is often at the forefront of the building of new mosques, especially where the Muslims are a minority; so in the lanes of Sri Lanka and the backstreets of Liverpool, England, will be found new structures, often subsidized by oil money. Islam is at a vigorous global stage.

The Colonial Impact in the Pacific

The Opening Up of the Pacific by Europeans

In the early sixteenth century the Spaniards were able to sail west to the Indies from Mexico. By the end of the century they had pioneered the return voyage eastward. The Portuguese Magellan pioneered the southern route around Cape Horn. In the eighteenth century a second great wave of voyages of discovery occurred, the chief explorer being Captain James Cook (1728–79), who explored the coasts of Australia and New Zealand and touched at many of the Pacific islands, including Hawaii, where he met his death. Subsequently, whalers and colonists affected most of the Pacific, as it lay open to European imperialism. Missionaries spread through the region, especially during the nineteenth century, and Christianity came to be the dominant religion.

The Spanish spread Catholicism to the Mariana Islands in the latter part of the seventeenth century, missions coming from the Philippines which had previously been evangelized. The London Missionary Society began to work in Tahiti in 1797. Thence they moved on to the Cook Islands, Samoa, Tuvalu, and the Gilberts (Kiribati). American missionaries started work in Hawaii in 1820, and Christianity fairly soon became the official religion under the queen of Hawaii. Methodism took over in Tonga after the king (who took the name George) converted, and likewise in Fiji the islands were united under Methodism. The Presbyterians became dominant in Vanuatu. Catholic missionaries, chiefly from France, were active in many of the islands, and Catholicism became dominant in New Caledonia. New Guinea, because of its size and multitude of cultures, was not so unified as many other areas in the region: it has a patchwork of Christianities, especially in the highlands, which were not missionized until the 1950s and 1960s. In the British and German parts (taken over by Australia after World War I), Anglicanism and Lutheranism were strongly established, but there were other Protestant denominations as

A traditionalist in Papua New Guinea shares in a mass performed by Pope John Paul II in 1984.

well, and Catholicism is numerically the strongest of the groups now. Much of the mission work in the Pacific region was undertaken by indigenous missionaries.

It is interesting that in so many regions the whole population of a given area converted to Christianity, and of a particular sort. This helped to preserve social solidarity when the preceding religion was repudiated. But there are smaller Churches which are strong in proselytization, and they may spread vigorously at the expense of established forms of Christianity. Most notable among these is the Mormon Church, which has spread out from Hawaii; it has a great interest in, and a desire to promote, the culture of the Pacific.

The cultural effect of the missions was dramatic, chiefly through the translation of the Bible into the indigenous languages. This gave a new dimension to language, and conferred great power on the imagery and models of the Bible. So it became deeply entrenched in the thinking of many in the Pacific region. There were other outcomes: the adoption of modified dress patterns, especially by the women, the opening up of trade to the West, and most dramatically and tragically the devastating consequences of relatively mild European diseases such as measles on a population with no acquired immunity. Up to a point the introduction of Western medicine moderated the effects of this new plague.

A complication experienced in the whole region was World War II, in which many of the islands came under the rule of the Japanese and were then exposed to American, Australian, and other troops as they set about the bloody business of reconquering the Pacific region.

Also important to note is that in some areas the indigenous population itself became a minority because of the coming of settlers. Notable was Hawaii, with its Japanese and American Whites; New Caledonia, with an influx of French; and Fiji, where a large migration of Indians occurred, brought in to work the sugar plantations, and by 1980 having a slight majority of the population. Among indigenous inhabitants such inflows have caused, naturally enough, quite a lot of resentment. New Caledonia remains under French control, while Hawaii has been absorbed as a State in the United States. In Fiji an indigenous *coup d'état* threw out the new, Indian-dominated government which was elected in 1987.

Australia and New Zealand

Australia and New Zealand, being relatively large, have had a rather different history from that of the islands. They both became subject to a deliberate policy of colonial settlement from Britain.

Australia started as a penal colony. The American Revolution cut off the penal areas of America, and the prevailing ideology in Britain at this time was that one could cure the disease of criminality by excising the criminals from the body politic, by shipping them overseas: since many thought that there was some kind of hereditary basis to criminality, this might actually effect a permanent cure.) New South Wales, therefore, came to be a convict settlement, first begun at Sydney Cove in 1788. After 1813 the colonists found their way across the Great Dividing Range, and spread out into the pastures and farmlands to the west. Other colonies were founded, such as Newcastle in 1801, Hobart in 1804, and Brisbane in 1824, all at first penal settlements. But gradually Australia became a place for settlement rather than punishment, and this was boosted by the discovery of gold in the 1850s.

It is a paradoxical country. Though as vast as the continental United States, it is heavily urban. Much of it is blank. The settlers started from the coasts and worked their way inland; but they did not have that optimism which marked the great American drive to the West at the same time. The inner vastness of Australia is barren, blindingly hot, adapted to only the most cunning lifestyle, ill suited to Whites. As the Australian settlers moved toward the heart of Australia their hope petered out. They became more preoccupied with the mere task of surviving than with conquering any Eldorado. And so the Australian myth is more of existing than of gaining the Golden West. Moreover for much of its history Australia has unconsciously existed with its back to the ocean. It was not till World War II that Australians had to become conscious of being in the Pacific. Their shops, their customs, their suburban gardens, their beer, their religion, their language—all derived from "Home," that is to say Britain: not England, because they had a good intermixture of Irish, Welsh, and Scots. They built a British suburb on a foreign shore. The Australian mix came to be something like the British scene without the same class system.

Moreover, though the Church of England had some status in the early days of the penal colonies, it did not have an established position as in England. The major denominations all became well established in Australia, as well as others such as the Mormons, the Seventh-Day Adventists, and the Salvation Army. The Roman Catholics were always a highly significant minority, up to twenty-five percent in the second half of the twentieth century. At first they were chiefly the Irish. But since World War II Australia has become a more variegated society with the arrival of so-called New Australian migrants, such as Poles, Yugoslavs, and Italians; then, in the 1970s, Vietnamese and other Asians, who had previously been kept out through the White Australia immigration policy.

A rather florid evangelical line of preaching and thinking has been strong in Australia since the latter part of the nineteenth century, advocating prohibition, a stop on gambling, and Sunday observance. There was often, especially before Vatican II, a lot of tension between Roman Catholics and Protestants, and this was a factor to take into account in Australian politics: Catholics gravitated to the Labor Party.

New Zealand was settled in a very different manner, by planning. In Christchurch, for instance, an Anglican-style community was settled; and in Otago (capital Dunedin) there was a settlement led by the Scottish Free Church, which was a reforming breakaway from the established Calvinist Church of Scotland. But New Zealand also had its gold rush, in Otago, and for this and other reasons labor became high-priced, and with that the incipient class system broke down. New Zealand had a like system to Australia, with no Church being established, though there were arrangements made for religious education in the schools. New Zealand remained rather sparsely populated, especially in the South Island, and this gave an appearance of relative prosperity, once the export of mutton to Europe became organized.

The chief difference between Australia and New Zealand had to do with the respective fates of the indigenous inhabitants. Although the Maoris came to be deprived of much of their land, they fought bitter wars with the White settlers in the 1860s. Their position was greatly weakened, but in theory they came out of it with equal rights, and partly by leaning on constitutional principle they had by the 1980s greatly improved their position. Many are by now of mixed descent; but those who have Maori descent (up to one-eighth) and wish to be Maori can be so: a point of importance partly because the close physical resemblance between Europeans and Proto-Polynesians makes merging of the races especially easy. At any rate, the Maoris at least were strong enough to fight back, and the two races can exist on a basis of equal respect (though racism of course persists in the White population). In Australia, the Aborigines were too weak and scattered, and too different in habits and culture from the White settlers. They were driven largely out of the richer parts of Australia and concentrated mostly in the north and center of the country. In Tasmania they were deliberately wiped out. Much genocidal activity took place, and many of the Whites refused to regard them as fully human.

Australian Aborigine Religion Today

It is against this rather melancholy background that we have to see the evolution of modern Aborigine religion. This is divided into two or three forms. First there is the indigenous religion of the Dreaming and the sacredness of the land. Second there is mission Christianity of different hues. Then there are some mixes of the two.

One may include in the latter the form of resurgent Aborigine religion during the 1970s and 1980s, when the Aborigines took a more overt and

A Maori wooden carving of an ancestor figure. Ancestor worship is widespread throughout the Polynesian islands, including New Zealand, and the dead and other spirits are included within the bounds of everyday society.

vigorous stance on land rights, in part encouraged by the Australian Labor Party. There is beginning to emerge a pan-Aborigine platform which has some analogies to the Native American movement in the United States. Though Aborigine religions represent a network which in the past covered the great continent in overlapping sacralities and a maze of traveled paths, nevertheless religions were also localized. Under the hammer blows of White culture, Aborigines need unity if they are to survive and gain their relevant rights; and it is from this point of view that we can think of a new pan-Aborigine ideology which is starting to emerge, emphasizing especially the tenderness with which Aborigines view the land and the total environment. There is a tendency for such views to be expressed in modern Western categories, and so to produce a mix of values, of which ecology forms a vital component. But we are only at the beginning of a process of discovering how an Australia-wide movement will shape itself.

It may be added that the concept of the time of the Dreaming is not by itself very well suited to explain change, for it fixes rites and customs in a kind of timelessness which is well suited to those who wish to maintain continuity. But the modern period, since the Aborigines' land was invaded by such potent outsiders, is more one of discontinuities. So far there have been rather few blends and reshapings of the tradition, though one can mention one or two. Thus, on Elcho Island, off the northeast coast, there was started in the late 1950s a movement which synthesized Aborigine ancestors with the prophets taught about in Christianity. More importantly, those who started the movement tried a rather desperate expedient: to make public the traditional secret holy objects. The rationale behind this was that their knowledge could be used to confront and combine with the knowledge displayed by the missionaries and the Whites. Aborigines had been held at a disadvantage by their very initiatory system, which helped to keep their most important powers secret. But of course the desired effect did not occur: outsiders were singularly unimpressed by the putative knowledge displayed. There were signs of adaptation: the holy objects were shown to women for the first time, a recognition that women had important rights not accorded in traditional Aborigine society. But since they were not briefed on the meanings of the objects, their status was still not equal.

The new movement petered out in the face of a strong fundamentalist Christian revival in the area, which has made strong inroads into Aborigine life, with its security, its modernizing methods and its moderate asceticism, important in combating prevalent alcoholism and other social diseases. Indeed, like other forms of Christianity, it often forms a religious net of values to take the place of the shattered webs of the old religion. For one of the effects of contact with Whites has been to alienate many of the young from tradition and to sap the morale of the elders, and through them the whole group. It is in such a situation of cultural disintegration that alcoholism becomes rampant: and one of the cures is a new universe of positive meanings.

In the Western Desert of Australia there have grown up from the 1970s and

1980s new cults which greatly simplify rituals, which are appropriate to mixed groups living in various settlements, which admit women into initiation, and which are somewhat politically active in relation to land rights. None of these has yet taken off to form a viable pan-Aboriginal complex, but no doubt the Aborigines are on the verge of such a new all-embracing reaffirmation of values, helped too by the interpretations of Aborigine religion created by writers on them, such as Mircea Eliade in his *Australian Religions: an Introduction* (1973).

Maori Religious Life After the Coming of the Whites

In the latter part of the nineteenth century a variety of missions were active in the North Island, especially, where most Maoris were concentrated. The result was a great success from the Christian point of view. The Maoris, like the other Polynesians, converted virtually en masse to the new religion. The tradition did not have much resilience. However, two Maori Christian movements did emerge: the Ringatu, which was founded in the 1860s by a Maori warrior turned preacher; and the much more important and vital Ratana movement, named after its founder, who had experienced conversion after grappling with alcoholism. Here was a Maori-controlled Church which could also play a part in the political arena and in the struggle for human dignity and social justice.

There has also in recent times been interest in whether the old Maori religion, though now virtually dead, can supply the materials for the background to Christian faith, that is, as a kind of alternative Old Testament. This move is of course very widespread in differing forms throughout the Third World. The mainstream White-dominated Churches, too, have been open to an egalitarian approach in religious matters: one former Archbishop of New Zealand is a Maori, who became Governor-General (that is, honorific President of the country and representative of the Queen in the Commonwealth system).

Auckland, New Zealand, has also become the largest Polynesian city in the world with an influx of non-Maori Polynesians from the islands, partly because some of these territories were mandated to New Zealand after World War I, and partly because of the relative magnetism of the city. Very traditionalist forms of Christianity prevail—no doubt giving a sense of certainty and rootedness in the flux of immigrant life.

Melanesia and the Cargo Cults

The impact of German, Dutch, Australian, and Japanese rule at different times in New Guinea and outlying islands (where also British and French rule came into play) was great. The emergence, from the 1890s onward, of so-called Cargo cults was a major response. These movements, based essentially on indigenous categories, but often mingled with Christian mythic and eschatological elements, looked to have access to the god or gods who were

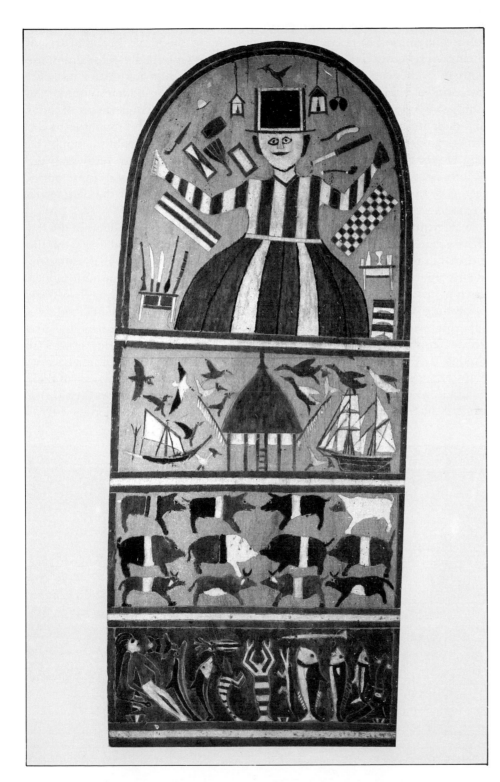

Cargo cults, especially common in Melanesia, are well illustrated in this votive offering from the Nicobar islands in the Bay of Bengal (which have possible linguistic connections with the South Pacific). Here, the white man at the top is surrounded by goods, such as guns, pens, mirrors, etc. The next level shows a hut with a traditional and a Western ship on either side. Further down is traditional currency, namely pigs, and at the bottom, there are various creatures of the sea.

the source of the cargoes brought in by the Europeans. The goods, ranging from canned food to radios, were eye-opening to the locals. In the matrix of their own religious tradition, vegetables and other crops had their origin in the gods: they knew about the god who brought taro to humankind, for instance. By parity of reasoning there must be a transcendental or hidden source of the Europeans' cargoes. World War II helped to increase the wonderment of locals and their amazement at the prodigious supply of everything brought in by the Americans. Again, in terms of their ritual categories it should no doubt be possible for them too to have direct access to the divine source of these. If the Whites denied that there was such a source, or said that the goods came out of factories, no doubt they were dissembling in order to keep the cargoes to themselves.

Sometimes this kind of cult has attracted the amused contempt of the Whites. The idea that you could get lots of baked beans by building symbolic airfields in the New Guinea scrub and by performing various rituals can seem at first sight somewhat ludicrous. But the cults had a deeper meaning not so obvious to the eye of the outside beholder. The canned goods and so forth were only the concrete manifestations of what the locals perceived as a superior power and a greater knowledge. They knew the knowledge was greater, and sometimes therefore thought of the invaders as being gods. But though they knew the knowledge was more powerful, they did not have it, and so they did not know on what basis it rested: how were they, out of their civilizational horizons, to imagine the industrial revolution, the division of labor, Newton's physics, capitalism, and the thought of Adam Smith and J. M.

The old rituals tamed: Fijians perform a wardance in front of a Christian church.

Keynes? The incoming cargoes were signs of power and they tried to have access to it in the only way in which they knew how, by ritual means. After all, their rites worked well enough when it came to taro.

Though the conceptual apparatus of such new religious movements is indigenous, the forms vary, from purely indigenous cults, through Christian versions, to syncretic Christian-indigenous movements. In the process, awareness of tradition becomes self-conscious, and so you can have a fourth kind—the conscious return to tradition, or what may be called neotraditionalism. The importance of rites is marked throughout. In the case of Christian movements, there is emphasis on right behavior as well as the appropriate kind of revivalist services. Sometimes, especially among syncretic movements, people may destroy their own fruits and agricultural products, felling trees and digging out crops. This prepares the way for the millennium: the future myth is important in movements which have been affected strongly by Christianity. The destruction of crops not only smooths the path to a rich future, miraculously brought, but also it represents a great sacrifice, and is a hidden way of repudiating the gods who provided the old fare, in face of the arrival of the new fare.

Like many other new religious movements arising at the point of meeting of small-scale societies and powerful colonial powers, the cargo cults represent a first experiment using the old categories. But they will not be ultimately viable as new religions without a better appreciation of the concepts on the other side of the divide. Here the impact of Western-style education, including higher education at Port Moresby and in the University of the South Pacific in Fiji, is bound to be profound, and may introduce some newer form of syncretic blend. There are signs that this is happening, for instance in the Moro movement on Guadalcanal, which mingles Christian, traditional, and capitalist themes together. This is, so to say, "beyond cargoism," because the leap to the "other side" has been made.

The Pacific Way

It remains true however that the overwhelmingly predominant religion of the Pacific region is Christian, and for the most part Protestant. As we have seen, in many areas conversion was by group and from the top down. This has helped to give stability to societies throughout the region. They are of course mainly very small societies, scattered in islands, from Micronesia to Polynesia. They are thus highly susceptible to the "logic of islands," which is that they are especially vulnerable to outside forces.

Because they are small-scale, and because the modern world is a place of greater amalgamations of economic and organizational forces, it is important for the islanders to combine: and to this end there is a Pacific Forum for the leading politicians of the South Seas, including New Zealand and Australia. This also leads to the question of whether there is some spiritual counterpart to this, and some have written of the "Pacific Way" to represent the values of

Opposite The experiential dimension: an evangelical preacher on Waikiki Beach, Hawaii, hoping to induce conversions.

the region. This Way seeks to incorporate some pre-Christian values; and in some ways it has undertones of revival. Thus it is often thought by people in the region that Northern Christianity has largely lost its way and will be revitalized by the fresher and more vigorous Christianity of the Pacific region. Such people are right, of course, in holding that the center of gravity in Christianity is surely moving south.

With the awakened consciousness of Maoris and Australian Aborigines in the larger southern states, and the welding of a new polity in Papua New Guinea, the region is likely to play an important part in the struggle of small-scale peoples for dignity. The western part of New Guinea was given over to Indonesia, as inheritor of the Dutch empire: this has already begun to spark another national struggle, since colonialism is of course not solely a White preserve. With its blue ocean and lovely islands, its rugged lands and beautiful bush, the South Pacific is a region not without deep problems, but with a call to shape its values to contribute to the welfare of humankind as a whole.

1917 ОКТЯБРЬ 1920

Товарищ! Утроив энергию свою,
Сквозь строй орудий, штыков щетину
Радостно встретим в кровавом бою
Октябрьской Революции Третью годовщину!

Она—залог нашей близкой победы,
Рабами нам больше не быть никогда!
Чрез временные неудачи и беды
Мы шествуем в светлое царство Труда.

Мечем пролетарским сражен издыхая
Дракон империализма разинул пасть...
Советская, федеративная, социалистическая, мировая
Республика—да здравствует ея власть!

Eastern Europe and the Soviet Union

CHAPTER 22

Russia: Expansion and Revolution

The Russians have played an important part in global colonialism, but it is not always noticed because their empire spread across the land; being in the great hinterland behind European Russia (itself vast enough not to be easily grasped by those further to the west), it is often conceived by outsiders in the vaguest possible terms. Even in the late nineteenth century, when Britain, for instance, was much preoccupied by the Russian threat, it was a threat which moved south from Central Asia toward India and in the direction of the warm waters of the Arabian Sea. The great extent of Russian advance to the east into Siberia was little comprehended. And in the twentieth century, when other colonial powers have been on the defensive, the Russian empire, suitably modernized and reshaped as the Soviet Union, scarcely seems to count as a colonial power at all.

By the end of the seventeenth century, virtually all of Siberia was in Russian hands. The vast territories were fairly thinly occupied by various Siberian peoples such as the Yakuts and the Tunguz. In Central Asia, the drive south had begun, and by 1900 Russia was up against the frontiers of Persia and Afghanistan, having subdued the Kazakhs, Uzbeks, and Tadjiks, together with several other peoples. By 1800, moreover, their drive through the Ukraine to the Black Sea and the Crimea was complete, and in Odessa they built an important harbor. There were to be more gains in the late nineteenth and early twentieth century at the expense of China, but the basic shape of Russia had formed. It was this empire which the Bolsheviks were to take over.

It had in the meantime been modernizing—through for instance the abolition of serfdom in 1861; the building of great railways, including the Trans-Siberian, started in 1891; the opening up of mineral and industrial development; and the consolidation of large towns, from St. Petersburg to the

Opposite The new Saint George: a Marxist ikon slaying the dragon of capitalism.

A crowd of farmers celebrating the anniversary of the foundation of Rural Solidarity, their free union, and giving the V for Victory sign outside Warsaw Cathedral.

Urals. Russia was on the brink of great economic advances in 1914; but the rigid bureaucracy and centralized Tsardom were unable eventually to cope with the hammer blows of war. Liberal revolution in 1917 was swiftly followed by the Bolshevik seizure of power and the beginning of the Russian Revolution under the initial guidance of Vladimir Ilyich Lenin (1870–1924). In due course the direction of the revolution was taken over by Joseph Stalin (1879–1953), who took the path of "Socialism in one country"; he collectivized agriculture, promoted intense industrialization at a headlong pace through various five-year plans, erected the apparatus of a thorough police State, and pursued for the most part a policy of suppressing religion. After World War II, which Stalin prosecuted with overwhelming, ultimate success, Soviet armies controlled most of Eastern Europe, and the Marxism which he espoused was imposed on Poland, East Germany, Hungary, Romania, and Bulgaria; but not on Yugoslavia and Albania, which had not in the same way been occupied by Soviet forces. But in all of them Marxism became the State ideology, often in place of a previous State religion.

Varieties of Marxism

The Stalinist model, though much criticized since Stalin's death, was long regarded as the pattern wherein a Communist State should be developed and organized. The Yugoslav and Albanian parties provided initial alternative modes of operating in the European context. Albania pursued a policy of strong isolationism with an alliance with the Chinese for a period, as a counterweight to Soviet power. It laid claim to be the only fully atheist State in the world, having crushed Islam, which was the majority faith, as well as Christianity. Its claim was scarcely true, since religion survived even in such an oppressive environment, as also in Muslim parts of the Soviet empire, through the clandestine work of Sufi orders and by other means. In Yugoslavia the chief preoccupation was with maintaining the unity of its federation of diverse peoples. But it also experimented with a nonaligned Communism and close commercial relations with the West.

The varying patterns of the period that followed World War II in part reflect the ways in which religion is present in the different countries. Poland is a dominantly Catholic country, the more so after the terrors of the Holocaust which wiped out virtually all of Poland's large prewar Jewish population. Also the move of the boundary westward has meant that the Ukrainian part, with its Orthodox and Uniate (that is, Vatican-affiliated Orthodox) populations, was absorbed in the Soviet Union. Poland is thus monolithically Catholic. Before the War the Catholicism often was right-wing politically; but in the events of the 1970s, culminating in the Solidarnosc or Solidarity movement, it has taken up roughly a social democratic posture. Though Solidarity is not itself a Church organization and is keen to demonstrate its independence and religious openness in practice, there is a great overlap between it and the Church, and often it is at or after Masses that important meetings and rallies

Map 19 Eastern Europe after the collapse of the Soviet Empire.

took place, under the leadership among others of Lech Waleska, a pious churchman.

The strength of this ultimately successful attempt to achieve independence for Poland was reinforced by the election of Cardinal Karol Wojtyla (b. 1920) as Pope John Paul II, the first Polish Pope, and the first non-Italian for nearly five hundred years, in 1978. The Polish Church has survived and indeed flourished while on the whole maintaining a conservative stance in matters of doctrine and ethics, but its social policy has converged with those who have wanted a more genuinely democratic way of running the unions and beyond that the State.

The other East European country where religion flourished is Romania, but the faith here is primarily Orthodoxy (though there is a substantial minority of Catholics among the Hungarians of Transylvania). After initial persecution in the 1950s and 1960s the Church had considerable financial support from the State, during the regime especially of Nicolae Ceausescu (1918–89) from 1966 onward. Romania was independent somewhat from the Soviet Union, but in a way very different from Poland. In the latter country the government and the party had great problems keeping a lid on popular movements from below. In Romania there was a somewhat independent foreign policy, but it was imposed from above. Romania was run in a rather Stalinist manner, with centralized planning and the pervasive presence of the secret police, to keep the population in line. But because the regime emphasized nationalism and the glories of the Romanian heritage, and because the Church played such an historic role in keeping alive the Romanian tongue and Romanian national identity during the Ottoman period, it was useful and possible to let the Church flourish. It was also a safety valve: the gleam of heaven could distract people from the rigors of earth.

However, the official ideology of the regime was still Scientific Socialism, as it is called, and party members, teachers, and other professionals were not expected to attend Church nor were they expected to be members of congregations. Religious dissent was banned. You could not convert a person from one religion to another, and the system was closely watched by the relevant ministry in Bucharest. Baptists and other wandering evangelists were dealt with severely.

The Contribution of Eliade

Romania, as it has happened, produced the most important religious intellectual to come out of Eastern Europe since World War II, Mircea Eliade (1907–86). As a precocious and brilliant young scholar in prewar Romania he plunged into Renaissance studies and from there branched out into Oriental learning, for he went to India and studied at the feet of India's best-known historian of philosophy, Surendranath Dasgupta (1885–1952) from 1928 to 1932. It was there that he began his work on yoga. But on his return to Romania he engaged in a wide range of literary activity, from scholarly works

Opposite Secular ritual: Stalin replaces the Christmas star; from the cover of *Ogonek* magazine.

to novels. He saw the consonance between varieties of folk religion the world over, and sought a new humanism which would do justice to the universal archetypes and symbols which well up from the human unconscious cross-culturally. He was in some ways a Romanian populist, seeking salvation among the peasantry whose intuitive knowledge and values were of the widest human significance. He therefore was not distant from the Romanian right wing and the so-called Iron Guard, part of which later collaborated with the Nazis. During World War II he was in the Romanian diplomatic service, and after the occupation of his country he stayed in exile. Between 1945 and 1955 he wrote his major works, and in 1957 he became a professor in Chicago and extended his influence widely over the American continent.

His orientation was Orthodox, a religion which combined the eternal values of human archetypal religion and the Christian break with timelessness and the plunge into the historical process. In a way all his writings, even those that seem on the surface the most detached and scholarly, are aimed at a kind of redemption in which something is done to remedy the exile which deprives us of the saving symbols.

Democratic Socialism as an Alternative

In Poland in 1980 (with the formation of Solidarity), in Hungary in the revolution of 1956, and in Czechoslovakia in 1968, there were spontaneous movements which can be represented as the demand for "Socialism with a human face," or in other words democratic Socialism. They were crushed by the reality or threat of Soviet tanks. These impulses combined nationalism and the desire for freedom in ordinary life, both of which were conspicuously crushed by the regimes imposed after World War II by Stalin.

Czechoslovakia had been a democracy before the war, so there was some rootage of these desires in nostalgia: before the cruel events of the Nazi and then the Communist regimes there existed something of a golden age for the well-organized Czechs. But the other States had been politically right-wing. Indeed, the prevalence of such thinking in Poland, Hungary, Romania, Yugoslavia, and Bulgaria was a reflection of the nationalism which had been given free rein by the Treaty of Versailles. It was very much a charter for a new, nationally oriented Eastern Europe. These more rampant forms of national politics lent themselves ultimately to takeover by a hard-line regime from Moscow which was bent on making Eastern Europe an extension of its empire. Meanwhile, however, Catholicism had become politically more mature in Western Europe through its espousal of a new and moderate Christian democracy, and to some degree therefore became the bearer of democratic ideals in the East. The Orthodox Church in the countries of Bulgaria, Romania, and Yugoslavia used its experience under the Muslim Ottomans to bow its head and weather the storms of Communist rule.

Thus throughout the whole of Eastern Europe and in the Soviet Union, the

Communist Party in effect became the true Church. Those who wished to gain promotion and do well in life, and to take part in the ruling of the country, needed to join. Citizens had to subscribe to the official ideology. And so it is that instead of the old Lutheran arrangement whereby the ruler's religion is made into that of the subjects, according to the old tag of *cuius regio eius religio*, we now have *cuius regio eius ideologia*, "Of whom the rule, of that person the ideology." It is only because we tend to draw a line, rather arbitrarily, between religions and ideologies that we did not notice how the old Protestant–Catholic carve-up was repeated in a new form in Eastern Europe.

The Eastern bloc countries were not pluralist. Marxism became the *de rigueur* religion, which is yet other than religion, much as State Shinto was entrenched in the Japanese Constitution before World War II. But even that was less pervasive, because it had no doctrines: now in Marxist countries there was an attempt to make the official line a set of ideas which has to be internalized. So the religion began to reach down into academic life, science, the arts, and every intellectual activity.

The Anti-religious crusade: ikons being carried away in 1930.

527

Religion in the Soviet Union

The European End

We have already in Chapter 20 noted some of the vicissitudes of Islam in the Soviet Union: and we shall a little later on say something about the position of small-scale religions in Siberia, both before and after Soviet predominance. Meanwhile let us look briefly at the situation in European Russia, amid the traditional Christian Churches and other groups. The Revolution itself in 1917 altered the picture greatly, since all private property was nationalized and this included the landholdings of the Orthodox Church. Religious education was at the same time banned. But it was not until 1929, during a period when peasant and religious resistance to the new measures of collectivization was at its height, that the severest restriction was placed on religion: the only right which a religious organization had was to conduct worship.

In 1926 the League of the Militant Godless had been set up, which carried on vigorous propaganda against religion. It charged that traditional religion was unscientific because it rejected Evolutionary Theory and thought that God was in the sky, and so forth (this was more an attack on literalism than anything). It also charged that traditional religion was right-wing politically and anti-revolutionary. It was superstitious, corrupt, manipulated by priests, hypocritical, and so on. Meanwhile, campaigns to close churches or turn them into grain stores, museums of atheism, and the like were vigorously pursued, so that the number of buildings still operative and the number of priests declined by up to ninety percent by World War II.

However, World War II posed new problems. Many Russians thought of Holy Russia as the focus of their loyalty. The Orthodox Church particularly had in its bones a nationalism which Stalin had need of. There were memories of Russian Orthodox beating off attacks by Teutonic Knights and Polish Catholic chauvinists. So for patriotic reasons, Stalin allowed the Churches greater latitude, and this period of greater relaxation lasted until about 1956.

But the Uniate Churches of Belorussia and the Ukraine were forcibly suppressed and had to merge with the Orthodox: in other words they had to renounce their ties to the Vatican. The Catholic Church always had the stigma of being a translational organization, and so its adherents were therefore looked on with suspicion as being possibly unpatriotic. So, too, Judaism was seen as an international faith. Generally speaking nonpracticing Jews have been able to do reasonably well within the structures of Soviet society (despite a beginning of pogrom in the last days of Stalin). But practicing Jews have had great obstacles placed in their path. Persecution has been the norm, with, however, a certain proportion being granted exit visas to go to Israel. Also, toleration, such as it is, has never been extended to the evangelists of Baptists and other Protestant organizations. The wandering and underground evangelical Christians are subject to severe persecution because they break the

Soviet norms. These imply a publicly controlled and evident form of religious organization.

The leaders of the official Churches have had to walk a tightrope in trying to keep the limited independence of their flocks and at the same time to adhere to the official Soviet line in world affairs. All these remarks apply not only to the mainstream Russian groups but also to national minority Churches such as the ancient Armenian Church.

The Small-Scale Religions of Siberia

The Russian spread eastward had its profound effects, of course, on the peoples of the vast regions of Siberia. European contact, as elsewhere, could spell disease. Many of the peoples were subject to Orthodox missionary activity. The 1917 Revolution had rather ambiguous effects. The Bolshevik ideology was sympathetic to these peoples as the objects of prior Tsarist repression. The Communists were keen on the expression of national sentiment through folklore, the language, indigenous art, and so on. On the other hand, they were opposed to religion and wished to impose a Marxist ideology on these peoples. Part of the problem was how to detach folklore and the like from religion.

Some customs, such as that of the domestic hearth, can survive in the new conditions of Soviet society. In the Soviet Far East there are still evidences of shamanism among the Tunguz people, while the Buryats have effected some kind of synthesis of Buddhism, shamanism, and Marxism, retaining thus a mélange of customs in the life of the State farms and collectives. (In some respects the collective character of Soviet agricultural life helped the identity of tribal groups.) As elsewhere, much of the older shamanic worldview persists, sometimes disguised in Orthodox language – where Christianity and indigenous religions have merged – and sometimes by itself.

In more recent times Soviet anthropologists made more sympathetic investigations of Siberian religions and uncovered a much greater survival of religious ideas than had been thought. Here again, Soviet atheism was not an all-conquering force.

Soviet Atheism

Atheism did, however, represent an important branch of the human array of worldviews. Probably we can say that Marxist atheism was the most important of the various worldviews of the Soviet Union, and despite the vigor of traditional religions in Eastern Europe it still had an important following there too. For many it expressed revolt against the corruptions of the older world which the Revolution replaced. Admittedly much unnecessary suffering occurred after the Revolution; but nevertheless the Communist system had its achievements, and so could express in its own way a sense of Soviet and in particular Russian patriotism. Despite a lot of disillusion with the system, it would not have worked if it were not for the fact that Soviet-style Marxist

Crowds lining up to see Lenin lying in state, 1924.

atheism did represent a worldview to which many citizens could be loyal, no doubt with many critical qualifications. Let us sketch briefly this worldview in its dimensions.

Doctrinally, scientific Marxism persuasively puts a form of materialism at the center. It has two important characteristics. First, it is not a crude materialism in saying that conscious events and mental products are simply material: they are derived from the material, but their existence can and does have important reflexive effects on the material world, ranging from the way my mental state may affect the health of my body to the manner in which revolutionary consciousness may build up the material production of society. This materialism is also highly dynamic, containing its contradictions which, so to say, propel it into motion. Lenin could argue that this inescapable dynamism is what gives the universe its independent life and so causes us to dispense with the idea of an outside God who imparts motion to the cosmos.

In terms of *mythic* history, the Soviet system had a crucial part to play in the whole pattern of events which will ultimately issue in world revolution and the achievement of universal human social justice. The Revolution of 1917 was the forerunner of others, and so countries such as China should recognize the seniority of the Soviet example.

In the *ethical* dimension, the Soviet system in eliminating unemployment achieved great social justice which was not evident in the capitalist countries, still less in the colonialized peoples of the Third World. The lack of certain individual rights was unimportant beside the great steps that were made in Marxist countries to give workers a dignity and status that they had not had before. The new Soviet person was hardworking, cultured, forward-looking, and devoted to science and to the realization of Marxist ideals.

In the *ritual* dimension, the Marxist rejected the old mumbo-jumbo, but there were the courtesies and ceremonies of the new State. In the pilgrimage to the tomb of Lenin, the rites of Marxism merged imperceptibly into those of the nation-State. As to the *material* dimension of the new order: Soviet art was supposed to reflect the nature of the new society, and so was rather iconographical, showing the heroisms of daily life and achievements of the party and State. With a shining and luminous kind of literalism, it may not figure greatly as art; but like religious painting it was meant to inspire. Similarly, the great writers were supposed to be Social Realists; although it happens that most critical opinion favors the achievements of the dissident writer, the Soviets found no way to regiment great art into existence. Their great musicians, Prokofiev and Shostakovich, managed to survive the system since their craft was less easily controllable. But the achievements of the material dimension were also to be seen in hydroelectric power, rocket technology, factories, and all the buildings and inventions which can be ascribed to the Soviet State.

All this adds up to a still credible worldview. Often it was this worldview which was the focus of criticism, but often too, the criticism itself started from within the worldview. It is not to be neglected as a major form of atheism in today's world, and its variations are held in Beijing, Pyongyang, and Havana. *Organizationally*, Marxism remains strongly embedded in China, North Korea, Vietnam, and Cuba.

In Western countries the Marxist strand is often carried on in a very vigorous (and sometimes very intolerant) way by those who follow that stormy petrel and theoretician of the Revolution, the great hero of the early Red Army, Leon Trotsky (1897–1940). His more fluid account of revolution attracted many in the West who were disillusioned by the heavy centralism and bureaucratic sluggishness of the Soviet system.

Finally, it was fairly obvious to Soviet sociologists as well as to outside observers that religions by no means withered away in the Soviet State. The modern intellectuals of the Soviet Union had by no means always conformed to Marxist orthodoxy; and the two most vital of recent writers, Boris Pasternak (1890–1960) and Alexander Solzhenitsyn (b. 1918), expressed an Orthodox viewpoint in the face of militant atheism. Even Buddhism, which was the religion most heavily hit, seemed to have staying power. Statistics

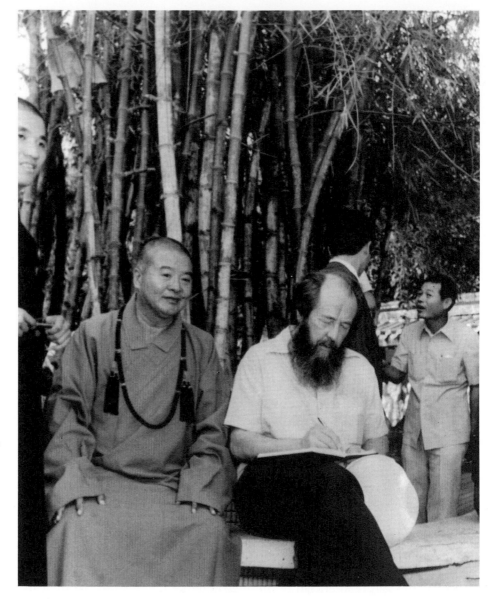

Alexander Solzhenitsyn (b.1918) visits a Buddhist temple in Taiwan after his exile from the Soviet Union in 1974 for his exposure of the labor camps in his native country. The spirituality of Russian Orthodoxy has something cognate with Mahāyāna Buddhist faith.

varied, but as many as twenty percent of European Soviet citizens continued to attend churches. As we saw in regard to Islam, the rate of belief remained very high indeed.

The Collapse of the Soviet Union and Subsequent Events

The collapse of the Marxist system in Eastern Europe, Central Asia, Russia, and Siberia was effectively complete by 1991. The Soviet Union simply disintegrated. Mikhail Gorbachev (b. 1931) came into power in 1985, and his reforms led to greater openness, which in turn revealed the sheer inefficiency and dreariness of the old system. Marxism lost its persuasiveness: many saw that seventy years of revolution, coercion, and central planning yielded largely bitter fruits. The two forces which had been at all productive were the defense industry and establishment on the one had and the propaganda enterprise on the other. Moreover, the system had suppressed the various nationalisms which were bound to arise in such a variegated overland empire as the Soviet Union's; and also in Eastern Europe. These were ready to reemerge in the late 1980s and the 1990s. They were accompanied by the reinvigoration of religions. The two combined in part through the role played by a Polish Pope, John Paul II (b. 1920), in the resurgence of Polish nationalism and in due course the destruction of the Berlin Wall, which had helped to keep the Eastern nations in thrall.

In general the former Soviet dependencies in Eastern Europe eventually adopted democratic forms of government—Poland, the Czech Republic, Hungary, Lithuania, Latvia, Estonia, Romania, Bulgaria, Albania, Ukraine, Slovakia; though Belorussia remained unreformed. Georgia, Armenia, and Azerbaijan in the Caucasus underwent wars and civil wars. The Central Asian states of Turkmenistan, Uzbekistan, Kyrgyzstan, and Kazakhstan became independent, with varying forms of dictatorships, but Islam was largely rehabilitated after its long period of suppression. In Chechnya a war supervened on the demise of the Soviet era, fueled in part by Muslim resistance to Russian rule.

Partly because the Soviet (and before it the Russian) Empire was an overland affair there is a tendency to ignore the fact that the period from 1989 onward was one of decolonialization. As elsewhere, religion played a significant role in this. Since it was an important element in each nation's tradition it combined with nationalism to form a powerful force replacing the Marxist ideology which had been dominant. In Eastern Europe various kinds of Christianity played their part; in Azerbaijan and Central Asia, it was Islam; in Mongolia, Buddhism. Meanwhile, Muslim guerrillas played a large part in the defeat of Soviet troops in Afghanistan: they evacuated the country in 1988.

Religion also was important in the break-up of Yugoslavia. Croatia and Serbia shared much of a common heritage and language: but Croatia is Catholic and Serbia is Orthodox. From 1991 the countries fought a bitter civil war. This was complicated by the disintegration of Bosnia-Herzegovina. There a third force, the Muslims, who under Tito's rule had been recognized as a separate nationality, were drawn into a three-way conflict. Substantially, the three ethnic groups were differentiated by religion. South of Serbia the region of Kosovo is peopled by Albanians (many Muslim), who are largely repressed by their Serbian rulers. The Balkans are an explosive area because minorities are found in many areas, and in an age of nationalism this leads to instability.

Russia itself emerged from the Soviet era with regions of possible conflict. There are Islamic enclaves of quite substantial size, such as Tatarstan, with its capital at Kazan, some 560 miles [900 kilometers] east of Moscow, and

Bashkiristan, in the South West Urals. There are many such pockets huge and small, with foreign ethnic populations, scattered within the fabric of the Russian Federation. The dominant Orthodox faith is affected by minority and evangelical groups which have made headway in the recent period. But the attitudes of the hierarchy are not pluralist, and there are attempts to impose a uniform religious education.

One should inquire as to why it was that Marxism failed, and so spectacularly and suddenly. First, it was an orthodoxy which was imposed by a heavy system of police, censorship, and propaganda. Often it ran up against the nationalisms of the peoples on whom it was imposed. The system was a centralist one, and in effect was a Russian system, so minority peoples felt oppressed. Moreover, the cruelties inflicted by Stalin were horrendous: he was responsible for many more deaths than even Hitler; and his prison system, immortalized by Alexander Solzhenitsyn in his novel *The Gulag Archipelago*, was extraordinary and vast. Even after his death, the regime remained oppressive. From time to time Soviet tanks had to be called in—in East Berlin, in Hungary, in Czechoslovakia and in Azerbaijan—and they left a trail of bitterness.

It is, interestingly enough, odd that even after the facts of Stalin's oppression became well known and after the glories of the Soviet fight against the Nazis were over, intellectuals who supported the Soviet system in the West were never castigated to the degree that those who supported Fascism were. The Communist tradition was more rigorously totalitarian than Hitler's Germany, and was more comprehensive in its manipulation of the truth.

Because of its centralist rigidity it was on the whole massively incompetent, and its scant regard for the interests of the consumer led it to a bleakness of life which its high-flown rhetoric did little to allay. If we look back on the dimensions of Soviet atheism we may moreover perceive why it could dissolve so rapidly.

Doctrinally, the dynamic materialism it displayed remained plausible; but there was no reason why spiritual forces in the world should be so neglected, nor was there any need to neglect alternative beliefs, such as those of Buddhism. While the system was represented as scientific, developments such as those of modern physics could be thought to contradict a straightforward materialism, such as that of Lenin. Also, the mythic sense of the centrality of the Soviet Union in revolutionary history wore thin, with the history of errors and oppressions since 1917.

Ethically, while the Communist ideal was fine, in practice there was no justice in an arrangement where the party functionaries lived like lords and the ordinary citizens scraped along, and where millions were locked up as slaves.

Perhaps it is in the *ritual* dimension that the greatest weaknesses appeared. While churches and mosques and synagogues were closed or restricted in their activities, depriving folk of the traditional color of ritual life, the rites of passage in a Communist society, such as weddings and funerals, were austere, and public holidays often celebrated abstractions. The warmth which gives significance to individual and family life was often lacking from the State's rituals; and the glorification of work could be oppressive.

This was linked to the fact that the Marxist system had no place for the *experiential* dimension of religion, beyond perhaps the emotions of patriotism. The inner poetry of living, the sense of the numinous, the strong sense of love—these were largely meaningless within the framework of Soviet philosophy. No wonder protest and dissent were found among artists and writers. In the background Russians could look back to their great authors, such as Dostoyevsky, Tolstoy, and Bulgakov.

The *material* dimension of Soviet Marxism is typified by the wedding-cake architecture that Stalin loved, and the utilitarian blocks of flats marching across the urban landscape. Socialist realism was scarcely experimental: and the variety which a rich artistic life can produce was singularly absent. In this, maybe, it mimicked the traditionalism of Orthodoxy.

And so, in the end, the Soviet system had little appeal. Its defects were not simply those of a command economy, but pervaded the living dimensions of the Marxist State. One of its main effects was the privatization of personal and family life. The strong ties that bound individuals together were a product of the spying and surveillance which demanded that you should trust only an intimate circle. And even then, as later turned out from the records of the Stasi (the State Police in East Germany), some friends and family still might betray you.

But beyond 1991 and the collapse of the system, something similar still persisted in China, North Korea, Vietnam, and Cuba. In China, however, different conditions developed: a greater freedom in the economy and a loosening up in regard to religions gave a certain ease, though adherence to the rule of the Communist Party was required.

CHAPTER 23

Africa in the Modern World

The European Impact

The Slave Trade

In 1800 Africa was still substantially unaffected by foreign conquest. There were some Portuguese trading posts on the coast, and some other settlements of European powers involved in the slave trade. There were Dutch farmers and settlers, not to mention Indonesians imported by them for labor, around the Cape, and British influence there was about to expand. But the great bulk of Black Africa retained its traditional powers and social patterns.

In a number of areas social life was disrupted by the slave trade, carried on by various Western nations and also substantially by the Arabs, especially in East Africa and across the Sahara. The profits of the trade were great. Its origin lay in plantations, of tobacco, sugar, and later cotton, which became vital ingredients of the economy of the New World—in Brazil, in the Caribbean, and in North America. Over ten million slaves arrived in these and other territories, mainly from Senegambia and the Gold Coast, but also from East Africa, and in the nineteenth century from Madagascar and Mozambique. The numbers of arriving slaves (for many, maybe up to thirty percent, perished in the crossing) were about a million and a half each for Spanish America, the British Caribbean, and French America; a bit over three and a half million for Brazil; half a million for Dutch America; four hundred thousand for British North America and the United States combined; and something under two hundred thousand for Europe. It was a great movement of human beings for those days. Its effects in West and Southwest Africa were by no means negligible, and it left a quite new stamp on the cultures of the American South, the Caribbean, and Brazil particularly. Reflexively it affected Africa because many of the new ideas which underlay the independence movements in Africa came from across the seas in the New World.

In some degree the religious effects of slavery were deeply shaped by whether the importing culture was Catholic or Protestant. If it was Catholic, as in Haiti and Brazil, then it was possible in some degree to integrate African religions with the cult of saints. On the other hand, in Protestant North America saints were disapproved; and it had to be in other ways that African values were brought into the practice of Christianity. The ritual of baptism, the idea of being possessed by God, and the imagery of spirituals were ways of expressing a mixed culture. In North America the increase in the population was predominantly natural, rather than by the importation of successive waves of slaves, and this brought distance from the African experience. Of course, elements of folklore and music would persist and enter into creative synthesis with White culture.

Catholicism, in providing a more hospitable context for the transmission of African religious values, also helped to create new religions, to which we shall return in the next chapter.

The Settlement of South Africa

In 1652 the Dutch East Indies Company, wishing to establish a staging post for the resupply of ships on the way to the East Indies, started a small base at the Cape of Good Hope. The settlement became Cape Town. At first there was no thought of a colony. But, as Dutch settlers came and undertook farming, the occupied zone was gradually extended beyond the bounds of Cape Town into the wild areas beyond. By the late eighteenth century the farmers had extended as far as the Kei river.

The British took over the Cape as a result of the Napoleonic wars, and later sent a substantial number of settlers to Natal. The Dutch-speaking farmers (or Boers) engaged in wars beyond the Kei, along the Fish River, and became at the same time greatly annoyed by what they thought of as outside interference, especially with the missionary lobby urging the abolition of slavery. In 1835 the Boers began the movement known as the Great Trek, and in due course occupied the regions known as the Orange Free State and the Transvaal, which became independent republics. Meanwhile the genius of Shaka (1787?–1832) had welded together a new nation, the Zulus, with whom the Boers and later the British came into collision. Their defeat in 1879 brought British control over the whole of Natal.

The British now faced two wars with the Boers, the second very bitter, from 1899 to 1902. The Boers were incensed by the methods by which the British confined their women and children in concentration camps—the origin of the term—and by the destruction of their homesteads and farms. Their revenge was to work away politically within the new State which the British set up in 1910, comprising Transvaal, the Orange Free State, Natal, and the Cape Province. Britain's interest in the first two was gold and diamonds. The vision of Cecil Rhodes (1853–1902) had seen British rule stretching from the Cape to Cairo. The South African system in fact extended somewhat into Rhodesia, though this stayed a separate colony (later it was renamed Zimbabwe, after the massive ruins of a prior African culture).

By 1948 the Boers (now Afrikaners) had gained power democratically within the chiefly White electorate, and began to implement the policy of separateness or *apartheid*. That is, they tried to separate as far as possible the different races, namely Black, so-called Colored (or mixed race), Asian, and White. The assumption of White control and superiority was at best thinly veiled. This system greatly deprives Blacks of educational, business, and other opportunities, and rests in part on an ideology of separateness entangled in Dutch Reformed Church theology.

This theology was Calvinist. The Afrikaners derived part of their Calvinism from their Dutch heritage, but there was also a good infusion of French Huguenot religious refugees, who added strong commitment to the traditional beliefs. In addition after the Trek—which had not, by the way, been much approved by the Church, and the Trekkers had no ministers with them—Scottish Calvinist ministers worked in South Africa with the Boers. Calvinism preached predestinationism and encouraged the Afrikaners to believe that they were a chosen people, who modeled their life and warfare on that of the ancient Israelites. Their defeat of the Zulus at the battle of Blood River in 1838 they saw as due to divine help, and made a covenant to remember the day ever afterward. They thought their own culture to be unique and free, and they did not want contamination from other races. All this was welded into a powerful myth for their edification; but it also justified racial superiority and the system in which the Black and Colored populations, plus the Asians (Indians and others, mainly in Natal), would have a much lesser stake in South Africa than the Whites. Later we shall see some of the Black reactions to all this.

The Colonial Scramble

The early settlement of South Africa preceded the main colonial conquest of African territories. Much of the initiative in this came from the French, who stimulated the British to rival action. The Germans and Belgians also put their hands into the tub. The partition of Africa was virtually complete by 1900. It remained for the Italians to take over Libya and the French and Spaniards to divide Morocco between them. Only Ethiopia remained free, having seriously defeated the Italians at Adowa in 1896. Germany lost her share of Africa after World War I; Tanganyika was taken over by the British and Namibia (Southwest Africa) by South Africa.

In 1881 the Mahdi, a messianic leader, mixing Islamic eschatology and the politics of revolt, had started his struggle in the Sudan, then under Egyptian control, and the British intervened. But in 1885 Khartoum fell and General Gordon (1833–85) was killed; it was not till 1898 that the Mahdi was crushed at the Battle of Omdurman, when Egypt and Britain jointly took over the Sudan as a condominium.

The scramble for Africa grew out of European rivalries. The boundaries were drawn for the most part without any regard to the linguistic and cultural divisions of the continent. When Africa became decolonized in the 1950s and

1960s these boundaries were held by the Organization for African Unity to be sacrosanct (mainly because of their absurdity: call one into question and the whole house of cards might come tumbling down). The successor States have had to fashion their myths of identity as best they can.

The Penetration of Christianity into Black Africa

Undoubtedly the greatest change to come over the African continent, and that was primarily in the twentieth century, was the massive spread of Christianity. It is now the majority religion of Black Africa. One might at some preceding stage have expected that Islam would become the dominant faith. It has indeed made some progress, but rather small compared with that of Christianity.

In the eighteenth century, apart from the relatively few Christians around the coasts where Europeans had settled or established trading posts, there was little Christianity at all, except in the ancient kingdom of Ethiopia. But toward the end of the century Christian opponents of the slave trade arranged for a group of emancipated slaves of African origin to be settled in Sierra Leone, at Freetown, and thirty years later a college, Fourah Bay College, was set up, to be Africa's first modern institution of higher education. It became a center for the spread of Christianity, as Black missionaries went out into the region. The most important of these was a Yoruba, from what is now Nigeria, Samuel Ajayi Crowther (1809?–91), who became Anglican Bishop on the Niger.

Already before the main partition of Africa missionaries were making progress, though the most famous White missionary in Africa, David Livingstone (1813–73), was more successful as an explorer than as a winner of souls (he only converted one person, who fell away). But during the colonial period there was especially strong activity in the translation of the Bible into vernacular languages, and this had a powerful influence on people. Christianity and education were closely connected, not just because in fact so many schools were run by missionaries, but because African societies saw the need for modernizing—if only often intuitively—and school was the main agency for this. And more than this: Christianity did supply something to rely on in a period of sudden and disturbing change. As classical African religion wilted, so Christianity provided an alternative.

The Bible seems to have had great potency. The missionaries were rather short-handed, and made much use of local catechists who were often poorly trained. But they could carry the Bible around with them: for most Africans the first and often the only book in their own language that they knew. Its power was the more numinous in that it could bring forth the very sounds of language—it was a miraculous score from which the person who could read could play a wonderful set of musical pieces. Also, its themes rang true to the African condition. It spoke of circumcision; of the witch of Endor; of Mount Carmel and the contest in rainmaking; of prophecy, healing, and the sufferings of the people of Israel. With much of this the Black African could easily identify.

Opposite A float at the carnival in Rio de Janeiro, Brazil, a festival held each year in the five days preceding Lent. (see Chapter 24).

As has happened at other times and places in Christian history the Bible was at odds with perceived practice. It had revolutionary potential. The mission Churches were almost completely in the control of Whites until the end of the 1950s; and it was not surprising if many Blacks saw in this some contradiction with the spirit of the Gospel. Part of the expression of Black resentment at injustices was found in the independent Churches, which proved to be so potent a phenomenon in most of Black Africa. It should on the other hand be noted that many missionaries supported independence movements. Still, there was until the 1960s a feeling of paternalism which was pervasive. Vatican II on the Catholic side, and various revolutionary changes "back home" among Protestants, altered this picture.

The Mainstream Churches in Black Africa

In virtually all of Africa, Catholicism has come to be the majority religion, and not only in territories formerly colonized by, say, France or Portugal. But it is, in most areas, very short of priests. Similarly, Protestant Churches are short of trained people. The result is that much of African Christianity follows on with the use of catechists, as in the days of the missionaries. This has meant that even when the Whites were in control at the top, at the bottom things were more fluid and not easy to keep a strict eye on. The strength of the system is that it leaves much of the work of the laity, and so it engenders a lot of active piety. Increasingly the leadership has become Black, with six African Cardinals. South Africa, with many White Anglicans and Catholics, has Black Church leaders, Archbishop Desmond Tutu, of Cape Town, being the best known example. Such figures have begun to play leading roles in Church policy-making through ecumenical and other global organizations.

Some differing strands of thought are evident in these Churches. On the one hand there is a greater interest in Liberation Theology, because of the struggle in South Africa and also elsewhere, insofar as the Churches are concerned with global injustices and a possible Marxist analysis both of how things are and of what should be done. More conservatively, there is interest in an African theology, which is the effort to make use of classical African categories in the statement of Christianity. It is the attempt to see in indigenous ideas something of a forerunner of the Gospel, and so to find in them an alternative or a supplement to the Old Testament. Some make the distinction between African theology and Black theology, the latter being a version of Liberation Theology.

The Notion of Africanness: A Modern Phenomenon

It is notable that much of African and Black theology is based on the sense that there is a common African or Black experience. This was scarcely true before the colonial period. The lack of communications in many areas, the divisions of language, the lack of a living "other" to promote a sense of solidarity among Blacks—these and many other factors worked against any unitary vision of Africa. It was above all through the colonial experience, and

The social dimension: the churches play a notable role in both sides of the South African struggle. Here Bishop Desmond Tutu, later Anglican Archbishop of Cape Town, addresses a press conference about a government ban on a conference on religion and peace.

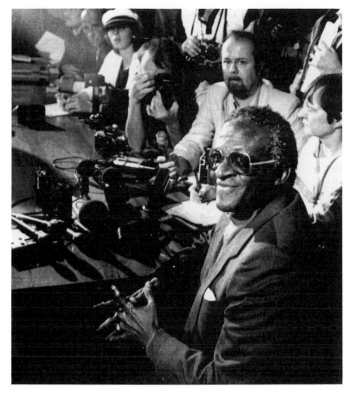

the growing realization of the nature of Black history and the sufferings and contempt so often lavished on Africans, that such a new sense of identity grew.

This is where of course the contributions of the Churches are ambiguous, for the fact of the matter is that many missionaries came to Africa with an ideology which was something like this: the Africans are inferior; they need Christianity and civilization; the means to this will be conversion and education; and then the African will be able to take his place proudly with the White person. Images were projected of "darkest Africa," and European and American readers thrilled to pursue the voyages and hardships of Livingstone or the adventures of the ebullient H. M. Stanley (1844–1904). Africans were represented as savages, sometimes noble no doubt.

These images have not gone away: though racism is everywhere to be found, it is especially strong against the Blacks. So it was not unnatural that, with self-consciousness, Africans should seek to define an African identity. A major contribution in this was the school of writers, somewhat under the stimulus of Jean-Paul Sartre (1905–1980) and Leopold Sedar Sengthor (b. 1906), who defined Négritude.

It was in the same milieu of a more embracing consciousness that indeed conceptions of African religion as a whole emerged. Thus in 1945 a Franciscan, Placide Tempels (1906-77), published his *La Philosophie bantoue*, which described a pan-Bantu worldview, seeing the universe as a dynamic system flowing from God and animated by a whole hierarchy of vital forces, some benevolent and others hostile, which play upon each other and appear at differing times as weakened and strengthened. Other writers, and not just from the region where the Bantu live (equatorial and southern Africa), saw this same structure. After World War II, especially, classical African religions thus came to be seen as an integrated whole. In this sense African religion is, so to speak, a modern invention, and itself a way of looking at classical religious phenomena from a new point of view.

The advantage of a pan-African approach is that it combines values in a large enough unit to deal with the influx of such forces as science, capitalism, theories of economic development, Christianity, etc. And yet an indigenous African worldview has not yet emerged which has quite the edge and complexity needed to embrace modern social and technological change. On the whole, the process of modernization has occurred through conversion to the Christian Churches, and to a lesser extent to Islam.

Islam South of the Sahara

During the colonial period Islam continued to spread into Black Africa from the north. Important agents of conversion were the various Sufi orders and the marabouts, who played a leading role in West Africa especially. One of them, from Senegal, Ibrahim Niass (1900–75), was especially important in stressing the universal character of Islam, as against the particularist trends which often emerged in the blends of Muslim and local cultures and values. But it was especially the Salafiya movements, led by men who were educated in Cairo

The ritual dimension: implanting the Qur'an in the hearts and minds of the young, in the Western Sudan, under the guidance of a religious leader or sheikh.

and in North Africa, who introduced the more radical anticolonial and anti-Western impulses. They were highly critical of marabout and Sufi leadership in tending to play upon the ignorance of the masses: they wanted a reformed, neofoundationalist Islam firmly rooted in the Qur'an. At the same time, they saw this Islam as able to stand up to the West both in values and in intellectual strength.

In East Africa, Islam played little political role. But Swahili culture was important: the language itself reflected a mixed Afro-Arab society, fluid at its edges, which established itself in various centers along the coast and inland, partly as a result of the vigorous trade in slaves conducted by the Arabs in the nineteenth century. Islam got a foothold too in Uganda, among the Baganda nobility, and this was one area of fierce struggle between Islam and Christianity—with more power going to the Christian missions since they were aided by the British.

Though syncretism between rituals particularly is widespread in Black Islam, this tends to be a temporary phenomenon, as Muslims on the *hajj* to Mecca come to perceive orthodox Islam and return with ideas of reform. The Salafiya movement, too, has tended to root out moves toward syncretism.

Another ingredient in Islam in Africa comes from the migrant populations of Asians in East Africa and South Africa, brought in to work in the plantations during the colonial period. A minority of these are Muslims, as are some of the Indonesian settlers who are a part of the so-called Colored or mixed race population in the Cape Province of South Africa. There have been tensions between Asians and Blacks, notably in the events of the 1970s leading to the emigration of most Indians from Uganda under the rule of Idi Amin; and in the Zulu-Asian riots of 1947 in Durban, South Africa, and sporadically since that time. Such tensions partly explain why the example of Gandhi, who was a very effective fighter for rights in South Africa during his twenty-year period there from 1893, has not been easy to popularize among the Black populations of South Africa.

Ethiopia and its Ancient Christian History

Of special fascination to many Africans, particularly in overseas revival movements, is the heritage of Ethiopia. The situation has however been complicated by the overthrow of the imperial system under Haile Selassie (1892–1975) in 1974 by a Marxist revolution. (Marxism, incidentally, has had some appeal in Africa, since Marxist regimes were set up not only in Ethiopia but in the former Portuguese territories of Angola and Mozambique, and in one or two other places.) Ethiopia's long Christian history and independence over nearly all its history from foreign domination creates a vital myth in Africa. Ethiopian Christianity dates from the fourth century or earlier. It has strong Semitic connections. The monarchy is traced back to Menelik, who was supposed to be son of Solomon the Great and the queen of Sheba; the use of dance in its ceremonial and the vital role of the Psalms recall consciously the minstrelsy of the period of David; circumcision of males is practiced; and the Sabbath is kept on Saturday. The attempt in the seventeenth century by Portuguese Jesuits to change the religion and romanize it was at first seemingly successful, through the conversion of the emperor in 1621. But his effort to impose the new religion was ultimately a failure: it met too much resistance. So it was that Ethiopian Christianity kept its independence, with its ancient structures. It retained its archaic language of Ge'ez in which the scriptures were written, its hierarchy, linked to the Coptic Church of Egypt, its scribes, painted shrines, monks in high rocky hermitages and monasteries, its magical rites, its ancient and particular saints, above all St. George and the Virgin Mary, its music and dancing, its minstrelsy and psalms: it was essentially *theirs*, and this familiarity arose from its integration into the culture and bones of the Christian Ethiopians. The dynamic Jesuits left an imprint on Ethiopian literature and architecture: but the ultimate prize managed to elude them.

Because Ethiopia has such a long history of Black Christianity it has often been looked on as a model for new Black movements both in Africa and overseas. There are Churches in America and the Caribbean which use the prefix Abyssinian or Ethiopian, and sometimes conduct liturgy in a mixture of Ge'ez and English. The mix is complicated by the emergence since 1974 of refugees from the new Marxist regime in Ethiopia itself, which has established its control over the Church.

New Religious Movements in Modern Africa

By far the most dynamic phenomenon in the modern period has been the growth of independent Churches or new religious movements in a number of regions, which have produced variations chiefly on Christian themes but have tried to adapt religion to the African condition rather than accept the foreign structures of Western missionary religion. They form a bridge between classical African religions and Western thought, and between indigenous values and those of the modern world. Estimates of the number of new religions vary, but probably there are about 10,000, spread over such regions as Nigeria, Ghana, central Kenya, Zaire, and South Africa, but less evident in Uganda and Tanzania. Perhaps fifteen percent of all Christians in Africa belong to such groups, though as we have noted the situation at the edges of Christianity is very fluid in Africa.

There were a number of problems in Africa for Blacks in regard to the White religion. One was the general question of control: mission Churches tended to be very paternalistic. Another was the role of ancestor cults, which were important socially in the African scene, but seen as superstitious or idolatrous by the missionaries. Another was the problem of polygamy, which was fairly widespread and built into social structures. There were great injustices caused if a man had to give up all but one wife. Another very potent issue was that of health. In some matters so-called Western medicine was seen to be effective, but in other areas it was much less so, and so a reversion to classical African modes of treatment was reasonable. There were analogies, too, with faith-healing in the Christian context.

In some degree the new religious movements dealt with these problems, by for instance splitting off from mainstream Churches under Black leadership; or by focusing on a Black Prophet or Messiah figure; or by otherwise establishing Black control. They could incorporate methods of faith-healing or more traditional medicine; and they could allow polygamy (with the Bible at their disposal Africans could easily see that polygamy was part of the fabric of ancient Israelite religion). They could reintegrate other features of African society and religious practice.

The first example we shall look at is the one founded through the example of the Prophet Simon Kimbangu (1889–1951). It is an interesting case, because it was a breakaway movement which nevertheless became a member of the World Council of Churches in 1969, thus attaining a kind of ecumenical "respectability." It is a case of Christianity rejoining the mainstream.

Kimbangu

Simon Kimbangu (1889–1951) was the founder of the Church of Jesus Christ on Earth through the Prophet Simon Kimbangu. He was the son of traditional healers, living in M'Kamba in the lower Belgian Congo (later Zaire and in 1997 Democratic Congo). It was a major and early independent African church. Other churches were, of course, led by Western missionaries and under their control. Kimbangu was educated at a Baptist school and as a young adult became a Christian, together with his wife. He failed, however, his examination to become a pastor. But he received a different call. He heard a voice which said, "I am Christ. My servants are unfaithful. I have chosen you to bear witness before your brothers and convert them. Tend my flock." Kimbangu was fearful and fled to Léopoldville (now Kinshasa) where he worked briefly at an oil refinery. He went back to his village and there received another calling to heal. There had been severe epidemics in previous years. It was in early April of 1921 that he performed his first public healing: he laid hands on a seriously sick woman and cured her.

It must be realized that the colonial and church authorities kept a fairly strict grip on the population. Kimbangu's healing did not fit in with this. As his movement spread, Kimbangu was perceived as a threat to the colonial order. An attempt to have him arrested failed and the prophet went to ground with a few followers. But another vision in September caused him to give himself up voluntarily. He was tried in October and sentenced to death by 130 lashes. But the Belgian monarch reprieved him on the urging of some missionaries. He was confined for life in Elisabethville (later Lumumbashi), where he died in 1951. Meanwhile, over two thousand of his followers were rounded up and imprisoned in a number of detention centers. This, if anything, reinforced the denomination. It was the first of such independent churches to be admitted to the World Council of Churches, in 1969.

The Church of Jesus Christ on Earth Through the Prophet Simon Kimbangu

Simon Kimbangu was born in what was then the Belgian Congo, later to be named Zaire, and was baptized a Baptist after his marriage. He was not able to become a pastor, failing his examinations, though he was trained as a catechist. He received visionary calls to be a healer, and eventually started to heal. He rapidly gained converts, and the colonial administration saw in this a threat. His arrest was ordered in 1921, but he eluded his would-be captors, until later in that year he voluntarily surrendered. Though he was sentenced to death for possible/alleged subversion against Belgian rule, the sentence was commuted by the Belgian king on the petition of missionaries, who favored more lenient treatment. He stayed in prison for the rest of his life and died in 1951. His imprisonment in some ways increased his appeal as a Prophet, and the movement continued to spread despite the exile and imprisonment of many of his followers (over two thousand). After his death his Church was reorganized by his youngest son in accordance with his wishes, and eventually came to join the World Council and to be one of the officially recognized Churches of Zaire, with over four million members.

In some ways of course Simon Kimbangu's career reminded his followers of the life of Jesus: here too there was a call, a healing ministry, a large following, condemnation to death by a colonial regime. It is notable that the themes of

The experiential dimension: the prophetic and shamanistic experiences of this man, Isaiah Shembe, drove him to form the Nazarite Church in Natal province in South Africa. Such independent forms of Christianity are a marked feature of the Black African scene.

the Bible could reverberate in this way, and cause the Prophet to recognize in his own healing powers the work of the Holy Spirit.

The Prophet Shembe and South African Zionism

Many of the new religious movements in South Africa have to do with healing. They also emphasize the charismatic powers of their leaders. They were influenced to a greater or lesser degree by an American Church which had some presence in South Africa, the Evangelical Christian Catholic Church of Zion City, Illinois: for this reason these new movements are often classified as Zionist. Since they often look forward to earthly liberation, the name has a deeper significance too.

One of the most notable of these was founded among the Zulu by the Prophet Isaiah Shembe (1870?–1935). At a time when the Zulu people had been deprived of much of its land, and not long after the Zulu rebellion of 1906, Shembe had visionary experiences; in one of these, at the mountain of Inhlangakazi, he underwent twelve days of retreat, temptations, and final victory, through which he got new powers both of casting out evil spirits and of healing. He set up his center at another mountain, Ekuphakameni, outside Durban, which is the scene of a great annual gathering. Shembe's career made many of his followers look on him as Messiah. At any rate the Nazarite Church which he founded was deeply imbued by his remarkable creativity in composing a body of hymns, which welled up from him, and which he committed to writing, having learned to read in his early forties for this purpose. This body of hymns was embedded in lovely rituals of solemn dancing and singing, with his followers dressed in the Zulu style. It was a religion of renewal and revival, among a people who had been crushed in war and deprived by colonial rule.

Some Catholic Separatist Movements

The two examples we have taken of revived Africanism and Christianity draw on Protestant sources. Father Placide Tempels, whom we have noted as a writer on Bantu philosophy, helped to found a movement known as the Jamaa (a word which means "family" in Swahili). It was intended to express a sort of African Catholicism from within the Church, but came under unfavorable judgment by the authorities, and part of the group became a separatist organization, which is still working in some areas of Shaba and Kasai in Zaire. In both Kenya and in Zambia there were other breakaway Catholic movements. But Vatican II, with its great encouragement of vernaculars, its call for dialogue with other religions rather than their repression, and its call to indigenization, made it less important for groups to try to break away.

Some Other Movements

An important strand of African religiosity is represented by those Churches which stem from the Aladura movement founded in the 1920s in Nigeria and prominent along the West African coast, stressing the importance of prayer and

Alice Lenshina of Zambia formed her own movement known as the Lumpas: another instance of new indigenous religions in the twentieth century.

spiritual healing. They incorporate charismatic visions and the virtues of an ethos of Biblical self-reliance.

A more eschatologically oriented movement was that founded by the Prophetess Alice Lenshina (1919?–78) in Zambia. She, too, had a vision in which she believed that she had been especially favored by God. She broke away from the Presbyterian mission to baptize her own followers. She emphasized forms of music that were attuned to her and her followers' ethnic background. Eventually they got into conflict, first with colonial authority and then with the new government of independent Zambia. The Lumpa Church (Excellent Church) saw the end of the world as near, and refused to pay taxes. In battles with the authorities her followers with their primitive weapons were easily overcome. Their very puritanical communes, outside of the sphere of the Devil who controls the world, were totalistic organizations that were bound to come into conflict with the new authorities. Though Christian in much of its ethos, the movement did not deny the existence of witchcraft, which it regarded as evil but as something which the Lumpa Church afforded protection against. By contrast, the rationally minded Presbyterians simply denied the very existence of witchcraft.

Some other movements were revivalist of classical African religion, using mission means of organization and propaganda in order to express their ideas, such as the Église de Dieu de Nos Ancêtres (The Church of God of Our Ancestors) in the southwest Belgian Congo (Zaire), founded in the 1950s.

In the various new Churches and movements we can see several patterns. One is where traditional functions are transferred but traditional content is rigidly rejected: for instance in movements where healing, but not traditional methods or theories, is prominent. Another mode is more explicitly syncretist, where classical motifs such as belief in ancestors are woven into Biblically based teachings. In many of the movements visionary experience is important. This is something that is hard for Protestant groups, especially, to control. It has brought to prominence many folk, both men and women, who are looked on by their followers as Prophets and sometimes as Suffering Servants who have followed the path of Jesus. The similarity of many of the motifs in the new movements to those which are found in the New Testament is quite striking.

As responses to the various powerful forces coming into African society the new movements are often effective within a limited context. They have produced some striking and beautiful forms of piety. Their great weakness, which in some degree the Kimbanguists have overcome, is that these new religions, as well as the classical forms, need some kind of doctrinal or philosophical underpinning if they are to digest successfully the impact of modern science, economic change, urbanization, and Christianity. They have a choice to turn back toward the mainstream Churches, in which case they will become distinctive African contributions within that context: or they will more explicitly turn away in order to create a new African synthesis which draws both on African classical religion and on Western concepts, including Christian ones.

All this bears on the general question of whether a pan-African philosophy is in the making. Or is it that Africa is too quickly being sucked into a global situation in which the dominant Western modes of thinking and organization will constitute a new form of mental colonialism? This is where Négritude and other forms of the search for an African philosophy are important. The new movements have great force in welling up and boiling around the frontiers of Christianity and Islam. But their very number does represent a fragmentation inherent both in the plurality of African societies and in the diversity of Biblical Christianity.

Reflections on Black Africa

The scene in Africa is one of great dynamism. The future will no doubt see the continued spread of Christianity and Islam at the expense of classical African religious forms. The societies in which they are based are on the whole too small to be able to bear the full impact of modern social changes, especially the magnetism of the cities. This last phenomenon will no doubt favor those new movements which can give people a new sense of identity in larger, more impersonal contexts. The struggle over the colonial heritage is largely over; and from 1989 the *apartheid* in South Africa collapsed and a new South Africa was born under the leadership of Nelson Mandela (b. 1918). But Africans still have to put up with the low value placed on their cultural achievements and styles of life by the West. An important ingredient in the attempt to break free from these limitations, and to spell out Africa's distinctive contributions to a world civilization both in the future and from the past, will be the formation of a philosophical framework in which we can view African ideas and institutions. Meanwhile Africa overseas is important, in South America, the Caribbean, and North America particularly. There, too, religious dynamism is evident.

Dimensions of African Spirituality

We can finish by looking briefly at the dimensions of African, and especially Christian, religion. Naturally there is great variety, as we have seen, but some patterns emerge.

First, as to *ritual*: forms of Christianity, both mainstream and new religions, have stressed African forms of worship. This is most notable in the hymns and devotionalism of some of the new movements, in the dance of Shembe's Church, for instance, and in the use of vernacular languages. Impetus to indigenization was given by Vatican II. For many Africans, because of the shortage of priests and pastors among the mainstream Churches, and for other reasons, the Eucharist is not so central. Vital is the imagery of baptism, partly because of the purificatory symbolism of water in the classical African background and partly because of the often numinous character of streams.

In the *experiential* dimension, there remains an important place for dreams and visions in the formation of new movements; and because of the affinity between African classical religion and Pentecostalism the latter has widespread life. Commitment becomes more important in the shifting choices of urban life and transformations of rural economies, and in these circumstances conversion experiences are important.

As for *ethics*, there is still heart-searching about marriage customs and the role of polygamy in African society. There are also issues about duties toward the ancestors. Very important in the African scene is a sense of solidarity, brotherhood and sisterhood, which some of the new religious communities wish to express with intensity.

As for the *doctrinal* dimension, there is some way to go in formulating the characteristic African holism in its modern cosmological setting: how can we combine some traditional African views of the interrelation of forces in the universe with a modern scientific worldview? There is also the problem of providing the philosophical basis for religious pluralism in the African setting.

Opposite The ritual dimension: water has played a prominent part in classical African religion and is given added significance in new forms of African Christianity.

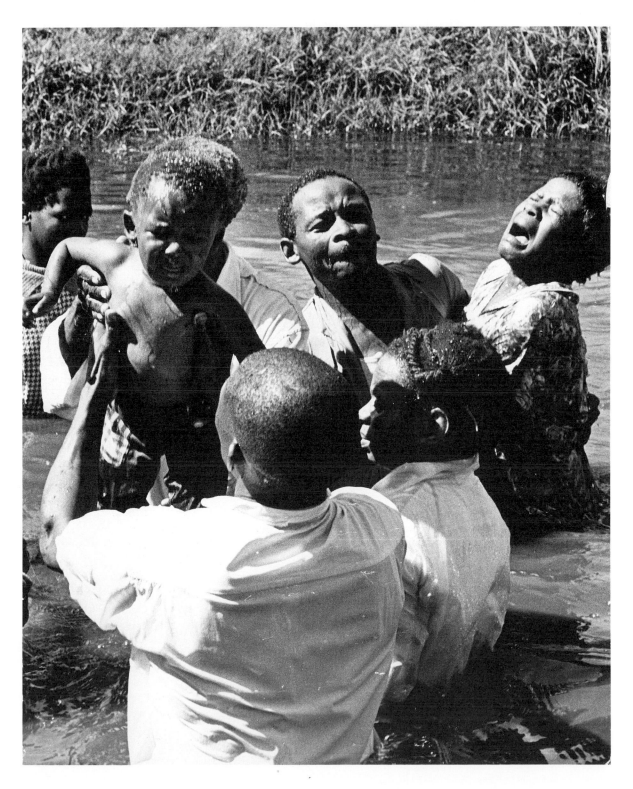

The dimension of *myth* leaves much to reflect on in telling the story of Africa in the perspectives of world history, and the relation of Christianity in Africa to that. It looks as if there is a story emerging which emphasizes the sufferings of Blacks, through the slave trade and the colonial era, as providing a parallel with the life of the Israelites in the Old Testament and the role of the Suffering Servant.

In *art*, African carving and painting have already made their first major impact on Western imagination, and are poised to express more deeply the new spiritualities which are flourishing in Africa.

Africa is an exuberant as well as a problem-haunted continent. The dimensions of its religious life match the contributions of other areas, but it may be that deeper creativities are yet to come.

Latin America and the Caribbean

CHAPTER 24

The Spirit of the Conquest

Although the original aim of sailing west from the Iberian peninsula was to reach Asia, and it was not until about 1520, nearly thirty years after Columbus' first landing, that the Spaniards were fully convinced that what they had found was really a New World, the discovery of these vast lands and their exploitation were taken up with a kind of crusading zest. The expulsion of the Muslims from Spain had been an arduous business, but it fired the Spaniards, and to a lesser degree the Portuguese, with a Catholic zeal. And to complicate matters, there was the Reformation, causing Europe to disintegrate religiously but reinforcing the value of commitment to the Catholic cause. The fact that the Spaniards acted in the New World with great cruelty and greed should not blind us to the fact that they thought themselves to be doing God's will. The Church followed on the heels of the Conquistadores, and there was held up before the eyes of the faithful the prospects of a great extension of Christ's work.

The general attitude to indigenous religions, such as the Aztec and the Inca systems, was one of horror and disdain. The Aztec practice of human sacrifice was not easy to take. But the true horrors lay in the general idolatry of the New World's inhabitants. The gods were often seen by Catholics as creatures of the Devil. So a great deal, therefore, of the native culture had to be rooted out. Disentangling culture from religion was itself a problem, and so much of the indigenous literatures and creations were simply destroyed.

The spirit of the conquest was one of dedication to a sacred cause at the same time as the opportunity for hugely exploiting the conquered population. And because of the advent of the Counter-Reformation the Church had the motivation and the apparatus to carry orthodox Catholic faith to the New World. The conquest was then in its own way a crusade.

The astonishing ease of some of the conquests was uncanny. It lay in the fact that the two great empires the Spaniards encountered were so centralized. The Spaniards struck at the brain of these empires and paralyzed their bodies. Their superiority lay in their horses and muskets, and their ships and cannons. The rapidity and glory of the conquests boosted the self-confidence of the victors and their belief that their civilization and religion were immensely superior to those of the peoples they had come to dominate.

By 1700 the Spanish domains in the New World were immense, running all the way from from California and Texas to Patagonia and from Ecuador to the Caribbean. The Portuguese ruled over the huge area of Brazil, after some fighting with the rival Dutch (who kept a base in Surinam). But certain areas were highly important and others thinly populated and marginal. The rich and densely populated places were Peru and Mexico (known as New Spain), together with part of the Caribbean. It was during the period leading to the consolidation of power over so great an area that the way of life of the New World was worked out and in this the Church played a leading part.

Disputes Over the Treatment of the Indians

For better or worse the natives were called *indios*, or Indians, because the theory was that Columbus and his successors had reached India. Indians the native populations would remain. The effect on the Indians of the conquest and its aftermath was to be devasting. This was not merely because so many were virtually enslaved, and worked in unspeakable conditions in the silver mines of Peru and elsewhere. It was also because of the incidence of European diseases, and above all smallpox. Estimating populations from the data available is not an easy job, but it may be that by 1700 the population of New Spain had fallen to only a tenth of what it had been in 1500. An important question was how the Indians were to be treated, both by the Church and by the civil powers. Were they to be regarded as even fully human?

In this debate a crucial role was played by Bartolomé de Las Casas (1474–1566). He had been born in Seville and gone overseas to take part in the subjugation of the large island of Hispaniola (now divided between Haiti and the Dominican Republic). He became a priest, but went on to take part in the bitter conquest of Cuba. In both islands he got lands under the *encomienda* system. It was a kind of feudalism, in which land with villages would be acquired by a Spaniard, usually as a reward for campaigning and conquest. At the age of forty, however, he was converted to a deep concern over the plight of the Indians and from that time on became their unwavering defender, speaking out boldly and plainly against the atrocities being committed against them. He gave up his own estates. His energies were considerable, and he was involved in various struggles and projects, including a colony in Venezuela that unsuccessfully tried to blend Spanish and Indians in agricultural work.

Opposite Africa meets Catholicism in the Voodoo of Haiti.

Las Casas was successful in his advocacy of Indian rights at the court, and agitated against a number of abuses. He was a force for adopting the New Laws in 1542, which in some measure protected Indian rights. He passionately advocated the equality of all human beings, and in his great *History of the Indies* he catalogued some of the major cruelties and hypocrisies that had been used in the extension of the faith: for him, mission should be a matter of preaching and gentle exhortation, not of violence and enslavement. There were those who argued, on a nakedly racist basis, that the Indians were inferior and as one put it "almost as monkeys to humans." He with vehement passion argued that the Indians had souls as much as the Whites. His career, and his tireless hostility to the abuses of colonialism, helped somewhat to mitigate the plight of the indigenous peoples of the New World.

A Religion for Both Peoples

The New World was a place for many Spaniards to settle. It gave vast opportunities for them. It was also of course the place of the Indians, and much of later history concerns the relations between these parties. But there was also a growing class of people of mixed descent. These *mestizos* were differentiated from the Whites, who held control over much of Latin American history. The latter themselves were divided into *criollos*, that is, those who were born and raised in the New World, and home-born Spaniards. Essentially, the liberation of the New World from Spain at the beginning of the nineteenth century was a *criollo* revolt against metropolitan control, and largely left the institutions in place.

The pattern which emerged in much of Mexico and Peru was that the Indians were organized into their own villages, where missionaries from various orders—Franciscans, Dominicans, and others—would labor, teaching them by means of vernacular languages. The secular priests (that is, ordinary priests not belonging to any of the orders) would minister to the Whites, and, after a generation or two, to the *mestizos*. So a form of segregation was practiced. It had the advantage from the colonists' point of view that the Indians if settled into villages were easier to control. They could also be the more easily incorporated into the system of *encomiendas*, and so into the pattern of forced labor. In outlying areas priests and monks would wander from village to village preaching Christianity, and this corresponded to the Church's growing ideal of mission work, following the prescription of Las Casas.

Much in the conversion of Indians was forced, and little compunction was shown in uprooting indigenous religion and destroying the gods of the conquered. In some degree the Catholic cult of saints helped to cover the reemergence of some of the old gods, however: or at least to provide alternatives to them. The most important saint in Mexico came to be Our Lady of Guadalupe: here, just outside Mexico City, the Virgin had appeared to an Indian and spoken to him in the native language of Nahuatl. She became a symbol of a religion which was now itself *mestizo*: the Mary of the Spaniards also spoke the language of the Indians. Throughout the great regions of Latin

Opposite Revolutionary impulses are important in much of Latin America, as is indicated in this mural by the Mexican painter Diego Rivera (1886–1957) celebrating the Mexican revolution.

America there remain pockets of indigenous culture and religion which have not much been touched by the missionary enterprise; but it is remarkable, even so, how wide the net of Catholicism was cast. Much of the conversion took place after the Council of Trent, so a kind of reformed Catholicism could work with greater effectiveness, and it was a highly ornate baroque style of art and architecture which was brought to the New World. Some of the great edifices of Catholic cathedrals in the many cities were built over pre-Christian sites, such as the site of the Templo Mayor in Mexico City, where once the Aztec emperor had performed his human sacrifices.

The Indians came to perceive that, great as was the catastrophe of the arrival of the Spaniards, it was not the end of the world. Were the old sacrifices really necessary? The invaders seemed to trample the gods with impunity. In the second half of the sixteenth century the Inquisition was also at work in the New World, rooting out idolatry, heresy, and Judaism. It was able to deal with captured Protestant seamen among others, and initially was somewhat directed at backsliders among the Indians; but a more paternalistic spirit later prevailed, for they were reckoned to be too native to be held fully responsible. For a long period, indeed, it was impossible for non-Spaniards to be priests, so that what was institutionalized was a thoroughly paternalistic system.

Paternalism in Paraguay and California

This paternalism can be illustrated by a Jesuit and a Franciscan example. The Jesuits had been admitted to the New World from the mid-sixteenth century on, and in the seventeenth and eighteenth centuries they began to organize what were called Reductions, or regimented villages, on great estates that had been given to the Order either by royal grant or in some other way. In these settlements the Indians were taught useful crafts and skills. Schools were opened and the local languages preserved and reduced to writing. It was a kind of benevolent dictatorship: complete obedience to the Jesuit fathers was enforced, and for the rest the Indians shared everything in common, on a basis of equality. It was religious communism. The Indians were there, not by choice on the whole, but because they had been born into the system or put there in recompense for some wrongdoing.

The great discipline of the Jesuits was matched by their devotion to education, but this was very narrowly conceived. In their universe education was a matter of hierarchy. The Church had the *magisterium* or teaching function. As soldiers of the Pope, they would hand down the truth. It was not a mode which in any way encouraged self-reliance, independent judgment, or free expression. Consequently, when the Jesuits were expelled from the New World (for European political reasons), the Indians of the Jesuit Reductions were at a great loss and the whole system fell apart. The most famous part of that system was the area of modern Paraguay, which had been a mini-State handed over to the Jesuits in deference to their marvelous method of control.

Opposite The mythic dimension: a narrative of significance for Indians focused upon the Virgin of Guadalupe who spoke in the indigenous language, Nahuatl, and thus became a reminder of how the Divine speaks to the Indians as well as to the Spaniards. Here she is seen returning after being taken in procession through Sucre, Bolivia.

In California a chain of mission stations, from San Diego in the south through to beyond San Francisco, was set up from the late eighteenth century onward, on the initiative of a Franciscan, Junípero Serra (1713–84). These mission stations gathered in the local Indians, such as the Chumash, in order that they should pursue agricultural and other pursuits. The missions would often have a place for a small garrison of troops, who would help to keep order and pacify the regions of Alta California which had hitherto been scarcely occupied by the Spanish. With independence for Mexico in the early nineteenth century, and the subsequent takeover by the United States, the system fell apart. The concentration of Indians, and their exposure to White people's diseases, had a devastating effect on Indian life, as did also the destruction of their traditional culture.

One of the ironies of the Franciscan mission chain is how in the Spanish-style churches (which are in their own way pleasing) there is fake marble painted on by Indians who did not know what it was they were imitating. But Our Lady of Guadalupe is also present here and there: a symbol of the inherent worth of Indian life, though that life was culturally despised by the Whites.

The Layering of Latin America

The net effect of the population and religious policies of the New World was that the people were arranged in three or four layers. There were the two kinds of Spaniards, European-born and *criollo*, on the top; then a swath of *mestizos*; then the Indians. In parts of the area the Indians had virtually gone, from some islands of the Caribbean for instance, and slaves from Africa had been introduced. Much of the importation of Blacks was in the nineteenth century: slavery was not abolished in Brazil until 1888. We may also note that in the nineteenth and twentieth centuries there was massive immigration from Europe in some countries.

This has produced a variety of racial patterns. The classic pattern is an ascending scale of population between Whites, *mestizos*, and Indians, of roughly the proportions 1:2:4 or 1:2:3. This applies in Mexico, Central America, and Peru. Then there are areas where the larger number are *mestizos*, as in Colombia and Venezuela. Then there are countries with a predominance of Blacks, such as Brazil and Cuba (the latter has lost its Indian population, however; and in Brazil it is the smallest section of the population). Then there are countries, notably Chile and Argentina, which are overwhelmingly White. In Argentina, more than half the migrants were from Italy, but there are significant Spanish, French, and other groups; while Brazil has a fair number of Germans and a significant group of Japanese descent: of all the countries of Latin America Brazil is the most colorfully variegated. In some areas, such as Amazonia, part of Central America, central Argentina, and southern Chile, there are extant unconquered Indian populations. In (formerly British) Guiana, a substantial population was brought in from India as indentured laborers in the latter part of the nineteenth century, and there are East Indians elsewhere in the English-speaking Caribbean.

Central America and the northern states of South America have the classic layered pattern, with the Indians at the bottom. This has made economic and social struggles all the more acute, as also in a different way in Brazil with its great Black population. This situation was not affected by the wars of independence, which lasted from 1810 to 1826. The resultant political pattern has with relatively minor changes persisted till modern times.

The Liberation of Latin America

The revolts of the colonies were essentially organized by the White elite. There had of course been independence wars on behalf of the Indians, but they had been crushed—most notably the campaign fought by the Inca prince Tupac Amarus (1742–81), who led a large Andean uprising which was put down with great cruelty. The motives of the colonial Whites in seeking independence were similar to those of the North American colonists a generation earlier. There was also strong influence from the liberal thinking of the Enlightenment, and the pervasion of British support for a new system which would widen the possibilities of trade and investment. But the change in government did not as yet involve any essential change in the system of land tenure, or in the primary facts of a kind of race-oriented class structure.

In Brazil no war was necessary: a separate monarchy in Brazil was established in 1815, later turning into an empire, and giving way in due course to a republic in 1889. In Cuba independence from Spain did not arrive till 1888. In the British Caribbean the islands achieved independence only after World War II. In Haiti, however, a slave rebellion established Black rule in 1804. Panama was not created till 1903, mainly as the bread of a sandwich of which the Canal was the filling.

The dominant motif of the anticolonial struggle among the elites of Latin America was liberal, and often this involved some anticlerical sentiment. But mostly the Church still exercised its traditional functions, even if in some countries religious orders were expelled. In a number of constitutions the nominal separation of Church and State was effected. The growth of various forces, such as the influence of Freemasonry, the work of Protestants, positivistic philosophy from Europe, liberal theories of government, and the arrival of large numbers of migrants from Europe, put pressure on the Catholic Church, which remained remarkably conservative up to World War II. Because of population increase, Latin American influence also grew within the Catholic worldwide community.

Protestantism, which was often effective in proselytizing tribal groups, and had its footholds in many new immigrant communities, was sometimes looked on as alien and even as an agent of North American imperialism. There was indeed quite a lot of traditional hostility against the Yankees or Gringos, as they were called, both among the elite—because of aesthetic philosophies stressing the superior culture of the Latin South, such as the philosophy known as Arielism, at one time moderately fashionable—and among the ordinary populations, because of the perceived exploitation of the masses by the forces of modern capitalism, emanating by the twentieth century chiefly from the United States.

Before World War II the Catholic Action movement, coming from France and Italy, stimulated new concerns for democratic action and service to the poor: a moderate social reformism spread its ideas through the creation of Christian Democratic parties. But many Churchmen wished to see a solidarity between Church and society, harking back to the old days: such dreams were helped by organizations such as Opus Dei, a new clerical and lay movement with extreme right-wing leanings. Such dreams of going back to a harmonious body of Catholic Christians (which may never have existed) were, however, interrupted by Vatican II. After this period there was an explosive period of doctrinal innovation and new social thinking, identified with what is known as Liberation Theology.

Liberation Theology

This set of ideas was heavily influenced by Marxism. It blended a Marxist analysis of the social situation with the Catholic and Christian values evident in the New Testament. Vatican II had given a great impetus to Biblical scholarship, and the new thinkers saw in the New Testament especially a revolutionary concern for the poor on the part of Christ. They argued that the Church's prime duty was to raise the life of the poor. They were often critical of older attitudes which glossed over present miseries because the faithful could be sure of the joys of heavenly bliss in the life after this one. The movement was thus very critical socially, revolutionary in spirit, concerned with altering the structures of existence, and anticapitalist. It led some priests into actively participating in revolutionary struggle, as in the case of the Sandinista revolution in Nicaragua.

The Liberation Theology movement also emphasized some other things, apart from the analysis of the present condition of the poor of the Third World. They were very keen on a practical approach (they used the Marxist world "praxis" here as a slogan for their commitment to realizing ideas in practice); and they were keen on starting at the grass roots, thus inverting the traditional Church approach, which was from the top down. They wanted to raise the consciousness of the poor (and this often meant the Indians), who too often were imbued with a kind of fatalism which traditional Catholicism did very little to puncture. So it was with "base communities" that the movement realized its ideas—the creation of small communities of lay and clerical people organizing social betterment, Bible-reading, and the raising of local consciousness. Over two hundred thousand such communities have been set up in Brazil and elsewhere in the continent.

Liberation Theology has come to have a wide influence beyond the Latin American scene, being of some especial attraction in the Third World and also among those involved in the Church struggle in South Africa. Among the prominent exponents are Gustavo Gutiérrez of Peru, Juan Luis Segundo of

Uruguay, Leonardo Boff of Brazil, Hugo Assmann of Costa Rica, and (among Protestants) José Miguel Bonino of Argentina.

Protestantism in Latin America

Protestantism has had a spectacular increase during the twentieth century. Its three roots are, first, migrant Churches in such countries as the Argentine, Chile, and Brazil, with a large number of German and other European

Oscar Romero (1917–80), a traditionalist, was appointed archbishop of San Salvador in 1977. The repression of the poor and the political violence led him to make more and more outspoken criticisms of the government. He was assassinated on 24 March 1980, while preaching, a year after being nominated for the Nobel Peace prize.

565

immigrants; second, more important, Protestant missions especially out of the United States, who have worked both among Catholics and among Indian tribes, where Biblical evangelical preaching has made large inroads; third, spontaneously arising Protestant groups from within Latin America, especially Pentecostals. Pentecostalism has also had some prominence within Catholicism, as elsewhere in the world after Vatican II. There may be as many as eighteen million Protestants in the Latin American region, compared with a few hundred thousand a century ago. But the statistics are hard to find.

The success of Protestant preaching was worrying enough at one time to be put on the agenda for Catholic Bishops' conferences, together with the impact of Freemasonry and other matters: until fairly recently relations between Catholics and Protestants have often been bitter, with Catholics trying to hold onto old monopolies and Protestants often taking a severe evangelical line against Catholic superstitions (as they saw them). The reasons for Protestant success, in Latin America as elsewhere in the Catholic world, are varied. One is that the individualism of Protestant religion makes sense in a capitalist, urban environment. Second, Protestant emphasis on religious experience and conversion is direct, appealing, and promising for togetherness, for feeling becomes the glue of new communities. Third, it is natural that people should awake to the essential pluralism of the religions and within the religions of the world. Catholicism can no longer claim to be the sole possibility.

All this is part of an increasing ferment in the Latin American scene. Among Catholics the meeting of bishops at Medellin in 1968 is commonly regarded as a turning point, when the voices which roused the social conscience of the Church were significant and loud, and when the Church seemed to acknowledge the need for new structures both in Christian life and in society. This call, with the attendant Liberation Theology, has made the Latin American Christian scene central to the religious history of the world.

Religion and Race

The Churches in the Caribbean Region

The islands of the Caribbean are culturally really a creation of the colonial era. The major part of the indigenous Indian populations in the region was wiped out by disease and oppression. Economically the islands came to depend on plantations, especially sugar, and to work the fields Blacks were imported from Africa. So in differing regions we have peoples of whom a rather small minority are settlers from Europe—Spain, France, Holland, Denmark, and Britain above all. The majority are Blacks; and there is a mixed-race intervening layer of folk. But as we have noted, some colonial powers also later imported Indians and Chinese as indentured laborers. On the mainland the colonial possessions of British Guiana, French Guiana, and Dutch Surinam were important too, and contained Indians as well; and similarly with Belize (formerly British Honduras) on the Central American mainland.

Because the island populations were so much a creation of European colonialism, they are predominantly Christian: but there were other influences than settlement and mission at work. For one thing, in one or two areas, notably Barbados, it was for long illegal to try to convert the Blacks. In other areas there were African ideas and rituals mingled in with Catholic practices, as in Haiti. There was a large trend in the British-dominated islands for Church of England (for a time established as the official Church) to be interested only in the White settlers, and from the 1800s on the void among the Blacks was largely filled by nonconformist Churches of varying kinds, Baptists, Methodists, and others. In the last twenty years or so the fastest-growing group in the Caribbean has been Pentecostalism, fired in part through fundamentalist American missionaries.

In Cuba, the victory of Fidel Castro (b. 1927) in 1959 led to pressures against religion. By 1980 only about a third of Cubans claimed to be Catholics, and there was a big overlap with the movement known as the Santería. This compares with a large majority claiming to be Catholic during the pre-Castro years. No doubt there is a feeling that certain answers are favored or expected in such polls, and the results reflect the change in ethos and regime. Castro's is the only genuinely successful Marxist regime in the Western hemisphere, though Nicaragua's Sandinista government, dating from 1979, may eventually attain like stability.

Black Religions in Latin America and the Caribbean

There are a number of religions in the Caribbean which serve to express some Africanness. In some ways the Santería in Cuba (and, since Castro, in various centers in the United States, among exiles) is the most interesting because it has imported so directly so many features of Yoruba religion and Yoruba rites. Its deities are Yoruba, but are also identified with Catholic saints: Shango, god of thunder, becomes St. Barbara; Orunmila, of divination, becomes St. Francis; Obatala is Our Lady of Mercy; Elegba is St. Peter. In this way the two religious traditions are integrated, and the Catholic saints no doubt provide a kind of cover for the other faith, which has persisted thus after the dislocations of forcible removal to the plantations. Similar remarks apply to the rather similar group of cults known as Shango (from the god) in Trinidad.

Interesting also is a kind of holding together of religious traditions, which however is not syncretistic in the proper sense, as represented by the system known as Winti in Surinam. It may be that because of the predominance of Protestantism, derived in part from Moravian missions, there was less ease in blending traditions. In any case, those who practice Winti most often behave in other contexts as straightforward Christians, whether Protestant or Catholic. Winti conceives the world as being shot through with various spirits and forces—gods of the air and earth and water, presided over by a High God—very much in the classical African way. Various rites both evoke and propitiate the varied gods, with spirit possession being a marked feature of the religion: it deals with everyday affairs including illness, and involves shamanistic cures.

Two forms of spiritism have been powerful in Brazil. One is known as Kardecism, after the French thinker Allan Kardec (1804–69). He propounded a view that there are spirits who are in process of reincarnation, and one can have communication with them through mediums. There is a hierarchy of such spirits, who ultimately derive from God. Happiness and unhappiness are the result of previous actions. The greatest virtue is Christian love, and we should cultivate this and other means to spiritual perfection: we are free agents and can alter our destinies, therefore. The belief-system of Kardecism ruled out miracles and a magical view of the world: for Kardec it was all based on science. His ideas were introduced into Brazil in the 1870s and 1880s and began to attract a large following among the urban middle class. It continued to gain support, despite a Catholic campaign against it in the 1950s.

Kardecism came to have a lot of influence upon an earthier, more symbol-laden movement which started in Rio de Janeiro in the 1920s, the Umbanda religion, a loose, African-based conglomeration of cults led by shamanistic women and men with their own groups. There is a strong Yoruba admixture here also. The groups are especially important in the great and often squalid urban shanty-towns, because they give a sense of belonging. The gods often are identified with Catholic saints, and there is a strong overlap between membership of the Church and of Umbanda.

Before and during World War II the government made attempts to stamp out the cults, but without success. In the period after World War II some blending between Kardecism and Umbanda occurred, because Kardecism provided a good doctrinal and intellectual framework for the cults, while the latter helped to give color and force to an otherwise too polite religion.

A somewhat analogous system to the Santería of Cuba is Haitian Voodoo (so-called: it is a term applied by outsiders). In this belief system and practical way of ritual, Catholicism is not rejected, but used as a framework within which the African gods and spirits (some from Nigeria, others from Benin and Zaire) may be approached to help with the ordinary problems and tribulations of life. The Christian God, the Bondye in Haitian Creole, presides and sends down his angels, the spirits, nearer to human beings on earth: but generally speaking we do not seek for him to do anything. He functions therefore very much as the High God of classical African religion. More immediate concerns are taken to more immediate spirits. Rituals range from the simplicity of lighting candles to animal sacrifices, and in the cities small temples are available. Drumming and singing are designed to bring on spirit-possession, which is an important function, for it serves as a main means of communication between spirits and humans, and enables spirits to participate in the celebrations. In general this religious system was created by slaves out of African materials, supplemented by some of the categories of Catholicism.

All the systems considered here give Black people dignity, insofar as they emphasize African roots. But some others also project connections to the future. Important among these is the Rastafari movement, which had some of its origin in the work of the Jamaican leader Marcus Garvey (1887–1940), in forming the Universal Negro Improvement Association in 1914. The coronation of Haile Selassie in 1930, coinciding too with the miseries of the Depression, helped to stimulate interest in a millennial return to the paradise of Ethiopia, a symbol of the riches of the Black tradition.

Rastafarianism by the early 1950s was strongly anti-White. It saw Whites as inferior to Blacks, thought of the coming of the Blacks to the West Indies as some kind of punishment, looked to the hope of return to Ethiopia, saw Haile Selassie as the living God, and believed that Blacks will soon be able to rule over Whites. Some of these beliefs have been modified: and some externals have been acquired since that time by the Rastafarians, such as the wearing of dreadlocks (which however, in a polite form, have become fashionable in a wider circle, as has the Rastafari music) and the smoking of marijuana. There came to be a greater emphasis on self-help among the Blacks of Jamaica, and less reliance on the actual help of Haile Selassie, especially as he was overthrown in 1974 and died in the following year.

Problems for South American Small-Scale Groups

In some areas of Latin America—in Nicaragua, for instance, but above all in the Amazon basin—the opening up of the areas to government control or commercial exploitation causes severe distress to the independent groups of Indians still subsisting outside of Latin culture and society. Logging and mining in Amazonia, and its development for pasturing cattle and growing crops, have had a severe impact on the environment of tribal peoples. Also, there are widespread evangelizations by Protestant groups which are changing patterns of life. It is doubtful whether many tribal communities will long survive in the present ways of life. On the other hand many who were long ago loosely integrated into Catholicism, such as the Quechua speakers of the high Andes, retain much of their preconquest culture and religion, but with a Catholic superstructure.

Reflections on the Latin American and Caribbean Scene

The dynamism of this highly varied region of the world is evident. There remain social problems which are most severe in those countries which have a high number of Indians. But some of the stratification into race-based classes has been overcome. Thus, in Mexico, the Revolution of 1910 harked back to leaders who were themselves Indians, most of all Benito Juárez (1806–72); and it commissioned the great murals of Diego Rivera (1886–1957), which combined a vision of indigenous liberation with Socialism (p. 558). The Institutional Revolutionary Party (a nice contradiction, some think) has provided Mexico with stability and a secular anticlerical State, despite the Catholicism of most of the population. But poverty remains.

The role of the Catholic Church has bifurcated between its old conservative support for established regimes and elites to the new revolutionary cast depicted by and encouraged through the new Liberation Theology. In many areas, Protestant evangelization is making progress, while Black populations have devised religions which in one way or another link to African roots. In the great republics of the far south, White societies have struggled with political problems and options, but the desire for pluralistic democracy seems stronger than ever after the dreadful killings of the military regime in Argentina in the 1970s and the violence and militarism of contemporary Chile, particularly during the Pinochet regime in Chile after 1973.

Dimensions of Caribbean and Latin Religion

We can perhaps single out some of the most significant items from the different developments as a sampling of the Latin American and Caribbean spirit. In regard to *doctrine*, the most vital contribution has been Liberation Theology; but it may also turn out that Kardecism too will spread, because "Spiritismo" is also well developed among Mexicans and Hispanics in the United States.

A native Guatemalan waits in line to greet Pope John Paul II in Guatemala City in 1983.

As to *myth* and the narrative dimension, there is a growing sense of Latin America's having a special part to play in human civilization; and there is the great popularity of Our Lady of Guadalupe, who supplied a mythic missing link between the religion of the conqueror and that of the conquered.

In regard to the *experiential* dimension, there is as elsewhere an emergence of emphasis on Pentecostal experience and the religion of being "born again." We may note, too, the persistence of shamanism at the level of the small-scale societies; and this wells up in the concern with mediums among the Black religions. The interest in hallucinogens also continues, for instance in the use of coca among Andean Indians and in the employment of marijuana among the Rastafaris.

As to the *ritual* dimension, the greatly simplified Catholic rites after Vatican II, and the use of the vernacular languages, represent a great shift away from the older colonial Baroque style. The setting up of "base communities" under the influence of Liberation Theology has revived the use of the Bible as a central element in the *practical* dimension of religion.

As to *ethics*, there is too a growing sense of identification with the poor, as in the preaching of John Paul II, and through the more revolution-oriented aspects of Catholicism. Protestantism imports a more individualistic ethos, which is encouraged too by the growth of capitalism and the beginnings of consumerism in the southern republics and elsewhere.

Organizationally, there are greater conflicts in some areas between Church and State—latently in Mexico, more overtly in Cuba and Nicaragua—and a general weakening of the authority of the Church in a period of more obvious pluralism; but again, Liberation Theology's concern with the grass roots gives a vivification of Church organization from below.

At the *material* level, the gradual diminution of the external signs of Counter-Reformation Catholicism does not remove the vast church buildings which are a glory of the Spanish colonial period, brooding over the cities which the Spaniards above all loved to found, to bring their own version of Christian civilization, in a highly confident period, to a whole great continent. It is this Spanish and Portuguese architecture, and that of the dusty towns in the plains and the Andes, on river sides and by the great oceans, that stands as the largest testament to the colonial spirit which is now beginning to fade.

CHAPTER 25

Reflections on the Twentieth Century

The twentieth century was the first when the religions came to know one another, by and large. It was the first era when the fruits of the comparative study of religion and of the dialogue among religions really appeared. While this led to positive relations between them, it was also a sign of a darker force. For it was part of the process of globalization, and this was partly a byproduct of the two World Wars.

The two great wars were also in part responsible for other great upheavals. There was the Revolution in Russia, brought about by Germans, indeed covering the whole former Tsarist Empire. The First World War also sparked the Second. The Treaty of Versailles imposed a harsh peace on Germany, stimulating the rise of Hitler and the Nazis, and also encouraged nationalisms of varying kinds. The Second World War weakened the European imperial powers and so was a major cause of the release of most of the world's countries from colonial bondage. It also helped in the making of the Chinese Revolution. In all these changes, religious and ideological elements played a significant role.

Let us concentrate first on the darker side of our story. The black truth is that Nazism and various forms of Marxism have sparked the worst massacres in human history. The wholesale destruction of Jews and Slavs and others under Hitler owed itself to a fanatical nationalism arguing that non-Aryans were inferior. The long drawn-out suffering in the Soviet Union (with even more killed and starved to death than under Hitler) was due to an illiberal Marxism-Leninism which dealt in dangerous and dreary abstractions. Again this was accompanied by a suppression of religious values and widespread cruelty to human beings. Likewise the Cultural Revolution in China proved lethal. The mass killings in Cambodia under Pol Pot drew on an ideology which mandated the murder of all those who had been infected by education or religion in the wider world of capitalism. A mad ideology had been cooked up by Khieu Sampan in the Sorbonne. Other murderous episodes can be put down to religious and national differences: the chaos of killing in India at Partition; before that the Armenian genocide in World War I in Turkey; later the massacres of Hutus and Tutsis in Central Africa, and so on.

Broadly, the evils of the century can be ascribed to largely ideological or nationalist factors. Where religions are combined with national identity they create a powerful cocktail. On the whole, however, religions have been at the receiving end of persecution in the twentieth century at the hands of these powerful ideologies: Eastern Orthodoxy and Catholicism under European and Soviet Marxism; the traditional religions of China under Maoism, as well as Christianity and Islam; Buddhism under the Khmer Rouge; Judaism under the Nazis; Islam in Central Asia under the Soviet Union.

In addition, the religions of the Tibetans, of the Uighurs, and of Inner Mongolia in China have been caught in the repression of these peoples by the Han Chinese under the cloak of Marxism. One should also contemplate South Africa, whose ideology of *apartheid* was a polite form of Nazism (softened by a form of British liberalism). This vanished with the release of Nelson Mandela in 1990 and the framing of a new constitution.

Pope John Paul II praying before Our Lady of Peace in Stoczek. Poland, in 1983.

The greatest ideological force in the twentieth century has been nationalism. It spread from Europe to Asia, Africa, and elsewhere, and helped to fuel the anticolonial movement. Nations created their historic myths, often garnished through their languages, and provided the separate frameworks for creating modern nations. National entities provided systems of education, welfare, bureaucratic systems, and so on; and their often overlapping populations were frequently a cause of intense conflict. Modern wars and guerilla struggles have supplied the pattern for mutual antagonisms. Often religions have provided the markers for differences between traditions.

The fourth great ideology has been liberal democracy, and this has been antithetical to the totalitarian ideologies of Communism and Fascism, and has an uneasy relationship to nationalism. It is, as it happens, the only philosophy fully compatible with science. For this reason Marxism could get entangled with Lysenko's wayward biology and find Einstein's Theory of Relativity awkward. Liberalism stands for the open society, which also stresses the critical approach to theories. Science is constantly subject to revision. Liberalism could combine with religion, but not with the strictest view of revelation or scripture. Consequently there has been a move toward polarization in religion: between trends toward a liberal or what is often called a modernist version, and trends toward a more conservative or fundamentalist variety. We may look upon the evolution of a faith as being toward modernism with conservatism as a reaction. There are intermediate positions, and dimensionally these trends are not necessarily in parallel. For instance, Anglo-Catholicism in Christianity is often liberal in thought but conservative in ritual and ethics.

In a number of Western countries liberal democracy has weakened tradition. In Scotland, Sweden, and Finland, for instance, Church attendance is small. It is often thought that a process of secularization is taking place, with the erosion of religiosity being an almost inevitable consequence of modern living. Certainly liberalism makes people less willing to listen to traditional authorities. For instance, Italy has the lowest birth rate in the world at the end of the twentieth century, despite the Pope's preaching against artificial methods of birth control. But a substantial proportion of the population still goes to Mass. It seems that the Pope still functions as a focus of ritual, but not as an ethical teacher. Nevertheless, secularization is not universal: the United States has a relatively high rate of Church attendance, and also there is a tendency for individuals to make up their own religions. This often means that they are serious about spirituality, but not about tradition.

Two Japanese Adventures

In reflecting on the twentieth century, we have seen how two dark empires collapsed—the Soviet and the Nazi, and less oppressive colonial systems crumbled in the aftermath of World War II. Another Empire made a spectacular debut, namely the Japanese, and this was an example of a cocktail of nationalism and religion. The Shinto-flavored nationalism of twentieth-century Japan was highly effective, in that a large part of the East was

The Gion Matsuri Shinto festival at Kyoto. A figure dressed as the goddess Amaterasu is paraded in the street.

Buddhist monks performing a ceremonial for the installation of a relic at a peace temple in Battersea Park, London.

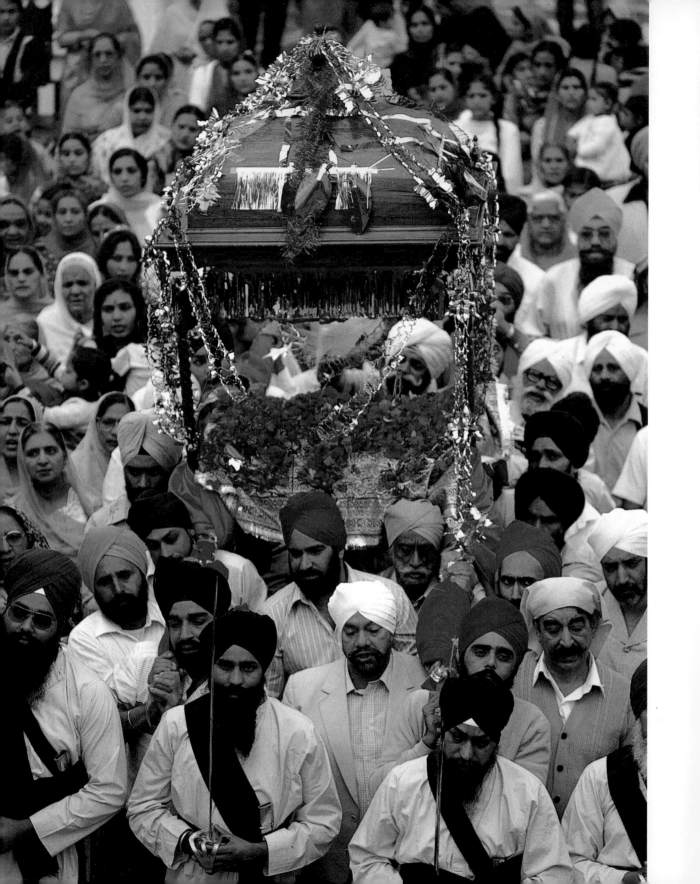

subjugated: Korea, Manchuria, parts of China, Southeast Asia, Burma, Malaya, Indonesia, and sundry parts of the Pacific islands. To some extent the Japanese were racists during this period, and as always it could mean the heartless treatment of those subjected to them. Racism is itself an extension of nationalism, and is a large force in the twentieth century, though it is hard to define, partly because it is an unscientific conception. The success of Japan militarily helped to undermine older colonialisms, and therefore was a factor in the spread of nationalisms throughout the Asian world.

Japan's second adventure saw the large abolition of Shinto-motivated nationalism and the substitution of liberal democracy under the aegis of the American occupation. Similar developments, at a slower pace, occurred in South Korea, Taiwan, Singapore, and Malaysia. Hong Kong partially took over this pattern, though its handing back to China in 1997 left some question marks. In all these countries there are substantial Buddhist minorities, and generally this is a religion which has an individualist tendency. This is one area where the dialogue between liberal Christians and Buddhists has proved very fruitful.

The Question of Islam

The twentieth century saw the reemergence of Islam as a powerful force: but it is nevertheless unable fully to resolve the problem of modernity. By the end of the century it presided over very few countries which had anything like a democratic regime—perhaps Turkey (where it had been partially banned), Pakistan and Malaysia. None of the Arab states were democratic, and a number of them entertained fairly cruel regimes (notably Syria, Iraq, and Libya). While Malaysia and Indonesia had had to come to terms with pluralism, some—particularly Iran and Sudan—had not. The Islamic and Arabic countries were, of course, throughout the latter part of the century preoccupied with Israel and the attempt to create a Palestinian state.

While Egypt, for example, has built a modern country, it has had at the same time to contend with Islamist forces, which gather strength both from the poverty of the masses and from a philosophy of struggle. Such fundamentalism aims to purify Islam and if possible reestablish the ancient law, the *shari'a*. The theory is that Islam's sad contemporary state arises from the corruption of the faith, notably through Sufism and through Western example. While Islamism often is vigorous and militant, it does not resolve the problem of a renewed Islam. The answer most likely lies in a form of the faith which is pluralist, democratic, and in tune with modern knowledge. The prescription is much the same as that for other religions.

The need for pluralism arises from the fact that in the majority of countries there are minorities of other religions. The overriding assumption of Islam is that there is only a single community. Again, modern societies demand freedom of religion, and this is not honored in traditional Islamic society. Moreover, as the case of Salman Rushdie shows, there are severe limitations on freedom of opinion, according to one interpretation of the *shari'a*. The need for democratic institutions arises from the nature of capitalist society in

Opposite Sikhs at the dedication of a temple in Kenya.

modern times: its freedoms go with the projects of business. But more than that, democracy enshrines certain human rights, and while differing religions may place a differing gloss on the notion, the safeguarding of them becomes imperative today. Finally, while Islam has little difficulty with modern science, especially in relation to cosmology, a dilemma is posed by it in relation to education. Traditional Islamic education needs to live side by side with the modern research university: yet the latter needs to bulge with questions and criticisms of existing theories, and this is in tension with the appeal to a literalist education. Therefore it seems plausible to say that Islam needs a form of modernism to come to terms with modernity (and postmodernity, which is not so very different).

In respect of this last point particularly, namely the relationship to science, Sufism is undervalued by Islamist tendencies. The mystical path within Islam moderates its literalist proclivities and has often evolved a metaphysical view of the divine and of the world which could live in harmony with the speculations of the day.

It is also worth noting that in the twentieth century Islam has made itself an important presence in North America and Europe. Migrant workers from Turkey, Pakistan, and Algeria particularly are important in Germany, Britain, and France. There are now more Muslims than Jews in Southern California. They are often well educated, and need a form of faith which combines both contemporary and traditional thinking.

Nevertheless, during the latter part of the twentieth century most attention is captured by the fundamentalist or Islamist groups, which have been resurgent in the Middle East above all and in North Africa. Their enthusiasm is sparked especially by the continuing struggle against Israel. They look back to a situation in which the Dar al-Islam incorporated Palestine, and from this perspective the Jews represent an alien intrusion, backed by a powerful United States. For them too the present state of Islam is sad: this once glorious civilization has been overrun first of all by Western colonialism and now by Western influences which need to be combated. Yet it is hard to distinguish between the struggle for the liberation of Islam and the struggle for political freedom. At any rate, the symbol of the *jihad* is powerful for Islamists, and militant groups among the Arabs and Iranians are prone to use the tactics of the guerrilla in fighting Israel.

Israel, of course, is a strange mixture. First of all it is a land devoted to a nation defined by reference to a religion, though that group, namely the Jews, is largely secularist. Moreover, the founding movement, Zionism, was secular and to a great extent Socialist. Nevertheless, a strong component within the nature is Orthodox, while others are Conservative or Reform Jews. A large part of their support comes from the United States where Reform and Conservative Judaism is powerful and influential. The religious factor therefore cannot be ignored in Israel, partly too because the voting system gives the religious parties undue influence, and from the founding days of the nation a traditionalist emphasis has been strong. Because at the same time the victory in the 1967 war particularly has given Israel large control over many Palestinians and a fair slice of Palestinian territory, the question of the liberation of Palestine has been a prominent part of the Arab agenda, and more generally of the Muslim agenda.

This has only encouraged the longevity of military and royal dictatorships among the Arab nations and the ideological entrenchment of the new Islamic regime in Iran. Therefore, it is to be hoped that in the end a Palestinian State may be created and peace with Israel brought into being among the Arab and other nations.

Elsewhere, of course, similarly military and authoritarian regimes are to be found in the Muslim world—in the Central Asian states which have inherited the closedness of the Soviet Union, in ravaged Afghanistan, even in relatively pluralist Indonesia, in the Sudan, and in much of North Africa.

Meanwhile, in South Asia there is a mass of Muslims that represents a great swath of the world's Muslim population. Those in India and Bangladesh enjoy something of a democratic regime, while Pakistan valiantly struggles toward it. Unfortunately in India the B.J.P. (Bharatiya Janata Party) version of Hindu militancy threatens to disturb the balance between the Hindu and Islamic traditions; and without the loyalty of its Muslim citizens—numerous roughly as the respective populations of Pakistan and Bangladesh—India would be in trouble.

Although fundamentalist-type Islam is conservative in many ways it also has a socially conscious tendency and is often modern in practice. Perhaps, therefore, it will pave the way for a more liberal orthodoxy. Moreover, the fact that Islam has penetrated substantially into Western countries will mean greater influences flowing from this diaspora to the main regions of Islam. At the end of the century there are, thus, developments which may yield a modernist Islam more in dialogue with its neighboring religions.

The Chinese Question

As the century ends, China is going through massive changes. The dominance of Deng Xiaoping (1904–97) saw the success of the "socialist market economy" he encouraged. China's productivity greatly improved, though not without problems, such as the plight of her eight hundred million farmers, whose income lagged behind that of the booming communities along the coast. One effect of Deng's leadership was a loosening up of the clampdown on religions, and some considerable revival of Buddhism and Islam. Periodically, however, there have been demonstrations by Muslims in Sichuan and Xinjiang. The less rigorous attitude to religion has not been permitted in Tibet, where attempts to demand independence or at least autonomy for Tibetan Buddhism have been harshly dealt with.

In 1997 the joining of Hong Kong to China heralded a new phase of development: perhaps the convergence of the two systems, between Hong Kong capitalism and the Socialist market economy. Perhaps China will move toward political reform after the relative success of the economic reform.

Chinese regimented health: a consequence of the Maoist revolution.

Consolidations

It is primarily in the twentieth century that new concepts have emerged, partly as a result of anti-colonial struggles and partly in recognition of overlapping phenomena. Thus, there has developed the notion of African religion, relating to the sub-Saharan form of classical African religion. The sense of kinship among Black Africans gives this idea extra reality. Similarly, Native American religion is now very widely accepted and is beginning to acquire a canon (see Black Elk, p. 389). Likewise Australian Aboriginal religion, Polynesian religion and other area categories have been consolidated. Perhaps the latest to be clearly recognized is Circumpolar religion. To some degree this book reflects some of these consolidations.

Another thing beginning to happen in the twentieth century is alliances between tribal and other groups across borders. Realizing the weakness of each group by itself there is more incentive to promote cooperation, as is happening among the ethnic pockets within India and in Myanmar (Burma), and among the so-called *indios* of Mexico and Central America.

New Religions

The globalization of the world has meant that religions have encountered one another as never before. A consequence is the creation of many new religious

580

movements. When Religion A meets Religion B, they can blend and influence one another. They might become Religion Ab and Religion Ba, and then, by purist reaction, Aa and Bb. They might also mutate into a separate form, namely Religion C. The permutations are numerous. Thus in Africa, differing forms blend with Christianity in the New Independent Churches, combining elements of indigenous practices and beliefs with New Testament teachings, and so on. In the nineteenth century, Anglo-Catholicism blended Church of England teachings and those of the Catholic tradition. Evangelical Christianity and Confucianism blend in the Unification Church.

Moreover, original new religions, like Mormonism, arise from within the milieu of nineteenth-century revivals; and the twentieth century has seen many transformations of faiths within the small-scale traditions of the world, from New Guinea to Siberia. There are also notable numbers of new religions in Japan, within the Hindu tradition, in America, Europe, and elsewhere.

Ecumenism

The major world religions, beginning with Christianity, have meanwhile drawn somewhat closer together. The twentieth century saw the formation of the World Council of Churches and the reformation of Catholicism in the Vatican II Council. In many ways significant differences between Christians were eliminated, except for the divide between literalists and liberals. Similarly Buddhism has formed the World Fellowship of Buddhists. While Islam has often practiced mutual tolerance, it is true that rifts between Sunni and Shi'a Muslims have continued.

But as well as the ecumenical feelings in the major religions, sometimes the divisions have been bitter. In Judaism, the splits between Orthodoxy and the Conservative and Reform movements have proved severe, especially in Israel.

There is, as well as these tensions, a wider ecumenism: that between religions. The modern era has seen a positive emphasis, perhaps beginning with the Parliament of Religions in 1993. The most eloquent form was that of Vivekānanda, as we have already seen, in which the ultimate unity of all faiths was affirmed. In the last resort not all, or perhaps any, religions really believe in this. Still the question of the possible unity of all religions has to be faced.

The Unity of Religions?

We can see how the question develops against the background of the various dimensions. (It may be observed that it is because of the comparative study of religions, chiefly in the twentieth century, that the truth has become clearer. Indeed, because of much narrow-mindedness in Western religion and a certain lack of interest, the field only became fully developed in the latter half of the century.)

First, it is remarkable that in *doctrine* a number of faiths have a virtual similarity in regard to the idea of Creation. This notion is that the world is not only created by a Divine Being, but continuously so: in other words it is continuously sustained by Him (or Her or It). This idea is found in Judaism, Islam, Christianity, theistic Hinduism, essentially in Daoism and Confucianism, in Sikhism, and among the Zoroastrians. It is also found among African and other religions. Nevertheless, in Buddhism and Jainism there is no idea that the world is dependent on a Creator. And so here is a major respect in which the unity of all religions cannot be maintained.

Second, in relation to human life there are significant divergences. A number of faiths, both ancient and modern, maintain that there is rebirth and reincarnation, but others do not.

In regard to the *mythic* or narrative dimension, each religion is somewhat particular: whether they venerate one character or another makes a lot of difference. The stories of Krishna, Christ, and Muhammad are rather diverse, even apart from the implications of their frameworks (as to incarnation, etc.). Again, insofar as some beliefs concentrate on one individual, there are differences where other faiths concentrate on whole peoples, and so on.

In regard to the *experiential* dimension there are both overlaps and divergences. Thus in Sufism, medieval mysticism, Daoism, and Buddhism there is a coincidence of mystical experience, though with differing flavors. But in certain phases of religion, the emphasis is different, on the numinous experience, and the sense of distance between subject and object. The separation of a tradition from others is clearest of all in the Theravāda, where the contemplative life is most starkly presented.

Although in relation to the *ethical* dimension there is a considerable overlap, even so there are important differences both of detail and of emphasis. The prescriptions for virtue contain diverse marriage clauses in Islam, Judaism, and Christianity; the social fabric is diversely conceived in Confucianism and Hinduism; the treatment of animals is different in Sikhism and Jainism; andso on.

With regard to *ritual* the requirements differ: sacrifices are demanded here and there, pilgrimages here, the contemplative life, without worship there. Again the Theravādin life differs profoundly from that of the psalm-singing Christian on the one hand, and the Brahmin rituals differ deeply from the rites of the Quaker. In some religions they are regarded sacramentally, and in others they are not.

Though perhaps *organization* is less important than other dimensions of religion in considering the unity of religions, nevertheless some organizations stamp their mark on salvation. *Extra ecclesiam nulla salus* ("There is no salvation outside the Church"): would that Church be so without a Pope? And the Brahmins are a sacred vivifying order. The Buddhist Order is an authoritative community taking one to *nirvāṇa* or at least a better life. Again, the divergences are fairly deep.

Finally, even the material dimension is differently conceived, according to whether material representations of the Transcendent are allowed or not. Are gods incorporated in their representations?

So we see in all this considerable difference, and even here and there severe clashes between ideals.

It therefore appears unrealistic to hold out for a fundamental unity of all religions. There are admittedly those like Vivekānanda and Guenon who have argued for this. It has mainly been on the basis of an underlying mysticism, that is to say, the contemplative life as understood in a number of religions. But that again is with the assumption that as in an overlying belief in union is the figure of God. That assumption does not hold in the Theravāda. Moreover, the various Divine Beings would be unified by the Real, not the unreal. How does Mahāyāna ontology fit into this?

Still, might there not be a looser fit between faiths? It might be thought of as follows—that all the major religions tend to converge. For instance, they all come to settle on a rhythm of both numinous and mystical experience, and to stress the union between subject and other on the one hand and the powerful grace-giving polarity between God and the worshipper on the other hand. There are similarities between Mahāyāna and Sufism and Christianity in some of its phase.

This might lead us to a further kind of speculation. We might discern in all of this patterns that hint at some future transformations. Perhaps in the long run there *will* be a convergence. The religions have already over the centuries changed a good deal. Why should they not evolve toward a unity? It is not that they have achieved this yet. Perhaps they have imperfectly understood their own messages anyway and distorted the revealed truth. It could be that in the next millennium they will more perfectly understand it and each other.

Of course, part of what we should be asking is: Why do we need some kind of unity? It rather assumes that we cannot be in harmony if we disagree. Also, human beings are such that even if some people pressed clearly for some unity in religions there would always be others who would resist that thesis. In short, disunity is always to some degree a property of human mingling.

Nevertheless, a certain hope in unity is worth having, partly because strife between faiths is unfortunate and as we have seen dialogue has developed during this century. We need as far as possible to avoid hostility. Let us now take a somewhat different tack, and address these matters through the path of knowledge, or rather of the theory of knowledge.

A Question of Knowledge

It is, I suppose, reasonable enough to ask how it is that we know what we claim to know, but the question is difficult to answer in the case of religion. Many of the replies are appeals to revelation, authority, or personal experience. Yet what is to be done if you appeal to one revelation and I to another? We can be persuaded by personal experience: and this may indeed be spiritually convincing, but it is a 'soft' reason for belief, in as much as a differing revelation can attract a similar proof. From a public point of view, however much my belief is hedged by certitude, it is still (and I repeat, from a public point of view) a matter of opinion.

In other words, an affirmation of faith expresses certitude; but it can hardly express objective certainty. From this perspective, faith is not something about which to dogmatize, and again it is a matter about which we may enter into dialogue, and should.

It is, moreover, a consequence of this position that religions are matters of openness: they are not to be imposed, but neither should their teachings be banned. It follows both from the theory of knowledge and from the demands of a democratic or open society that all major (and also many non-major) religions should be given a tolerant hearing in a modern state, never mind what the traditional lore may be. This in fact is what has tended to happen increasingly in the twentieth century, though there are exceptions: in China, in Iran and in some other places, the logic of modern democracy has not taken hold.

There are other trends that emerge out of the modern world. There is, for instance, a tendency for the simplification of rituals. The press of time, the need for intelligibility, the demands of contemporary life—these have alike tended in this direction. It is true that a certain traditionalism, for instance in Orthodox Judaism, has moved in the other direction. It emphasizes again an internal polarization through many religions as to both belief and practice. The liberal wings or varieties of religion have tended in one direction, the new conservatism in another.

A New Time

We have already noted that in the Western world in particular, where individualism is most developed, there are a large number of people who, as it were, make up their own religion. They often link spirituality to various kinds and conditions of health, and give themselves over to private rituals. These people are delineated in various types of end-of-the-century sociological literature; and they are sometimes linked, too, to those concerns loosely dubbed "New Age". Such individuals have often highly eclectic beliefs, and may have a loose and wandering loyalty to groups and churches. It is easy for those more solidly bound to a religious tradition to underestimate the seriousness of such individuals: they may look to some a bit wild or sometimes even flippant. But they do represent a growing trend in religion. In one sense they are the ultimate in Protestantism, in that they rely, not so much upon their own faith, as upon their own judgment. They also exhibit the fact that they are seekers, trying to find the mysterious key to life.

Communication on the Internet will no doubt facilitate this process, and generally speaking because it is worked on individually, it will contribute to the lonely aspect of the medium and therefore of those religions that can be conveyed thereby.

Secular Ideologies—a Reflection

Meanwhile, a fairly important segment of the Western population, not to mention those in South and Southeast Asia, and the Arab and African worlds, are effectively secular in their beliefs. A vital strand in this group belongs to the professional classes and intelligentsia. Many of these people are secular humanists, and were Marxists of one sort or another. They often combine beliefs, as Socialists, Marxist humanists, or liberal atheists. There are also other motifs worked in: for instance, Freudian ideology remains fairly strong.

As we look back across the century, especially having taken care to understand and delineate the nature of the world's beliefs, we should express a fair degree of skepticism about Freudian, or for that matter Jungian, analysis. On the whole, Freud himself, and subsequent Freudians, have been remarkably ignorant about the details of the world's myths, while Jung's analysis was selectively derived from a vast mass of material, and therefore hard to falsify. Moreover, myth has been ill-defined in these areas and indeed covers a wide genre of stories. Nevertheless, differing varieties of psychoanalysis fit into a broadly humanistic framework, and remain influential in the Western world. More important is the general framework of scientific humanism, buttressed by the ethical doctrine known as utilitarianism. This, with semi-Marxist variants (left over in particular from the former Soviet Union), probably accounts for the great majority of humanists in the contemporary world. With its usual rejection of religions, it is a formidable intellectual force at the end of the twentieth century. Scientific humanism appeals, of course, to science and is always revisionary and as such it keeps up with the times in a way that religion sometimes does not. On the other hand, it does not always explore what may be called the spiritual side of life. Yet there is no reason, apart from prejudice, why it should not.

The humanist worldview naturally sees the world as being empirical—to be estimated experimentally and as it is. On the other hand, this does not precisely exclude the Transcendent. The Big Bang, let us say, saw the beginning and evolution of the Universe. The empiricist does not postulate anything more. But the theist (for instance) may ascribe the Big Bang to a First Cause. There might have been no cosmos, no universe. The universe, it might be said, was brought into being by a conscious Cause. Such a view cannot be proved, but it does allow for the idea of a Transcendent Being. So in this argument, which follows the so-called Cosmological Argument, in the theistic tradition of Aquinas among others, the compatibility of a scientific and a theistic worldview is indicated.

Nevertheless, scientific humanism is a self-sufficient philosophy which has become increasingly important during the twentieth century, partly on its own merits and partly because of disillusion with some existing beliefs and traditions. The latter are sometimes presented in literalistic ways which seem to deny the findings of scientific inquiry.

One of the major shifts during the last half century has been to an environmentalist outlook. The way living beings are integrated into their environment and into the workings of the planet earth are not only fascinating and revealing. They also indicate the desperate dangers we run as a consequence of loading the Earth with pollutants and byproducts of our increasingly masterful activities as human beings. The heating up of the planet may be arising naturally, but indications are that it is due to us. Small countries like the Maldive Islands may just disappear, and cities on the sea may be swamped: all sorts of deleterious effects may occur. This new concern with environmentalism is something which traditional religions and scientific humanism may share. Indeed, the traditions have sometimes raised some major issues in the field: the Jain tenderness for animal life and the Buddhist view of all animal life as interconnected have been influential. Much has been learned, too, from the way Aboriginal or other indigenous peoples manage their surroundings and live in balance with their fellow animals. But, of course, for various reasons such peoples are losing their traditional way of life, from the Inuit who have given up hunting, to the people of Papua New Guinea who have moved to Port Moresby.

In 1969 the writer and scientist James Lovelock used the name Gaia (from the Greek word for the earth) to signify our planet as a united, interacting entity with all its life forms, as if it were a single organism. The imagery of this vision was strengthened by those vivid and beautiful pictures of the earth taken from space on the way to the moon. It is something which is beginning to enter our consciousness. Perhaps the cosmos is similarly to be regarded as a huge interaction of heavenly bodies. In any case, it seems that environmentalism is well established at the end of the century, and can function as one element in scientific humanism and in religious philosophy.

Finally, primarily in America to begin with, feminism has made a great impact on the social world of the West and increasingly outside. The enhancement of the rights of women is a logical extension of all the battles fought in the democracies for human rights. It is also something contained in the Marxist perspective. Sometimes conservative religion has resisted it. But as we have already seen, women are increasingly having a role in religions where in the past a patriarchal perspective has prevailed. Moreover, throughout the world this elementary thought is only now being learned—that in educating a girl you educate a generation. But like other social reforms it involves a long struggle to change well entrenched attitudes, and in some cultures there is the fear of undermining customs that have worked reasonably in the past. Yet freedom is impossible ultimately to resist, and the globalized world of communication makes it swifter to take hold.

Diasporas in the Modern World

We have noted how religions have spread into one another through migrations. In the period since World War II, upheavals caused by war as well as voluntary migrations have meant that much of Europe has experienced Islamic influxes, Hinduism particularly in Britain (and Sikhism), and African forms of Christianity and new religious movements. Throughout Central Asia and in the Caucasus, Russian settlement has occurred; and Chinese migrations in Southeast Asia: and so forth. Consequently, large numbers of countries have people of mixed religion. There are minorities everywhere. These various diasporas dictate a pluralist ethos.

Since the flow of money on the whole is from the richer countries to the poorer, that is, from the lands that receive these emigrants to those that send them, the new diasporas tend to influence the homelands a lot. The new areas challenge the religion more than the old, and they therefore in some degree prepare the religion for a more pluralistic attitude. On the other hand they may help to fuel radical minority groups. Thus, the movement among the Sikhs for Khalistan is energized by support from Canada, Britain, and elsewhere. The struggle against Sinhalese Buddhist hegemony in Sri Lanka is waged in Europe particularly by Tamil refugees.

In Israel there is a strange reversal of the old diaspora. The new homeland is back there, looked at nostalgically. It was just before the twentieth century, in 1896, that Theodor Herzl published his seminal book on Israel, *Der Judenstaat* (*The Jewish State*), which argued for a Jewish nation-state, on the grounds that the anti-Semitism of the Vienna of his day (which influenced, of course, the virulent politics of the young Adolf Hitler) would never let Jews live at peace, even if assimilated, in a country dominated by others. As it was he was proved right, and though Hitler never thought that the dream of a Jewish state would be realized, he ensured its realization because of the Holocaust. But Israel's stability is still not guaranteed, even now at the end of the century. The peace process with the Palestinians is at best sickly. The massive support by the United States of America is not easily able to overcome the still-hostile intentions of their neighbors, including the Palestinians with whom they overlap. Bombings continue, or are threatened still. Yet Jews, Palestinians, Arabs of all kinds, and Iranians live together peacefully within a pluralistic society like the United States. It is a lesson in the bitternesses which can (though need not) grow out of nationalism.

Tibetan Buddhist monks at a makeshift temple near Greenham Common, Newbury, Berkshire, England, the site of a prolonged peace demonstration against the siting of nuclear weapons at the U.S. air base. The camp was established in September 1981; the last Cruise missiles were withdrawn from Greenham Common

Western devotees of Krishna in the Hare Krishna movement.

But even in a pluralist society it is necessary to educate people into tolerance; and this in turn needs knowledge. It is no use saying "Tolerate these people," if we remain ignorant about them. I remarked at the beginning of this survey that ours is the first century when the religions really came to know one another—and this was largely during the second half, since World War II. The techniques for doing this are largely by introducing Religious Studies into high schools, and even before this into primary schools. Progress has been made in this, but there are often difficulties in overcoming deep prejudices, for instance in Western countries among Christians who wrongly feel that introducing young people to alternative faiths is somehow to betray loyalty and truth. Further, there are other voices which attest that because religion is false there is no point in inculcating any religious education. But the answer to these points is that if we are to understand the world, we must understand its worldviews. It is vulgar ignorance not to understand the values of our neighbors. The issue is not whether what they say is true but whether it is forceful. It is not its truth but its power that counts. And, of course, that in part depends on its emotional impact, independently of its evidence. So we shall finish this book with some thoughts on religious education. Partly, we do this because increasingly in the modern world the exploration of religion in a systematic way helps to soften the tensions which are almost inevitably bound to arise in pluralistic societies.

Worldview Analysis and Plural Societies

Traditionally religious education (or its secular parallel in Marxist societies) was conceived as inculcating the official faith or ideology, and sometimes perhaps two systems: for instance in Germany there were parallel Catholic and Protestant schools, and likewise in Northern Ireland. But recently, under the influence of pluralism and with the recognition of an educational (rather than simply an instructional) perspective, a multifaith approach has grown and developed. In Britain this was evident from the 1960s, and in Scandinavia, Germany, Canada, and elsewhere from a similar period. In the United States, especially in California, such an approach has been taken on from the 1980s. In South Africa with the death of *apartheid,* a like pluralism in religious education has developed. The nature of Christian education has also softened, taking in a positive attitude to other religions, and being open-ended in posing questions—this has been for the most part in liberal circles and to some degree in Catholic education, especially since Vatican II.

The logic behind this is that in order to understand the various religions, or some of them, you need to see them from their point of view, and from the standpoint of their feelings. Or, since this is put a little abstractly, you need to understand the people of such other faiths, and so you need to have empathy for them. Empathy does not necessarily mean sympathy: but you have to be able to begin to feel your way into their perspective. This requires imagination, and we shall later see how this can be cultivated. But empathy by itself is not enough. You need a lot of information too. If you are to understand what Shabbat means to the Jew, you have to know a bit about how in particular it is celebrated. You should know the story of the creation of the world and that story's relation to the Shabbat. You have to know something of how the family works among the Jews and its role in the wider community. You also have to know some of the varieties of different practice among differing communities of Jews (Orthodox, Conservative, Reform, and so forth). In other words a key to religious education is informed empathy.

Traditionally, religious education in Europe and North America leaned heavily on the Bible. No doubt there are advantages in inculcating the scripture. But it does not by itself tell you fully about the faith or the religion, and it only samples religious experience. You cannot learn what people do, nor does it spell out doctrine. For a fuller understanding of Christianity as it is practiced you need much more than the Bible. Similar remarks apply to the Qur'an or the Talmud, or the *Analects*, though this is not to say that induction into relevant scriptures is unimportant. And, of course, considerable experience has been gained in the study of foreign religions in how to explore them meaningfully. A pluralistic milieu makes this all the more important, so that young people can learn about the faiths of their surroundings, as well as of the wider world.

This last point is worth dwelling upon: the question of the wider world. The globe has undergone a dramatic change in the last half-century. The process of the drawing together of cultures has been accompanied by an increase in tensions. Religions have been seen to play an important part in the determination of events. Even if you are living in, say, Australia, where there are relatively few Muslims, knowledge of Islam is important, because the world's largest Muslim population lives next door in Indonesia. So knowing about the wider world means, then, knowing about religions. The same applies to history: to grasp traditions you need to grasp faiths.

Traditional religious education, based on scriptures, can leave young people both ignorant and prejudiced about alternative faiths. Indeed, it is often a major consequence of religious segregation. One of the most interesting cases is in Northern Ireland. By and large, education is indeed segregated there, ever since it became a separate entity and even before then. It is amazing that such separation is allowed. Had all Catholics been Black and all Protestants White, would such segregation have been allowed? But because the division is labeled "religious" it is tolerated. Catholic children grow up not knowing any Protestant children. It might be replied that the Churches want this to happen. Yet a Church can interfere with democracy and human rights as well as anyone else.

In general, then, a pluralistic approach to religious education is best. As I noted earlier, it is in the twentieth century and especially in its second half that the comparative study of religion has made the greatest advances. We can therefore take advantage of this fact in trying to stimulate exciting practice in the exploration of religion.

We have mentioned the importance of informed empathy. This does not, of course, tell you about the truth of religion (or its falsity): its purpose is to provide knowledge as to how a religion works and feels. It can also tell you how it has worked and used to feel, though this is not as easy: you can always get to know about a living religion better than a dead one. You can always ask people what they believe, and how they feel, something you cannot do with the dead.

After you have come to some understanding of a religion or worldview, then you may, if you will, judge it—whether it is mainly true or mainly false, or whatever. But you cannot judge if you do not understand, or misunderstand. During the greater part of history and among most people, religions have been misunderstood. This is one of the ongoing scandals of the human condition. Ignorance has been normal, understanding scarce. This is a great breakthrough of the twentieth century: the determination to understand other cultures and traditions, though again it is a value shared by a minority. There is also among some, as we have seen, the wish to enter into genuine dialogue with other traditions. This at least signifies the desire to go beyond merely understanding another faith, but also agreeing on values where this is at all possible. This desire has not been altogether absent in the past, but it is somewhat more prevalent in the twentieth century.

The present "mixing up" of the world—the pluralistic condition—has the advantage that it renders the empathy much more practical. You may make friends with Buddhists, with Jews, with Christians, with Hindus, with Muslims, wherever you live. You can accompany them to a temple, or mosque, or synagogue, and so on. This stimulates the imaginative side of your nature. It can vivify your empathy. When I was in Durban, South Africa, I was taken by a friend to a strongly evangelical chapel populated wholly by Indians (apart, that evening, from myself and my friend). I could get a strong feel for the occasion and for the kind of spirituality being celebrated. They even asked me to say a word to them after the service. I said that there would be a little piece of Durban there in California, and thanked them for their hospitality. I did not agree with quite a bit of what they said: but I could honestly say that I understood that kind of religion a bit better, and I appreciated their having invited us.

Also, of course, ours is an age of tourism. You can see Buddhism in practice if you travel to Sri Lanka. When I was young, more than 50 years ago, hardly anyone could go to Ceylon (as it then was). Now it is fairly commonplace. Seeing the monuments of another culture again stimulates empathy, and gets you to see into another tradition, and conversing with Buddhist monks can help you to penetrate into another tradition.

It is possible also to move into another culture or cultural circle by means of a novel: say Dostoyevsky's *The Brothers Karamazov*, or Antonio Fogazzaro's *The Saint*, or R. K. Narayan's *The Guide*. After all, a novelist incorporates a sort of empathy, for the narrative encapsulates a point of view and the elements of feelings. Similar remarks apply to movies and TV presentations. The thirteen-part series *The Long Search* presents various of the major world's religions, and was a sign of the twentieth century's increasing commitment to understanding religions.

It is worth also reflecting that understanding is a matter of degree. It may be that we can never understand any person perfectly. The question is whether you can understand him or her better, or more deeply than before. It is not our ambition to achieve anything very profound: but it is an advance on what has gone on through much of human history and in most societies for us to have a positive attitude toward understanding other cultures and points of view. Often people have been afraid that opening up our minds leads to slackness of belief and that this in turn undermines the fabric of society.

A World Worldview

Finally, we may ask: even if there is not a unity in regard to religion, could there be some kind of world worldview, perhaps at some higher level? I would argue that a global society, such as we are now developing, needs some guidelines as to how religions and ideologies are to treat one another. It is implicit in our discussion, and at times explicit, that our total society should be pluralistic. This implies that we should not suppress any religious manifestation except for good reason. As far as possible, differing customs should be held together. Differing expressions of spirituality should be allowed. There is little call for drab conformism in behavior. Even now there is probably too much conformity. There is no strong reason to banish polygamy where there is a substantial population of Muslims, and bureaucratic problems could be worked around.

The norm in religious education should be toward understanding, and governments might encourage dialogue between the differing worldviews. A democratic public should be sensitive in matters of religion, and verbal and other clashes should be discouraged. There are areas of the world where a relatively idyllic picture is to be seen—for instance in Scandinavia. Elsewhere, the democracies are struggling with outbreaks of hatred, but are making progress. There are regions, Iran for instance, where religious intolerance leads to the throttling of human rights. But overall we can say that the last half century has brought considerable change for the better, compared with previous years. This is especially so in the ex-Soviet Union and also in Western Europe from rather earlier. So the global picture is surely brightening.

Perhaps in a period of increased tolerance a new religious age is dawning. It is extraordinary how some of the great figures of our age are religious persons: Mahātma Gandhi, Archbishop Tutu, John XXIII, and Mother Teresa. The most influential figures of all ages have been so: Confucius, the Buddha, Jesus, Muhammad, Kabīr, Zarathustra…

So a world worldview is emerging. We can call it global pluralism for short.

East comes West: a child practicing a form of Indian yoga in America.

Glossary

Adi Granth   The Sikh scriptures, sometimes called Guru Granth, which succeeds the last human Guru, namely Gobind Singh.

Adur or Atar   Fire, regarded as purified, and ritually tended in Zoroastrian temples.

ahiṃsā   Non-injury, harmlessness: a virtue in Jainism and found also in the Hindu and Buddhist traditions; given a political meaning by Gandhi.

Ahura Mazda   Zoroastrian term for the good God and Creator: later Ohrmazd

ajīva   Non-life or inert matter (as opposed to *jivas* or souls) in Jainism.

akh   The glorious aspect of the human being, capable of appearing after death, in ancient Egyptian religion.

Allah   (Islam) The one true God.

Amesha Spentas   The seven Holy Immortals regarded as offshoots or emanations of God, in Zoroastrian doctrine.

Amrit   Sweetened water in which a Sikh is baptized.

Anabaptists   Movement in early Reformation, which held that only adults should be baptized, since it postulated the faith of the person baptized, and only grown people could have faith.

anekāntavāda   The doctrine known as relativism in Jainism.

Angas   The earliest texts in the Jain tradition.

angas   The stages or parts of the Eightfold Path in Buddhism

Angra Mainyu   The evil counterforce to God in Zoroastrianism; later Ahriman.

arca   Image or icon in Hinduism.

ātman   Permanent self or supreme Self in Hinduism.

atonement   Doctrine of reconciliation in Christianity, when God and humans are once more 'at one' through sacrifice of Christ

atua   A God in Polynesian religion: the Creator or any lesser deity.

Avatāra   (Hinduism) Descent or incarnation of God (notably Viṣṇu) in such figures as Rama, Kṛṣṇa and the future Kalki.

ba   the human soul (with *akh*) in ancient Egyptian religion.

baptism   The sacrament of immersion in water, or being sprinkled with water, whereby a person is initiated into the Christian Church.

Baptists   The denomination in Christian Protestantism which stresses the sacrament of Baptism and which follows on from the Anabaptists: powerful in America and in particular in the South.

bhakti   Devotionalism in Hindu and some Buddhist traditions.

Bible   The collection of books which are treated by Christians as the record of God's revelation.

Bodhisattva   Buddha-to-be who puts off his final liberation to work tirelessly for the sake of other living beings. The most famous bodhisattva figure is Avalokiteśvara who became Guanyin in China and Kannon in Japan.

bosatsu   Japanese term for Bodhisattva or Being destined for Enlightenment.

Brahman   The power in the sacrifice and in the Brahmin class in Hinduism: extrapolated as the Holy Power sustaining the universe: Sacred Reality, God.

Buddha   An enlightened being who has seen the truth of dharma.

Bundahishn   The original creation of the world, in Zoroastrianism: also the title of a scripture.

butsudan   A shrine with a Buddha statue in a Japanese household, parallel to a *kamidan* with a representation of a *kami*.

Caliph   The leader of Islam, most recently based in Istanbul: modern nationalism and prior movements split the Islamic area, and modern attempts to spread a Pan-Islamic philosophy have revived the call for a reinstitution of the Caliphate.

Calumet   French expression applied to instrument for smoking in the Native American tradition from Canada to South America.

Chiao   A religious movement, teaching or sect.

Chinvat   The bridge (in Islamic doctrine) which leads to heaven or hell. A beautiful maid leads the soul across if good. If bad it is found to be razor thin and he slides into hell.

Christ   The anointed one or Messiah who is the agent of salvation.

Church   The community of Christians on earth and in heaven.

Communion   The Eucharist or Mass or Lord's Supper. In a separate usage the Communion of Saints comprises those who are saved and have passed away.

Corroboree   Australian aboriginal festival get together, often reenacting myths.

Cosmos   The orderly world: came to be used in ancient Greece for the universe.

Daimoku   Japanese title of the Lotus Sutra, which is invoked in Nichiren Buddhism to ensure salvation.

Dao   (Tao) The Way, the ruling principle of the cosmos in Daoism (Taoism).

Dharma   The law or principle underlying social and physical life in the Hindu and Buddhist traditions.

Dhyāna   Meditation: usually in eight stages of ascending purity of consciousness.

dhyāna   (Pali: *jhāna*) Meditation in Buddhism, later in China rendered as Qān (Korean Son, Japanese, Zen).

Digambara   One main branch of the Jaina tradition, referring to ascetics who are nudist (literally 'sky-clad').

ecopsychism   The view that there are spirits in the environment (hunting and gathering peoples often are involved with this outlook).

Existentialism   A philosophical view espoused by Jean-Paul Sartre, Martin Heidegger and many others emphasizing human freedom (hence its name: human existence precedes essence: he make up his nature as he goes along).

Fascism Totalitarian or strongly authoritarian system of extremely romantic nationalist type; not necessarily racist, but certainly so in the case of Nazism.

Filioque 'And from the son'—a phrase inserted into the creed by the Roman Catholic Church and seen by the Orthodox as a wrongful intrusion. It helped exacerbate the rift between the Orthodox and Catholic Churches.

frashokereti The act of creation, resurrection and final judgment: renewal of things, in Zoroastrian myth and doctrine.

fravashis The eternal spirits of human beings, residing in heaven (our being here is a matter of choice); in Zoroastrianism.

Fundamentalism A term used loosely: usually of conservative Christians; sometimes used of Islamists, that is rather reducal Muslims; and also of Hindus (say, the B.J.P.). It is best confined to Christians of a fairly literal bent in regard to the Bible.

Grace The power of God entering into humans to empower them to good deeds and salvation.

Granth See *Adi Granth*.

gurudwara Sikh temple.

Guru Spirirual preceptor in the Hindu tradition; also the ten leaders of the Sikh community culminating in Guru Gobind Singh.

Ḥadīth Certified stories about the life of the Prophet Muḥammada and therefore the basis for rules and hints about conduct.

hajj Pilgrimage to Mecca, enjoined on all Muslims if he or she reasonably can. One who has been is a *Hajji*.

Hasidim (or Chasidim) A movement founded in Eastern Europe (Ukraine and Southern Poland) in the late 18th century, with an emphasis on mysticism.

Haskalah The Jewish Enlightenment in Europe: mainly during the late 18th and 19th centuries. It generated new thinking and ethical and ritual practice among Jews.

Hesychasm Orthodox style of mysticism, especially in early medieval Greece (based on the word *hesyche* or peace) and involving breathing techniques.

High God The idea of a Deity who is not necessarily heavily engaged with humankind, but presides distantly over our fate (the idea is attributed to Wilhelm Schmidt). Small scale tribes often believe in such a Being.

Holocaust Greek word for whole burnt offering (literally 'whole burnt'). Later used for the Nazi massacre of vast numbers of Jews (and others).

hubris Based on the Greek *hybris*, referring to the kind of arrogance which leads humans to claim equality with the gods (or God).

ikon An Eastern Orthodox ikon (or icon) which portrays a saint or Christ, and usually placed on the main partition in an Orhodox church, to be reverenced and kissed, and regarded as a 'window onto heaven'.

Imam A prayer-leader in a mosque; also used as a title for the twelve great leaders of Shi'a Islam.

Israel The land which is the focus of Jewish aspiration.

Īśvara The Lord God (literally the Lord), in Hinduism: the usual term for the personal God (Viṣṇu, Śiva, etc.)

Janamsakhi Sikh writings celebrating the life of Guru Nanak.

jāti Caste; within the larger framework of *varṇa* headed by Brahmins (followed by *kṣatriya*, *vaiśya* and *śudra* classes, after which come untouchables or *dalits*).

jhāna see *dhyāna*.

jihād Holy struggle (in Islam): either a spiritual or a military struggle.

jina Victor, title given to Mahāvīra. His followers are called *jainas*. The title was also afforded the Buddha.

jing A classical text, usually used for the ancient Confucian collection of five classics, but also applied to some other fundamental sources such as the Platform Sutra of Qān tradition.

Jōdō The Pure Land (in Japanese), a heaven on the way to *nirvāṇa*.

Kabbalah The "received tradition" of Jewish mysticism expressed in such texts as the *Zohar* (13th century Spain).

kachina A sacred mask used by the Hopi in the American Southwest.

kāma Love or pleasure (Sanskrit, Pāli).

kami God or spirit in Shinto.

Kannon (Japan) The *bodhisattva* Avalokiteśvara in female form (Chinese Guanyin).

karma Literally 'act': also refers to the effects of acts, together with the law governing them.

Kashrut Jewish dietary requirements, i.e. what is "kosher" or unpolluted, pure.

Kevala (Jainism) State of liberation in which the *jīva* exists motionless at the summit of the universe, pictured as a colossal human.

Khalsa The Sikh community or order, the "pure ones" started by Gobind.

Khilafat The Caliphate movement, seeking the restoration of the Caliph.

Kojiki Scripture of Shinto, codified in the 7th century C.E.

Kokutai (Japan) The national essence: so the Shinto of the pre-World War II period is sometimes referred to as Kokutai Shinto.

li Proper behavior, prized by Confucius, including ceremonious and ritual behavior.

li Principle or spiritual substance or energy, combining with qi (*ch'i*) or material energy (Neo-Confucian philosophy).

Liberal Protestantism The kind of Protestantism that interprets the Bible in the light of scholarship, science and democratic principles.

Liberation Theology Catholic movement interpreting the Gospel in Marxist terms: influential in South and Central America from the 1970s.

Logos Human reason, sometimes identified as the principle governing the cosmos and with Christ.

Love Greek *agapē*, the reverential affection for other human beings which is the primary Christian virtue.

mahāvrata The great vow taken by a Jain monk or nun, pledging to practise non-injury and to avoid lying, sex, stealing and owning anything.

Mahāyāna The Great Vehicle: the Buddhist movement stressing the way of the Buddha, and relying on the philosophy of Emptiness: includes such new thrusts as Pure Land Buddhism.

mana The concept of sacred force: a Melanesian term adopted by anthropologists and historians of religion.

maṇḍala A sacred diagram used in the Vajrayāna and in Hinduism, sometimes identifying the cosmic directions with great Bodhisattvas.

manes The shades of the dead in Roman religion.

Manthras Words of power: prayers drawn mainly from the earliest scriptures attributed to Zarathustra.

mantra a sacred formula in the Indian tradition and in later Buddhism.

mappō The period when the Dharma is no longer possible to follow, and so schools like the Pure Land arise.

marabout In North African Islam, a saint or holy person.

marae Polynesian sacred area with shrine.

masalai Papua–New Guinea word for a demon or spirit liable to haunt humans.

mashiaḥ Messiah: person who will come in the future to restore Israel and usher in period of peace. It was a title applied to Jesus.

matsuri Shinto festival.

Mennonites   Followers of Menno Simons, who settled largely in Eastern Europe and North America, and were successors of the Anabaptists.

Messiah   See *mashiaḥ*.

Miko   Shinto shamans or priestesses, brought up strictly as virgins and dedicated to the cult of the local *kami*.

millet system   The Ottoman arrangement for Christians and Jews to have a degree of autonomy.

Mitzvah (plural *Mitzvot;* Judaism)   Commandment: there are ten main ones and traditionally 613 in all.

Mizimu (Bantu)   The spirits of the dead: ancestors.

modernism   A modernizing standpoint in any religious tradition, represented by such positions as those of Reform Judaism, liberal Protestantism, Buddhist modernism, Islamic modernism, etc.

Mool Mantra (Sikhism)   The "basic verse," a brief statement of belief composed by Nanak affirming the oneness of God.

mysteria   Mysteries or mystery religions involving the revelation of truth in dramatic form by initiation.

mythos   Story of the gods in authoritative mode.

nabi   Prophet in Islam, including Abraham and Jesus, as well as Muḥammad

nembutsu   Calling on the Buddha in faith, in Japanese Pure Land Buddhism: the formula is 'Homage to the Buddha'.

Neoconfucianism   The medieval Confucian revival in China and Korea.

Neo-Platonism   The religious philosophy pioneered by Plotinus.

Nganga   Specialist in healing with sickness and various evils, in Central and Southern African traditions: a so-called witch-doctor.

nirvāṇa   (*Nibbana* in Pali) The cessation of rebirth brought on by greed, hatred and delusion.

numen   Spirit or god in Roman religion: from it the adjective 'numinous' was derived by Rudolf Otto.

numinous   characterized by being awe-inspiring mysterious and fearful.

Ohrmazd   See Ahura Mazda.

pancasīla   The five precepts in Buddhism—to refrain from taking life, stealing, wrong sex, wrong speech and drugs and intoxicants.

panth   Literally the path, viz. the Sikh community (who follow the path).

pentecostalism   A movement which is usually conservative Biblically but is animated by speaking in tongues and other experiences inspired by the Holy Spirit (so it is claimed): strong in Latin America.

philosophia   The love of wisdom: in former times, in particular in the Hellenistic and Roman worlds a philosophy was more like a religion than it is now.

Prajñā (Pali:*Praññā*)   Buddhist term for insight or vision.

Pratītyasamutpāda (Buddhism)   Codependent origination of events, the law which links together all the events of the world in sequences of saṃsāra.

Presbyterianism   A denomination which is affiliated with the Reformed Churches, and ruled by elected presbyteries according to a mode laid down by Calvin.

Pūjā (Hinduism)   Worship.

Pure Land movement   Originally found in India and from there developed in China and Japan, so-called from the Pure Land projected by Amitabha Buddha (Japanese Amida), it took a radical form in Japan.

Qabbalah   See Kabbalah.

qalandars   Muslim ascetics, often adopting Hindu means of self-mortification.

Qān (Ch'ān)   Meditation (a Chinese version of Sanskrit *dhyāna*) and name of an important school known in Japanese as Zen.

qi (ch'i)   material energy, which combines with *li* or principle to make up things in the world.

Qur'ān (Islam)   The sacred revelation or word of God, being eternal, and revealed to the Prophet.

Rabbi (Judaism)   A teacher of the traditional Torah, and learned teacher and spiritual counselor of a community.

Rahit   The code of ethics and rituals laid upon Sikhs, including the wearing of the five K's: uncut hair, dagger, breeches, comb and iron bangle.

Reconstructionist Movement   The modern Jewish movement founded by Mordecai Kaplan in 1935, stressing the vitality of Jewish culture and underplaying belief in an anthropomorphic God.

Reform Judaism   Liberal Judaism of the modern period, strong especially in America under the influence of Isaac Wise among others.

Religio   That which binds us to the gods, religion (Latin).

ren (jen)   Humane-heartedness, in the Confucian tradition; benevolence towards other human beings.

ṛṣi (rishi)   A Vedic seer, or visionary.

ṣalat   Islamic prayer.

sannyāsin   A recluse, often an elderly person giving up the world after

having trodden the various stages of life (in the Hindu tradition).

Saṃsāra (Buddhism)   The living flux of existence in which individuals are involved in the process of rebirth.

sangha   The community of Buddhist monks.

sant   A North Indian belonging to a devotional tradition in North India, typically viewing God as without attributes. The two most important (in that they gave rise to Sikhism) were Kabīr and Nānak.

Sat Guru   The name most given to God in Sikhism, "Being, the Teacher."

satori   Realization or enlightenment in Zen Buddhism.

saum   Fasting (in Islam) especially during the holy month of Ramadan.

Shabbat (Judaism)   The "rest" day, from Friday sundown to sundown on Saturday.

Shaman   (Tungus word from Siberia) a visionary who can, in sharing experimentally in the vicissitudes of the sick, help to cure them and who can locate resources (such as fish and game) in a hunting society; often experiences death and rebirth.

shari'a   Islamic law, interpreted according to diverse schools.

Shi'a   The denomination other than Sunni or the traditional form of Islam. The Shi'i or Shi'a believe in a differing tradition of Caliphs; and in an occult or hidden Imam who will manifest himself in the future.

Shinto   The way of the *kami*, a strong element in Japanese religion and for a while in modern times expressing the mandatory ethos of the Japanese nation.

Sikh   Literally "disciple," member of the Sikh Panth.

Śīla   Virtue or a precept encouraging a virtue, such as the five precepts summing up Buddhist morality.

Sin (Christianity)   The estrangement of humans from God, thought to be due to the actions of Adam and Eve in the first instance.

Sufism   The mystical or contemplative path within Islam.

starets   Russian holy man.

Stūpa (Buddhism)   A mound for containing relics, formalized into the central feature of temples and pagoda.

sūnyatā   Emptiness: the major philosophical doctrine of the Mahāyāna.

Śvetambara   White-clad ones: those Jains belonging to the group which does not practice monastic nudity. Each monk or nun has three pieces of white cloth to wear.

tabu or *tapu*   A Polynesian word meaning dangerous or forbidden: great *mana* generates *tabu*.

Taiping (T'ai P'ing)   The heavenly peace, looked forward to as an eschatological kingdom in Daoist literature; name of mid–19th-century rebellion in China.

Taizhi (T'ai Chi)   The Great Ultimate in Neo-Confucianism: the Source of All Things.

Talmud   A major text of the Jewish tradition, in Aramaic, being in two forms, the Babylonian and Palestinian. The former is in principle binding, as to its legal and ethical or halakhic provisions, on all orthodox Jews.

Tantra   Ritualistic form of Buddhism and Hinduism, sometimes emphasizing the female power of God.

tapas   Literally heat: term for austerity in the Indian tradition, specially emphasized in Jainism and parts of Hinduism.

Tathāgata   Title of the Buddha, meaning 'Thus-gone'.

Tathatā   Mahayana word meaning 'Suchness', used for ultimate reality.

temenos   A sancruary or sacred area (Greek).

Tendai   A sacramental and esoteric movement within Japanese Buddhism, originally based on the Lotus Sutra.

Tian (T'ien)   Heaven or personalized God residing above, whose cult was that of the Emperor.

Tirthankara   Ford-maker – a title of the supreme leaders of Jainism.

theos   Greek word for God or a god.

theosis   Divinization, becoming divine or god-like (Greek Orthodox).

Torah   (Judaism) The teaching or law, handed down in both written and oral form to Moses on Sinai: identified in written form with the first five books of the Hebrew Bible.

totem   Algonquin word from North America: a natural species of animal or plant which is affiliated to a clan, which does not hunt or gather it.

Trinity   God in Christianity conceived as consisting of three persons (Father, Son and Holy Spirit) united in one substance.

umma   The community in Islam.

Unitarianism   A movement which rejects the Trinity doctrine.

Utilitarianism   The ethical theory that a good or evil action is determined by its propensity to cause human happiness or unhappiness.

Yahweh   (Judaism) The chief name of God in Hebrew.

Yazatas   (Zoroastrianism) Heavenly beings or angels thought worthy or worship. The most popular is Mithra.

yin-yang   The female and male principles in Chinese religion.

yoga   The practice of inner meditation in Indian traditions.

yasasna   worship in the Zoroastrian tradition.

zakat   Giving alms to the poor: one of the pillars of Islam.

Zen   Literally "meditation". The name of Japanese forms of yogic Buddhism, exploiting fresh techniques of contemplation.

Zurvan   Time: focus of a later Zoroastrian deviation in which Ohrmazd and Ahriman derive from it, looked on as a divinity.

Bibliography

Walter Capps, *Religious Studies: The Making of a Discipline*, Minneapolis, 1995

S. Cromwell Crawford, ed., *World Religions and Global Ethics*, New York, 1991

Mircea Eliade, ed., *The Encyclopedia of Religion*, 15 vols., New York, 1987

E. E. Evans-Pritchard, *Theories of Primitive Religion*, Oxford, 1965

John R. Hinnells, ed., *A Handbook of Living Religions*, Baltimore, 1985

G. van der Leeuw, *Religion in Essence and Manifestation*, Princeton, 1987

Rudolf Otto, *The Idea of the Holy*, London, 1950

Sabrina P. Ramet and Donald W. Treadgold, eds., *Render under Caesar: The Religious Sphere in World Politics*, Washington, 1995

Eric J. Sharpe, *Comparative Religion – A History*, London, 1976

Ninian Smart, *Dimensions of the Sacred: An Anatomy of the World's Beliefs*, San Francisco, 1997

Ninian Smart, *The Religious Experience of Mankind*, 5th edn., Upper Saddle River, NJ, 1996

Ninian Smart and Richard Hecht, eds., *Sacred Texts of the World*, London, 1982

R. J. Z. Werblowsky, *Beyond Tradition and Modernity: Changing Religions in a Changing World*, London, 1976

Earliest Religion

E. O. James, *The Beginnings of Religion*, Westport, Conn., 1973

Johannes Maringer, *The Gods of Prehistoric Man*, New York, 1960

Alexander Marshack, *The Roots of Civilization*, New York, 1972

Elizabeth Shee Twohig, *The Megalithic Art of Western Europe*, Oxford, 1981

South Asia

Paul Bowen, ed., *Themes and Issues in Hinduism*, London, 1997

E. O. Cole and P. S. Sambhi, *The Sikh Tradition*, London, 1978

Edward Conze, *Buddhism: Its Essence and Development*, New York, 1984

S. N. Dasgupta, *A History of Indian Philosophy*, 5 vols., Delhi, 1976

M. David Eckel, *To See the Buddha: A Philosopher's Quest for the Meaning of Emptiness*, San Francisco, 1992

Mircea Eliade, *Yoga: Immortality and Freedom*, 2nd ed., Princeton, 1969

Gavin Flood, *An Introduction to Hinduism*, Cambridge, 1996

Melvyn C. Goldstein and Matthew T. Capstein, *Buddhism in Contemporary Tibet*, Berkeley, 1988

Richard Gombrich, *Theravada Buddhism*, London, 1988

Friedholm Hardy, *The Religious Culture of India: Power, Love and Wisdom,* Cambridge, 1994

Peter Harvey, *An Introduction to Buddhism*, Cambridge, 1994

P. S. Jaini, *The Jaina Path of Purification*, Berkeley, 1979

Winston L. King, *Buddhist Meditation*, Philadelphia, 1980

Klaus K. Klostermaier, *A Survey of Hinduism*, Albany, NY, 1994

Julia Leslie, *Roles and Rituals for Hindu Women*, London, 1997

Wendy Doniger O'Flaherty, ed., *Karma and Rebirth in Classical Indian Traditions*, Berkeley, 1980

Walpola Rahula, *What the Buddha Taught*, New York, 1962

Ninian Smart, *Doctrine and Argument in Indian Philosophy*, London, 1964

John S. Strong, *The Experience of Buddhism: Sources and Interpretations*, Belmont, CA, 1995

Giuseppe Tucci, *The Religions of Tibet*, Berkeley, 1980

Steven Vertovec, *Hindu Trinidad*, London, 1992

Benjamin Walker, *Hindu World*, 2 vols., London, 1968

A. K. Warder, *Indian Buddhism*, Delhi, 1970

Heinrich Zimmer, *Myths and Symbols in Indian Art and Civilization*, Princeton, 1972

China and Korea

D. Bodde, *Festivals in Classical China*, Princeton, 1975

Julia Ching, *Chinese Religions*, New York, 1993

Kenneth Ch'en, *Buddhism in China*, Princeton, 1973

F. H. Cook, *Hua-yen Buddhism*, Philadelphia, 1977

Theodore de Bary and JaHyun Kim Maboush, eds, *The Rise of Neo-Confucianism in Korea*, New York, 1985

Daniel K. Gardner, *Chu Hsi and the Ta Hsueh*, Cambridge, MA, 1986

Stuart R. Schram, *The Political Thought of Mao Tse-tung*, rev. edn., New York, 1969

D. Howard Smith, *Confucius*, New York, 1973

L. C. Thompson, *Chinese Religion: An Interpretation*, 4th edn., Encino, Ca., 1989

Holmes Welch, *The Practice of Chinese Buddhism*, New York, 1967

Holmes Welch and Anna Siedel, eds., *Facets of Taoism: Essays in Chinese Religion*, New Haven, 1979

Feng Yu-lan, *A History of Chinese Philosophy*, 2 vols., Princeton, 1952–3

Japan

Carmen Blacker, *The Catalpa Bow: A Study of Shamanistic Practices in Japan*, London, 1975

H. Dumoulin, *History of Zen Buddhism*, New York, 1965

H. Byron Earhart, *Japanese Religion*, 3rd edn., Belmont, Ca., 1982

Joseph M. Kitagawa, *Religion in Japanese History*, New York, 1990

S. Murakami, *Japanese Religion in the Modern Century*, Tokyo, 1980

D. T. Suzuki, *Shin Buddhism*, New York, 1970

South East Asia

Georges Coedes, *The Indianized States of Southeast Asia*, Canberra, 1968

Clifford Geertz, *The Religion of Java*, Glencoe, Ill, 1960

Melford E. Spiro, *Burmese Supernaturalism*, 2nd edn., Philadelphia, 1978

Donald Swearer, *The Buddhist World of Southeast Asia*, Albany, NY, 1995

Keith W. Taylor, *The Birth of Vietnam*, Berkeley, 1983

Oceania and Australasia

Mircea Eliade, *Australian Religions: An Introduction*, Ithaca, New York, 1973

Peter Lawrence and M. J. Meggitt, eds., *Gods, Ghosts and Men in Melanesia*, Melbourne, 1965

Albert C. Moore, *Arts in the Religions of the Pacific*, London, 1997

Roslyn Poignant, *Oceanic Mythology: Myths of Polynesia, Micronesia, Melanesia, Australia*, London, 1967

Jean Smith, *Tapu Removal in Maori Religion*, Wellington, 1976

Indigenous American Religions

Walter H. Capps, ed., *Seeing with a Native Eye*, New York, 1976

Michael Coe, Dean Snow and Elizabeth Benson, *Atlas of Ancient America*, New York and Oxford, 1989

Ake Hultkrantz, *The Religions of the North American Indians*, Berkeley, 1979

Walter Krickeberg, et al, *Pre-Columbian American Religions*, New York, 1968

J. H. Steward, ed., *Handbook of South American Indians*, vol. 1, Washington, D.C., 1949

Ancient Near East

W. F. Albright, *From the Stone Age to Christianity*, Baltimore, 1958

J. Gray, *Near Eastern Mythology*, London, 1969

S. N. Kramer, *History Begins at Sumer*, New York, 1963

S. Morena, *Egyptian Religion*, New York, 1973

Persia and Central Asia

Mary Boyce, *Zoroastrians: Their Beliefs and Practices*, London and Boston, 1984

Mircea Eliade, *Shamanism*, Princeton, 1965

John R. Hinnells, *Persian Mythology*, New York, 1971

John R. Hinnells, *Zoroastrianism and the Parsees*, London, 1981

Geo Widengren, *Mani and Manicheism*, New York, 1965

R. C. Zaehner, *The Dawn and Twilight of Zoroastrianism*, New York, 1961

The Hellenistic World and Northern Europe

Peter Brown, *The Making of Late Antiquity*, Cambridge, Mass., 1979

Hilda Davidson, *Gods and Myths of Northern Europe*, Baltimore, 1964

E. R. Dodd, *Pagan and Christian in an Age of Anxiety*, New York, 1970

G. S. Kirk, *The Nature of Greek Myths*, New York, 1975

M. P. Nilsson, *A History of Greek Religion*, New York, 1964

A. D. Nock, *Conversion*, New York, 1961

A. and B. Rees, *Celtic Heritage*, London, 1975

H. J. Rose, *Ancient Roman Religion*, New York, 1948

Kyrosslava T. Znayenko, *The Gods of the Ancient Slavs*, Columbus, Ohio, 1980

Judaism

Joseph Blau, *Modern Varieties of Judaism*, New York, 1966

Richard Hecht and Roger Friedland, *To Rule Jerusalem*, Cambridge, 1995

Louis Jacobs, *The Jewish Religion: A Companion*, Oxford, 1995

E. Kedourie, ed., *The Jewish World*, New York, 1979

Nicolas de Lange, *Judaism*, Oxford, 1987

C. G. Monterfiore and H. Loewe, eds., *A Rabbinic Anthology*, new edn., New York, 1974

J. Neusner, *Early Rabbinic Judaism*, Leiden, 1975

H. Rabinowicz, *The World of Hasidism*, Hartford, Conn., 1970

D. Rudavsky, *Modern Jewish Religious Movements*, 3rd edn., New York, 1979

G. G. Sholem, *Major Trends in Jewish Mysticism*, New York, 1961

Juliet Steyn, *The Jew: Assumptions of Identity*, London, 1998

Alan Unterman, *Jews: Their Religious Beliefs and Practices*, Boston, 1981

J. Weingreen, *From Bible to Mishna*, New York, 1976

Christianity

Catherine Albanese, *America: Religion and Religions*, Belmont, Ca., 1981

A. S. Atiya, *A History of Eastern Christianity*, New York, 1970

D. B. Barrett, ed., *World Christian Encyclopedia*, Nairobi, 1982

Peter Brown, *Augustine of Hippo: A Biography*, Berkeley, 1967

Owen Chadwick, *The Popes and European Revolution*, New York, 1981

C. H. Dodd, *The Founder of Christianity*, New York, 1970

Enrique Dussel, ed., *The Church in Latin America, 1492-1992*, Maryknoll, NY, 1992

R. S. Ellwood, *Religious and Spiritual Groups in Modern America*, Englewood Cliffs, N. J., 1973

W. H. C. Frend, *The Early Church*, Philadelphia, 1966

Judith Herrin, *The Formation of Christendom*, Princeton, 1987

W. J. Hollenberger, *The Pentecostals*, London, 1972

Paul Johnson, *A History of Christianity*, New York, 1976

J. N. D. Kelly, *Early Church Doctrines*, New York, 1978

C. Lane *Christian Religion in the Soviet Union*, New York, 1979

John McManners, ed., *The Oxford Illustrated History of Christianity*, Oxford, 1992

Y. Meyendorff, *Byzantine Theology*, 2nd edn., 1978

Marta Sordi, *Christians and the Roman Empire*, Norman, OK, and London, 1994

Timothy Ware, *The Orthodox Church*, Baltimore, 1980

Islam

Clinton Bennett, *Muhammad: An Interpretative Study*, London, 1988

Clifford Geertz, *Islam Observed*, New Haven, Conn., 1968

Ernest Gollner, *Muslim Society*, Cambridge, 1981

S. Hussain M. Jagri, *Origins and Early Development of Shi'a Islam*, London, 1979

Bernard Lewis, *The Emergence of Modern Turkey*, London, 1963

Richard C. Martin, *Islam: A Cultural Perspective*, Englewood Cliffs, N. J., 1982.

Marmaduke M. Pickthall, *The Meaning of the Glorious Koran*, New York, 1930

Fazlur Rahman, *Islam*, 2nd edn., Chicago, 1979

Anne-Marie Schimmel, *Mystical Dimensions of Islam*, Chapel Hill, N. C., 1975

Wilfred C. Smith, *Islam in Modern History*, Princeton, 1957

H. Montgomery Watt, *Muhammad: Prophet and Statesman*, London, 1974

David Waynes, *An Introduction to Islam*, Cambridge, 1975

African Religions

Roger Bastide, *The African Religions of Brazil*, Baltimore, 1978

David Chidester, *Religions of South Africa*, London, 1992

Adrian Hastings, *A History of African Christianity*, 1950–1975, New York, 1979

Irving Hexham and Karla Poewe, *New Religions as Global Cultures*, Boulder, CO, 1997

Elizabeth Isichei, *A History of Christianity in Africa: From Antiquity to the Present*, Grand Rapids, MI, 1995

J. S. Mbiti, *Concepts of God in Africa*, New York, 1970

Thomas Pakenham, *The Scramble for Africa*, London, 1991

E. G. Parrinder, *African Traditional Religion*, 3rd edn., London, 1979

Benjamin C. Ray, *African Religions*, New York, 1976

H. W. Turner, *Religious Innovations in Africa*, Boston, 1980

E. M. Zuesse, *Ritual Cosmos: The Sanctification of Life in African Religions*, Athens, Ohio, 1979

Secular Worldviews

Frederick Copleston, *A History of Philosophy*, Vol. VIII, London, 1966

Leszcek Kolokowski, *Main Currents of Marxism*, 3 vols., Oxford, 1978–1981

John Macquarrie, *Twentieth Century Religious Thought*, 2nd edn., New York, 1981

David Martin, *A General Theory of Secularization*, San Francisco, 1979

Peter Merkl and Ninian Smart, eds., *Religion and Politics in the Modern World*, New York, 1984

David Roberts, *Existentialism and Religious Belief*, N.Y., 1960

T. L. S. Sprigge, *Theories of Existence*, Harmondsworth, 1985

Credits

The author, publishers and Calmann & King Ltd wish to thank the following institutions and individuals who have provided photographic material for use in this book:

Colour illustrations

65 G. Bauer/Barbara Heller Archive; 66, 117, 136 Victoria and Albert Museum/Michael Holford; 83, 135, 575 (top) M. Macintyre/Alan Hutchinson Library; 84 (bottom) National Gallery of Prague, W. Forman/Barbara Heller Archive; 84 (top), 293 British Library/Michael Holford; 118(1.) Wellcome Musuem/Michael Holford; 118 (r.) British Museum; 153, 399, 451, 452, 501 Douglas Dickens; 154 G. Clyde/Michael Holford; 171 (top) Christine Osborne Pictures, London; 171 (bottom) Bridgeman Art Library; 172 A. Singer/Alan Hutchison Library; 189, 208, 249 Michael Holford; 190 Museum für Völkerkunde, Basel/W. Forman/Barbara Heller Archive; 207 (bottom), W. Forman/Barbara Heller Archive; 207 (top), 312 (top), 433 (bottom), 519, 539 (top and bottom), 575 (bottom), 576 Alan Hutchison Library; 250 British Library/Fotomas Index; 251 (top) Bibliothèque Nationale, Paris/Sonia Halliday; 251 (bottom) Bibliothèque Nationale, Paris/S. Corr; 252 Sonia Halliday; 294, 557 Barnaby's Picture Library; 311 (top) Wallace Collection, London; 311 (bottom) Museum of Mankind, London/Michael Holford; 312 (bottom) S. Errington/Alan Hutchison Library; 337 The Toledo Museum of Art, Toledo, Ohio; Gift of Edward Drummond Libbey; 340 Kunsthistorisches Museum, Vienna; 381 (top) Popperfoto, London; 381 (bottom left) Corbis UK Ltd; 381 (bottom right) Topham Picturepoint, London; 382 Charles Walker Collection/Images; 400 Ann and Bury Peerless; 433 (top) P. Goycolea/Alan Hutchison Library; 434 (top) Charles Walker Collection/Images; 434 (bottom) Popperfoto, London; 502 (top) AKG London; 502 (bottom) Christine Osborne Pictures, London; 520 David King Collection; 540, 558 Tony Morrison/South American Pictures.

Black-and-white illustrations

FRONTISPIECE E. T. Archive

INTRODUCTION

12 Novosti Press Agency; 15 Alan Hutchison Library; 16, 20 Victoria and Albert Museum; 17 Sarnath Museum/JCK Archive; 18 John Topham Library; 19 I. W.M./Robert Hunt Library.

Chapter 1 33, 34 C&K Archive; 37 Institut für Urgeschichte Universität Tübingen; 38 Mansell Collection; 39 AKG London; 41 Jerico Excavation Fund/C&K Archive.

Chapter 2 47, 57, 70, 86 (l. and r.) Douglas Dickens; 47 Musee Guimet, Paris; W. Forman/Barbara Heller Archive; 61 Freer Gallery of Art, Washington/JCK Archive; 71, 88, 93 (l. and r.), 96, 103 Victoria and Albertr Museum; 73 Alan Hutchison Library; 79 Ann and Bury Peerless; 89 W. Forman/Barbara Heller Archive; 92 C&K Archive; 104 Metropolitan Museum of Art, New York.

Chapter 3 110, 122, 127 Victoria and Albert Museum; 111 John Topham Library; 113 Visual Arts Library; 115 Mansell Collection; 123 Barnaby's Picture Library.

Chapter 4 139 P. Montagnon/Alan Hutchison Library; 143 Barnaby's Picture Library; 146 John Topham Picture Library; 150 Robert Hunt Library; 152 Douglas Dickens; .

Chapter 5 158 Douglas Dickens; 161, 162 Barnaby's Picture Library.

Chapter 6 170, 175 Museum of Mankind, London; 175 Alan Hutchison Library; 180 Australian News and Information Bureau.

Chapter 7 184 Rietburg Museum, Zurich Collection: von der Heydt; 185 British Museum/Mansell Collection; 187 (bottom left) Harvard University Museum; 187 (top and bottom right) Douglas Dickens; 193 Photo James Mooney/Smithsonian Institution; National Anthropological Archives; 195 mithsonian Institution; National Anthropological Archives; 196 John Topham Library/C&K Archive.

Chapter 8 198, 202 Mansell Collection; 204 W. Forman/Barbara Heller Archive; 206 Alan Hutchison Library; 209 Giraudon/Mansell Collection; 211 British Library/Mansell Collection.

Chapter 9 222 Edinburgh University Library; 225 Douglas Dickens.

Chapter 10 235 Mansell Collection; 237 Mary Evans Picture Library; 239 Ronald Sheridan Library; 240 London Museum/Mansell Collection; 244, 253 Anderson/Mansell Collection; 246 C&K Archive; 248 Pont. Comm. di Arch. Sacra, Rome.

Chapter 11 258 Alinari/Mansell Collection; 263 C&K Archive; 266, 273 Mansell Collection; 267 Christine Osborne Pictures, London; 274 N. D. McKenna/Alan Hutchison Library; 275, 277 C&K Archive; 280 British Library/Mansell Collection.

Chapter 12 291 (l. and r.) Victoria and Albert Museum.

Chapter 13 309 Black Star/Robert Hunt Library; 316 John Topham Library; 317 W. Forman/Barbara Heller Archive; 318 J. Highet/Alan Hutchison Library; 321 Barnaby's Picture Library.

Chapter 14 327 Anderson/Mansell Collection; 329, 342, 351, 354 Mansell Collection; 333, 348, 355 Fotomas Index; 334 Mary Evans Picture Library; 343 Rijksmuseum, Amsterdam; 357 Popperfoto.

Chapter 15 368 Fotomas Index; 369 Mansell Collection; 371 Barnaby's Picture Library; 379, 388 John Topham Library; 394 Popperfoto.

Chapter 16 402 Victoria and Albert Museum; 409 Ann and Bury Peerless; 418 Popperfoto; 421 John Topham Library; 424, 431 Douglas Dickens; 429 Barnaby's Picture Library.

Chapter 17 437 Mary Evans Picture Library, London; 442, 446 Alan Hutchison Library; 447 Douglas Dickens; 450 John Topham Library; 454 Topham Picturepoint, London.

Chapter 18 461 Hulton Getty, London; 463 Robert Hunt Library; 464 Popperfoto; 466 Black Star/Robert Hunt Library.

Chapter 19 470 Mansell Collection; 473, 480 Barnaby's Picture Library; 482, 483 John Topham Library.

Chapter 20 490, 492, 506 Barnaby's Picture Library; 493, 496 Popperfoto; 494 Black Star/Robert Hunt Library; 504 Mohammed Amin/Camerapix.

Chapter 21 509 John Topham Library; 512 National Museum of New Zealand; 515 Rijksmuseum voor Volken-Kunde, Leiden/W. Forman/Barbara Heller Archive; 516 Black Star/Robert Hunt Library.

Chapter 22 524, 530 David King Collection; 522, 532 John Topham Library; 527 Popperfoto.

Chapter 23 519, 544 John Topham Library; 548, 550 Popperfoto; 553 Black Star/Robert Hunt Library.

Chapter 24 561 Barnaby's Picture Library; 565 Popperfoto; 570 John Topham Library.

Chapter 25 573, 587 John Topham Library; 580 Alan Hutchison Library; 588 Barnaby's Picture Library; 592 J. Highet/Alan Hutchison Library

Index

Figures in italics refer to captions